Introduction to Digital Communications

Introduction to Digital Communications

Ali Grami

AMSTERDAM • BOSTON • HEIDELBERG • LONDON
NEW DELHI • NEW YORK • OXFORD • PARIS • SAN DIEGO
SAN FRANCISCO • SINGAPORE • SYDNEY • TOKYO
Academic Press is an imprint of Elsevier

ELSEVIER

Introduction toDigital Communications
Ali Grami

Academic Press
An imprint of Elsevier
125 London Wall, London, EC2Y 5AS, UK
525 B Street, Suite 1800, San Diego, CA 92101–4495, USA
225 Wyman Street, Waltham, MA 02451, USA
The Boulevard, Langford Lane, Kidlington, Oxford OX5 1GB, UK

Original ISBN: 978-0-12-407682-2

First Printed in India 2015

Indian Reprint ISBN: 978-93-5107-319-2

Published by Elsevier, a division of Reed Elsevier India Private Limited.
Registered Office: 818, 8th Floor, Indraprakash Building, 21 Barakhamba Road, New Delhi-110001
Corporate Office: 14th floor, Building No. 10B, DLF Cyber City Phase-II, Gurgaon-122 002, Haryana, India.

Printed and bound in India by Sai Printo Pack, Okhla, New Delhi (India)

To the loves of my life:
Shirin, Nickrooz, and Neeloufar

Contents

Preface

This is an undergraduate-level textbook that lucidly provides the basic principles in the analysis and design of digital communication systems. Since digital communications is an advanced topic, the treatment here is more descriptive and explanatory rather than merely rigorous. However, it is not devoid of mathematical analyses, as all relevant results are presented. Although the mathematical level of the book is intentionally constrained, the intuitive level of it is not. The premise is that complex concepts are best conveyed in the simplest possible context. The goal, at every step of the way, is to provide big picture through analysis, description, example, and application. In taking a systems approach to digital communications, the text hardly considers actual physical realizations of the devices (i.e., the systems are presented in block diagram form).

There is intentionally much more in this book than can be taught in one semester (of 36 lecture hours). The book consists of 12 chapters focused on digital communications. Chapters 1 & 2 provide an overview of the fundamentals of digital communications. Since digital communications at the physical layer involves the transmission of continuous-time signals where the channel noise is also in the form of continuous time, Chapters 3 & 4 cover deterministic and random signals in detail, and should serve as review materials. Chapters 5 to 12, inclusive, discuss the critical elements and major topics in the broad field of digital communications. In addition, there is an appendix with a summary of analog communications.

As this text is primarily written at a level that is most suitable for junior and senior students, the coverage of the book, in terms of depth and breadth as well as tone and scope, lends itself very well to distinct audiences in an electrical engineering program. In a third-year course on digital communications, the coverage may include Chapters 3 & 4 (review of select sections), Chapters 1, 2, 5, 6, 7, 9 & 10 (all sections). In a third-year course on communication systems, the coverage may include Chapters 3 & 4 (review of select sections), Appendix (all sections), Chapters 1, 2, 5 & 6 (all sections), Chapters 7, 9

& 10 (a couple of sections in each chapter). In a fourth-year course on digital communications, with a third-year course on communication systems as a prerequisite, the coverage may contain a review of Chapters 1, 2, 5, 6 and a complete coverage of Chapters 7 to 12, inclusive.

There is also a secondary target audience that can include undergraduate students in the software engineering and information technology programs. In teaching such a course, it is important not to get mired in too many theoretical details, and the focus, instead, must be almost exclusively on the descriptive aspects of systems and intuitive explanations of analytical results and design objectives. This book can also be used by professionals, such as practicing engineers, project leaders, and technical managers, who already have familiarity with the standards and systems and are seeking to advance their knowledge of the fundamentals of the field. It may also serve graduate students as a reference.

Upon request from the publisher, a Solutions Manual can be obtained only by instructors who use the book for adoption in a course.

Acknowledgements

Acknowledgements are a bore for the reader, but a source of true pleasure for the author. All writing is in some sense collaborative. This book is no exception, as it builds upon the ideas, approaches, and insights of teachers, students, and colleagues in both academia and industry. In the course of writing a textbook of this nature, one is bound to lean on the bits and pieces of materials developed by others. I would therefore like to greatly thank the many authors and researchers in the field of digital communications whose writings and findings helped me one way or the other.

I am truly grateful to Dr. J.F. Hayes, my master's supervisor at McGill University, and Dr. S. Pasupathy, my PhD supervisor at the University of Toronto, who both taught and inspired me about communications. Their broad knowledge, valuable insights, and research excellence in the area of digital communications helped shape my foundation in the field. I owe them a great deal of gratitude for their advice and perspectives on numerous occasions.

I am heavily indebted to many people for their contributions to the development of this text as well as their reviews of some chapters, including Dr. I. Dincer, Dr. X. Fernando, Dr. M. Nassehi, Dr. A. Sepasi Zahmati, Dr. H. Shahnasser, and Dr. M. Zandi, as well as the anonymous reviewers who provided many valuable comments. I would also like to express my appreciation to all the students I have had over the years at various universities. A reflection of what I learned from them is on every page of this book. I would like to thank Lucas Huffman who commented on many parts of the book and prepared some of the figures. A special thanks is due to Ahmad Manzar who provided helpful comments on the entire manuscript and prepared the solutions to the computer exercises.

We have used trademarks in this book without providing a trademark symbol for each mention. We acknowledge the trademarks, and express that their use reflects no intention of infringing upon them. The financial support of Natural

Sciences and Engineering Research Council (NSERC) of Canada was also crucial to this project. I am grateful to the staff of Elsevier for their support in various phases of this project, namely Stephen Merken, Nate McFadden, and Anusha Sambamoorthy as well as other members of the production team. No book is flawless, and this text is certainly no different from others. Your comments and suggestions for improvements are always welcomed. I would greatly appreciate it if you could send your feedback to idc.grami@gmail.com.

CHAPTER 1

Introduction

CONTENTS

1.1 HISTORICAL REVIEW OF COMMUNICATIONS

Due to a host of well-conceived ideas, indispensable discoveries, crucial innovations, and important inventions over the past two centuries, information transmission has evolved immeasurably. The technological advances in communications and their corresponding societal impacts are moving at an accelerating pace. To understand today's modern communication systems, networks, and devices, and to help obtain a sense of perspective about future breakthroughs, it may be insightful to have a glance at the historical developments in the broad field of communications.

A number of people have made significant contributions to help pave the way for a multitude of technological revolutions in the arena of communications. The array of collective, and sometimes collaborative, achievements made in communications are, in essence, due to a team effort, a team whose knowledgeable, talented, and ingenious members lived at different times and in different places; however, we can only afford to mention a select few here. The nineteenth century witnessed scientists and discoverers, such as Oersted, who showed that electric currents can create magnetic fields, Faraday, who discovered that electric current can be induced in a conductor by a changing magnetic field, as well as Maxwell who developed the theory of electromagnetic waves and Hertz who experimentally verified it. Their collective contributions led to the foundation of wireless communications, more specifically, that an electric signal is transmitted by varying an electromagnetic field to induce current change in a distant device. The twentieth century brought researchers and theoreticians, such as Nyquist and Reeves, who respectively contributed to signal sampling process and pulse code modulation, as well as others, such as North, Rice, Wiener, and Kolmogorov, who made contributions to optimal signal and noise processing. Finally, it was Shannon, with his exceptional contribution to the mathematical theory of communications, who laid the unique foundation for digital transmission and today's information age [1]. Table 1.1 highlights some of the major events in the history of telecommunications [2–4].

Introduction to Digital Communications

Table 1.1 Some of the major events in the history of telecommunications

Year	Event
1820	Orested showed electric currents cause magnetic fields
1831	Faraday showed magnetic fields produce electric fields
1844	Morse perfected line telegraphy
1864	Maxwell developed the theory of electromagnetism
1866	First transatlantic telegraph cable became operational
1876	Bell invented telephone
1887	Hertz verified Maxwell's electromagnetic theory
1896	Marconi demonstrated wireless telegraphy
1907	First transatlantic radio telegraphy service implemented
1915	First continental telephone service (in US) deployed
1918	Armstrong devised superheterodyne radio receiver
1920	First commercial AM radio broadcasting began
1920s	Contributions on signal and noise by Nyquist, Hartley, and others
1933	Armstrong demonstrated FM radio
1936	First commercial TV broadcasting by BBC in England resumed
1937	Reeves proposed PCM
1941	NTSC black and white TV standard developed
1945	Clarke proposed geostationary satellite
1948	Shannon published the mathematical theory of communications
1948	Brattain, Bardeen, and Shockley invented transistor
1940s	Contributions on optimal filtering by Kolmogorov, Wiener, and others
1953	NTSC color TV standard developed
1953	First transatlantic telephone cable deployed
1957	First satellite (Sputnik I) launched
1960	Laser developed
1962	First dial-up (300-bps) modem developed
1962	First communication satellite (Telstar I) launched
1966	First facsimile (fax) machine developed
1969	ARPANET (precursor to Internet) developed
1970	Low-loss optic fiber developed
1971	Microprocessor invented
1976	Personal computers developed
1979	First (analog) cellular mobile telephone system (in Japan) deployed
1989	GPS developed
1992	First digital cellular mobile telephone system (in Europe) deployed
1993	HDTV standard developed
1997	Wireless LAN developed
1990s	Ubiquitous use of the Internet accelerated

The ***telegraph***, which provides communications at a distance by coded signals, is considered as the first invention of major significance to communications. The first commercial electrical telegraph was constructed by Wheatstone and Cooke, and perfected by Morse. The telegraph was the forerunner of digital transmission in that ***Morse code*** was used to represent a variable-length binary code, where short sequences of dots (short beeps) and dashes (long beeps) represent frequent letters and long ones represent infrequent letters. In the mid-nineteenth century, the first permanent transatlantic telegraph cable became operational, and at the outset of the twentieth century, Marconi and others demonstrated ***wireless telegraphy***, and the first transatlantic radio message was sent. The telegraph is hardly present today.

The ***telephone***, which provides two-way voice communications, was invented by Bell. Like telegraphy, the telephone was first viewed as a point-to-point communication system. But shortly after, the first telephone exchange was established. With the first transcontinental telephone service in the early twentieth century and the first transatlantic telephone cable in the mid-fifties, as well as inventions of the diode, triode, transistor, digital switch, and fiber optic cables, the telephone and the telephone network steadily evolved toward what it is today. Voice communications by telephone at its inception was analog in its entirety. However, half a century later, the transmission of speech signals over the backbone networks along with the switching of the signals became digital, yet the local loop remained analog. And now, for mobile telephones, even the signal between the mobile device and the network is in digital and hence, is an all-digital network.

Radio broadcasting, a one-way wireless transmission of audio signals over radio waves intended to reach a wide audience, grew out of the vacuum tube and early electronics. Following the earlier work on radio, the first amplitude modulation (AM) radio broadcasting was introduced, and grew rapidly across the globe. Shortly after, Armstrong invented the superheterodyne radio receiver and the first frequency modulation (FM) system, and was the first to advocate the principle of power-bandwidth trade-off. FM radio broadcasting gained popularity in the mid-twentieth century, especially with the introduction of FM stereo.

Television is a medium that is used for transmitting and receiving video and sound. TV technology was based on the evolution of electronics that began with the invention of the vacuum tube. TV was invented in the United States in 1929, BBC began the first commercial TV broadcasting in monochrome in 1936, the NTSC color TV was introduced in 1953, and the first commercial HDTV broadcasting began in 1996. Today, there is no analog TV transmission, and TV signals are now exclusively digital.

In 1945, Clarke published his famous article to propose the idea of a ***geostationary satellite*** as a relay for communications between various points on Earth. In the late fifties, the former Soviet Union launched the first satellite, Sputnik I, and then the United States launched Explorer I. In 1962, the US launched Telstar I, the first satellite to relay TV programs across the Atlantic. Today, there are several hundreds of satellites employing various frequency bands (e.g., L-band, C-band, X-band, Ku-Band, and Ka-band) in various orbits (LEO, MEO, and GEO) to provide a multitude of services, such as radio and TV broadcasting, mobile and business communications, and GPS.

Following the earlier radio systems, the first public mobile telephone service was introduced in the mid-forties. The system had an interface with the public-switched telephone network (PSTN), the landline phone system. Each system in a city used a single, high-powered transmitter and large tower in order to cover distances of over 50 km. It began as a push-to-talk system (i.e., half-duplex mode) employing FM with 120 kHz of radio-frequency (RF) bandwidth. By the sixties, it had become a full-duplex, auto-dial system, but due to advances in RF filters and low-noise amplifiers, the FM bandwidth transmission was cut to 30 kHz. This mobile radio communication system, which lasted until the early eighties, was very spectrally inefficient, as very few in a geographical area could subscribe to it. These non-cellular mobile systems could now be referred to as ***0G systems***. Due to a vast level of basic research, in the fifties and sixties, companies such as AT&T and Motorola, NTT in Japan, and Ericson in Europe developed and demonstrated various cellular mobile systems in the seventies. These systems were all analog, and employed FM. In North America, the analog cellular mobile system, known as the advanced mobile phone system (AMPS), which used 30-kHz channels to employ frequency-division multiple access (FDMA), was deployed in 1983. The analog cellular mobile systems are referred to as ***1G systems***. Due to the lack of mobile roaming capability across Europe and the severe shortage of system capacity in North America, the need for digital cellular mobile systems was born. In North America, IS-54, which was based on a three-slot time-division multiple access (TDMA) scheme using a 30-kHz channel, and IS-95, which was based on many users employing a 1.25 MHz-channel using code-division multiple access (CDMA) scheme, were introduced. In Europe, the GSM, through which eight users employ a 200-kHz TDMA channel, was developed, and became the most widely-used mobile system in the world. ***Digital cellular mobile systems***, such as the IS-54, IS-95, GSM, and some others, introduced in the nineties, are referred to as ***2G systems***. After that, ***3G systems***, which provided data transmission at high rates in addition to voice transmission, began to emerge. Figure 1.1 presents the trends in mobile communications.

The ***Internet***, composed of thousands interconnected networks, is a classic example of an innovation that originated in many different places. To connect computers with their bursty traffic, the sixties witnessed the birth of packet-switched networks and the development of the Advanced Research Projects Agency Network (ARPANET). After Vint Cerf and Bob Kahn, known as the Internet pioneers,

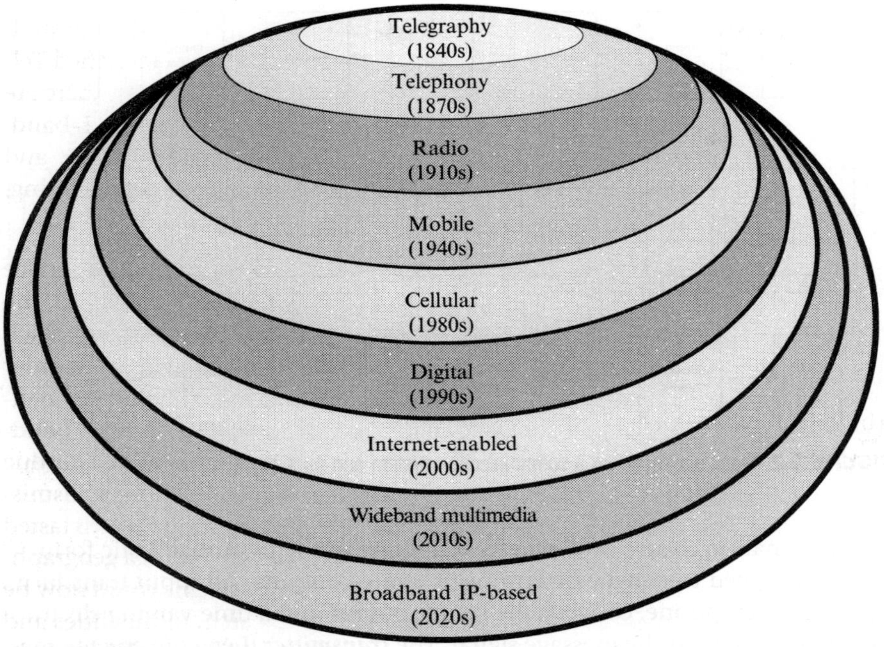

FIGURE 1.1 Evolution of telecommunications with a focus on mobile communications.

devised the protocols to achieve end-to-end delivery of computer data in the mid-seventies, the transmission control protocol and Internet protocol (TCP/IP) became the official protocol for the ARPANET, and ARPANET was renamed the Internet in the mid-eighties. In the early nineties, a hypermedia software interface to the Internet, named the ***World Wide Web*** (WWW), was proposed by Tim Berners-Lee. This was the turning point that resulted in the explosive growth of the Internet and yielded numerous commercial applications for the Internet. The Internet has evolved at a faster rate and become more widely-used than any other innovation, invention, or technology in the history of telecommunications. The set of cultural, educational, political, and financial impacts of the Internet on our way of lives is and will remain unparalleled for many years to come.

1.2 BLOCK DIAGRAM OF A DIGITAL COMMUNICATION SYSTEM

Figure 1.2a shows the basic functional blocks of a typical communication system. Regardless of the particular application and configuration, all information transmission systems involve three major subsystems: the transmitter, the channel, and the receiver.

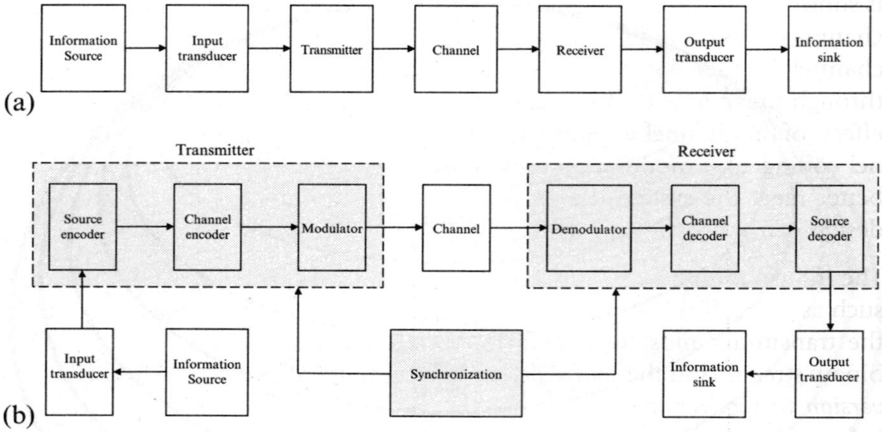

FIGURE 1.2 Block diagrams: (a) a communication system and (b) a digital communication system.

The information source produces its output, which is in probabilistic form, as there is no need to convey deterministic source outputs. An input transducer, such as a microphone, converts the source output into a time-varying electrical signal, referred to as the message signal. The ***transmitter*** then converts the message signal into a form suitable for transmission through a physical channel, such as a cable. The transmitter generally changes the characteristics of the message signal to match the characteristics of the channel by using a process called modulation. In addition to modulation, other functions, such as filtering and amplification, are also performed by the transmitter.

The ***communication channel*** is the physical medium between the transmitter and the receiver, where they are physically separated. No communication channel is ideal, and thus a message signal undergoes various forms of degradation. Sources of degradation may include attenuation, noise, distortion, and interference. As some or all of these degradations are present in a physical channel, a paramount goal in the design of a communication system is to overcome the effects of such impairments.

The function of the ***receiver*** is to extract the message signal from the received signal. The primary function is to perform the process of demodulation, along with a number of peripheral functions, such as amplification and filtering. The complexity of a receiver is generally more significant than that of the transmitter, as a receiver must additionally minimize the effects of the channel degradations. The output transducer, such as a loudspeaker, then converts the receiver output into a signal suitable for the information sink.

Figure 1.2b shows the basic functional elements of a digital communication system. In a simple, yet classical fashion, the transmitter or the receiver each is subdivided into three blocks. The transmitter consists of the source encoder, channel encoder, and modulator, and the receiver consists of the demodulator, channel decoder, and source decoder. At the receiver, the received signal passes through the inverse of the operations at the transmitter, while minimizing the effects of the channel impairments. The three functions of source coding, channel coding, and modulation may be designed in concert with one another to better meet the system design goals, yet accommodating the overall system design constraints.

The information may be inherently digital, such as computer data, or analog, such as voice. If the information is in analog form, then the source encoder at the transmitter must first perform ***analog-to-digital conversion*** to produce a binary stream, and the ***source decoder*** must then perform ***digital-to-analog conversion*** to recover the analog signal. The ***source encoder*** removes redundant information from the binary stream so as to make efficient use of the channel. Source coding, also known as data compression, leads to bandwidth conservation, as the spectrum is always at a premium. The important parameters associated with source coding are primarily the efficiency of the coder (i.e., the ratio of actual output data rate to the source information rate) and the encoder/decoder complexity.

The ***channel encoder*** at the transmitter introduces, in a controlled fashion, redundancy. The additional bits are used by the ***channel decoder*** at the receiver to overcome the channel-induced errors. The added redundancy serves to enhance the performance by reducing the bit error rate, which is the ultimate performance measure in a digital communication system. The important parameters associated with channel coding are primarily the efficiency of the coder (i.e., the ratio of data rate at the input of the encoder to the data rate at its output), error control capability, and the encoder/decoder complexity.

The modulator at the transmitter and the demodulator at the receiver serve as the interface to the communication channel. The ***modulator*** accepts a sequence of bits, and maps each sequence into a waveform. A sequence may consist of only one or several bits. At the receiver, the ***demodulator*** processes the received waveforms, and maps each to the corresponding bit sequence. The important parameters of modulation are the number of bits in a sequence represented by a waveform, the types of waveforms used, the duration of the waveforms, the power level and the bandwidth used, as well as the demodulation complexity.

There are, of course, other functional blocks, not shown in Figure 1.1b, that are required in a practical digital communication system. They may include synchronization, an essential requirement for all digital commination systems, as well equalization, amplification, and filtering, to name a few.

1.3 ORGANIZATION OF THE BOOK

This textbook provides a comprehensive introduction to digital communications at a level that undergraduate students can grasp all important concepts and obtain a fundamental understanding of digital communication system analysis and design. This book consists of 12 chapters and an appendix, and is organized as follows:

Chapter 2 briefly offers a descriptive overview of major aspects of digital communications with a view to set the stage for what will be covered in the rest of the book. The focus is on the rationale behind digital (vis-à-vis analog), network models, transmission media and impairments, and radio transmission and spectrum. An array of inter-related, inter-dependent design objectives and a host of interacting and conflicting design constraints are identified.

Chapter 3 provides an extensive discussion of signals, systems, and spectral analysis. Humans appreciate time and its continuous and irreversible flow, and above all the impact of its changes. Signals are therefore always defined in the time domain. Physical signals are quite distinct in the time domain, so are many analytical signals. However, in the frequency domain, which is the key measure of how slowly or rapidly signals change in the time domain, a group of distinct signals may share common characteristics. This commonality in turn allows us to design communication systems to transmit, receive, and process a very wide range of signals.

Chapter 4 introduces the basic concepts of probability, random variables, and random processes, with the sole focus of their applications in digital communications, as time-varying, information-bearing signals from the receiving viewpoint are unpredictable. In addition, there are major sources of channel degradation that are random functions of time. This chapter helps pave the way for the performance assessments of digital communication systems with nondeterministic imperfections.

Chapter 5 presents a detailed discussion on how analog signals can be converted into their digital representations. Since humans produce and perceive audio and visual signals in analog form, for the transmission, processing, and storage of audio and visual signals as well as other analog information-bearing signals in digital form, analog-to-digital conversion in the transmitter and digital-to-analog conversion in the receiver are indispensable operations.

Chapter 6 details digital transmission over a baseband channel in the context of pulse amplitude modulation. We first introduce intersymbol interference and the Nyquist criterion to eliminate it, discuss pulse shaping and eye patterns, present the optimum system design to minimize the effect of noise, make a comparison of systems using binary and M-ary signaling, and expand means to combat intersymbol interference using various equalization techniques.

Chapter 7 focuses on digital continuous-wave (CW) binary and M-ary modulation schemes. Digital passband modulation is based on variation of the amplitude, phase, or frequency of the sinusoidal carrier, or some combination of these parameters. As there are a host of reasons why modulation may be required, including transmission of digital data over bandpass channels, a number of digital modulation techniques that have some common characteristics and yet distinct features are discussed.

Chapter 8 highlights synchronization, since in every digital communication system, some level of synchronization is required, without which a reliable transmission of information is not possible. Of the various levels of synchronization, the focus here is on symbol synchronization and carrier recovery, as the role of the former is to provide the receiver with an accurate estimate of the beginning and ending times of the symbols and the latter aims to replicate a sinusoidal carrier at the receiver whose phase is the same as that sent by the transmitter.

Chapter 9 expands on the fundamental relationships between the bit error rate performance and the information rate. Information theory leads to the quantification of the information content of the source, as denoted by entropy, the characterization of the information-bearing capacity of the communication channel, as related to its noise characteristics, and consequently the establishment of the relationship between the information content of the source and the capacity of the channel.

Chapter 10 is concerned with error-control coding, as coding can accomplish its purpose through the deliberate introduction of redundant bits into the message bits. The redundancy bits, which are derived from the message bits as well as the code features and parameters, can provide a level of error detection and correction; however, it cannot guarantee that an error will always be detectable or correctable. At the expense of the channel bandwidth, error-control coding can reduce the bit error rate for a fixed transmitted power and/or reduce the transmit power for a fixed bit error rate.

Chapter 11 describes the major facets of communication networks in an overview fashion, with a focus on multiuser communications, which includes many aspects of wireless communications, such as multiple access methods, and some aspects of wired communications, such as network topology, and public and local area networks. The concepts of cryptography and digital signature are also briefly discussed.

Chapter 12 gives and overview of some aspects of wireless communications, including radio link analysis, mobile radio propagation characteristics, and diversity techniques. As the field of wireless communications has been exponentially expanding and has led to the introduction of versatile mobile/portable devices with their high-data-rate capabilities and numerous mobile applications, there is also a mention of what the future holds.

The appendix summarizes analog continuous-wave modulation namely amplitude modulation, including double sideband (DSB), single sideband (SSB), and vestigial sideband (VSB) schemes, each with and without a carrier, along with narrowband and wideband frequency modulation. In addition, the bandwidth and power requirements, along with methods of their generation and demodulation, are briefly discussed. Detailed derivations are avoided, but the results of the analyses along with intuitive explanations are provided.

References

[1] C.E. Shannon, A mathematical theory of communication, *Bell Syst. Tech. J.* 27 (July, October, 1948) 379–423, 623–656.

[2] S. Verdu, Fifty years of Shannon theory, *IEEE Trans. Inform. Theor.* 44 (October 1998) 2057–2078.

[3] A. Huurdeman, *The Worldwide History of Telecommunications*, Wiley-IEEE Press, July 2003, ISBN: 978-0-471-20505-0.

[4] http://en.wikipedia.org.

CHAPTER 2

Fundamental Aspects of Digital Communications

INTRODUCTION

In today's world, communications are essential and pervasive, as the age of communications with anyone, anytime, anywhere has arrived. The theme is multimedia—the confluence of voice, data, image, music, text, graphics, and video warranting simultaneous transmission in an integrated fashion. With the push of advancing digital technology and the pull of public demand for an array of innovative applications, it is highly anticipated that every aspect of digital communications will continue to broaden so as to usher in even more achievements. The emerging trend is toward low-cost, high-speed, high-performance, utterly-secure, highly-personalized, context-aware, location-sensitive, and time-critical multimedia applications. After studying this chapter on the fundamental aspects of digital communications and understanding all relevant concepts, students should be able to do the following:

1. State the numerous merits of digital and its dominance in communications.
2. Know the few drawbacks of digital and how they can be mitigated.
3. Understand how text can be represented.
4. Expand on the audio characteristics and the impact of digitization on speech and music.
5. Explain the attributes of image and video and the impact of compression on them.
6. Identify how computers form packets to send them over communication networks.
7. Distinguish between the various characteristics associated with wired transmission media.
8. Highlight the benefits and shortcomings associated with radio communications.
9. Assess various modes of radio wave propagation.
10. Define the modulation process.

CONTENTS

11. Identify the principal reasons signals may need to be modulated.
12. Describe signal attenuation.
13. Differentiate among different types of distortions along with their possible remedies.
14. Discuss various sources of interference and how to mitigate them.
15. Summarize various sources of noise.
16. Grasp the limiting factors of a band-limited Gaussian channel.
17. Appreciate the relationship among power, bandwidth, and capacity.
18. Outline digital communication design objectives.
19. List digital communication design constraints.
20. Connect the fundamental aspects of digital communications.

2.1 WHY DIGITAL?

The telegraph, invented in the mid-nineteenth century, was the forerunner of digital communications. However, it is now that we can emphatically say digital is the pervasive technology of the twenty-first century and beyond, as the first generation of cellular phones in the late seventies was the last major analog communication invention. During the past three decades, communication networks, systems, and devices have all moved toward digital. The primary examples are wireless networks, Internet, MP3 players, smartphones, HDTV, GPS, and satellite TV and radio. Digital communication technology will continue to bring about intelligent infrastructures and sophisticated end-user devices, through which a host of applications in entertainment (e.g., wireless video on demand), education (e.g., online interactive multimedia courses), information (e.g., 3-D video streaming), and business (e.g., mobile commerce) will be provided. The burgeoning field of digital communications will thus continue to affect almost all aspects of our contemporary life.

A basic definition of ***digital*** is the transmission of a message using binary digits (***bits***) or symbols from a finite alphabet during a finite time interval (bit or symbol duration). A bit or symbol occurring in each interval is mapped onto a continuous-time waveform that is then sent across the channel. Over any finite interval, the continuous-time waveform at the channel output belongs to a finite set of possible waveforms. This is in contrast to analog communications, where the output can assume any possible waveform. Digital can bring about many significant benefits, of course, at the expense of few shortcomings, for there is no free lunch in digital communications.

2.1.1 Advantages of Digital

Design efficiency: Digital is inherently more efficient than analog in exchanging power for bandwidth, the two premium resources in communications. Since an essentially unlimited range of signal conditioning and processing options are available to the designer, effective trade-offs among power, bandwidth, performance, and complexity can be more readily accommodated. For any required performance, there is a three-way trade-off among power, bandwidth, and complexity (i.e., an increase in one means the other two will be reduced).

Versatile hardware: The processing power of digital integrated circuits continues to approximately double every 18 months to 2 years. These programmable processors easily allow the implementation of improved designs or changed requirements. Digital circuits are generally less sensitive to physical effects, such as vibration, aging components, and external temperature. They also allow a greater dynamic range (the difference between the largest and the smallest signal values). Processing is now less costly than precious bandwidth and power resources. This in turn allows considerable flexibility in designing communication systems.

New and enhanced services: In today's widely distributed way of life, Internet services, such as web browsing, e-mailing, texting, e-commerce, streaming and interactive multimedia services, have all become feasible and some even indispensable. It is also easier to integrate different services, with various modalities, into the same transmission scheme or to enhance services through transmission of some additional information, such as playing music or receiving a phone call with all relevant details.

Control of quality: A desired distortion level can be initially set and then kept nearly fixed at that value at every step (link) of a digital communication path. This reconstruction of the digital signal is done by appropriately-spaced regenerative repeaters, which do not allow accumulation of noise and interference. On the other hand, once the analog signal is distorted, the distortion cannot be removed and a repeater in an analog system (i.e., an amplifier) regenerates the distortion together with the signal. In a way, in an analog system, the noises add, whereas in a digital system, the bit error rates add. In other words, with many regenerative repeaters along the path, the impact in an analog system is a reduction of many decibels (dBs) in the signal-to-noise ratio (SNR), whereas the effect in a digital system is a reduction of only a few dBs in the SNR.

Improved security: Digital encryption, unlike analog encryption, can make the transmitted information virtually impossible to decipher. This applies especially to sensitive data, such as electronic banking and medical information transfer. Secure communications can be achieved using complex cryptographic systems.

Flexibility, compatibility, and switching: Combining various digital signals and digitized analog signals from different users and applications into streams of different speeds and sizes—along with control and signaling information—can be much easier and more efficient. Signal storage, reproduction, interface with computers, as well as access and search of information in electronic databases can also be quite easy and inexpensive. Digital techniques allow the development of communication components with various features that can easily interface with a different component produced by a different manufacturer. Digital transmission brings about the great ability to dynamically switch and route messages of various types, thus offering an array of network connectivities, including unicast, multicast, narrowcast, and broadcast.

2.1.2 Disadvantages of Digital

Signal-processing intensive: Digital communication systems require a very high degree of signal processing, where every one of the three major functions of source coding, channel coding, and modulation in the transceiver—each requiring an array of sub-functions (especially in the receiver)—warrants high computational load and thus complexity. Due to major advances in digital signal processing (DSP) technologies in the past two decades, this is no longer a major disadvantage.

Additional bandwidth: Digital communication systems generally require more bandwidth than analog systems, unless digital signal compression (source coding) and *M*-ary (vis-à-vis binary) signaling techniques are heavily employed. Due to major advances in compression techniques and bandwidth-efficient modulation schemes, the bit rate requirement and thus the corresponding bandwidth requirement can be considerably reduced by a couple of orders of magnitude. As such, additional bandwidth is no longer a critical issue.

Synchronization: Digital communication systems always require a significant share of resources allocated to synchronization, including carrier phase and frequency recovery, timing (bit or symbol) recovery, and frame and network synchronization. This inherent drawback of digital transmission cannot be circumvented. However, synchronization in a digital communication system can be accomplished to the extent required, but at the expense of a high degree of complexity.

Non-graceful performance degradation: Digital communication systems yield non-graceful performance degradation when the SNR drops below a certain threshold. A modest reduction in SNR can give rise to a considerable increase in bit error rate (BER), thus resulting in a significant degradation in performance.

2.2 COMMUNICATIONS MODALITIES

The main sources of information are broadly categorized as follows: text (e.g., alphanumeric characters), audio (e.g., speech, music), and visual (e.g., image, video). The confluence of voice, data, image, music, text, graphics, and video has led to what is widely known as ***multimedia***. The characteristics of all these modalities and their transmission requirements are distinct. Humans produce and perceive audio and visual signals in an analog form. To this effect, in digital transmission of audio and visual signals, both analog-to-digital and digital-to-analog conversions are required.

After converting analog sources into digital, they are compressed with a high compression ratio. Compression is achieved by exploiting redundancy to the largest extent possible and associating the shortest binary codes with the most likely outcomes. There are fundamentally two types of compression methods: i) ***lossless compression*** used in texts and sensitive data, so the original data can be reconstructed exactly (i.e., the compression is completely reversible) and ii) ***lossy compression*** used in audio and visual signals, in that permanent loss of information in a controlled manner is involved, and it is therefore not completely reversible. Lossy compression is, however, capable of achieving a compression ratio higher than that attainable with lossless compression. Lossy compression is employed only when degradation in performance to the end user is either unnoticeable or noticeable, but acceptable.

In a ***discrete memoryless source*** (DMS), the output symbols are statistically independent and the goal is to find a source code that gives the minimum average number of bits per symbol. Shannon's source coding theorem states there can be no lossless source code for a DMS whose average codeword length can be less than its source entropy (i.e., the average information content per symbol). In short, for a DMS, the source entropy provides a bound for the best lossless data compression that can be done.

2.2.1 Text

By ***text***, we mean a collection of alphanumeric characters representing, say, English text, software programs, information data, and mathematical formulas. In digital transmission, each character is converted to a sequence of bits. The text transmitted by a computer is usually encoded using American Standard

Code for Information Interchange (ASCII). Each character in ***ASCII*** is represented by seven bits constituting a unique binary sequence made up of 1s and 0s. Therefore, there are 128 different characters to include all symbols and control functions produced by a typical keyboard or a keypad. An eighth bit, also known as a parity bit, is added for error detection and to make it a byte.

A widely-used compression technique for text is the ***Lempel-Ziv (LZ) algorithm***, which is intrinsically adaptive and capable of encoding groups of characters that occur frequently, while not requiring any advance knowledge of the message statistics. The LZ algorithm is based on parsing the source data stream into segments that are the shortest sequences not encountered previously. The new sequence is encoded in terms of previously seen sequences that have been compiled in a code book (dictionary). An impressive compression of about 55% of ordinary English text can be achieved.

The target BER is a function of the content of the text. For ordinary English text, say a newspaper article, a BER of 10^{-4} may be acceptable, but for a bank statement and fund transfer, a BER of 10^{-10}, or even lower, may be required.

2.2.2 Audio

Audio primarily includes speech and music. Speech is the primary method of human communication. Speech, both produced and perceived, is in analog form. Uttered speech thus needs to be digitized for digital transmission or storage, and converted back to analog to be perceived. The power spectrum (i.e., the distribution of long-term average power versus frequency) of ***speech*** approaches zero for zero frequency and reaches a peak in the neighborhood of a few hundred Hertz (Hz). Therefore, speech processing (i.e., production, transmission, storage, and perception) is very sensitive to frequency. More specifically, the power in speech concentrates in the frequencies 100–800 Hz, above which it declines quite drastically. Only about 1% of the power in speech lies above 4 kHz, and humans can hardly hear voice frequencies outside the 100–4000 Hz range. The power content in 100–800 Hz range generally allows speaker recognition and that in the 800–4000 Hz range allows speech recognition (intelligibility).

Telephone speech requires a bandwidth of about 100–3100 Hz and the analog speech quality typically requires an SNR of about 27–40 dB. Analog speech at the 40-dB quality can be converted into a 64 kilobits per second (kbps) digital signal using an 8-bit pulse-code modulation (PCM) technique. The measure of quality for the bits is BER. As long as the BER falls in the range of 10^{-4} to 10^{-5} or less, it is considered high-quality speech, also known as toll quality. A high-performance, low-rate speech compression technique is based on the human physiological models involved in speech generation. Using digital compression techniques, such as linear prediction coding (LPC), the bit rate requirements for digital speech can be significantly reduced. The 64-kbps rate can be reduced to a range of 1.2 kbps to 13 kbps, depending on the required speech quality. In principle, the resulting bit rate reduction is a function of the complexity of the speech compression method, which in turn is a function of the target application, such as toll-quality voice in telephony and low-quality voice in search and rescue operations. Various LPC techniques now form the basis of many modern cellular vocoders, voice over Internet protocol (VoIP), and other audio ITU-T G-series standards.

A note made by a musical instrument may last for a short time, such as pressing a key on a piano or hitting a prolonged note on a French horn. Typically, music has two structures, a melodic structure consisting of a time sequence of sounds, and a harmonic structure consisting of a set of simultaneous sounds. High-fidelity ***music*** requires a bandwidth of 20–20,000 Hz. We perceive both loudness and musical pitch more or less logarithmically, so a power ratio of 1 dB between two sounds may sound quite small to us. Our most acute hearing takes place over 800–3000 Hz, and it is here that we distinguish different musical instruments and perceive the direction of sound. The two elements that are important in high-fidelity music are the SNR value and the dynamic range.

The bit rate requirement for standard stereo CD-quality music is 1.411 Mbps using a 16-bit PCM technique, which in turn results in an SNR of about 90 dB. A waveform representing music varies relatively slowly, and as such past music samples can be used to rather strongly predict the present sample. Sophisticated digital-conversion methods, such as perceptual encoding employed in MP3 with frequency and temporal masking techniques, can take advantage of this predictability to reduce 1.411 Mbps to tens of kbps. The BER requirement for CD-quality music is about 10^{-9} or less.

2.2.3 Visual

An ***image*** is a two-dimensional array of values that must be reduced to a one-dimensional waveform. This is typically accomplished by the scanning process. The widely-used raster scanning consists of successive lines across the image. Consider scanning, printing, or faxing a standard black-and-white 8.5″ × 11″ page with a modest resolution of 600 dots per inch, where a dot represents a bit one or zero. The number of bits in a page is then about 4.2 megabytes (MB). Well-known compression techniques, such as the Huffman coding—where the number of bits for each outcome is roughly equal in length to the amount of information conveyed by the outcome in question—can be used. Using Huffman coding, the number of bits required for transmission or storage of such a page can be greatly reduced by one to two orders of magnitude. For an 8″ × 10″ color print, with 400 × 400 pixels per square inch and 24 bits per pixel (8 bits for each of the three primary colors of red, green, and blue), the number of bits is then about 38.4 MB. By using image-compression techniques, such as the JPEG image-coding standard for compression of still images, it can be reduced by about two orders of magnitude.

Video is a moving picture, and from a signal-processing standpoint, video is actually a succession of still images. The North American NTSC-TV signal has a bandwidth of 4.2 MHz, which extends down to zero frequency, and requires a 6-MHz channel allocation. Use of direct sampling and quantization leads to an uncompressed digital video signal of about 250 Mbps, provided that there are 30 frames per second, 720 × 480 pixels per image frame, and 24 bits per pixel. The HDTV signal requires an uncompressed digital video stream of about 1.5 Gbps, provided that there are 30 frames per second, 1920 × 1080 pixels per frame, and 24 bits per pixel.

The power of video compression is staggering, as the key to video compression is based on human visual perception. MPEG-2 is a widely-used standard for video compression that supports diverse video-coding applications for a wide range of quality, from VCR to HDTV, depending on the transmission rate. MPEG-2 is a highly popular standard that is used in DVD, HDTV, terrestrial digital video broadcasting (DVB-T), and digital video broadcasting by satellite (DVB-S). MPEG-2 exploits both temporal (inter-frame) and spatial (intra-frame) compression techniques, as a relatively small number of pixels changes from frame to frame and there is a very strong correlation among neighboring pixels on a given frame. Using MPEG-2, the uncompressed digital video for the NTSC-TV and HDTV can be reduced to about 6 Mbps and 19.4 Mbps, respectively, and both can then utilize the allocated 6-MHz bandwidth.

In addition to MPEG standards, there are the ITU-T H-series standards, which compress video at a rate of multiples of 64 kbps in applications such as videophone and videoconferencing. For instance, a close variant of one of these standards, designed for very low bit rate coding applications, is now used in Flash video, a highly popular format for video sharing on Internet sites, such as YouTube. Another example is a versatile standard, developed jointly by ITU-T (International Telecommunications Union-Telecommunication) and MPEG (Moving Picture Experts Group), that supports compressed video applications for a wide range of video quality and bit rates, with applications such as mobile phone service (50–60 kbps), Internet standard-definition video (1–2 Mbps), and Internet high-definition video (5–8 Mbps).

2.3 COMMUNICATION NETWORK MODELS

Communication networks are needed to support a wide range of services, while allowing diverse devices to communicate seamlessly. A fundamental feature to all network architectures is the grouping of communications and related-connection functions into ***layers***. The principles of layering consist of bidirectional communication (i.e., each layer can perform two opposite tasks, one in each direction). Layering simplifies design, implementation, and testing by partitioning the overall communication process into distinct, yet related, parts. Protocols in each layer can be designed separately from those in other layers. Between each pair of layers, there is an interface. It is the interface that defines the services offered by the lower layer to the upper layer. Layering provides flexibility for modifying and evolving protocols and services without having to change layers below.

2.3.1 Layered Architectures

The various important concepts in protocol layering, such as those in the widely-known OSI model and TCP/IP protocol suite, are as follows:

Encapsulation/decapsulation: A technique in which a data unit consisting of a number of bits from one layer is placed within the data field portion of the data unit of another layer is called encapsulation. Encapsulation is done at the source and decapsulation at the destination, whereas at the intermediate points, such as routers, both decapsulation and encapsulation are carried out. The process of encapsulation only narrows the scope of the dependencies between adjacent layers, and the details of the implementation of the other layers are irrelevant.

Addressing: Any communication that involves two parties needs two addresses: a source address and a destination address. Apart from the physical layer, which only consists of bits and does not need addresses, each layer has a pair of addresses. Depending on the layer, some addresses are locally defined and some are global in scope.

Multiplexing/demultiplexing: Multiplexing involves the sharing of a layer by several next-higher layer protocols, one at a time, and demultiplexing means that a layer can decapsulate and deliver a data unit to several next-higher layer protocols.

Before we embark on a brief discussion of the two well-known layered architectures of the OSI model and the TCP/IP protocol suite, as shown in Figure 2.1, a word on the lack of the OSI model's success is in order. The OSI model appeared after the TCP/IP model was fully in place and a lot of resources had been spent, so changing it would cost a great deal. In addition, some of the OSI layers were not fully defined, and the corresponding software was not fully developed. Also, it did not show a high enough level of performance to convince those involved to switch from the TCP/IP protocol suite to the OSI model.

2.3.2 OSI Model

The ***Open Systems Interconnection*** (OSI) model was an international effort by the ***International Organization for Standardization*** (ISO) to enable multivendor computer interconnection over public communication networks. The purpose of the OSI reference model was to provide a framework for the development of protocols. OSI provided a unified view of layers, protocols, and services that is still in use in the development of new protocols. Detailed standards were developed for each layer, but some of these are not in use. It is important to highlight that the roles of certain layers have overlapped. For instance, error detection and correction or encryption and compression, originally assigned to other layers, may be found at the physical layer. The OSI model, as shown in Figure 2.1a, describes a seven-layer abstract reference model

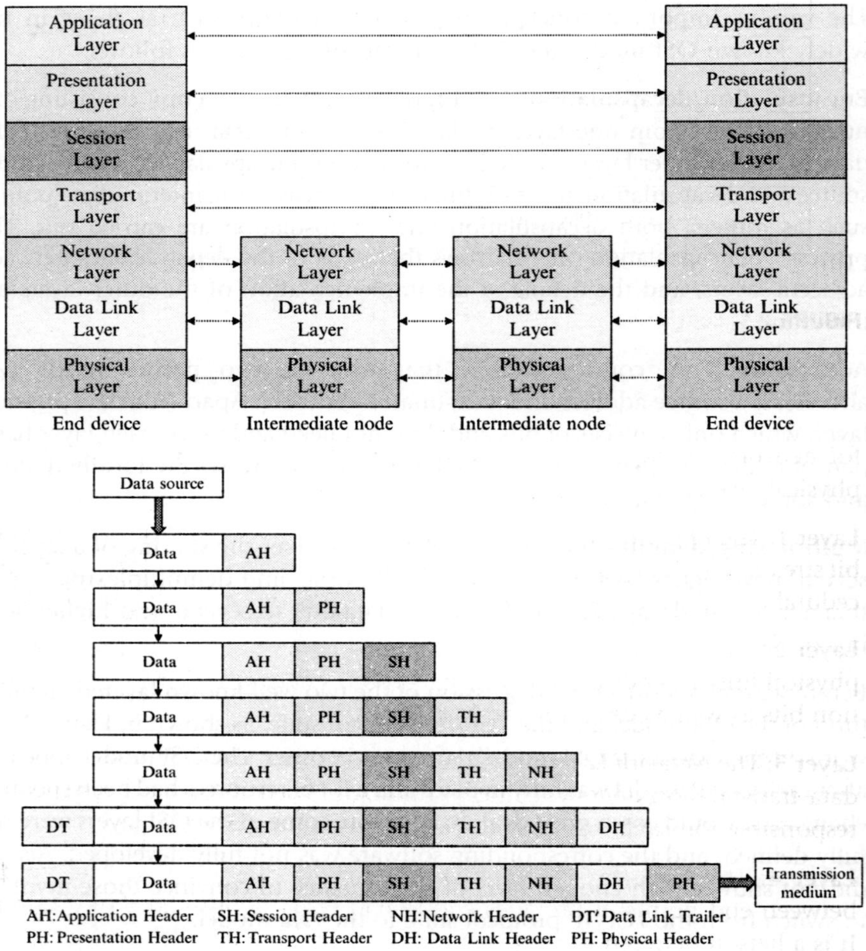

(a)

FIGURE 2.1 Communication network models: (a) the OSI model and

(Continued)

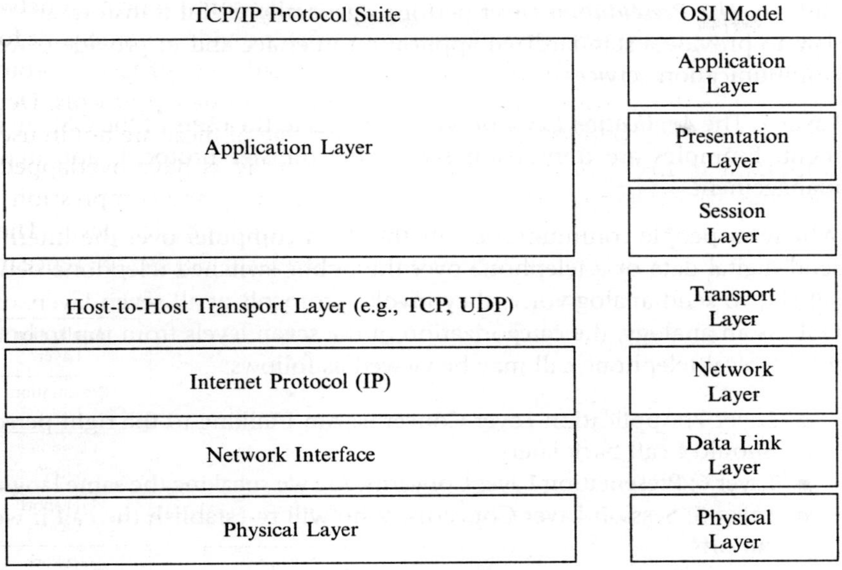

(b)

FIGURE 2.1, cont'd (b) the TCP/IP model.

for network architecture. The focus of this book is primarily on Layer 1, the physical layer.

Layer 1: The ***Physical Layer*** is concerned with the transmission of unstructured bit streams over a physical link; it deals with the mechanical, electrical, and procedural characteristics to establish, maintain, and deactivate the physical link.

Layer 2: The ***Data Link Layer*** provides the reliable transfer of data across the physical link; it sends blocks of data (frames) with the necessary synchronization bits as well as error and flow control bits.

Layer 3: The ***Network Layer*** provides upper layers with independence from the data transmission and switching technologies used to connect systems; it is responsible for establishing, maintaining, and terminating connections.

Layer 4: The ***Transport Layer*** provides reliable, transparent transfer of data between end points; it provides end-to-end error recovery and flow control. It is a liaison between the upper three layers and the lower three layers.

Layer 5: The ***Session Layer*** provides the control structure for communication between applications; it establishes, manages, and terminates connections (sessions) between cooperating applications, and also provides recovery.

Layer 6: The ***Presentation Layer*** performs generally useful transformations on data to provide a standardized application interface and to provide common communication services.

Layer 7: The ***Application Layer*** provides services to the users of the OSI environment. Examples are transaction server, file transfer protocol, and network management.

Whenever people communicate, whether by a computer over the Internet to send digital data or a telephone over the public-switched telephone network (PSTN) to send analog voice, they invoke protocols at all seven layers of the OSI. As an analogy, the categorization of the seven levels from top to bottom for a typical telephone call may be viewed as follows:

- Layer 7: Application Layer Concerns: Am I talking to the right person? Should I call back later?
- Layer 6: Presentation Layer Concerns: Are we speaking the same language?
- Layer 5: Session Layer Concerns: Who will re-establish the call if we are cut off?
- Layer 4: Transport Layer Concerns: What is the most cost-effective way to handle this call?
- Layer 3: Network Layer Concerns: Redial for a busy signal. Disconnect when it is completed.
- Layer 2: Data Link Layer Concerns: Talk or listen when you are supposed to. Ask for a repeat, if needed.
- Layer 1: Physical Layer Concerns: These are the actual sounds spoken and heard.

2.3.3 TCP/IP Protocol Suite

The ***TCP/IP protocol*** suite is the dominant commercial architecture used on the Internet today, and its layers do not match those in the OSI layer, as shown in Figure 2.1b. The TCP/IP consists of four layers in addition to hardware devices. The application layer in the TCP/IP protocol suite is usually considered to be the combination of three layers in the OSI model. The TCP/IP application layer programs are generally run directly over the transport layer. Two basic types of services are offered in the transport layer. The first service consists of a reliable connection-oriented transfer of a stream of bits, which is provided by the ***Transmission Control Protocol (TCP)***, such as e-mail delivery. The second service consists of the best-effort connectionless transfer of individual messages, which is provided by the ***User Datagram Protocol (UDP)***, as used for VoIP. This service provides no mechanisms for error recovery or flow control, so UDP is used for applications that require quick, but not necessarily reliable delivery.

The network layer handles the transfer of information across multiple networks using routers. This layer corresponds to the part of the OSI network layer that is concerned with the transfer of packets between nodes that are connected to different networks. It must therefore deal with the routing of packets from router to router across these networks. The network layer includes the main protocol, the ***Internet Protocol (IP)***, which defines the format of the packet, called a datagram, as well as the format and structure of addresses used in this layer. The IP is responsible for routing a packet from its source to its destination through routers in its path. The IP also has the unicasting and multicasting routing capabilities. The IP is a connectionless protocol that provides no flow control (lack of a mechanism to prevent buffer overflow), no error control (absence of means to reduce errors), and no congestion control (inability to limit packets in transit) services. Should any of these services be required for an application, the application should rely only on the transport layer protocol.

2.4 GUIDED-TRANSMISSION MEDIA

Information transmission across a communication network is accomplished in the physical layer by means of a transmission medium to convey the energy of a signal from a transmitter to a receiver. In telecommunications, transmission media can be divided into two broad categories: guided (wired) and unguided (radio). Guided-transmission media include twisted-pair cable, coaxial cable, and fiber-optic cable, as shown in Figure 2.2, and the unguided-transmission medium is the atmosphere or free space, through which electromagnetic waves are propagated to convey information.

2.4.1 Twisted-Pair Cable

Twisted-pair was designed and built mainly for speech communications. As shown in Figure 2.2a, a twisted-pair cable consists of two insulated conducting (typically copper) wires, closely twisted together to reduce the susceptibility to crosstalk (electrical signals from other adjacent wires) and noise. One of the wires is used to carry signals to the receiver, and the other is used only as a ground reference. The receiver detects the information signal by the voltage difference between the two.

A twisted-pair cable can pass a wide range of frequencies. At a given frequency, a higher gauge (thicker) wire yields a higher signal attenuation. The attenuation for twisted-pair, measured in dB per distance, sharply increases with frequencies above 100 kHz. Since the attenuation per distance is higher for higher frequencies, the bandwidth of twisted-pair decreases with distance. Depending on

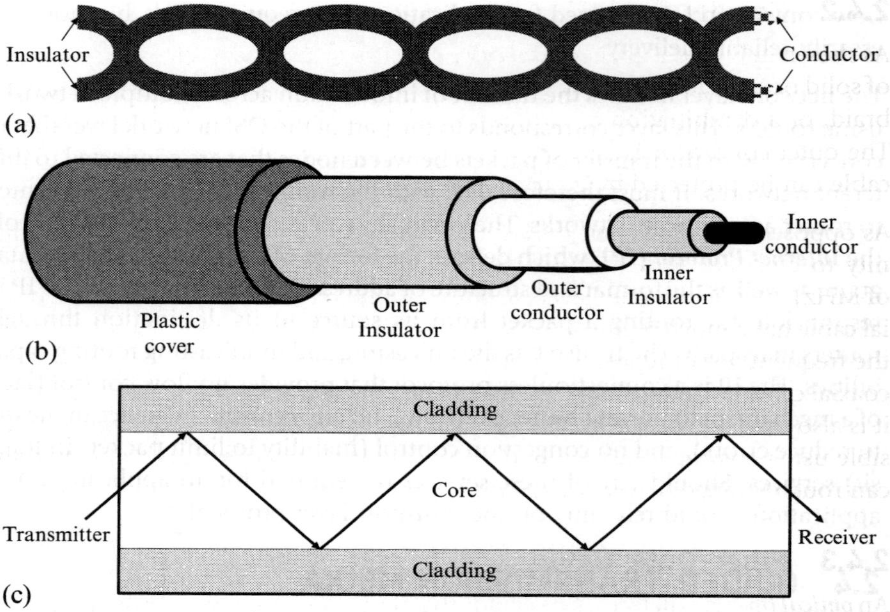

FIGURE 2.2 Guided-transmission media: (a) twisted-pair cable, (b) coaxial cable, and (c) fiber-optic cable.

the gauge of the unshielded twisted-pair, the attenuation can roughly range between 1–4 dB/km at 4 kHz, between 5–10 dB/km at 100 kHz, and 10–20 dB/km at 1 MHz. For digital transmission over a twisted-pair cable, repeaters are required every couple of kilometers.

Twisted-pair cables are used in the telephone network to transmit voice. The ***local loop***, the line connecting subscribers to the central office, consists of unshielded twisted-pair (UTP) cables. To improve voice transmission, the transmission frequencies are limited to 4 kHz to reduce the crosstalk and loading coils are added to provide a flatter transfer function. These factors, not the inherent bandwidth of twisted-pair, limit the digital transmission rate over telephone lines to below approximately 40 kbps.

However, a ***digital subscriber line*** (DSL), which uses a UTP cable, can provide much higher rates for short distances, provided that the user equipment and the interface at the central office are both changed to match the DSL transmission requirements. Besides distance, there are other factors, such as the size of the wire, the signaling type, crosstalk interference from other lines, and the SNR value, which can affect the available bandwidth and in turn the transmission rate. Moreover, twisted-pair cables are used in Ethernet LANs, such as 10Base-T at 10 Mbps, 100Base-TX at 100 Mbps, 1000Base-T at 1 Gbps, capable of carrying various modalities.

2.4.2 Coaxial Cable

As shown in Figure 2.2b, a ***coaxial cable*** consists of an inner (central) conductor of solid or stranded wire (usually copper) and an outer conductor of metal foil, braid, or a combination of two, separated by a dielectric insulating material. The outer conductor is also enclosed in an insulating sheath, and the whole cable can be protected by a plastic cover.

As opposed to twisted-pair cables, coaxial cables provide much better immunity to crosstalk and interference, offer much larger bandwidths (hundreds of MHz), but yield higher levels of attenuation. In other words, although coaxial cable has a much higher bandwidth, the signal weakens rapidly and requires the frequent use of repeaters, roughly every kilometer or so. The widest use of coaxial cable is for the distribution of television signals in cable TV systems, and it is also used for local area networks (LANs). Rates up to tens of Mbps are feasible using coaxial cables, with 10 Mbps being the standard. The attenuation can roughly range between 7–27 dB/km at 10 MHz.

2.4.3 Fiber-Optic Cable

An ***optical fiber*** is a dielectric waveguide that transports light signals just as metallic (twisted-pair or coaxial) cable transports electrical signals. As shown in Figure 2.2c, an optical fiber consists of a very fine cylinder of glass (core) surrounded by a concentric layer of glass (cladding). The core has a slightly higher optical density (index of refraction) than the cladding. Therefore, when a ray of light from the core approaches the cladding, the ray is completely reflected back into the core, and the ray of light is guided within the fiber. Information is transmitted by varying the intensity of the light source with the message signal. The light in the fiber is periodically amplified and regenerated by repeaters along the transmission path, and at the receiver, the light intensity is detected by a photodiode.

There are two types of optical fibers, the low-cost multimode fibers and the low-loss single-mode fibers. A ***multimode fiber*** has a ray of light that can reach the receiver over multiple paths. Since each path has its own delay, the differences in delays cause interference. This limits the maximum bit rates that are achievable using multimode fibers. In a ***single-mode fiber*** where the core of fiber is much narrower, the single mode propagates with low loss and dispersion, thus requiring much fewer repeaters. Sources of noise in fiber-optic cables are photodiodes and electronic amplifiers. Optical fibers have unique characteristics, such as an enormous potential bandwidth, low transmission losses, immunity to electromagnetic interference, small size and weight, ruggedness, and flexibility. Optical fiber transmission systems are widely deployed in backbone networks, and can provide nearly error-free transmission rates up to several hundred Gbps over tens of kilometers, as typical attenuation is about 0.2–0.5 dB/km.

2.5 RADIO TRANSMISSION

Radio encompasses the electromagnetic spectrum in the range of 3 kHz to 300 GHz. Radio transmission uses an unguided medium, and may possess principal benefits, but at the expense of some major shortcomings.

2.5.1 Advantages of Radio

Salient benefits of radio transmission are as follows:

- Radio uniquely allows the realization and deployment of mobile systems with a multitude of diverse wireless applications and services.
- Radio inherently possesses broadcast, narrowcast, and multicast capabilities.
- Radio networks can be quickly implemented or reconfigured and extra terminals can be easily introduced or removed.
- Radio systems do not require right-of-way and can be deployed by procuring only the sites where the antennas are located.
- Signal level can be maintained over much longer distances in radio systems than in wired systems, as with an increase in the distance, the attenuation in decibels increases only logarithmically in radio systems but linearly in wired systems.

2.5.2 Disadvantages of Radio

The major drawbacks of radio transmission are as follows:

- The radio spectrum is finite and scarce and, unlike wired media, it is not possible to procure additional capacity. An operating frequency in a radio band can be reused only in sufficiently-distant geographical areas or by certain multiple access schemes.
- To maximize its utility, the radio spectrum is mainly regulated by government agencies, as regulatory bodies apply strict requirements on the emission characteristics of radio communication equipment, and frequency coordination is generally required when planning radio systems.
- Interference, which is the energy that appears at the receiver from sources other than its own transmitter, is a major degradation in radio systems.
- Path characteristics (i.e., attenuation and distortion) tend to vary with time, often in an unpredictable way. Multipath fading, a significant impairment in radio communications especially in mobile systems, occurs when the transmitted signal arrives at the receiver via propagation paths at different delays.
- Signals can be much more easily intercepted in wireless systems than in wired systems; it is thus a more challenging task to make radio-based systems more secure.

2.5.3 Radio Spectrum

It is imperative to highlight that spectrum is a very scarce commodity, and efficient use of any part of spectrum is of paramount importance. ***Radio spectrum*** refers to the part of the electromagnetic spectrum corresponding to radio frequencies—i.e., frequencies lower than around 300 GHz (or, equivalently, wavelengths longer than about 1 mm). Frequency assignments and technical standards are set internationally by the ***International Telecommunications Union*** (ITU). The Radiocommunication Sector of ITU (ITU-R) provides frequency assignments and is concerned with the efficient use of the radio frequency spectrum.

Table 2.1 shows the frequency bands and some of their major aspects. The frequency bands are designated in logarithmic frequency and the progression of frequency bands has increasingly larger bandwidths. For instance, the MF band (from 0.3–3 MHz) has a bandwidth of 2.7 MHz, whereas the VHF band (from 30–300 MHz) has a bandwidth of 270 MHz. Higher bandwidths can generally lend themselves to higher system capacities and transmission rates as well as lower levels of interference and bit error rates, but at the expense of higher signal attenuation and equipment complexity.

Table 2.1 Frequency bands

Frequency band	Frequency range	Wavelength range	Transmission media	Propagation mode
Extra-Low Frequency (ELF)	3–30 Hz	100,000–10,000 km	Wire pairs	Ground wave
Super-Low Frequency (SLF)	30–300 Hz	10,000–1,000 km	Wire pairs	Ground wave
Ultra-Low Frequency (ULF)	300–3 kHz	1,000–100 km	Wire pairs	Ground wave
Very-Low Frequency (VLF)	3–30 kHz	100–10 km	Wire pairs	Ground wave
Low Frequency (LF)	30–300 kHz	10–1 km	Wire pairs	Ground wave
Medium Frequency (MF)	0.3–3 MHz	1–0.1 km	Wire pairs & coaxial cable	Ground wave & sky wave
High Frequency (HF)	3–30 MHz	100–10 m	Coaxial cable	Sky wave
Very-High Frequency (VHF)	30–300 MHz	10–1 m	Coaxial cable	Sky wave & line of sight
Ultra-High Frequency (UHF)	0.3–3 GHz	1–0.1 m	Coaxial cable & waveguide	Line of sight
Super-High Frequency (SHF)	3–30 GHz	100–10 mm	Waveguide	Line of sight
Extra-High Frequency (EHF)	30–300 GHz	10–1 mm	Waveguide	Line of sight
Infrared	0.3–430 THz	1 mm–700 nm	Optical fibers	Laser beams
Visible Light	430–750 THz	700–400 nm	Optical fibers	Laser beams
Ultraviolet	0.75–30 PHz	400–10 nm	Optical fibers	Laser beams

Some parts of spectrum have been designated as ***industrial, scientific, and medical (ISM) bands***. There are a dozen ISM bands, such as 2.4–2.5 GHz and 5.725–5.875 GHz. These bands allow limited power transmission from various transmitting devices as well as unintentional radiations, such as microwave ovens, and short-range, low-power communication systems, including Wi-Fi, Bluetooth devices, and cordless phones. The communication equipment operating in ISM bands must tolerate any interference generated by other ISM equipment as users have no regulatory protection.

The energy in a radio frequency (RF) current can radiate off a conductor into space as electromagnetic waves (radio waves). This is the basis of radio technology. In radio communications, the signal is transmitted using an antenna that radiates energy at some carrier frequency and is received by another antenna. The propagation characteristics of electromagnetic waves used in radio channels are highly dependent on the operating frequency. Under similar conditions of propagation, the higher-frequency signal attenuates faster than the lower-frequency signal and becomes too weak to be detected at the receiver. An RF power amplifier is used to amplify the power level of such a transmitted signal, so that it can travel larger distances with less attenuation. Also, the higher the operating frequency is, the more directive the antenna beam becomes.

2.5.4 Wave Propagation

Like light waves, radio signals by nature travel in a straight line, and therefore propagation beyond line of sight requires a means of deflecting the radio waves. The available methods are ***reflection*** (when the radio signal is bounced off a surface), ***refraction*** (when the radio signal bends due to a change in medium), ***diffraction*** (when the radio signal meets a sharp edge and redirects), and ***scattering*** (when the radio signal spreads out). For any type of radio communications, the signal disperses with distance. The signal attenuation in free space is inversely related to the square of the distance that the radio signal must travel as well as the square of the frequency that the radio signal is operating at.

Depending on the frequency and antenna, the radiated energy can propagate in either a unidirectional or omnidirectional fashion. In the former case, a properly-aligned antenna can receive the modulated signal, and in the latter case, any antenna in the area of coverage can receive the signal. In general, radio frequencies below 1 GHz or so are more suitable for omnidirectional applications and above 1 GHz or so are typically tailored for unidirectional applications. Also, at low and medium frequencies, radio waves can penetrate walls. This is viewed as an advantage when a signal is required to be received inside a building and is regarded as a disadvantage when it is required to isolate a communication to just inside or outside a building to reduce the level of interference.

The range of 300 MHz to 300 GHz is known as ***microwave radio frequencies***. Rain attenuation, which refers primarily to the absorption of a microwave frequency signal by atmospheric rain, snow, or ice, is a dominant source of signal degradation. Rain attenuation is a function of many factors, such as location, distance, elevation angle, and frequency. Rain attenuation is directly related to frequency (i.e., the higher the operating frequency, the more severe the rain attenuation can be).

Radio waves at different frequencies propagate in different ways. As shown in Figure 2.3, there are three distinct methods for the transmission of radio signals: ground-wave propagation, sky-wave propagation, and line-of-sight propagation.

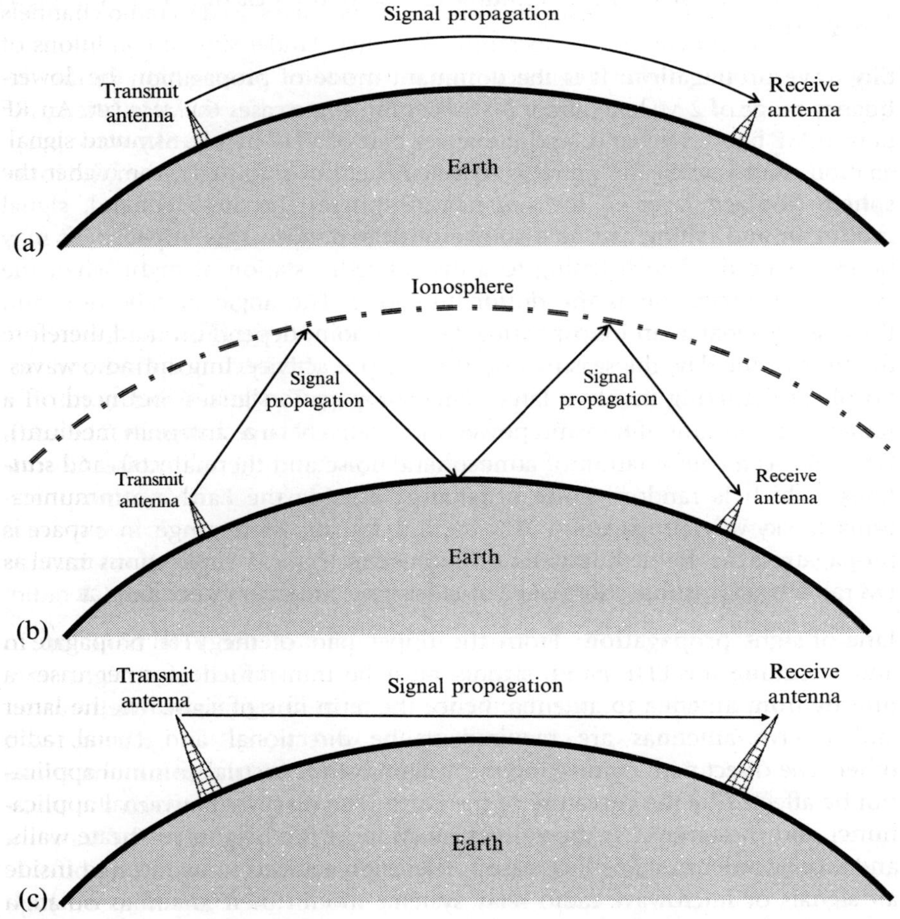

FIGURE 2.3 Radio propagation modes: (a) ground-wave propagation, (b) sky-wave propagation, and (c) line-of-sight propagation.

Ground-wave propagation: It is the dominant mode of propagation for frequencies below 2 MHz (all bands up to and including the lower part of MF band). In this frequency range, the Earth and the ionosphere (the layer of atmosphere where particles exist as ions) act as a waveguide for radio wave propagation. These low-frequency signals propagate (by diffraction) in all directions around the curved surface of the Earth for thousands of kilometers. Distance depends on the amount of power in the signal. Since the ground is not a perfect electrical conductor, ground waves are attenuated rapidly as they follow the Earth's surface. The signal attenuation is a function of time and the frequency band. Also, the atmospheric noise level is rather high. The channel bandwidths available in these frequency bands are rather modest and in turn yield rather low transmission speeds. Typical applications include long-range navigation and maritime communications, radio beacon, and AM radio broadcasting.

Sky-wave propagation: It is the dominant mode of propagation in the frequency range of 2 MHz to about 30 MHz or in some cases 60 MHz (the upper part of MF band, HF band, and the lower part of VHF band). Sky-wave propagation results when the signal is reflected (bent or refracted) from the ionosphere (ionized layer of the upper atmosphere). In the HF band, signal multipath and fading can be a source of degradation. This impairment may be experienced when listening to a distant radio station at night when the sky-wave propagation is the dominant mode. The angle of reflection and the loss of signal at an ionospheric reflection point depend on the frequency, the time of the day, the season, and the sunspot activity. Ionosphere and troposphere scattering involves large signal propagation losses and requires a rather large amount of transmit power and relatively large antennas. The additive noise is a combination of atmospheric noise and thermal noise. Cosmic noise, which is random noise originating outside the Earth's atmosphere, impacts sky-way propagation. The typical transmission range in sky-wave propagation can be in hundreds of kilometers. Typical applications include FM radio broadcasting, short-wave broadcasting, amateur radio, and CB radio.

Line-of-sight propagation: From the upper part of the VHF band up to and including the EHF band, signals must be transmitted in straight lines directly from antenna to antenna, hence the term line of sight. The transmit and receive antennas are required to be directional and facing each other. The direct path connecting the antennas in terrestrial communications can be affected by the curvature of the Earth. The distance between the transmitter and the receiver is therefore a function of the heights of the transmit and receive antennas. For this reason, television stations transmitting off-the-air signals or microwave radio relay systems mount their antennas on high towers or buildings to reach a broad coverage area. Specifically, for terrestrial communications, the maximum distance between transmit and receive antennas for direct line-of-sight radio propagation is about $D=\sqrt{17}\left(\sqrt{H_T}+\sqrt{H_R}\right)$, where H_T and H_R are the heights of transmit and receive antennas in meters, respectively, and D is the maximum distance in kilometers over which communications between them can take place by direct line-of-sight radio signals. Applications include off-the-air (VHF and UHF) TV broadcasting, which are examples of line-of-sight terrestrial communications, and satellite TV broadcasting and VSAT networks, which are examples of line-of-sight satellite communications.

2.6 TRANSMISSION IMPAIRMENTS

Signals travel though transmission media that are not perfect. The received signal is therefore different from the transmitted one. There are a few major causes for transmission impairments. Figure 2.4 shows an example of various degradations.

2.6.1 Attenuation

Every channel introduces some transmission ***attenuation (loss)***. By increasing the physical distance between the transmitter and the receiver, the signal power (strength) at the receiver decreases. This loss is due to overcoming the resistance of the medium. For wired media, attenuation has an exponential dependence on distance, i.e., the attenuation in dB increases linearly with the distance, whereas for wireless systems the attenuation in dB increases logarithmically with the distance.

As an example, suppose for a given distance the loss in a guided medium and an unguided medium are both x dB. If we increase the distance by a factor of 1000, then the loss in the guided medium is $1000x$ dB, whereas that in the unguided medium is only $x + 10\log 1000 = x + 30\,\text{dB}$. Thus, the signal level is more attenuated in wired systems than in wireless systems. To compensate for transmission loss, amplifiers must be used to enhance the signal level; however, amplification can then boost other types of degradations, such as noise and interference levels, as well.

2.6.2 Distortion

Due to the non-ideal channel, the transmitted signal changes its form or shape, thus resulting in signal perturbation. This is known as ***distortion***. Unlike noise

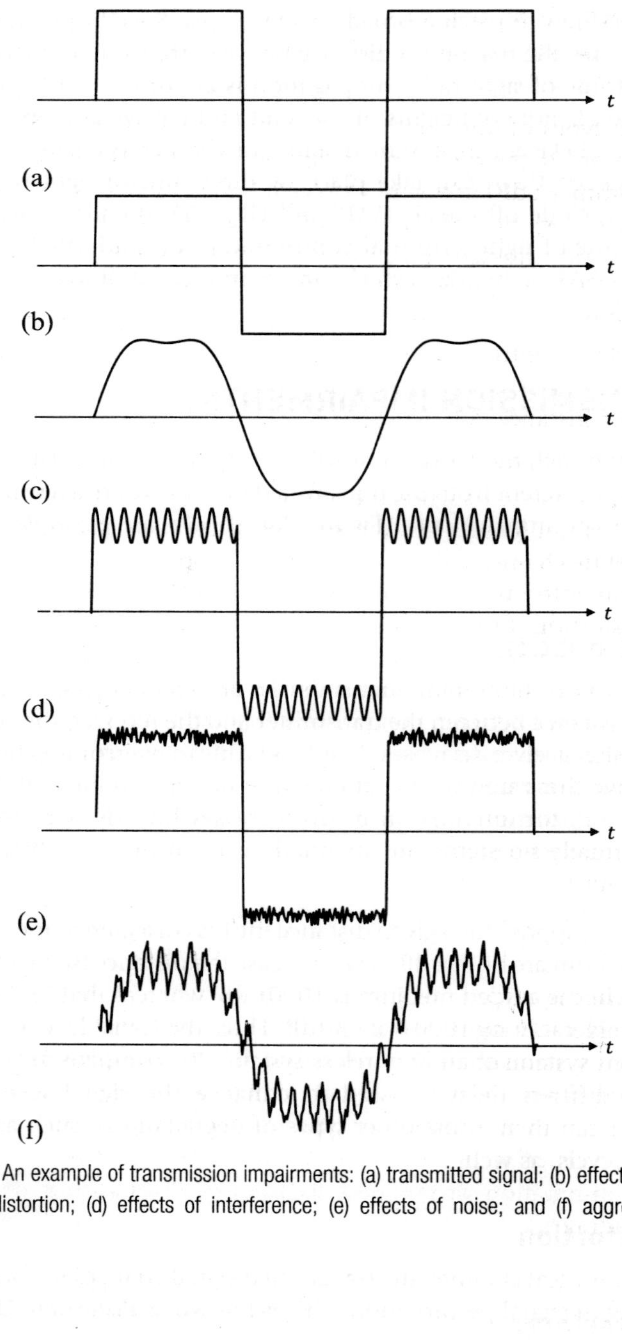

FIGURE 2.4 An example of transmission impairments: (a) transmitted signal; (b) effects of attenuation; (c) effects of distortion; (d) effects of interference; (e) effects of noise; and (f) aggregate effects of impairments.

and interference, distortion disappears when the signal is turned off. The distinct types of distortion are linear distortion, nonlinear distortion, and multipath fading.

There are two types of ***linear distortions***: amplitude distortion and phase (or delay) distortion. If the amplitude response of the channel is not constant (or almost within ± 1 dB) in the message band, the result is ***amplitude distortion*** and if the phase response of the channel is not linear (i.e., various frequency components of the message signal suffer different amounts of delay), the result is then ***phase (delay) distortion***. Delay distortion is a critical problem in data and video transmission, but the human ear is surprisingly insensitive to it. Wired telephone channels introduce linear distortion, which can result in intersymbol interference. However, equalizers can significantly mitigate the impact of linear distortion. For instance, adaptive equalization is employed in all high-speed voice-band data modems.

Nonlinear distortion occurs when the relationship between the input signal and output signal is not linear (i.e., the superposition principle is not held). For instance, satellite channels, due to the use of high-power amplifiers (e.g., SSPA or TWTA) can introduce nonlinear distortion. Practical amplifiers produce nonlinear distortion if the input amplitude is large. In practice, the output of the amplifier becomes saturated at some value as the amplitude of the input signal is increased. Nonlinear distortion brings about ***intermodulation*** (i.e., the output has new frequency components that are not present in the spectrum of the input signal but now lie inside the signal bandwidth). Filtering therefore cannot remove these unwanted frequency components. One method to mitigate nonlinear distortion is to employ input signals that have a constant envelope (i.e., virtually no signal fluctuations). Another one is to keep the signal amplitude within the linear operating range of the transfer characteristic by using companding (i.e., a compressor before the nonlinear channel and an expander right after it).

Multipath fading is a type of degradation that occurs in radio communications, and it is considerably more prevalent in mobile radio systems. It occurs when more than one version of the transmitted signal arrives at the receiver, generally all with very different delays. Multipath fading can result in very wide fluctuations in the random amplitude and phase of the received signal and generally yield a severe amount of intersymbol interference. The receiver must thus employ a combination of complex techniques to minimize the impact of multipath fading.

2.6.3 Interference

Interference refers to energy that appears at the receiver from sources other than its own transmitter. It can manifest itself in wired cables in the form of crosstalk and echo, but it is significantly more dominant in radio communications. Interference can be generated by other users of the same frequency or by equipment that inadvertently transmits energy outside its band and into the bands of adjacent channels or systems.

There are various ways to practically remove or significantly minimize radio interference in most cases. They include appropriate filtering with stringent requirements, appropriately-placed physical barriers, transmit and receive antennas with high directivity, spatial (geographical) separation between wanted and interfering sources, and strict requirements set by regulatory bodies on the emission properties of equipment.

2.6.4 Noise

Noise refers to unwanted, ever-present, random waves that tend to disturb the transmission and processing of signals in a communication system, thus yielding a corrupted version of the transmitted signal. There are several types of noise, such as ***thermal noise*** (due to the random motion of electrons in a conductor), ***shot noise*** (due to the discrete nature of current flow in electronic devices), and ***impulse noise*** (due to natural sources, such as lightning, and man-made sources, such as high-voltage power lines).

Noise is generally assumed to be added to the signal. Filtering can be used to maximize SNR at the receiver (i.e., it can reduce noise contamination), but there inevitably remains some amount of noise that cannot be eliminated. Moreover, due to the central limit theorem, the aggregate of a number of different noises can be assumed to have a Gaussian distribution. It is also generally assumed that noise is white and thus emanates an equal amount of noise power per unit bandwidth at all frequencies. To this effect, ***additive white Gaussian noise*** (AWGN) is the most common type of noise considered in digital communication systems, and constitutes one of the most fundamental system limitations. The effects of noise cannot be eliminated, but by appropriate filtering the SNR value can be maximized.

2.7 MODULATION PROCESS

Modulation is defined as a process through which an information-bearing message (i.e., modulating) signal is used to modify (i.e., modulate) some parameter (e.g., amplitude, frequency, phase) of a periodic (such as a high-frequency sinusoidal) signal known as a carrier wave, individually or in combination, to produce the modulated signal for transmission. This is similar to when a musician modulates a tone by varying its volume (amplitude), its timing (phase), and its pitch (frequency).

We have three distinct modulation categories: ***amplitude modulation*** (AM), ***frequency modulation*** (FM), and ***phase modulation*** (PM). However, in the context of digital communications, the term ***shift keying*** is generally used instead of the word modulation. To this effect, we have ***amplitude-shift keying*** (ASK), ***frequency-shift keying*** (FSK), and ***phase-shift keying*** (PSK). There is also another category in digital communications, which is a hybrid of ASK and PSK, known as ***quadrature amplitude modulation*** (QAM). It is important to note that PSK and QAM are used in digital communication systems far more often than ASK and FSK. In some cases, the modulated signal is simply related to the message signal, such as with ASK, and in some cases, the relationship is rather complicated, such as with QAM.

A ***modem*** is a device that provides two-way communications, and thus performs both modulation in the transmitter and demodulation (i.e., the inverse operation of modulation) in the receiver. Modulation is performed to achieve one or more of the following objectives:

Modulation for efficient radio transmission: For radio communications, antennas are needed to radiate (transmit) and receive the modulated signal. The size of the antenna depends on the wavelength and the application. Modulation helps translate the message signal with low frequency components into a signal with much higher frequency components. The resulting modulated signal can thus possess a much smaller wavelength, and that in turn allows much smaller antennas. The signal wavelength λ can be found using $\lambda = \frac{c}{f}$, where f is the signal frequency in Hertz (Hz), c is the speed of light in meters per second (mps), and λ in meters (m). As an example, efficient electromagnetic radiation for line-of-sight radio propagation generally requires antennas whose physical dimensions are at least 10% of the signal's wavelength. Therefore, an audio signal with frequency components up to 100 Hz requires an antenna about 300 km, but with modulation at 300 MHz, the antenna needs to be only about 10 cm long. Another example is that for cellular mobile telephones, antennas are typically 25% of the signal wavelength, so for the above-mentioned audio signal, an antenna spanning 750 km would be required, but with modulation at 900 MHz, the equivalent antenna diameter would be only about 8 cm.

Modulation to match channel characteristics: Modulation allows modification of the message signal to a form suited to the characteristics of the transmission channel. The majority of practical channels have bandpass characteristics and modulation translates the frequency components of the lowpass message signal to the passband range, so the spectrum of the transmitted signal can match the characteristics of the channel. Applications may include satellite TV, in which baseband video signals with frequency components up to 6 MHz are converted into RF signals operating at 14 GHz, and cellular phones, in which baseband speech signals with frequency components up to 4 kHz are converted into RF signals operating at 900 MHz.

Modulation for frequency assignment: Modulation allows many radio and television stations to broadcast simultaneously in a given geographical area. Since each station has a different assigned carrier frequency, the desired broadcast signals can be separated from others by tuning the receiver to select different stations as required.

Modulation for multiplexing: When more than one signal needs to utilize a single channel, modulation may be used to translate different signals to different spectral locations. Applications include FM stereophonic broadcasting, in which the sum of the right-hand and left-hand signals and their differences are accommodated into a single channel, and cable TV, in which a number of TV channels along with the upstream and downstream Internet traffic are all integrated into a single channel.

Modulation to allow common processing: Sometimes the frequency range of the signal to be processed and the frequency range of the processing device do not match, and the processing device is complex. Modulation allows the processing equipment to operate in some fixed frequency range and instead translate the frequency range of the signal to correspond to the fixed frequency range of the processing equipment. This is the case when in a system, such as AM radio, all RF signals coming from various AM radio stations are converted to a certain intermediate-frequency (IF) in a receiver.

Modulation to overcome hardware limitations: The performance, design, and cost of some signal-processing devices, such as filters and amplifiers, often depend on the signal spectral location and the ratio of the highest to lowest signal frequencies. It is generally desirable to keep the ratio of signal bandwidth to its center frequency within 1–10%. Modulation can be therefore used to translate the signal to a location in the frequency domain where design requirements can be better met.

Modulation to reduce noise and interference: The effect of noise and interference cannot be completely eliminated in a communication system. However, by significantly expanding the bandwidth of the transmitted signal, the noise and interference immunity in some cases can be considerably enhanced. In other words, bandwidth increase is traded for noise and interference reduction. Applications include FM radio and spread spectrum techniques.

Modulation to allow design trade-offs: Modulation techniques, employing digital *M*-ary (vis-à-vis binary) signaling, can provide a balancing act to optimally achieve digital communication design objectives, such as higher transmission rate, lower transmit power, smaller signal bandwidth, lower bit error rate, and more modest complexity. By increasing *M*, bandwidth can be saved at the expense of an increase in bit error rate. By using trellis-coded modulation, transmission rate can be enhanced, not with an increase in bandwidth but at the expense of increased modem complexity.

2.8 FUNDAMENTAL LIMITS IN DIGITAL TRANSMISSION

The quality of digital transmission can be determined by two parameters: the ***transmission bit rate*** and the ***bit error rate*** (i.e., the fraction of bits that are received in error). Obviously, the smaller the bit error rate is, the more reliable the digital communication system is. In principle, it is possible to design a system that operates with zero bit error rate even though the channel is noisy. These two parameters in turn can be determined by the channel bandwidth W, measured in Hz, and the signal-to-noise ratio at the receiver input, where the average signal power S and the average noise power N are both measured in watts (W). Shannon addressed the question of determining the maximum achievable bit rate at which essentially error-free transmission is possible over an ideal channel of bandwidth W Hz and of a given signal-to-noise ratio, i.e., $\left(\frac{S}{N}\right)$, by using sufficiently complex channel coding. Shannon stated that the channel capacity for a band-limited, power-limited channel with additive white Gaussian noise (AWGN) is given by the following formula:

$$C = W\log_2\left(1 + \frac{S}{N}\right) = W\log_2\left(1 + \left(\frac{E_b}{N_o}\right)\left(\frac{R}{W}\right)\right) \tag{2.1}$$

Note that the capacity C is in bits per second (bps), the limited bandwidth W is in Hz, the signal-to-noise ratio $\frac{S}{N}$ is in a linear (not logarithmic) scale, and the logarithm is to the base 2. We also have $N = N_0 W$, where N_0 represents the noise power spectral density in Watts/Hz, and $S = RE_b$, where R represents the bit rate in bps and E_b is the bit energy in Joules (J). The bit error rate can be made arbitrarily small only if the transmission rate R is less than the channel capacity C. However, the Shannon's information capacity theorem does not say how to design the system. The larger the ratio $\frac{R}{C}$ is, the more efficient the system is.

2.9 DIGITAL COMMUNICATION DESIGN ASPECTS

In a communication system, whether analog or digital, there are two primary resources: transmitted power and channel bandwidth. The transmitted power is the average power of the transmitted signal. The channel bandwidth reflects the band of significant frequency components allocated for the transmission of the input (message) signal. One of these two resources may be more precious than the other; hence communication channels are generally classified as band-limited, such as the plain old telephone system (POTS), or power-limited, such as optical fiber links and satellite channels. Each of these two premium resources can have a very significant bearing on many system aspects.

The digital communication ***design objectives*** are many, but not all of equal importance; some are required and some are desirable. Some are more difficult than others to achieve, so further resources and additional complexities are needed to accommodate them. Table 2.2 provides a list of digital communication design objectives.

It is virtually impossible to achieve all digital communication design objectives simultaneously, because they are all inherently inter-related and in fact some are clearly in conflict with other design imperatives, so difficult trade-offs must be made. For instance, high-speed transmission is in conflict with low channel bandwidth, and low bit error rate is in conflict with low transmit power.

There are some unyielding ***design constraints*** that necessitate the trading off of any one system requirement with each of the others. Some constraints must be satisfied, such as those dictated by theorems in communication theory or required by governments, and some are desirable, such as those required by the users. Table 2.2 also provides a list of digital communication design constraints.

Design of digital communication systems and networks thus present many challenges, as it is a multidimensional, nonlinear, constrained optimization problem. It is imperative to emphasize that there are many system variables and parameters representing a multitude of constraints, some of which cannot be easily quantified and directly factored into a design, and there are a host of conflicting design objectives that all need to be fully met, and only some, but not all, can be accommodated.

Table 2.2 Digital communication design objectives and constraints

Design objectives	Design constraints
▪ Maximize transmission rate (bps)	▪ The Shannon capacity theorem (and the Shannon limit)
▪ Minimize bit error rate	▪ The Nyquist theoretical minimum bandwidth requirement
▪ Minimize signal bandwidth (Hz)	▪ Source entropy for lossless compression
▪ Minimize transmit power (W)	▪ Subjective perception for lossy compression
▪ Maximize system throughput	▪ Government regulations (e.g., frequency allocations and coordination)
▪ Minimize overhead and signaling bits	▪ Technological limitations (e.g., state-of-the-art components)
▪ Minimize noise and interference (W)	▪ Laws of nature (e.g., multipath fading, ionospheric propagation)
▪ Minimize overall delay (s)	▪ De jure and de facto standards (e.g., IEEE, ISO, Bluetooth)
▪ Minimize jitter (s)	▪ User device specifications (e.g., aesthetics, size, weight, cost)
▪ Maximize system security	▪ User interface requirements (e.g., user-friendly features)
▪ Maximize system flexibility	▪ Mass, power and real estate envelopes (e.g., satellite buses)
▪ Maximize system capacity (bps)	▪ Networking requirements (e.g., mobile service coverage)
▪ Minimize computational load	▪ Radiation restrictions (e.g., acceptable health hazard in mobile devices)
▪ Minimize system complexity	▪ Service and traffic differentiation (e.g., user and application priority)
▪ Maximize system utilization	▪ Maintainability (e.g., ease of testing, monitoring and control)
▪ Maximize system reliability	▪ Upgrade requirements (e.g., forward and backward compatibility)
▪ Minimize system cost ($)	▪ Application requirements (e.g., traffic patterns and characteristics)
▪ Minimize access/usage fee ($)	▪ Market considerations (e.g., risks, economies of scale, affordability)

Summary and Sources

In this chapter, the emphasis was on highlighting major aspects of digital communications. We thus briefly provided some to-the-point descriptions and intuitive explanations of various concepts involved in an end-to-end digital communication system. The crux of what was briefly discussed here, though a bit abstract in tone and coverage, will be expanded later. Before embarking on a quantitative discussion and detailed analysis of essential components of digital communication systems, some basic mathematical tools to understand, analyze, and design digital communication systems are needed, which are provided in the subsequent two chapters.

The current status of the pervasive digital communication application and technology is due to the cumulative impacts of the significant contributions made, by quite many for so long, to the field of digital communications from both transmission and networking aspects. It is a well-known fact, however, that the Shannon's exceptional contribution [1] laid the unique foundation for the field, and the impact of his extraordinary work will always remain unparalleled. There are many excellent books, in both areas of digital transmission systems and communication networks, which discuss in detail the topics briefly highlighted in this chapter, including references [2–5] on digital transmission and [6–9] on communication networks.

[1] C.E. Shannon, A mathematical theory of communication, *Bell Syst. Tech. J.* 27 (July, October, 1948) 379–423, 623–656.

[2] R.W. Lucky, J. Salz, and E.J. Weldon Jr., *Principles of Data Communication*, McGraw-Hill, ISBN: 007-038960-8, 1968.

[3] R.D. Gitlin, J.F. Hayes, and S.B. Weinstein, *Data Communications Principles*, Plenum Press, ISBN: 0-306-43777-5, 1992.

[4] B. Sklar, *Digital Communications Fundamentals and Applications*, second ed., Prentice-Hall, ISBN: 0-13-084788-7, 2001.

[5] J.G. Proakis and M. Salehi, *Digital Communications*, fifth ed., McGraw-Hill, ISBN: 978-0-07-295716-7, 2008.

[6] A. Leon-Garcia and I. Widjaja, *Communication Networks - Fundamental Concepts and Key Architectures*, second ed., McGraw-Hill, ISBN: 0-07-119848-2, 2004.

[7] B.A. Forouzan, *Data Communications and Networking*, fifth ed., McGraw-Hill, ISBN: 978-0-07-337622-6, 2013.

[8] W. Stallings, *Data and Computer Communications*, ninth ed., Prentice-Hall, ISBN: 978-0-13-139205-2, 2011.

[9] G.E. Friend, J.L. Fike, C. Baker, and J. Bellamy, *Understanding Data Communications*, Longman Higher Education, ISBN: 9780672270192, 1987.

CHAPTER 3

Signals, Systems, and Spectral Analysis

INTRODUCTION

This chapter begins with basic operations on signals. Signals and systems from various points of interest are classified and their applications in digital communications are highlighted. Sinusoidal signals and signals through which practical signals can be formed are reviewed. To introduce the important concepts of frequency and bandwidth, an extensive discussion of the Fourier series and transform, along with their properties and applications, is presented. Time and frequency relations are discussed and various definitions of bandwidth are provided. We then turn our focus on transmission of lowpass and bandpass signals, as well as various types of distortions and filters. After studying this chapter and understanding all relevant concepts and examples, students should be able to do the following:

1. Know how to scale up/down, add, multiply, differentiate, and integrate signals.
2. Understand how to time shift and time scale signals.
3. Apply the precedence rule in operations performed on independent variables.
4. Classify signals from different perspectives.
5. Describe analog and digital signals and their sources.
6. Determine the period and fundamental frequency of a periodic signal.
7. Evaluate the energy and power of a signal.
8. Discuss the classification of systems from different perspectives.
9. Differentiate between the concepts of system analysis and system design.
10. Grasp all relevant aspects of linear time-invariant systems.
11. Appreciate sinusoidal signals and their unique roles in communications.
12. Identify various representations of the Fourier series.
13. State how to find the Fourier transform of a signal.
14. Connect the concepts of the Fourier series and Fourier transform.

CONTENTS

15. Summarize the importance and applications of the Fourier transform properties.
16. Provide various definitions of bandwidth and time-bandwidth product.
17. Characterize the impact of systems on signals.
18. Analyze the effects of various types of distortions and communication filters.
19. Define autocorrelation and spectral density functions.
20. Outline various representations of bandpass signals.

3.1 BASIC OPERATIONS ON SIGNALS

In communications, any time-varying physical phenomenon that conveys information is referred to as a ***signal***. Examples include signals with useful information, such as human voices, MP3 music, JPEG images, seismic signals, CT scans, ECG signals, and MPEG videos, or signals that are considered useless and unwanted, such as noise and interference.

Our focus here is on one-dimensional signals defined by single-valued functions of time; that is, for every instant of time, there is a unique value of the function. In our analysis, signals are functions of the independent variable time, but they can also be considered as functions of the independent variable space. In other words, the following discussion can be viewed as both temporal signal analysis and spatial signal analysis. Furthermore, we assume $g(t)$ represents a continuous signal, where the vertical axis represents $g(t)$ and the horizontal axis represents t, a real number, and $g(n)$ represents a discrete signal, where the vertical axis represents $g(n)$ and the horizontal axis represents n, an integer. The basic operations on signals are divided into two distinct categories: i) operations performed on the dependent variable $g(t)$ or $g(n)$, and ii) operations performed on the independent variable t or n. In addition, a mixed set of operations from both categories can be simultaneously applied to signals.

3.1.1 Operations Performed on Dependent Variable

In ***amplitude-scaling operations***, the signal $g(t)$ is multiplied by a scaling factor k to form $y(t)$, and thus defined by

$$y(t) = k g(t) \tag{3.1}$$

If $k > 0$, then the resulting product $y(t)$ is a scaled up or down version of $g(t)$. Note that for $k > 1$, the signal is amplified (e.g., by an audio amplifier), and for $0 < k < 1$, the signal is attenuated (e.g., due to the free space propagation). However, if $k < 0$, then $y(t) = |k|(-g(t))$ is a scaled up or down version of $-g(t)$. Note that $-g(t)$ is the flipped version of $g(t)$ with respect to the horizontal axis (i.e., about the line $g(t) = 0$).

EXAMPLE 3.1

Suppose the signal $h_1(t)$ is defined as follows:

$$h_1(t) = \begin{cases} 0, & t<0 \\ t, & 0\leq t\leq 1 \\ 1, & 1<t \end{cases}$$

Determine $h_2(t)=1.5h_1(t)$, $h_3(t)=0.5h_1(t)$, and $h_4(t)=-0.5h_1(t)$.

Solution

Using (3.1), we can obtain $h_2(t)$ and $h_3(t)$, as they are amplitude-scaled versions of $h_1(t)$, and $h_4(t)$, as it is an amplitude-scaled version of $-h_1(t)$. Figure 3.1 shows all signals.

In *addition operations,* two signals $g_1(t)$ and $g_2(t)$ are added to form the sum $y(t)$, and thus are defined by

$$y(t)=g_1(t)+g_2(t) \tag{3.2}$$

A physical example of a device that adds signals is an audio mixer, which combines music and voice signals. Note that the difference between two signals $g_1(t)$ and $g_2(t)$ can be viewed as the sum of $g_1(t)$ and $(-1)g_2(t)$. An example to determine the difference between two signals is when an estimate of the echo signal is subtracted from the received signal.

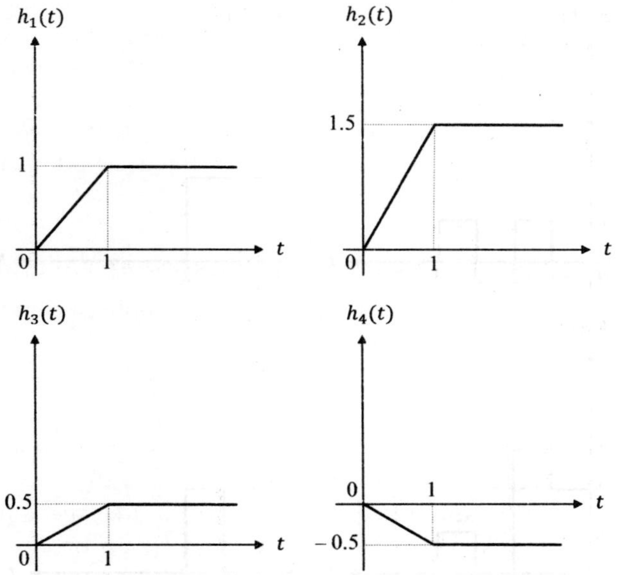

FIGURE 3.1 Signals in Example 3.1.

In ***multiplication operations***, two signals $g_1(t)$ and $g_2(t)$ are multiplied to form the product $y(t)$, and thus are defined by

$$y(t) = g_1(t)g_2(t) \tag{3.3}$$

A physical example of a device that multiplies signals is an AM radio transmitter, in which a signal consisting of the sum of a scaled-down version of an audio signal and a constant component is multiplied by a signal, known as a carrier wave.

EXAMPLE 3.2

Suppose the signals $k_1(t)$ and $k_2(t)$ are defined as follows:

$$k_1(t) = \begin{cases} 0, & t<1 \\ 1, & 1 \le t \le 2 \\ 0, & 2<t<3 \\ 1, & 3 \le t \le 4 \\ 0, & 4<t \end{cases}$$

and

$$k_2(t) = \begin{cases} 0, & t<0 \\ 2, & 0 \le t \le 2 \\ 0, & 2<t \end{cases}$$

Determine $k_3(t) = k_1(t) + k_2(t)$ and $k_4(t) = k_1(t)\,k_2(t)$.

Solution

Using (3.2) and (3.3), we can obtain, in a piecewise fashion, $k_3(t)$ and $k_4(t)$, respectively. All signals are shown in Figure 3.2.

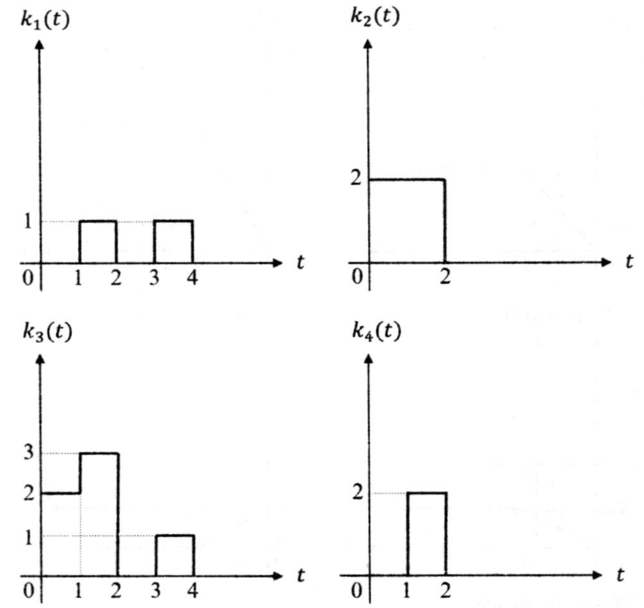

FIGURE 3.2 Signals in Example 3.2.

In *differentiation operations,* the derivative of the signal $g(t)$ with respect to time t is taken, and thus defined by

$$y(t) = \frac{d}{dt}g(t) = g'(t) \tag{3.4}$$

A physical example is an inductor, as the voltage across the inductor with inductance L is equal to L times the derivative of the current flowing through it.

In *integration operations,* the integral of the signal $g(t)$ with respect to time t is taken, and thus is defined by

$$y(t) = \int g(t)\,dt \tag{3.5}$$

A physical example is a capacitor, as the voltage across the capacitor with capacitance C is equal to $\frac{1}{C}$ times the integral of the current flowing through it.

EXAMPLE 3.3

Consider the signals $w_1(t) = |t|$ and $w_2(t) = 1$, and determine $w_3(t) = w_1'(t)$ and $w_4(t) = \int w_2(t)\,dt$.

Solution

Using (3.4) and (3.5), we can easily obtain $w_3(t)$ and $w_4(t)$, respectively. All signals are shown in Figure 3.3.

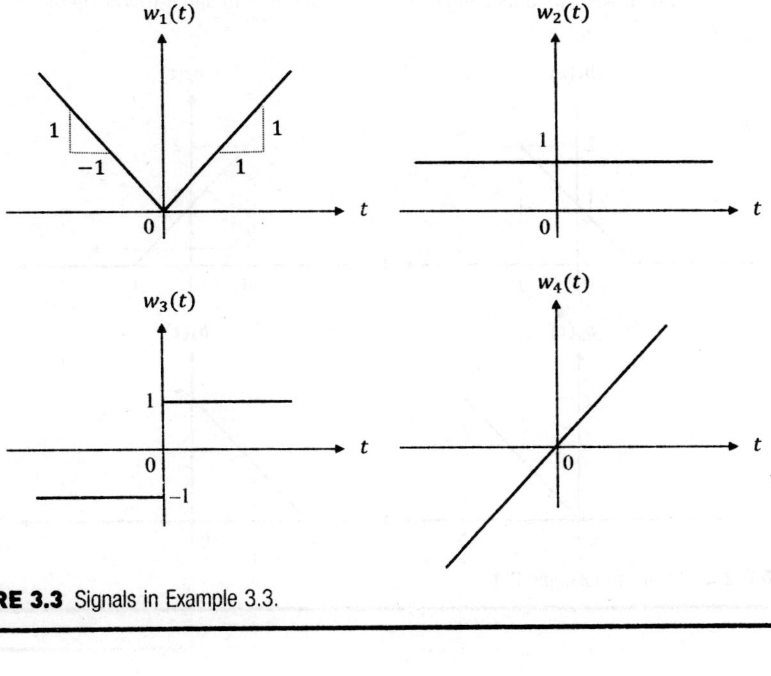

FIGURE 3.3 Signals in Example 3.3.

3.1.2 Operations Performed on Independent Variable

In ***time-reversal operations***, also known as time-inversion, time-folding and time-reflection operations, the flipped version of the signal $g(t)$ around the vertical axis (i.e., about the line $t=0$) is obtained, and thus is defined by

$$y(t)=g(-t) \tag{3.6}$$

In ***time-shifting operations***, the time-shifted version of the signal $g(t)$ is obtained, and thus is defined by

$$y(t)=g(t-\tau) \tag{3.7}$$

where τ is a real number representing a time shift. If $\tau>0$, then $y(t)$ is obtained by shifting $g(t)$ toward the right (i.e., $y(t)$ is a time-delayed version of the signal $g(t)$). If $\tau<0$, $g(t)$ is shifted toward the left (i.e., $y(t)$ is a time-advanced version of the signal $g(t)$).

EXAMPLE 3.4

Suppose the signal $b_1(t)$ is defined as follows:

$$b_1(t)=\begin{cases} t+1, & |t|\le 1 \\ 0, & |t|>1 \end{cases}$$

Determine $b_2(t)=b_1(-t)$, $b_3(t)=b_1(t-1)$, and $b_4(t)=b_1(t+1)$.

Solution

Using (3.6), we can obtain $b_2(t)$, and using (3.7), we can obtain $b_3(t)$ and $b_4(t)$. All signals are shown in Figure 3.4.

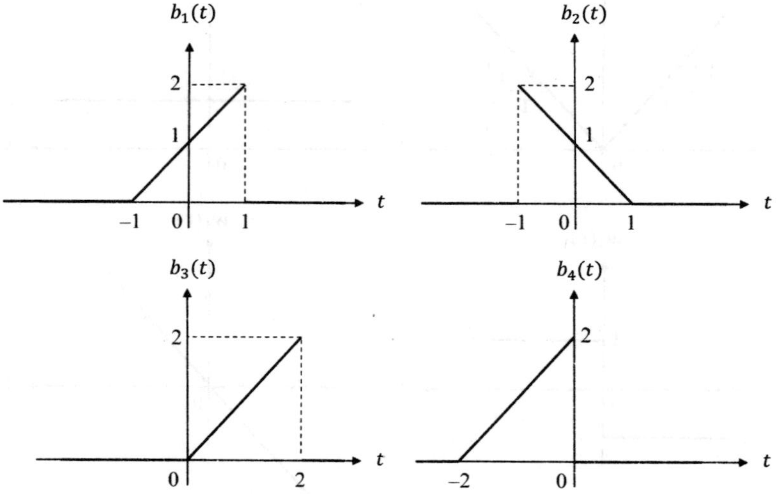

FIGURE 3.4 Signals in Example 3.4.

In *time-scaling operations*, the time-scaled version of the signal $g(t)$ is obtained, and thus is defined by

$$y(t) = g(\beta t) \tag{3.8}$$

where $\beta \neq 0$ is a real number representing a time-scaling factor. If $\beta > 1$, the signal $y(t)$ is a compressed (contracted) version of $g(t)$, and if $0 < \beta < 1$, the signal $y(t)$ is an expanded (stretched) version of $g(t)$. Note that if $\beta = 1$, then the signal remains unchanged, and if $\beta < 0$, then the signal $y(t)$ is the time-scaled version of $g(-t)$ (i.e., $y(t) = g(-|\beta|\, t)$, with $|\beta|$ as the time-scaling factor).

EXAMPLE 3.5

Suppose the signal $c_1(t)$ is defined as follows:

$$c_1(t) = \begin{cases} -t+1, & |t| \leq 1 \\ 0, & |t| > 1 \end{cases}$$

Determine $c_2(t) = c_1(2t)$, $c_3(t) = c_1(t/2)$, and $c_4(t) = c_1(-2t)$.

Solution

Using (3.8), we can easily obtain $c_2(t)$ and $c_3(t)$, and using (3.6) and then (3.8), we can obtain $c_4(t)$. All signals are shown in Figure 3.5.

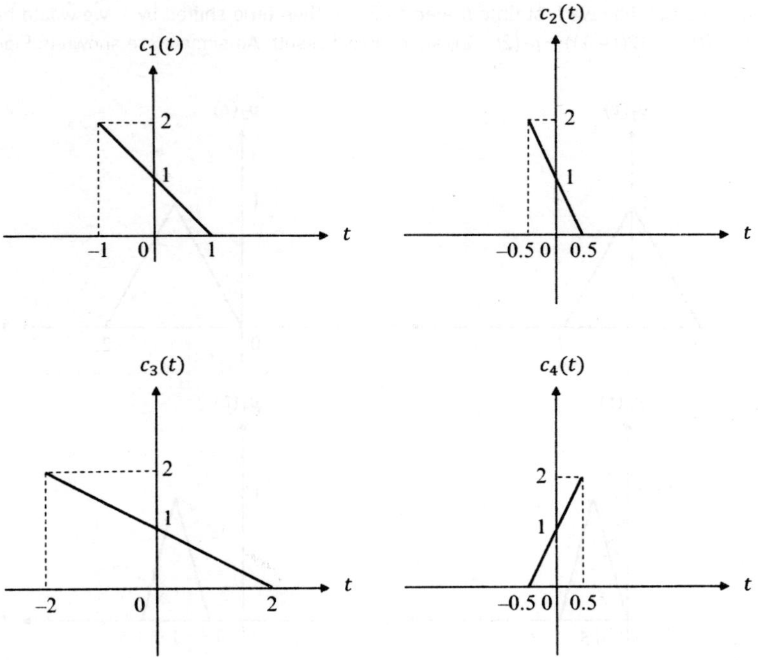

FIGURE 3.5 Signals in Example 3.5.

It is possible that a combination of both time-shifting and time-scaling operations is required (e.g., $y(t)=g(\beta t-\tau)$, where $\tau \neq 0$ and $\beta \neq 0$ are both real numbers, and represent the time shift and time scale, respectively). It is thus imperative to follow the precedence rule for time-shifting and time-scaling operations. The proper order to perform both operations is to carry out first the time-shifting operation (i.e., replacing t by $t-\tau$) and then the time-scaling operation (i.e., replacing t by βt). It is worthwhile to highlight that this relation between $y(t)$ and $g(t)$ must satisfy the conditions $y(0)=g(-\tau)$ and $y(\tau/\beta)=g(0)$. These conditions can in turn provide useful checks on $y(t)$ in terms of $g(t)$.

EXAMPLE 3.6

Determine the signal $p_3(t)=p_1(2t-1)$, if the signal $p_1(t)$ is defined as follows:

$$p_1(t)=\begin{cases}1-|t|, & |t|\leq 1\\ 0, & |t|>1\end{cases}$$

Solution

We must first time shift the signal $p_1(t)$ and then time scale it. Using (3.7), we first time shift $p_1(t)$ to the right by a shift of 1 to get $p_2(t)=p_1(t-1)$. Using (3.8), we then time scale $p_2(t)$ by a factor of 2 to get $p_3(t)=p_2(2t)=p_1(2t-1)$. As a check, the conditions $p_3(0)=p_1(-1)$ and $p_3\left(\frac{1}{2}\right)=p_1(0)$ are both satisfied. Note that had we first time scaled by 2 and then time shifted by 1, we would have then obtained $p_4(t)=p_1(2(t-1))=p_1(2t-2)$, an incorrect result. All signals are shown in Figure 3.6.

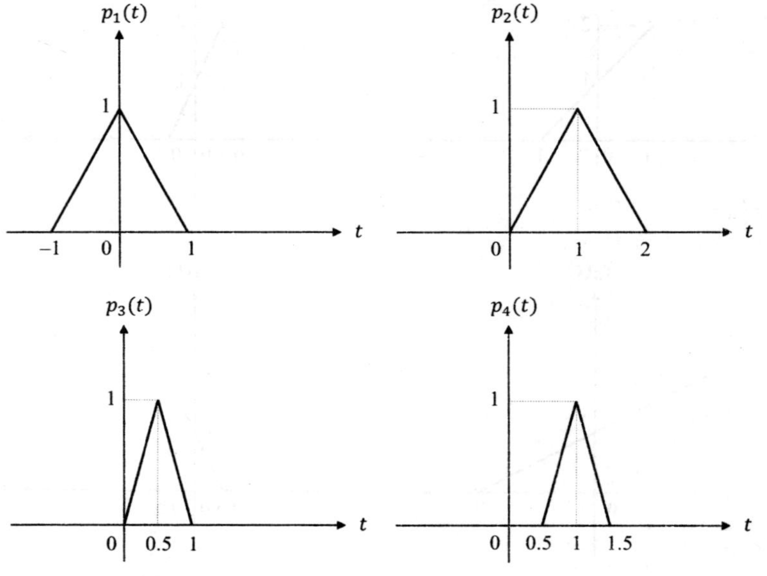

FIGURE 3.6 Signals in Example 3.6.

3.2 CLASSIFICATION OF SIGNALS

Representation and processing of a signal highly depends on the type of signal being considered. Signals can be broadly classified into a number of different ways.

3.2.1 Continuous-Value and Discrete-Value Signals

A ***continuous-value signal*** is one that may have any value within a continuum of allowed values; the continuum on the vertical axis can be finite or infinite. An analog speech transmitted over a twisted-pair telephone line can be categorized as a continuous-value signal, as the signal level over time can continuously range from a quiet whisper to a deafening scream.

A ***discrete-value signal*** can only have values taken from a discrete set consisting of a finite number of values. A discrete-value signal may be derived from a continuous-value signal when the signal value is quantized (rounded). Figure 3.7 shows continuous-value and discrete-value signals.

3.2.2 Continuous-Time and Discrete-Time Signals

A signal is said to be a ***continuous-time signal*** if it is defined for all time *t*, a real number. Continuous-time signals arise naturally when a physical signal, such

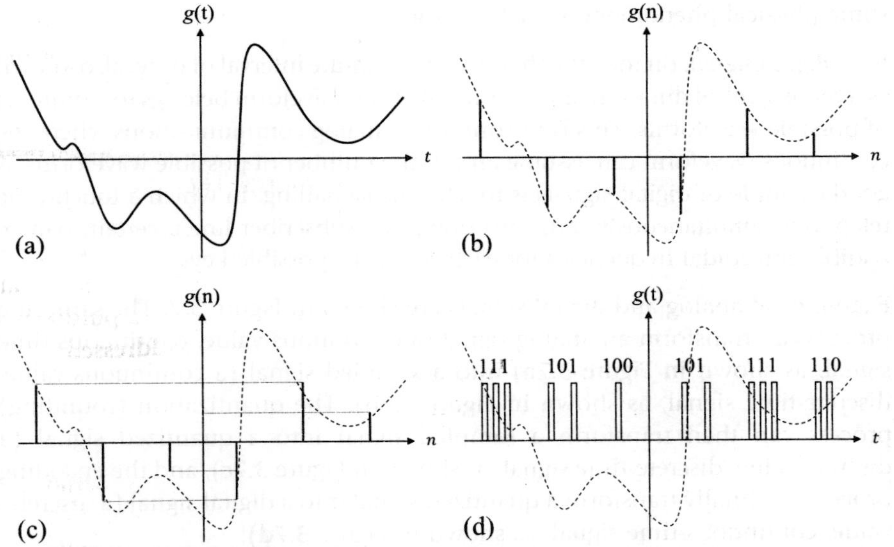

FIGURE 3.7 Continuous/discrete-value, continuous/discrete-time signals: (a) continuous-value, continuous-time signal; (b) continuous-value, discrete-time signal; (c) discrete-value, discrete-time signal; and (d) discrete-value, continuous-time signal.

as a light wave, is converted by a transducer, such as a photoelectric cell, into an electrical signal. A continuous-time signal can have zero value at certain instants of time or for some intervals of time.

A signal is said to be a ***discrete-time signal*** if it is defined only at discrete instants of time n. In other words, the independent variable on the horizontal axis has discrete values only (i.e., it takes its value in the set of integers). Note that it does not mean a discrete-time signal has zero value at nondiscrete (noninteger) instants of time, it simply implies we do not have (or probably we do not care to have) the values at noninteger instants of time. A discrete-time signal $g(n)$ is often derived from a continuous-time signal $g(t)$ by the sampling process. Figure 3.7 shows continuous-time and discrete-time signals.

3.2.3 Analog and Digital Signals

The terms analog and digital describe the nature of the signal amplitude on the vertical axis, as analog and digital signals are both continuous-time signals defined for all time t. For an ***analog signal***, the dependent variable on the vertical axis can be any real number $(-\infty, \infty)$. Humans produce and perceive audio and visual signals in an analog form. Examples of analog signals include signals representing light and sound intensity and multidimensional position. Analog signals arise when a physical signal is converted by a transducer, such as the conversion of an acoustic wave by a microphone into an electrical signal. The variation of the analog signal with time is analogous (proportional) to some physical phenomenon, such as voice.

For a ***digital signal***, on the other hand, over any finite interval of time, also known as a bit or symbol duration, the continuous-time waveform belongs to a finite set of possible waveforms. This is in contrast to analog communications where the continuous waveform can assume an infinite number of possible waveforms. A good example of digital signals is touch-tone signalling, in which a touch-tone telephone simultaneously transmits down the subscriber line a certain pair of audible sinusoidal frequencies for each of the 12 possible keys.

Examples of analog and digital signals are shown in Figure 3.7. The sampling process can transform an analog signal (a continuous-value, continuous-time signal, as shown in Figure 3.7a) into a sampled signal (a continuous-value, discrete-time signal, as shown in Figure 3.7b). The quantization (rounding) process can then transform a sampled signal into a quantized signal (a discrete-value, discrete-time signal, as shown in Figure 3.7c), and the encoding process can finally transform a quantized signal into a digital signal (a discrete-value, continuous-time signal, as shown in Figure 3.7d).

In an analog communication system, the objective at the receiver is to reproduce the transmitted waveform with enough precision for an acceptable and subjective perception. However, in a digital communication system, the objective is to determine which one of the finite set of waveforms have been sent by the transmitter. To this effect, the figure of merit for the performance of analog communication systems is a fidelity criterion, namely, the signal-to-noise ratio (SNR), whereas the figure of merit for the performance of digital communication systems is the average bit error rate (BER).

3.2.4 Deterministic and Random Signals

A ***deterministic signal*** is a fully-defined (completely-specified) function of the independent variable time. A deterministic signal is a signal about which there is no uncertainty with respect to its value, and we can thus determine the exact value of the signal at any given time. Signals characterizing linear distortions in communication channels or sinusoidal signals used as local oscillators in transmitters are all deterministic.

If a signal is known only in terms of statistical averages and probabilistic description—such as its mean value, mean square value, and distribution—rather than its full mathematical equation or complete numerical table or exact graphical description, it is then a ***random signal***. In other words, for a random signal, there is some degree of uncertainty before it actually occurs, as amplitudes of random signals must be described probabilistically.

In digital communications, a random signal may belong to a group of signals, with each signal in the group having a different waveform as well as having a certain probability of occurrence. The ensemble of signals is referred to as a random (stochastic) process. Message signals, interference at all levels, and noise of all types are considered as random signals.

It is imperative to emphasize that the essence of communications is randomness. In communications, message signals are almost never deterministic, as deterministic signals carry no information. Any signal that conveys information must have uncertainty in it. The message signals from the receiving viewpoint are unpredictable; otherwise, their transmissions will serve no purpose, and thus become unnecessary.

3.2.5 Real and Complex Signals

In both real and complex signals, the independent variable is real-valued. A ***real signal*** at any given time takes its value in the set of real numbers, and a ***complex signal*** takes its value in the set of complex numbers. A complex signal can in turn be represented by two real signals, such as the real and imaginary parts or equivalently magnitude (amplitude) and phase values. Signals that we observe physically (using voltmeters, ammeters, oscilloscopes, etc.) are all real signals, as complex signals have no physical meaning. Certain mathematical models and calculations can be greatly simplified if we use complex notation. In communications, a complex signal is often used to convey information about the magnitude and phase of a signal in the frequency domain.

3.2.6 Periodic and Nonperiodic Signals

A ***periodic signal*** repeats itself in time. A periodic continuous-time signal $g(t)$ is a function of time that satisfies the periodicity condition $g(t)=g(t \pm T_0)$ for all time t, where t starts from minus infinity and continues forever, and T_0 is a positive number. The smallest value of T_0 that satisfies this condition is called the ***period***. Note that a time-shift to the right or to the left by T_0 results in exactly the same periodic signal $g(t)$. Assuming $p(t)$ is a time-limited signal that defines only one period of the signal $g(t)$, then $g(t)$ can be analytically expressed as follows:

$$g(t)=g(t \pm T_0)=\sum_{k=-\infty}^{\infty} p(t-kT_0) \tag{3.9}$$

The reciprocal of the period is called the ***fundamental frequency*** of the periodic signal, and its multiples are called ***harmonics***. Any signal for which no value of T_0 satisfies the above condition is then a ***nonperiodic signal***.

No physical signal can be truly categorized as periodic, as no physical signal can start from minus infinity and continue forever. However, for very long enough observation intervals, and of course, for the analysis and design purposes, it is reasonable to assume to have periodic signals.

For a discrete-time signal to be periodic, the period must be a positive integer; otherwise, it is called nonperiodic. It is worth noting that a discrete-time signal obtained by uniform sampling of a periodic continuous-time signal may or may not be periodic, as it highly depends on the sampling rate.

A continuous-time signal consisting of the sum of two time-varying functions is periodic, if and only if both functions are periodic and the ratio of these two periods is a rational number. In such a case, the least common multiple of the two periods is the period of the sum signal. Alternatively, the fundamental frequency of each of the two periodic signals can be found and the greatest common factor of the two fundamental frequencies is then the fundamental frequency of the sum signal. This is in contrast to discrete-time signals, where the sum of two periodic discrete-time signals is always periodic.

Note that we have defined periodic functions in the time domain. However, it is also possible to define a periodic function in the frequency domain. For instance, a continuous-time signal sampled in the time domain is periodic in the frequency domain, as will be discussed in the context of sampling theorem.

3.2.7 Even and Odd Signals

A real signal is said to be an ***even signal*** if we have the following:

$$g(t) = g(-t) \tag{3.10}$$

for all time t, even signals are thus symmetric about the vertical axis (i.e., around the line $t = 0$). A signal is said to be an ***odd signal*** if we have the following:

$$g(t) = -g(-t) \tag{3.11}$$

for all time t. Odd signals are thus symmetric about the origin. If two signals are both even, their sum and difference are both even, and if they are both odd, their sum and difference are both odd. The derivative of an odd signal is an even signal and the derivative of an even signal is an odd signal. If two signals are both even or both odd, then their product and quotient are both even, but if one is even and the other is odd, then their product and quotient are both odd. A signal, which is by definition a single-valued function, cannot be both odd and even. A real physical signal is rarely an even or an odd signal.

An arbitrary real signal can always be decomposed into an ***even part*** $g_e(t)$ and an ***odd part*** $g_o(t)$. In other words, we have the following:

$$\begin{aligned} g(t) &= g_e(t) + g_o(t) \\ g_e(t) &= \frac{g(t) + g(-t)}{2} \\ g_o(t) &= \frac{g(t) - g(-t)}{2} \end{aligned} \tag{3.12}$$

EXAMPLE 3.7

Determine whether the signal $z(t) = t^3 + t^2$ is an odd signal or an even signal or neither; if it is neither, then determine the odd and even parts of it.

Solution

From $z(t)$, we find $z(-t) = -t^3 + t^2$. Since we have $z(t) \neq z(-t)$, $z(t)$ is not an even function, since we have $z(t) \neq -z(-t)$, $z(t)$ is not an odd function. We therefore have to find the odd and even parts of $z(t)$. Using (3.12), the even and odd parts of $z(t)$ are, respectively, as follows:

$$z_e(t) = \frac{z(t) + z(-t)}{2} = \frac{t^3 + t^2 - t^3 + t^2}{2} = t^2$$

$$z_o(t) = \frac{z(t) - z(-t)}{2} = \frac{t^3 + t^2 + t^3 - t^2}{2} = t^3$$

Figure 3.8 shows $z(t)$, $z_e(t)$, and $z_o(t)$.

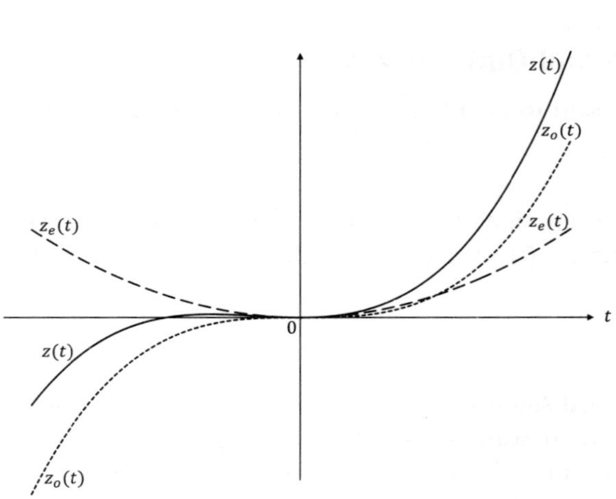

FIGURE 3.8 Signals in Example 3.7.

3.2.8 Energy and Power Signals

In signal analysis, it is customary to assume a $1-\Omega$ resistor, so regardless of whether $g(t)$ represents a voltage across it or a current through it, we may express the instantaneous power $p(t)$ associated with the signal $g(t)$ as $p(t) = |g(t)|^2$. The magnitude squared is used in the instantaneous normalized power to allow the possibility of $g(t)$ being a complex-valued signal. For real signals, we therefore have $p(t) = g^2(t)$. It is important to highlight that mathematically, power is the derivative of energy with respect to time, and physically, it is the rate at which energy is supplied or consumed. In a digital communication system, power determines the voltage applied to the transmitter, and the system performance directly depends on the received signal energy.

Table 3.1 presents the total-energy and average-power formulas. Note that for a nonperiodic signal, the time average spans over all time t or n, whereas for a periodic signal, the time average spans over only one single period. This means that the power content of a periodic signal is equal to the average power in one period (cycle).

A signal is referred to as an ***energy signal*** if and only if its total energy E is finite; in other words, when we have $0 < E < \infty$. A necessary condition for the energy to be finite is that the signal amplitude must approach zero as time approaches plus or minus infinity (i.e., $g(t) \to 0$ as $t \to \pm\infty$). If the signal energy is infinite, the time average of the energy (if it exists), i.e., the average power, is more meaningful.

Table 3.1 Energy and power of signals

	Continuous-time signals	Discrete-time signals
Total energy of the nonperiodic signal $g(t)$ or $g(n)$	$E=\int_{-\infty}^{\infty}\lvert g(t)\rvert^2 dt$	$E=\sum_{n=-\infty}^{\infty}\lvert g(n)\rvert^2$
Average power of the nonperiodic signal $g(t)$ or $g(n)$	$P=\lim_{S\to\infty}\left(\frac{1}{2S}\right)\int_{-S}^{S}\lvert g(t)\rvert^2 dt$	$P=\lim_{N\to\infty}\left(\frac{1}{2N}\right)\sum_{n=-\infty}^{\infty}\lvert g(n)\rvert^2$
Average power of the periodic signal $g(t)$ or $g(n)$	$P=\left(\frac{1}{T_0}\right)\int_{-T_0/2}^{T_0/2}\lvert g(t)\rvert^2 dt$	$P=\left(\frac{1}{N}\right)\sum_{n=0}^{N-1}\lvert g(n)\rvert^2$

A signal is referred to as a ***power signal***, if and only if the average power of the signal is finite; in other words, when we have $0<P<\infty$. An energy signal has zero average power, whereas a power signal has infinite energy. The definitions of energy signal and power signal can be then summarized as follows:

$$\textbf{Energy signal: } 0<E<\infty \text{ (finite total energy) and } P=0 \text{ (zero average power)}$$

$$\textbf{Power signal: } 0<P<\infty \text{ (finite average power) and } E=\infty \text{ (infinite total energy)} \qquad (3.13)$$

A signal cannot be both an energy signal and a power signal; if it is one, it cannot be the other. However, a signal with infinite power, such as a unit ramp signal (i.e., $g(t)=t$ for $t\geq 0$ and $g(t)=0$ for $t<0$) can be neither an energy signal nor a power signal. No physical signal can have infinite energy or infinite average power, but in signal analysis, according to strict mathematical definitions, signals, such as sinusoidal, have infinite energy. Every signal observed in real life is an energy signal. It is practically impossible to generate a power signal because such a signal would have an infinite duration and infinite energy. Periodic signals and random signals are usually viewed as power signals, whereas signals that are deterministic and nonperiodic are usually viewed as energy signals. Signal energy and power are generally measured in Joules (J) and Watts (W), respectively. Due to a very wide range of values for power in communication systems, it is the common practice to use the logarithmic scale to represent signal power.

EXAMPLE 3.8

Classify the following signals as energy signals or power signals or neither: a) $f_1(t) = e^{-t}$ for $t \geq 0$ and $f_1(t) = 0$ for $t < 0$, b) $f_2(t) = \cos(t)$, and c) $f_3(t) = e^{-t}$.

Solution

We use the results in the second column of Table 3.1, as these three signals are all continuous-time signals; moreover, they are all real, so we can use $g^2(t)$ rather than $|g(t)|^2$.

(a) $f_1(t)$ is a nonperiodic signal whose energy is as follows:

$$E = \int_{-\infty}^{\infty} |f_1(t)|^2 dt = \int_{0}^{\infty} e^{-2t} dt = 0.5 < \infty$$

Since its energy is finite, it is an energy signal.

(b) $f_2(t)$ is a periodic signal (with period of 2π) whose power is as follows:

$$P = \left(\frac{1}{T}\right) \int_{-\frac{T}{2}}^{\frac{T}{2}} |f_2(t)|^2 dt = \left(\frac{1}{2\pi}\right) \int_{-\pi}^{\pi} \cos^2(t) dt = 0.5 < \infty$$

Since its power is finite and nonzero, it is a power signal.

(c) The energy and power of $f_3(t)$ are, respectively, as follows:

$$E = \int_{-\infty}^{\infty} |f_3(t)|^2 dt = \int_{-\infty}^{\infty} e^{-2t} dt = \infty$$

$$P = \lim_{S \to \infty} \left(\frac{1}{2S}\right) \int_{-S}^{S} e^{-2t} dt = \infty$$

Since its power and energy are both infinite, it is neither a power signal nor an energy signal.

3.2.9 Causal and Noncausal Signals

A ***causal signal*** is zero for negative time ($t < 0$); otherwise, it is called a ***noncausal signal***. All real (physically-realizable) signals are causal.

3.2.10 Time-Limited and Band-Limited Signals

An (absolutely) ***time-limited signal*** is exactly zero outside a finite interval of time and an (absolutely) ***band-limited signal*** has no spectrum (frequency contents) outside a finite band of frequencies. An absolutely band-limited signal cannot be absolutely time-limited, and vice versa. However, a signal may be neither time-limited nor frequency-limited, such as a Gaussian pulse. All real (physical) signals are time-limited, as such they are not absolutely band-limited. However, a real signal may be considered to be band-limited for all practical purposes in the sense that its amplitude (magnitude) spectrum may have a negligible level above a certain frequency.

3.2.11 Baseband and Bandpass Signals

The term baseband is used to designate the band of frequencies representing the original signal as delivered by a source of information. A ***baseband signal*** generally has nonzero frequency content from around zero up to a certain frequency. An example of a baseband signal is an audio signal. A ***bandpass signal***, on the other hand, has non-negligible frequency content only in a finite band of frequencies centered about a certain frequency much greater than zero. An example of a bandpass signal is a radio signal transmitted over the air, such as off-the-air radio and TV signals.

3.3 CLASSIFICATION OF SYSTEMS

Signals are operated on by systems. An understanding of systems is therefore important in the analysis and design of communication systems. A ***system*** is defined mathematically as a unique transformation that maps an input (an excitation) into an output (a response). A system—made up of various inter-related, inter-dependent, and interacting components—may transform a signal into another signal with properties and characteristics different from those of the input signal, usually with the objective to shape the input signal characteristics or transfer and extract some information. A system can process a set of input signals to produce a set of output signals, where the output must be uniquely defined for any reasonably acceptable (legitimate) input.

It is important to highlight that ***system analysis*** is the determination of the output signal when the input signal and the system characteristics (what fully defines the system) are known, whereas ***system synthesis*** is the identification (characterization) of the system when the input and output signals are both known. System synthesis is generally much more difficult than system analysis. Moreover, in analysis, the solution is always unique, whereas in synthesis, there may exist infinitely many solutions or sometimes none at all.

It is worth noting that sometimes the words synthesis and design may be used interchangeably. The term synthesis is generally used to describe analytical procedures that can usually be methodically carried out step by step. On the other hand, the term ***design*** includes analytical methods, along with practical heuristic procedures—mainly based on all or a combination of trial-and-error techniques, parametric simulations, limited experimentations, numerical analysis, optimization/sub-optimization of subsystems, and above all the experience of the designer. In design, the goal is to carry out, in an iterative fashion, a plethora of design trade-offs through a host of system parameters and variables, so as to accommodate a multitude of conflicting design constraints to the extent possible.

Mathematically, a system is a functional relationship between the system input and output. Depending on the properties of the functional relationship, we can broadly classify systems into a number of different ways.

3.3.1 Baseband and Passband Systems

A ***baseband system***, like a lowpass filter, passes the low-frequency components of the input signal. An example of a baseband system is the twisted-pair wires forming the local access of the public switched telephone network. A ***passband system***, like a bandpass filter, can pass certain frequencies inside some frequency band, and reject frequencies outside that band. The majority of practical channels have bandpass characteristics. Modulation must thus be employed to translate the frequency of the lowpass message signal, so the spectrum of the transmitted passband signal can match the bandpass characteristics of the channel. An example of a passband channel is a cellular mobile system.

3.3.2 Invertible and Noninvertible Systems

In an ***invertible system***, the input of the system can be recovered from the output. There must be a one-to-one mapping between input and output signals for a system to be invertible; otherwise, it is a ***noninvertible system***. Invertibility requires a second system in cascade with the first system, such that the output signal of the second system becomes the same as the input signal applied to the first system. The property of invertibility is important in digital communication design. For example, a system called an equalizer is put at the receiver in cascade with the channel so as to compensate the distortion due to the physical characteristics of the channel. This makes the received signal as similar as possible to the transmitted signal.

3.3.3 Lumped and Distributed Systems

A ***lumped system*** is one in which the dependent variables are all functions of time only. In a lumped system, the travel time of the signal is assumed to be negligible. In general, to characterize a lumped system, a set of ordinary differential equations must be solved. A ***distributed system*** is one in which all dependent variables are functions of time and one or more spatial variables. A distributed system is one for which the travel time of the signal between the components cannot be neglected and the voltages and currents are functions of position as well as time. In general, to characterize a distributed system, a set of partial differential equations must be solved. If the physical dimensions of the system components are smaller than the wavelength of the highest of the signal frequency applied to the system, it is called a lumped system; otherwise, it is referred to as a distributed system. As a rough engineering rule of thumb, if no parts of the structure can exceed one tenth of the wavelength of the highest signal frequency, then the system can be assumed to consist of lumped elements. Electronic circuits are lumped systems, and power transmission lines and microwave circuits are generally categorized as distributed systems.

3.3.4 Adaptive and Fixed Systems

In an ***adaptive system***, some of the system parameters, based on some specified criterion, are adjusted iteratively over time so as to make the system operate in, or as close as to, an optimum fashion. An adaptive system is generally employed where complete knowledge of the relevant input characteristics is not available or when there are some slow variations in the statistics of the input. Examples may include adaptive equalizers and echo cancelers used in high-speed dial-up data modems. On the other hand, a ***fixed system*** is a time-invariant system whose parameters do not change, such as analog filters consisting of passive elements.

3.3.5 Systems with or without Feedback

In a ***feedback system***, a portion of the system output is fed back into the system, thus introducing a level of dependencies among input and output signals in the system. With the use of feedback in communication systems, satisfactory response and robust performance can generally be achieved. In a system with no feedback, also known as an ***open-loop control system***, the present output has no bearing on the future output, and these systems do not generally exhibit instability. Physical examples may include scalar quantizers and modulators. In a system with feedback, also known as a ***closed-loop control system***, the past output may influence the present or future outputs. Most physical systems embody some form of feedback. Examples may include tracking systems, compensation of nonideal elements, and adaptive decision-feedback equalizers. In a system with feedback, a closed sequence of cause-and-effect relations exists between system variables.

There are two types of feedback systems. In a ***positive feedback system***, the feedback is used to increase the input signal level, thus generally making the system unstable. Positive feedback is widely used in oscillatory circuits such as oscillators and timing circuits. In a ***negative feedback system***, the feedback is used to decrease the input signal level to ensure system stability. Tendency toward oscillation or instability is an important characteristic of feedback, and the issue of instability in all feedback systems thus needs to be fully addressed. Physical examples in communication systems may include amplifiers and phase-locked loops. Combination of feed-forward and feedback control can significantly improve performance over only feedback control whenever there is a major disturbance that can be measured and compensated for before it affects the process output, such as adaptive decision-feedback equalizers.

3.3.6 Systems with or without Memory

In a ***system with memory***, the output at a given time also depends on the preceding and/or succeeding values of the input signal. In other words, the present output value is also a function of the past and/or future values of the input signal. The earliest past input or the most distant future input define how far the memory of the system extends. In contrast, in a system with no memory, also known as a ***memoryless system***, the present output value depends only on the present value of the input signal. A resistive circuit is considered as a memoryless system, whereas a reactive circuit can be an example of a system with memory.

3.3.7 Systems with Single/Multiple Inputs and Single/Multiple Outputs

A system can have one or more input signals and one or more output signals. We can thus have four different systems: i) single input, single output (SISO), ii) single input, multiple outputs (SIMO), iii) multiple inputs, single output (MISO), and iv) multiple inputs, multiple outputs (MIMO). SISO systems are employed in all wired communication systems as well as in many wireless communication systems. However, the other three different types of systems are almost exclusively employed in radio transmission, where more than one antenna in the transmitter and/or in the receiver may be employed.

In a ***SISO system***, the transmitter or receiver each has a single radio frequency (RF) chain. SISO systems are used in radio and TV broadcast, and Wi-Fi and Bluetooth technologies.

In a ***SIMO system***, a receive diversity technique is employed to improve transmission reliability and coverage by employing space-time block coding. This can be achieved by selecting the best antenna to receive a stronger signal or combine signals from all antennas in such a way that the SNR is maximized.

A ***MISO system*** allows the transmitter to transmit signals both in time and space (i.e., the signal is transmitted by several antennas at different times). The advantage of using MISO is that the multiple antennas and the additional processing are moved from the receiver to the transmitter. For instance, the complexity of the transmit subsystem of a base station is increased, so the receive complexity of the cell phones can be reduced. This results in a reduction in size, cost, and power requirements for cell phones.

In a ***MIMO system***, by employing the same number of antennas both at the transmitter and the receiver, the throughput can be multiplied by the same factor as the number of antennas. MIMO is employed in WiMAX wireless systems.

3.3.8 Passive and Active Systems

A ***passive system*** consists of circuit elements, such as resistors, capacitors, and inductors, which are capable of dissipating or storing energy. An ***active system*** may include not only passive elements, but also active elements, such as batteries, operational amplifiers, and transistors, which are capable of generating (supplying) energy.

3.3.9 Causal and Noncausal Systems

A system is said to be causal if it does not respond before the input is applied. In other words, in a ***causal system***, the output at any time depends only on the values of the input signal up to and including that time and does not depend on the future values of the input. In contrast, the output signal of a ***noncausal system*** depends on one or more future values of the input signal. All physically realizable systems are causal. Note that all memoryless systems are causal, but not vice versa. If delay can be incorporated in a system, then a noncausal system may become physically realizable.

3.3.10 Stable and Unstable Systems

In a ***stable system***, the output signal is bounded for all bounded input signals. This requirement is known as the ***bounded-input bounded-output (BIBO) stability*** criterion. The output of such a stable system does not diverge if the input does not diverge. A system is stable if its impulse response approaches zero as time approaches infinity. A system that is not stable is known as an ***unstable system***.

3.3.11 Continuous-Time and Discrete-Time Systems

A ***continuous-time system*** has continuous-time signals as its input and continuous-time signals as its output. Continuous-time systems are characterized by differential equations. Examples include analog filters and amplifiers. A ***discrete-time system*** has discrete-time signals as its input and discrete-time signals as its output. Discrete-time systems are characterized by difference equations. Examples include digital filters, adaptive equalizers, and echo and noise cancellers.

3.3.12 Power-Limited and Band-Limited Systems

In a communication system, there are two primary resources: transmitted power and channel bandwidth. The transmitted power is the average power of the transmitted signal. The channel bandwidth reflects the band of significant frequency components allocated for the transmission of the input (message) signal. One of these two resources may be more precious than the other; hence communication channels are generally classified as ***band-limited***, such as the local access of the public switched telephone network, or ***power-limited***, such as satellite channels.

3.3.13 Linear and Nonlinear Systems

In a ***linear system***, the superposition principle holds. The ***superposition principle*** is based on the additivity and homogeneity properties. The ***additivity property*** requires that the system output to a number of different inputs all applied simultaneously is equal to the sum of the outputs when each input is applied individually, and the ***homogeneity property*** entails whenever the input is scaled by a constant factor, the output is also scaled by the same constant factor. In other words, the system output to a linear combination of some inputs is the same linear combination of the outputs, where each output corresponds to a particular input. As shown in Figure 3.9, a system is linear if and only if the following is satisfied:

Linearity:

$$\text{If } x_1(t) \rightarrow y_1(t) \text{ and } x_2(t) \rightarrow y_2(t), \text{ then } \alpha x_1(t) + \beta x_2(t) \rightarrow \alpha y_1(t) + \beta y_2(t) \tag{3.14}$$

in which α and β are some nonzero constants. Surprisingly, if an input-output characteristic of a system is defined mathematically by a linear equation (i.e., $y(t) = mx(t) + b$, where $m \neq 0$ and $b \neq 0$), then the system is not linear, as it does not satisfy (3.14). Examples of linear systems include AM radio broadcasting and communication filters. In a linear system, the output to a zero input is always zero (for linearity, this is a necessary condition, but not a sufficient condition). It is important to highlight that linearity allows the decomposition of a complex input signal into a linear combination of some fundamental, probably well-known, signals whose outputs can be derived rather easily.

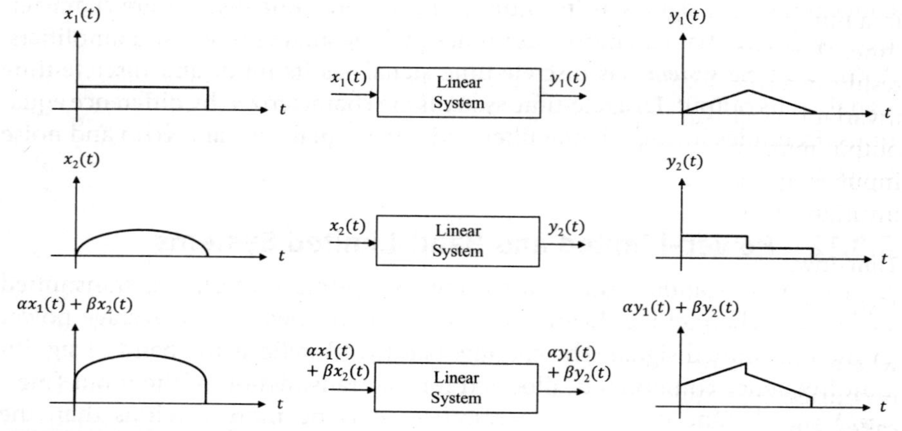

FIGURE 3.9 A linear system.

When a system is not linear, it is called a ***nonlinear system***. Linearity is a conceptual ideal and mathematical definition that cannot be strictly realized in practice in all cases. The reason lies in the fact that almost any device behaves in a nonlinear fashion, if its input amplitude is large enough. Also, many nonlinear systems can behave in an almost linear fashion, if their input signals are small enough. Examples of nonlinear systems include FM radio broadcasting and amplifiers operating at saturation. Nonlinearity may give rise to nonlinear distortion, which in turn can bring about intermodulation distortion. This means that the output has new frequency components that are not present in the input band, but do lie inside the input band and cannot thus be filtered out. It is thus essential to ensure that communication channels and devices operate in a linear region.

EXAMPLE 3.9

Classify the following systems as linear or nonlinear systems:

a) $y(t) = t^2 x(t)$ and b) $y(t) = t x^2(t)$.

Solution

To classify a system as linear, (3.14) must be satisfied.

(a) If we apply $x_1(t)$ and $x_2(t)$, we get $y_1(t) = t^2 x_1(t)$ and $y_2(t) = t^2 x_2(t)$, respectively. If we apply $\alpha x_1(t) + \beta x_2(t)$, we get $t^2(\alpha x_1(t) + \beta x_2(t))$, which is the same as $\alpha y_1(t) + \beta y_2(t)$, and the system is thus linear.

(b) If we apply $x_1(t)$, we get $y_1(t) = t x_1^2(t)$, and if we apply $x_2(t)$, we get $y_2(t) = t x_2^2(t)$. Now if we apply $\alpha x_1(t) + \beta x_2(t)$, we get $t(\alpha x_1(t) + \beta x_2(t))^2$, which is not the same as $\alpha y_1(t) + \beta y_2(t)$, and the system is thus nonlinear.

3.3.14 Time-Invariant and Time-Varying Systems

In a ***time-invariant system***, the input-output relationship does not change with time. This means that a time shift (i.e., time delay or time advance) in the input results in a corresponding time shift in the output. The characteristics of a time-invariant system do not change with time. In other words, for a given input, the output remains the same (i.e., its shape does not change), no matter when the input is applied to the system. As shown in Figure 3.10, a system is time-invariant if and only if the following is satisfied:

Time-Invariance:

$$\text{If } x(t) \rightarrow y(t), \text{ then } x(t-\tau) \rightarrow y(t-\tau) \tag{3.15}$$

where $\tau \neq 0$ is a real constant. A landline (fixed) telephone system during a call is considered a time-invariant system. A system that is not time-invariant is called a ***time-varying system***. A mobile telephone system is a time-varying system and modulation is a time-varying process.

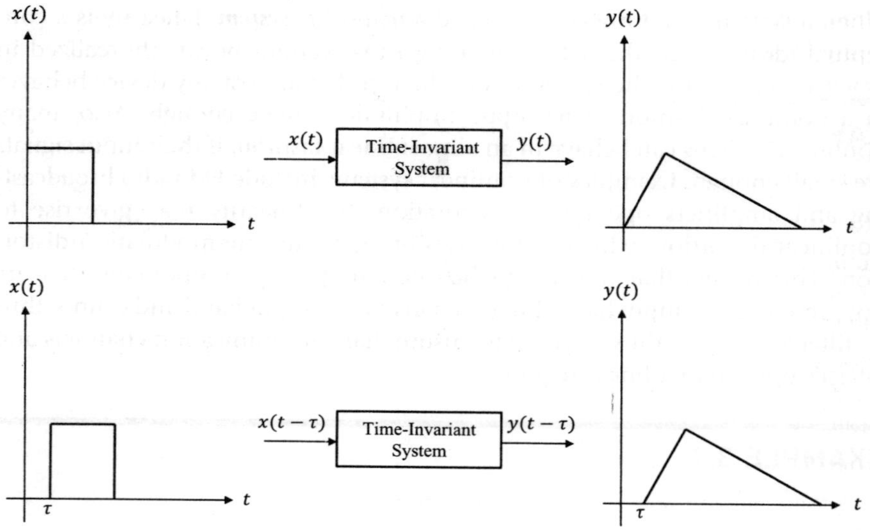

FIGURE 3.10 A time-invariant system.

To check a system for time-invariance, you need to compare the output produced by the shifted input with the shifted output, where the shifted output can be obtained by making a global change from t to $t-\tau$ in the input-output relation. If they are the same, the system is then a time-invariant system; otherwise, it is a time-varying system.

EXAMPLE 3.10

Classify the following systems as time-invariant or time-varying systems:

a) $y(t)=t^2x(t)$ and b) $y(t)=x^2(t)$.

Solution – To classify a system as time-invariant, (3.15) must be satisfied (i.e., we need to check if the output produced by the shifted input and the shifted output are the same).

(a) The output produced by the shifted input is $t^2x(t-\tau)$ and the shifted output $y(t-\tau)$ is $(t-\tau)^2x(t-\tau)$. These two are not the same and the system is therefore time-varying.

(b) The output produced by the shifted input is $x^2(t-\tau)$ and the shifted output $y(t-\tau)$ is $x^2(t-\tau)$. These two are the same, and the system is therefore time-invariant.

3.3.15 Linear Time-Invariant (LTI) Systems

In a ***linear time-invariant (LTI) system***, both linearity and time-invariance conditions must be satisfied. For LTI systems, the input-output relationship is straightforward. In an LTI system, the system impulse response, i.e., the system output when the system input is an impulse (a signal with extremely short duration and extremely large amplitude), can completely characterize the system and provide all relevant information to describe the system behavior for any input.

EXAMPLE 3.11

Classify the following systems into LTI and non-LTI systems:
a) $y(t)=x(t)\cos(t)$, b) $y(t)=(x(t+1)+x(t)+x(t-1))/3$, and c) $y(t)=\cos(x(t))$.

Solution

For each of these systems, we first determine if a system is linear by using (3.14), if it is, we then determine if it is time-invariant by using (3.15).

(a) When we have $y_1(t)=x_1(t)\cos(t)$ and $y_2(t)=x_2(t)\cos(t)$, then a linear combination of $x_1(t)$ and $x_2(t)$ as the input can give rise to an output that is the same linear combination of $y_1(t)$ and $y_2(t)$. It is thus linear.

The shifted output $y(t-\tau)=x(t-\tau)\cos(t-\tau)$ is not the same as the output produced by the shifted input $x(t-\tau)\cos(t)$. It is thus time-varying. We can therefore conclude it is not an LTI system.

(b) When we have $y_1(t)=(x_1(t+1)+x_1(t)+x_1(t-1))/3$ and $y_2(t)=(x_2(t+1)+x_2(t)+x_2(t-1))/3$, then a linear combination of $x_1(t)$ and $x_2(t)$ as the input results in an output that is identical to the same linear combination of $y_1(t)$ and $y_2(t)$. It is therefore linear.

The shifted output $y(t-\tau)=(x(t-\tau+1)+x(t-\tau)+x(t-\tau-1))/3$ is the same as the output produced by the shifted input $(x(t-\tau+1)+x(t-\tau)+x(t-\tau-1))/3$. It is therefore time-invariant. We can thus conclude it is an LTI system.

(c) When we have $y_1(t)=\cos(x_1(t))$ and $y_2(t)=\cos(x_2(t))$, then a linear combination of $x_1(t)$ and $x_2(t)$ as the input cannot give rise to an output that is the same linear combination of $y_1(t)$ and $y_2(t)$. It is thus a nonlinear system, and as such it cannot be an LTI system.

3.4 SINSUOIDAL SIGNALS

It is of paramount importance to state that the sinusoidal signal is the most widely-used signal in the analysis, design, and operation of communication systems. The sinusoidal signal may be viewed as a simple oscillating curve with smooth and consistent changes, where each period consists of a single arc above the time axis followed by a single arc below it.

3.4.1 Characteristics of Sinusoidal Signals

Continuous-time and discrete-time versions of a ***sinusoidal signal***, in the form of the cosine or sine functions, are respectively defined as follows:

$$\begin{aligned} g(t) &= A\cos(2\pi f_0 t+\varphi)=A\sin(2\pi f_0 t+\varphi') \\ g(n) &= A\cos(2\pi f_0 n+\varphi)=A\sin(2\pi f_0 n+\varphi') \end{aligned} \quad (3.16)$$

where $A\neq 0$ is the ***amplitude*** representing the peak deviation from zero, measured in volts or amperes, $f_0>0$ is the ***fundamental frequency*** measured in Hertz

(Hz), and $-\pi \leq \varphi \leq \pi$ and $-\pi \leq \varphi' \leq \pi$, each is the ***initial phase*** (i.e., when $t=0$ or $n=0$) measured in radians. In a continuous-time or a discrete-time sinusoidal signal, nf_0 (i.e., the integral multiple of the fundamental frequency) is referred to as the ***n^{th}-harmonic frequency***, where n is a positive integer.

A continuous-time sinusoidal signal is periodic and its ***period*** is the inverse of its fundamental frequency (i.e., $T_0 = 1/f_0$ seconds). The discrete-time version of a sinusoidal signal, where n is an integer, may or may not be periodic. The signal $g(n)$ is periodic with a period N/f_0 provided that N is the smallest integer that can make N/f_0 an integer. If f_0 is not a rational number, then there can be no N that can make N/f_0 an integer (i.e., $g(n)$ is not a periodic signal).

The sinusoidal signal $x(t) = A\cos(2\pi f_0 t + \varphi)$, where $\varphi \neq 0$, is the time-shifted version of the sinusoidal signal $y(t) = A\cos(2\pi f_0 t)$ by $\varphi/2\pi f_0$ seconds. A negative value of φ represents a ***delay*** (a shift to the right), i.e., $x(t)$ lags $y(t)$, and a positive value of φ represents a ***head-start*** (a shift to the left), i.e., $x(t)$ leads $y(t)$.

By using the trigonometric identities $A\cos(2\pi f_0 t + \varphi) \equiv -A\cos(2\pi f_0 t + \varphi + \pi)$ and $A\sin(2\pi f_0 t + \varphi) \equiv -A\sin(2\pi f_0 t + \varphi - \pi)$, a negative amplitude can always be turned into a positive one, provided that the initial phase is changed by $-\pi$ or π, depending on whether the sinusoidal signal is in the form of a cosine or a sine function, respectively. Positive amplitudes can be called magnitudes. Figure 3.11 shows the sinusoidal signal $x(t) = A\cos(2\pi f_0 t + \varphi)$ for various values of A, f_0, and φ.

EXAMPLE 3.12

Classify the following sinusoidal signals as periodic or nonperiodic signals:

a) $z_1(t) = \sin\left(8\pi t + \frac{\pi}{2}\right)$, b) $z_2(n) = \sin\left(8\pi n + \frac{\pi}{2}\right)$, c) $z_3(t) = 7\sin(2t)$, and d) $z_4(n) = 5\sin(2n)$.

Solution

The period of a periodic continuous-time or discrete-time sinusoidal signal is independent of the values of its amplitude and initial phase. In order to find the period of a sinusoidal signal, we set the independent-variable term in the argument of the sinusoidal signal equal to $2\pi f_0 t$, if the sinusoidal is a continuous-time signal, or equal to $2\pi f_0 n$, if the sinusoidal is a discrete-time signal.

(a) $z_1(t)$ is a continuous-time signal, and we thus have $8\pi t = 2\pi f_1 t$ (i.e., we have $f_1 = 4$ Hz or equivalently $T_1 = 1/f_1 = 0.25$). The period of $z_1(t)$ is thus 0.25 seconds.

(b) $z_2(n)$ is a discrete-time signal, and we thus have $8\pi n = 2\pi f_2 n$ (i.e., we have $f_2 = 4$ Hz or equivalently $T_2 = N/f_2 = 0.25N$). Since $N=4$ is the smallest integer that can make $0.25N$ an integer, $z_2(n)$ is a periodic signal whose period is 1 second.

(c) $z_3(t)$ is a continuous-time signal, and we thus have $2t = 2\pi f_3 t$ (i.e., we have $f_3 = 1/\pi$ Hz or equivalently $T_3 = 1/f_3 = \pi$). The period of $z_3(t)$ is thus π seconds.

d) $z_4(n)$ is a discrete-time signal, and we thus have $2n = 2\pi f_4 n$ (i.e., we have $f_4 = 1/\pi$ Hz or equivalently $T_4 = N/f_4 = N\pi$). Since π is not a rational number, there is no N that can make N/f_4 an integer, and $z_4(n)$ is therefore not periodic.

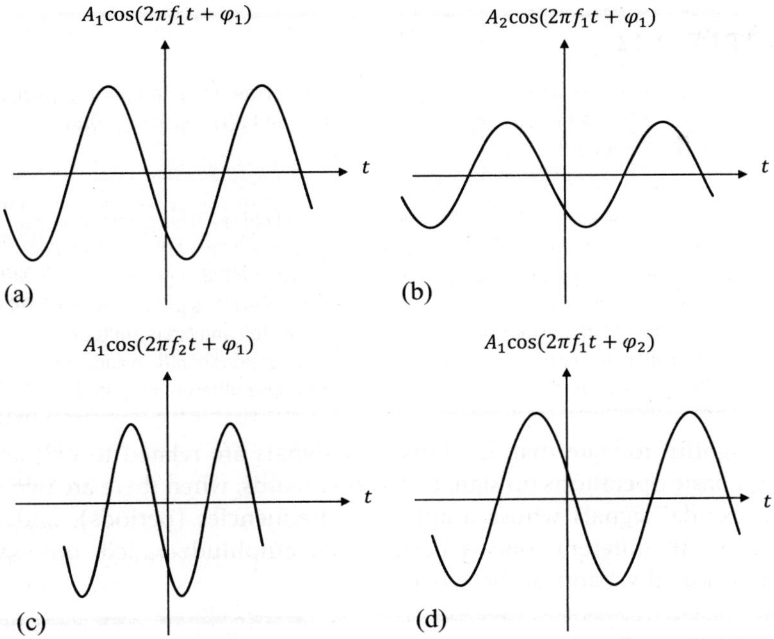

FIGURE 3.11 Sinusoidal signals with various amplitudes, frequencies, and initial phases: (a) a generic sinusoidal signal; (b) a sinusoidal signal whose amplitude is different from that in (a); (c) a sinusoidal signal whose frequency is different from that in (a); and (d) a sinusoidal signal whose initial phase is different from that in (a).

EXAMPLE 3.13

Classify the following signals as periodic or nonperiodic:

a) $x(t) = 2\cos(6t) + 3\sin(4t)$ and b) $x(t) = 5\cos(5\pi t) + \sin(2t)$.

Solution

A signal consisting of two sinusoidal signals is considered to be periodic, if the ratio of their periods is a rational number.

(a) The period of 2 cos(6*t*) (i.e., T_1) can be obtained by solving the equation $6t = 2\pi t/T_1$. We then have $T_1 = \pi/3$. The period of 3 sin(4*t*) (i.e., T_2) can be obtained by solving the equation $4t = 2\pi t/T_2$. We then have $T_2 = \pi/2$. The least common multiple of $\pi/3$ and $\pi/2$ is π. The period of $x(t)$ is thus π seconds. Note that $x(t)$ has a period of π during which 2 cos(6*t*) has a duration equal to three periods and 3 sin(4*t*) has a duration equal to two periods.

(b) The signal 5 cos($5\pi t$) is periodic whose period is 0.4 and sin(2*t*) is periodic whose period is π. Since the ratio of the two periods is not a rational number, $x(t)$ is not periodic.

EXAMPLE 3.14

Consider the following three different sinusoidal signals in terms of their amplitudes, frequencies, and initial phases: $h(t)=4\sin(2\pi t)$, $k(t)=2\sin(4\pi t+0.2)$, and $b(t)=6\sin(\pi t-0.8)$. Comment on $k(t)$ and $b(t)$ in relation to $h(t)$.

Solution

The period of $h(t)$ is 1, the period of $k(t)$ is 0.5, and the period of $b(t)$ is 2. This points to the fact that $k(t)$ is a compressed version of $h(t)$, where the time-scaling factor is 2, and $b(t)$ is a stretched version of $h(t)$, where the time-scaling factor is 0.5. In other words, since $h(t)$ is a periodic signal, $k(t)$ is also periodic with a fundamental frequency twice that of $h(t)$, whereas $b(t)$ is periodic with a fundamental frequency half of that of $h(t)$. Furthermore, $k(t)$ is shifted to the left and $b(t)$ is shifted to the right. It is clear that $k(t)$ and $b(t)$ both are time-shifted and time-scaled versions of $h(t)$. In addition, $h(t)$, $k(t)$, and $b(t)$ are amplitude-scaled versions of one another, as they have different amplitudes.

It is insightful to state that all sinusoidal signals are related to one another through basic operations on signals. In other words, when there are two different sinusoidal signals whose amplitudes, frequencies (periods), and initial phases are all different, one is basically an amplitude-scaled, time-shifted, and time-scaled version of the other.

EXAMPLE 3.15

Consider a sinusoidal signal $g(t)=A\cos(2\pi f_0 t+\varphi)$, where the parameters A, f_0 and φ are nonzero constants representing the amplitude, frequency, and initial phase of the sinusoidal signal, respectively. Determine if it is an energy signal or a power signal or neither.

Solution

The signal $g(t)$ is a real, periodic continuous-time signal with period $T_0=1/f_0$ and is therefore a power signal. Using Table 3.1, we have:

$$P=\left(\frac{1}{T_0}\right)\int_{-\frac{T_0}{2}}^{\frac{T_0}{2}}|g(t)|^2dt=(f_0)\int_{-\frac{1}{2f_0}}^{\frac{1}{2f_0}}(A\cos(2\pi f_0 t+\varphi))^2dt$$

$$=\left(\frac{A^2 f_0}{2}\right)\int_{-\frac{1}{2f_0}}^{\frac{1}{2f_0}}(1+\cos(4\pi f_0 t+2\varphi))\,dt=\left(\frac{A^2 f_0}{2}\right)\left(\tfrac{1}{2f_0}-\left(-\tfrac{1}{2f_0}\right)\right)=\frac{A^2}{2}$$

Note that the power of a sinusoidal signal is a function of its amplitude A only, and thus independent of its period T_0, fundamental frequency f_0, and initial phase φ.

3.4.2 Benefits and Applications of Sinusoidal Signals

From both theoretical and practical points of view, the sinusoidal signal is regarded as the most dominant signal in communication theory. We now briefly summarize the importance of sinusoidal signals from various perspectives.

Nature itself is characteristically sinusoidal, such as sound and light waves, seismic waves, and the ripples of the ocean surface. Man-made devices can have sinusoidal motions, such as sinusoidal variation in the motion of a pendulum, the oscillation of a spring around the equilibrium, and the vibration of a string. A clear whistle is an example of a sinusoidal change of pressure at a single frequency. A simple physical example in electric circuits includes an ideal charged capacitor connected in parallel to an ideal inductor, where the voltage across the capacitor in the steady state is a sinusoidal signal. A sinusoidal signal is easy to generate, transmit, and distribute and it is the form of electricity generated throughout the world and supplied to consumers.

A sinusoid is also easy to handle mathematically. For instance, the derivative, integral, and power functions of a sinusoid as well as the time-scaled and time-shifted versions of a sinusoid are themselves sinusoids. A sinusoidal signal is the only periodic signal where it retains its wave shape when added to another sinusoidal signal of the same frequency with arbitrary initial phase and amplitude. Through Fourier analysis, any practical nonsinusoidal periodic signal can be represented by the sum of sinusoids, each with its own amplitude, frequency, and initial phase.

It is crucial to highlight the fact that in an LTI system, for a sinusoidal input signal, the output is also a sinusoidal signal. However, the amplitude and initial phase of the output signal may be different from those of the input signal, but their frequencies remain the same (i.e., LTI systems hold the property of sinusoidal signal in, sinusoidal signal out), as shown in Figure 3.12.

3.4.3 Relation between Sinusoidal and Complex Exponential Signals

We first introduce the well-known Euler's identity and its two resulting identities:

$$
\begin{aligned}
e^{j\theta} &\equiv \cos(\theta) + j\sin(\theta) \\
\cos(\theta) &\equiv \frac{e^{j\theta} + e^{-j\theta}}{2} \\
\sin(\theta) &\equiv \frac{e^{j\theta} - e^{-j\theta}}{2j}
\end{aligned}
\tag{3.17}
$$

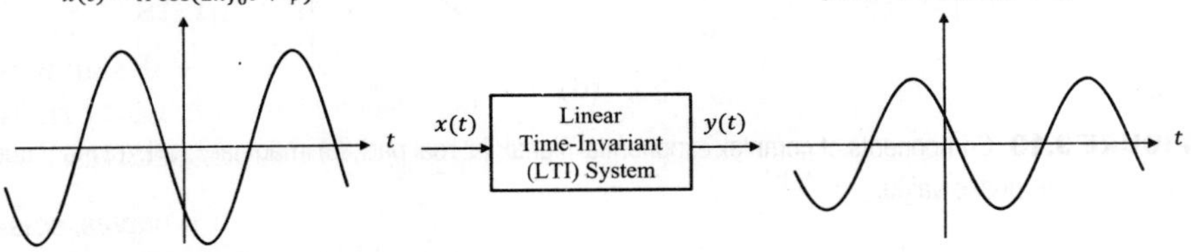

FIGURE 3.12 Sinusoidal signals in LTI systems.

where $j = \sqrt{-1}$. The continuous-time version of the ***complex exponential signal*** is then defined as follows:

$$g(t) = A\ \exp(j(2\pi f_c t + \varphi)) = A\ \cos(2\pi f_c t + \varphi) + jA\ \sin(2\pi f_c t + \varphi) \tag{3.18}$$

where A, f_c, and φ are known as the amplitude, frequency, and initial phase of the complex exponential signal, respectively, and both the real and imaginary parts are also periodic functions. $g(t)$ is a complex signal and therefore has no physical meaning. The reason for using it is to provide a compact mathematical description. Since $g(t)$ is complex, we can also describe it in terms of its magnitude and phase, and we thus have $|g(t)| = |A|$ and $\measuredangle g(t) = 2\pi f_c t + \varphi$. Figure 3.13 shows the real part $A\cos(2\pi f_c t + \varphi)$, the imaginary part $A\sin(2\pi f_c t + \varphi)$, the magnitude value $|A|$, and the phase value $(2\pi f_c t + \varphi)$ of the complex exponential signal $g(t)$. Moreover, for $\varphi = 0$, $g(t)$ is an example of a signal with complex conjugate symmetry (i.e., its real part is even and its imaginary is odd, or equivalently, its magnitude is even and its phase is odd).

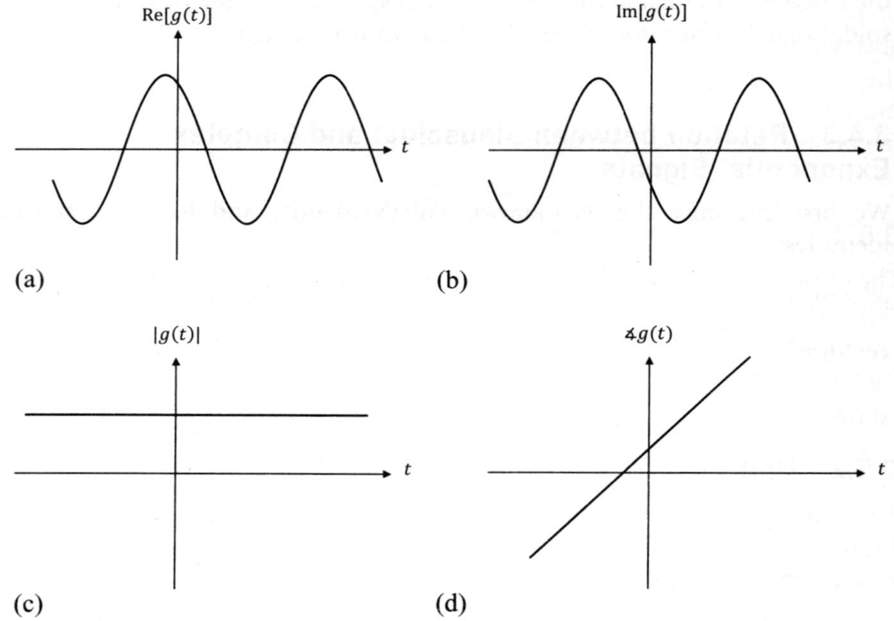

FIGURE 3.13 Components of complex exponential signal: (a) real part; (b) imaginary part; (c) magnitude value; and (d) phase value.

3.5 ELEMENTARY SIGNALS

Elementary or basic signals can be viewed as building blocks for the construction of more complex and practical signals, and may be used to help model some physical signals that occur in nature. The focus here is on continuous-time signals, but the discussion can be easily extended to discrete-time signals as well. All these signals are defined mathematically, and may be divided into two distinct groups. One group of signals are all continuous and differentiable at every point in time, such as sinusoidal and exponential signals. These two signals are important in the system analysis, for they can arise naturally in the solutions of the differential equations. Moreover, linear combinations of these signals can also be used to express many other real signals, thus giving rise to Fourier analysis.

Another group of signals is ***singularity functions*** that are not continuous or differentiable everywhere. In signal and system analysis, singularity functions, also known as generalized functions, are related to each other through integrals and derivatives and they can be used to mathematically describe signals with discontinuities or discontinuous derivatives. A singularity function may be defined piecewise and may exhibit a sudden change at some instants of time. Singularity functions are often used as standard inputs in checking the response of an LTI system in the time domain. Singularity functions are mathematical abstractions and, strictly speaking, do not occur in physical systems. However, they are useful in approximating certain conditions in physical systems. By multiplying some singularity functions and signals that are continuous and differentiable, we can get signals that are used widely in practical systems.

3.5.1 DC Signal

The values of a ***DC signal*** remain the same for all time t (i.e., $g(t) = k$, where k is a real number). Note that DC stands for direct current, and implies a constant value regardless of time. A physical example includes the voltage across an alkaline battery, such as 1.5-V AA batteries.

3.5.2 Unit Step Function

The ***unit step function*** is a singularity function. The unit step function multiplied by any signal produces a causal version of that signal. As shown in Figure 3.14, it is generally defined by

$$u(t) = \begin{cases} 1, & t \geq 0 \\ 0, & t < 0 \end{cases} \tag{3.19}$$

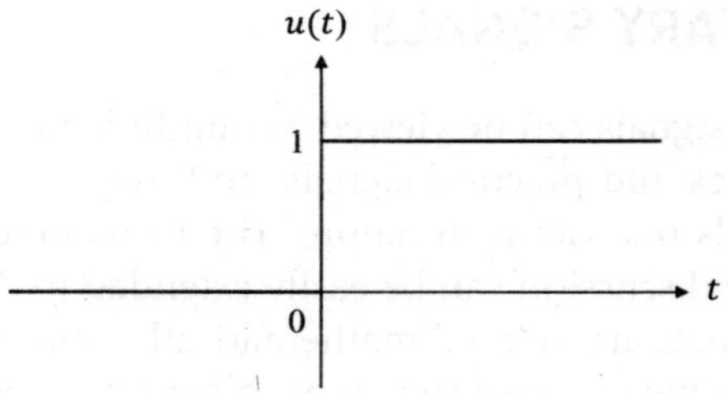

FIGURE 3.14 Unit step function.

3.5.3 Exponential Signal

The ***one-sided exponential signal*** is defined as follows:

$$g(t) = \begin{cases} k\exp(bt), & t \geq 0 \\ 0, & t < 0 \end{cases} \tag{3.20}$$

where $k \neq 0$ and b are both real numbers. k is the value of the signal measured at time $t = 0$. If $b > 0$, we have a growing exponential, and if $b < 0$, we have a decaying exponential. Note that if $b = 0$, then $g(t)$ reduces to a DC signal equal to the constant k. The voltage across a capacitor in a transient state when it is being discharged is in the form of a decaying exponential. The ***double exponential signal***, also known as the tent signal, may be viewed as the sum of a truncated decaying exponential signal and a truncated rising (growing) exponential signal, and is defined as follows:

$$g(t) = k\left(e^{bt}u(-t) + e^{-bt}u(t)\right) \tag{3.21}$$

where $b > 0$ and k is a real number. The ***exponentially-damped sinusoidal signal*** is defined as follows:

$$g(t) = ke^{-bt}\cos(2\pi f_c t + \varphi)u(t) \tag{3.22}$$

where $b > 0$ and k is a real number. Note that by increasing time t, the amplitude of the sinusoidal oscillation decreases in an exponential fashion, eventually approaching zero for infinite time.

3.5.4 Sinc Function

The ***sinc function***, as shown in Figure 3.15, is defined as follows:

$$g(t) = \frac{\sin(\pi t)}{\pi t} \triangleq \text{sinc}(t) \tag{3.23}$$

A sinc function is an even function with unity area. A sinc pulse passes through zero at all positive and negative integers (i.e., $t = \pm 1, \pm 2, \ldots$), but at time $t = 0$,

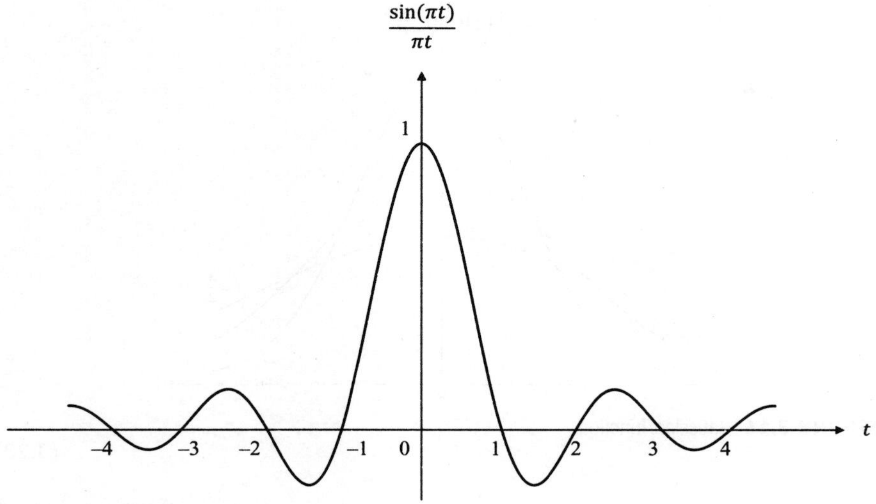

FIGURE 3.15 Sinc function.

it reaches its maximum of 1. This is a very desirable property in a pulse, as it helps to avoid intersymbol interference, a major cause of degradation in digital transmission systems. The product of a sinc function and any other signal would also guarantee zero crossings at all positive and negative integers.

3.5.5 Gaussian Pulse

The ***Gaussian pulse***, as shown in Figure 3.16, is defined as follows:

$$g(t) = \left(\frac{1}{\alpha}\right)\exp\left(-\frac{\pi t^2}{\alpha^2}\right) \tag{3.24}$$

where $\alpha > 0$. This pulse has a unit area, and dies down very rapidly. This pulse is neither time-limited nor frequency-limited. The Gaussian pulse is employed in GSM cellular systems.

3.5.6 Unit Ramp Function

The ***unit ramp function***, as shown in Figure 3.17, is defined as follows:

$$g(t) = tu(t) \tag{3.25}$$

The unit ramp function can be viewed as the integral of the unit step function (i.e., $g(t) = \int u(t)dt$).

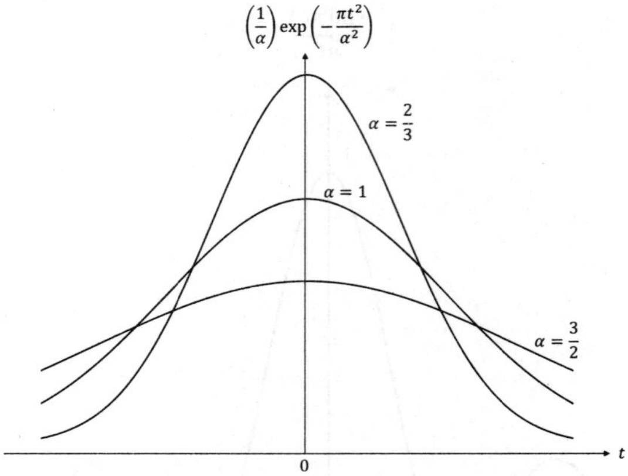

FIGURE 3.16 Gaussian function.

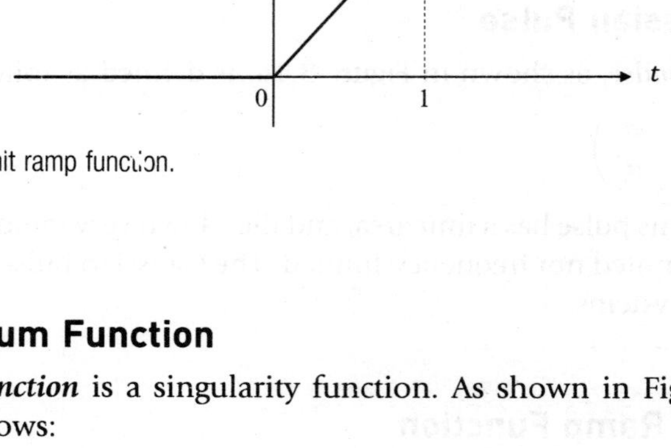

FIGURE 3.17 Unit ramp function.

3.5.7 Signum Function

The ***signum function*** is a singularity function. As shown in Figure 3.18, it is defined as follows:

$$\text{sgn}(t) \triangleq \begin{cases} 1, & t > 0 \\ 0, & t = 0 \\ -1, & t < 0 \end{cases} \tag{3.26}$$

A signum function can be used to generate the Hilbert transform of single-sideband modulated signals in amplitude modulation.

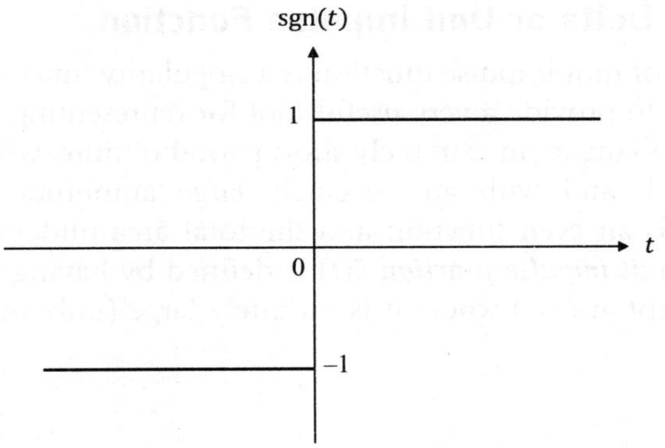

FIGURE 3.18 Signum function.

3.5.8 Rectangular Pulse

The ***rectangular pulse*** can be viewed as a singularity function. As shown in Figure 3.19a, it is defined as follows:

$$p(t) = Au\left(t + \frac{T}{2}\right) - Au\left(t - \frac{T}{2}\right) = \begin{cases} A, & |t| \le \frac{T}{2} \\ 0, & |t| > \frac{T}{2} \end{cases} \tag{3.27}$$

It is an even pulse whose width is T, height is A, and area is thus AT. If $AT = 1$, then it is a unit rectangular pulse. The ***radio frequency pulse*** is defined by the product of a rectangular pulse and a sinusoidal signal. A radio-frequency (RF) pulse is shown in Figure 3.19b. If a bit is represented by a rectangular pulse, then an RF pulse is a frequency-shifted version of the rectangular pulse.

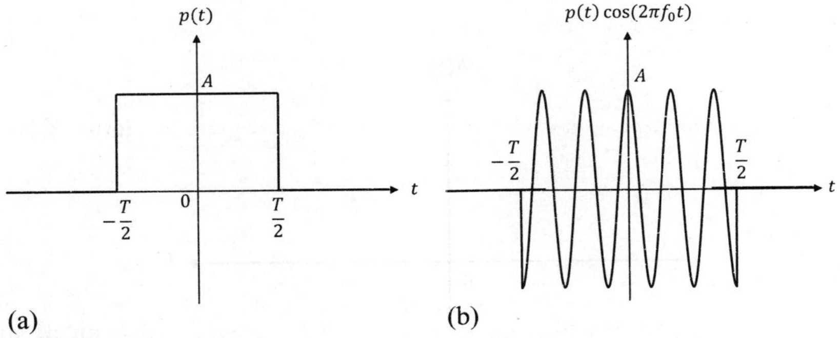

FIGURE 3.19 (a) Rectangular pulse and (b) radio frequency pulse.

3.5.9 Dirac Delta or Unit Impulse Function

The Dirac delta or unit impulse function is a singularity function, and defined mathematically to provide a very useful tool for representing a physical phenomenon that occurs in an extremely short period of time, which is too short to be measured, and with an extremely large amplitude. As shown in Figure 3.20, it is an even function and the total area under it is unity. The ***Dirac delta*** or ***unit impulse function*** $\delta(t)$ is defined by having zero amplitude everywhere except at $t=0$ where it is infinitely large (unbounded). We thus have:

$$\delta(t)=0,\ t\neq 0$$
$$\int_{-\infty}^{\infty}\delta(t)dt=\int_{0^-}^{0^+}\delta(t)dt=1 \tag{3.28}$$

The derivative of a unit step function is a delta function. The value of a unit step function is zero for $t<0$, hence its derivative is zero, and the value of a unit step function is one for $t>0$, hence its derivative is zero. However, a unit step function has a discontinuity at $t=0$. The derivative of a discontinuity is thus represented by an impulse function.

It is also important to point out that the delta function $\delta(t)$ can be defined as a limiting form of the Gaussian pulse or the unit rectangular pulse or the double exponential pulse, as each of these pulses can become infinitely narrow in duration and infinitely large in amplitude, and yet the area remains finite and fixed at unity. Also, note that (3.28) can give rise to the following well-known properties:

Shifting property: $$g(m)=\int_{-\infty}^{\infty}g(t)\delta(t-m)dt \tag{3.29a}$$

Convolution property: $$g(t)=\int_{-\infty}^{\infty}g(s)\delta(t-s)ds \tag{3.29b}$$

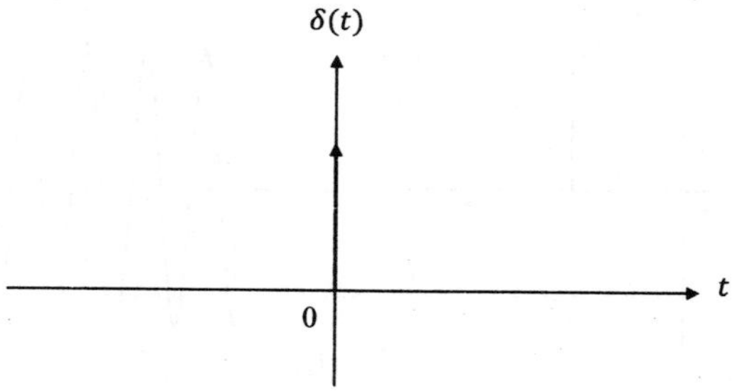

FIGURE 3.20 Unit impulse function.

3.5.10 Periodic Pulse and Impulse Trains

A ***periodic pulse train*** with period T_0 consists of rectangular pulses of duration T. The duty cycle of a periodic pulse train is defined by T/T_0. An application of the periodic pulse train is in the practical sampling process. An even periodic pulse train, as shown in Figure 3.21a, can be analytically expressed as follows:

$$g(t) = \sum_{k=-\infty}^{\infty} p(t - kT_0) \tag{3.30}$$

where $p(t)$ is a rectangular pulse, as defined in (3.27). A ***periodic impulse train*** consists of impulses (delta functions) uniformly spaced T_0 seconds apart. An application of a periodic impulse train is in the ideal sampling process. Using (3.28), an even periodic impulse train, as shown in Figure 3.21b, can be analytically expressed as follows:

$$g(t) = \sum_{k=-\infty}^{\infty} \delta(t - kT_0) \tag{3.31}$$

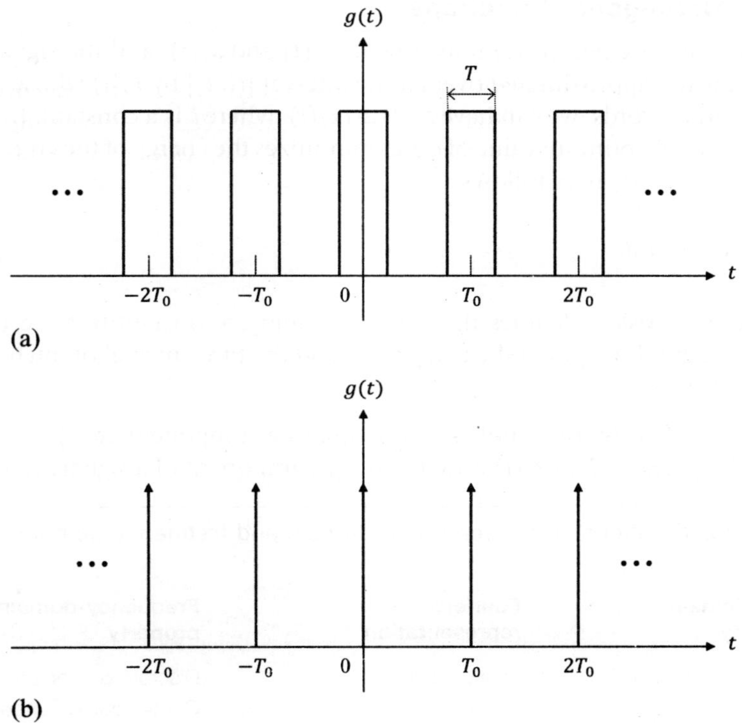

FIGURE 3.21 Periodic trains: (a) pulse train and (b) impulse train.

3.6 FOURIER SERIES

Utilizing sinusoidal functions to represent arbitrary signals is commonly referred to as ***Fourier analysis***. Fourier analysis, which is at the core of spectral analysis, allows a signal to be equivalently represented in the time domain or in the frequency domain. Table 3.2 presents time-domain properties of a signal and its frequency-domain properties using the appropriate Fourier representation. Table 3.2 reveals the following two interesting properties: i) continuous and discrete time-domain signals have nonperiodic and periodic frequency-domain representations, respectively, and ii) periodic and nonperiodic time-domain signals have discrete and continuous frequency-domain representations, respectively.

The focus of Fourier analysis in this chapter is on the Fourier transform, which is the frequency-domain representation of continuous-time nonperiodic signals, such as speech, music, image, and video. However, an introduction of the Fourier series is a necessary stepping stone toward a detailed discussion of the Fourier transform, as the Fourier series is easy to understand, and also has applications in analyzing communication circuits and designing communication filters.

3.6.1 Orthogonal Functions

Suppose there are two continuous signals $x_1(t)$ and $x_2(t)$, and the signal $x_1(t)$ can be linearly approximated over a time interval $[t_1, t_2]$ by $x_2(t)$ whose energy is E_2. In other words, we can have $x_1(t) \cong cx_2(t)$, where c is a constant. It can be shown that the optimum value of c that minimizes the energy of the error signal $e(t) = x_1(t) - cx_2(t)$ is as follows:

$$c = \frac{1}{E_2}\int_{t_1}^{t_2} x_1(t)x_2^*(t)dt \tag{3.32a}$$

where the asterisk * denotes the complex conjugate operation. Note that in (3.32a), both the shapes of the two signals and the time interval of interest play important roles.

Equation (3.32a) in turn implies $x_1(t)$ contains a component $cx_2(t)$, and $cx_2(t)$ is thus the projection of $x_1(t)$ on $x_2(t)$. If the component of a signal $x_1(t)$ of the

Table 3.2 Relationship between time-domain and frequency-domain properties

Time-domain property	Fourier representation	Frequency-domain property
Continuous & periodic	Fourier series	Discrete & nonperiodic
Continuous & nonperiodic	Fourier transform	Continuous & nonperiodic
Discrete & periodic	Discrete-time Fourier series	Discrete & periodic
Discrete & nonperiodic	Discrete-time Fourier transform	Continuous & periodic

form $x_2(t)$ is zero (i.e., we have $c = 0$), meaning there is zero contribution from one signal to the other, then $x_1(t)$ and $x_2(t)$ are said to be orthogonal over an interval $[t_1, t_2]$. Mathematically, $x_1(t)$ and $x_2(t)$ are ***orthogonal signals*** over a time interval $[t_0, t_0 + T_0]$, of duration T_0, if and only if we have the following:

$$c = \int_{t_0}^{t_0 + T_0} x_1(t) x_2^*(t) dt = 0 \tag{3.32b}$$

As a vector can be represented as a sum of orthogonal (perpendicular) vectors, which form the coordinate system of a vector space, a signal can be represented as a sum of orthogonal signals, which form the coordinate system of a signal space. A signal can be linearly approximated by a set of N mutually orthogonal signals over a certain interval. An orthogonal set of time functions is said to be a complete set if the approximation can be made into equality. The set of orthogonal functions, which are all linearly independent, is called a set of ***basis functions***. A vector can be represented as a sum of its vector components in various ways, depending on the choice of a coordinate system. Similarly, a signal can be represented as a sum of its signal components in various ways, depending on the choice of a set of basis functions. It can be shown that for a periodic signal, with period T_0, the sinusoids or complex exponentials of all harmonics of the fundamental frequency (i.e., n/T_0, where n is a positive integer) are an orthogonal complete set over the period, and form a set of basis functions.

3.6.2 Dirichlet's Conditions

Fourier series is an expansion of a periodic signal in terms of the summing of an infinite number of sinusoids or complex exponentials, as any periodic signal of practical nature can be approximated by adding up sinusoids with the properly chosen frequencies, amplitudes, and initial phases. To apply the Fourier series representation to an arbitrary periodic signal $g(t)$ with the period T_0, it is sufficient, but not strictly necessary, that the following conditions, known as ***Dirichlet's conditions***, are satisfied:

i) The periodic signal is single-valued, with a finite number of maxima and minima and at most a finite number of discontinuities within the interval of one period.
ii) The signal is absolutely integrable over the interval of one period, i.e.,

$$\int_{-T_0/2}^{T_0/2} |g(t)| dt < \infty \tag{3.33}$$

Note that although a periodic pulse train does not satisfy these conditions, it has a Fourier series representation. The signals usually encountered in communication systems meet the Dirichlet's conditions, as the physical possibility of a periodic signal, like those generated in a communications lab, is a sufficient condition for the existence of a converging Fourier series.

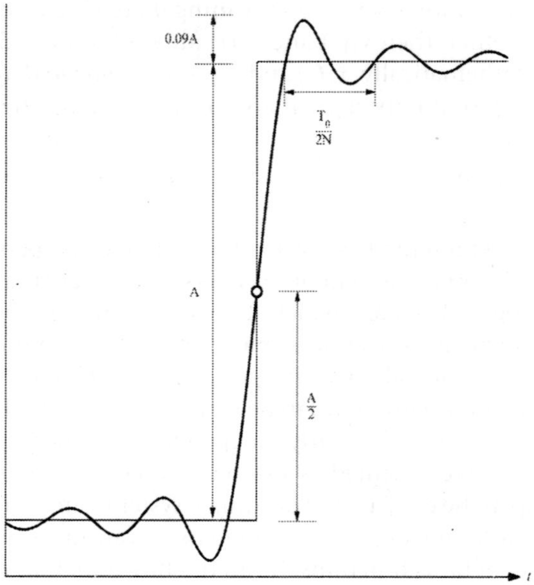

FIGURE 3.22 Gibbs phenomenon.

When there is a discontinuity in a piecewise continuously differentiable periodic signal $g(t)$, the series exhibits a behavior known as ***Gibbs phenomenon***, as shown in Figure 3.22. In that, the Fourier series at the point of discontinuity converges to an average of the left-hand and right-hand limits of $g(t)$ at the instant of discontinuity (i.e., to the arithmetic mean of the signal value on either side of the discontinuity). However, on each side of the discontinuity, the Fourier series has oscillatory overshoot with a period of $T_0/2N$, where T_0 is the signal period and N represents the number of terms included in the Fourier series, and a peak value of almost 9% of the amplitude of the discontinuity. The peak is independent of N, though the period of the oscillatory overshoot is a function of N. Since all real signals are continuous, Gibbs phenomenon does not occur, and we can thus assume the Fourier series representation is identical to the periodic signal. However, some mathematically defined signals, such as rectangular pulse train, have discontinuities, as such Gibbs phenomenon needs to be addressed.

3.6.3 Quadrature Fourier Series

In the ***quadrature Fourier series***, also known as ***trigonometric Fourier series***, the orthogonal functions are an infinite number of sine and cosine functions, representing the first and the remaining harmonics. The periodic signal, in which the period is T_0 and the quantity n/T_0 represents the nth harmonic of the fundamental frequency, may be expressed as follows:

$$g(t) = a_0 + \sum_{n=1}^{\infty}\left(a_n \cos\left(\frac{2\pi nt}{T_0}\right) + b_n \sin\left(\frac{2\pi nt}{T_0}\right)\right), \quad -\frac{T_0}{2} \leq t \leq \frac{T_0}{2} \tag{3.34a}$$

Note that each of the terms $\cos(2\pi nt/T_0)$ and $\sin(2\pi nt/T_0)$ is called a basis function. The term a_0, which represents the average value of the periodic signal $g(t)$, is also known as the DC component, and the summation term, known as the AC component, comprises an infinite series of harmonic sinusoids. In representing a periodic signal by sum of sinusoids, generally only the first few terms play a significant role in providing a very close approximation. The coefficients a_0 as well as a_n and b_n, representing the unknown amplitudes of the cosine and sine functions, are, respectively, as follows:

$$a_0 = \left(\frac{1}{T_0}\right)\int_{-T_0/2}^{T_0/2} g(t)dt \tag{3.34b}$$

$$a_n = \left(\frac{2}{T_0}\right)\int_{-T_0/2}^{T_0/2} g(t)\cos\left(\frac{2\pi nt}{T_0}\right)dt, \; n = 1, 2, \ldots \tag{3.34c}$$

$$b_n = \left(\frac{2}{T_0}\right)\int_{-T_0/2}^{T_0/2} g(t)\sin\left(\frac{2\pi nt}{T_0}\right)dt, \; n = 1, 2, \ldots \tag{3.34d}$$

Since $g(t)$ is periodic with period T_0, sometimes it may be more convenient to carry out the integrations from 0 to T_0 instead. When the periodic signal $g(t)$ is real, a_0, a_n, and b_n are then all real. If $g(t)$ is real and even, then $b_n = 0$ and its Fourier series contains only cosine terms, and if $g(t)$ is real and odd, then $a_n = 0$ and its Fourier series contains only sine terms.

EXAMPLE 3.16

Consider a periodic square wave $g(t)$ whose period is $2L$ seconds, as shown in Figure 3.23. This odd signal is described analytically over one period as follows:

$$g(t) = \begin{cases} -1, & -L < t \leq 0 \\ 1, & 0 < t \leq L \end{cases}$$

Determine the quadrature Fourier series coefficients, and sketch the signal in terms of its Fourier series coefficients.

Solution

Using (3.34b) and noting $T_0 = 2L$, we have the following:

$$a_0 = \left(\frac{1}{2L}\right)\int_{-L}^{L} g(t)dt = \left(\frac{1}{2L}\right)\left(\int_{-L}^{0} -dt + \int_{0}^{L} dt\right) = 0$$

Since $g(t)$ is an odd signal, $a_n = 0$, and the Fourier series consists of only sine functions. Using (3.34d), we have the following:

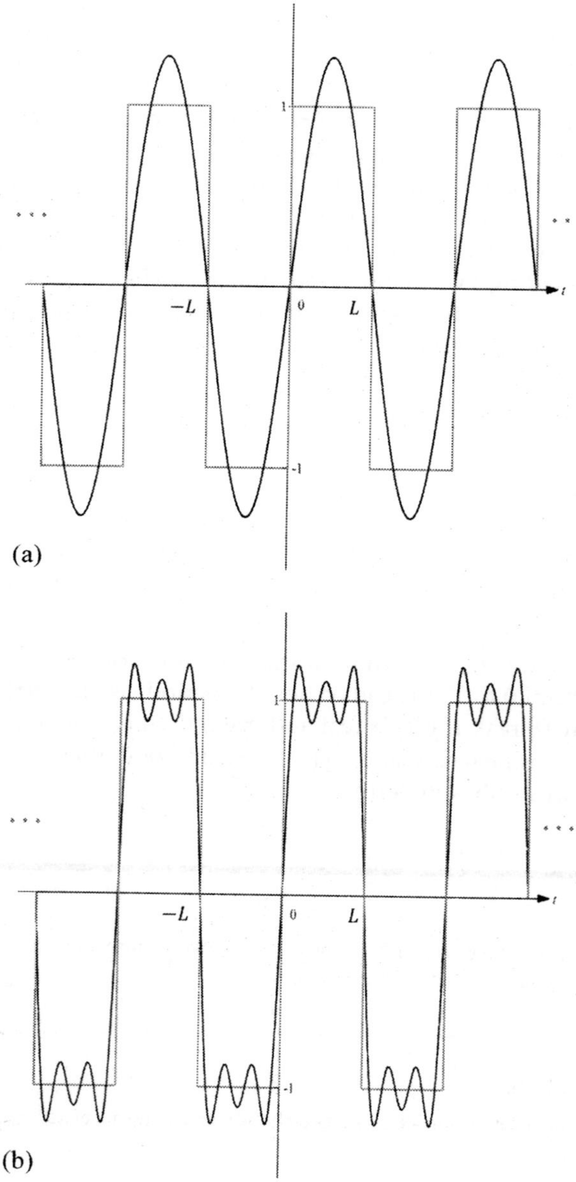

FIGURE 3.23 Signals in Example 3.16: (a) Fourier series approximation using first term; (b) Fourier series approximation using first five terms; and

(Continued)

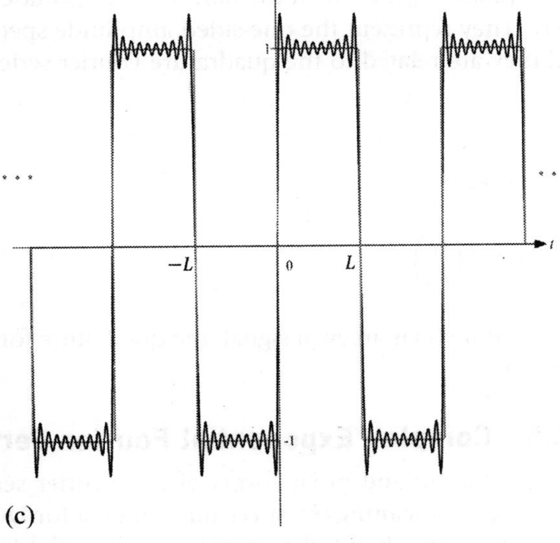

FIGURE 3.23, cont'd (c) Fourier series approximation using first twenty terms.

$$b_n = \left(\frac{1}{L}\right)\left(\int_{-L}^{0} - \sin\left(\frac{\pi nt}{L}\right)dt + \int_{0}^{L} \sin\left(\frac{\pi nt}{L}\right)dt\right) = \frac{2(1-\cos(\pi n))}{\pi n}$$

Note that for even values of n, we have $b_n = 0$. Using (3.34a), we thus get the following:

$$g(t) = \sum_{\substack{n=1 \\ n=odd}}^{\infty} \left(\frac{4}{\pi n}\right) \sin\left(\frac{\pi nt}{L}\right)$$

Figure 3.23 also shows the signals represented by the first term, the first five terms, and the first 20 terms in the above summation. It is important to note that only the first few terms play a critical role in providing a close approximation to the original square wave.

3.6.4 Polar Fourier Series

The *polar Fourier series* is a compact representation of the quadrature Fourier series, using the following trigonometric identity:

$$A\cos x + B\sin x \equiv \sqrt{A^2+B^2}\cos\left(x - \tan^{-1}\left(\frac{B}{A}\right)\right) \tag{3.35}$$

Using (3.35), (3.34a) can be transformed into the following:

$$g(t) = d_0 + \sum_{n=1}^{\infty} d_n \cos\left(\frac{2\pi nt}{T_0} + \theta_n\right), \ -\frac{T_0}{2} \le t \le \frac{T_0}{2} \tag{3.36a}$$

where d_0 is the DC component (average value), and the coefficients d_n and the initial phases θ_n are called the harmonic amplitudes and phase angles, respectively. They represent the one-sided amplitude spectrum and phase spectrum, and they are related to the quadrature Fourier series coefficients as follows:

$$d_0 = a_0 \tag{3.36b}$$

$$d_n = \sqrt{a_n^2 + b_n^2} \tag{3.36c}$$

$$\theta_n = -\tan^{-1}\left(\frac{b_n}{a_n}\right) \tag{3.36d}$$

Note that if $g(t)$ is an even signal, the quadrature form and polar form are then identical.

3.6.5 Complex Exponential Fourier Series

The quadrature and polar forms of the Fourier series are one-sided spectral components, meaning the spectrum can exist for DC and positive frequencies, but on the other hand, the complex exponential Fourier series has two-sided spectral components. The ***complex exponential Fourier series*** is a simple form, in which the orthogonal functions are the complex exponential functions. Using (3.17), (3.34a) can thus be transformed into the following:

$$g(t) = \sum_{n=-\infty}^{\infty} c_n \exp\left(\frac{j2\pi nt}{T_0}\right), \quad -\frac{T_0}{2} \le t \le \frac{T_0}{2} \tag{3.37a}$$

where c_n is defined as follows:

$$c_n = \left(\frac{1}{T_0}\right) \int_{-T_0/2}^{T_0/2} g(t) \exp\left(-\frac{j2\pi nt}{T_0}\right) dt, \; n = 0, \pm 1, \pm 2, \ldots \tag{3.37b}$$

The coefficient c_n is, in general, a complex number. It is important to note that the presence of negative frequencies and complex-valued basis functions has no physical meaning, and from a system analysis standpoint they just provide a compact mathematical expression. When $g(t)$ is real, then $c_{-n} = c_n^*$, where the asterisk * denotes the complex conjugate operation. If $g(t)$ is real and even, c_n is then a real number (i.e., its imaginary part is zero), and if $g(t)$ is real and odd, c_n is then a pure imaginary number (i.e., its real part is zero).

3.6.6 Spectrum of Periodic Signals

The objective to expand a periodic signal by a Fourier series is to obtain a representation in the frequency domain consisting of its various harmonic components. At each harmonic frequency, the signal has a magnitude and a phase that can be obtained from the complex exponential Fourier series coefficients c_n.

Using the complex exponential Fourier series, $g(t)$ has frequency components at all positive and negative multiples of the fundamental frequency $1/T_0$. The frequency-domain description consisting of frequency components is called a ***spectrum***. Because a periodic signal contains only discrete frequency components, the spectrum is referred to as a ***discrete spectrum***.

A periodic signal therefore has a dual representation: the time-domain representation that shows the signal repeats itself and the frequency-domain representation that shows the spectrum is discrete. The discrete spectrum gives an alternative representation of a periodic signal as it allows to synthesize the signal, to filter the undesired components of the signal, and to determine the approximate channel bandwidth required to pass the signal undistorted. In system analysis, the Fourier series can also be used to calculate the steady-state output of an LTI system responding to an arbitrary periodic signal. The Fourier coefficient c_n in (3.37b) may be expressed as follows:

$$c_n = |c_n| \exp(j\varnothing_n) \tag{3.38a}$$

where $|c_n| \geq 0$ and $\varnothing_n$ are the amplitude (or magnitude) and the phase of the nth harmonic component of the periodic signal $g(t)$, respectively. A plot of $|c_n|$ versus frequency yields the ***discrete amplitude spectrum*** of the signal and a plot of $\varnothing_n$ versus frequency is called the ***discrete phase spectrum***. These two are referred to as ***discrete spectra*** or ***line spectra***. For a real-valued periodic signal $g(t)$, we have the following:

$$|c_n| = |c_{-n}| \tag{3.38b}$$

$$\varnothing_n = -\varnothing_{-n} \tag{3.38c}$$

(3.38b) and (3.38c) indicate that for a real-valued periodic signal, the amplitude spectrum is symmetrical about the vertical axis (i.e., it is an even function of frequency) and the phase spectrum is symmetrical about the origin (i.e., it is an odd function of frequency). The coefficients a_n and b_n in the quadrature Fourier series are related to the coefficients c_n in the complex exponential Fourier series as follows:

$$c_n = \begin{cases} \dfrac{(a_n - jb_n)}{2}, & n > 0 \\ a_0, & n = 0 \\ \dfrac{(a_n + jb_n)}{2}, & n < 0 \end{cases} \tag{3.39}$$

It is important to also note that a DC component in a signal shifts the signal upward or downward, depending on if the DC component is positive or negative. The presence of a DC component has no impact on the definition of the fundamental frequency and its harmonics. However, its presence may make it harder to detect if the signal has any type of symmetry.

EXAMPLE 3.17

Consider the signal $g(t)$, which is an even periodic train of unit-amplitude rectangular pulses of duration T and period T_0, as shown in Figure 3.24a. Determine the complex exponential Fourier

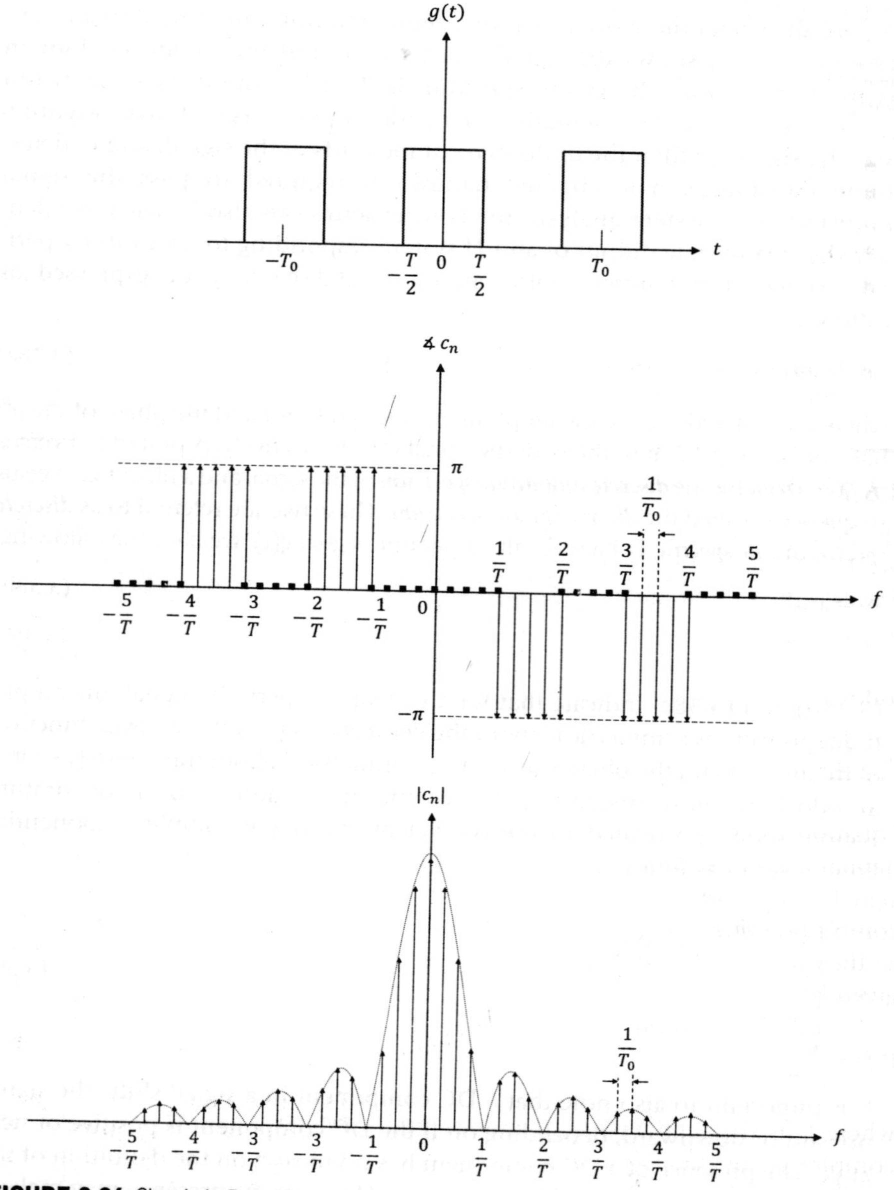

FIGURE 3.24 Signals in Example 3.17.

series coefficients, and sketch the magnitude spectrum $|c_n|$. Discuss the impacts of T and T_0 on the coefficients, and in turn on the discrete spectra.

Solution

Using (3.37b), we have the following:

$$c_n = \left(\frac{1}{T_0}\right) \int_{-T/2}^{T/2} \exp\left(-\frac{j2\pi nt}{T_0}\right) dt = \left(\frac{1}{\pi n}\right) \sin\left(\frac{\pi nT}{T_0}\right) = \frac{T}{T_0} \text{sinc}\left(\frac{nT}{T_0}\right)$$

The amplitude and phase spectra are also shown in Figure 3.24. We can thus draw the following conclusions:

- The amplitude and phase spectra are both discrete, for all duty cycles.
- Since $g(t)$ is a real signal, the amplitude spectrum is an even function and the phase spectrum is an odd function.
- The envelope of the amplitude spectrum is determined by the duty cycle $\frac{T}{T_0}$.
- The line spacing in the amplitude spectrum is inversely related to the period of the signal T_0. For a given pulse duration T, an increase in T_0 can thus bring about smaller line spacing (i.e., more discrete components).
- Zero-crossings (nulls) occur in the envelope of the amplitude spectrum at frequencies that are multiples of $1/T$. For a given period T_0, a decrease in T yields a broader main lobe.

3.6.7 Power of Periodic Signals

The power expression in general is not linear. However, for certain signals, such as a Fourier series that is an example of a set of orthogonal functions, the total power is the sum of the individual power values. Using the average power of a period signal introduced in Table 3.1 and the complex exponential Fourier series presented in (3.37a), the power content of a periodic signal is then as follows:

$$P = \sum_{n=-\infty}^{\infty} |c_n|^2 \tag{3.40a}$$

Equation (3.40a), which is a consequence of the orthogonality of the exponential basis functions, indicates that the average power content of a periodic signal is the sum of the power contents of its harmonic components in the complex exponential Fourier series of the signal. The above equation is known as the ***Parseval's power theorem***. For a periodic signal, the ***power spectrum*** is given by

$$P(f) = \sum_{n=-\infty}^{\infty} |c_n|^2 \, \delta(f - nf_0) \tag{3.40b}$$

where f_0 is the fundamental frequency and c_n represents the corresponding complex exponential Fourier series coefficients. Equation (3.40b) can also be used to define the power content as a function of the bandwidth of interest.

EXAMPLE 3.18

Consider the signal $g(t)$, a periodic train of rectangular pulses of duration 0.25 seconds and period of 1 second. This even signal is described analytically over one period as follows:

$$g(t)=\begin{cases}2, & 0\leq t\leq 1/8\\ 0, & 1/8<t<7/8\\ 2, & 7/8\leq t\leq 1\end{cases}$$

(a) Using the complex exponential Fourier series coefficients, determine the amplitude spectrum and the power spectrum of $g(t)$.
(b) Determine what portion of the power lies within the main lobe and also find the frequency W, where W is an integer, so about 96% of the power lies in the frequency range $[-W, W]$.

Solution

(a) Using (3.37b) and the result in Example 3.17, the amplitude spectrum is thus $|c_n|=|0.25\text{sinc}(\frac{n}{4})|$. Using (3.40b), we thus get the power spectrum as follows:

$$P(f)=\sum_{n=-\infty}^{\infty}\left(\frac{1}{16}\right)\text{sin c}^2\left(\frac{n}{4}\right)\delta(f-nf_0)$$

(b) Using Table 3.1, the total average power is then as follows:

$$P=\left(\frac{1}{T_0}\right)\int_{-T_0/2}^{T_0/2}|g(t)|^2dt=\int_{-1/8}^{1/8}4\,dt=1$$

Figure 3.25 shows the power content in terms of the number of power components. There are nine power components in the frequency range [−4, 4], whose sum is thus as follows: $\sum_{n=-4}^{4}(1/16)\text{sin c}^2(n/4)=0.904$ (i.e., over 90% of the total power in the main lobe). By considering a wider range than the frequency range [−4, 4], the portion of power can be beyond 90%. To this end, we now need to solve

$$\sum_{n=-W}^{W}\left(\frac{1}{16}\right)\text{sin c}^2\left(\frac{n}{4}\right)\geq 0.96$$

for W, where W is an integer. For $W=13$ Hz, more than 96% of the total power lies in the frequency range [−13, 13] (i.e., a total of 27 power components).

3.7 FOURIER TRANSFORM

The Fourier series is used to represent the frequency components of a periodic signal. However, in most applications, signals are not periodic. To represent the frequency components of a nonperiodic deterministic signal, the Fourier

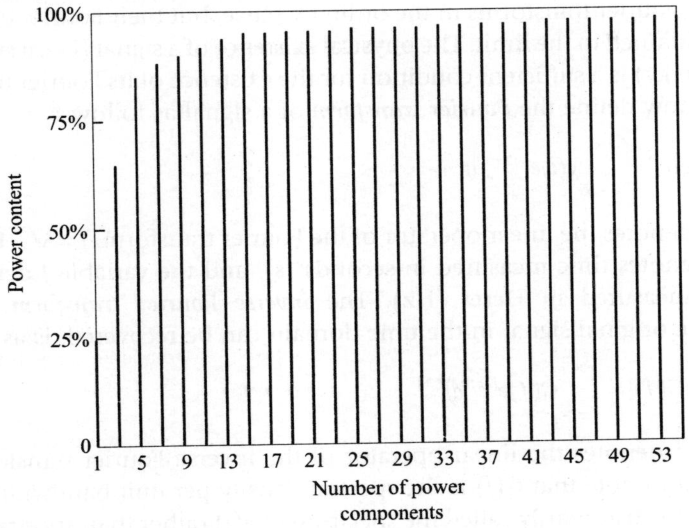

FIGURE 3.25 Signals in Example 3.18.

transform is employed. The Fourier transform of a nonperiodic signal can be viewed as the complex exponential Fourier series of a periodic signal whose period is approaching infinity, and one cycle of this periodic signal is defined by the nonperiodic signal. The spectrum thus becomes so dense that the spectral components are spaced at infinitesimal interval. Since the fundamental frequency is approaching zero, the discrete frequency approaches the continuous frequency and the summation becomes an integral. The resulting spectrum consists of a continuous range of frequencies, and may include a continuum of frequencies ranging from $-\infty$ to ∞.

3.7.1 Fourier Transform Pair

A signal is Fourier transformable if it satisfies the ***Dirichlet's conditions***. These conditions, which are sufficient but not strictly necessary, are as follows:

i) The signal is single-valued, with a finite number of maxima and minima and a finite number of discontinuities in any finite time interval.

ii) The signal is absolutely integrable over the entire time, i.e.,

$$\int_{-\infty}^{\infty} |g(t)|dt < \infty \tag{3.41}$$

Note that a sinc function does not satisfy Dirichlet's condition, as it is not absolutely integrable, yet it possesses the Fourier transform. Also, certain signals do not have Fourier transforms in the ordinary sense, but their Fourier transforms can be obtained in the limit. The physical existence of a signal (i.e., a signal with finite energy) is a sufficient condition for the existence of its Fourier transform. We can now define the ***Fourier transform*** of a signal as follows:

$$G(f) = F[g(t)] = \int_{-\infty}^{\infty} g(t)e^{-j2\pi ft}\,dt \tag{3.42a}$$

where F denotes the linear operator of the Fourier transform, $j = \sqrt{-1}$, the variable t denotes time measured in seconds (s), and the variable f denotes frequency measured in Hertz (Hz). The ***inverse Fourier transform,*** through which the original signal in the time domain can be recovered, is as follows:

$$g(t) = F^{-1}[G(f)] = \int_{-\infty}^{\infty} G(f)e^{j2\pi ft}\,df \tag{3.42b}$$

where F^{-1} denotes the linear operator of the inverse Fourier transform. It is important to note that $G(f)$ is the spectral density per unit bandwidth, but in practice it is customarily called the spectrum of $g(t)$ rather than spectral density of $g(t)$. We call $G(f)$, the Fourier spectrum of $g(t)$, as a lowercase letter denotes a time function and an uppercase letter denotes a function in frequency. A signal is uniquely defined by either its time-domain representation or its frequency-domain representation; a change in one results in a change in the other. A shorthand notation for the Fourier-transform pair is as follows:

$$g(t) \leftrightarrow G(f) \tag{3.42c}$$

3.7.2 Fourier Spectra

The Fourier transform $G(f)$ may be a complex function, even when $g(t)$ is real. It can thus be represented as follows:

$$G(f) = |G(f)|e^{j\theta(f)} \tag{3.43}$$

where $G(f)$ is known as the continuous spectrum of the signal $g(t)$, $|G(f)|$ is known as the ***magnitude spectrum*** (even though amplitude density spectrum would be more correct, as its dimension is amplitude per frequency), and $\theta(f)$ is known as the ***phase spectrum***, and they are both defined for all frequencies. Unless the inverse Fourier transform needs to be computed or some phase-sensitive process, such as the design of an all-pass filter, is to be carried out, the magnitude spectrum is usually more important than the phase spectrum. When $g(t)$ is a real signal, its Fourier transform has the following property:

$$G(f) = G^*(-f) \tag{3.44a}$$

where the asterisk * denotes the complex conjugation operation. From (3.44a), we can show that for a real signal, its Fourier transform is complex and

Hermitian (i.e., the magnitude spectrum is even and the phase spectrum is odd), and we therefore have the following:

$$|G(f)| = |G(-f)| \tag{3.44b}$$

$$\theta(f) = -\theta(-f) \tag{3.44c}$$

If $g(t)$ is real and even, $G(f)$ is then real and even, and if $g(t)$ is real and odd, $G(f)$ is then imaginary and odd.

To provide insight into the relationship between a time function and its Fourier transform, it is important to underscore that for a time-limited signal $g(t)$, which exists only over the interval $[a, b]$ and is zero everywhere outside this interval, the spectrum $G(f)$ consists of an infinite number of exponentials that all exist at all times $(-\infty, \infty)$. The amplitudes and phases of these components, as required, are such that they add up exactly to $g(t)$ over the interval $[a, b]$ and add up to exactly zero outside this interval.

EXAMPLE 3.19

Consider the signal $g(t) = \exp(-mt)\,u(t)$. Determine and sketch the Fourier transform of $g(t)$ when $m \neq 0$.

Solution

For $m < 0$ (growing exponential), the Fourier integral for $g(t) = \exp(-mt)\,u(t)$ does not converge. Hence, when $m < 0$, the Fourier transform of $g(t)$ does not exist. When $m > 0$ (decaying exponential), using (3.42a), we get

$$G(f) = \frac{1}{m + j2\pi f}$$

The amplitude spectrum $|G(f)|$ and the phase spectrum $\theta(f)$, as shown in Figure 3.26, are thus as follows:

$$|G(f)| = \frac{1}{\sqrt{m^2 + (2\pi f)^2}}$$

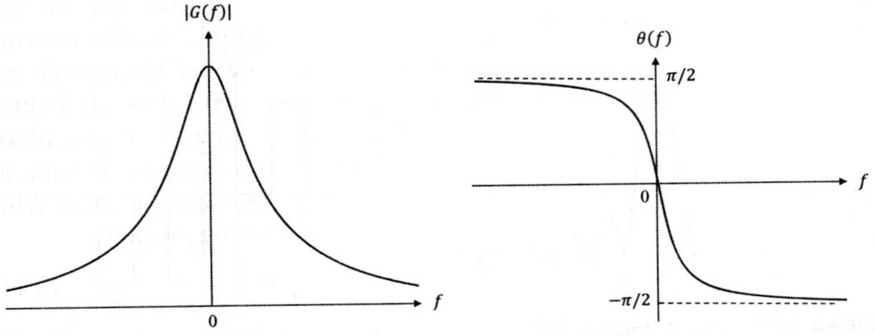

FIGURE 3.26 Signals in Example 3.19.

and

$$\theta(f) = -\tan^{-1}\left(\frac{2\pi f}{m}\right)$$

Since $g(t)$ is a real signal, $|G(f)|$ is an even function of f and $\theta(f)$ is an odd function of f.

EXAMPLE 3.20

Consider the signal $g(t)$, which is a rectangular even pulse of duration T and amplitude A, defined as follows:

$$g(t) = A(u(t+T/2) - u(t-T/2))$$

Determine the Fourier transform $G(f)$, and sketch its magnitude and phase spectra.

Solution

Using (3.42a), the Fourier transform $G(f)$ is determined as follows:

$$G(f) = \int_{-T/2}^{T/2} A\exp(-j2\pi ft)\,dt = AT\left(\frac{\sin(\pi fT)}{\pi fT}\right) = AT\,\text{sinc}(fT)$$

Since $g(t)$ is real and even, $G(f)$ is real and even. Figure 3.27 shows the magnitude spectrum $|G(f)|$ and the phase spectrum $\theta(f)$. The phase spectrum takes on the values 0° and + 180°, depending on the polarity of sinc(fT). We have used both + 180° and −180° to preserve the odd symmetry. The amplitude spectrum has a main lobe with a width of $2/T$ Hz, centered on the origin. The amplitudes of the side lobes decrease with increases in frequency.

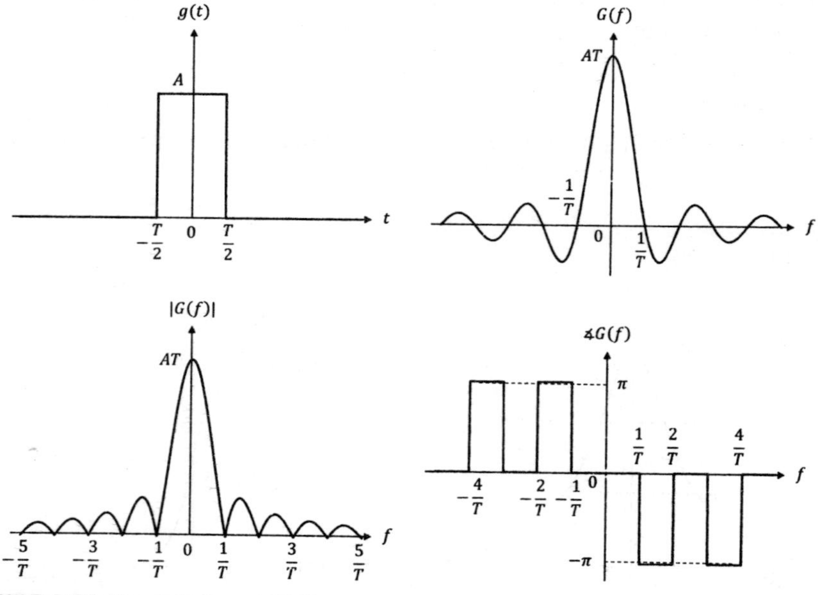

FIGURE 3.27 Signals in Example 3.20.

EXAMPLE 3.21

Determine the Fourier transform of $\delta(t - t_0)$, where t_0 is a constant time shift, and the inverse Fourier transform of $\delta(f - f_0)$, where f_0 is a constant frequency shift.

Solution

Using (3.42a), we get the following:

$$G(f) = \int_{-\infty}^{\infty} \delta(t - t_0)\, e^{-j2\pi ft}\, dt$$

Using (3.29a), the sifting property, we obtain the following:

$$\delta(t - t_0) \leftrightarrow e^{-j2\pi f t_0}$$

Note that when $t_0 = 0$, we get the following well-known Fourier transform pair, as shown in Figure 3.28a:

$$\delta(t) \leftrightarrow 1$$

Using (3.42b), we get the following:

$$g(t) = \int_{-\infty}^{\infty} \delta(f - f_0)\, e^{j2\pi ft}\, df$$

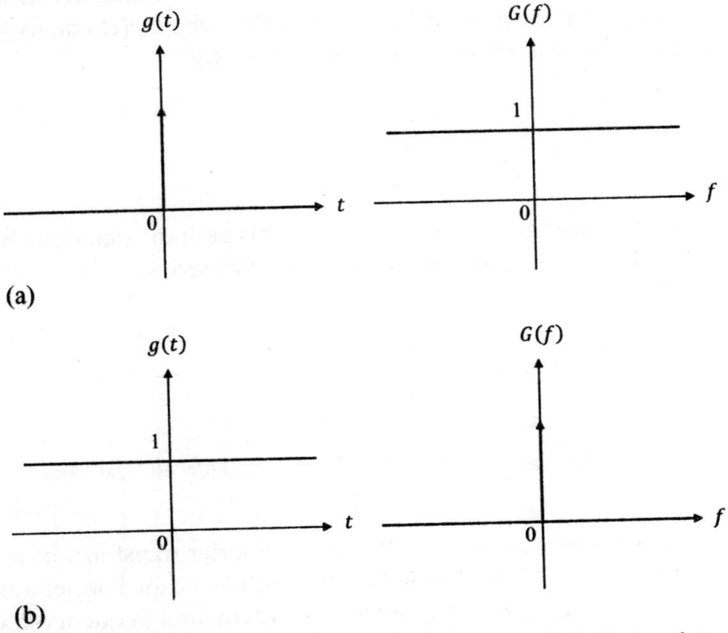

FIGURE 3.28 Signals in Example 3.21: (a) Dirac delta function and its Fourier transform and (b) DC signal and its Fourier transform.

Using (3.29a), the sifting property, we obtain the following:

$e^{j2\pi f_0 t} \leftrightarrow \delta(f - f_0)$

Note that when $f_0 = 0$, we get the following well-known Fourier transform pair, as shown in Figure 3.28b:

$1 \leftrightarrow \delta(f)$

3.7.3 Fourier Transform for Periodic Signals

The Fourier transform of a periodic signal, in a strict mathematical sense, does not exist, as periodic signals are not energy signals. In a limiting sense, Fourier transform can be defined for complex exponentials. As such, the Fourier transform of a periodic signal can be obtained through the Fourier transform of its complex exponential Fourier series term by term. To this effect, all periodic signals have a common feature in that their Fourier transforms consist of delta functions. Thus, the delta (impulse) function, which does not exist physically and is not defined explicitly, can provide a unified method of describing periodic signals in the frequency domain.

Consider the periodic signal $g(t)$ with period T_0. We can then define the periodic signal $g(t)$ using the generating function $p(t)$, where $p(t)$ equals $g(t)$ over one single period and is zero elsewhere, as shown by:

$$g(t) = \sum_{m=-\infty}^{\infty} p(t - mT_0) \tag{3.45}$$

On the other hand, using (3.37a) and (3.37b), this periodic signal can be represented in terms of the complex exponential Fourier series:

$$g(t) = \sum_{n=-\infty}^{\infty} c_n \exp\left(\frac{j2\pi nt}{T_0}\right) \tag{3.46a}$$

$$c_n = \left(\frac{1}{T_0}\right)\int_{-T_0/2}^{T_0/2} g(t)\exp\left(-\frac{j2\pi nt}{T_0}\right)dt = f_0\int_{-\infty}^{\infty} p(t)\exp(-j2\pi nf_0 t)dt = f_0 P(nf_0) \tag{3.46b}$$

where c_n is the complex coefficient, $P(f)$ is the Fourier transform of $p(t)$, and $f_0 = 1/T_0$. As the RHS of (3.46b) indicates, the samples of the Fourier transform of the generating function at multiples of the fundamental frequency f_0 and the complex exponential Fourier series coefficients of the periodic function are linearly related. Substituting (3.46b) into (3.46a) and combining the result with (3.45) yields the following:

$$g(t) = \sum_{m=-\infty}^{\infty} p(t - mT_0) = f_0 \sum_{n=-\infty}^{\infty} P(nf_0) \exp(j2\pi nf_0 t) \tag{3.47}$$

where (3.47) is known as ***Poisson's sum formula.*** Noting the Fourier transform of an exponential function is a delta function, the Fourier transform of the periodic signal $g(t)$ in (3.47) is then as follows:

$$g(t) = \sum_{m=-\infty}^{\infty} p(t - mT_0) \leftrightarrow G(f) = f_0 \sum_{n=-\infty}^{\infty} P(nf_0)\delta(f - nf_0) \tag{3.48}$$

Equation (3.48) highlights the fact that the Fourier transform of a periodic signal consists of delta functions occurring at integer multiples of the fundamental frequency, including the origin, and each delta function is scaled by a factor equal to the corresponding value of $P(nf_0)$. Note that the nonperiodic generating function $p(t)$, constituting one period of $g(t)$, has a continuous spectrum, but the periodic $g(t)$ has a discrete spectrum. In other words, periodicity in the time domain results in a discrete spectrum defined at integer multiple of the fundamental frequency.

Note that for an infinite sequence of uniformly spaced delta functions, we have $p(t) = \delta(t)$ and we thus have $P(f) = 1$. Using (3.48), we can have the following interesting relation:

$$\sum_{m=-\infty}^{\infty} \delta(t - mT_0) \leftrightarrow f_0 \sum_{n=-\infty}^{\infty} \delta(f - nf_0) \tag{3.49}$$

Note that if $T_0 = 1$ (i.e., $f_0 = 1$), then an infinite sequence of uniformly spaced delta functions in the time domain is its own Fourier transform.

EXAMPLE 3.22

Determine the Fourier transforms of $\cos(2\pi f_c t)$ and $\sin(2\pi f_c t)$.

Solution

The signal $\cos(2\pi f_c t)$ is periodic with period $1/f_c$, and the generating function $p(t)$ is as follows:

$$p(t) = \begin{cases} \cos(2\pi f_c t), & |t| \le \dfrac{1}{2f_c} \\ 0, & |t| > \dfrac{1}{2f_c} \end{cases}$$

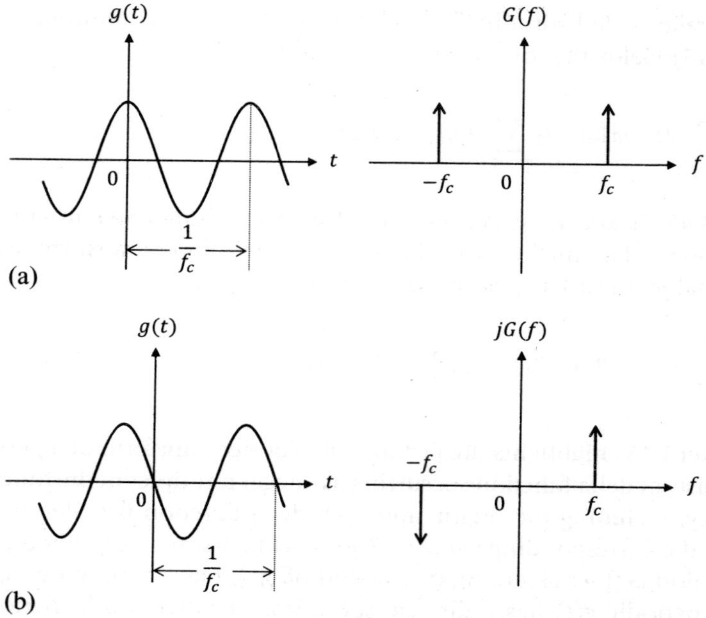

FIGURE 3.29 Signals in Example 3.22: (a) cosine function and its Fourier transform and (b) sine function and its Fourier transform.

Using (3.17) and (3.42a), the Fourier transform of $p(t)$ is as follows:

$$P(f)=\int_{-\frac{1}{2f_c}}^{\frac{1}{2f_c}} \cos(2\pi f_c t)e^{-j2\pi ft}\,dt=\int_{-\frac{1}{2f_c}}^{\frac{1}{2f_c}}\left(\frac{e^{j2\pi f_c t}+e^{-j2\pi f_c t}}{2}\right)e^{-j2\pi ft}\,dt=\frac{\sin(\pi f/f_c)}{2\pi(f_c-f)}+\frac{\sin(\pi f/f_c)}{2\pi(-f_c-f)}$$

$P(f)$ at multiples of f_c is then as follows:

$$P(nf_c)=\frac{\sin(\pi n)}{2\pi f_c(1-n)}+\frac{\sin(\pi n)}{2\pi f_c(-1-n)}$$

Using L'Hôpital's rule, we have $P(\pm f_c)=1/2f_c$, and for all other values of n (i.e., $n\neq\pm1$), we have $P(nf_c)=0$. Using (3.48), we thus have the following important Fourier transform pair:

$$\cos(2\pi f_c t)\leftrightarrow 0.5(\delta(f-f_c)+\delta(f+f_c))$$

With the same line of reasoning, we can get the Fourier transform of $\sin(2\pi f_c t)$ as follows:

$$\sin(2\pi f_c t)\leftrightarrow -0.5j(\delta(f-f_c)-\delta(f+f_c))$$

Figure 3.29 shows $\cos(2\pi f_c t)$ and $\sin(2\pi f_c t)$ and their Fourier transforms.

3.7.4 Properties of Fourier Transform

The Fourier transform possesses many important and useful properties through which the tedious mathematical work of finding the Fourier transform or the inverse Fourier transform can be significantly simplified. Effective applications of these properties, along with possible exploitation of signal symmetries, can provide a valuable check on the final results. The Fourier transform properties are summarized in Table 3.3.

Table 3.3 Fourier transform properties

Property	Mathematical description
Linearity	$g_1(t) \leftrightarrow G_1(f) \,\&\, g_2(t) \leftrightarrow G_2(f) \Rightarrow \alpha g_1(t) + \beta g_2(t) \leftrightarrow \alpha G_1(f) + \beta G_2(f)$
Time-frequency duality	$g(t) \leftrightarrow G(f) \Rightarrow G(t) \leftrightarrow g(-f)$
Time scaling	$g(t) \leftrightarrow G(f) \Rightarrow g(\alpha t) \leftrightarrow \left(\frac{1}{\lvert\alpha\rvert}\right) G\left(\frac{f}{\alpha}\right)$
Time reversal	$g(t) \leftrightarrow G(f) \Rightarrow g(-t) \leftrightarrow G(-f)$
Time shifting	$g(t) \leftrightarrow G(f) \Rightarrow g(t-t_0) \leftrightarrow G(f)e^{-j2\pi f t_0}$
Frequency translation	$g(t) \leftrightarrow G(f) \Rightarrow e^{j2\pi f_c t} g(t) \leftrightarrow G(f-f_c)$
Linear modulation	$g(t) \leftrightarrow G(f) \Rightarrow g(t)\cos(2\pi f_c t) \leftrightarrow 0.5(G(f+f_c) + G(f-f_c))$
Time convolution	$g_1(t) \leftrightarrow G_1(f) \,\&\, g_2(t) \leftrightarrow G_2(f) \Rightarrow g_1(t) * g_2(t) \leftrightarrow G_1(f)G_2(f)$
Time multiplication	$g_1(t) \leftrightarrow G_1(f) \,\&\, g_2(t) \leftrightarrow G_2(f) \Rightarrow g_1(t)g_2(t) \leftrightarrow G_1(f) * G_2(f)$
Conjugate functions	$g(t) \leftrightarrow G(f) \Rightarrow g^*(t) \leftrightarrow G^*(-f)$
Time autocorrelation	$g(t) \leftrightarrow G(f) \,\&\, R_g(\tau) = \int_{-\infty}^{\infty} g^*(t)g(t-\tau)dt \Rightarrow R_g(\tau) \leftrightarrow \lvert G(f)\rvert^2$
Time differentiation	$g(t) \leftrightarrow G(f) \Rightarrow \frac{d}{dt} g(t) \leftrightarrow j2\pi f G(f)$
Time integration	$g(t) \leftrightarrow G(f) \Rightarrow \int_{-\infty}^{t} g(\tau)d\tau \leftrightarrow \frac{G(f)}{j2\pi f} + \frac{G(0)}{2}\delta(f)$
n^{th} moments	$g(t) \leftrightarrow G(f) \Rightarrow t^n g(t)dt \leftrightarrow \left(\frac{j}{2\pi}\right)^n + \frac{d^n}{df^n} G(f)$
Time average	$g(t) \leftrightarrow G(f) \Rightarrow \int_{-\infty}^{\infty} g(t)dt = G(0)$
Frequency average	$g(t) \leftrightarrow G(f) \Rightarrow \int_{-\infty}^{\infty} G(f)df = g(0)$
Parseval's relation	$g_1(t) \leftrightarrow G_1(f) \,\&\, g_2(t) \leftrightarrow G_2(f) \Rightarrow \int_{-\infty}^{\infty} g_1(t)g_2^*(t)dt = \int_{-\infty}^{\infty} G_1(f)G_2^*(f)df$

Note: 1) $\leftrightarrow$ *implies Fourier transform pair*

2) *"$A \Rightarrow B$" implies "If A, then B"*

3) *$\lvert\,\rvert$ denotes magnitude of the complex quantity contained within*

4) *α and β are some real constants and n is some positive integer*

5) *$*$ implies the complex conjugate operation when left as an exponent and implies the convolution operation when inserted between two signals*

Linearity Property:
Let $g_1(t) \leftrightarrow G_1(f)$ and $g_2(t) \leftrightarrow G_2(f)$, then for constants α and β, we have (3.50)
$\alpha g_1(t) + \beta g_2(t) \leftrightarrow \alpha G_1(f) + \beta G_2(f)$

The proof of this property directly follows from the linearity of integrals defining the Fourier transform and the inverse Fourier transform.

This extremely important property underscores the fact that the Fourier transform is a linear operation. In other words, the Fourier transform of a linear combination of a number of Fourier transformable signals is equal to the same linear combination of the Fourier transforms of the signals, and vice versa.

EXAMPLE 3.23

Determine the Fourier transforms of the even and odd parts of the rectangular pulse $g(t)$ defined as follows: $g(t) = A\,u(t) - A\,u(t-T)$.

Solution

Using (3.12), we have $g_e(t) = (g(t) + g(-t))/2$ and $g_o(t) = (g(t) - g(-t))/2$. Using the linearity property, we can get the Fourier transforms of $g_e(t)$ and $g_o(t)$ as follows:

$$\begin{aligned}
G_e(f) &= \int_{-\infty}^{\infty} g_e(t)\exp(-j2\pi ft)\,dt = 0.5\int_{-\infty}^{\infty} (g(t)+g(-t))\exp(-j2\pi ft)dt \\
&= 0.5\int_{-\infty}^{\infty} g(t)\exp(-j2\pi ft)\,dt + 0.5\int_{-\infty}^{\infty} g(-t)\exp(-j2\pi ft)dt \\
&= 0.5\int_{0}^{T} A\exp(-j2\pi ft)\,dt + 0.5\int_{-T}^{0} A\exp(-j2\pi ft)\,dt \\
&= \left(\frac{A}{2}\right)\left(-\frac{1}{j2\pi f}\right)(\exp(-j2\pi fT)-1) + \left(\frac{A}{2}\right)\left(-\frac{1}{j2\pi f}\right)(1-\exp(j2\pi fT)) \\
&= \left(\frac{A}{2}\right)\left(-\frac{1}{j2\pi f}\right)[\exp(-j2\pi fT) - \exp(j2\pi fT)] = \left(\frac{A}{2}\right)\left(-\frac{1}{j2\pi f}\right)(-2j\sin(2\pi fT)) = AT\,\mathrm{sinc}(2fT)
\end{aligned}$$

$$\begin{aligned}
G_o(f) &= \int_{-\infty}^{\infty} g_o(t)\exp(-j2\pi ft)\,dt = 0.5\int_{-\infty}^{\infty} (g(t)-g(-t))\exp(-j2\pi ft)\,dt \\
&= 0.5\int_{-\infty}^{\infty} g(t)\exp(-j2\pi ft)\,dt - 0.5\int_{-\infty}^{\infty} g(-t)\exp(-j2\pi ft)\,dt \\
&= 0.5\int_{0}^{T} A\exp(-j2\pi ft)\,dt - 0.5\int_{-T}^{0} A\exp(-j2\pi ft)\,dt \\
&= \left(\frac{A}{2}\right)\left(-\frac{1}{j2\pi f}\right)(\exp(-j2\pi fT)-1) - \left(\frac{A}{2}\right)\left(-\frac{1}{j2\pi f}\right)(1-\exp(+j2\pi fT)) \\
&= \left(\frac{A}{2}\right)\left(-\frac{1}{j2\pi f}\right)[\exp(-j2\pi fT) + \exp(j2\pi fT) - 2] \\
&= \left(\frac{A}{2}\right)\left(-\frac{1}{j2\pi f}\right)(2\cos(2\pi fT)-2) = j\left(\frac{A}{2\pi f}\right)(-2\sin^2(\pi fT)) = -jAT\,\mathrm{sinc}(fT)\sin(\pi fT)
\end{aligned}$$

EXAMPLE 3.24

Determine the Fourier transform of the unit step function $u(t)$.

Solution

The unit step function can be viewed as a limit of the following exponential function:

$$g(t) = \begin{cases} \dfrac{(1+e^{-at})}{2}, & t>0 \\ \dfrac{(1-e^{at})}{2}, & t<0 \end{cases}$$

We can thus define the unit step function as follows:

$$u(t) = \lim_{a\to 0} g(t)$$

The Fourier transform of $g(t)$ is then as follows:

$$\begin{aligned} G(f) &= \int_{-\infty}^{0} \frac{(1-e^{at})}{2}\exp(-j2\pi ft)\,dt + \int_{0}^{\infty} \frac{(1+e^{-at})}{2}\exp(-j2\pi ft)\,dt \\ &= 0.5\left\{\int_{-\infty}^{0} -e^{at}\exp(-j2\pi ft)\,dt + \int_{0}^{\infty} e^{-at}\exp(-j2\pi ft)dt\right\} + 0.5\int_{-\infty}^{\infty} \exp(-j2\pi ft)\,dt \\ &= 0.5\left\{-\frac{1}{a-j2\pi f} + \frac{1}{a+j2\pi f}\right\} + 0.5\,\delta(f) = \frac{-j4\pi f}{2(a^2+4\pi^2 f^2)} + 0.5\,\delta(f) \end{aligned}$$

We therefore have:

$$U(f) = \lim_{a\to 0} G(f) = \lim_{a\to 0}\left\{\frac{-j4\pi f}{2(a^2+4\pi^2 f^2)} + 0.5\,\delta(f)\right\} = \frac{1}{j2\pi f} + \frac{\delta(f)}{2}$$

EXAMPLE 3.25

Determine the Fourier transform of sgn(t).

Solution

We know that the signum function can be written in terms of the unit step function, as follows:

$$\text{sgn}(t) = 2u(t) - 1$$

Using the linear property of the Fourier transform, we have:

$$F[\text{sgn}(t)] = F[2u(t) - 1] = 2F[u(t)] - \delta(f)$$

After substituting the Fourier transform of $u(t)$, we have:

$$F[\text{sgn}(t)] = 2\left\{\frac{1}{j2\pi f} + \frac{\delta(f)}{2}\right\} - \delta(f) = \frac{1}{j\pi f}$$

Duality Property: (3.51)
If $g(t) \leftrightarrow G(f)$, then $G(t) \leftrightarrow g(-f)$

The proof of this property follows from replacing t by $-t$ in the definition of the inverse Fourier transform, i.e.,

$$g(-t) = \int_{-\infty}^{\infty} G(f) \exp(-j2\pi ft)\, df$$

and then interchanging the variable t and f, we thus get the following:

$$G(t) \leftrightarrow g(-f) = \int_{-\infty}^{\infty} G(t) \exp(-j2\pi ft)\, dt$$

This property portrays that there is a consistent symmetry between the time-domain and frequency-domain representations of a signal. With caution, we may interchange time and frequency.

EXAMPLE 3.26

Determine the Fourier transform of $g(t) = \text{sinc}(t)$.

Solution

We know we have the following transform pair:

$$\left(u\left(t+\frac{1}{2}\right) - u\left(t-\frac{1}{2}\right)\right) \leftrightarrow \text{sinc}(f)$$

By using the duality property of the Fourier transform, we get the following:

$$\text{sinc}(t) \leftrightarrow \left(u\left(-f+\frac{1}{2}\right) - u\left(-f-\frac{1}{2}\right)\right)$$

Since $\left(u\left(-f+\frac{1}{2}\right) - u\left(-f-\frac{1}{2}\right)\right)$ is an even function, we then have the following:

$$\text{sinc}(t) \leftrightarrow \left(u\left(f+\frac{1}{2}\right) - u\left(f-\frac{1}{2}\right)\right)$$

EXAMPLE 3.27

Assuming we have $G(f) = e^{-2|f|}$, determine its inverse Fourier transform $g(t)$. Note that the Fourier transform of $e^{-2|t|}$ is $1/\left(1+(\pi f)^2\right)$.

Solution

By using the duality property, we thus get

$$g(t) = F^{-1}\left[e^{-2|f|}\right] = \frac{1}{1+(\pi t)^2}$$

Time-Scaling Property:

Let $g(t) \leftrightarrow G(f)$, then for real constant $a \neq 0$, we have

$$g(at) \leftrightarrow \left(\frac{1}{|a|}\right) G\left(\frac{f}{a}\right) \tag{3.52}$$

To prove this property, we first take the Fourier transform of $g(at)$, and then make a change of variable (i.e., set $s = at$, where $ds = a\,dt$). Depending on the sign of a, we can therefore have the following two cases:

$$F[g(at)] = \int_{-\infty}^{\infty} g(at)e^{-j2\pi ft}dt = \left(\frac{1}{a}\right)\int_{-\infty}^{\infty} g(s)e^{-j2\pi\left(\frac{f}{a}\right)s}ds = \left(\frac{1}{a}\right)G\left(\frac{f}{a}\right), \quad a > 0$$

$$F[g(at)] = \int_{-\infty}^{\infty} g(at)e^{-j2\pi ft}dt = -\left(\frac{1}{a}\right)\int_{-\infty}^{\infty} g(s)e^{-j2\pi\left(\frac{f}{a}\right)s}ds = -\left(\frac{1}{a}\right)G\left(\frac{f}{a}\right), \quad a < 0$$

Combining the above two equations gives rise to (3.52).

This property highlights the fact that compression in one domain brings about expansion in another. In other words, the compression in the time domain by some factor is equivalent to the expansion of its frequency domain by the same factor, and vice versa. For instance, if a signal is contracted in the time domain (i.e., the signal duration becomes shorter and the changes in the signal appear more abrupt), its frequency content is increased. This property provides a valuable insight in signal duration and its bandwidth, as they are inversely proportional (i.e., by making a signal narrower, its spectrum becomes wider, and vice versa). For the special case of time reversal (i.e., $a = -1$), we have $g(-t) \leftrightarrow G(-f)$.

EXAMPLE 3.28

Consider the signal $g(t) = A\,u\left(t + \frac{T}{2}\right) - A\,u\left(t - \frac{T}{2}\right)$, where $A > 0$ is the amplitude and T is the duration of the rectangular pulse, as shown in Figure 3.30a.Determine the Fourier transform $G(f)$. Assuming the area of the pulse remains a constant, discuss the impact of changes in T on $G(f)$.

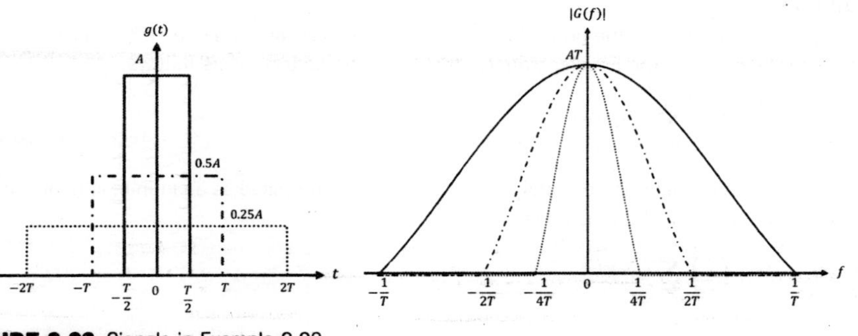

FIGURE 3.30 Signals in Example 3.28.

Solution

Using (3.40a), the Fourier transform $G(f)$ is determined as follows:

$$G(f) = \int_{-T/2}^{T/2} A \exp(-j2\pi ft)dt = AT\left(\frac{\sin(\pi fT)}{\pi fT}\right) = AT\,\mathrm{sinc}(fT)$$

Since $g(t)$ is real and even, $G(f)$ is real and even. The amplitude spectrum has a main lobe with a width of $2/T$ Hz, centered on the origin. The amplitudes of the side lobes decrease with increases in frequency. Assuming AT, the area of a pulse in the time domain, is a constant, Figure 3.30b shows the main lobe of $|G(f)|$ for various values of T. Note that a time compression (i.e., a decrease in T) brings about a frequency expansion (i.e., an increase in main lobe). As $T \to 0$, then $|G(f)| \to A$ (i.e., as the pulse becomes the narrowest, the main lobe becomes the widest, and as $T \to \infty$, then $|G(f)| \to A\delta(f)$ (i.e., as the pulse becomes the widest), the main lobe becomes the narrowest).

Time-Shifting Property:

If $g(t) \leftrightarrow G(f)$, then for a constant t_0 as a time shift, we have (3.53)

$g(t-t_0) \leftrightarrow G(f)e^{-j2\pi ft_0}$

To prove this property, we first take the Fourier transform of $g(t-t_0)$, and then make a change of variable (i.e., set $s = t - t_0$, where $ds = dt$). We therefore have the following:

$$F[g(t-t_0)] = \int_{-\infty}^{\infty} g(t-t_0)e^{-j2\pi ft}dt = \int_{-\infty}^{\infty} g(s)e^{-j2\pi f(s+t_0)}ds = e^{-j2\pi ft_0}\int_{-\infty}^{\infty} g(s)e^{-j2\pi fs}ds$$
$$= G(f)e^{-j2\pi ft_0}$$

This property underlines the fact that when a signal is shifted in time, which in turn leaves its shape unchanged, its magnitude spectrum completely remains unaffected by the time shift, but its phase is shifted by a linear factor proportional to the time shift.

EXAMPLE 3.29

Determine the Fourier transform of the following impulse train:

$$\sum_{i=-\infty}^{\infty} \delta(t-iT)$$

Solution

Noting $\delta(t) \leftrightarrow 1$ and using the time-shifting property, we have $\delta(t-t_0) \leftrightarrow e^{-j2\pi ft_0}$. Therefore, using the linearity property, the Fourier transform of the impulse train is as follows:

$$F\left[\sum_{i=-\infty}^{\infty} \delta(t-iT)\right] = \sum_{m=-\infty}^{\infty} e^{-j2\pi fmT}$$

The impulse train is a periodic signal, and it can thus be expressed as an infinite sum of complex exponential functions. We thus have:

$$\sum_{i=-\infty}^{\infty} \delta(t-iT) = \left(\frac{1}{T}\right)\sum_{n=-\infty}^{\infty} e^{j2\pi nt/T}$$

By replacing t by f, T by $1/T$, and n by $-m$, and then dividing both sides by T, we get the following:

$$\left(\frac{1}{T}\right)\sum_{i=-\infty}^{\infty}\delta(f-i/T)=\sum_{m=-\infty}^{\infty}e^{-j2\pi mfT}$$

We thus have the following:

$$F\left[\sum_{i=-\infty}^{\infty}\delta(t-iT)\right]=\left(\frac{1}{T}\right)\sum_{i=-\infty}^{\infty}\delta\left(f-\frac{i}{T}\right)$$

The Fourier transform of impulse train, spaced T seconds, is thus another impulse train, spaced $1/T$ Hz apart.

Frequency-Shifting Property:

If $g(t)\leftrightarrow G(f)$, then for a constant f_c as a frequency shift, we have (3.54)

$$e^{j2\pi f_c t}g(t)\leftrightarrow G(f-f_c)$$

To prove this property, we take the Fourier transform of $\exp(j2\pi f_c t)g(t)$, as follows:

$$F\left[e^{j2\pi f_c t}g(t)\right]=\int_{-\infty}^{\infty}e^{j2\pi f_c t}g(t)e^{-j2\pi ft}dt=\int_{-\infty}^{\infty}g(t)e^{-j2\pi(f-f_c)t}dt=G(f-f_c)$$

This property brings to light the fact that a multiplication in the time domain by a complex exponential results in a shift in the frequency domain. Note that the frequency-shifting property is the dual of the time-shifting property. This property is also called the ***linear modulation theorem***. Since exponential $e^{j2\pi f_c t}$ is not a real function, it cannot be physically generated, as such frequency shifting in practice is achieved by multiplying the signal by a sinusoidal function.

EXAMPLE 3.30

Determine the Fourier transforms of $\cos(2\pi f_c t+\theta)$ and $\sin(2\pi f_c t+\theta)$, where f_c and θ are the frequency and initial phase, respectively.

Solution

Using (3.17), we get the following:

$$\cos(2\pi f_c t+\theta)=0.5\,e^{j\theta}e^{j2\pi f_c t}+0.5\,e^{-j\theta}e^{-j2\pi f_c t}$$

Using the linearity property and the frequency-shifting property, and noting $1\leftrightarrow\delta(f)$, we get the following:

$$\begin{aligned}\cos(2\pi f_c t+\theta)\leftrightarrow F[\cos(2\pi f_c t+\theta)]&=0.5\,e^{j\theta}F\left[e^{j2\pi f_c t}\right]+0.5\,e^{-j\theta}F\left[e^{-j2\pi f_c t}\right]\\&=0.5\left(e^{j\theta}\delta(f-f_c)+e^{-j\theta}\delta(f+f_c)\right)\end{aligned}$$

Using (3.17), we get the following:

$$\sin(2\pi f_c t+\theta)=-0.5j\,e^{j\theta}e^{j2\pi f_c t}+0.5j\,e^{-j\theta}e^{-j2\pi f_c t}$$

Similarly, we can find the Fourier transform of a sine function as follows:

$$\sin(2\pi f_c t+\theta) \leftrightarrow F[\sin(2\pi f_c t+\theta)] = -0.5je^{j\theta}F\left[e^{j2\pi f_c t}\right] + 0.5je^{-j\theta}F\left[e^{-j2\pi f_c t}\right]$$
$$= -0.5j\left(e^{j\theta}\delta(f-f_c) - e^{-j\theta}\delta(f+f_c)\right)$$

The spectrum of the cosine function or the sine function consists of a pair of delta functions occurring at $f=\pm f_c$. As expected, their magnitude spectra remain the same, but their phase spectra are different.

EXAMPLE 3.31

Determine the Fourier transform of the radio-frequency pulse:

$$g(t) = \left(Au\left(t+\frac{T}{2}\right) - Au\left(t-\frac{T}{2}\right)\right)\cos(2\pi f_c t).$$

Solution

Noting we have $\left(Au\left(t+\frac{T}{2}\right) - Au\left(t-\frac{T}{2}\right)\right) \leftrightarrow AT\,\text{sinc}(fT)$, and using (3.17), the Fourier transform of $g(t)$ is then as follows:

$$\left(Au\left(t+\frac{T}{2}\right) - Au\left(t-\frac{T}{2}\right)\right)\cos(2\pi f_c t) = \left(Au\left(t+\frac{T}{2}\right) - Au\left(t-\frac{T}{2}\right)\right)\left(\frac{e^{j2\pi f_c t}+e^{-j2\pi f_c t}}{2}\right) \leftrightarrow$$
$$\frac{AT}{2}\left(\text{sinc}(f-f_c) + \text{sinc}(f+f_c)\right)$$

Convolution Property:

Let $g_1(t) \leftrightarrow G_1(f)$ and $g_2(t) \leftrightarrow G_2(f)$, then we have (3.55)

$$\int_{-\infty}^{\infty} g_1(\tau)g_2(t-\tau)d\tau = g_1(t) * g_2(t) \leftrightarrow G_1(f)G_2(f)$$

where the symbol * denotes the convolution operation. To prove this property, we first take the Fourier transform of the convolution integral, and then make a change of variable (i.e., set $s=t-\tau$, where $ds=dt$). We therefore have the following:

$$F\left[\int_{-\infty}^{\infty} g_1(\tau)g_2(t-\tau)d\tau\right] = \int_{-\infty}^{\infty}\int_{-\infty}^{\infty} g_1(\tau)g_2(t-\tau)d\tau e^{-j2\pi ft}dt$$
$$= \int_{-\infty}^{\infty} g_1(\tau)\left(\int_{-\infty}^{\infty} g_2(t-\tau)e^{-j2\pi f(t-\tau)}dt\right)e^{-j2\pi f\tau}d\tau$$
$$= \int_{-\infty}^{\infty} g_1(\tau)\left(\int_{-\infty}^{\infty} g_2(s)e^{-j2\pi fs}ds\right)e^{-j2\pi f\tau}d\tau$$
$$= \int_{-\infty}^{\infty} g_1(\tau)G_2(s)e^{-j2\pi f\tau}d\tau = \left(\int_{-\infty}^{\infty} g_1(\tau)e^{-j2\pi f\tau}d\tau\right)G_2(s)$$
$$= G_1(f)G_2(f)$$

This property stresses that the convolution of two signals in the time domain is transformed into the product of their individual Fourier transforms. This allows us to exchange a complex convolution operation in the time domain for a simple multiplication operation in the frequency domain and then an inverse Fourier transform operation.

EXAMPLE 3.32

Determine the Fourier transform of the following triangular pulse:

$$g(t) = \begin{cases} -|t|+1, & |t| \le 1 \\ 0, & |t| > 1 \end{cases}$$

Solution

The convolution of a unit-amplitude unit-wide rectangular pulse with itself results in a triangular pulse, i.e. $g(t) = g_1(t) * g_1(t)$, where $g_1(t) = u\left(t+\frac{1}{2}\right) - u\left(t-\frac{1}{2}\right)$. By using the convolution property, the Fourier transform of $g(t)$ can be viewed as the product of the Fourier transform of the rectangular pulse and itself. In other words, we have the following:

$$G(f) = \text{sinc}(f)\,\text{sinc}(f) = \text{sinc}^2(f)$$

EXAMPLE 3.33

Determine $g(t) = \cos(2\pi t) * e^{-|t|}$.

Solution

The Fourier transforms of $e^{-|t|}$ and $\cos(2\pi t)$ are, respectively, as follows:

$$F\left[e^{-|t|}\right] = \int_{-\infty}^{\infty} e^{-|t|} e^{-j2\pi ft}\,dt = \int_{-\infty}^{0} e^{t} e^{-j2\pi ft}\,dt + \int_{0}^{\infty} e^{-t} e^{-j2\pi ft}\,dt = \frac{2}{1+(2\pi f)^2}$$

$$F[\cos(2\pi t)] = 0.5\,(\delta(f+1) + \delta(f-1))$$

Using the convolution property, we thus have the following:

$$F\left[e^{-|t|} * \cos(2\pi t)\right] = 0.5\,(\delta(f+1) + \delta(f-1))\left(\frac{2}{1+(2\pi f)^2}\right) = \left(\frac{\delta(f+1) + \delta(f-1)}{\left(1+(2\pi)^2\right)}\right)$$

We now take the inverse Fourier transform, and thus have:

$$e^{-|t|} * \cos(2\pi t) = F^{-1}\left[\left(\frac{\delta(f+1) + \delta(f-1)}{\left(1+(2\pi)^2\right)}\right)\right] = F^{-1}\left[\left(\frac{\delta(f+1)}{\left(1+(2\pi)^2\right)}\right)\right] + F^{-1}\left[\left(\frac{\delta(f-1)}{\left(1+(2\pi)^2\right)}\right)\right]$$

$$= \frac{1}{1+(2\pi)^2}\left(e^{-j2\pi t}\right) + \frac{1}{1+(2\pi)^2}\left(e^{j2\pi t}\right) = \frac{2\cos(2\pi t)}{1+(2\pi)^2}$$

Multiplication Property:
Let $g_1(t) \leftrightarrow G_1(f)$ and $g_2(t) \leftrightarrow G_2(f)$, then we have (3.56)

$$g_1(t)g_2(t) \leftrightarrow \int_{-\infty}^{\infty} G_1(s)G_2(f-s)ds = G_1(f) * G_2(f)$$

where * denotes the convolution operation. To prove this property, we first take the Fourier transform of $g_1(t)\, g_2(t)$, then substitute the inverse Fourier transform for $g_2(t)$, and finally make a change of variable (i.e., set $s=f-\rho$, where $ds=d\rho$). We therefore have the following:

$$F[g_1(t)g_2(t)] = \int_{-\infty}^{\infty} g_1(t)g_2(t)e^{-j2\pi ft}\,dt = \int_{-\infty}^{\infty} g_1(t)\left(\int_{-\infty}^{\infty} G_2(\rho)e^{j2\pi\rho t}d\rho\right)e^{-j2\pi ft}dt$$

$$= \int_{-\infty}^{\infty}\int_{-\infty}^{\infty} g_1(t)G_2(\rho)e^{-j2\pi(f-\rho)t}d\rho\, dt = \int_{-\infty}^{\infty} G_2(f-s)ds\int_{-\infty}^{\infty} g_1(t)e^{-j2\pi st}\,dt$$

$$= \int_{-\infty}^{\infty} G_2(f-s)G_1(s)ds = G_1(f) * G_2(f)$$

This property, also known as ***multiplication theorem***, points to the fact that the Fourier transform of the multiplication of two signals in the time domain is the convolution of their individual Fourier transforms. Note that if $g_1(t)$ and $g_2(t)$ have bandwidths W_1 and W_2 Hz, then their product, i.e., $g_1(t)g_2(t)$, has a bandwidth equal to the sum of their bandwidths, i.e., (W_1+W_2) Hz. Moreover, if one of the two signals, say $g_1(t)$, is a sinusoidal signal with frequency f_c, then the Fourier transform of the product is in fact the frequency-shifted version of $G_2(f)$ by $\pm f_c$.

EXAMPLE 3.34

Determine the Fourier transform of $g(t)=\text{sinc}(t)\cos(2\pi f_c t)$.

Solution

$g(t)$ is the product of two signals. We thus find the Fourier transform of each of the two signals and then find the convolution of their Fourier transforms. We have the following Fourier transforms:

$$\text{sinc}(t) \leftrightarrow u\left(f+\frac{1}{2}\right) - u\left(f-\frac{1}{2}\right)$$

$$\cos(2\pi f_c t) \leftrightarrow 0.5(\delta(f+f_c)+\delta(f-f_c))$$

We therefore have the following:

$$F[g(t)] = F[\text{sinc}(t)] * F[\cos(2\pi f_c t)] = \left(u\left(f+\frac{1}{2}\right) - u\left(f-\frac{1}{2}\right)\right) * 0.5\,(\delta(f+f_c)+\delta(f-f_c))$$

Noting the convolution of any function with a delta function results in a function shifted to the location of the delta function. We therefore have:

$$G(f) = 0.5\left(u\left(f+\frac{1}{2}+f_c\right) - u\left(f-\frac{1}{2}+f_c\right) + u\left(f+\frac{1}{2}-f_c\right) - u\left(f-\frac{1}{2}-f_c\right)\right)$$

Conjugate Functions: (3.57)
If $g(t) \leftrightarrow G(f)$, then $g^*(t) \leftrightarrow G^*(-f)$

To prove this property, we start with the definition of the inverse Fourier transform:

$$g(t) = \int_{-\infty}^{\infty} G(f) e^{j2\pi ft} df$$

We then take the complex conjugate of the inverse Fourier transform, and replace f by $-s$ and df by $-ds$. We thus have:

$$g^*(t) = \int_{-\infty}^{\infty} G^*(f) e^{-j2\pi ft} df = -\int_{\infty}^{-\infty} G^*(-s) e^{j2\pi st} ds = \int_{-\infty}^{\infty} G^*(-f) e^{j2\pi ft} df \leftrightarrow G^*(-f)$$

This property displays that the Fourier transform of a complex-valued time function $g(t)$ is the complex conjugate of the Fourier transform of $G(-f)$. Note that if $g(t)$ is a real-valued time function, i.e., $g(t) = g^*(t)$, we then have $G(f) = G^*(-f)$, which in turn means the magnitude response is an even function and the phase response is an odd function.

EXAMPLE 3.35

Assuming $g(t)$ is a complex-valued function, determine the Fourier transform of its real and imaginary parts.

Solution

The real part and the imaginary part of $g(t)$ are, respectively, as follows:

$$g_r(t) = \frac{g(t) + g^*(t)}{2}$$

$$g_i(t) = \frac{g(t) - g^*(t)}{2j}$$

Using the linear property based on conjugate functions, we have:

$$G_r(f) = \frac{G(f) + G^*(-f)}{2}$$

$$G_i(f) = \frac{G(f) - G^*(-f)}{2j}$$

Autocorrelation Property:

Let $R_g(\tau) = g(\tau) * g^*(-\tau)$ and $g(t) \leftrightarrow G(f)$, then we have (3.58)

$R_g(\tau) \leftrightarrow |G(f)|^2$

To prove this property, we take the Fourier transform of $g(\tau) * g^*(-\tau)$, using the convolution property. The result is thus the product of the Fourier transform of $g(\tau)$ (i.e., $G(f)$) and the Fourier transform of $g^*(-\tau)$ (i.e., $G^*(f)$). We therefore have:

$$F[g(\tau) * g(-\tau)] = G(f)\, G^*(f) = |G(f)|^2$$

This property reflects the point that the Fourier transform of the time autocorrelation function of the signal $g(t)$ is the magnitude squared of the Fourier transform $G(f)$, a real-valued, nonnegative function. The autocorrelation provides a measure of similarity between a signal and its time-delayed version. The time-delayed versions of a signal all have the same autocorrelation function, as the Fourier transform of the autocorrelation function has no information about phase. For a given time-domain function, there is therefore a unique autocorrelation function. The converse, however, is not necessarily true.

EXAMPLE 3.36

Determine the autocorrelation function of the signal $g(t)=e^{-t}u(t)$.

Solution

We first find the Fourier transform of the signal $g(t)$:

$$G(f)=\int_{-\infty}^{\infty} g(t)e^{-j2\pi ft}dt=\int_{0}^{\infty} e^{-t}e^{-j2\pi ft}dt=\frac{1}{1+j2\pi f}$$

By taking the inverse Fourier transform of the magnitude squared, we get the autocorrelation function:

$$R_g(\tau)=\int_{-\infty}^{\infty} |G(f)|^2 e^{j2\pi ft}dt=\int_{0}^{\infty}\frac{1}{1+(2\pi f)^2}e^{j2\pi ft}dt=0.5e^{-|\tau|}$$

EXAMPLE 3.37

Determine the autocorrelation function of the periodic signal $g(t)=\cos(2\pi f_c t)$.

Solution

We first find the square of the magnitude spectrum as follows:

$$|G(f)|^2=|0.5(\delta(f+f_c)+\delta(f-f_c))|^2=0.25(\delta(f+f_c)+\delta(f-f_c))$$

Taking the inverse Fourier transform results in the autocorrelation function as follows:

$$R_g(\tau)=0.5\cos(2\pi f_c\tau)$$

As expected, the autocorrelation function is also periodic with the same period.

Differentiation Property:

If $g(t)\leftrightarrow G(f)$, then (3.59

$$\frac{d}{dt}g(t)\leftrightarrow j2\pi f G(f)$$

To prove this property, we take the first derivative of the inverse Fourier transform as follows:

$$\frac{d}{dt}g(t)=\frac{d}{dt}\int_{-\infty}^{\infty} G(f)e^{j2\pi ft}df=\int_{-\infty}^{\infty}(j2\pi f\,G(f))e^{j2\pi ft}df\leftrightarrow j2\pi f\,G(f)$$

This property indicates that if the first derivative of a signal is Fourier transformable, then the differentiation of a time function has the effect of multiplying i

Fourier transform by the factor $j2\pi f$. Assuming that the Fourier transform of the higher-order derivative exists, with the repeated application of this property, we can then have the following relation:

$$\frac{d^n}{dt^n}g(t) \leftrightarrow (j2\pi f)^n G(f).$$

EXAMPLE 3.38

Determine the Fourier transform of the signal $g(t)$ defined by

$$g(t)=\begin{cases} 0, & t<-2 \\ t+2, & -2\le t\le -1 \\ 1, & -1<t<1 \\ -t+2, & 1\le t\le 2 \\ 0, & t>2 \end{cases}$$

Solution

The derivative of $g(t)$ is as follows:

$$\frac{d}{dt}g(t)=u(t+2)-u(t+1)-u(t-1)+u(t-2)$$

The second derivative of $g(t)$ is then as follows:

$$\frac{d^2}{dt^2}g(t)=\delta(t+2)-\delta(t+1)-\delta(t-1)+\delta(t-2)$$

Note that the derivative of a discontinuity is an impulse function whose amplitude is equal to the magnitude of the discontinuity. We now take the Fourier transform of both sides as follows:

$$(j2\pi f)^2\, G(f)=e^{j4\pi f}-e^{j2\pi f}-e^{-j2\pi f}+e^{-j4\pi f}$$

We can therefore find $G(f)$ as follows:

$$G(f)=\frac{\cos(2\pi f)-\cos(4\pi f)}{2\pi^2 f^2}$$

Integration Property:

If $g(t)\leftrightarrow G(f)$, then

$$\int_{-\infty}^{t} g(\tau)d\tau \leftrightarrow \frac{G(f)}{j2\pi f}+\left(\frac{G(0)}{2}\right)\delta(f) \tag{3.60}$$

To prove this property, we take advantage of the fact that the definite integral of a function may be viewed as the convolution of that function and the unit step function. In other words, we have:

$$\int_{-\infty}^{t} g(s)ds = g(t)*u(t)$$

We know that the convolution in the time domain results in the multiplication in the frequency domain, so we therefore have:

$$F\left[\int_{-\infty}^{t} g(s)ds\right] = F[g(t)]\,F[u(t)] = G(f)\left(\frac{1}{j2\pi f} + \frac{\delta(f)}{2}\right) = \frac{G(f)}{j2\pi f} + \frac{G(0)\,\delta(f)}{2}$$

This property shows that the integration of a time function has the effect of dividing its Fourier transform by the factor $j2\pi f$, but an additional term is needed to account for a possible DC component in the integrator output. This property can be generalized to multiple integrations.

EXAMPLE 3.39

Using $g(t) = \delta(t+1) - 2\,\delta(t) + \delta(t-1)$, determine the Fourier transform of $k(t)$, where

$$k(t) = \begin{cases} 1 - |t|, & |t| \le 1 \\ 0, & |t| > 1 \end{cases}$$

Solution

By integrating $g(t)$ twice, we can get $k(t)$. Noting that we have

$$G(f) = \exp(-j2\pi f) - 2 + \exp(j2\pi f) = 2\cos(2\pi f) - 2 = -4\sin^2(\pi f)$$

we use the integration property twice to obtain the Fourier transform of $k(t)$. We thus get:

$$K(f) = \frac{G(f)}{(j2\pi f)^2} = \frac{-4\sin^2(\pi f)}{(j2\pi f)^2} = \text{sinc}^2(f).$$

n^{th}-Moment Property:

If $g(t) \leftrightarrow G(f)$, then (3.61)

$$\int_{-\infty}^{\infty} t^n g(t)dt = \left(\tfrac{j}{2\pi}\right)^n \frac{d^n}{df^n} G(f)_{|f=0}$$

To prove this property, we differentiate the Fourier transform with respect to frequency, and we thus have:

$$\frac{d}{df}G(f) = \frac{d}{df}\int_{-\infty}^{\infty} g(t)\,e^{-j2\pi ft}dt = \int_{-\infty}^{\infty} (-j2\pi t)\,g(t)\,e^{-j2\pi ft}\,dt$$

We repeat the process n times, and we thus get the following:

$$\frac{d^n}{df^n}G(f) = \int_{-\infty}^{\infty} (-j2\pi t)^n\,g(t)\,e^{-j2\pi ft}\,dt$$

We divide both sides by $(-j2\pi)^n$ and we set $f = 0$. We therefore get the following:

$$\int_{-\infty}^{\infty} t^n g(t)dt = \left(\frac{j}{2\pi}\right)^n \frac{d^n}{df^n} G(f)_{|f=0}$$

EXAMPLE 3.40

Noting that the Fourier transform of a Gaussian pulse is a Gaussian pulse, i.e., we have:

$e^{-\pi t^2} \leftrightarrow e^{-\pi f^2}$

Determine the second moment of the Gaussian pulse.

Solution

We find the first and the second derivatives of the Fourier transform as follows:

$$\frac{d}{df}G(f) = -2\pi f e^{-\pi f^2}$$

$$\frac{d^2}{df^2}G(f) = -2\pi e^{-\pi f^2} + (2\pi f)^2 e^{-\pi f^2}$$

We now set $f = 0$ in the second derivative, multiply it by $\left(\frac{j}{2\pi}\right)^2$, and thus obtain the following:

$$\left(\frac{j}{2\pi}\right)^2 \frac{d^2}{df^2}G(f)_{|f=0} = \left(\frac{j}{2\pi}\right)^2 (-2\pi) = \frac{1}{2\pi}$$

We therefore have the following:

$$\int_{-\infty}^{\infty} t^2 e^{-\pi t^2} dt = \frac{1}{2\pi}$$

Time-Average Property:

If $g(t) \leftrightarrow G(f)$, then

$$\int_{-\infty}^{\infty} g(t)dt = G(0) \tag{3.62}$$

To prove this property, we simply put $f = 0$ in the definition of the Fourier transform.

This property states that the area under a time function is equal to the value of its Fourier transform $G(f)$ at $f = 0$. In other words, the time average of a signal is equal to its DC value.

EXAMPLE 3.41

Determine the time-average of $g(t) = e^{-t}\sin(2\pi f_c t)u(t)$.

Solution

Noting we have $e^{-t}u(t) \leftrightarrow \frac{1}{1 + j2\pi f}$, and using the Euler's identity and the frequency shifting property, the Fourier transform $G(f)$ is then as follows:

$$G(f) = \frac{1}{2j}\left(\frac{1}{(1 + j2\pi(f - f_c)} - \frac{1}{(1 + j2\pi(f - f_c)}\right) = \frac{2\pi f_c}{(1 + j2\pi f)^2 + (2\pi f_c)^2}$$

We therefore have

$$\int_{-\infty}^{\infty} g(t)dt = G(0) = \frac{2\pi f_c}{1 + (2\pi f_c)^2}$$

Frequency-Average Property:

If $g(t) \leftrightarrow G(f)$, then (3.63)

$$\int_{-\infty}^{\infty} G(f)df = g(0)$$

To prove this property, we simply put $t=0$ in the definition of the inverse Fourier transform.

This property reveals that the area under the Fourier transform of a signal is equal to the value of its time function $g(t)$ at $t=0$.

EXAMPLE 3.42

Determine the frequency average of the signal $G(f) = 0.5\,(\text{sinc}(f-f_c) + \text{sinc}(f+f_c))$.

Solution

Using $\left(u\left(t+\frac{1}{2}\right) - u\left(t-\frac{1}{2}\right)\right) \leftrightarrow \text{sinc}(f)$ and the frequency shifting property, $g(t)$ is as follows:

$$g(t) = \left(u\left(t+\frac{1}{2}\right) - u\left(t-\frac{1}{2}\right)\right)\cos(2\pi f_c t)$$

We therefore have:

$$\int_{-\infty}^{\infty} G(f)df = g(0) = 1$$

Parseval's Relation:

If $g_1(t) \leftrightarrow G_1(f)$ and $g_2(t) \leftrightarrow G_2(f)$, then we have (3.64)

$$\int_{-\infty}^{\infty} g_1(t)g_2^*(t)dt = \int_{-\infty}^{\infty} G_1(f)G_2^*(f)df$$

To prove this property, we substitute for the inverse Fourier transforms of $g_1(t)$ and $g_2^*(t)$, and rearrange the terms:

$$\int_{-\infty}^{\infty} g_1(t)g_2^*(t)dt = \int_{-\infty}^{\infty}\left\{\int_{-\infty}^{\infty} G_1(f)e^{j2\pi ft}df\right\}\left\{\int_{-\infty}^{\infty} G_2^*(s)e^{-j2\pi st}ds\right\}dt$$

$$= \int_{-\infty}^{\infty} G_1(f)\int_{-\infty}^{\infty} G_2^*(s)\int_{-\infty}^{\infty} e^{j2\pi t(f-s)}dt\,ds\,df$$

The above expression can be simplified by the fact that the inverse Fourier transform of an exponential function is a delta function, i.e., we have the following:

$$\int_{-\infty}^{\infty} e^{j2\pi t(f-s)}dt = \delta(f-s)$$

We therefore have:

$$\int_{-\infty}^{\infty} g_1(t)g_2^*(t)dt = \int_{-\infty}^{\infty} G_1(f)\left(\int_{-\infty}^{\infty} G_2^*(s)\delta(f-s)ds\right)df$$

Using the sifting property in (3.29a), we get the following:

$$\int_{-\infty}^{\infty} g_1(t)g_2^*(t)dt = \int_{-\infty}^{\infty} G_1(f)G_2^*(f)df$$

This property also illustrates the fact that if $g_1(t) = g_2(t) = g(t)$, then we have the following:

$$\int_{-\infty}^{\infty} |g(t)|^2 dt = \int_{-\infty}^{\infty} |G(f)|^2 df.$$

This is known as ***Rayleigh's energy theorem***, in which the squared magnitude spectrum represents the energy spectral density. We can thus conclude that the signal energy can be calculated through either $g(t)$ or $G(f)$.

EXAMPLE 3.43

Determine the area under $g(t) = \text{sinc}^2(t)$.

Solution

Noting that we have $\text{sinc}(t) \leftrightarrow \left(u\left(f+\frac{1}{2}\right) - u\left(f-\frac{1}{2}\right)\right)$, by using the Rayleigh's energy theorem, we have the following:

$$\int_{-\infty}^{\infty} \text{sinc}^2(t)\, dt = \int_{-\infty}^{\infty} \left(u\left(f+\frac{1}{2}\right) - u\left(f-\frac{1}{2}\right)\right)^2 df = 1$$

3.7.5 Numerical Computation of Fourier Transform: Discrete Fourier Transform

When $g(t)$ is mathematically known, its Fourier transform can be determined by using (3.42a), either analytically or through numerical integration. However, if $g(t)$ cannot be defined mathematically, we cannot use (3.42a) and we then need to compute $G(f)$ numerically. To compute $G(f)$ numerically, we have to use the samples of $g(t)$. However, $G(f)$ can be determined only at some finite number of frequencies (i.e., at samples of $G(f)$ only). We therefore need to find the relationships between samples of $g(t)$ and samples of $G(f)$, i.e., to define the ***discrete Fourier transform*** (DFT) and its ***inverse discrete Fourier transform*** (IDFT). The DFT provides an approximation to the Fourier transform. In any numerical computation, the input data must be finite, so the number of samples of $g(t)$ and $G(f)$ must be both finite. To this effect, if $g(t)$ is not time-limited, we truncate it to make its duration finite, so we can find its DFT, and if $G(f)$ is not frequency-limited, we filter it to make it band-limited, so we can find its IDFT.

Figure 3.31 shows the relation between the samples of $g(t)$ and samples of $G(f)$ and all relevant parameters. We consider the duration of $g(t)$ to be $T_0 > b$, i.e., $g(t) = 0$ in the interval $b < t \leq T_0$. We sample $g(t)$ at uniform intervals of T_s seconds, then the number of samples N is as follows:

$$N = \frac{T_0}{T_s} = \frac{f_s}{f_0} \tag{3.65}$$

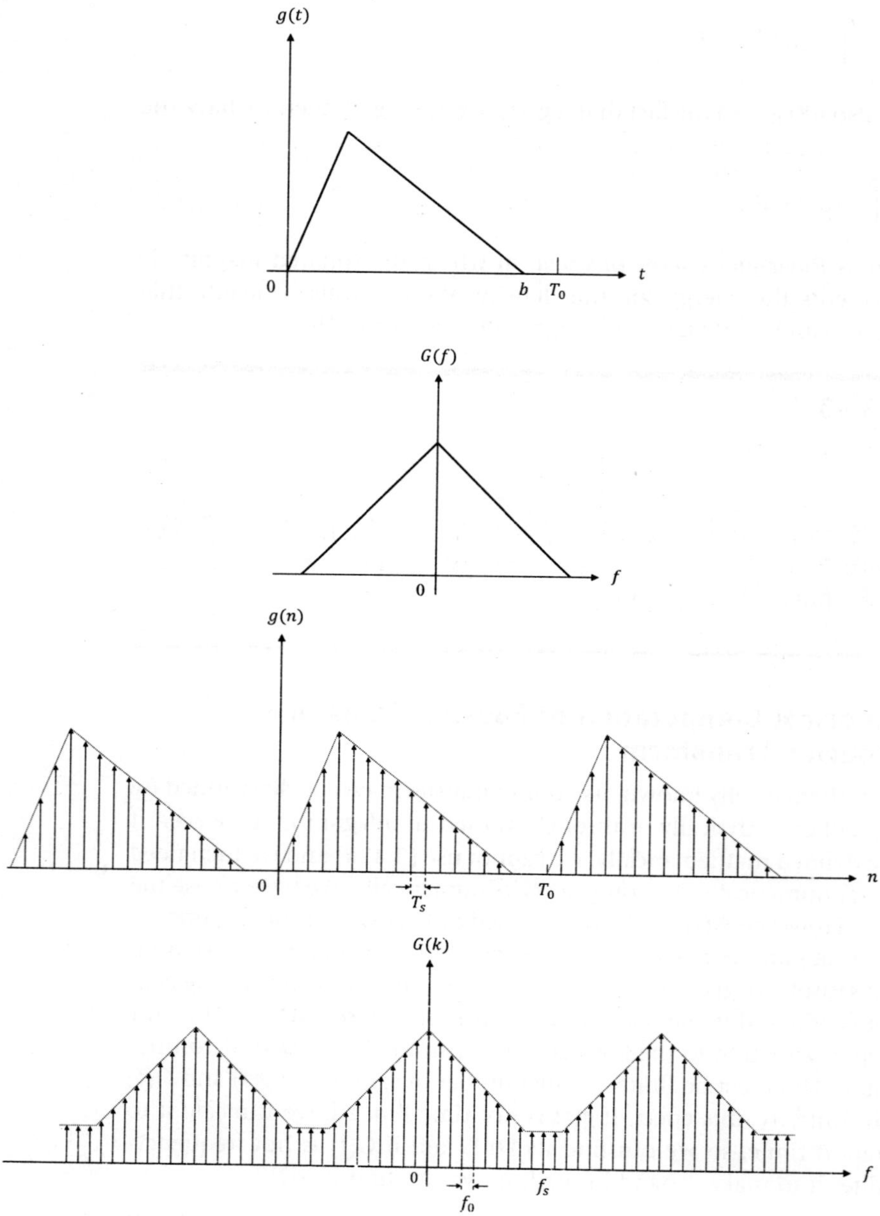

FIGURE 3.31 Relation between the samples of $g(t)$ and samples of $G(f)$.

where $f_0 = \frac{1}{T_0}$ is the spectral sampling interval and $f_s = \frac{1}{T_s}$ is the sampling frequency of $g(t)$. Consider a finite data sequence $\{g(0), g(1), \ldots, g(N-1)\}$, which is the result of sampling an analog signal $g(t)$. With T_s as the sampling interval in the time domain, the Fourier transform sequence $\{G(0), G(1), \ldots, G(N-1)\}$ is the result of sampling $G(f)$, with f_s as the sampling interval in the frequency domain. The ***discrete Fourier transform*** and the ***inverse discrete Fourier transform***, which are both linear operations, are respectively as follows:

$$G(k) = \sum_{n=0}^{N-1} g(n) \exp\left(-\frac{j2\pi nk}{N}\right), \quad k = 0, 1, 2, \ldots, N-1, \tag{3.66a}$$

$$g(n) = \left(\frac{1}{N}\right) \sum_{k=0}^{N-1} G(k) \exp\left(\frac{j2\pi nk}{N}\right), \quad n = 0, 1, 2, \ldots, N-1 \tag{3.66b}$$

Figure 3.32 shows the implementation of DFT and IDFT. Note that the DFT is a periodic sequence of length N, with period f_s, and the IDFT is a periodic sequence of length N, with period T_0. The periodic repetition of the discrete Fourier transform can cause overlapping of spectral components, resulting in error. This error, however, can be made as small as possible by decreasing the sampling interval T_s (i.e., increasing the sampling frequency f_s). Also, when $g(t)$ is not time-limited, its truncation will cause further error. This error can be reduced by increasing the truncating interval T_0. When $T_0 > b$, we have several zero-valued samples in the interval $[b, T_0]$. Thus, by increasing the number of zero-valued samples, we reduce f_0. This process is called ***zero padding***, through which, we can have more closely spaced samples of $G(f)$. For a given sampling

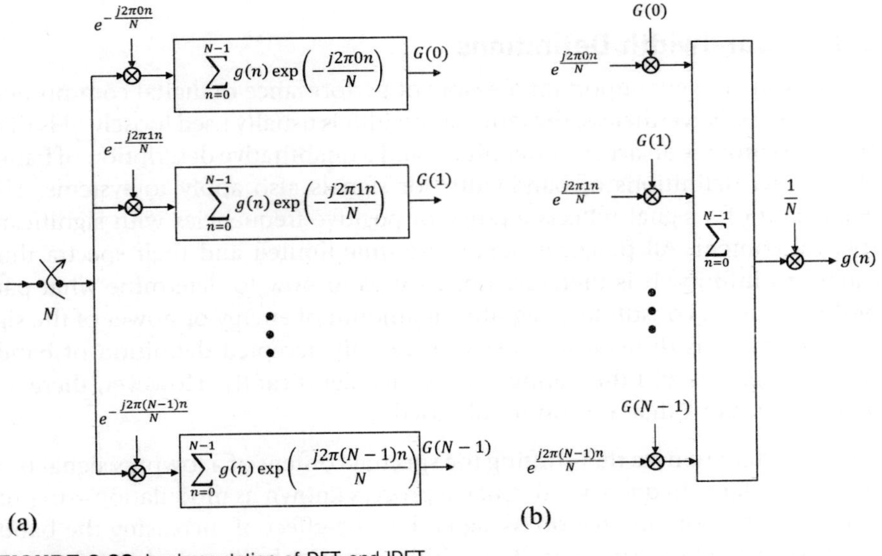

FIGURE 3.32 Implementation of DFT and IDFT.

interval T_s, larger T_0 implies larger N. In short, by choosing a reasonably large value of N, we have samples of $G(f)$ as close as possible.

Sequences of numbers defined at uniformly spaced points in time and frequency are used to compute DFT. The signal $g(n)$ and its spectrum $G(k)$ are both periodic with the period of N. To compute DFT, we require N^2 complex operations. Note that each complex signal generator actually consists of a pair of generators that outputs a cosine signal and a sine signal. For large N, the processing time may become quite excessive. There is a well-known algorithm called the ***fast Fourier transform*** (FFT) that can significantly reduce the number of computations. The FFT is very efficient as it follows the divide-and-conquer strategy, whereby the original DFT computation is decomposed successively into smaller DFT computations.

3.8 TIME AND FREQUENCY RELATIONS

A signal can be fully defined either in the time domain or in the frequency domain, but not in both. Using the Fourier transform pair, a signal defined in one domain can be completely determined in the other domain. The time duration and frequency spectrum of a signal are inversely related, as a contraction in one domain results in an expansion in the other domain. Noting that the spectral width of signals can have a direct bearing on the communication system capacity as well as on the equipment design accommodating the desired signal while rejecting noise, we need to focus on definitions of bandwidth. Since the effective time duration of a signal can have an impact on the interference level, the time-bandwidth product needs to be also defined and thus examined.

3.8.1 Bandwidth Definitions

Bandwidth is a very important measure of performance in digital communication systems. Nevertheless, the term bandwidth is usually used loosely. It is thus critical to provide an accurate definition and a quantitative description of bandwidth. The definitions of bandwidth for signals also apply to systems. The ***bandwidth*** of a signal reflects a range of positive frequencies with significant spectral content. All practical signals are time-limited and their spectra thus extend to infinity. It is therefore not clear as to how to determine what part of the spectrum constitutes a significant amount of energy or power of the signal. Clearly, it is difficult to have a universally accepted definition of bandwidth, as signals and their applications vary significantly. However, there are many definitions that are commonly used.

It is important to note that shifting the spectral content of a lowpass signal by a sufficiently large frequency—through a process known as modulation—to produce its corresponding bandpass signal has the effect of increasing the bandwidth of the signal. The term bandwidth, denoted by B, may be defined, as the difference (in Hz) between two nominal frequencies, f_2 and f_1, i.e., $B = f_2 - f_1$, where $f_2 \geq f_1 \geq 0$, and f_2 and f_1 are determined by one of the following definitions of bandwidth.

Absolute Bandwidth – Absolute bandwidth provides a theoretical definition. Assuming the spectrum is zero beyond $f_2 \geq f_1 \geq 0$, we have $B = f_2 - f_1$. Absolute bandwidth can be applied to frequency-limited signals and ideal lowpass and bandpass filters. No absolute bandwidth can be defined for high-pass filters, as $f_2 \to \infty$, and consequently $B \to \infty$. In essence, for all realizable signals and filters, the absolute bandwidth is infinite.

3-dB (or Half-Power) Bandwidth – The 3-dB (or half-power) bandwidth is one of the widely-used definitions. Assuming the maximum (peak) value of the magnitude spectrum occurs at a frequency inside the band $[f_1, f_2]$, we have $B = f_2 - f_1$, where the magnitude spectrum at any frequency inside the band falls no lower than $1/\sqrt{2}$ times the peak value. The signal power at f_1 or f_2 is thus 3 ($\cong -20 \log_{10}(1/\sqrt{2})$) dB lower than the peak signal power. However, this definition becomes ambiguous when the magnitude spectrum has multiple peaks. With this definition, the bandwidth can be easily read from a plot of magnitude spectrum. However, it may not be quite representative when the magnitude spectrum has slowly decreasing tails.

Fractional-Power Bandwidth – The occupied bandwidth, as adopted by FCC, defines a band of frequencies with 99% of the signal power, where 0.5% of the signal power is above the upper-frequency limit and 0.5% of the signal power is below the lower-frequency limit. This definition is primarily focused on passband signals and filters. However, for lowpass signals and filters, the definition may be modified to include 1% of the signal power above the upper-frequency limit (f_2), as the signal power below the lower-frequency limit ($f_1 = 0$) is zero.

Null-to-Null (Zero-Crossing) Bandwidth – The null-to-null (zero-crossing) bandwidth is a commonly-used definition. For bandpass signals, when the magnitude spectrum has a main lobe (the lobe with the peak value) bounded by nulls (the frequencies f_1 and f_2 at which the magnitude spectrum is zero), we have $B = f_2 - f_1$, as the main lobe is centered on the frequency $f_c = (f_2 + f_1)/2$. For lowpass signals, we have $f_1 = 0$ (i.e., only one half of the width of the main spectral lobe is the bandwidth). Note that the null-to-null bandwidth can be easily read from a plot of magnitude spectrum.

Bounded-Power Bandwidth – The level of power at every frequency outside the power bandwidth has fallen at least to a certain level below its maximum level. This relative level is usually specified in negative decibels. For instance, a power bandwidth of –50 dB indicates the signal outside the power bandwidth is attenuated by a factor of 100,000, say from a maximum of 1000 W to a level not exceeding 10 mW.

Root-Mean-Square (rms) Bandwidth – It is defined as the square root of the second moment of the squared magnitude spectrum of the signal taken about the origin ($f = 0$), and then normalized to the signal energy. The root-mean square bandwidth B_{rms} for a lowpass signal is defined mathematically in (3.67a). Although the mathematical evaluation of the rms bandwidth is rather simple, its measurement in the lab is not straightforward.

Amplitude-Equivalent Bandwidth – It is an equivalent rectangular pulse whose height is the maximum of magnitude spectrum and its bandwidth is B_{AEB}, so the rectangular pulse and the magnitude spectrum of the signal have the same area. The amplitude equivalent bandwidth for a lowpass signal is defined mathematically in (3.68a).

Noise-Equivalent Bandwidth – It is an equivalent rectangular bandwidth with the same mid-band gain (the maximum value of the squared magnitude spectrum over all frequencies) that will have as much power as the signal over all frequencies. The power equivalent bandwidth B_{NEB} for a lowpass signal is defined mathematically in (3.69a).

Note that a bandwidth definition, such as those of root-mean-square, amplitude-equivalent, and noise-equivalent, can be easily extended to band-pass signals and filters, if instead of the zero frequency, the center frequency $f_c \gg 0$ is considered.

3.8.2 Time-Bandwidth Product

As the scaling property of the Fourier transform clearly indicates, a time reduction in the duration of a signal (i.e., time compression) gives rise to an increase in its spectrum (i.e., bandwidth expansion), and vice versa. More specifically, if the duration of a signal is increased by a certain factor, the bandwidth of the signal is then decreased by the same factor. It is thus mutually exclusive for a signal to be both time-limited and band-limited. The ***time-bandwidth product*** is therefore always infinite, unless time duration and bandwidth duration of a signal are defined in a way that their product is finite. For any class of signals, such as exponential and Gaussian pulses, the product of the signal's duration and its bandwidth is a constant. It is important to note that for a class of signals, the choice of a particular definition for bandwidth merely changes the value of the constant. The time-bandwidth product is lower bounded, and highlights the uncertainty principle that both the time duration and the bandwidth of a signal cannot be made arbitrarily small simultaneously. In here, we assume $g(t)$ is a real even signal with its maximum value at $t = 0$, and its even magnitude spectrum $|G(f)|$ has its maximum value at $f = 0$.

Root-mean square bandwidth and time duration – The bandwidth, corresponding time duration, and the resulting time-bandwidth product for a low-pass signal are respectively as follows:

$$B_{rms} = \sqrt{\frac{\int_{-\infty}^{\infty} f^2|G(f)|^2 df}{\int_{-\infty}^{\infty} |G(f)|^2 df}} = \left(\frac{1}{E}\right)\sqrt{\int_{-\infty}^{\infty} f^2|G(f)|^2 df} \tag{3.67a}$$

$$T_{rms} = \sqrt{\frac{\int_{-\infty}^{\infty} t^2|g(t)|^2 dt}{\int_{-\infty}^{\infty} |g(t)|^2 dt}} = \left(\frac{1}{E}\right)\sqrt{\int_{-\infty}^{\infty} t^2|g(t)|^2 dt} \tag{3.67b}$$

$$T_{rms}\, B_{rms} \geq \frac{1}{4\pi} \tag{3.67c}$$

where E is the signal energy and the equality holds for the Gaussian pulse. This in turn means with respect to the rms bandwidth definition, the Gaussian pulse occupies the least possible bandwidth.

Amplitude-equivalent bandwidth and time duration – The bandwidth, corresponding time duration, and the resulting time-bandwidth product for a low-pass signal are respectively as follows:

$$B_{AEB} = \frac{\int_{-\infty}^{\infty} |G(f)| df}{2G(0)} \tag{3.68a}$$

$$T_{AEB} = \frac{\int_{-\infty}^{\infty} |g(t)| dt}{2g(0)} \tag{3.68b}$$

$$T_{AEB}\, B_{AEB} \geq \frac{1}{4} \tag{3.68c}$$

Noise-equivalent bandwidth and time duration – The bandwidth, corresponding time duration, and the resulting time-bandwidth product for a low-pass signal are respectively as follows:

$$B_{NEB} = \frac{\int_{-\infty}^{\infty} |G(f)|^2 df}{2|G(0)|^2} \tag{3.69a}$$

$$T_{NEB} = \frac{\left(\int_{-\infty}^{\infty} |g(t)| dt\right)^2}{\int_{-\infty}^{\infty} |g(t)|^2 dt} \tag{3.69b}$$

$$T_{NEB}\, B_{NEB} \geq \frac{1}{2} \tag{3.69c}$$

It is important to note that regardless of the definition employed for the bandwidth and time duration, the bandwidth of a signal and the corresponding time duration of the signal are inversely proportional.

EXAMPLE 3.44

Consider the well-known tent signal $g_1(t) = e^{-m|t|}$, where m is a positive constant, and the widely-used Gaussian signal $g_2(t) = e^{-bt^2}$, where b is a positive constant. Figure 3.33 shows the time and frequency representations of these two lowpass signals. By using the definitions provided in (3.67), (3.68), and (3.69), determine the time-bandwidth product for each of these two signals.

Solution

The results, as shown in Table 3.4, indicate that the time-bandwidth product for all cases is independent of the parameters m and b.

3.9 SIGNAL TRANSMISSION THROUGH SYSTEMS

Our main focus here is on LTI systems and their impacts on signals, and not so much concerned with the actual system elements. We view a system in terms of the operation it performs on an input $x(t)$ to produce an output $y(t)$.

3.9.1 Signal Transmission through LTI Systems

In the time domain, a linear system is described by its impulse response (i.e., the response of the system with zero initial condition when its input is a unit impulse or delta function $\delta(t)$). For a time-invariant system, the shape of the impulse response remains the same no matter when the unit impulse is applied to the system. Assuming the unit impulse $\delta(t)$ is applied to an LTI system at $t=0$, the ***impulse response*** is represented by $h(t)$ in the time domain or equivalently by its ***frequency response*** $H(f)$ (i.e., the Fourier transform of $h(t)$). In other words, for $x(t)=\delta(t)$, we have $y(t)=h(t)$, or equivalently, if $X(f)$ and $Y(f)$ represent the Fourier transforms of the input and output of an LTI system, respectively, then for $X(f)=1$, we have $Y(f)=H(f)$. In an LTI system, a frequency component is present at the output if it is present at the input. In other words, LTI systems cannot introduce new frequency components, as only nonlinear and/or time-varying systems can produce new frequency components.

The necessary and sufficient condition for an LTI system to be causal is to have a zero impulse response for negative time. We thus have the following:

Causality criterion in an LTI system: $h(t)=0, \text{ for } t<0$ (3.70)

The necessary and sufficient condition for an LTI system to have the bounded-input-bounded-output (BIBO) stability is to have an absolutely integrable impulse response. We thus have the following:

Stability criterion in an LTI system: $\int_{-\infty}^{\infty} |h(t)|dt < \infty$ (3.71)

An LTI system can be described by a linear differential equation (for continuous-time signals) or a linear difference equation (for discrete-time

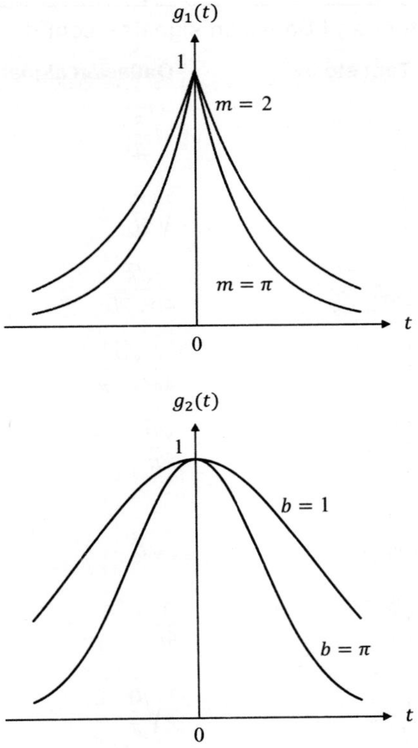

FIGURE 3.33 Signals in Example 3.44.

Table 3.4 Time-bandwidth product for tent and Gaussian signals

Terms of interest	Tent signal	Gaussian signal
$g(t)$	$e^{-m\|t\|}, m > 0$	$e^{-bt^2}, b > 0$
$G(f)$	$\frac{2m}{m^2 + 4\pi^2 f^2}$	$\sqrt{\frac{\pi}{b}} e^{-\pi^2 f^2 / b}$
$g(0)$	1	1
$G(0)$	$\frac{2}{m}$	$\sqrt{\frac{\pi}{b}}$
$\int_{-\infty}^{\infty} \|g(t)\| dt$	$\frac{2}{m}$	$\sqrt{\frac{\pi}{b}}$
$\int_{-\infty}^{\infty} \|G(f)\| df$	1	1

(Continued)

Table 3.4 Time-bandwidth product for tent and Gaussian signals—cont'd

Terms of interest	Tent signal	Gaussian signal
$\int_{-\infty}^{\infty} \lvert g(t)\rvert^2 dt = E$	$\frac{1}{m}$	$\sqrt{\frac{\pi}{2b}}$
$\int_{-\infty}^{\infty} \lvert G(f)\rvert^2 df = E$	$\frac{1}{m}$	$\sqrt{\frac{\pi}{2b}}$
$\int_{-\infty}^{\infty} t^2 \lvert g(t)\rvert^2 dt$	$\frac{1}{2m^3}$	$\frac{\sqrt{\pi}}{4b\sqrt{2b}}$
$\int_{-\infty}^{\infty} f^2 \lvert G(f)\rvert^2 df = \frac{1}{4\pi^2}\int_{-\infty}^{\infty} (g'(t))^2 dt$	$\frac{m^2}{4\pi^2}$	$\frac{b\sqrt{b}}{4\pi^2\sqrt{2\pi}}$
$B_{rms} = \left(\frac{1}{E}\right)\sqrt{\int_{-\infty}^{\infty} f^2 \lvert G(f)\rvert^2 df}$	$\frac{m}{2\pi}$	$\frac{\sqrt{b}}{2\pi}$
$T_{rms} = \left(\frac{1}{E}\right)\sqrt{\int_{-\infty}^{\infty} t^2 \lvert g(t)\rvert^2 dt}$	$\frac{1}{m\sqrt{2}}$	$\frac{1}{2\sqrt{b}}$
$T_{rms}B_{rms} \geq 1/4\pi$	$\frac{\sqrt{2}}{4\pi}$	$\frac{1}{4\pi}$
$B_{AEB} = \frac{\int_{-\infty}^{\infty} \lvert G(f)\rvert df}{2G(0)}$	$\frac{m}{4}$	$\frac{1}{2}\sqrt{\frac{b}{\pi}}$
$T_{AEB} = \frac{\int_{-\infty}^{\infty} \lvert g(t)\rvert dt}{2g(0)}$	$\frac{1}{m}$	$\frac{1}{2}\sqrt{\frac{\pi}{b}}$
$T_{AEB}B_{AEB} \geq 1/4$	$\frac{1}{4}$	$\frac{1}{4}$
$B_{NEB} = \frac{\int_{-\infty}^{\infty} \lvert G(f)\rvert^2 df}{2\lvert G(0)\rvert^2}$	$\frac{m}{8}$	$\frac{0.5\sqrt{b}}{\sqrt{2\pi}}$
$T_{NEB} = \frac{\left(\int_{-\infty}^{\infty} \lvert g(t)\rvert dt\right)^2}{\int_{-\infty}^{\infty} \lvert g(t)\rvert^2 dt}$	$\frac{4}{m}$	$\frac{\sqrt{2\pi}}{\sqrt{b}}$
$T_{NEB}B_{NEB} \geq 1/2$	$\frac{1}{2}$	$\frac{1}{2}$

signals). LTI systems play a significant role in digital communication system analysis and design, as an LTI system can be easily characterized either in the time domain using the system impulse response $h(t)$ or in the frequency domain using the system transfer function $H(f)$.

3.9.2 Time Response and Convolution in LTI Systems

Convolution is the input-output relationship in the time domain. By convolution, the output $y(t)$ in an LTI system can be derived from the input $x(t)$ and the impulse response $h(t)$. It can be shown that the output $y(t)$ can be derived as follows:

$$y(t)=\int_{-\infty}^{\infty} x(\tau)h(t-\tau)d\tau = x(t)*h(t)=\int_{-\infty}^{\infty} h(\tau)x(t-\tau)d\tau = h(t)*x(t) \tag{3.72}$$

where * denotes the convolution operation. Equation (3.72) is called the ***convolution integral***, and shows that $y(t)$, which is the response to $x(t)$, is the convolution of the input $x(t)$ and the impulse response $h(t)$. Note that $y(t)$ is nonzero for the interval that is the sum of the intervals during which $x(t)$ and $h(t)$ are nonzero. In other words, if $x(t)$ is limited to the time interval $[a, b]$ and $h(t)$ is limited to the time interval $[c, d]$, $y(t)$ is then limited to the time interval $[a+c,\ b+d]$. Equation (3.72) reflects the fact that the present value of the output signal is a weighted integral over the past history of the input signal, weighted according to the impulse response of the system. In a way, the impulse response $h(t)$ acts as a memory function for the system. For a causal LTI system, there can be no output prior to the time $t=0$. Therefore, the lower limit of the integration in (3.72) can be changed to zero. For an LTI system, the impulse response $h(t)$ contains all the information needed, and thus completely characterizes the system.

EXAMPLE 3.45

Suppose the impulse response of an LTI system is as follows:

$h(t)=u(t)-u(t-2)$

Determine the output signal $y(t)$ provided that the input signal is as follows:

$x(t)=u(t)-u(t-3)$

Solution

After substituting $h(t)$ and $x(t)$ in (3.72), the signal output is then as follows:

$$y(t)=\int_{-\infty}^{\infty} x(\tau)h(t-\tau)d\tau$$

$$=\int_{-\infty}^{\infty} u(\tau)u(t-\tau)d\tau-\int_{-\infty}^{\infty} u(\tau)u(t-2-\tau)d\tau-\int_{-\infty}^{\infty} u(\tau-3)u(t-\tau)d\tau+\int_{-\infty}^{\infty} u(\tau-3)u(t-2-\tau)d\tau$$

$$=t\,u(t)-(t-2)\,u(t-2)-(t-3)\,u(t-3)+(t-5)\,u(t-5).$$

$x(t)$, $h(t)$ and $y(t)$ are all shown in Figure 3.34.

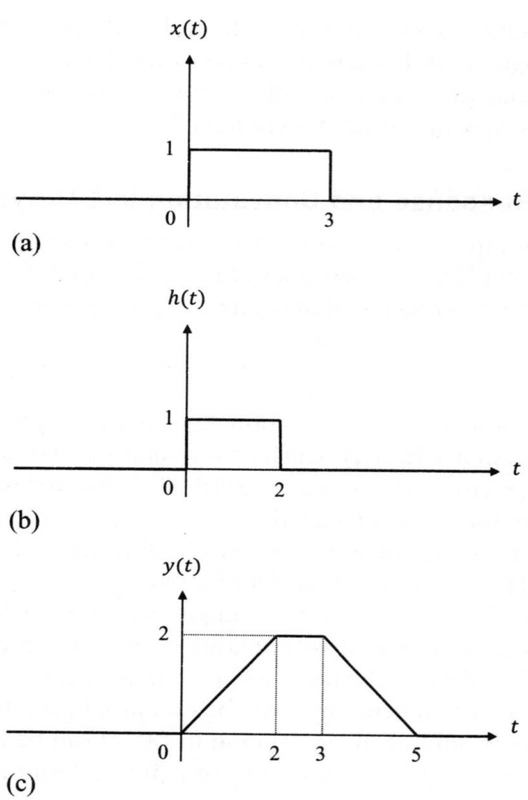

FIGURE 3.34 Signals in Example 3.45.

3.9.3 Frequency Response and Transfer Function in LTI Systems

We know, from the discussion on the Fourier transform, that convolution in the time domain implies multiplication in the frequency domain. Using (3.72), we can therefore have the following:

$$Y(f)=X(f)H(f) \tag{3.73}$$

Equation (3.73) implies that the Fourier transform of the output signal is equal to the product of the transfer function of the system and the Fourier transform of the input signal. $H(f)$, the Fourier transform of $h(t)$, is generally referred to as the ***transfer function*** or the ***frequency response*** of the LTI system, and contains all relevant information about the system. If $X(f)$ is limited to the frequency band $[x_1, x_2]$ and if $H(f)$ is limited to the frequency band $[h_1, h_2]$, $Y(f)$ is then limited to the frequency band $[y_1, y_2]=[x_1, x_2]\cap[h_1, h_2]$. In other words, if at a certain frequency, the Fourier transform of the input signal or the transfer function is zero, the Fourier transform of the output signal at that frequency is also zero. To find $y(t)$, it is sometimes much easier to find $Y(f)$ by using (3.73) and then find its inverse Fourier transform. The frequency response $H(f)$ is generally complex and can thus be written as follows:

$$H(f) = |H(f)| \exp(j\beta(f)) \tag{3.74}$$

where $|H(f)|$ is called the ***amplitude (magnitude) response***, and $\beta(f)$ is called the ***phase response***. In a linear system with a real-valued impulse response $h(t)$, we have the following:

$$|H(f)| = |H(-f)| \tag{3.75a}$$

$$\beta(f) = -\beta(-f) \tag{3.75b}$$

We can therefore conclude that for a real-valued impulse response the magnitude response is an even function and the phase response is an odd function. Since $X(f)$ and $Y(f)$ may be complex, using (3.73) and (3.74), we have the following:

$$|Y(f)| = |X(f)||H(f)| \tag{3.76a}$$

$$\measuredangle Y(f) = \measuredangle X(f) + \beta(f) \tag{3.76b}$$

The magnitude response of the output signal is thus the product of the magnitude response of the input and the magnitude response of the transfer function, and the phase response of the output signal is the sum of the phase response of the input signal and the phase response of the transfer function. In other words, an input signal of frequency f is modified, as its magnitude response is scaled by a factor $|H(f)|$ and its phase response is shifted by a factor $\beta(f)$. Clearly, during the transmission, some frequency components may be amplified, while others may be attenuated, and the relative phases of the various components may also change, thus resulting in an output signal that may be different from the input signal.

By using a sine-wave generator at the input of an LTI system and an oscilloscope at its output, the system frequency response can be easily measured in a communication laboratory, and thus plotted. For the system input $x(t) = A\cos(2\pi f_0 t)$, the system output will be $y(t) = A|H(f_0)|\cos(2\pi f_0 t + \beta(f_0))$. For the frequency range of interest, f_0 is varied, and at each step, the amplitude and phase at the output are both measured. The ratio of the magnitude of the output to that of the input represents the magnitude (amplitude) response of the LTI system and the difference between the phase of the output and that of the input represents its phase response.

EXAMPLE 3.46

Suppose the frequency response of an LTI system is as follows:

$$H(f) = \frac{1}{2 + j2\pi f}$$

Determine the output signal in the time domain provided that the input signal is as follows:

$$x(t) = e^{-t}u(t)$$

Solution

Using (3.42a), the Fourier transform of the input signal is as follows:

$$X(f) = \frac{1}{1 + j2\pi f}$$

Using (3.73), we then determine the Fourier transform of the output signal:

$$Y(f) = X(f)\,H(f) = \left(\frac{1}{2 + j2\pi f}\right)\left(\frac{1}{1 + j2\pi f}\right) = \frac{1}{(2 + j2\pi f)(1 + j2\pi f)} = \frac{1}{1 + j2\pi f} - \frac{1}{2 + j2\pi f}$$

Using (3.42b), the inverse Fourier transform is as follows:

$$y(t) = e^{-t}u(t) - e^{-2t}\,u(t) = (e^{-t} - e^{-2t})\,u(t)$$

3.9.4 Application of Periodic Signals to LTI Systems

The response of an LTI system to a complex exponential is a complex exponential with the same frequency and a possible change in its magnitude and/or phase. With $H(f)$ as the LTI system transfer function, the response to the exponential $\exp(j2\pi f_0 t)$ is $\exp(j2\pi f_0 t)H(f_0)$. Note that $H(f)$ is a complex function that can be characterized by its magnitude response $|H(f)|$ and phase response $\measuredangle H(f)$. Suppose the input $x(t)$ is periodic with period $T_0 = 1/f_0$, and has the following Fourier series representation:

$$x(t) = \sum_{n=-\infty}^{\infty} x_n \exp\left(\frac{j2\pi nt}{T_0}\right) \tag{3.77}$$

where $\{x_n\}$ represents the complex exponential Fourier series coefficients for the input $x(t)$. The output $y(t)$ is also periodic with period $T_0 = 1/f_0$, and has the following Fourier series representation:

$$y(t) = \sum_{n=-\infty}^{\infty} x_n H\left(\frac{n}{T_0}\right) \exp\left(\frac{j2\pi nt}{T_0}\right) = \sum_{n=-\infty}^{\infty} y_n \exp\left(\frac{j2\pi nt}{T_0}\right) \tag{3.78}$$

where $\{y_n\}$ represents the complex exponential Fourier series coefficients for the output $y(t)$. For the amplitude and phase of the nth harmonic of the output signal, we thus have the following:

$$y_n = x_n H\left(\frac{n}{T_0}\right) \Leftrightarrow \begin{cases} |y_n| = |x_n|\left|H\left(\frac{n}{T_0}\right)\right| \\ \measuredangle y_n = \measuredangle x_n + \measuredangle H\left(\frac{n}{T_0}\right) \end{cases} \tag{3.79}$$

EXAMPLE 3.47

Consider an LTI system whose frequency response is as follows:

$H(f) = -j\left(\frac{\pi}{4}\right)\operatorname{sgn}(f)$

Suppose the input signal $x(t)$ is an odd periodic square wave of period 1, where $x(t)=1$, for $0<t\leq 0.5$, and $x(t)=-1$, for $0.5<t\leq 1$. Determine the output signal in the time domain.

Solution

We first determine the magnitude and phase frequency responses, which are as follows:

$|H(f)| = \frac{\pi}{4}$ and $\measuredangle H(f) = -\left(\frac{\pi}{2}\right)\operatorname{sgn}(f)$

Using (3.37), we thus have:

$$\begin{aligned} x(t) &= \left(\frac{4}{\pi}\right)\sum_{n=1}^{\infty}\frac{1}{2n-1}\sin(2(2n-1)\pi t) \\ &= \left(\frac{1}{j}\right)\left(\frac{2}{\pi}\right)\sum_{n=1}^{\infty}\frac{1}{2n-1}(\exp(j2(2n-1)\pi t) - \exp(-j2(2n-1)\pi t)) \end{aligned}$$

To determine the output corresponding to each frequency, we use (3.79):

$$\begin{aligned} y(t) &= \left(\frac{1}{j}\right)\left(\frac{\pi}{4}\right)\left(\frac{2}{\pi}\right)\sum_{n=1}^{\infty}\frac{1}{2n-1}(\exp(j2(2n-1)\pi t - \pi/2) - \exp(-j2(2n-1)\pi t) + \pi/2) \\ &= \sum_{n=1}^{\infty}\frac{1}{2n-1}\sin\left(2(2n-1)\pi t - \frac{\pi}{2}\right) = -\sum_{n=1}^{\infty}\frac{1}{2n-1}\cos(2(2n-1)\pi t) \end{aligned}$$

3.9.5 Distortionless Transmission

It is of paramount interest that in a communication channel the output signal be an exact replica of the input signal; after all, that is the ultimate goal in signal transmission. It is therefore important to determine the characteristics of a communication system that allows no distortion. In a ***distortionless transmission***, the input and output signals in the time domain have identical shapes, except for a possible change of amplitude and a constant delay. In other words, for the input signal $x(t)$ transmitted through a distortionless channel, the output signal $y(t)$ is defined by:

$$y(t) = kx(t - t_d) \tag{3.80}$$

where the constant $k<1$ reflects the ***transmission attenuation***, and the constant $t_d>0$ accounts for the ***transmission delay***, as a transmission medium always introduces an attenuation, no matter how small, and a delay, no matter how short. By applying the Fourier transform to (3.80), we get the following:

$$Y(f) = kX(f)e^{-j2\pi f t_d} \tag{3.81}$$

The transfer function of a distortionless channel $H(f)$ is then defined as follows:

$$H(f) = \frac{Y(f)}{X(f)} = ke^{-j2\pi f t_d} \tag{3.82a}$$

Equation (3.82a) indicates that in order to achieve distortionless transmission through a channel, the magnitude response of the channel must be a constant and the phase response must be a linear function of frequency that passes through the origin. In other words, the following two requirements must be satisfied over the frequency band of interest (the band of frequencies that the spectrum of the transmitted signal exists):

$$|H(f)| = k \tag{3.82b}$$

$$\measuredangle H(f) = \beta(f) = -2\pi f t_d \tag{3.82c}$$

Equations (3.82b) and (3.82c) provide the requirements for distortionless transmission, as shown in Figure 3.35.

When the magnitude response of the channel $|H(f)|$ is not constant over the frequency band of interest, we have magnitude distortion (i.e., the frequency components of the input signal experience different amounts of attenuation, or possibly gain). Also, when the phase response of the channel $\beta(f)$ is not linear with respect to the frequency inside the band of interest, we have phase distortion (i.e., the components of different frequencies undergo different amounts of delay). Interestingly, the human ear is insensitive to phase distortion, but relatively sensitive to amplitude distortion. However, the human eye is more sensitive to time delay, rather than amplitude distortion.

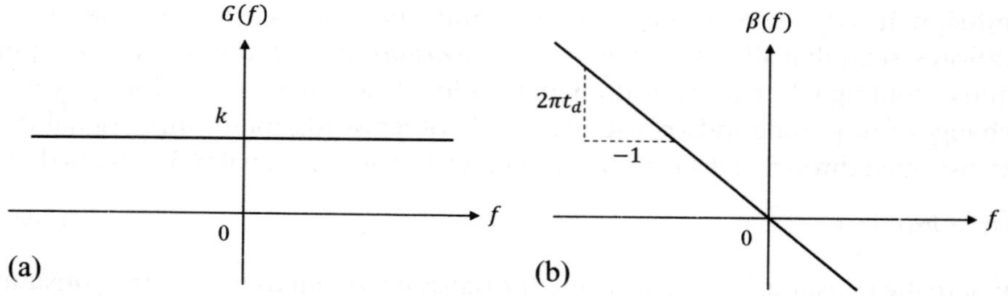

FIGURE 3.35 Frequency response of an ideal distortionless channel: (a) magnitude response and (b) phase response.

EXAMPLE 3.48

Consider an LTI system whose impulse response is as follows:

$h(t) = \exp(-t)u(t)$

Determine the system output $y(t)$ if its input is $x(t) = \cos(t) + \cos\left(\sqrt{3}t\right)$.

Solution

Using (3.42a), the magnitude and phase spectra of the system frequency response is as follows:

$$|H(f)| = \frac{1}{\sqrt{1+(2\pi f)^2}}$$

and

$$\measuredangle H(f) = \beta(f) = -\tan^{-1}(2\pi f)$$

Using (3.42a), the Fourier transform of the input is as follows:

$$X(f) = 0.5\left(\delta\left(f - \frac{1}{2\pi}\right) + \delta\left(f + \frac{1}{2\pi}\right)\right) + 0.5\left(\delta\left(f - \frac{\sqrt{3}}{2\pi}\right) + \delta\left(f + \frac{\sqrt{3}}{2\pi}\right)\right)$$

Note that the input signal has only two distinct frequency components. Using (3.73), the Fourier transform of the output is then as follows:

$$Y(f) = \left(\frac{\sqrt{2}}{4}\right)\left(\delta\left(f - \frac{1}{2\pi}\right)\exp\left(-\frac{j\pi}{4}\right) + \delta\left(f + \frac{1}{2\pi}\right)\exp\left(\frac{j\pi}{4}\right)\right)$$
$$+\left(\frac{1}{4}\right)\left(\delta\left(f - \frac{\sqrt{3}}{2\pi}\right)\exp\left(-\frac{j\pi}{3}\right) + \delta\left(f + \frac{\sqrt{3}}{2\pi}\right)\exp\left(\frac{j\pi}{3}\right)\right)$$

Using (3.42b), the output $y(t)$ is as follows:

$$y(t) = \frac{\sqrt{2}}{2}\cos\left(t - \frac{\pi}{4}\right) + \frac{1}{2}\cos\left(\sqrt{3}t - \frac{\pi}{3}\right)$$

The linear distortion has impacted the input signal, where the amounts of attenuation and delay are both different at the two frequencies.

3.9.6 Nonlinear Distortion

A nonlinear system cannot be described by a transfer function, as a change in the input signal may not directly produce a corresponding change in the output signal. We assume here the system is memoryless in the sense that the output $y(t)$ depends only on the input $x(t)$ at time t. To evaluate the ***nonlinear distortion***, the common procedure is to approximate the input-output relation, also known as the transfer characteristics, by a power series of the input $x(t)$:

$$y(t) = a_1x(t) + a_2x^2(t) + a_3x^3(t) + \ldots \tag{3.83}$$

Assuming $X(f)$ is the Fourier transform of $x(t)$, the Fourier transform of (3.83) becomes as follows:

$$Y(f) = a_1X(f) + a_2X(f) * X(f) + a_3X(f) * X(f) * X(f) + \ldots \tag{3.84}$$

where * denotes the convolution operation. Assuming $x(t)$ is band-limited to W Hz, $x^2(t)$ is band-limited to $2W$ Hz, $x^3(t)$ is band-limited to $3W$ Hz, and so on and so forth. The nonlinearities have thus created new output frequency components that are not present in the input. With appropriate filtering, these out-of-band frequency components ($|f| \geq W$) can be suppressed. However, the second-, third-, and the higher-order nonlinearities all produce undesirable in-band frequency components ($|f| \leq W$). Since these frequency components, which lie in the frequency band of interest, cannot be removed, we have nonlinear distortion.

EXAMPLE 3.49

In a nonlinear system, the input-output characteristic is as follows:

$y(t) = x(t) + x^2(t)$

Determine the output signal in time and frequency domains, if the input signal is as follows:

$x(t) = 2\cos(2000\pi t) + 2\cos(3000\pi t)$

Solution

The output signal $y(t)$ is therefore as follows:

$y(t) = 2\cos(2000\pi t) + 2\cos(3000\pi t) + (2\cos(2000\pi t) + 2\cos(3000\pi t))^2$

Using trigonometric identities, the output signal can then be simplified as:

$y(t) = 2\cos(2000\pi t) + 2\cos(3000\pi t) + 4 + 2\cos(4000\pi t) + 2\cos(6000\pi t) + 4\cos(5000\pi t) + 4\cos(1000\pi t)$

As shown in Figure 3.36, the system has produced frequencies in the output other than the input frequencies of 1 and 1.5 kHz. They include harmonic distortion terms at harmonics of the input frequencies (i.e., 2 and 3 kHz) and intermodulation distortion terms involving the sum and difference of the harmonics of the input frequencies (i.e., 0, 0.5 and 2.5 kHz).

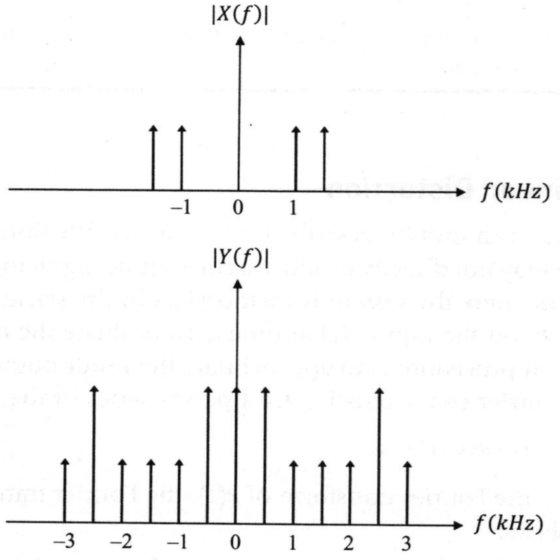

FIGURE 3.36 Signals in Example 3.49.

Although there is no correcting measure for nonlinear distortion, it can be minimized by careful design to make sure the input signal does not exceed the linear operating range of the channel's transfer characteristics. Keeping the signal amplitude within the linear operating range is accomplished by using two nonlinear devices, a compressor and an expander. A compressor essentially reduces the amplitude range of an input signal so that it falls within the linear range of the channel. Since reducing the input range results in reducing the output range, an expander is required to increase the output to the appropriate level. The combined operation of compressing and expanding is called ***companding***.

3.10 COMMUNICATION FILTERS

In communication systems, filters are widely used to process signals. A ***communication filter*** is a frequency-selective system that can shape and limit the spectrum of a signal. The characteristics of a filter are determined by its frequency response (i.e., the magnitude and phase responses). Filtering is thus the process by which the relative magnitude and phase of the frequency components in a signal are changed.

3.10.1 Ideal Filters

An ***ideal filter*** exactly passes signals at certain sets of frequencies and completely rejects the rest. In order to avoid distortion in the filtering process, a filter should ideally have a flat magnitude characteristic and a linear phase characteristic over the passband of the filter (the frequency range of interest). The most common types of filters are the ***low-pass filter*** (LPF), ***high-pass filter*** (HPF), ***band-pass filter*** (BPF), and ***band-stop filter*** (BSF), which pass low, high, intermediate, and all but intermediate frequencies, respectively. Figure 3.37 shows the magnitude and phase responses of ideal LPF, HPF, BPF, and BSF. Most communication filters are of LPF and BPF types.

For a physically-realizable filter, its impulse response $h(t)$ must be causal. In the frequency domain, this condition is equivalent to the ***Paley-Wiener criterion***, which states that the necessary and sufficient condition for $|H(f)|$ to be the magnitude response of a causal (realizable) filter is as follows:

$$\int_{-\infty}^{\infty} \frac{|\ln|H(f)||}{(1+f^2)} df < \infty \tag{3.85}$$

This condition is not met if $|H(f)|=0$ over a finite band of frequencies (i.e., a filter cannot perfectly reject any band of frequencies). However, if $|H(f)|=0$ at a single frequency (or a set of discrete frequencies), the condition may be met.

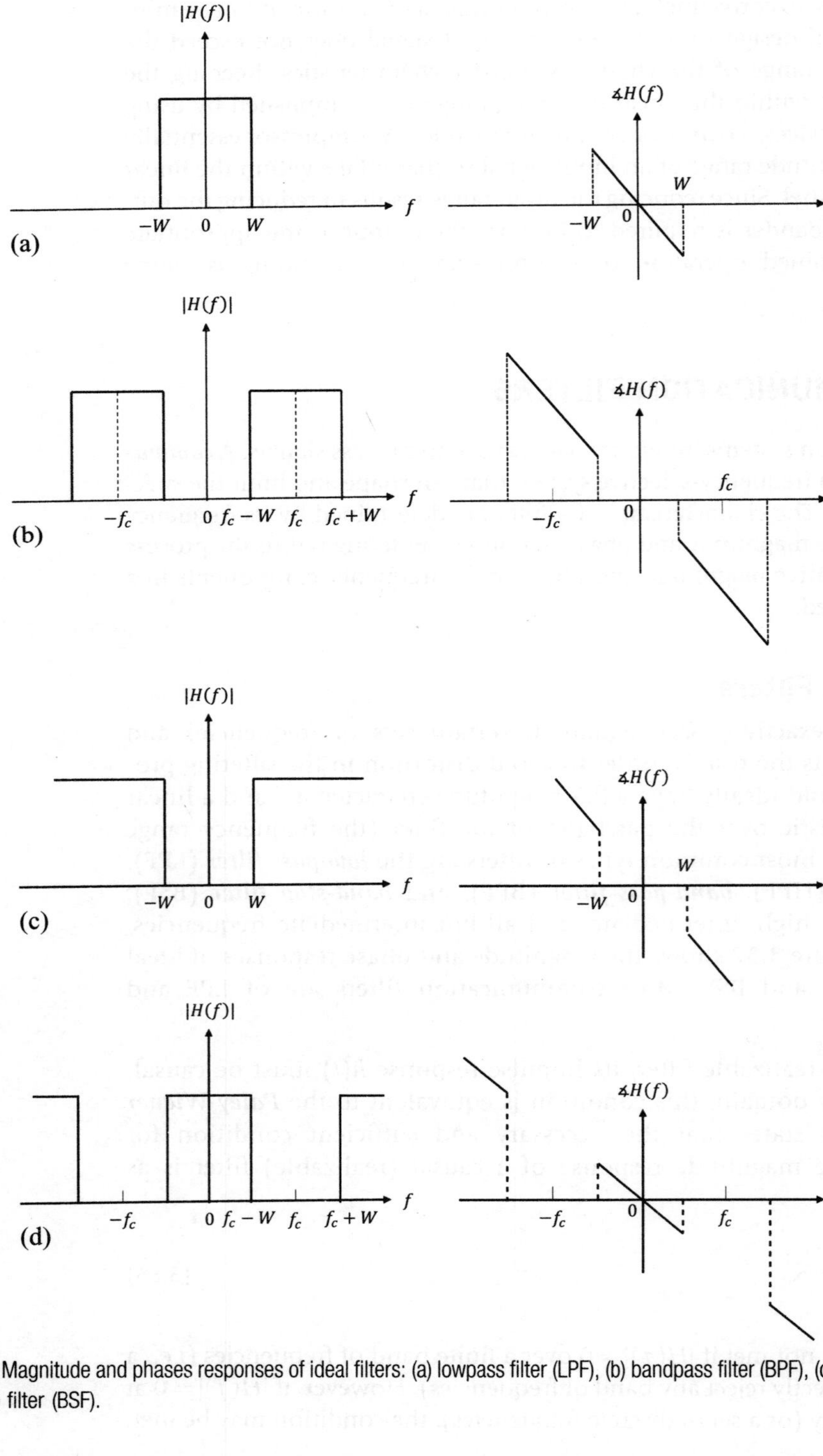

FIGURE 3.37 Magnitude and phases responses of ideal filters: (a) lowpass filter (LPF), (b) bandpass filter (BPF), (c) highpass filter (HPF), and (d) bandstop filter (BSF).

According to this criterion, ideal filters are clearly noncausal. Some continuous magnitude responses, such as $|H(f)| = \exp(-|f|)$, are not allowable magnitude responses for causal filters because the integral in (3.85) does not give a finite result.

EXAMPLE 3.50

Determine the frequency responses and impulse responses of an ideal LPF and BPF, and discuss the causality issue.

Solution

The frequency response of an ideal LPF with a bandwidth of W Hz and its impulse response are respectively defined as follows:

$$H_{LPF}(f) = (u(f+W) - u(f-W))\exp(-j2\pi f t_0)$$

and

$$h_{LPF}(t) = 2W\text{sinc}(2W(t-t_0))$$

The impulse response for $t_0 = 0$ is shown in Figure 3.38a. As reflected in (3.85), $|H(f)|$ does not meet the Paley-Wiener criterion, and $h(t)$ is thus not causal. One practical approach to filter design is to cut off the tail of $h(t)$ for $t < 0$. In order to have the truncated version of $h(t)$ as close as possible to the ideal impulse response, the delay t_0 must be as large as possible. Theoretically, a delay of infinite duration is needed to realize the ideal characteristics. But practically, a delay of just a few times $\frac{1}{2W}$ can make the truncated version reasonably close to the ideal one. As an example, for an audio LPF filter with a bandwidth of 20 kHz, a delay of 0.1 milliseconds would be a reasonable choice.

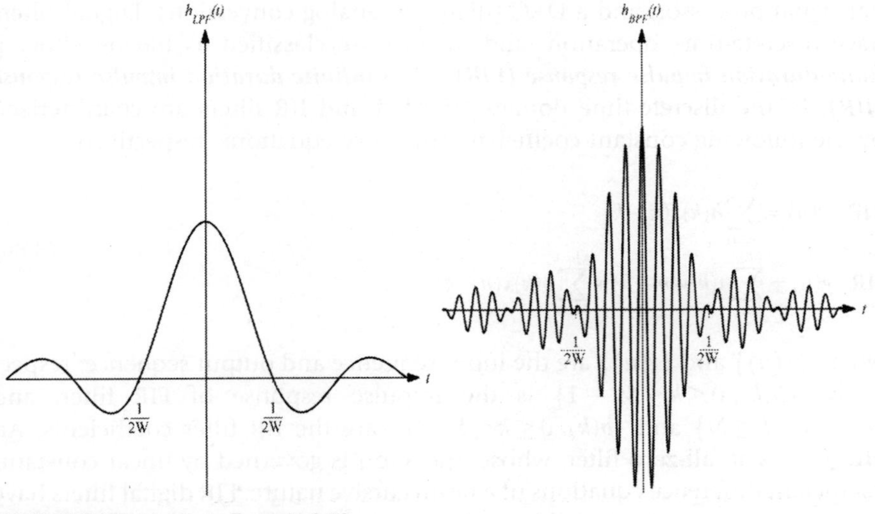

FIGURE 3.38 Signals in Example 3.50.

The frequency response of an ideal BPF, with a bandwidth of $2W$ Hz and centered around the frequency f_c, as well as its impulse response are respectively defined as follows:

$$H_{BPF}(f) = (u(f+W+f_c) - u(f-W+f_c) + u(f+W-f_c) - u(f-W-f_c))e^{-j2\pi f t_0}$$

and

$$h_{BPF}(t) = 4W\,\mathrm{sinc}(2W(t-t_0))\cos(2\pi f_c(t-t_0))$$

The impulse response for $t_0 = 0$ is shown in Figure 3.38b. If $f_c \gg 2W$, it is reasonable to view $h_{BPF}(t)$ as the slowly-varying envelope sinc$(2Wt)$ modulating the high-frequency oscillatory signal $\cos(2\pi f_c t)$ and shifted to the right by t_0.

3.10.2 Filter Types

There are two distinct categories of filters: analog filters and digital filters. An ***analog filter*** has a continuous-time operation and is characterized by an impulse response of infinite duration. Analog filters are divided into passive filters and active filters. A ***passive filter*** consists of passive circuit elements, such as resistors, inductors, and capacitors. An ***active filter*** consists of active elements, such as operational amplifiers, in addition to passive elements. Passive filters are useful at high frequencies, but active elements can eliminate the need for using bulky and expensive inductors, particularly in low-frequency applications, and generate gain greater than unity. Also, switched-capacitors can be used to replace resistors that would take up too much space in integrated circuits. Analog filters offer the benefits of continuous-time operation and reduced complexity.

A typical ***digital filter*** consists of an ADC (analog-to-digital conversion), a digital signal processor, and a DAC (digital-to-analog conversion). Digital filters have discrete-time operation, and in turn are classified as having either a ***finite-duration impulse response (FIR)*** or an ***infinite-duration impulse response (IIR)***. In the discrete-time domain, the FIR and IIR filters are characterized by the following constant coefficient difference equations, respectively:

$$\begin{aligned} &\textbf{FIR}: y(n) = \sum_{k=0}^{M-1} h(k)x(n-k) \\ &\textbf{IIR}: y(n) = \sum_{k=1}^{N} a(k)y(n-k) + \sum_{k=0}^{M-1} b(k)x(n-k) \end{aligned} \tag{3.86}$$

where $\{x(n)\}$ and $\{y(n)\}$ are the input sequence and output sequence, respectively, $\{h(k), 0 \le k \le M-1\}$ is the impulse response of FIR filter, and $\{a(k), 1 \le k \le N\}$ and $\{b(k), 0 \le k \le M-1\}$ are the IIR filter coefficients. An FIR filter is an all-zero filter, whose operation is governed by linear constant-coefficient difference equations of a nonrecursive nature. FIR digital filters have finite memory, are always stable, and can realize a desired magnitude response with an exactly linear phase response (i.e., with no phase distortion). An IIR filter has poles and zeros, whose operation is governed by linear constant-coefficient difference equations of a recursive nature. IIR filters have a lower computational complexity, but at the expense of phase distortion. FIR filters are employed in communication systems, when phase distortion is undesirable.

3.10.3 Filter Design

The frequency response of a filter is characterized by the following frequency bands: ***passband***, as input signals with frequencies inside it are passed with little or no distortion, ***stopband***, as input signals with frequencies inside it are attenuated or blocked, and ***transition band***, as it separates the passband from the stopband.

An ideal filter has no transition band (i.e., the transition from the passband to stopband is abrupt and occurs at a single frequency). These characteristics result in a nonimplementable filter. Therefore, from a practical standpoint, an acceptable level of deviation from ideal specifications is permitted. Practical (realizable) filter characteristics are gradual, without jump discontinuities in the magnitude response.

Figure 3.39 presents the tolerance diagram for a physically-realizable analog (continuous-time) LPF. Analogous specifications are used for digital (discrete-time) filters, with the added provision that the response is always periodic in the frequency domain. Note that the magnitude response in the passband must lie between 1 and $1-\varepsilon_p$ (i.e., $1-\varepsilon_p < |H(f)| < 1$) for $0 < |f| < f_p$, where f_p is the ***passband cut-off frequency*** and $0 \ll \varepsilon_p < 1$ is a tolerance parameter. The magnitude response in the stopband must not exceed $0 < \varepsilon_s \ll 1$ (i.e., $|H(f)| < \varepsilon_s$) for $|f| > f_s$, where f_s is the ***stopband-edge frequency***. The magnitude response in the transition bandwidth must lie between $1-\varepsilon_p$ and ε_s (i.e., $\varepsilon_s < |H(f)| \le 1-\varepsilon_p$) for $f_p \le |f| \le f_s$. The frequency response of a filter usually has a large dynamic range, as such it is common practice to use a logarithmic scale for the magnitude response $|H(f)|$. Therefore, the fluctuation in the passband is $-20\log(1-\varepsilon_p)$ dB and the fluctuation in the stopband is $20\log(\varepsilon_s)$ dB.

After specifying the filter parameters ($\varepsilon_p, \varepsilon_s, f_p, f_s$), the design of the filter consists of the following two steps: i) the ***approximation of a frequency response*** (i.e., magnitude response or phase response or both) by a realizable transfer function that represents a stable and causal system, and ii) the ***realization of the approximating transfer function*** by a physical system. Both these two steps can be implemented in a variety of ways, thus highlighting the nonuniqueness of the filter design problem.

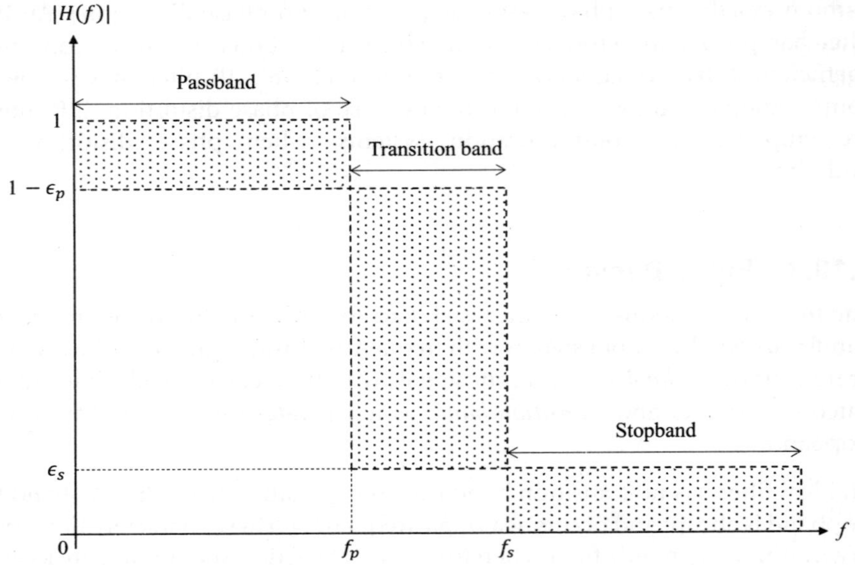

FIGURE 3.39 Tolerance diagram for a physically-realizable analog (continuous-time) LPF.

The two optimality criteria commonly used in filter design are the maximally-flat magnitude response, and the equiripple magnitude response. The ***Butterworth filter*** has a maximally-flat passband response, which is ideal for passing the amplitude of a signal with little distortion. The ***Chebyshev filter*** provides faster roll-off than the Butterworth by allowing ripple in the passband response. A common alternative to both the Butterworth and Chebyshev filters is the ***Elliptic filter***, which provides the fastest roll-off at the expense of ripple in both the passband and the stopband. Another type of filter that is suitable for data communications is the ***Bessel filter***, which has a maximally-flat group delay (approximately linear in-band phase response), but has a wider transition band.

3.11 SPECTRAL DENSITY AND AUTOCORRELATION FUNCTIONS

Autocorrelation represents the correlation of a signal with itself, and thus provides a measure of similarity between the signal and its own delayed version. Autocorrelation provides valuable spectral information about the signal, and may be viewed as the time-domain counterpart of spectral density, defined as the distribution of signal energy or power per unit of bandwidth. The focus of the following discussion is on real-valued signals.

3.11.1 Energy Spectral Density

According to Rayleigh's energy theorem discussed earlier, for real-valued signals, we have the following:

$$E=\int_{-\infty}^{\infty} g^2(t)dt=\int_{-\infty}^{\infty} |G(f)|^2 df \tag{3.87}$$

The energy of signal can be thus calculated through either $g(t)$ or $G(f)$. The magnitude squared is called the ***energy spectral density*** (ESD), and is as follows:

$$\Psi_g(f)=|G(f)|^2 \tag{3.88}$$

Energy spectral density, which is always an even, nonnegative, real-valued function of frequency, represents the distribution of the energy of the signal in the frequency domain. The ESD of an energy signal for any frequency can be interpreted as the energy per unit bandwidth, which is affected by frequency components of the signal around that frequency. Substituting (3.88) into (3.87) highlights the fact that the total area under the energy spectral density function of an energy signal equals the total signal energy.

When an energy signal is transmitted through an LTI system, the ESD of the output equals the ESD of the input multiplied by the squared magnitude response of the system. In other words, for an LTI system with the transfer function $H(f)$, we have the following:

$$\Psi_y(f)=|H(f)|^2\,\Psi_x(f) \tag{3.89}$$

The ESD of an energy signal can be measured by using a variable narrowband bandpass filter to scan the frequency band of interest and determining the energy of the filter output for each mid-band frequency setting of the filter.

3.11.2 Autocorrelation of Energy Signals

The ***autocorrelation function*** for a real-valued energy signal is defined as follows:

$$R_g(\tau)=\int_{-\infty}^{\infty} g(t)g(t-\tau)dt=g(\tau)*g(-\tau) \tag{3.90}$$

$R_g(\tau)$ is the autocorrelation function of an energy signal, which measures the similarity between the signal $g(t)$ and its delayed version $g(t-\tau)$. The time lag (or delay) is the scanning parameter that helps measure the autocorrelation function. The autocorrelation function is a real-valued, even function, whose maximum represents the energy of the signal and occurs at the origin

$(\tau = 0)$. For an energy signal $g(t)$, the autocorrelation function and energy spectral density form a Fourier transform pair, i.e., we have:

$$R_g(\tau) \longleftrightarrow \Psi_g(f) \tag{3.91}$$

If the real-valued signal is passed through an LTI system with the impulse response $h(t)$, the autocorrelation function of the output signal is as follows:

$$R_y(\tau) = R_x(\tau) * h(\tau) * h(-\tau) \tag{3.92}$$

where $R_x(\tau)$ and $R_y(\tau)$ are the input and output autocorrelation functions, respectively.

EXAMPLE 3.51

The energy signal $x(t) = 2\pi e^{-2\pi t} u(t)$ is applied to a lowpass filter whose squared magnitude response is as follows: $|H(f)|^2 = (1 + f^2)(u(f + 1/2) - u(f - 1/2))$. Determine the autocorrelation function and energy spectral density at both input and output.

Solution

Using (3.42), we first find the Fourier transform of $x(t)$, which is as follows:

$$X(f) = \frac{1}{1 + jf}$$

Using (3.88), the input energy spectral density $\Psi_x(f)$ is thus as follows:

$$\Psi_x(f) = \frac{1}{1 + f^2}$$

Using (3.91), the input autocorrelation function $R_x(\tau)$ is thus as follows:

$$R_x(\tau) = \pi e^{-2\pi|\tau|}$$

Using (3.89), the output energy density function $\Psi_y(f)$ is thus as follows:

$$\Psi_y(f) = u(f + 1/2) - u(f - 1/2)$$

Using (3.91), the output autocorrelation function $R_y(\tau)$ is thus as follows:

$$R_y(\tau) = \text{sinc}(\tau).$$

3.11.3 Power Spectral Density

The average power of a real-valued signal $g(t)$ is defined as follows:

$$P = \lim_{T \to \infty} \frac{1}{2T} \int_{-T}^{T} |g(t)|^2 dt \tag{3.93}$$

Power signals have infinite energy; they are not therefore Fourier transformable. To circumvent this problem, we define $g_T(t)$ as a truncated version of the signal $g(t)$, whose time duration is very long, but finite. $g_T(t)$ is thus an energy signal and has the Fourier transform $G_T(f)$. The ***power spectral density*** (PSD) of the power signal $g(t)$, which is the time average of the energy spectral density of the truncated version $g_T(t)$, is defined as follows:

$$S_g(f) = \lim_{T\to\infty} \frac{1}{2T} |G_T(f)|^2 \tag{3.94}$$

Power spectral density, which is always an even, nonnegative, real-valued function of frequency, represents the distribution of the power of the signal in the frequency domain. The following highlights the fact that the total area under the power spectral density function of a power signal $g(t)$ equals the average signal power.

$$P = \int_{-\infty}^{\infty} S_g(f)df \tag{3.95}$$

When a power signal is transmitted through an LTI system, the PSD of the output equals the PSD of the input multiplied by the squared magnitude response of the system. In other words, for an LTI system with transfer function $H(f)$, we have the following:

$$S_y(f) = |H(f)|^2 S_x(f) \tag{3.96}$$

The PSD of a power signal can be measured by using a variable narrow-band bandpass filter to scan the frequency band of interest and determine the power of the filter output for each mid-band frequency setting of the filter.

3.11.4 Autocorrelation of Power Signals

The ***autocorrelation function*** for a real-valued power signal is defined as follows:

$$R_g(\tau) = \lim_{T\to\infty} \frac{1}{2T} \int_{-T}^{T} g(t)g(t-\tau)dt \tag{3.97}$$

$R_g(\tau)$ is the autocorrelation function of the power signal, which measures the similarity between the signal $g(t)$ and its delayed version $g(t-\tau)$. The time lag (or delay) is the scanning parameter that helps measure the autocorrelation function. The autocorrelation function is a real-valued, even function, whose maximum represents the power of the signal and occurs at the origin ($\tau = 0$). If $g(t)$ is periodic, then its autocorrelation function is also periodic with the same period as $g(t)$. For a power signal $g(t)$, the autocorrelation function and power spectral density form a Fourier transform pair, i.e.,

$$R_g(\tau) \longleftrightarrow S_g(f) \tag{3.98}$$

If a real-valued signal is passed through an LTI system with the impulse response $h(t)$, the autocorrelation function of the output signal is as follows:

$$R_y(\tau) = R_x(\tau) * h(\tau) * h(-\tau) \tag{3.99}$$

where $R_x(\tau)$ is the input autocorrelation function and $R_y(\tau)$ is the output autocorrelation function.

EXAMPLE 3.52

The power signal $x(t) = \cos(2\pi t)$ is applied to an ideal differentiator whose transfer function is as follows: $H(f) = j2\pi f$. Determine the autocorrelation function and power spectral density at both the input and output.

Solution

Using (3.97), we first find the input autocorrelation function,

$$R_x(\tau) = \left(\frac{1}{2}\right)\cos(2\pi\tau)$$

Using (3.98), we then find the input power density function,

$$S_x(f) = \left(\frac{1}{4}\right)(\delta(f+1) + \delta(f-1))$$

Using (3.96), we then find the output power density function,

$$S_y(f) = (4\pi^2 f^2)\left(\left(\frac{1}{4}\right)(\delta(f+1) + \delta(f-1))\right) = \pi^2(\delta(f+1) + \delta(f-1))$$

Using (3.98), we then determine the output autocorrelation function,

$$R_y(\tau) = 2\pi^2\cos(2\pi\tau).$$

It is important to note that a signal, defined in the time domain or frequency domain, has unique autocorrelation and spectral density functions. However, the converse is not true, as several different signals may have the same autocorrelation and spectral density functions. The reason lies in the fact that the autocorrelation function of a signal has no information about the time of the original signal and the spectral density function has no information about the phase spectrum of the signal.

3.12 LOWPASS AND BANDPASS SIGNALS

A ***lowpass signal*** has frequency content around the zero frequency and the non-negligible frequency content is limited by $|f| < W$. On the other hand, a ***bandpass signal*** has non-negligible frequency content far from the zero frequency, and centered around some frequency $\pm f_c$, known as the carrier frequency. When the carrier frequency is much higher than the bandwidth of the bandpass signal, i.e., $f_c \gg 2W$, the signal is referred to as ***narrowband bandpass signal***.

3.12.1 Lowpass Representation of Bandpass Signals

A real-valued bandpass signal $g(t)$ with nonzero spectrum $G(f)$ in the vicinity of $\pm f_c$ may be expressed as follows:

$$g(t) = a(t)\cos(2\pi f_c t + \theta(t)) = Re\left[a(t)\, e^{j(2\pi f_c t + \theta(t))}\right] \qquad (3.100)$$

where $a(t)$ and $\theta(t)$ are called the ***envelope and phase of the bandpass signal*** $g(t)$, respectively. Note that the envelope is always nonnegative. They are both real-valued lowpass signals (i.e., they are slowly time-varying signals). Expanding (3.100) yields the following:

$$g(t) = g_I(t)\cos(2\pi f_c t) - g_Q(t)\sin(2\pi f_c t) \qquad (3.101)$$

where the real-valued lowpass signals $g_I(t)$ and $g_Q(t)$ are known as the ***in-phase component*** and ***quadrature component*** of the bandpass signal $g(t)$, respectively, and are defined by

$$g_I(t) = a(t)\cos(\theta(t)) \qquad (3.102a)$$

$$g_Q(t) = a(t)\sin(\theta(t)) \qquad (3.102b)$$

As reflected below, the envelope and phase components can be obtained from the in-phase and quadrature components:

$$a(t) = \sqrt{g_I^2(t) + g_Q^2(t)} \qquad (3.103a)$$

$$\theta(t) = \tan^{-1}\left(\frac{g_Q(t)}{g_I(t)}\right) \qquad (3.103b)$$

Since both $g_I(t)$ and $g_Q(t)$ are lowpass signals, they may be derived from the bandpass signal $g(t)$ using the scheme shown in Figure 3.40a, where both lowpass filters are identical with a bandwidth of W Hz. Figure 3.40b shows how the bandpass signal $g(t)$ can be reconstructed from its in-phase and quadrature components.

3.12.2 Quadrature Amplitude Modulation

Figures 3.40b and 3.40a can also represent the generic structures of linear modulation schemes, known as ***quadrature amplitude modulation*** (QAM) or ***quadrature-carrier modulation***. QAM allows the transmission of two independent message signals on the same carrier frequency and conserves bandwidth, as the two signals occupy the same transmission bandwidth and yet the two messages can be separated at the receiver.

The two signals $m_1(t)$ and $m_2(t)$, which are both lowpass signals with bandwidth W, are applied to the modulator shown in Figure 3.41a. Using two

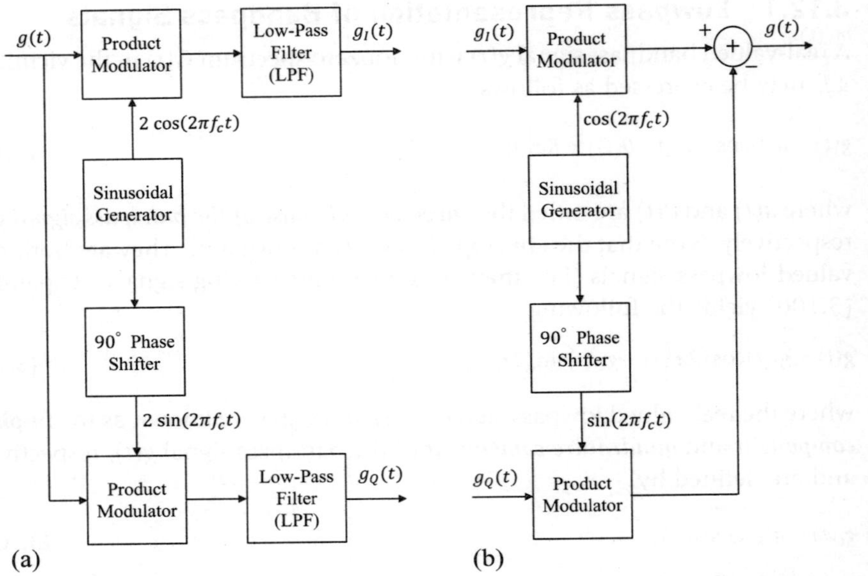

FIGURE 3.40 Bandpass signal from/to lowpass signal conversion: (a) derivation of in-phase and quadrature components from bandpass signal and (b) reconstruction of bandpass signal from in-phase and quadrature components.

quadrature carriers $A_c\cos(2\pi f_c t)$ and $A_c\sin(2\pi f_c t)$, the transmitted signal $s(t)$ is then as follows:

$$s(t) = m_1(t)\cos(2\pi f_c t) + m_2(t)\sin(2\pi f_c t) \tag{3.104}$$

This modulated signal occupies a transmission bandwidth of $2W$, centered at the carrier frequency f_c. A comparison of (3.101) and (3.104) reveals that $m_1(t)$ is the in-phase component and $-m_2(t)$ is the quadrature component.

At the receiver, a synchronous demodulator, as shown in Figure 3.41b, is required to separate and recover the original message signals. Synchronization ensures the correct phase and frequency relationships between the local oscillators used in the transmitter and receiver. At the outputs of the product modulators, the signals with high-frequency components are removed by lowpass filters with bandwidth W. It is required that QAM modulation system be totally synchronous; otherwise, an error in the phase or the frequency of the carrier at the demodulator in QAM will result in loss and interference between the two channels.

3.12.3 Phase and Group Delay

Consider the bandpass signal $x(t) = x_I(t)\cos(2\pi f_c t) - x_Q(t)\sin(2\pi f_c t)$, where $x_I(t)$ and $x_Q(t)$ are lowpass signals, each with a bandwidth of $W \ll f_c$. This

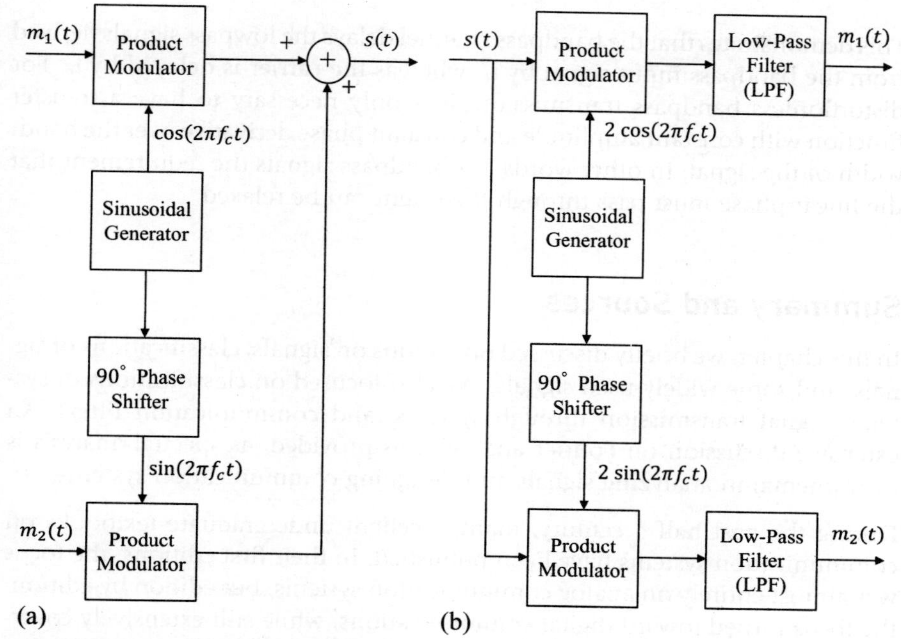

FIGURE 3.41 Quadrature amplitude modulation: (a) modulator and (b) demodulator.

bandpass signal passes through a channel, which introduces no amplitude distortion but has a linear phase. However, if we assume the linear equation in (3.82c) does not pass through origin, we then have:

$$\beta(f) = -2\pi f t_g + C = -2\pi f t_g - 2\pi f_c(t_p - t_g) \tag{3.105}$$

where t_p is known as the ***phase delay*** or ***carrier delay*** and t_g is known as the ***group delay*** or ***envelope delay***. The group delay is known as the derivative of the phase response, i.e., we have:

$$t_g = \left(-\frac{1}{2\pi}\right)\frac{d\beta(f)}{df} \tag{3.106}$$

In the case of linear phase, the group delay t_g is a constant. Group delay is the delay that a group of two or more frequency components undergoes in passing through a linear system. Using (3.82), we have the following:

$$H(f) = k\exp(j(-2\pi f t_g - 2\pi f_c(t_p - t_g))) \tag{3.107}$$

Using the inverse Fourier transform as well as the time shifting and convolution properties of the Fourier transform, the output is then as follows:

$$y(t) = k(x_I(t - t_g)\cos(2\pi f_c(t - t_p)) - x_Q(t - t_g)\sin(2\pi f_c(t - t_p))) \tag{3.108}$$

This demonstrates that the bandpass channel delays the lowpass signals derived from the bandpass input signal by t_g, whereas the carrier is delayed by t_p. For distortionless bandpass transmission, it is only necessary to have a transfer function with constant amplitude and constant phase derivative over the bandwidth of the signal. In other words, for bandpass signals the requirement that the linear phase must pass through the origin can be relaxed.

Summary and Sources

In this chapter, we briefly discussed operations on signals, classifications of signals, and some widely-used signals. We also focused on classifications of systems, signal transmission through systems, and communication filters. An extensive discussion on Fourier analysis was provided, as spectral analysis is instrumental in analyzing signals and designing communication systems.

During the past half a century, many excellent undergraduate textbooks on communication systems have been published. In their first editions, the focus was almost entirely on analog communication systems, but edition by edition, the focus turned toward digital communications, while still extensively covering analog modulation techniques [1–9]. There are also some good books that cover signals and systems in great detail [10–13].

[1] S. Haykin, *Communication Systems,* John Wiley & Sons, 1978. ISBN 0-471-02977-7, 1978.

[2] B.P. Lathi and Z. Ding, *Modern Digital and Analog Communication Systems,* fourth ed., Oxford, 2009. ISBN 978-0-19-533145-5, 2009.

[3] K.S. Shanmugam, *Digital and Analog Communication Systems,* John Wiley & Sons, 1979. ISBN 0-471-03090-2, 1979.

[4] R.E. Ziemer and W.H. Tranter, *Principles of Communications,* sixth ed., John Wiley & Sons, 2009. ISBN 978-0-470-25254-3, 2009.

[5] A.B. Carlson and P.B. Crilly, *Communication Systems,* fifth ed., McGraw-Hill, 2002. ISBN 978-0-07-338040-7, 2002.

[6] H. Taub and D.L. Schilling, *Principles of Communication Systems,* second ed., McGraw-Hill, 1986. ISBN 0-07-062955-2, 1986.

[7] L.W. Couch II., *Digital and Analog Communication Systems,* eighth ed., Pearson, 2013. ISBN 978-0-13-291538-0, 2013.

[8] S. Haykin and M. Moher, *Communication Systems,* fifth ed., John Wiley & Sons, 2009. ISBN 978-0-471-69790-9, 2009.

[9] J.G. Proakis and M. Salehi, *Fundamentals of Communication Systems,* second ed., Pearson, 2014. ISBN 0-13-147135-X, 2014.

[10] A.V. Oppenheim and A.S. Willsky, S. Hamid, *Signals and Systems,* second ed., Prentice Hall, 1996. ISBN 978-0138147570, 1996.

[11] S. Haykin and B. Van Veen, *Signals and Systems,* second ed., John Wiley & Sons, 2003. ISBN 0471-37851-8, 2003.

[12] M.J. Roberts, *Fundamentals of Signals and Systems,* McGraw-Hill, 2008. ISBN 0-07-340454-3, 2008.

[13] H.P. Hsu, *Signals and Systems,* McGraw-Hill, 1995. ISBN 0-07-030641-9, 1995.

Problems

3.1 Consider the doublet pulse $x(t)$ consisting of two rectangular pulses: one of amplitude 1, defined for the interval $-1 \le t \le 0$, and the other of amplitude -1, defined for the interval $0 \le t \le 1$. Determine the following signals in terms of $x(t)$:

(a) $g(t) = x(t) + x(t-1) + x(-t)$

(b) $g(t) = \frac{dx(t)}{dt}$

(c) $g(t) = \int x(t)dt$

(d) $g(t) = x(2t)$

(e) $g(t) = x(2t-1)$

3.2 Assuming the amplitude A, the frequency f_c, and the initial phase θ are all known constants, and $x(t)$ and $y(t)$ are the system input and output, respectively, classify the following systems as linear or nonlinear systems:

(a) $y(t) = A\,(x(t))\cos(2\pi f_c t + \theta)$

(b) $y(t) = A\left(\frac{dx(t)}{dt}\right)\cos(2\pi f_c t + \theta)$

(c) $y(t) = A\left(\int_0^t x(t)dt\right)\cos(2\pi f_c t + \theta)$

(d) $y(t) = A\cos(2\pi f_c t + \theta + x(t))$

(e) $y(t) = A\cos\left(2\pi f_c t + \theta + \frac{dx(t)}{dt}\right)$

(f) $y(t) = A\cos\left(2\pi f_c t + \theta + \int_0^t x(t)dt\right)$

3.3 Classify the following signals as periodic signals or nonperiodic signals; if a signal is periodic, then determine its period:

(a) $f(t) = \sin(6\pi t) + \cos(4\pi t)$

(b) $f(t) = 1 + \cos(t)$

(c) $f(t) = \exp(-|t|)\cos(2\pi t)$

(d) $f(t) = (u(t) - u(t-1))\cos(7\pi t)$

(e) $f(t) = \sin\left(\sqrt{2}\pi t\right) + \cos(2t)$

3.4 Classify the following signals as energy signals or power signals, or signals that are neither energy signals nor power signals:

(a) $z(t) = A\exp(j(2\pi t + \theta))$

(b) $z(t) = \mathrm{sgn}(t)$

(c) $z(t) = \exp(-2|t|)$

(d) $z(t) = tu(t)$

(e) $z(t) = 1 + \cos(t)$

3.5 Classify the following systems as linear or nonlinear systems, and time-varying or time-invariant systems, where $x(t)$ and $y(t)$ represent the system input and output, respectively:

(a) $y(t) = 0.2x(t-1)$

(b) $y(t) = tx(t)$

(c) $y(t) = x(t) + t$

(d) $y(t) = x(t) + 1$

(e) $y(t) = x(t)\cos(t)$

3.6 Classify the following signals as even or odd signals. If a signal is neither even nor odd, then determine its even and odd parts:
(a) $g(t) = \cos(t) + \sin(t) + \sin(t)\cos(t)$
(b) $g(t) = tu(t)$
(c) $g(t) = \sin(4\pi t + \pi/5)$
(d) $g(t) = \exp(-|t|)\sin(t)$
(e) $g(t) = u(t+1) - u(t-1)$

3.7 Classify the following systems as causal or noncausal systems, and memory or memoryless systems, where $x(t)$ and $y(t)$ represent the system input and output, respectively:
(a) $y(t) = x(t+1)\,x(t)\,x(t-1)$
(b) $y(t) = x(t)\cos(t+1)$
(c) $y(t) = 1 + x(t) + x^2(t)$
(d) $y(t-1) = 0.5(x(t) + x(t-1))$
(e) $y(t) = e^{-t}x(t-1)\,u(t)$

3.8 Design the following systems, i.e., provide examples for their input–output relations:
(a) A linear, time-invariant, causal system.
(b) A linear, time-invariant, noncausal system.
(c) A linear, time-varying, causal system.
(d) A linear, time-varying, noncausal system.
(e) A nonlinear, time-invariant, causal system.
(f) A nonlinear, time-invariant, noncausal system.
(g) A nonlinear, time-varying, causal system.
(h) A nonlinear, time-varying, noncausal system.

3.9 Design the following signals, i.e., provide examples for their time-amplitude relations:
(a) Two signals that are neither even nor odd, but their product is an even signal.
(b) A signal with unity power, which is periodic and odd.
(c) A signal with unity power, which is nonperiodic and even.
(d) A signal whose even part is periodic and odd part is nonperiodic.

3.10 Suppose we have $x(t) = \cos(t) + \sin(t)$. Show that $x(t)$ is periodic and determine its period, fundamental frequency, and average power. Also determine the minimum and maximum values of $x(t)$.

3.11 Suppose $g(t)$ is a real-valued energy signal with even and odd parts. Show that the energy of $g(t)$ is equal to the sum of the energies of its even and odd parts.

3.12 Show that in the complex exponential Fourier series, if the periodic signal $g(t)$ is real and even, then c_n is a pure real number (i.e., its imaginary part is zero) and an even function of n, and if the periodic $g(t)$ is real and odd, then c_n is a pure imaginary number (i.e., its real part is zero) and an odd function of n.

3.13 Show that in the complex exponential Fourier series for a real-valued periodic signal $g(t)$, the magnitude spectrum is even, i.e., $|c_n| = |c_{-n}|$ and the phase spectrum is odd, i.e., $\varnothing_n = -\varnothing_{-n}$.

3.14 Prove Parseval's power theorem, i.e., $P = \sum_{n=-\infty}^{\infty} |c_n|^2$, where $\{|c_n|\}$ are the complex exponential Fourier series coefficients.

3.15 Find the complex exponential Fourier series of the periodic signal $g(t) = \exp(t),\ 0 < t < 2\pi$ with $g(t + 2\pi) = g(t)$.

3.16 Find the complex exponential Fourier series for the signal $g(t) = 1 + \sin(2\pi t) + \cos^2(2\pi t)$.

3.17 Show that in the quadrature (trigonometric) Fourier series, if $g(t)$ is a periodic real and even signal, then $b_n = 0$ and its Fourier series contains only cosine terms, and if $g(t)$ is a periodic real and odd signal, then $a_n = 0$ and its Fourier series contains only sine terms.

3.18 Consider the periodic even signal $g(t)$ whose period is $2L$ seconds. The signal over one period is defined as follows:

$$g(t) = \begin{cases} -\dfrac{L}{2} + t, & 0 \le t \le L \\ -\dfrac{L}{2} - t, & -L \le t \le 0 \end{cases}$$

Determine the quadrature (trigonometric) Fourier series coefficients.

3.19 If $g(t)$ is a real-valued function of time and $G(f)$ is the Fourier transform of $g(t)$, then show that the amplitude (magnitude) response $|G(f)|$ is an even function, and the phase response $\measuredangle G(f)$ is an odd function.

3.20 Assuming $g(t)$ is an arbitrary time-limited energy signal, then by using the singularity functions and the Fourier transform properties, determine the Fourier transform of $v(t) = \gamma + \mu g(\alpha t + \beta)$, where α, β, γ and μ are all known nonzero constants.

3.21 Prove that an absolutely band-limited signal cannot be absolutely time-limited, and vice versa.

3.22 Show that if a signal in time domain is odd, its Fourier transform is then pure imaginary, and if it is even, then its Fourier transform is pure real.

3.23 Noting that the Fourier transform of $g(t)$ is $G(f)$, determine the Fourier transform of $g^n(t)$, where n is a positive integer. If $G(f)$ is band-limited to W Hz, find the bandwidth of the Fourier transform of $g^n(t)$.

3.24 Assuming $x(t)$ is the input and $y(t)$ is the output, we have a communication channel with the following relation: $y(t) = Ax(t - c) + Bx(t - d)$, where $A \neq 0$ and $B \neq 0$ representing the amplitude scaling factors, and $c > 0$ and $d > 0$

representing the transmission delays. Evaluate the channel transfer function (i.e., frequency response) $H(f)$ in terms of A, B, c and d.

3.25 (a) Assuming $a > 0$, find the Fourier transform of the signal $g(t) = e^{-a|t|}$ and the inverse Fourier transform of the signal $h(t) = \frac{1}{b^2 + t^2}$.
(b) Consider the time-limited parabolic signal $g(t) = t^2(u(t+1) - u(t-1))$. Determine its Fourier transform.

3.26 Suppose we have an LTI system whose output $y(t)$ and input $x(t)$ are related by

$$4y(t) + 3\frac{dy(t)}{dt} = x(t)$$

Determine the Fourier transform of the output when we have the input signal as follows: $(t) = e^{-t}u(t)$.

3.27 Assuming $x(t)$ and $y(t)$ are the input and output signals, and we have in a communication channel the following nonlinear relation: $y(t) = x(t) + x^2(t)$. Assuming the input signal is $x(t) = m(t)\cos(2\pi f_c t)$ and $m(t)$ is a lowpass message signal with bandwidth $W \ll f_c$, find $y(t)$. Is it possible to retrieve $m(t)$?

3.28 Design (i.e., determine) a low-pass signal $g(t)$ in the time domain, so its Fourier transform $G(f)$ has only discrete components at multiples of 5 kHz, and design (i.e., determine) a low-pass signal $h(t)$ in the time domain, so its Fourier transform $H(f)$ is continuous and has a bandwidth of 5 kHz.

3.29 Let the input to an LTI system be the signal $x(t) = \text{sinc}(4t)$ and the system impulse response be $h(t) = \text{sinc}(2t)$. Determine the output signal.

3.30 Determine the Fourier transform of the normalized Gaussian pulse $g(t) = \exp(-\pi t^2)$.

3.31 Show that the response of an LTI system with a transfer function $H(f)$ to the complex exponential $x(t) = x_0 \exp(j(2\pi f_0 t + \theta_0))$ is a complex exponential with the same frequency, where x_0, f_0, and θ_0 are known constants.

3.32 Using the rms definitions of bandwidth and time duration, show that $T_{rms}W_{rms} \geq \frac{1}{4\pi}$. You may use the Cauchy-Schwartz inequality, which states for real functions $f(t)$ and $g(t)$, we have $\left(\int_a^b g^2(t)dt\right)\left(\int_a^b f^2(t)dt\right) \geq \left(\int_a^b f(t)g(t)dt\right)^2$.

3.33 Using the rms definitions of bandwidth and time duration, show that $T_{rms}W_{rms} = \frac{1}{4\pi}$ holds for the normalized Gaussian pulse.

3.34 Using the noise-equivalent definitions of bandwidth and time duration, show that $T_{NER}W_{NER} \geq \frac{1}{2}$. You may use a special form of Cauchy-Schwartz inequality, which states for a function $g(t)$, we have $\int_{-\infty}^{\infty} |g(t)|dt \geq \left|\int_{-\infty}^{\infty} g(t)dt\right|$.

3.35 Using the noise-equivalent definitions of bandwidth and time duration, show the condition under which the equality holds.

3.36 Using the amplitude-equivalent definitions of bandwidth and time duration, show that $T_{NER}W_{NER} \geq \frac{1}{4}$.

3.37 Using the amplitude-equivalent definitions of bandwidth and time duration, show the condition under which the equality holds.

3.38 The magnitude of the transfer function of a filter is given by $H(f) = \left(1 + \left(\frac{f}{10000}\right)^2\right)^{-0.5}$. Determine the filter type and its 3-dB bandwidth. Determine the output $y(t)$ if the input is as follows: $x(t) = 7\cos\left(40000\pi t + \frac{\pi}{4}\right)$.

3.39 In a nonlinear system, the input $x(t)$ and the output $y(t)$ are related as follows:

$$y(t) = x(t) + x^2(t)$$

If we have $x(t) = 2\text{sinc}(2t)$, then determine the Fourier transform $Y(f)$.

3.40 The autocorrelation function of a nonperiodic power signal is $R(\tau) = \exp\left(-\frac{\tau^2}{2\sigma^2}\right)$. Find the power spectral density and the average power content of the signal.

3.41 Find the power spectral density and autocorrelation functions of $g(t) = \cos(10\pi t) + \cos(20\pi t)$.

3.42 Show that if the carrier at the demodulator in the QAM system is not completely synchronous, then the co-channel interference results.

3.43 Quadrature Amplitude Modulation (QAM) is the most widely used digital modulation scheme in communication systems. Assume that $m_1(t)$ and $m_2(t)$ are both lowpass signals, whose Fourier transforms $M_1(f)$ and $M_2(f)$ have bandwidths of W_1 and W_2, respectively. Write the output signal $s(t)$ in terms of $m_1(t)$ and $m_2(t)$, and write $S(f)$ in terms of $M_1(f)$ and $M_2(f)$. Determine the output of the lowpass filters in terms of $m_1(t)$ and $m_2(t)$, assuming LPFs have cut-off frequencies which are much less than f_c and greater than both W_1 and W_2.

Computer Exercises

3.44 Suppose $f(t)$ is a periodic signal whose period is 2π, and $f(t) = -1$ when $-\pi < t \leq 0$ and $f(t) = 1$ when $0 < t \leq \pi$. Draw $f(t)$ accurately as well as each of the following four functions in the time domain for $-6\pi \leq t \leq 6\pi$. What conclusions can you draw by comparing $f(t)$ to the set of signals $s_1(t)$, $s_2(t)$, $s_3(t)$, and $s_4(t)$?

$$s_1(t) = \left(\frac{4}{\pi}\right)\sin(t).$$

$$s_2(t) = s_1(t) + \left(\frac{4}{3\pi}\right)\sin(3t).$$

$$s_3(t) = s_2(t) + \left(\frac{4}{5\pi}\right)\sin(5t).$$

$$s_4(t) = s_3(t) + \left(\frac{4}{7\pi}\right)\sin(7t).$$

3.45 Plot $h(t) = -\text{sinc}(t+1) + \text{sinc}(t) + \text{sinc}(t-1) - \text{sinc}(t-2) + \text{sinc}(t-3)$, where $\text{sinc}(t) = \frac{\sin(\pi t)}{\pi t}$. Determine the values of $h(t)$ at $t = k/2$, where k is an integer between -5 and 5. Can you draw any conclusions?

3.46 Determine the impulse responses $h(t)$ of ideal LPF, BPF, and HPF, where the cut-off frequencies of the LPF and HPF are both 1 kHz and the cut-off frequencies of the BPF are 1 kHz and 2 kHz.

3.47 Determine the Fourier transform of a Gaussian pulse, assuming it has a zero mean, but various values for its variance.

3.48 Determine the Fourier transform of $\text{sinc}^2(t)$, and compare it with the analytical result.

3.49 Determine the autocorrelation function and power spectral density function of the following signal:

$$g(t) = 2\cos(t-2) + 3\sin(2t+1).$$

3.50 Determine the system output in both time and frequency domains, if the system input is $x(t) = \text{sinc}(t)$, and $y(t)$ and $x(t)$ are related as follows:

$$y(t) = x(t) + x^2(t).$$

3.51 Design a LPF whose magnitude response in the passband ranges between 1 and 0.99 and in the stopband does not exceed 0.01, with a transition band between 1 kHz and 1.1 kHz. Also, determine its impulse response.

CHAPTER 4

Probability, Random Variables, and Random Processes

CONTENTS

INTRODUCTION

We first present the fundamentals of probability, along with the axioms of probability and their implications. We then focus on random variables, where the outcomes of random experiments are real numbers, and mathematically describe continuous and discrete random variables, while highlighting their properties and applications. Finally, we introduce stochastic processes and their impacts on linear time-invariant systems. To introduce the abstract notions and complex concepts of probability, random variables, and random processes, a plethora of diverse examples is presented. After studying this chapter and understanding all relevant concepts and examples, students should be able to do the following:

1. Know the axioms of probability and their resulting properties.
2. Understand the concept of conditional probability and the application of Bayes' rule.
3. Appreciate the distinct concepts of mutual exclusivity and statistical independence.
4. Describe the cumulative distribution function (cdf) and probability density function (pdf).
5. Identify the properties of cdf and pdf, and how to use them to calculate probabilities.
6. Define the important continuous and discrete random variables.
7. Grasp all relevant aspects of the Gaussian distribution.
8. Determine the expected value and variance of a random variable.
9. Explain the fundamentals and applications of the conditional cdf and pdf.
10. Evaluate the Chebyshev bound.
11. State the joint cdf and pdf and their corresponding properties.
12. Differentiate among the concepts of independence, uncorrelatedness, and orthogonality.

Introduction to Digital Communications

13. Relate the concepts of the sum of random variables and the central limit theorem.
14. Connect the concept of random variables to the concept of random processes.
15. Discuss the wide-sense and strict-sense stationary processes.
16. Gain insight into the ergodic processes.
17. Find autocorrelation and power spectral density functions.
18. Analyze random processes through linear time-invariant systems.
19. Characterize the additive white Gaussian noise.
20. Apply the sampling operation to random signals.

4.1 PROBABILITY

Probability represents the chance that a given event will occur. Almost everyone has an intuitive notion about probability from experience. The study of probability stems from the analysis of certain games of chances. Probability has many important applications in most branches of science and engineering. However, our focus is solely on communications, as randomness is the essence of communications.

4.1.1 Basic Definitions

An experiment is a measurement procedure or observation process in which conditions are known. The outcome is the end result of an experiment. In a ***random experiment***, the outcome may unpredictably vary when the experiment is repeated, as the conditions under which it is performed cannot be predetermined with sufficient accuracy. In a random experiment, the outcome is not uniquely determined by the causes and cannot be known in advance, because it is subject to chance.

The ***sample space*** S of a random experiment is defined as the set of all possible ***outcomes*** of an experiment. In a random experiment, the outcomes, also known as ***sample points***, are mutually exclusive (i.e., they cannot occur simultaneously). An ***event*** is a subset of the sample space of an experiment (i.e., a set of sample points). Two ***mutually exclusive*** (also known as ***disjoint***) events have no common outcomes (i.e., the occurrence of one precludes the occurrence of the other). The ***union*** of two events is the set of all outcomes that are in either one or both of the two events. The ***intersection*** of two events, also known as the joint event, is the set of all outcomes that are in both events. A ***certain (sure) event*** consists of all outcomes, and thus always occurs. A ***null (impossible) event*** contains no outcomes, and thus never occurs. The ***complement*** of an event contains all outcomes not included in the event.

EXAMPLE 4.1

In a random experiment that constitutes rolling a typical (i.e., fair, six-sided cubic shape) die provide specific examples to highlight the above definitions.

Solution

The sample space *S* includes six sample points 1, 2, 3, 4, 5, and 6. An event may be one with even outcomes (i.e., 2, 4, and 6), one with odd outcomes (i.e., 1, 3, and 5), or one whose outcomes are divisible by 3 (i.e., 3 and 6). Two mutually exclusive events may be an event with even outcomes and an event with odd outcomes. The union of two events, where one is with odd outcomes and the other is with outcomes that are divisible by 3, consists of 1, 3, 5, and 6, and their intersection consists of only 3. A certain event consists of outcomes that are equal to or greater than 1 and equal to or less than 6. A null event consists of outcomes that are less than 1 or greater than 6. The complement of the event, whose outcomes are divisible by 3, is an event that contains 1, 2, 4, and 5 as its outcomes.

When the sample space *S* is countable, such as when it includes all integers between 1 and 9, it is known as a ***discrete sample space***. When the sample space *S* is uncountably infinite, such as when it includes all real numbers between 1 and 9, it is known as a ***continuous sample space***.

4.1.2 Axioms of Probability

The ratio that represents the number of times a particular event occurs over the number of times the random experiment has been repeated is defined as the ***relative frequency*** of the event. When the number of times the experiment being repeated approaches infinity, the relative frequency of the event, which approaches a limit because of statistical regularity, is called the ***probability*** of the event. For instance, if we have a fair coin, and we toss it infinitely many times, then the probability of heads is $\frac{1}{2}$. Probability is therefore a real number assigned to an event, indicating how likely it is that the event will occur when an experiment is performed. Note that a probability *P* is a function that assigns a value to an event *A*, and *P*(*A*) thus represents the ***probability of A***. The ***axioms of probability*** are as follows:

- Axiom I:

  $P(A) \geq 0$

- Axiom II:

  $P(S) = 1$ (4.1)

- Axiom III:

  If $A_1, A_2, A_3, \ldots$ is a countable sequence of events such that $A_i \cap A_j = \emptyset$ for all $i \neq j$, where $\emptyset$ is the empty set (null event), then

  $P(A_1 \cup A_2 \cup A_3 \cup \ldots) = P(A_1) + P(A_2) + P(A_3) + \cdots$

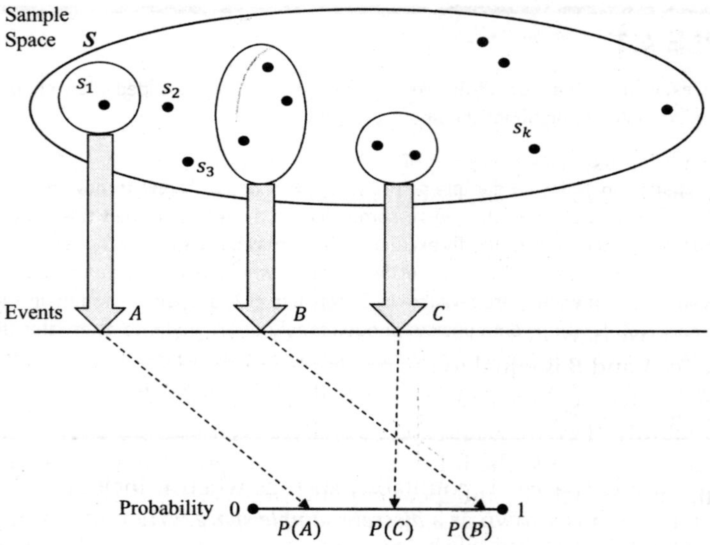

FIGURE 4.1 Relationship among sample space, events, and probability.

Figure 4.1 shows the relationship among sample space, events, and probability. These axioms satisfy the intuitive notion of probability, as Axiom I highlights that the probability of an event is nonnegative, Axiom II emphasizes that the probability of all possible outcomes is one, and Axiom III underscores that the total probability of a number of disjoint (mutually exclusive) events is the sum of the individual probabilities. From these three axioms, the following important properties, also known as corollaries, can be derived:

- $P(A^c) = 1 - P(A)$, where event A^c is the complement of event A.
- $P(A) \leq 1$.
- $P(\emptyset) = 0$, where $\emptyset$ is the null event. (4.2)
- If A and B are not disjoint events, then $P(A \cup B) = P(A) + P(B) - P(A \cap B)$.
- if $A \subset B$, then $P(A) \leq P(B)$.

4.1.3 Conditional Probability and Bayes' Rule

Suppose there are two events A and B with probabilities $P(A)$ and $P(B)$, respectively. If we assume the probability of event B is influenced by the outcome of event A and we also know that event A has occurred, then the probability that event B will occur will no longer be $P(B)$. The probability of event B when it is known that event A has occurred is defined as the ***conditional probability***, denoted by $P(B/A)$ and read as probability of B given A. The conditional probability $P(B/A)$ and the conditional probability $P(A/B)$ are, respectively, defined as follows:

$$P(B/A) = \frac{P(A \cap B)}{P(A)}, \quad P(A) \neq 0$$
$$P(A/B) = \frac{P(A \cap B)}{P(B)}, \quad P(B) \neq 0 \tag{4.3}$$

where $P(A \cap B)$, also denoted by $P(A, B)$, is known as the ***joint probability*** of events A and B. Equation (4.3) then gives rise to the following:

$$P(A \cap B) = P(B/A)P(A) = P(A/B)P(B) \tag{4.4}$$

If the knowledge of event A does not change the probability of the occurrence of event B, then we have $P(B/A) = P(B)$. Under this condition, the joint probability of events A and B is equal to the product of probabilities of events A and B, and these events are then said to be ***statistically independent***. Moreover, if the joint probability of events A and B is zero, these events are then said to be ***mutually exclusive*** or ***disjoint***. The following highlights the conditions under which two events are statistically independent and mutually exclusive:

$$P(A \cap B) = P(A)P(B) \Leftrightarrow \text{Statistically independent events}$$
$$P(A \cap B) = 0 \Leftrightarrow \text{Mutually exclusive events} \tag{4.5}$$

It is important to differentiate between the concept of statistical independence and the concept of mutual exclusivity. Note that if events A and B are mutually exclusive, then events A and B cannot occur at the same time (i.e., the occurrence of one implies that the other has zero probability of happening). Hence, mutually exclusive events are dependent events. If two events A and B are both mutually exclusive and statistically independent, then it implies that at least one of the two events A and B has zero probability (i.e., we have $P(A \cap B) = P(A)P(B) = 0$).

EXAMPLE 4.2

In rolling a pair of fair dice, event A denotes when the sum of the values of the two dice is equal to 3 and event B is when the value of one of the dice is 3. Are the events A and B mutually exclusive? Are they statistically independent?

Solution

A and B are mutually exclusive, because they cannot occur together (i.e., we have $P(A \cap B) = 0$). The event A, with the sum of 3, occurs when the outcome is either {1, 2} or {2, 1}. Noting that the total number of possible outcomes is 36 ($= 6 \times 6$), we thus have

$$P(A) = \frac{2}{36} = \frac{1}{18}$$

We also have:

$$P(B) = 1 - P(\overline{B}) = 1 - \left(\frac{5}{36}\right)\left(\frac{5}{36}\right) = \frac{11}{36}$$

We therefore have:

$$P(A \cap B) = 0 \neq \frac{1}{18} \times \frac{11}{36} = P(A)P(B)$$

This clearly points to the fact that the events A and B are not independent, because they do not satisfy (4.5).

The notion of statistically independence can be exploited to compute probabilities of events that involve noninteracting, independent sub-events.

EXAMPLE 4.3

As shown in Figure 4.2, between points A and B, there are two parallel links, and between points B and C, there are also two parallel links. Assume the probability of failure over any one link is p, and the failure in one link is statistically independent of that in another link. Determine the probability of link failure between points A and C in terms of the probability of failure p.

Solution

There is a failure between points A and B, if both links fail. The probability of failure between points A and B is thus p^2. Similarly, the probability of failure between points B and C is p^2. We can therefore conclude that the probability of no failure between points A and B or that between points B and C each is $1-p^2$.

In order to have no failure between points A and C, there must be no failure between points A and B, nor must there exist a failure between points B and C. In other words, the probability of no failure between A and C is $(1-p^2)^2$. The probability of failure between points A and C is thus $1-(1-p^2)^2 = p^2(2-p^2)$. For practical communication links, we always have $p \ll 1$, the probability of failure between points A and C thus becomes approximately $2p^2$.

In order to determine the probability of event A, it is sometimes best to separate all possible causes leading to event A. If events $B_1, B_2, \ldots, B_n$ are all mutually exclusive events whose union makes the entire sample space S, as shown in Figure 4.3, we can then use the set of joint probabilities to obtain $P(A)$, i.e., we can have the following:

$$P(A) = P(A \cap B_1) + P(A \cap B_2) + \cdots + P(A \cap B_n) \tag{4.6}$$

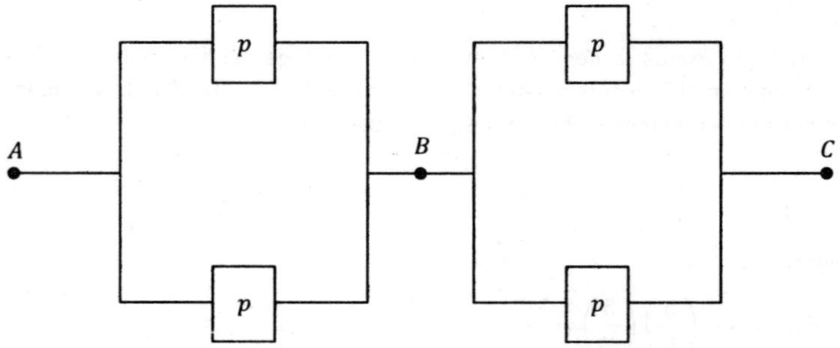

FIGURE 4.2 Link configuration between points A and C.

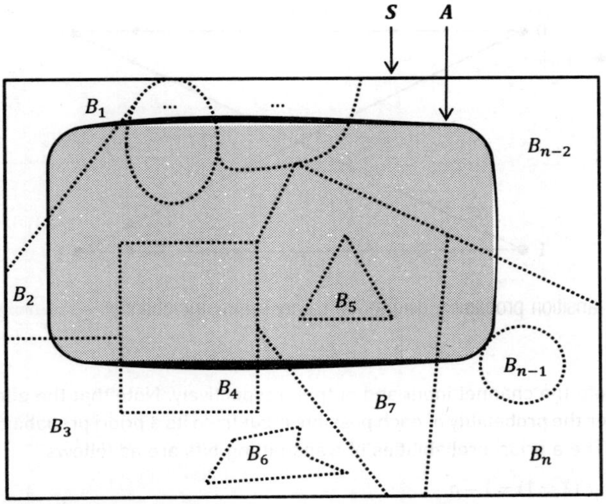

FIGURE 4.3 A partition of sample space S into n disjoint sets.

Applying (4.4), (4.6) then leads to the well-known ***theorem on total probability***, as follows:

$$P(A) = P(A/B_1)\,P(B_1) + P(A/B_2)\,P(B_2) + \cdots + P(A/B_n)\,P(B_n) \tag{4.7}$$

This divide-and-conquer approach is a practical tool to determine the probability of event A. The total probability theorem thus highlights the probabilities of effects given causes when causes do not deterministically select effects.

When one conditional probability is given, but the reversed conditional probability is required, the following relation, known as ***Bayes' rule***, which is based on (4.3), (4.4), and (4.7), can be used:

$$P(B_1/A) = \frac{P(A \cap B_1)}{P(A)} = \frac{P(A/B_1)\,P(B_1)}{P(A/B_1)\,P(B_1) + P(A/B_2)\,P(B_2) + \cdots + P(A/B_n)\,P(B_n)} \tag{4.8}$$

In short, Bayes' rule highlights inference from an observed effect. It is also important to note that the probability of an event before any experiment is performed is referred to as ***a priori probability*** and after the experiment is performed is called ***a posteriori probability***.

EXAMPLE 4.4

In a binary symmetric communication (BSC) channel, the input bits transmitted over the channel are either 0 or 1 with probabilities p and $1 - p$, respectively. Due to channel noise, errors are made. As shown in Figure 4.4, the channel is assumed to be symmetric, which means the probability of receiving 1 when 0 is transmitted is the same as the probability of receiving 0 when 1 is transmitted. The conditional probabilities of error are assumed to be each ϵ. Determine the average probability of error, also known as the bit error rate, as well as the a posteriori probabilities.

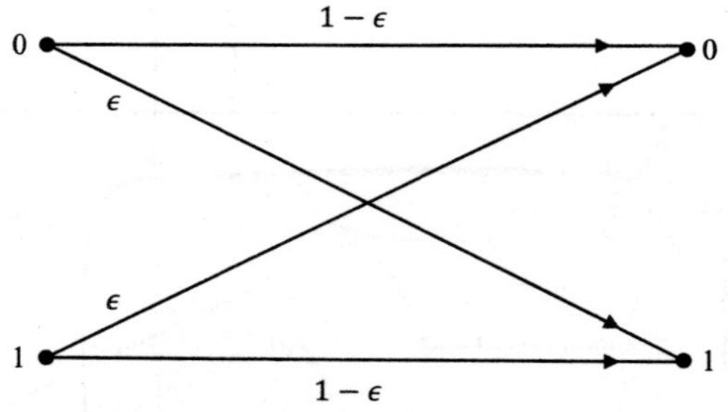

FIGURE 4.4 Transition probability diagram of binary symmetric channel.

Solution

Let X and Y denote the channel input and output, respectively. Note that the effect of the transmission is to alter the probability of each possible input from its a priori probability to its a posteriori probability. The a priori probabilities of transmitting bits are as follows:

$P(X=0)=p$ and $P(X=1)=1-p$.

With the transition probabilities of

$P(Y=1/X=0)=P(Y=0/X=1)=\epsilon$

and applying (4.7), the average probability of error can be calculated as follows:

$$\begin{aligned}P(e)&=P(Y=1,X=0)+P(Y=0,X=1)=P(Y=1/X=0)P(X=0)+P(Y=0/X=1)P(X=1)\\&=\epsilon p+\epsilon(1-p)=\epsilon\end{aligned}$$

Using Bayes' rule in (4.8), the a posteriori probabilities are then as follows:

$$\begin{aligned}P(X=0/Y=0)&=\frac{P(Y=0/X=0)P(X=0)}{P(Y=0)}=\frac{P(Y=0/X=0)P(X=0)}{P(Y=0/X=0)P(X=0)+P(Y=0/X=1)P(X=1)}\\&=\frac{(1-\epsilon)p}{(1-\epsilon)p+\epsilon(1-p)}=\frac{p-\epsilon p}{p+\epsilon-2\epsilon p}\end{aligned}$$

and

$$\begin{aligned}P(X=1/Y=1)&=\frac{P(Y=1/X=1)P(X=1)}{P(Y=1)}=\frac{P(Y=1/X=1)P(X=1)}{P(Y=1/X=0)P(X=0)+P(Y=1/X=1)P(X=1)}\\&=\frac{(1-\epsilon)(1-p)}{(1-\epsilon)(1-p)+\epsilon p}=\frac{1-p-\epsilon+\epsilon p}{1-p-\epsilon+2\epsilon p}.\end{aligned}$$

The following interesting observations regarding BSC channels can now be made:

- For $\epsilon=0$, i.e., when the channel is ideal, both a posteriori probabilities are one.
- For $\epsilon=\frac{1}{2}$, the a posteriori probabilities are the same as the a priori probabilities.
- For $\epsilon=1$, i.e., when the channel is most destructive, both a posteriori probabilities are zero.

It is very insightful to note that in the absence of a channel, the optimum receiver, which minimizes the average probability of error $P(e)$, would always decide in favor of the bit whose a priori probability was the greatest. Moreover, if $P(e)>\frac{1}{2}$, that is more often than not an error is made, an inverter can then be employed to reduce the bit error rate to $1-P(e)>\frac{1}{2}$, simply by turning a 1 into a 0 and a 0 into a 1.

EXAMPLE 4.5

As shown in Figure 4.5a, a network connecting the end points A and D has five identical links. The links are assumed to fail independently and the probability of failure in a link is p. Determine the probability of failure between the end points A and D in terms of the probability p.

Solution

We first define $P(F_i)$ as the probability that link $\#i$ fails, for $i = 1, 2, 3, 4, 5$, and $P(F)$ as the probability that the entire network fails. One way to find the probability of network failure is to include all

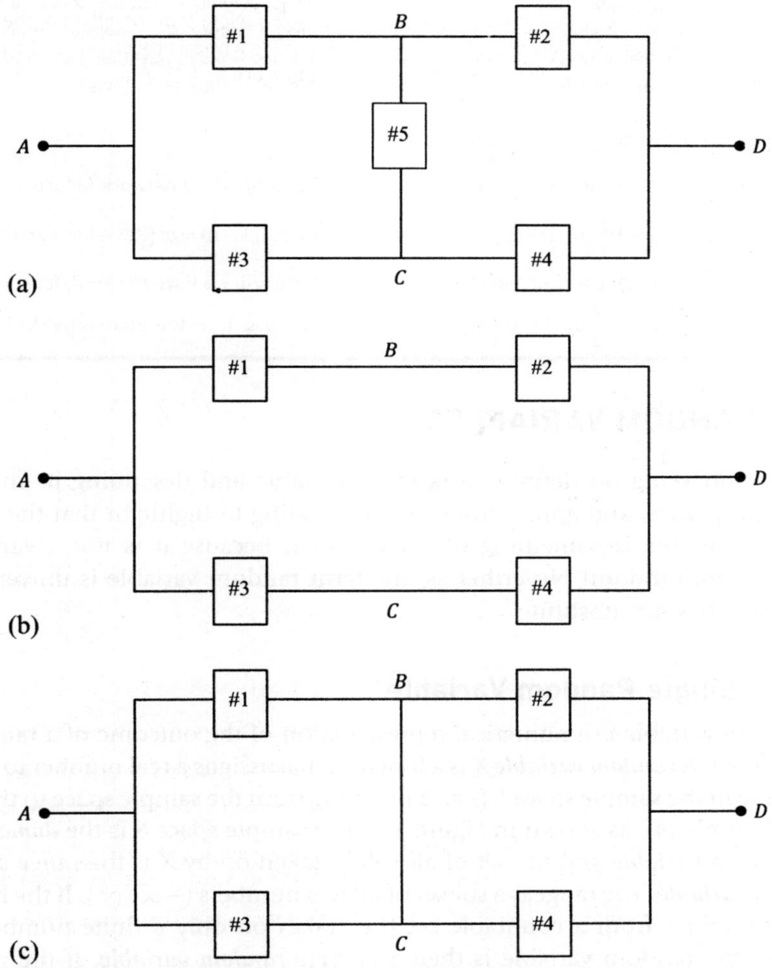

FIGURE 4.5 (a) Link configuration between points A and D, (b) link configuration with permanently-failed link #5, and (c) link configuration with never-failing link #5.

$32\left(=2^5\right)$ possible events that involve in the failure or nonfailure of the five links. However, the total probability theorem offers a simpler approach.

Link #5 (the link between B and C) makes this problem complex, because it is causing the network not to be consisting of just series and parallel links. We therefore find the conditional probability of failure under two mutually exclusive conditions.

In one condition, link #5 has failed and can thus be viewed as nonexistent; this in a way is similar to the concept of open circuit in the context of circuit theory. As shown in Figure 4.5b, we then have two branches in parallel and in each branch there are two links in series. The conditional probability that the network fails given that link #5 has failed is thus as follows:

$$P(F/F_5)=P((F_1 \cup F_2)\cap(F_3 \cup F_4))=\left(1-(1-p)^2\right)^2=p^2(2-p)^2$$

In the other condition, link #5 is a permanent link with no possibility of failure; this in a way is similar to the concept of short circuit in the context of circuit theory. As shown in Figure 4.5c, we then have two parts in series and in each part there are two links in parallel. The conditional probability that the network fails given that link #5 never fails is thus as follows:

$$P(F/\overline{F_5})=P((F_1 \cap F_3)\cup(F_2 \cap F_4))=1-\left(1-p^2\right)^2=p^2\left(2-p^2\right)$$

Using (4.7), the total probability theorem determines the probability of network failure:

$$P(F)=P(F/F_5)\,P(F_5)+P(F/\overline{F_5})P(\overline{F_5})=p^2(2-p)^2p+p^2\left(2-p^2\right)(1-p)=p^2\left(2p^3-5p^2+2p+2\right)$$

Note that $P(F)$ is not a linear function of p. As expected, for $p=0$, we have $P(F)=0$, for $p=1$, we have $P(F)=1$, and for $p=\frac{1}{2}$, we have $P(F)=\frac{1}{2}$. In practice, $0<p\ll 1$, we therefore have $P(F)\approx 2p^2$.

4.2 RANDOM VARIABLES

Before embarking on defining a random variable and describing its importance, properties, and applications, it is interesting to highlight that the term random variable is something of a misnomer, because it is not a variable and it is not random! Nevertheless, the term random variable is universally used, as it has no substitute.

4.2.1 Single Random Variable

A random variable is a numerical representation of the outcome of a random experiment. A ***random variable*** X is a function that assigns a real number to each outcome in the sample space S (i.e., a mapping from the sample space to the set of real numbers), as shown in Figure 4.6. The sample space S is the ***domain of the random variable*** and the set of all values taken on by X is the ***range of the random variable***. The range is a subset of all real numbers $(-\infty, \infty)$. If the range assumes values from a countable set (i.e., takes on only a finite number of values), the random variable is then a ***discrete random variable***. If the range can take infinitely many real values (i.e., takes on values that vary continuously

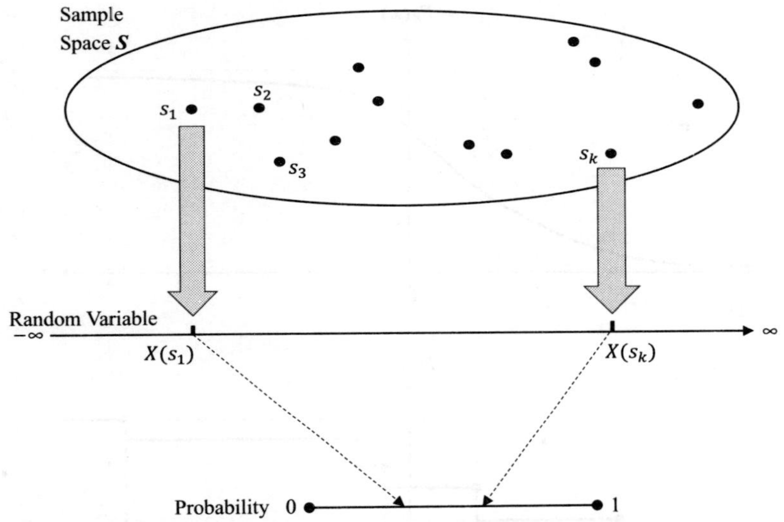

FIGURE 4.6 Relationship among sample space, random variable, and probability.

within one or more real intervals), it is then a ***continuous random variable***. The number of calls made by a cell phone during a finite interval of time is an example of a discrete random variable, whereas the exact time when a phone call is made is an example of a continuous random variable.

The ***cumulative distribution function*** (cdf) $F_X(x)$ of a random variable X is defined as follows:

$$F_X(x) = P(X \leq x), \quad \text{for } -\infty < x < \infty. \tag{4.9}$$

The event $\{X \leq x\}$ and its probability vary as x is varied (i.e., $F_X(x)$ is a function of the variable x). The cdf of a random variable always exists, and has the following basic properties:

- $0 \leq F_X(x) \leq 1$.
- $F_X(x)$ is a nondecreasing function of x, i.e., if $a < b$, then $F_X(a) \leq F_X(b)$.
- $\lim_{x \to \infty} F_X(x) = 1$.
- $\lim_{x \to -\infty} F_X(x) = 0$.
- $F_X(x)$ is continuous from the right, i.e., for $h > 0, F_X(b) = \lim_{h \to 0} F_X(x+h) = F_X(b^+)$.
- $P(a < X \leq b) = F_X(b) - F_X(a)$.
- $P(X = b) = F_X(b) - F_X(b^-)$.
- $P(X > x) = 1 - F_X(x)$.

(4.10)

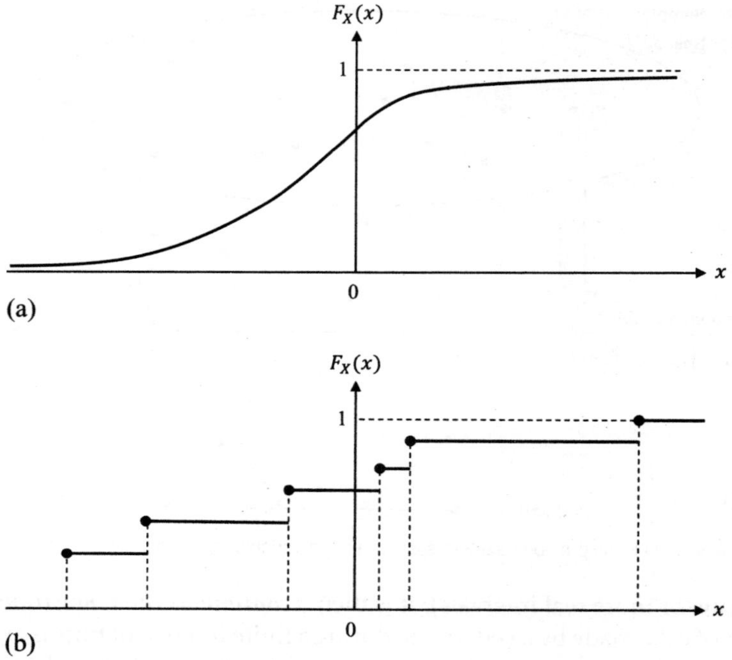

FIGURE 4.7 (a) Continuous cdf and (b) discrete cdf.

Figure 4.7 shows cdf examples for continuous and discrete random variables. $F_X(x)$ is a continuous function for a continuous random variable. It is important to note that if the cdf is continuous at a point c, then $P[X=c]=0$. This is an example of an event with probability zero that is not necessarily an impossible event.

The ***probability density function*** (pdf) $f_X(x)$ of a random variable, if it exists, is defined as the derivative of the cdf $F_X(x)$:

$$f_X(x)=\frac{dF_X(x)}{dx}. \tag{4.11}$$

However, the definition of pdf allows placing a delta function of weight $P[X=x]$ at the point x where the cdf is discontinuous. The pdf properties are as follows:

- $f_X(x)\geq 0.$
- $P(a\leq X\leq b)=\int_a^b f_X(x)dx.$
- $\int_{-\infty}^{\infty} f_X(x)dx=1.$ (4.12)
- $F_X(x)=\int_{-\infty}^{x} f_X(s)ds.$

EXAMPLE 4.6

Let X be a continuous random variable whose pdf is as follows:

$$f_X(x) = \begin{cases} kx, & 0 \le x \le 1 \\ 0, & \text{otherwise} \end{cases}$$

where k is a constant. Determine k, $F_X(x)$, and $P(0.25 < X \le 2)$.

Solution

Using (4.12), we solve the following equation:

$$\int_{-\infty}^{\infty} f_X(x)dx = \int_0^1 kx\,dx = 1.$$

We therefore obtain $k = 2$. Using (4.12), we thus have:

$$F_X(x) = \int_0^x 2s\,ds = \begin{cases} 0, & x \le 0 \\ x^2, & 0 < x \le 1 \\ 1, & 1 < x \end{cases}$$

$P(0.25 < X \le 2)$ can thus be found in two different ways:

$$P(0.25 < X \le 2) = F_X(2) - F_X(0.25) = 1 - \frac{1}{4} \times \frac{1}{4} = \frac{15}{16}$$

or

$$P(0.25 < X \le 2) = \int_{0.25}^{1} 2x\,dx = \frac{15}{16}$$

$F_X(x)$ is a staircase function for a discrete random variable, where the magnitude of any jump (discontinuity) at a point is equal to the probability at that point. It can therefore be represented by the weighted sum of unit-step functions. Since the pdf of a discrete random variable is the derivative of its cdf, it can be thus represented by the weighted sum of delta functions. The cdf and pdf of a discrete random variable are then defined as follows:

$$\begin{aligned} F_X(x) &= \sum_k p_X(x_k)\, u(x - x_k) = \sum_k P(X = x_k)\, u(x - x_k) \\ f_X(x) &= \frac{dF_X(x)}{dx} = \sum_k p_X(x_k)\, \delta(x - x_k) = \sum_k P(X = x_k)\, \delta(x - x_k) \end{aligned} \quad (4.13)$$

where $\{p_X(x_k)\}$ is known as the **probability mass function** (pmf).

EXAMPLE 4.7

Suppose we have a fair coin. Let X be the number of heads in three coin tosses. Find the pdf and cdf of the random variable X.

Solution

A fair coin implies the likelihood of tails is the same as the likelihood of heads. After tossing three times, there can be a total of eight equally-likely outcomes as follows:

$\{HHH, HHT, HTH, HTT, THH, THT, TTH, TTT\}$.

Noting X is the number of heads in three coin tosses, the pmf of X is therefore as follows:

$P(X=0)=\frac{1}{8}$, $P(X=1)=\frac{3}{8}$, $P(X=2)=\frac{3}{8}$, and $P(X=3)=\frac{1}{8}$.

The pdf and cdf of this discrete random variable are then as follows:

$$f_X(x)=\frac{1}{8}\delta(x)+\frac{3}{8}\delta(x-1)+\frac{3}{8}\delta(x-2)+\frac{1}{8}\delta(x-3)$$

$$F_X(x)=\frac{1}{8}u(x)+\frac{3}{8}u(x-1)+\frac{3}{8}u(x-2)+\frac{1}{8}u(x-3)$$

4.2.2 Important Single Random Variables

Table 4.1 and Table 4.2 summarize some of the basic properties of some well-known continuous and discrete random variables, respectively.

Bernoulli random variable is a discrete random variable. It takes the value of 1 with probability of p and 0 with probability of $1-p$, where $0 \le p \le 1$. Its pmf is then defined as follows:

$$P(X=k)=p_X(k)=\begin{cases} 1-p, & k=0 \\ p, & k=1 \end{cases} \tag{4.14}$$

A Bernoulli trial is equivalent to the tossing of a biased coin. A Bernoulli random variable may be used in modeling channel errors.

Binomial random variable is a discrete random variable. It is the number of times 1, with probability p, occurs in n independent Bernoulli trials, where $0 \le p \le 1$. Its pmf is then defined as follows:

$$P(X=k)=p_X(k)=\begin{cases} \binom{n}{k} p^k(1-p)^{n-k}, & k=0, 1, \dots, n \\ 0, & \text{otherwise} \end{cases} \tag{4.15}$$

Table 4.1 Important continuous random variables

Name	Probability Density Function	Mean	Variance
Uniform	$f_X(x)=\frac{1}{b-a}, \quad a \le x \le b$	$\frac{a+b}{2}$	$\frac{(b-a)^2}{12}$
Exponential	$f_X(x)=\lambda e^{-\lambda t}, \ x \ge 0, \ \lambda > 0$	$\frac{1}{\lambda}$	$\frac{1}{\lambda^2}$
Gaussian	$f_X(x)=\frac{1}{\sqrt{2\pi\sigma^2}}\exp\left(-\frac{(x-m)^2}{2\sigma^2}\right), \ -\infty < x < \infty$	m	σ^2
Rayleigh	$f_X(x)=\left(\frac{x}{\alpha^2}\right)\exp\left(-\frac{x^2}{2\alpha^2}\right), \quad x \ge 0, \quad \alpha > 0$	$\alpha\sqrt{\frac{\pi}{2}}$	$\left(2-\frac{\pi}{2}\right)\alpha^2$

Table 4.2 Important discrete random variables

Name	Probability Mass Function	Mean	Variance
Bernoulli	$p_0=(1-p),\ p_1=p,\ 0\le p\le 1$	p	$p(1-p)$
Binomial	$p_k=\binom{n}{k}p^k(1-p)^{n-k},\ k=0,1,\cdots,n$	np	$np(1-p)$
Geometric	$p_k=p(1-p)^{k-1},\ k=1,2,\cdots$	$\frac{1}{p}$	$\frac{1-p}{p^2}$
Poisson	$p_k=\frac{\alpha^k e^{-\alpha}}{k!},\ \alpha>0,\ k=0,1,\cdots$	α	α

where $\binom{n}{k}\triangleq\frac{n!}{k!(n-k)!}$. A Binomial random variable may be used to model the total number of erroneous bits when a sequence of n bits is transmitted over a channel with a bit error rate of p.

EXAMPLE 4.8

In a digital commutation system, bits are transmitted over a channel in which the bit error rate is assumed to be 0.0001. The transmitter sends each bit five times, and a decoder takes a majority vote of the received bits to determine what the transmitted bit was. Determine the probability that the receiver will make an incorrect decision.

Solution

Each bit transmission is viewed as a Bernoulli trial. Using (4.15), we find $P(X\ge 3)$, where $p=0.0001$:

$$P(X\ge 3)=\sum_{k=3}^{5}\binom{5}{k}(0.0001)^k(0.9999)^{5-k}\cong 9.99\times 10^{-12}$$

A uniform random variable can be discrete or continuous. Figure 4.8 shows the pdf and cdf for continuous and discrete uniform random variables. The ***discrete uniform random variable*** occurs when outcomes are equally likely, such as rolling a fair die. It takes on values in a set of L positive integers with equal probability. Its pmf is then defined as follows:

$$P(X=k)=p_X(k)=\frac{1}{L},\quad k=m+1,\ \ldots,\ m+L,\quad -\infty<m<\infty \tag{4.16}$$

The discrete random variable is used to generate random numbers in computer simulation models. Note that events that have an equi-probable finite number of outcomes form the basis upon which counting formulas, to find the number of combinations and permutations, are developed.

The ***continuous uniform random variable*** arises where all values in a known finite interval of the real line are equally likely. The continuous random variable in the interval $[a, b]$ has the following pdf:

$$f_X(x)=\begin{cases}\frac{1}{b-a}, & a<x\le b\\ 0, & \text{otherwise}\end{cases} \tag{4.17}$$

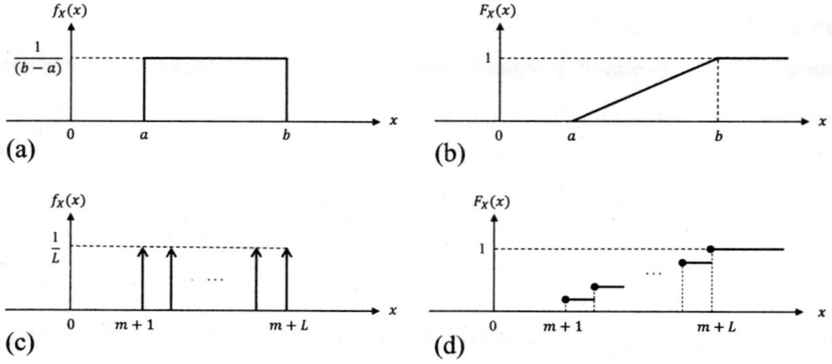

FIGURE 4.8 (a) pdf of a continuous random variable, (b) cdf of a continuous variable, (c) pdf of a discrete random variable, and (d) cdf of a discrete random variable.

The continuous uniform random variable is used when the range of the random variable is known, and we have no other knowledge about possible values that the random variable can have. This random variable is often used to model the random phase of a sinusoidal signal, in that a uniform distribution of phase between 0 and 2π (i.e., $[0, 2\pi]$) is frequently assumed. Also, in analog to digital conversion, this random variable is used to describe the errors due to rounding off in the quantization process.

The ***Gaussian (normal) random variable*** is the most widely used random variable in communications, simply because it can be used to approximate the sum of a large number of independent random variables. It represents the distribution of thermal noise in signal transmission. The Gaussian random variable is a continuous random variable whose pdf is as follows:

$$f_X(x) = \left(\frac{1}{\sqrt{2\pi\sigma^2}}\right)\exp\left(-\frac{(x-m)^2}{2\sigma^2}\right), \quad -\infty < x < \infty \tag{4.18}$$

where the parameter m, called the mean, can have any finite real value (i.e., $-\infty < m < \infty$), and the parameter σ^2, called the variance, can have any finite positive value (i.e., $0 < \sigma^2 < \infty$). As shown in Figure 4.9, the Gaussian pdf is a bell-shaped curve centered and symmetric about m and its width increases with σ, the standard deviation. The maximum value of the Gaussian pdf, also known as mode, occurs at the mean value m, and is inversely proportional to σ. The cdf of the Gaussian random variable is given as follows:

$$F_X(x) = \int_{-\infty}^{x}\left(\frac{1}{\sqrt{2\pi\sigma^2}}\right)\exp\left(-\frac{(t-m)^2}{2\sigma^2}\right)dt \tag{4.19}$$

By making a change of variable $x = \frac{t-m}{\sigma}$, (4.19) becomes as follows:

$$F_X(x) = \int_{-\infty}^{\frac{x-m}{\sigma}}\left(\frac{1}{\sqrt{2\pi}}\right)\exp\left(-\frac{x^2}{2}\right)dx \tag{4.20}$$

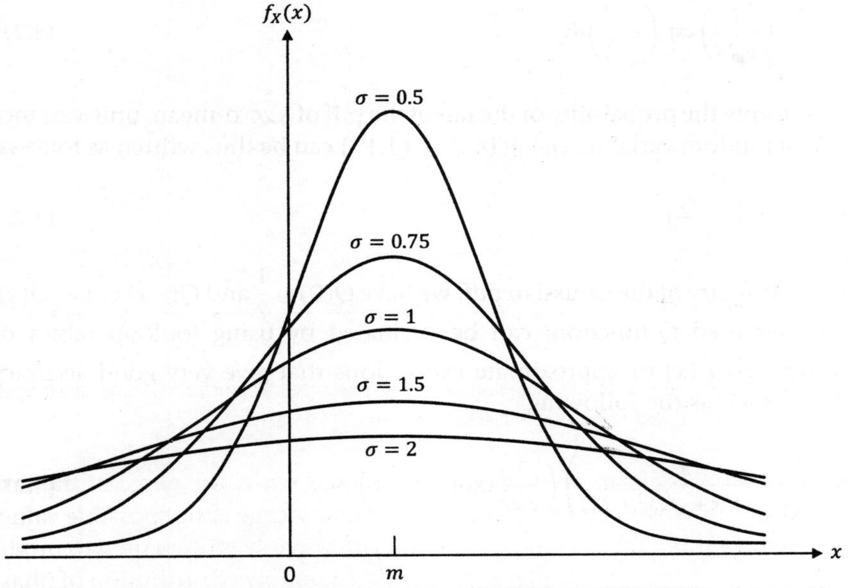

FIGURE 4.9 pdf of a Gaussian random variable with mean m and variance σ^2.

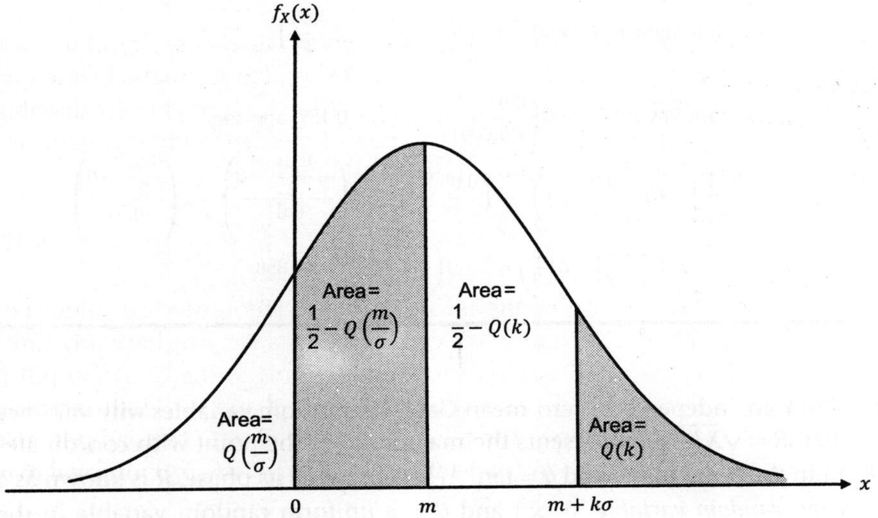

FIGURE 4.10 Area interpretation of $Q(x)$ for Gaussian pdf.

The integrand in (4.20) is known as a zero-mean (i.e., $m = 0$), unit-variance (i.e., $\sigma^2 = 1$) Gaussian pdf. Since the above integral cannot be solved analytically, a numerical solution is required. To determine (4.20), we can use the ***Q-function***, as shown in Figure 4.10 and defined below:

$$Q(x) = \int_x^{\infty} \left(\frac{1}{\sqrt{2\pi}}\right) \exp\left(-\frac{x^2}{2}\right) dx \tag{4.21}$$

$Q(x)$ is simply the probability of the tail of the pdf of a zero-mean, unit-variance Gaussian random variable. Using (4.21), (4.19) can be thus written as follows:

$$F_X(x) = 1 - Q\left(\frac{x-m}{\sigma}\right) \tag{4.22}$$

Due to symmetry of the Gaussian pdf, we have $Q(0) = \frac{1}{2}$ and $Q(-x) = 1 - Q(x)$. The widely-used Q-function, can be evaluated by using look-up tables or MATLAB's *qfunc*(x) or approximate expressions that give very good accuracy for $Q(x)$, such as the following:

$$Q(x) \approx \left(\frac{\pi}{(\pi-1)x + \sqrt{(x^2+2\pi)}}\right)\left(\frac{1}{\sqrt{2\pi}}\exp(-x^2/2)\right) \tag{4.23}$$

EXAMPLE 4.9

In a communication system, the noise level is modeled as a Gaussian random variable with $m = 0$ and $\sigma^2 = 0.0001$. Determine $P(X > 0.01)$ and $P\left(-\frac{0.04}{3} \leq X \leq \frac{0.05}{3}\right)$.

Solution

Using (4.22), we have $P(X > 0.01) = Q\left(\frac{0.01-0}{\sqrt{0.0001}}\right) = Q(1) = 0.159$, and also

$$P\left(-\frac{0.04}{3} \leq X \leq \frac{0.05}{3}\right) = P\left(-\frac{0.04}{3} \leq X\right) - P\left(\frac{0.05}{3} \leq X\right) = Q\left(\frac{-\frac{0.04}{3} - 0}{0.01}\right) - Q\left(\frac{\frac{0.05}{3} - 0}{0.01}\right)$$

$$= Q\left(-\frac{4}{3}\right) - Q\left(\frac{5}{3}\right) = 1 - Q\left(\frac{4}{3}\right) - Q\left(\frac{5}{3}\right) \cong 0.858.$$

If X and Y are independent zero-mean Gaussian random variables with variance σ^2, then $R = \sqrt{X^2 + Y^2}$ represents the magnitude of the point with coordinates (X, Y) in the polar plane and $\theta = \tan^{-1}\left(\frac{Y}{X}\right)$ represents its phase. R is known as a ***Rayleigh random variable*** $[0, \infty)$ and θ is a uniform random variable in the interval $[0, 2\pi]$. The pdf for the Rayleigh random variable X, as shown in Figure 4.11, is given by

$$f_X(x) = \begin{cases} \left(\frac{x}{\sigma^2}\right)\exp\left(-\frac{x^2}{2\sigma^2}\right), & x \geq 0 \\ 0, & x < 0 \end{cases} \tag{4.24}$$

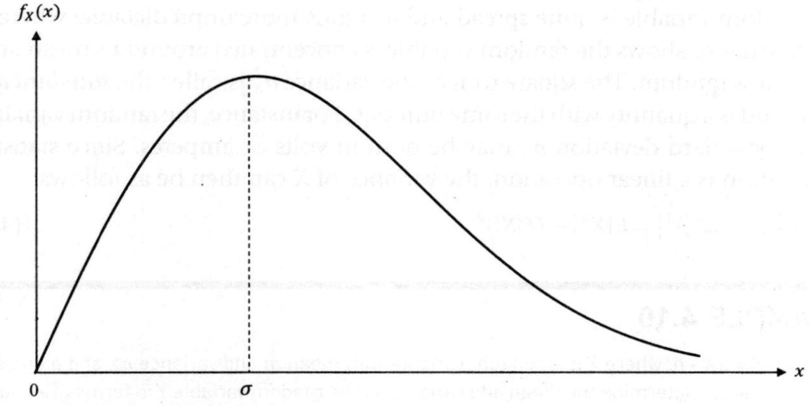

FIGURE 4.11 Rayleigh pdf with mean $\sigma\sqrt{\pi/2}$ and variance $\sigma^2(2-\pi/2)$.

where x is a nonnegative real number, as magnitude can never be negative. The mean, variance, and mode of the Rayleigh distribution are $\sigma\sqrt{\frac{\pi}{2}}$, $\sigma^2\left(2-\frac{\pi}{2}\right)$, and σ, respectively. Unlike the Gaussian random variable, the mean and variance depend on a single parameter σ and cannot thus be adjusted independently.

4.2.3 Expected Value

The ***expected value*** or ***mean*** of a random variable X represents a real number, and in a very large number of observations of X, corresponds to the average of X or the sample mean or the arithmetic mean. The expected value of a continuous random variable and that of a discrete random variable are, respectively, as follows:

$$\begin{aligned} E[X] &= \int_{-\infty}^{\infty} x f_X(x)dx \\ E[X] &= \sum_i x_i P(X=x_i). \end{aligned} \tag{4.25}$$

In other words, the mean locates the center of gravity of the area under the curve of the pdf. Let X be a random variable and let $Y=g(X)$ denote a real-valued function. Y is therefore a random variable as well. The expected value of the random variable Y when X is a continuous random variable and when it is a discrete random variable are, respectively, as follows:

$$\begin{aligned} E[g(X)] &= \int_{-\infty}^{\infty} g(x) f_X(x)dx \\ E[g(X)] &= \sum_i g(x_i)P(X=x_i). \end{aligned} \tag{4.26}$$

If we assume $Y=g(X)\triangleq(X-E[X])^2$, then $E[Y]$ is called the ***variance*** of the random variable X. The variance of X, denoted by σ_X^2, is the second moment of the difference between a random variable X and its mean $E[X]$, and is a measure of the width of the pdf of X. It is a measure of its randomness. For instance, a large variance indicates the random variable is quite spread and it is thus more unpredictable, whereas a small variance shows the random variable is concentrated around its mean and it is thus less random. The square root of the variance σ_X^2 is called the ***standard deviation***, and is a quantity with the same unit as X. For instance, the random variable X and its standard deviation σ_X may be both in volts or amperes. Since statistical expectation is a linear operation, the variance of X can then be as follows:

$$\sigma_X^2 = E\left[(X - E[X])^2\right] = E\left[X^2\right] - (E[X])^2 \tag{4.27}$$

EXAMPLE 4.10

Suppose $Y = aX + b$, where X is a random variable with mean m and variance σ_X^2, and a and b are fixed constants. Determine the mean and variance of the random variable Y in terms of a and b as well as the mean and variance of the random variable X.

Solution

Using (4.25) and noting statistical expectation is a linear operation, we obtain the mean of Y as follows:

$$E[Y] = E[aX + b] = a\,E[X] + b = a\,m + b$$

This in turn means the mean value of Y is linearly related to the mean value of X in the same way that the random variables Y and X are linearly related. We then find the mean-square value of Y as follows:

$$E\left[Y^2\right] = E\left[(aX + b)^2\right] = E\left[a^2x^2 + b^2 + 2abX\right] = a^2E\left[x^2\right] + b^2 + 2abE[X]$$

Using (4.27), we can now find the variance of Y, as follows:

$$\sigma_Y^2 = E\left[Y^2\right] - (E[Y])^2 = \left(a^2E\left[X^2\right] + b^2 + 2abE[X]\right) - (a\,E[X] + b)^2 = a^2E\left[X^2\right] - a^2E^2[X] = a^2\sigma_X^2$$

For certain values of a and b, we have the following interesting relations:

- If $b = 0$, i.e., Y is proportional to X, then $E[Y] = a\,E[X] = am$ and $\sigma_Y^2 = a^2\sigma_X^2$.
- If $a = 0$, i.e., Y is not a random variable, then $E[Y] = b$ and $\sigma_Y^2 = 0$.
- If $a = 1$, i.e., Y is a shifted version of X, then $E[Y] = E[X] + b = m + b$ and $\sigma_Y^2 = \sigma_X^2$.

EXAMPLE 4.11

Suppose we have a fair coin. Let X be the number of tails in four coin tosses. Determine the mean and variance of the random variable X.

Solution

Using (4.25), we first find the mean:

$$E[X] = (0)\left(\frac{1}{16}\right) + (1)\left(\frac{4}{16}\right) + (2)\left(\frac{6}{16}\right) + (3)\left(\frac{4}{16}\right) + (4)\left(\frac{1}{16}\right) = 2$$

and using (4.27), we have:

$$E\left[X^2\right] = (0)^2\left(\frac{1}{16}\right) + (1)^2\left(\frac{4}{16}\right) + (2)^2\left(\frac{6}{16}\right) + (3)^2\left(\frac{4}{16}\right) + (4)^2\left(\frac{1}{16}\right) = 5$$

We therefore have $\sigma_X^2 = 5 - (2)^2 = 1$.

EXAMPLE 4.12

We have $X = A\cos(2\pi f_c t + \theta)$, where the amplitude A and the frequency f_c are both known constants, and θ is a uniform random variable in the interval $[0, 2\pi]$. Find the expected value and variance of the random variable X.

Solution

Using (4.25), we get:

$$E[X] = \int_0^{2\pi} A\cos(2\pi f_c t + \theta)\left(\frac{1}{2\pi}\right) d\theta = 0.$$

Using (4.26) and a trigonometric identity, we get:

$$E[X^2] = \int_0^{2\pi} A^2(\cos(2\pi f_c t + \theta))^2\left(\frac{1}{2\pi}\right) d\theta = \frac{A^2}{2}\int_0^{2\pi}(1 + \cos(4\pi f_c t + 2\theta))\left(\frac{1}{2\pi}\right) d\theta = \frac{A^2}{2}.$$

Using (4.27), we thus obtain $\sigma_X^2 = \frac{A^2}{2}$.

4.2.4 Conditional cdf and pdf of a Random Variable

The ***conditional cdf*** and ***conditional pdf*** incorporate partial knowledge about the outcome of an experiment in the evaluation of probabilities of events. If there is some information about a random variable X, then its conditional cdf and pdf need to incorporate that. Suppose the event C, defined as $X \leq b$, is given, we thus have $P(C) = P(X \leq b) = \int_{-\infty}^{b} f_X(x)dx > 0$. Using (4.3) and (4.11), the conditional cdf and pdf of X given C are, respectively, defined as follows:

$$\begin{aligned} F_X(x/C) &= P(X \leq x/C) = \frac{P((X \leq x) \cap C)}{P(C)} = \frac{P(X \leq x, X \leq b)}{P(C)} \\ f_X(x/C) &= \frac{dF_X(x/C)}{dx} \end{aligned} \tag{4.28}$$

There are now two possible situations, depending on whether x or b is larger. If $x \geq b$, then the event that $X \leq b$ is contained in the event that $X \leq x$ and we thus have $P((X \leq x) \cap C) = P(X \leq x, X \leq b) = P(X \leq b) = P(C)$. On the other hand, if $x \leq b$, then the event that $X \leq x$ is contained in the event that $X \leq b$ and we thus have $P((X \leq x) \cap C) = P(X \leq x, X \leq b) = P(X \leq x)$. As a result, the conditional cdf and pdf in (4.28) can be simplified as follows:

$$\begin{aligned} F_X(x/C) &= \begin{cases} \dfrac{P(C)}{P(C)} = 1, & x > b \\ \dfrac{P(X \leq x)}{P(C)}, & x \leq b \end{cases} \\ f_X(x/C) &= \begin{cases} 0, & x > b \\ \dfrac{f_X(x)}{P(C)}, & x \leq b \end{cases} \end{aligned} \tag{4.29}$$

In (4.29), dividing the pdf of X, i.e., $f_X(x)$, by $P(C)$, which is less than one, ensures that the area under the conditional pdf $f_X(x/C)$ is one, an essential requirement for any pdf.

EXAMPLE 4.13

Assume X is a zero-mean unit-variance Gaussian random variable. Determine the conditional pdf $f_X(x/|X| \leq 1)$.

Solution

We know we have:

$$P(|X| \leq 1) = P(-1 \leq X \leq 1) = P(-1 \leq X) - P(1 \leq X) = Q(-1) - Q(1) = (1 - Q(1)) - Q(1) = 1 - 2Q(1) \\ = 0.683$$

Using (4.29), we have the following:

$$f_X(x/|X| \leq 1) = \begin{cases} \frac{f_X(x)}{0.683} = 1.464 f_X(x), & -1 < x \leq 1 \\ 0, & x \leq -1 \text{ or } x > 1 \end{cases}$$

Figure 4.12 shows the pdf of X and its conditional pdf. Note that for the range of the random variable X for which the condition is not met, the conditional pdf is zero, and for the range in which it is met, the conditional pdf is scaled up version of the pdf of X so as to ensure the area under it is unity.

4.2.5 Functions of a Single Random Variable

Let X be a random variable and let $g(X)$ be a real-valued function of X. If $Y = g(X)$, then Y is also a random variable. The cdf of Y depends on both the function $g(X)$ and the cdf of X. The probability of an event C involving Y is equal to the probability of the equivalent event B involving X such that $g(X)$ is in C (i.e., we have $P(Y \text{ in } C) = P(g(X) \text{ in } C) = P(X \text{ in } B)$).

To determine the pdf of Y, we solve the equation $y = g(x)$ for x in terms of y. Assuming there are n solutions $\{x_1, x_2, \ldots, x_n\}$ and for each solution x_i, the

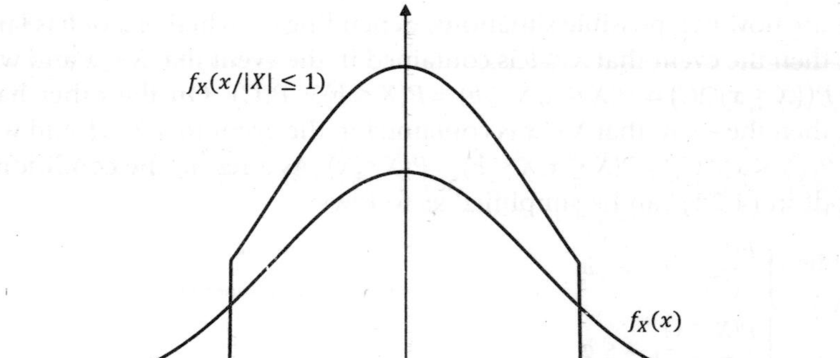

FIGURE 4.12 pdfs for Example 4.13.

derivative $y' = g'(x_i)$ exists, and is also nonzero, it can be shown that the pdf of $Y = g(X)$ is as follows:

$$f_Y(y) = \sum_{i=1}^{n} \frac{f_X(x_i)}{|g'(x_i)|} \tag{4.30}$$

EXAMPLE 4.14

The random variables X and Y are linearly related, i.e., $Y = aX + b$, where $a \neq 0$ and b are some fixed constants. Determine the cdf and pdf of Y in terms of the cdf and pdf of X.

Solution

Noting that the sign of the constant a plays a role, the cdf of Y can be determined as follows:

$$F_Y(y) = P(Y \leq y) = P(aX + b \leq y)$$

$$= \begin{cases} P\left(X \leq \dfrac{y-b}{a}\right) = F_X\left(X \leq \dfrac{y-b}{a}\right), & a > 0 \\ P\left(X \geq \dfrac{y-b}{a}\right) = 1 - F_X\left(X \leq \dfrac{y-b}{a}\right), & a < 0 \end{cases}$$

We differentiate the above equation to obtain the pdf of Y:

$$f_Y(y) = \begin{cases} \left(\dfrac{1}{a}\right) f_X\left(\dfrac{y-b}{a}\right), & a > 0 \\ \left(\dfrac{1}{-a}\right) f_X\left(\dfrac{y-b}{a}\right), & a < 0 \end{cases}$$

We thus have:

$$f_Y(y) = \frac{1}{|a|} f_X\left(\frac{y-b}{a}\right)$$

Of course, this last equation is in the format of (4.30), as we have $g(x) = ax + b$, $x_1 = \dfrac{y-b}{a}$, $g'(x) = a$ and $g'\left(\dfrac{y-b}{a}\right) = a$.

EXAMPLE 4.15

Let X be a random variable with a Gaussian pdf with mean m and standard deviation σ. Let $Y = aX + b$. Find the pdf of Y, and determine a and b in terms of m and σ, such that the random variable Y has a zero-mean and unit-variance.

Solution

Using the result in the previous example as well as (4.18), the pdf of Y is as follows:

$$f_Y(y) = \left(\frac{1}{|a|\sqrt{2\pi\sigma^2}}\right) \exp\left(-\frac{(y-b-am)^2}{2a^2\sigma^2}\right)$$

After comparing the above equation with (4.18), we can conclude that Y is also a Gaussian random variable whose mean is $b + am$ and variance is $a^2\sigma^2$. This highlights the important fact that a linear function of a Gaussian random variable is also a Gaussian random variable. We now need to solve the following system of linear equations for a and b:

$$\begin{cases} a^2\sigma^2 = 1 \\ b + am = 0 \end{cases} \rightarrow \begin{cases} a = \pm\dfrac{1}{\sigma} \\ b = \mp\dfrac{m}{\sigma} \end{cases}$$

EXAMPLE 4.16

Let X be a zero-mean unit-variance Gaussian random variable whose pdf $f_X(x)$ is known. Assuming $Y = X^2$, determine the pdf of the random variable Y, i.e., $f_Y(y)$.

Solution

We first solve the equation $y = x^2$, we thus obtain $x = \pm\sqrt{y}$, assuming $y > 0$. We then find the derivative $y' = 2x$. Using (4.30), we obtain the following result:

$$f_Y(y) = \begin{cases} \dfrac{f_X(\sqrt{y})}{2\sqrt{y}} + \dfrac{f_X(-\sqrt{y})}{2\sqrt{y}} = \left(\dfrac{1}{\sqrt{2\pi y}}\right)\exp\left(-\dfrac{y}{2}\right), & y > 0 \\ 0, & y \leq 0 \end{cases}$$

4.2.6 Chebyshev Inequality

To determine the probability of an event, the pdf or cdf of a random variable is required. However, when neither of them is known, then the mean and variance can be used to arrive at bounds on probabilities. A bound, by definition, encompasses all cases, including the worst case, therefore, when it is applied to a particular case, it may be quite weak (i.e., not very tight). The ***Chebyshev inequality***, which can be used to obtain lower bounds on the probability of finding the random variable X outside an interval, is as follows:

$$\begin{aligned} &P(|X - m| \geq a) \leq \frac{\sigma^2}{a^2}, && a > 0 \\ &P(|X - m| \leq c\sigma) \geq 1 - \frac{1}{c^2}, && c > 0 \end{aligned} \tag{4.31}$$

Note that m and σ^2 are the mean and the variance of the random variable X, respectively.

EXAMPLE 4.17

Calculate and estimate the width or spread of a Gaussian random variable using the Q-function and the Chebyshev inequality, respectively.

Solution

By using (4.22) and (4.31), the calculation and estimation results can be provided as follows:

Probability	Calculation	Estimation
$P[\|X-m\|\leq\sigma]$	$1-2Q(1)\approx 0.6826$	$1-\frac{1}{(1)^2}\cong 0$
$P[\|X-m\|\leq 2\sigma]$	$1-2Q(2)\approx 0.9444$	$1-\frac{1}{(2)^2}\cong 0.75$
$P[\|X-m\|\leq 3\sigma]$	$1-2Q(3)\approx 0.9973$	$1-\frac{1}{(3)^2}\cong 0.8889$
$P[\|X-m\|\leq 4\sigma]$	$1-2Q(4)\approx 0.99994$	$1-\frac{1}{(4)^2}\cong 0.9375$
$P[\|X-m\|\leq 5\sigma]$	$1-2Q(5)\approx 0.99999$	$1-\frac{1}{(5)^2}\cong 0.96$

This means that for a Gaussian random variable, the probability of observing X within a few standard deviations is very high. Although by increasing the width under consideration, the accuracy of an estimate can be improved, the estimate, however, always falls far short of its corresponding calculation, as the Chebyshev inequality is not a tight bound. Note the area under a Gaussian pdf, for instance, in the interval $(m-4\sigma, m+4\sigma)$ is 99.994% and a very negligible 0.006% of the area lies outside this interval. Such numbers are very important, as they can be used in defining our confidence in results based on measurements with random errors.

4.2.7 Pair of Random Variables

We now focus on two continuous random variables; however, the discussion can be easily extended to multiple continuous or discrete random variables. A pair of random variables X and Y represents a function that assigns a pair of real numbers to each outcome in the sample space S. In other words, it is a mapping from the sample space to the real plane, rather than to the real line as it is the case for a single random variable. The ***joint cdf*** of two-dimensional random variables X and Y is defined as follows:

$$F_{X,Y}(x,y)=P(X\leq x, Y\leq y) \tag{4.32}$$

The probability of the event $\{X\leq x, Y\leq y\}$ varies as x and y are varied, i.e., $F_{X,Y}(x, y)$ is a function of the variables x and y. The joint cdf has the following properties:

- $F_{X,Y}(x_1,y_1)\leq F_{X,Y}(x_2,y_2)$, if $x_1\leq x_2$ and $y_1\leq y_2$.
- $\lim_{x\to a^+} F_{X,Y}(x,y)=F_{X,Y}(a,y)$.
- $\lim_{y\to b^+} F_{X,Y}(x,y)=F_{X,Y}(x,b)$.
- $F_{X,Y}(x_1,-\infty)=0$.
- $F_{X,Y}(-\infty,y_1)=0$.
- $F_{X,Y}(\infty,\infty)=1$.
- $F_X(x_1)=F_{X,Y}(x_1,\infty)$.
- $F_Y(y_1)=F_{X,Y}(\infty,y_1)$.
- $P(x_1<X\leq x_2, y_1<Y\leq y_2)=F_{X,Y}(x_2,y_2)-F_{X,Y}(x_2,y_1)-F_{X,Y}(x_1,y_2)+F_{X,Y}(x_1,y_1)$ (4.33)

If X and Y are jointly continuous random variables, then the ***joint pdf***, which can be obtained from the joint cdf by differentiation, is as follows:

$$f_{X,Y}(x,y) = \frac{\partial^2 F_{X,Y}(x,y)}{\partial x \, \partial y} \tag{4.34}$$

Note that if X and Y are not jointly continuous, it is then possible that the above partial derivative does not exist. In view of this, we may need to invoke delta functions at the points where the cdf is jointly discontinuous. A two-dimensional joint pdf is analogous to a mass density distributed over a plane where the total mass is unity. The joint pdf properties are as follows:

- $F_{X,Y}(x,y) = \int_{-\infty}^{x}\int_{-\infty}^{y} f_{X,Y}(w,z)dwdz.$
- $\int_{-\infty}^{\infty}\int_{-\infty}^{\infty} f_{X,Y}(x,y)\,dx\,dy = 1.$
- $P(a < X \le b, c < Y \le d) = \int_{c}^{d}\int_{a}^{b} f_{X,Y}(x,y)dxdy.$ (4.35)
- $f_Y(y) = \int_{-\infty}^{\infty} f_{X,Y}(x,y)dx.$
- $f_X(x) = \int_{-\infty}^{\infty} f_{X,Y}(x,y)dy.$

The $f_X(x)$ and $f_Y(y)$ in (4.35) are each known as a ***marginal pdf***, and they are obtained by integrating over the variables that are not of interest. It is important to note that the joint pdf in general cannot be obtained from the marginal pdfs, as the marginal pdfs can only provide partial information about the joint pdf.

EXAMPLE 4.18

Suppose the joint pdf of X and Y is as follows:

$$f_{X,Y}(x,y) = \begin{cases} 2(1-x), & 0 \le x \le 1 \text{ and } 0 \le y \le 1 \\ 0, & \text{elsewhere} \end{cases}$$

Calculate the probability that $x \le 0.5$ and $0.4 \le y \le 0.7$, and find the marginal pdfs of X and Y.

Solution

Using (4.35), we can obtain the following:

$$P(0 \le x \le 0.5, 0.4 \le y \le 0.7) = \int_{0.4}^{0.7}\int_{0}^{0.5} 2(1-x)dxdy = 0.225.$$

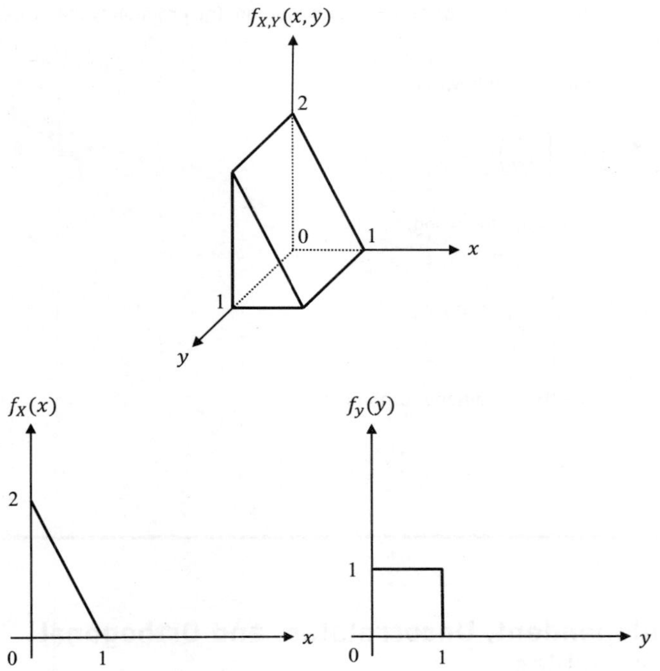

FIGURE 4.13 Joint pdf and marginal pdfs for Example 4.18.

$$f_X(x) = \int_{-\infty}^{\infty} f_{X,Y}(x,y)dy = \int_0^1 2(1-x)dy = 2(1-x),\ 0 \le x \le 1.$$

$$f_Y(y) = \int_{-\infty}^{\infty} f_{X,Y}(x,y)\,dx = \int_0^1 2(1-x)dx = 1,\ 0 \le y \le 1.$$

Figure 4.13 shows the joint pdf as well as the marginal pdfs.

Assuming X and Y are two dependent continuous random variables, the ***conditional pdf*** of Y given $X=x$, and the conditional pdf of X given $Y=y$ are, respectively, defined as follows:

$$\begin{aligned} f_{Y/X}(y/x) &= \frac{f_{X,Y}(x,y)}{f_X(x)} \\ f_{X/Y}(x/y) &= \frac{f_{X,Y}(x,y)}{f_Y(y)} \end{aligned} \tag{4.36}$$

EXAMPLE 4.19

Suppose $f_{X,Y}(x,y) = \begin{cases} \frac{1}{2}, & 0 \le x \le y \text{ and } 0 \le y \le 2. \\ 0, & \text{elsewhere} \end{cases}$

Determine the conditional pdf of X, given $Y=y$, and evaluate the probability that $X<\frac{1}{2}$, given $Y=1$.

Solution

Using (4.35), we first find the following:

$$f_Y(y)=\int_{-\infty}^{\infty} f_{X,Y}(x,y)dx=\int_0^y\left(\frac{1}{2}\right)dx=\frac{y}{2}.$$

Using (4.36), we then find the following:

$$f_{X/Y}(x/y)=\frac{f_{X,Y}(x,y)}{f_y(y)}=\frac{\frac{1}{2}}{\frac{y}{2}}=\frac{1}{y},\quad 0\le y\le 2$$

We can now determine the conditional probability:

$$P\left(X\le\frac{1}{2}/Y=1\right)=\int_0^{1/2} f_{X/Y}(x/y=1)\,dx=\int_0^{1/2}\left(\frac{1}{1}\right)dx=\frac{1}{2}.$$

4.2.8 Independent, Uncorrelated, and Orthogonal Random Variables

The random variables X and Y are ***independent*** if and only if their joint cdf is equal to the product of the marginal cdfs or equivalently if and only if their joint pdf is equal to the product of the marginal pdfs, as shown below:

$$\begin{aligned} F_{X,Y}(x,y)&=F_X(x)F_Y(y)\\ f_{X,Y}(x,y)&=f_X(x)f_Y(y)\end{aligned} \tag{4.37}$$

If X and Y are independent random variables, then the random variables defined by any pair of functions $g(X)$ and $h(Y)$ are also independent.

EXAMPLE 4.20

The joint pdf for the random variables X and Y is given by $f_{X,Y}(x,y)=x+y$ for $0\le x\le 1$ and $0\le y\le 1$. Are X and Y statistically independent?

Solution

Using (4.35), we obtain the marginal pdfs as follows:

$$f_X(x)=\int_{-\infty}^{\infty} f_{X,Y}(x,y)dy=\int_0^1(x+y)dy=x+0.5,\quad 0\le x\le 1.$$

$$f_Y(y)=\int_{-\infty}^{\infty} f_{X,Y}(x,y)dx=\int_0^1(x+y)dx=y+0.5,\quad 0\le y\le 1.$$

Since we have

$$f_{X,Y}(x,y) = (x+y) \neq (x+0.5)(y+0.5) = f_X(x)f_Y(y)$$

The random variables X and Y are not statistically independent.

The expected value of $g(X, Y)$, which is a function of two random variables X and Y, is defined as follows:

$$E[g(X,Y)] = \int_{-\infty}^{\infty}\int_{-\infty}^{\infty} g(X,Y) f_{X,Y}(x,y)\,dx\,dy \tag{4.38}$$

EXAMPLE 4.21

Let $Z = X + Y$. Find $E[Z]$.

Solution

Using (4.38), we have the following:

$$E[Z] = \int_{-\infty}^{\infty}\int_{-\infty}^{\infty} (x+y) f_{X,Y}(x,y)\,dx\,dy = \int_{-\infty}^{\infty}\int_{-\infty}^{\infty} x f_{X,Y}(x,y)\,dx\,dy + \int_{-\infty}^{\infty}\int_{-\infty}^{\infty} y f_{X,Y}(x,y)\,dx\,dy$$

$$= \int_{-\infty}^{\infty} x\left(\int_{-\infty}^{\infty} f_{X,Y}(x,y)\,dy\right)dx + \int_{-\infty}^{\infty} y\left(\int_{-\infty}^{\infty} f_{X,Y}(x,y)\,dx\right)dy$$

$$= \int_{-\infty}^{\infty} x f_X(x)\,dx + \int_{-\infty}^{\infty} y f_Y(y)\,dy = E[X] + E[Y].$$

Thus, the expected value of the sum of two random variables is equal to the sum of the individual expected values. This is an important result, especially in view of the fact that X and Y random variables need not to be independent.

EXAMPLE 4.22

Suppose the random variables X and Y are independent and we have $g(X, Y) = f(X)h(Y)$. Show that $E[g(X, Y)] = E[f(X)]\,E[h(Y)]$.

Solution

Using (4.38), we can obtain the following:

$$E[g(X,Y)] = \int_{-\infty}^{\infty}\int_{-\infty}^{\infty} f(x)h(y) f_{X,Y}(x,y)\,dx\,dy = \int_{-\infty}^{\infty}\int_{-\infty}^{\infty} f(x)h(y) f_X(x) f_Y(y)\,dx\,dy$$

$$= \left\{\int_{-\infty}^{\infty} f(x) f_X(x)\,dx\right\}\left\{\int_{-\infty}^{\infty} h(y) f_Y(y)\,dy\right\} = E[f(x)]\,E[h(y)].$$

Additionally, for the special case of $g(X, Y) = f(X)h(Y) = X^jY^k$, and for any real j and k, we have $E[X^jY^k] = E[X^j]E[Y^k]$. This is an important result for independent random variables.

The ***covariance*** of two random variables X and Y, which measures the degree of similarity between X and Y, is defined as follows:

$$COV(X, Y) = E[(X - E[X])(Y - E[Y]) = E[XY] - E[X]E[Y] \tag{4.39a}$$

The ***correlation coefficient***, which is the normalized version of the covariance, is defined as follows:

$$\rho_{X,Y} = \frac{COV(X, Y)}{\sigma_X \sigma_Y} = \frac{E[XY] - E[X]E[Y]}{\sigma_X \sigma_Y} \tag{4.39b}$$

The correlation coefficient provides a measure of the linear dependence between the random variables X and Y, and can be at most 1 in magnitude. It is insightful to know that a ***positive correlation coefficient*** implies X and Y both increase or decrease together, and a ***negative correlation coefficient*** indicates when X increases, Y decreases, and vice versa. If $\rho_{X,Y} = \pm 1$, then Y can be predicted by a linear function of X, i.e., $Y = aX + b$, where $a \neq 0$ and b are some constants. Note that for $\rho_{X,Y} = 1$, we have $a > 0$, and for $\rho_{X,Y} = -1$, we have $a < 0$.

The random variables X and Y are ***uncorrelated*** if and only if $E[XY] = E[X]E[Y]$, i.e., $\rho_{X,Y} = 0$, and they are ***orthogonal*** if and only if $E[XY] = 0$. As shown earlier, if X and Y are independent, we have $E[X^j Y^k] = E[X^j]E[Y^k]$, including when $j = k = 1$. It is then obvious that X and Y are uncorrelated (i.e., $E[XY] = E[X]E[Y]$) when they are independent. That is, independence indicates absence of correlation. However, the converse, in general, is not always true, i.e., it is possible for X and Y to be uncorrelated, but not independent. As discussed later, there is only one special case for which independence and uncorrelatedness are equivalent, and that is when the random variables X and Y are jointly Gaussian.

EXAMPLE 4.23

Let θ be uniformly distributed in the interval $[0, 2\pi]$. Let $X = \cos(\theta)$ and $Y = \sin(\theta)$. Are X and Y are independent? Are they uncorrelated? Are they orthogonal?

Solution

If X and Y were independent, the point (X, Y) would assume all values in the square $-1 \leq x \leq 1$ and $-1 \leq y \leq 1$. However, this is not the case. Since x and y are related according to $x^2 + y^2 = \cos^2(\theta) + \sin^2(\theta) = 1$, X and Y are not independent. We now find the following:

$$E[XY] = E[\cos(\theta)\sin(\theta)] = \int_0^{2\pi} (\cos(\theta)\sin(\theta))\left(\frac{1}{2\pi}\right) d\theta = \int_0^{2\pi} \frac{1}{2}\sin(2\theta)\left(\frac{1}{2\pi}\right) d\theta = 0$$

X and Y are thus orthogonal. Noting that $E[X] = E[Y] = 0$, we have $E[XY] = E[X]E[Y]$, X and Y are also uncorrelated.

4.2.9 Jointly Gaussian Random Variables

The random variables X and Y are ***jointly Gaussian*** if their joint pdf, for $-\infty < x < \infty$ and $-\infty < y < \infty$, has the following form:

$$f_{X,Y}(x,y) = \frac{\exp\left\{-\frac{1}{2\left(1-\rho_{X,Y}^2\right)}\left(\left(\frac{x-m_X}{\sigma_X}\right)^2 - 2\rho_{X,Y}\left(\frac{x-m_X}{\sigma_X}\right)\left(\frac{y-m_Y}{\sigma_Y}\right)+\left(\frac{y-m_Y}{\sigma_Y}\right)^2\right)\right\}}{2\pi\sigma_X\sigma_Y\sqrt{1-\rho_{X,Y}^2}} \tag{4.40}$$

where m_X and m_Y are the mean values, and σ_X and σ_Y are the standard deviations of the random variables X and Y, respectively, and $\rho_{X,Y}$ is the correlation coefficient between X and Y. To determine the probability, we need to find the volume under $f_{X,Y}(x,y)$ for the particular region of interest in the x-y plane. Some of the important properties of the jointly Gaussian random variables are as follows:

- If $\rho_{X,Y} = 0$, then the random variables X and Y are not only uncorrelated, but they are also statistically independent.
- If $\sigma_X = \sigma_Y$ and $\rho_{X,Y} = 0$, then the equal-pdf contour is a circle, otherwise it is an ellipse.
- The marginal pdf of X and that of Y are both Gaussian random variables.
- The conditional pdf of X given $Y = y$ and that of Y given $X = x$ are individually Gaussian random variables.

EXAMPLE 4.24

Suppose X and Y are jointly Gaussian random variables. Show that if they are uncorrelated (i.e., $\rho_{X,Y} = 0$), then they are statistically independent.

Solution

With $\rho_{X,Y} = 0$, (4.40) simplifies to the following:

$$f_{X,Y}(x,y) = \frac{1}{2\pi\sigma_X\sigma_Y}\exp\left\{-\frac{1}{2}\left[\left(\frac{x-m_X}{\sigma_X}\right)^2+\left(\frac{y-m_Y}{\sigma_Y}\right)^2\right]\right\}$$

Using (4.35), we can obtain the marginal pdfs $f_X(x)$ and $f_Y(y)$ as follows:

$$f_X(x) = \left(\frac{1}{\sqrt{2\pi\sigma_X{}^2}}\right)\exp\left(-\frac{(x-m_X)^2}{2\sigma_X{}^2}\right)$$

$$f_Y(y) = \left(\frac{1}{\sqrt{2\pi\sigma_Y{}^2}}\right)\exp\left(-\frac{(y-m_Y)^2}{2\sigma_Y{}^2}\right)$$

We thus have $f_{X,Y}(x,y) = f_X(x)f_Y(y)$, which implies X and Y are statistically independent.

4.2.10 Sum of Random Variables

If the random variable Z is the sum of n independent random variables x_1, x_2, ..., x_n, then the pdf of the sum Z is the convolution of the pdf of x_1, the pdf of x_2, ..., and the pdf of x_n.

EXAMPLE 4.25

A random variable is defined as the sum of four independent and identically-distributed random variables. Assuming the pdf of each has a uniform distribution in the interval $\left[-\frac{1}{2}, \frac{1}{2}\right]$, determine the pdf of the sum.

Solution

Note that the convolution of the two functions $f_{X_1}(x)$ and $f_{X_2}(x)$ is defined as follows:

$$f_{X_1}(x) * f_{X_2}(x) = \int_{-\infty}^{\infty} f_{X_1}(t) f_{X_2}(x-t)dt$$

where * denotes the convolution operation. We first find the pdf of the sum of two uniformly-distributed random variables. The pdf of $b = a_1 + a_2$ is the convolution of the pdfs of a_1 and a_2. It is well known that the convolution of two identical square-shape functions results in a triangular-shape function and is thus as follows:

$$f_B(b) = \begin{cases} 1-|b|, & |b| \leq 1 \\ 0, & |b| > 1 \end{cases}$$

We then find the pdf of the sum of three random variables. The pdf of $c = a_1 + a_2 + a_3 = b + a_3$ is the convolution of the pdfs of b and a_3, and is thus as follows:

$$f_C(c) = \begin{cases} 0.75 - c^2, & |c| \leq 0.5 \\ 0.5\,(1.5 - |c|)^2, & 0.5 \leq |c| \leq 1.5 \\ 0, & 1.5 \leq |c| \end{cases}$$

We finally find the pdf of the sum of four random variables. The pdf of $d = a_1 + a_2 + a_3 + a_4 = c + a_4$ is the convolution of the pdfs of c and a_4, and is thus as follows:

$$f_D(d) = \begin{cases} \frac{|d|^3}{2} - d^2 + \frac{2}{3}, & 0 \leq |d| < 1 \\ -\frac{|d|^3}{6} + d^2 - 2|d| + \frac{4}{3}, & 1 \leq |d| < 2 \\ 0 & 2 \leq |d| \end{cases}$$

Figure 4.14 shows the pdfs of one single variable, the sum of two variables, the sum of three random variables, and the sum of four random variables. The total interval of the convolution is the sum of the intervals of the functions being convoluted. To this effect, by adding more random variables, the pdf of the sum becomes wider and closer to that of a Gaussian random variable.

The variance of the sum of random variables is equal to the sum of the individual variances only if the random variables are statistically independent. However, the expected value of the sum of random variables is always equal to the sum of the individual expected values, whether the random variables are statistically independent or not. The sum of a number of independent Gaussian random variables with their respective means and variances is a Gaussian random variable whose mean is the sum of the means and variance is the sum of the variances.

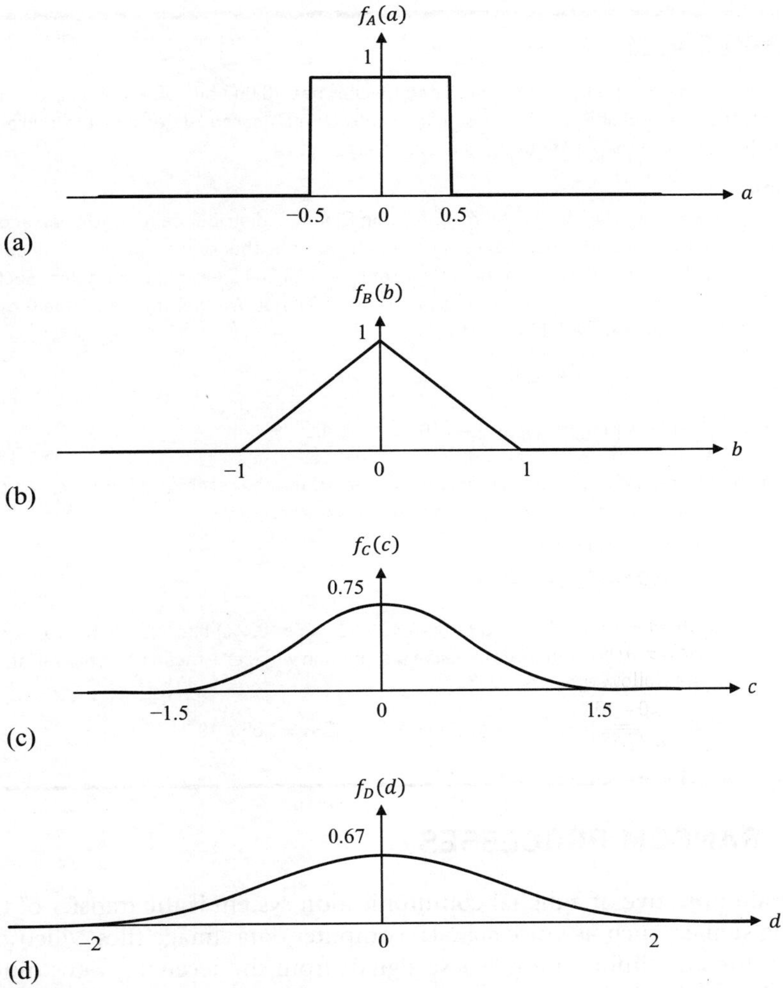

FIGURE 4.14 (a) pdf of one variable, (b) pdf of sum of two variables, (c) pdf of sum of three variables, and (d) pdf of sum of four variables.

Let S be the sum of n independent identically-distributed (iid) random variables, each with finite mean m and finite variance σ^2. Therefore, the mean of S is nm and its variance is $n\sigma^2$. Let V be the normalized sum with zero-mean and unit-variance, i.e., $V = (S - nm)/\sigma\sqrt{n}$. The ***central limit theorem*** states as $n \to \infty$, the pdf of V, regardless of the distribution of the n random variables, can be approximated by a Gaussian random variable with zero-mean and unit-variance. Based on the central limit theorem, thermal noise is assumed to have Gaussian distribution. The Gaussian distribution thus plays a central role in communications.

EXAMPLE 4.26

In a binary communication channel, each data packet has 10,000 bits. Each bit can be in error independently with probability of 10^{-3}. Using the central limit theorem, determine the approximate probability that more than 0.4% of the bits are in error.

Solution

There are two ways to solve this problem, one using Binomial distribution to provide an accurate, but time-consuming result, and one using the central limit theorem to provide a good quick approximation. The focus here is on the latter. There are 10,000 iid random variables. Each random variable is assumed to be 1 if the bit is in error and 0 if not. We therefore have the mean and variance for each random variable as follows:

$$\text{Mean} = 10^{-3}(1) + \left(1 - 10^{-3}\right)(0) = 10^{-3}$$

$$\text{Variance} = \left(10^{-3}(1)^2 + \left(1 - 10^{-3}\right)(0)^2\right) - \left(10^{-3}\right)^2 = 0.000999$$

Based on the central limit theorem, S is assumed to be the number of errors in the packet, and has a Gaussian distribution with the following mean and variance:

$$\text{Mean} = nm = 10000 \times 0.001 = 10$$

$$\text{Variance} = n\sigma^2 = 10000 \times 0.000999 = 9.99$$

The number of erroneous bits S is greater than 40 ($= 10000 \times 0.4\%$) bits. Noting the random variable $V = (S - nm)/\sigma\sqrt{n}$ is a standard Gaussian distribution with zero-mean and unit-variance, we can thus have the following:

$$P(S > 40) = P\left(V > \frac{40 - 10}{\sqrt{9.99}}\right) = P(V > 9.49158) = Q(9.49158) = 1.05 \times 10^{-21}$$

4.3 RANDOM PROCESSES

The main objective of a digital communication system is the transfer of time-varying signals, such as voice signals, computer data, image files, video clips, and multimedia information. These signals from the receiving viewpoint are unpredictable; otherwise their transmissions serve no purpose, and thus become unnecessary. In addition, there are sources of channel degradation, such as noise, interference, and fading that are random functions of time. Hence, the study of random processes is imperative to digital communications.

4.3.1 Basic Concepts

Each sample point in the sample space is a function of time, and the sample space comprising functions of time is called a ***random process*** or ***stochastic process***. The notion of a random process is an extension of the random variable concept; the difference is that in random processes, the mapping is done onto signals (functions of time) rather than onto constants (real numbers). The basic connection between the concept of a random process and the concept of a random variable is at any particular instant of time the value of a random process is a random variable.

To every outcome (sample point) w in the sample space S, according to some rule, a function of time is assigned. The graph of the function $X(t, w)$ versus t, for w fixed, is called a ***sample function*** of the random process. For a given $w = w_i$, a specific function of time t, i.e., $X(t, w_i)$, is produced, and for a specific time $t = t_k$, $X(t_k, w)$ is a random variable, as it maps w onto the real line. For a specific w_i and a specific t_k, $X(t_k, w_i)$ is simply a number. An ensemble of $X(t, w)$ is called a random process.

EXAMPLE 4.27

Suppose we have $X(t, \theta) = A\cos(2\pi f_c t + \theta)$, where the amplitude A and the frequency f_c are known constants, and θ is a discrete random variable with $P(\theta = 0) = 1/2$ and $P(\theta = \pi) = 1/2$. Is $X(t, \theta)$ a random process?

Solution

$X(t, \theta)$ is a random process because it comprises random time-varying functions. The value of the signal is a function of time and the random variable θ representing the random phase of the sinusoidal signal. The two sample functions of this random process are as follows: $X(t, 0) = A\cos(2\pi f_c t)$ and $X(t, \pi) = A\cos(2\pi f_c t + \pi) = -A\cos(2\pi f_c t)$.

EXAMPLE 4.28

Suppose we have $X(t, A) = A\cos\left(2\pi f_c t + \frac{\pi}{2}\right)$, where A is a uniform random variable in the interval $[-1, 1]$ and the frequency f_c is a known constant. Is $X(t, A)$ a random process?

Solution

$X(t, A)$ is a random process because it comprises random time-varying functions. The value of the signal is a function of time and the random variable A representing the random amplitude of the sinusoidal signal. This random process has infinitely many sample functions, a couple of which are as follows: $X(t, -1) = -1\cos\left(2\pi f_c t + \frac{\pi}{2}\right) = \sin(2\pi f_c t)$, $X(t, 0) = 0$, and $X(t, 1) = \cos\left(2\pi f_c t + \frac{\pi}{2}\right) = -\sin(2\pi f_c t)$.

It is common to suppress w, and simply let $X(t)$ denote a random process. As a random process at a given time is a random variable, it can thus be described with a pdf. In general, the form of the pdf of a random process is different for different instants of time. In most cases, it is not possible to determine the pdf of a random process at a certain time or the joint pdf at two or many different times, because all sample functions are generally not known.

A stochastic process is specified by the collection of kth ***-order joint cdfs or pdfs***, for any k and any choice of sampling instants $t_1, \ldots, t_k$. Let $X(t_1), \ldots, X(t_k)$ be the

k random variables obtained by sampling the random process $X(t)$ at times $t_1, \ldots, t_k$. Assuming the stochastic process is continuous-valued, then its joint cdf and pdf are, respectively, defined as follows:

$$F_{X(t_1),\ldots,X(t_k)}(x_1,\ldots,x_k) = P[X(t_1) \le x_1, \ldots, X(t_k) \le x_k]$$
$$f_{X(t_1),\ldots,X(t_k)}(x_1,\ldots,x_k) = \frac{\partial^k F_{X(t_1),\ldots,X(t_k)}(x_1,\ldots,x_k)}{\partial x_1 \ldots \partial x_k} \tag{4.41}$$

Note that for $k=1$, the cdf and pdf of the random process $X(t)$ at time t are then represented by $F_{X(t)}(x)$ and $f_{X(t)}(x)$, respectively.

4.3.2 Statistical Averages

The ***mean and variance functions of the random process*** $X(t)$ are, in general, both deterministic functions of time, and defined, respectively, as follows:

$$m_X(t) = E[X(t)] = \int_{-\infty}^{\infty} x f_{X(t)}(x)dx$$
$$\sigma_X^2(t) = E\left[(X(t) - E[X(t)])^2\right] = \int_{-\infty}^{\infty} (x - m_X(t))^2 f_{X(t)}(x)dx \tag{4.42}$$

The ***autocorrelation and autocovariance functions*** of the random process $X(t)$ are, in general, functions of t_1 and t_2, and are defined, respectively, as follows:

$$R_X(t_1,t_2) = E[X(t_1)X(t_2)] = \int_{-\infty}^{\infty}\int_{-\infty}^{\infty} x_1 x_2 f_{X(t_1),X(t_2)}(x_1,x_2)dx_1dx_2$$
$$\begin{aligned} C_X(t_1,t_2) &= E[(X(t_1) - m_X(t_1))(X(t_2) - m_X(t_2))] \\ &= \int_{-\infty}^{\infty}\int_{-\infty}^{\infty} (x_1 - m_X(t_1))(x_2 - m_X(t_2)) f_{X(t_1),X(t_2)}(x_1,x_2)dx_1dx_2 \\ &= R_X(t_1,t_2) - m_X(t_1)m_X(t_2) \end{aligned} \tag{4.43}$$

Note that $f_{X(t_1),X(t_2)}(x_1,x_2)$ is the joint pdf of random variables $X(t_1)$ and $X(t_2)$. The ***correlation coefficient***—defined as a measure of the extent to which a random variable $X(t_1)$ can be predicted as a linear function of the random variable $X(t_2)$ —is given as follows:

$$\rho_X(t_1,t_2) = \frac{C_X(t_1,t_2)}{\sqrt{C_X(t_1,t_1)}\sqrt{C_X(t_2,t_2)}} \tag{4.44}$$

EXAMPLE 4.29

Let $X(t) = R\cos(2\pi t)$, where R is a random variable whose mean and variance are m_R and σ_R^2, respectively. Determine the mean, variance, autocorrelation, and covariance functions, and correlation coefficient of $X(t)$.

Solution

At time t, $\cos(2\pi t)$ is a constant, and $X(t)$ is thus a random variable. Using (4.42), the mean and variance functions of $X(t)$ are then as follows:

$$m_X(t) = E[X(t)] = E[R\cos(2\pi t)] = E[R]\cos(2\pi t) = m_R\cos(2\pi t)$$

$$\begin{aligned}\sigma_X^2(t) &= E\left[X^2(t)\right] - (E[X(t)])^2 = E\left[R^2\cos^2(2\pi t)\right] - (E[R])^2\cos^2(2\pi t)\\ &= E\left[R^2\right]\cos^2(2\pi t) - (E[R])^2\cos^2(2\pi t)\\ &= \left(E\left[R^2\right] - (E[R])^2\right)\cos^2(2\pi t)\\ &= \sigma_R^2\cos^2(2\pi t)\end{aligned}$$

Note that the mean and variance of the random process are both functions of time. Using (4.43), the autocorrelation and autocovariance functions of $X(t)$ are, respectively, as follows:

$$\begin{aligned}R_X(t_1,t_2) &= E[X(t_1)X(t_2)] = E[R\cos(2\pi t_1)R\cos(2\pi t_2)] = E\left[R^2\right]\cos(2\pi t_1)\cos(2\pi t_2)\\ &= (\sigma_R^2 + m_R^2)\cos(2\pi t_1)\cos(2\pi t_2)\end{aligned}$$

$$\begin{aligned}C_X(t_1,t_2) &= E[(X(t_1) - m_X(t_1))(X(t_2) - m_X(t_2))] = R_X(t_1,t_2) - m_X(t_1)m_X(t_2) =\\ &= (\sigma_R^2 + m_R^2)\cos(2\pi t_1)\cos(2\pi t_2) - (m_R\cos(2\pi t_1))\,(m_R\cos(2\pi t_2))\\ &= \sigma_R^2\cos(2\pi t_1)\cos(2\pi t_2)\end{aligned}$$

Note that the autocorrelation and autocovariance functions are individually a function of t_1 and t_2. Using (4.44), the correlation coefficient is then as follows:

$$\begin{aligned}\rho_X(t_1,t_2) &= \frac{C_X(t_1,t_2)}{\sqrt{C_X(t_1,t_1)}\sqrt{C_X(t_2,t_2)}} = \frac{\sigma_R^2\cos(2\pi t_1)\cos(2\pi t_2)}{\sqrt{\sigma_R^2\cos(2\pi t_1)\cos(2\pi t_1)}\sqrt{\sigma_R^2\cos(2\pi t_2)\cos(2\pi t_2)}}\\ &= \frac{\cos(2\pi t_1)\cos(2\pi t_2)}{|\cos(2\pi t_1)||\cos(2\pi t_2)|}\end{aligned}$$

If t_1 and t_2 are chosen in such a way that $\cos(2\pi t_1)$ and $\cos(2\pi t_2)$ have different signs, then $\rho_X(t_1,t_2) = -1$ and if they have the same signs, we then have $\rho_X(t_1,t_2) = 1$.

4.3.3 Stationary Processes

A random process at a given time is a random variable and, in general, the characteristics of this random variable depend on the time at which the random process is sampled. A random process $X(t)$ is said to be ***stationary*** or ***strict-sense stationary*** if the pdf of any set of samples does not vary with time. In other words, the joint pdf or cdf of $X(t_1)$, …, $X(t_k)$ is the same as the joint pdf or cdf of $X(t_1 + \tau)$, …, $X(t_k + \tau)$ for any time shift τ, and for all choices of t_1, …, t_k. A ***nonstationary process*** is characterized by a joint pdf or cdf that depends on time instants t_1, …, t_k. For a stationary random process, the mean and variance are both constants (i.e., neither of them is a function of time).

In principle, it is difficult to determine if a process is stationary, moreover, stationary processes cannot occur physically, because in reality signals begin at some finite time and end at some finite time. Due to practical considerations, we simply consider the observation interval to be limited, and usually use the first and second order statistics rather than the joint pdfs and cdfs. Since it is difficult to determine the distribution of a random process, the focus usually becomes on a partial, yet useful, description of the distribution of the process, such as the mean, autocorrelation, and autocovariance functions of the random process.

A random process $X(t)$ is a ***wide-sense stationary process*** if its mean is a constant (i.e., it is independent of time), and its autocorrelation function depends only on the time difference $\tau = t_2 - t_1$ and not on t_1 and t_2 individually. In other words, in a wide-sense stationary process, the mean and autocorrelation functions do not depend on the choice of the time origin. All random processes that are stationary in the strict sense are wide-sense stationary, but the converse, in general, is not true. However, if a Gaussian random process is wide-sense stationary, then it is also stationary in the strict sense. If $X(t)$ is wide-sense stationary, we then have the following:

$$m_X(t) = E[X(t)] = \text{Constant}$$
$$R_X(t_1, t_2) = E[X(t_1)X(t_2)] = R_X(t_2 - t_1) = R_X(\tau) \tag{4.45}$$

In a wide-sense stationary random process, the autocorrelation function $R_X(\tau)$ has the following properties:

- $R_X(\tau)$ is an even function.
- $R_X(0) = E[X^2(t)]$ gives the average power (second moment) or the mean-square value of the random process.
- The maximum value of $R_X(\tau)$ occurs at $\tau = 0$, i.e., $|R_X(\tau)| \le R_X(0)$.
- The more rapidly $X(t)$ changes with time t, the more rapidly $R_X(\tau)$ decreases from its maximum $R_X(0)$ as τ increases, simply because the autocorrelation function is a measure of the rate of change of a random process.
- The autocorrelation function can have three types of components:
  - a component that approaches zero as $\tau \to \infty$ (e.g., an exponential function),
  - a periodic component (e.g., a sinusoidal function), and
  - a constant component representing the mean squared of the random process.

It is important to note that a wide-sense stationary random process yields a unique autocorrelation function, but the converse is not true (i.e., two different wide-sense stationary random processes may have the same autocorrelation function).

EXAMPLE 4.30

Consider a random process $X(t)$ defined as follows:

$X(t) = A\cos(t) + B\sin(t)$

where A and B are uncorrelated random variables with zero-mean and unit-variance. Is $X(t)$ wide-sense stationary?

Solution

We thus have $E[A]=E[B]=0$. Since A and B are uncorrelated, we have $E[AB]=E[A]E[B]=0$. Since $\sigma_A^2=E[A^2]-(E[A])^2=1$ and $\sigma_B^2=E[B^2]-(E[B])^2=1$, we have $E[A^2]=E[B^2]=1$. Using (4.42) and (4.43), the mean and autocorrelation functions are then as follows:

$$m_X(t)=E[X(t)]=E[A\cos(t)+B\sin(t)]=E[A\cos(t)]+E[B\sin(t)]=E[A]\cos(t)+E[B]\sin(t)=0$$

and

$$\begin{aligned}R_X(t,t+\tau)&=E[X(t)X(t+\tau)]=E[(A\cos(t)+B\sin(t))(A\cos(t+\tau)+B\sin(t+\tau))]\\&=E[A^2]\cos(t)\cos(t+\tau)+E[B^2]\sin(t)\sin(t+\tau)=\cos(t)\cos(t+\tau)+\sin(t)\sin(t+\tau)\\&=\cos(\tau)\end{aligned}$$

Since the mean is not a function of time and the autocorrelation is a function of the time difference τ, $X(t)$ is a wide-sense stationary random process.

In digital communications, we often need to deal with more than one random process at a time. For instance, when $X(t)$ is the input to a system and another process $Y(t)$ is the output of the system, we may need to assess the inter-relatedness between $X(t)$ and $Y(t)$. The joint behavior of two random processes is specified by the collection of joint cdfs for all possible choices of time samples of the processes. $X(t)$ and $Y(t)$ are ***independent random processes*** if the random vectors $\{X(t_1), \ldots, X(t_k)\}$ and $\{Y(t_1^{'}), \ldots, Y(t_j^{'})\}$ are independent for all k, j, and for all $t_1, \ldots, t_k$ and $t_1^{'}, \ldots, t_j^{'}$, i.e., the joint cdfs is equal to the product of the individual cdfs or equivalently, the joint pdfs is equal to the product of the individual pdfs.

The ***cross-correlation function*** of two random processes $X(t)$ and $Y(t)$ is defined by

$$R_{XY}(t_1, t_2)=E[X(t_1)Y(t_2)]=R_{YX}(t_2, t_1) \tag{4.46}$$

The random processes $X(t)$ and $Y(t)$ are ***jointly wide-sense stationary***, if $X(t)$ and $Y(t)$ are both wide-sense stationary and if their cross-correlation depends only on $\tau=t_1-t_2$, i.e., when we have:

$$R_{XY}(\tau)=E[X(t)Y(t+\tau)]=R_{YX}(-\tau) \tag{4.47}$$

The wide-sense stationary random processes $X(t)$ and $Y(t)$ are ***uncorrelated*** if the cross-correlation function is equal to the product of their means, and they are ***orthogonal*** if their cross-correlation is zero. In other words, we have the following:

$$\begin{aligned}&R_{XY}(\tau)=E[X(t)Y(t+\tau)]=E[X(t)]E[Y(t+\tau)] \Leftrightarrow \text{Uncorrelated processes}\\&R_{XY}(\tau)=E[X(t)Y(t+\tau)]=0 \Leftrightarrow \text{Orthogonal processes}\end{aligned} \tag{4.48}$$

EXAMPLE 4.31

Consider a pair of random processes $X(t)$ and $Y(t)$ that are defined as follows:

$$\begin{aligned}X(t)&=W(t)\cos(2\pi t+\theta)\\Y(t)&=W(t)\sin(2\pi t+\theta)\end{aligned}$$

where $W(t)$ is a wide-sense stationary process and the random variable θ, which is independent of $W(t)$, is uniformly distributed in the interval $[0, 2\pi]$. Determine the cross-correlation of $X(t)$ and $Y(t)$ as well as the conditions where $X(t)$ and $Y(t)$ can be orthogonal to each other.

Solution

Using (4.46), we have

$R_{XY}(t_1, t_2) = E[X(t_1)Y(t_2)] = E[W(t_1)\cos(2\pi t_1 + \theta)W(t_2)\sin(2\pi t_2 + \theta)]$

Since $W(t)$ and θ are independent, we can then have:

$R_{XY}(t_1, t_2) = E[W(t_1)W(t_2)]\,E[\cos(2\pi t_1 + \theta)\sin(2\pi t_2 + \theta)]$

Noting $W(t)$ is wide-sense stationary and using a trigonometric identity, we thus have:

$$\begin{aligned} R_{XY}(t_1, t_2) &= R_W(t_1 - t_2)E\left[\frac{1}{2}(\sin(2\pi t_1 + 2\pi t_2 + 2\theta) - \sin(2\pi t_1 - 2\pi t_2))\right] \\ &= \frac{1}{2}R_W(t_1 - t_2)(E[\sin(2\pi t_1 + 2\pi t_2 + 2\theta)] - E[\sin(2\pi t_1 - 2\pi t_2)]) \\ &= -\frac{1}{2}R_W(t_1 - t_2)\sin(2\pi t_1 - 2\pi t_2) = -\frac{1}{2}R_W(\tau)\sin(2\pi\tau). \end{aligned}$$

In order to have $X(t)$ and $Y(t)$ orthogonal to each other, the cross-correlation must be zero. In other words, the values of τ for which $R_W(\tau) = 0$ or $\sin(2\pi\tau) = 0$ (i.e., $\tau = \frac{k}{2}$, $k = 0, \pm 1, \pm 2, \ldots$) can ensure orthogonality of $X(t)$ and $Y(t)$.

4.3.4 Ergodic Processes

In a stationary process, the mean and autocorrelation functions are determined by ensemble averaging (i.e., averaging across all sample functions of the process). This in turn requires complete knowledge of the first-order and second-order joint pdfs of the process. In practice, it is difficult, if not impossible, to observe all sample functions of a random process at a given time. It is more likely to be able to observe a single sample function for a long period of time. We thus define the ***time-averaged mean, variance and autocorrelation functions*** of the sample function $x(t)$, respectively, as follows:

$$\begin{aligned} \langle x(t)\rangle &= \lim_{T\to\infty}\left(\frac{1}{2T}\right)\int_{-T}^{T} x(t)dt \\ \langle (x(t) - \langle x(t)\rangle)^2\rangle &= \lim_{T\to\infty}\left(\frac{1}{2T}\right)\int_{-T}^{T} (x(t) - \langle x(t)\rangle)^2 dt \qquad (4.49) \\ \langle x(t)x(t-\tau)\rangle &= \lim_{T\to\infty}\left(\frac{1}{2T}\right)\int_{-T}^{T} x(t)x(t-\tau)dt \end{aligned}$$

where $\langle\,\rangle$ is used to denote the time averaging operation. These averages are random variables, because their values depend on which sample function of the random process $X(t)$ is used in the time-averaging calculations. Except for the autocorrelation function, which is an ordinary function of the variable τ, the mean and the variance both turn out to be constants. In general, the time averages and ensemble averages are not equal.

If all statistical properties of the random process $X(t)$ can be determined from a single sample function, then the random process is said to be ***strict-sense ergodic***. For a random process to be ergodic, it must be strictly stationary, but the converse is not always true. For ergodic processes, the moments can be determined by time averages as well as ensemble averages, simply put, all time and ensemble averages are interchangeable, not just the mean, variance, and autocorrelation functions.

In general, we are not interested in estimating all the ensemble averages but rather only certain averages, such as the mean, variance, and autocorrelation functions. As such, our focus lies in the class of ***wide-sense ergodic*** processes. It is generally difficult, if not impossible, to prove that ergodicity is a reasonable assumption for a physical process, as only one sample function can be observed. Nevertheless, ergodicity is assumed unless there are compelling physical reasons for not doing so, that is the ergodic property holds whenever needed.

DC power and AC power as well the total power are all measurable quantities for ergodic processes in the sense that they can be replaced by the corresponding time averages and a finite-time approximation to these time averages can be measured in the laboratory. In the context of electrical engineering power estimation, assuming $X(t)$ is an ergodic random process that may correspond to either a voltage or a current waveform across a one-ohm resistor, the square of the mean value represents the ***DC power***, the variance represents the ***AC power***, the standard deviation represents the root mean-square (rms) value, and the mean-square value indicates the ***total power*** (= DC power + AC power).

EXAMPLE 4.32

Suppose we have $X(t) = A\cos(2\pi f_c t + \theta)$, where the amplitude A and the frequency f_c are known constants, and θ is a continuous uniform random variable in the interval $\left[-\frac{\pi}{4}, \frac{\pi}{4}\right]$. Determine if this random process is ergodic.

Solution

Using (4.42), the expected value of the random process at an arbitrary time t is as follows:

$$E[X(t)] = E[A\cos(2\pi f_c t + \theta)] = \int_{-\pi/4}^{\pi/4} A\cos(2\pi f_c t + \theta)\left(\frac{2}{\pi}\right) d\theta = \frac{2\sqrt{2}A}{\pi}\cos(2\pi f_c t)$$

The mean is a function of time and hence it is not stationary. This process cannot be ergodic, since ergodicity requires stationarity.

EXAMPLE 4.33

Suppose we have $X(t) = A\cos(2\pi f_c t + \theta)$, where the amplitude A and the frequency f_c are known constants, and θ is a continuous uniform random variable in the interval $[0, 2\pi]$. Determine if this random process is ergodic.

Solution

Using (4.42) and (4.43), it is easy to show that the mean and the autocorrelation function are as follows:

$$m_X(t) = E[X(t)] = 0$$

$$R_X(\tau) = [X(t_1)X(t_2)] = \frac{A^2}{2}\cos 2\pi f_c \tau$$

It is therefore wide-sense stationary. Using (4.49), we now determine the time-averaged mean and autocorrelation functions of $X(t)$, respectively:

$$\begin{aligned}
\langle x(t)\rangle &= \lim_{T\to\infty}\left(\frac{1}{2T}\right)\int_{-T}^{T} x(t)dt = \lim_{T\to\infty}\left(\frac{1}{2T}\right)\int_{-T}^{T} A\cos(2\pi f_c t + \theta)dt \\
&= \lim_{T\to\infty}\left(\frac{1}{2T}\right)\frac{A}{2\pi f_c}(\sin(2\pi f_c T + \theta) - \sin(2\pi f_c(-T) + \theta)) \\
&= \lim_{T\to\infty}\left(\frac{1}{2T}\right)\frac{A}{2\pi f_c}(2\sin(2\pi f_c T)\cos\theta) = 0
\end{aligned}$$

$$\begin{aligned}
\langle x(t)x(t-\tau)\rangle &= \lim_{T\to\infty}\left(\frac{1}{2T}\right)\int_{-T}^{T} x(t)x(t-\tau)dt \\
&= \lim_{T\to\infty}\left(\frac{1}{2T}\right)\int_{-T}^{T} A\cos(2\pi f_c t + \theta)A\cos(2\pi f_c(t-\tau) + \theta)dt \\
&= \lim_{T\to\infty}\left(\frac{A^2}{4T}\right)\int_{-T}^{T} (\cos(4\pi f_c t - 2\pi f_c\tau + 2\theta) + \cos(2\pi f_c\tau))dt \\
&= \frac{A^2}{2}\cos(2\pi f_c\tau)
\end{aligned}$$

We showed that the time-averaged mean and autocorrelation functions are identical with the ensemble-averaged mean and autocorrelation functions and hence the random process is ergodic in wide-sense.

4.3.5 Power Spectral Density

To analyze deterministic time-domain signals in the frequency domain, we use the Fourier transform. In case of random processes, we could use the Fourier transform of a sample function; however, a single sample function in general falls short of being a representative of the whole ensemble of sample functions in a random process. A random process is a collection of sample functions, and the spectral characteristics of these signals determine the spectral characteristics of the random process. A statistical average of the sample functions is thus a more meaningful measure to reflect the spectral components of the random signal.

For wide-sense stationary processes, the autocorrelation function is an appropriate measure for the average rate of change of a random process. Figure 4.15 shows two sets of sample functions for slowly-varying and rapidly-varying wide-sense stationary random processes, and their representative autocorrelation functions. If the random signals are slowly time-varying, then the random process will mostly possess low frequencies and its power will be mostly concentrated at low frequencies. For such signals, the autocorrelation function is long in duration, and decreases slowly as the time difference between two samples is increased. On the other hand, if the random signals change very fast, then most power in the random process will be at high frequencies. For such signals, the autocorrelation function is short in duration, and decreases rapidly as the time difference between two samples is increased.

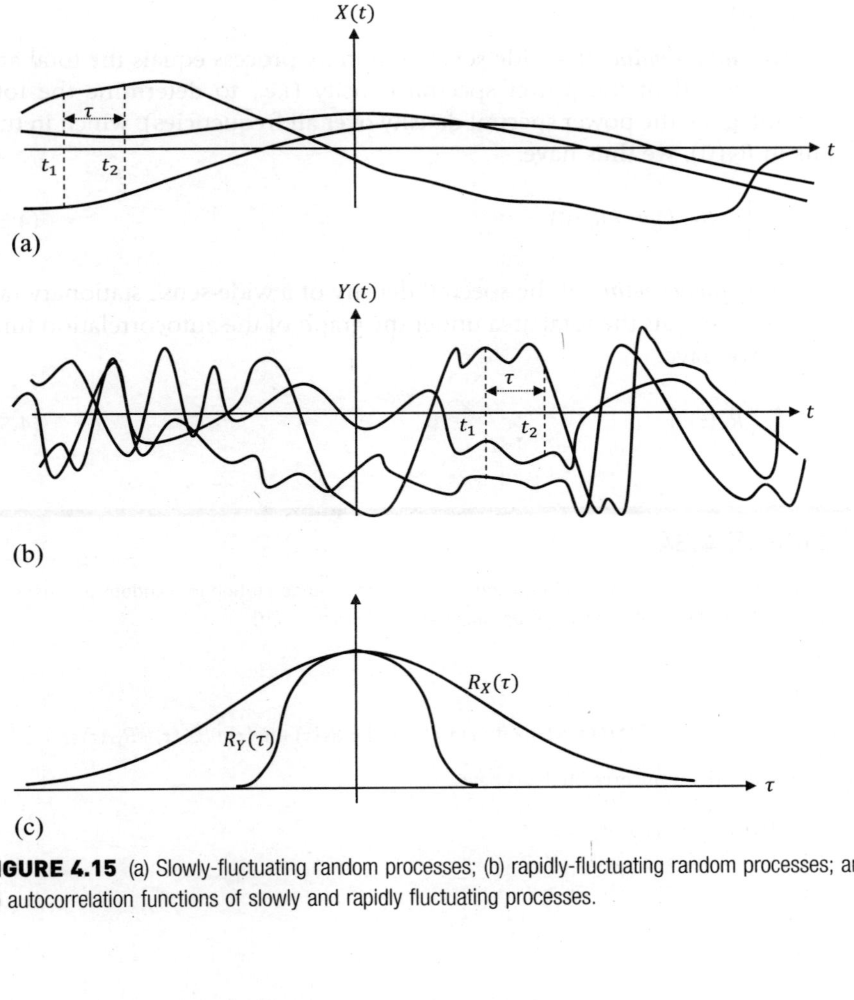

FIGURE 4.15 (a) Slowly-fluctuating random processes; (b) rapidly-fluctuating random processes; and (c) autocorrelation functions of slowly and rapidly fluctuating processes.

We now define the ***power spectral density*** or ***power spectrum*** of a random process which determines the distribution of the power of the random process at different frequencies. The power spectral density of a random process $X(t)$ is denoted by $S_X(f)$ and is measured by Watts per Hertz (W/Hz). ***Wiener-Khintchine theorem*** states that the power spectral density of a wide-sense stationary process and its autocorrelation function form a Fourier transform pair, as given by

$$\begin{aligned} S_X(f) &= F[R_X(\tau)] = \int_{-\infty}^{\infty} R_X(\tau) e^{-j2\pi f\tau} d\tau \\ R_X(\tau) &= F^{-1}[S_X(f)] = \int_{-\infty}^{\infty} S_X(f) e^{j2\pi f\tau} df \end{aligned} \tag{4.50}$$

The power spectral density of a wide-sense stationary random process is always real, nonnegative, and for a real-valued random process, it is an even function of frequency.

The ***mean-square value*** of a wide-sense stationary process equals the total area under the graph of the power spectral density (i.e., to determine the total power, integrate the power spectral density over all frequencies), which in turn results in $R_X(0)$, we thus have:

$$E[X^2(t)] = \int_{-\infty}^{\infty} S_X(f) df = R_X(0) \tag{4.51}$$

The ***zero-frequency value*** of the spectral density of a wide-sense stationary random process equals the total area under the graph of the autocorrelation function, i.e., we have:

$$S_X(0) = \int_{-\infty}^{\infty} R_X(\tau) d\tau \tag{4.52}$$

EXAMPLE 4.34

Suppose $X(t)$ and $Y(t)$ are uncorrelated, zero-mean, wide-sense stationary random processes. If $Z(t) = X(t) + Y(t)$, then determine the power spectral density of $Z(t)$.

Solution

Using (4.47), we have:

$$R_Z(\tau) = E[Z(t)Z(t+\tau)] = E[(X(t)+Y(t))(X(t+\tau)+Y(t+\tau))] = R_X(\tau) + R_Y(\tau) + R_{XY}(\tau) + R_{YX}(\tau)$$

Since $X(t)$ and $Y(t)$ are uncorrelated, we have:

$$R_{XY}(\tau) = E[X(t)]\, E[Y(t+\tau)] = R_{YX}(-\tau)$$

Since $X(t)$ and $Y(t)$ are zero-mean, their cross-correlation functions are zero (i.e., $R_{XY}(\tau) = 0$), we thus have:

$$R_Z(\tau) = R_X(\tau) + R_Y(\tau)$$

Noting that the Fourier transform is a linear operation, then by using (4.50), we can obtain the following:

$$S_Z(f) = S_X(f) + S_Y(f)$$

EXAMPLE 4.35

Let $X(t) = A\cos(2\pi t + \theta)$, where θ is uniformly distributed in the interval $[0, 2\pi]$. Find its power spectral density and the total power.

Solution

Using (4.45) and also a trigonometric identity, we have:

$$\begin{aligned} R_X(t_1, t_2) &= E[X(t_1)X(t_2)] = E[A\cos(2\pi t_1 + \theta)A\cos(2\pi t_2 + \theta)] \\ &= \frac{A^2}{2}E[\cos(2\pi t_1 + 2\pi t_2 + 2\theta) + \cos(2\pi t_1 - 2\pi t_2)] = \frac{A^2}{2}\cos(2\pi\tau) \end{aligned}$$

Using (4.50), we get:

$$S_X(f) = \frac{A^2}{4}(\delta(f+1) + \delta(f-1))$$

Using (4.51) and noting $X(t)$ has a zero mean, we can obtain the total power P as follows:

$$P = R_X(0) = \int_{-\infty}^{\infty} S_X(f)df = \frac{A^2}{2}$$

4.3.6 Response of Linear Time-Invariant Systems to Random Processes

Suppose a wide-sense stationary random process $X(t)$ is applied to a linear time-invariant (LTI) system whose impulse response is $h(t)$ and frequency response is $H(f)$, the system output is then a wide-sense stationary random process $Y(t)$. The ***mean of the output random process*** $Y(t)$, which is equal to the mean of the input random process $X(t)$ multiplied by the DC response of the system, is as follows:

$$E[Y(t)] = E[X(t)]\int_{-\infty}^{\infty} h(s)ds = E[X(t)]\,H(0) \tag{4.53}$$

Based on (4.53), if the system is not a lowpass filter or the input is a zero-mean random process, the output process is then zero-mean. The ***power spectral***

density of the output random process $Y(t)$ is equal to the power spectral density of the input $X(t)$ multiplied by the squared magnitude of the transfer function $H(f)$ of the system, hence we have:

$$S_Y(f) = |H(f)|^2 S_X(f) \tag{4.54}$$

As reflected in (4.54), the system phase response has no bearing on the output power spectral density. Note that the autocorrelation function of the output can be easily found through the inverse Fourier transform of the power spectral density of the output.

EXAMPLE 4.36

The power spectral density of a zero-mean wide-sense stationary random process is the constant $N_0/2$. This random process is passed through an ideal lowpass filter whose bandwidth is B Hz. Determine the autocorrelation function of the output, and the instants of time for which the samples of the output signal are uncorrelated.

Solution

Using (4.54), we get:

$$S_Y(f) = |H(f)|^2 S_X(f) = \begin{cases} |H(0)|^2 \left(\frac{N_0}{2}\right), & 0 \le |f| \le B \\ 0, & \text{otherwise} \end{cases}$$

The inverse Fourier transform of the output power spectral density gives rise to the output autocorrelation function, hence:

$$R_Y(\tau) = |H(0)|^2 B N_0 \,\text{sinc}(2B\tau)$$

Using (4.53) and noting the input mean is zero, the output mean is also zero. Using (4.48), we have uncorrelated samples at the output, if we have the following:

$$R_Y(\tau) = |H(0)|^2 B N_0 \left(\frac{\sin(2\pi B\tau)}{(2\pi B\tau)}\right) = 0$$

which means $\frac{\sin(2\pi B\tau)}{(2\pi B\tau)} = 0$, or equivalently, we have $2\pi B\tau = \pi k$, or $\tau = \frac{k}{2B}$, where $k = \pm 1, \pm 2, \ldots$

EXAMPLE 4.37

Suppose we have $Y(t) = AX(t)\cos(2\pi t + \theta)$, where the amplitude A is a known constant, $X(t)$ is a wide-sense stationary random process, and θ is a uniform random variable in the interval $[0, 2\pi]$. Moreover $X(t)$ and θ are assumed to be independent. Determine the power spectral density of $Y(t)$ in terms of the power spectral density of $X(t)$.

Solution

Using (4.45) and also a trigonometric identity, and noting $X(t)$ and θ are independent, we get the following:

$$R_Y(\tau) = E[Y(t+\tau)Y(t)] = E[AX(t+\tau)\cos(2\pi t + 2\pi\tau + \theta)AX(t)\cos(2\pi t + \theta)]$$
$$= 0.5A^2 R_X(\tau)E[\cos(2\pi\tau) + \cos(4\pi t + 2\pi\tau + 2\theta)] = \frac{A^2}{2}R_X(\tau)\cos(2\pi\tau)$$

We now find the Fourier transform of $R_Y(\tau)$, noting multiplication in one domain requires convolution in the other, the power spectral density of the output is then as follows:

$$S_Y(f) = \frac{A^2}{2}F[R_X(\tau)] * F[\cos(2\pi\tau)] = \frac{A^2}{2}S_X(f) * \left(\frac{1}{2}(\delta(f-1) + \delta(f+1))\right)$$

where * denotes the convolution operation. After carrying out the convolution operation, we then obtain the following:

$$S_Y(f) = \frac{A^2}{4}(S_X(f-1) + S_X(f+1)).$$

When a random process is transmitted through a linear system, the first two moments—mean, as well as autocorrelation and covariance functions—can generally provide an adequate statistical characterization of the system. However, when the system is nonlinear, valuable information may be contained in higher-order moments of the resulting random process.

4.3.7 Gaussian Random Process

The Gaussian random process makes mathematical analysis simple and analytic results possible. Moreover, due to the central limit theorem, a Gaussian random process is an appropriate model to describe many different physical phenomena, such as noise in a communication system. A random process $X(t)$ is a ***Gaussian random process*** if the samples $X(t_1), X(t_2), \ldots, X(t_k)$ are jointly Gaussian random variables for all k, and all choices of $t_1, t_2, \ldots, t_k$. The joint pdf of Gaussian random variables is determined by the vector of means and a covariance matrix. For a Gaussian random process $X(t)$, the joint pdf of two random variables resulting from sampling $X(t)$, i.e., $X(t_1), X(t_2)$, is completely specified by the set of means $m_X(t)$ and the set of autocovariance functions $C_X(t_1, t_2)$. A Gaussian process has some interesting properties, but they are not true in general for random variables that are not jointly Gaussian, they are as follows:

- The Gaussian process provides a good mathematical model for many physically-observed random phenomena.
- The Gaussian random process from which Gaussian random variables are derived can be completely specified, in a statistical sense, from all first and second moments only.
- If a Gaussian random process $X(t)$ is the input to a linear system, then the output $Y(t)$ is also a Gaussian random process, and $X(t)$ and $Y(t)$ are jointly Gaussian processes.
- If a Gaussian random process satisfies the conditions for wide-sense stationary, then the process is also strictly stationary.

- If a Gaussian random process is stationary, then it is also ergodic.
- If the set of random variables obtained by sampling a Gaussian random process are all uncorrelated, the set of random variables are then statistically independent.
- If the joint pdf of the random variables resulting from sampling the random process is Gaussian, then the resulting marginal densities and conditional densities are all individually Gaussian.
- Linear transformation of a set of Gaussian random variables, obtained by sampling a Gaussian random process, produces another set of Gaussian random variables.
- The linear combination of jointly Gaussian variables, resulting from sampling the random process, is also jointly Gaussian.
- For Gaussian random variables, nonlinear and linear mean-square estimates are identical.
- In system analysis, the Gaussian process is often the only one for which a complete statistical analysis can be carried out.

EXAMPLE 4.38

A stationary Gaussian random process $X(t)$ with zero-mean and power spectral density $S_X(f)$ is applied to a linear filter whose impulse response $h(t)$ is as follows:

$$h(t) = \begin{cases} \frac{1}{T}, & 0 < t < T \\ 0, & \text{otherwise} \end{cases}$$

A sample Y is taken of the random process at the filter output at time T. Determine the mean, variance, and pdf of the random variable Y.

Solution

Since $h(t)$ is a linear filter, the output $Y(t)$ is also a Gaussian random process, and a sample at time T is a Gaussian random variable. Also, the frequency response $H(f)$ is as follows:

$$H(f) = \int_{-\infty}^{\infty} h(t)\exp(-j2\pi ft)\,dt = \left(\frac{1}{T}\right)\int_0^T \exp(-j2\pi ft)\,dt = \text{sinc}(fT)\exp(-j\pi fT)$$

Using (4.53), we have

$$E[Y] = E[X]\,H(0) = 0$$

Using (4.27), (4.51), and (4.54), we then have:

$$\sigma_Y^2 = E\left[Y^2\right] - (E[Y])^2 = E\left[Y^2\right] = \int_{-\infty}^{\infty} |H(f)|^2 S_X(f)\,df = \int_{-\infty}^{\infty} S_X(f)\,\text{sinc}^2(fT)df$$

The filter output is therefore Gaussian with a zero mean and a variance that is a function of input power spectral density.

4.3.8 Noise

Noise refers to the unwanted and ever-present time-varying waves that can degrade the transmission of signals in communication systems. A major communication design objective is to minimize the effect of noise. There are two distinct categories of sources of noise, one is external to the system, such as atmospheric noise and man-made noise, and the other is internal to the system, such as the transmitting and receiving equipment causing shot and thermal noise.

White noise is ideally defined as a wide-sense stationary random process $n(t)$ whose frequency components all appear with equal power. White noise is a mathematical idealization and cannot exist as a physically realizable process. The adjective white is used in the sense that white light contains equal amounts of all frequencies within the visible frequency band. Since the power spectral density of white noise is a constant for all frequencies, its autocorrelation function consists of a delta (impulse) function. The power spectral density and autocorrelation functions of white noise, as shown in Figure 4.16, are as follows:

$$S_N(f) = \frac{N_0}{2}$$
$$R_N(\tau) = \frac{N_0}{2}\delta(\tau) \tag{4.55}$$

It is important to highlight that according to (4.55), any two different samples of white noise—no matter how closely together in time they are taken—are

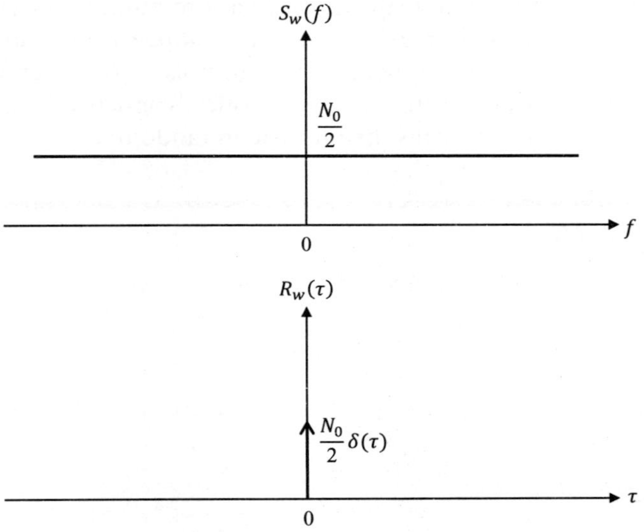

FIGURE 4.16 Power spectral density and autocorrelation function of white noise.

uncorrelated. Strictly speaking, white noise has infinite average power and, as such, it is not physically realizable. As long as the bandwidth of a noise process at the input of a system is significantly larger than that of the system itself, the noise process can be modeled as white noise.

EXAMPLE 4.39

Show that white noise is a zero-mean process.

Solution

The proof is by contradiction, in that we assume white noise $n(t)$ is not a zero-mean process. To this effect, it can be viewed as the sum of a zero-mean process $n_Z(t)$ and a constant K that represents the mean of white noise, i.e., we have:

$$n(t) = n_Z(t) + K$$

The autocorrelation function of $n(t)$ is then as follows:

$$\begin{aligned} R_N(\tau) &= E[n(t)\,n(t+\tau)] = E[(n_Z(t)+K)(n_Z(t+\tau)+K)] \\ &= E[n_Z(t)n_Z(t+\tau)] + K\,E[n_Z t] + K\,E[n_Z(t+\tau)] + K^2 \\ &= R_Z(\tau) + (K)(0) + (K)(0) + K^2 = R_Z(\tau) + K^2 \end{aligned}$$

Using (4.55), we must then have the following:

$$R_N(\tau) = R_Z(\tau) + K^2 = \frac{N_0}{2}\delta(\tau)$$

We thus conclude that we must have $K^2 = 0$, i.e., $K = 0$.

It is of great importance to note that noise in a communication system is generally assumed to be stationary, zero-mean, ***additive white Gaussian noise (AWGN)***. Any two samples of white Gaussian noise, no matter how closely together in time they are taken, are thus statistically independent. In a sense, white Gaussian noise represents the ultimate in randomness.

EXAMPLE 4.40

A linear time-invariant system works as a differentiator (i.e., its output is the derivative of its input). Determine the power spectral density of the output signal, if the input signal is an idealized white noise.

Solution

The frequency response of a differentiator is a linear function of frequency, and is thus as follows:

$$H(f) = j2\pi f$$

Using (4.54) and (4.55), we have:

$$S_Y(f) = |H(f)|^2 S_X(f) = (2\pi f)^2 \frac{N_0}{2} = 2\pi^2 N_0 f^2$$

4.3.9 Narrowband Bandpass Noise

In a communication receiver, a bandpass filter is generally employed as part of the demodulation process. The noise $n(t)$ at the output of such a filter is known as ***narrowband bandpass noise***. This filtered noise is a bandpass process whose power spectral density is mainly concentrated around some frequency f_c with a bandwidth of $2W$ Hz. To assess the impact of narrowband noise on the performance of a communication system, the narrowband bandpass noise is represented in the following two ways:

$$n(t) = n_I(t)\cos(2\pi f_c t) - n_Q(t)\sin(2\pi f_c t)$$
$$n(t) = R(t)\cos(2\pi f_c t + \theta(t)) \tag{4.56}$$

where $n_I(t)$ and $n_Q(t)$ are the **lowpass in-phase and quadrature components**, respectively, and $R(t) = \sqrt{(n_I(t))^2 + (n_Q(t))^2}$ and $\theta(t) = \tan^{-1}\left(\frac{n_Q(t)}{n_I(t)}\right)$ are the **lowpass envelope and phase components**, respectively. Figure 4.17 shows extraction of $n_I(t)$ and $n_Q(t)$ from $n(t)$ and generation of $n(t)$ from $n_I(t)$ and $n_Q(t)$. If $n(t)$ is filtered white Gaussian noise, the in-phase component $n_I(t)$ and the quadrature component $n_Q(t)$ are then zero-mean jointly Gaussian. As shown in Figure 4.18, $n_I(t)$ and $n_Q(t)$ have the same power spectral density, and are as follows:

$$S_{N_I}(f) = S_{N_Q}(f) = \begin{cases} S_N(f + f_c) + S_N(f - f_c), & |f| \le W \\ 0, & \text{otherwise} \end{cases} \tag{4.57}$$

$n_I(t)$ and $n_Q(t)$ components are uncorrelated with each other, and assuming $S_N(f)$ is symmetric around the mid-frequency f_c, $n_I(t)$ and $n_Q(t)$ components are statistically independent. When $n(t)$ is a Gaussian zero-mean random process, then $R(t)$ is Rayleigh-distributed and $\theta(t)$ is uniformly-distributed.

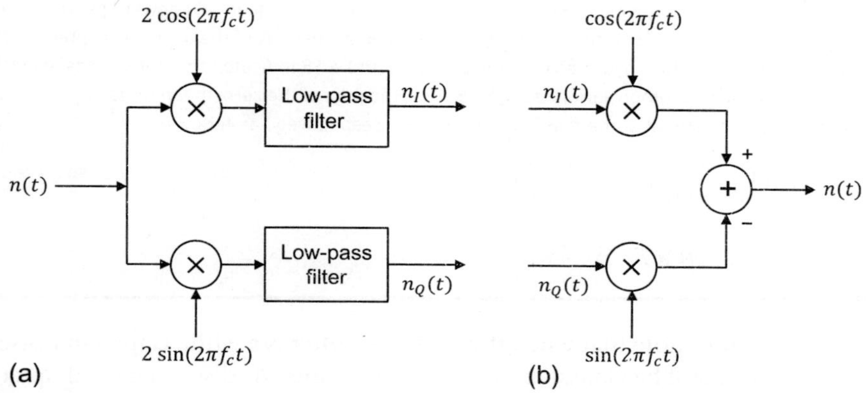

FIGURE 4.17 (a) Extraction of in-phase and quadrature components and (b) generation of narrowband bandpass process.

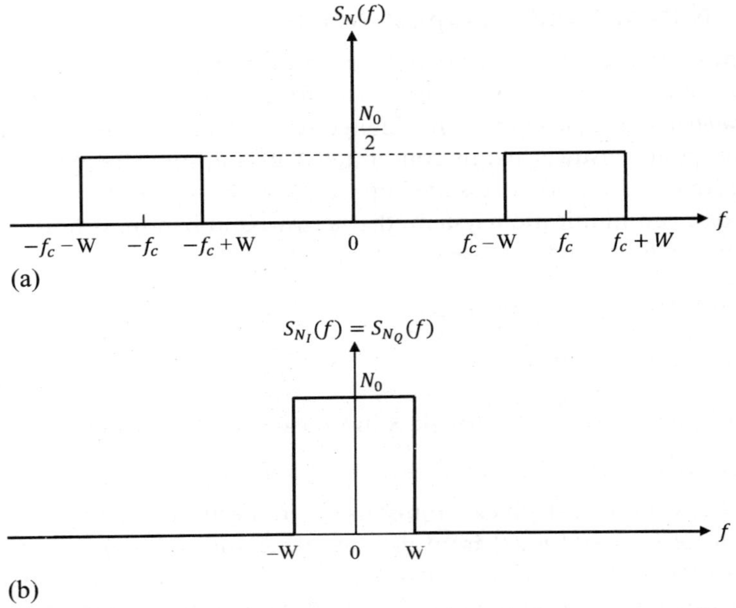

FIGURE 4.18 (a) Power spectral density of bandpass white noise and (b) power spectral density of in-phase and quadrature components.

EXAMPLE 4.41

Suppose a white Gaussian noise process of zero-mean and power spectral density $\frac{N_0}{2}$ is passed through an ideal narrowband bandpass filter. Determine the statistical characteristics of the in-phase and quadrature components of the filter output.

Solution

The filter output is a narrowband Gaussian process $n(t)$ with zero-mean and power spectral density as shown in Figure 4.18. Using (4.57), the power spectral density of the lowpass in-phase and quadrature components is symmetric around zero. Figure 4.18 indicates that the processes $n(t)$, $n_I(t)$ and $n_Q(t)$ have a common variance $2N_0W$. Hence, the pdfs of the zero-mean Gaussian random variables $n_I(t)$ and $n_Q(t)$, at some fixed time $t=t_1$, are, respectively, as follows:

$$f_{N_I(t)}(n_I(t_1)) = \left(\frac{1}{2\sqrt{\pi N_0 W}}\right)\exp\left(-\frac{n_I^2(t_1)}{4N_0W}\right)$$

$$f_{N_Q(t)}(n_Q(t_1)) = \left(\frac{1}{2\sqrt{\pi N_0 W}}\right)\exp\left(-\frac{n_Q^2(t_1)}{4N_0W}\right)$$

It is important to note that when the input to a filter is a white Gaussian noise, the output will still be Gaussian, but no longer white. As discussed in Chapter-3, the ***noise equivalent bandwidth*** of a nonideal filter, whose input is white noise, is defined as follows:

$$B_{NEB} = \frac{\int_0^\infty |H(f)|^2 df}{H_{\max}^2} \tag{4.58}$$

where $H(f)$ represents the transfer function of the filter and $H_{\max}$ denotes the maximum value of $|H(f)|$ in the passband frequencies of the filter. The equivalent noise bandwidth of a commercial filter is generally provided by the manufacturer.

EXAMPLE 4.42

Determine the noise equivalent bandwidth of a first-order lowpass RC filter.

Solution

The transfer function of the filter and its magnitude response are as follows:

$$H(f) = \frac{1}{1 + j2\pi fRC}$$

and

$$|H(f)| = \frac{1}{\sqrt{1 + (2\pi fRC)^2}}$$

Noting $H_{\max}^2 = 1$ and using (4.58), we thus obtain $B_{NEB} = \frac{1}{4RC}$.

4.3.10 Sampling Theorem of Random Signals

Sampling is an indispensable signal-processing tool to bridge between continuous-time signals and discrete-time signals and, in turn, paves the way for digital signal processing and transmission. A wide-sense stationary process $X(t)$ is called band-limited if its power spectral density vanishes for frequencies beyond a specific frequency W and it has finite power, as shown below:

$$S_X(f) = 0, \quad |f| > W$$
$$R_X(0) < \infty \tag{4.59}$$

$X(t)$ can be reconstructed from the sequence of its samples taken at a minimum rate of twice the highest frequency component (i.e., $2W$). The sampled version of the process equals the original in the mean-square sense for all time t, and it is as follows:

$$\hat{X}(t) = \sum_{n=-\infty}^{\infty} X\left(\frac{n}{2W}\right) \operatorname{sinc}(2Wt - n), \quad -\infty < t < \infty \tag{4.60}$$

where $X\left(\frac{n}{2W}\right)$ is the random variable obtained by sampling the process $X(t)$ at $t = \frac{n}{2W}$. It can be shown that the ***mean-square error*** between the original process and the sampled version is zero, i.e., we have the following:

$$\overline{e^2} = E\left[\left(X(t) - \hat{X}(t)\right)^2\right] = 0 \tag{4.61}$$

Suppose we have $S_X(f) \neq 0$, for $|f| > W$, i.e., $X(t)$ is not band-limited to W Hz. If $X(t)$ is applied to an ideal lowpass filter whose bandwidth is W Hz and the resulting output $Y(t)$ is sampled at a rate equal to $2W$, then the resulting mean-square error between the original (unfiltered) signal $X(t)$ and the sampled version $\hat{Y}(t)$ is as follows:

$$\overline{e^2} = E\left[\left(X(t) - \widehat{Y}(t)\right)^2\right] = 2\int_W^{\infty} S_X(f)df \neq 0 \tag{4.62}$$

EXAMPLE 4.43

The power spectral density of a wide-sense stationary random process is as follows:

$$S_X(f) = \begin{cases} -10^{-12}|f| + 10^{-6}, & |f| \leq 10^6 \\ 0, & \text{otherwise} \end{cases}$$

The signal is passed through an ideal lowpass filter whose bandwidth is W Hz, and its output is then sampled at $2W$ Hz. Determine the mean-square value of the sampling error for a) $W = 1$ MHz and b) $W = 500$ kHz.

Solution

This problem highlights the relationship between the bandwidth of a random signal and the sampling rate.

(a) Using (4.61), we have $\overline{e^2} = 0$, as the sampling rate is twice the highest frequency component.

(b) Since the sampling rate is not high enough, we must use (4.62) to find the mean-square error:

$$\overline{e^2} = 2\int_{\frac{10^6}{2}}^{10^6} \left(-10^{-12}f + 10^{-6}\right)df = 0.25.$$

Summary and Sources

In this chapter, we first introduced the basic concept of probabilities of random events, the conditional probability, which quantifies the effect of partial knowledge about the outcome of an event, and Bayes' rule, which gives the a posteriori probability of an event given that another event has occurred. The discussion of a single random variable was extended to two random variables, definitions of independent, uncorrelated, and orthogonal random variables were provided, and the jointly Gaussian random variables and the central limit theorem were introduced. We also developed models and procedures for characterizing random processes, highlighted the basic connection between the concept of a random process and the concept of a random variable, and introduced statistical averages, stationary processes, and ergodic processes. After introducing the Gaussian random process and its features, we characterized noise encountered in communication systems. The knowledge gained in this chapter will be utilized in the following chapters to assess digital communication systems with nondeterministic imperfections.

There are many good books on probability and statistics, and there are few good books on random processes. However, the book by Leon-Garcia [1] is one of the best books which covers probability, random variables, and stochastic processes very well, not only with a clear emphasis on electrical engineering applications, but with a focus on communications as well. There are other excellent books in the area that have been widely used during the past decades, including the widely-known book by Papoulis and Pillai [2]. Of course, there are other good sources which also deal with various aspects of random variables and random processes [3–11].

[1] Leon-Garcia, *Probability, Statistics, and Random Processes for Electrical Engineering,* third ed., Pearson, ISBN: 978-0-13-147122-1, 2008.

[2] Papoulis and S.U. Pillai, *Probability, Random Variables and Stochastic Processes,* fourth ed., McGraw-Hill, ISBN: 0-07-112256-7, 2002.

[3] W.L. Root and W.B. Davenport, *An Introduction to the Theory of Random Signals and Noise,* Wiley-IEEE Press, ISBN: 978-0-87942-235-6, 1987.

[4] G.R. Cooper and C.D. McGillem, *Probabilistic Methods of Signal and System Analysis,* third ed., Oxford University, ISBN: 0195123549, 1998.

[5] R.A. Johnson, *Probability and Statistics for Engineers,* eighth ed., Prentice Hall, ISBN: 978-0-321-64077-2, 2011.

[6] T.L. Fine, *Probability and Probabilistic Reasoning for Electrical Engineering,* Pearson, ISBN: 0-13-020591-5, 2006.

[7] H.P. Hsu, *Probability, Random Variables, and Random Processes,* McGraw-Hill, ISBN: 0-07-030644-3, 1996.

[8] A.H. Haddad, *Probabilistic Systems and Random Signals,* Pearson, ISBN: 0-13-009455-2, 2006.

[9] M.R. Spiegel, *Probability and Statistics,* McGraw-Hill, ISBN: 0-07-060220-4, 1975.

[10] R.L. Scheaffer and L.J. Young, *Introduction to Probability and its Applications,* third ed., Cengage Learning, ISBN: 978-0-534-38671-9, 2010.

[11] S. Kay, *Intuitive Probability and Random Processes Using MATLAB,* Springer, ISBN: 978-0-387-24157-9, 2006.

Problems

4.1 Given that $P(A)=0.9$, $P(B)=0.8$, and $P(A\cap B)=0.7$, determine $P(A^c\cap B^c)$. Note that A^c and B^c are the complements of A and B, respectively.

4.2 An experiment consists of rolling three fair six-sided dice at the same time. Event G is when the sum of the dots shown on the three dice is equal to 16. Find the probability of event G.

4.3 Consider rolling a single fair die, and define two events $H=\{1, 2, 3, 4\}$ and $J=\{3, 4, 5\}$. Are events H and J mutually exclusive? Are they statistically independent?

4.4 There are two identical bags. In each bag, there are 10 balls, numbered from 1 to 10. We randomly pick a ball from each bag. Determine the probability that the product of the two numbers on the two balls, picked from the two bags, is a multiple of 3.

4.5 Two numbers x and y are selected at random between 0 and 2. Let events A, B, and C be defined as follows: $A=\{1<x<2\}$, $B=\{1<y<2\}$, and $C=\{x>y\}$. Are there any two events which are statistically independent?

4.6 Assuming there are n events $A_1, A_2, \ldots, A_n$, write an expression to show when they are mutually exclusive events, and an expression to show when they are statistically independent events.

4.7 Suppose all four ways a family can have two children are equally likely. Let event A be a family with two children, but at least one is a girl, and event C be with two girls. Are events A and C statistically independent?

4.8 There are four devices, but one of them is defective. Two, one after the other, are to be selected at random for use. Find the probability that the second device selected is not defective, given that the first one was not defective.

4.9 The manufacturers A, B, and C have records of providing products with 10%, 5%, and 20% defective rates, respectively. Suppose 20%, 35%, and 45% of the current supply came from the manufacturers A, B, and C, respectively. If a randomly selected product is defective, what is the probability that it comes from the manufacturer B?

4.10 Suppose that 10% of all used computers need repairs. If four computers are randomly selected, find the probability that at least one computer in the sample of four is defective.

4.11 In pulse code modulation, to combat the accumulation of noise and distortion, regenerative repeaters are used to make decisions on bits. Consider a pulse code modulation system with $k \geq 1$ regenerative repeaters in series. Suppose the average probability of error incurred in each regeneration process is p. Assuming $kp \ll 1$, approximate the average probability of error for the entire end-to-end channel. Note that a bit is detected correctly over the entire channel, consisting of k regenerative repeaters, if either the bit is detected correctly over every link or errors on a bit are made over an even number of links only.

4.12 A system consists of n subsystems in series. Each of the n subsystems consists of parallel components, where the first subsystem consists of n_1 parallel components, the second subsystem consists of n_2 parallel components, and finally the nth subsystem consists of n_n parallel components. Assume that the probability of failure of a component is p and the components fail independently. Note that $n, n_1, n_2, \ldots, n_n$ are all positive integers and may be different from one another. Find the probability that the system functions.

4.13 A system consists of m subsystems in parallel. Each of the m subsystems consists of components in series, where the first subsystem consists of m_1 components in series, the second subsystem consists of m_2 components in series, and finally the mth subsystem consists of m_m components in series. Assume that the probability of failure of a component is p and the components fail independently. Note that $m, m_1, m_2, \ldots, m_m$ are all positive integers and may be different from one another. Find the probability that the system fails.

4.14 There are two urns. The first urn contains ten black and five white balls, whereas the second one contains three black and three white balls. If a ball selected at random from one of the urns is white, then determine the probability that it was drawn from the first urn.

4.15 Noting that n and r are both positive integers and $n \geq r$, the following table shows the formulas for permutations (i.e., the number of ordered selections of r elements from a set with n elements) and combinations (i.e., the number of unordered selections of r elements from a set with n elements), with and without repetition (replacement) of elements. Note that once an element is randomly picked with repetition, it is put back with the other elements and there is therefore a chance that it can be picked again. However, with no repetition (replacement), after an element is randomly picked, it is put aside and there is therefore no chance at all that it can be picked again.

Type	Repetition Allowed?	Formula
r-permutations	No	$\frac{n!}{(n-r)!}$
r-combinations	No	$\frac{n!}{r!(n-r)!}$
r-permutations	Yes	n^r
r-combinations	Yes	$\frac{(n+r-1)!}{r!(n-1)!}$

As a particular case, suppose there are 7 balls in an urn, numbered from 1 to 7 inclusive, and two balls from the urn are randomly picked, one after the other one, i.e., $n=7$ and $r=2$. Determine the number of permutations and combinations that two balls can be picked, with and without replacement (repetition).

4.16 This problem is widely known as Monty Hall problem. You are on a game show and you are given the choice of three doors and you will win what is behind your chosen door. Behind one door is a valuable prize, but behind the other two are worthless prizes. All prizes are placed randomly behind the doors before the show starts.

The rules of the game show are as follows: After you have chosen a door, the door remains closed for the time being. The game show host, who knows what is behind each door, now has to open one of the two remaining doors, and the door he opens must have a worthless prize behind it. If both remaining doors have worthless prizes behind them, he chooses one at random. After the host opens a door with a worthless prize, he will ask you to decide whether you want to stay with your first original door or to switch to the other closed door. In order to win the valuable prize, is it better for you to stay or to switch?

4.17 A Bayesian spam filter uses information about previously seen e-mails to guess whether an incoming e-mail is spam (an unwanted and unsolicited message). For a particular word or expression x, the probability that x appears in a spam e-mail is estimated by determining the ratio of the number of spam e-mails in which x appears to the number of spam e-mails. Also, the probability that x appears in a non-spam e-mail is estimated by determining the ratio of the number of non-spam e-mails in which x appears to the number of non-spam e-mails. A spam filter sometimes fails to identify a spam e-mail as spam, this is called a false negative, and it sometimes identifies an e-mail that is not spam as spam, this is called a false positive. The filter rejects an e-mail as spam if the probability of spam e-mail given it contains the word x is greater than the threshold $0<\eta<1$.

As a particular case, suppose the word "account" occurs in 500 of 4000 e-mail messages known to be spam and in 50 of 10000 e-mail messages known not to be spam, and the probability of a spam e-mail is 0.5, if the threshold is 0.9, will the spam filter reject such e-mails as spam?

4.18 This problem is known as false positives on diagnostic tests. Let event A be that the tested person has the disease ($\bar{A}$ is its complement). Let event B denote that the test result is positive. Suppose $P(B/A)$, the probability of having a positive test result given the person has the disease, $P(B/\bar{A})$, the probability of having a positive test result given the person does not have the disease, and $P(A)$, the probability that the tested person has the disease, are all known. The goal is to determine the probability that a person has the disease given that the test result is positive.

As a particular case, suppose we have $P(B/A)=0.999$, $P(B/\bar{A})=0.005$ and $P(A)=0.001$, determine the probability that a person has the disease given that the test result is positive.

4.19 This problem is known as how-to-make-the-best-choice. You are faced with a choice among n candidates who present themselves for evaluation in random order. How do you choose among them, or in probabilistic terms, what decision rule should you use to maximize the probability of choosing the best candidate? Note that the basic assumptions are as follows: i) you view candidates one at a time sequentially, and assign a score of x_i to the candidate, where $i = 1, \ldots, n$, ii) no two candidates have the same score, i.e., $P(x_i = x_j) = 0$ for $i \neq j$, iii) you wish to select the candidate with the highest score in $x_1, x_2, \ldots, x_n$, iv) it is necessary to come to a decision, whether to choose or reject each candidate immediately after the individual evaluation has been performed, and once made, that decision to accept or reject is final and absolute, i.e., you cannot go back in time, v) the order of arrival of candidates is random, and vi) if you have not made a decision by the time you view the nth candidate, i.e., the last candidate, you must then choose that last candidate. Consult the Internet to find the strategy as how to make the best choice.

As a particular case, suppose there are three candidates with three different scores, what is the strategy to make the best choice?

4.20 Algorithms that make random choices at one or more steps are called probabilistic algorithms. A particular class of probabilistic algorithms is Monte Carlo algorithms. Monte Carlo algorithms always produce answers to decision problems, but a small probability remains that these answers may be incorrect. A Monte Carlo algorithm uses a sequence of tests and the probability that the algorithm answers the decision problem correctly increases as more tests are carried out. Suppose there are $n \gg 0$ items in a batch and the probability that an item is defective is p when random testing is done. To decide all items are good, n tests are required to guarantee that none of the items are defective. However, a Monte Carlo algorithm can determine whether all items are good as long as some probability of error is acceptable.

A Monte Carlo algorithm proceeds by successively selecting items at random and testing them one by one, where the maximum number of items being tested is a pre-determined $k \ll n$. When a defective item is encountered, the algorithm stops to indicate that out of the n items in a batch, there is at least one defective. If a tested item is good, the algorithm goes on to the next item. If after testing k items, no defective item is found, the algorithm concludes that all n items are good, but with a modest probability of error which is independent of n. Assuming the events of testing different items are independent, determine that the probability not even one item is defective after testing k items. Analyze the impact of n, k, and p on the probability of finding not even a defective item.

As a particular case, suppose there are ten million IC chips made in a factory, where the probability that an IC chip is in a perfect condition is 0.99. Based on the Monte Carlo algorithm, determine the minimum number of IC chips which need to be tested so the probability of finding not even a defective IC chip among those tested is less than one in a million.

4.21 Noting the mode of a random variable X is defined to be the most probable value of X, i.e., the value x at which the pdf of X achieves its maximum, determine the mode of a Rayleigh random variable.

4.22 Noting the median of a random variable X is defined to be the value x for which the probability below it is the same as the probability above it, i.e., the value x which divides the area under the pdf into two halves, determine the median of an exponential random variable.

4.23 Determine the variance, mean, median, and mode of a Gaussian random variable.

4.24 Determine the mean and variance of a continuous uniform random variable.

4.25 Determine the mean and variance of a Bernoulli random variable.

4.26 Determine the mean and variance of a binomial random variable.

4.27 Determine the probability of the first error occurring at the 10,000th transmission in a digital transmission system where the average probability of error is one in a billion.

4.28 Suppose X is a Gaussian random variable with a mean of 4 and a variance of 9. Using the Q-function, determine $P(0 < X \leq 9)$.

4.29 Suppose the random variable X is uniformly distributed between 0 and 1 with probability 0.25, takes on the value of 1 with probability p, and is uniformly distributed between 1 and 2 with probability 0.5. Determine p as well as the pdf and cdf of the random variable X.

4.30 Assume 10,000 bits are independently transmitted over a channel in which the bit error rate (probability of an erroneous bit) is 0.0001. Using the binomial distribution, calculate the probability when the total number of errors is less than or equal to 2.

4.31 The variance of a discrete uniform random variable Z, which takes on values in a set of n consecutive integers, is 4. Determine the mean of this random variable.

4.32 Assuming X is a discrete random variable whose pmf is as follows: $p(X=0)=0.2$, $p(X=1)=0.3$, $p(X=2)=0.4$ and $p(X=3)=0.1$. Determine the mean and variance of X.

4.33 Let X be the number of dots shown on a fair six-sided die. If the random variable Y is defined as $Y = X + X^2$, then determine the pmf of Y, and also determine $P(10 < Y \leq 24)$.

4.34 Let Y be the sum of the dots shown on a pair of fair six-sided dice. Determine the pmf of Y and its mean. Also, determine the conditional pdf given that $5 \leq Y \leq 9$ and the mean of this conditional pdf.

4.35 The pdf of a Gaussian variable X is given by $f_X(x) = Ke^{-\frac{(x-4)^2}{18}}$. Find the value of K and determine the probability of X to be negative.

4.36 Determine the constant c if the cdf of the continuous random variable X is as follows:

$$F_X(x) = \begin{cases} 0, & x \le 0 \\ cx^2, & 0 < x \le 1 \\ 1, & x > 1 \end{cases}$$

Determine the pdf of X, i.e., $f_X(x)$, and also $P(0.1 < X \le 0.4)$.

4.37 Consider a random variable X whose pdf is $f_X(x) = 2e^{-b|x|}$, where $-\infty < x < \infty$ and $b > 0$. Determine b and find $P(1 < X \le 2)$.

4.38 Prove the exponential random variable satisfies the memoryless property, i.e., prove that $P[X > (t+h)/X > t] = P[X > h]$, for $h > 0$.

4.39 Suppose X is a random variable whose pdf is defined as follows:

$$f_X(x) = \left(\frac{2x}{9}\right)(u(x) - u(x-3))$$

where $u(.)$ is a unit step function. Determine the conditional pdf $f_X(x/1 < X \le 2)$ as well as its mean.

4.40 Let X be a Gaussian random variable whose mean is m and variance is σ^2. Determine the expected value of X given that $X < b$, i.e., $E[X/X < b]$, where b is a known constant.

4.41 Determine $E[X/X > 0.5]$, if the random variable X has the following pdf:

$$f_X(x) = \begin{cases} -|x| + 1, & 0 < x \le 1 \\ 0, & \text{elsewhere} \end{cases}$$

4.42 In a binary transmission system, 0's and 1's are equally-likely to be transmitted, and the symbol 0 is represented by -1 and the symbol 1 is represented by $+1$. The channel introduces additive zero-mean unit-variance Gaussian noise. As a result, there are erroneous bits at the receiver. Determine (i.e., write the integral expression for) the average probability of bit error (bit error rate).

4.43 A source of noise in a communication system is modeled as a Gaussian random variable with zero-mean unit-variance. Determine the probability that the value of the noise exceeds 1. Given that the value of the noise is positive, determine the probability that the value of the noise exceeds 1.

4.44 The input X to a communication channel takes values 1 or -1 with equal probabilities. The output of the channel is given by $Y = X + N$, where N is a zero-mean, unit-variance Gaussian random variable. Determine $P(X = 1/Y > 0)$.

4.45 Let X be a Gaussian random variable whose mean is zero and variance is σ^2. Determine the expected value and the variance of X given that $X > 0$.

4.46 A random variable has a zero-mean, unit-variance Gaussian distribution. A constant 1 is added to this random variable. Determine the probability that the average of two independent measurements of this composite signal is negative.

4.47 The mean of the random variable Y is twice the mean of the random variable X, and the standard deviation of Y is twice that of X. If $Y = aX + b$, then determine the values of the constants a and b.

4.48 The number of phone calls made by a cell-phone user during a day is a random variable. The mean and the variance of this random variable are 15 and 9, respectively. Using the Chebyshev inequality, estimate the probability that the number of calls is more than 5 from the mean.

4.49 Suppose the pdf of the random variable X is an even function and we also have the random variable $Y = X^4$. Are X and Y correlated? Are X and Y statistically independent?

4.50 Let X and Y be a pair of two random variables. Show that we have

$$(E[XY])^2 \le E[X^2]E[Y^2]$$

Note that this is known as the Cauchy-Schwarz inequality.

4.51 Assuming that X is a Gaussian random variable whose mean is 3 and variance is 4, Y is a Gaussian random variable whose mean is -1 and variance is 2, and X and Y are independent, determine the covariance of the two random variables $Z = X - Y$ and $W = 2X + 3Y$.

4.52 Assuming Θ is a uniform random variable in the interval $[-\pi, \pi]$, and $X = \cos\Theta$, determine the pdf of the random variable X.

4.53 Let the random variable Y be defined by $Y = aX + b$, where X is a Gaussian random variable whose mean is 5 and variance is 10, and a and b are both known nonzero constants. Determine the mean and variance of Y, as well as the probability of $Y > -1$.

4.54 X and Y are individually zero-mean unit-variance Gaussian random variables, and they are also jointly Gaussian with ρ as the correlation coefficient. Show the conditional pdf of X given $Y = y$ is Gaussian, and determine its mean and variance.

4.55 X and Y are two independent zero-mean unit-variance Gaussian random variables. Determine the probability that X is positive and Y is negative, i.e., $P(X > 0, Y < 0)$.

4.56 The joint cdf of a pair of random variables (X, Y) is as follows: $F_{X,Y}(X, Y) = (1 - e^{-x})(1 - e^{-y})$ for $x \geq 0$ and $y \geq 0$, and $F_{X,Y}(X, Y) = 0$, otherwise. Find the marginal cdf's of X and Y, and determine $P(X > x, Y > y)$.

4.57 The joint pdf of a pair of random variables (X, Y) is as follows: $f_{X,Y}(x, y) = 0.125\,(x + y)$, for $0 < x \leq 2$ and $0 < y \leq 2$, and $f_{X,Y}(x, y) = 0$, otherwise. Find the conditional pdf's $f_{Y/X}(y/x)$ and $f_{X/Y}(x/y)$, and determine the conditional probability $P(0 < Y \leq 0.5/X = 1)$.

4.58 Consider the joint pdf of a pair of random variables (X, Y) given by $f_{X,Y}(x, y) = K(x + y)$, for $0 < x \leq 1$ and $0 < y \leq 1$, and $f_{X,Y}(x, y) = 0$, otherwise. Are X and Y statistically independent?

4.59 The joint pdf of a pair of random variables (X, Y) is given by $f_{X,Y}(x, y) = 2$ for $0 < y \leq x < 1$, and $f_{X,Y}(x, y) = 0$, otherwise. Find the conditional means $E(Y/X = x)$ and $E(X/Y = y)$.

4.60 The joint pdf of a pair of random variables (X, Y) is given by $f_{X,Y}(x, y) = 1$ for $0 \leq x \leq 1$ and $0 \leq y \leq 1$, and $f_{X,Y}(x, y) = 0$, otherwise. Are the random variables X and Y statistically independent?

4.61 Let X and Y be statistically independent random variables, where their pdf's are as follows: $f_X(x) = 1$ for $0 < x \leq 1$, and $f_X(x) = 0$, otherwise, and $f_Y(y) = e^{-y}$ for $y \geq 0$, and $f_Y(y) = 0$, otherwise. Assuming $Z = X + Y$, determine the pdf of Z.

4.62 In a store, the purchases are independent and identically distributed random variables with mean of \$8 and standard deviation of \$2. Estimate the probability that the first 100 shoppers spend a total of \$780 to \$820.

4.63 Find the constant c such that the second moment of the difference of the random variable Y and c, i.e., the mean square error $E\left[(Y - c)^2\right]$, is minimum.

4.64 Assume that we have a signal generator that can generate one of the six possible sinusoids. The amplitude of all sinusoids is two, and the phase for all of them is $\frac{\pi}{4}$, but the frequencies can be 10, 20, ..., 60 kHz. We roll a fair six-sided die, and depending on its outcome, as denoted by f, we generate a sinusoidal signal whose frequency is 10000 times what the die shows. Write the equation for this random process $X(t)$.

4.65 Consider $X(t) = A\cos(2\pi f_0 t + \theta)$, where the amplitude A and frequency f_0 are known constants, and θ denotes the random phase uniformly distributed over the interval $[0, \pi]$. Is $X(t)$ a wide-sense stationary random process?

4.66 Show that the autocorrelation function $R_X(\tau)$ of a wide-sense stationary random process $X(t)$ is an even function, i.e., $R_X(\tau) = R_X(-\tau)$.

4.67 Show that the autocorrelation function $R_X(\tau)$ of a wide-sense stationary random process $X(t)$ has its maximum value at $\tau = 0$.

4.68 The autocorrelation function of a random signal is as follows: $R_X(\tau) = \exp(-2|\tau|)$. Determine its power spectral density.

4.69 Let $X(t)$ be a zero-mean wide-sense stationary Gaussian random process with the power spectral density $S_X(f) = \frac{3}{\pi^2}$ for $|f| \leq 500$ Hz, and $S_X(f) = 0$, otherwise. Suppose $X(t)$ is the input to a simple differentiator whose transfer function is as follows: $H(f) = j2\pi f$. Determine the distribution of the output process, its mean and variance.

4.70 Suppose the wide-sense stationary processes $X(t)$ and $Y(t)$ are related as follows: $Y(t) = X(t)\cos(2\pi f_c t + \theta) - X(t)\sin(2\pi f_c t + \theta)$, where the frequency f_c is a constant and the initial phase θ, which is independent of $X(t)$, is a continuous uniform random variable over the interval $[0, 2\pi]$. Suppose $S_X(f)$, the power spectral density of $X(t)$, is band-limited to W Hz. Determine $S_Y(f)$, the power spectral density of $Y(t)$, in terms of $S_X(f)$.

4.71 Let $Y(t) = A\cos(2\pi ft + \theta) + A\sin(2\pi ft + \theta)$, where the amplitude A and the frequency f are both known constants and the initial phase θ is a uniform random variable in the interval $[0, 2\pi]$. Determine the expected value and variance of $Y(t)$.

4.72 Suppose we have two random processes $X(t) = \cos(t + \theta)$ and $Y(t) = \sin(t + \theta)$, where θ is a uniform random variable over the interval $[0, 2\pi]$. Show that $R_{XY}(-\tau) = R_{YX}(\tau)$.

4.73 Let $X(t)$ be a nonstationary Gaussian random process whose mean and covariance function are as follows: $m_X(t) = t - 8$ and $C_X(t_1, t_2) = e^{|t_1 - t_2|}$. Find $P[X(3) < 6]$.

4.74 Let the random process $X(t)$ be defined by $X(t) = A + Bt$, where A and B are independent random variables, each uniformly distributed over the interval $[-1, 1]$, and t is the parameter of time. Determine the mean and the autocorrelation function of $X(t)$.

4.75 A zero-mean white Gaussian noise with the power spectral density 1 mW/Hz passes through an ideal LPF with bandwidth 5000 Hz. Assuming $Y(t)$ is the output random process, show that the random variables $Y(t)$ and $Y(t + 0.001)$ are statistically independent.

4.76 Assuming the input is white noise, determine the noise equivalent bandwidth of a LPF whose transfer function is as follows: $H(f) = \exp(-|f|)$.

4.77 The autocorrelation function of a wide-sense stationary process $X(t)$ is as follows: $R_X(\tau) = 1 + 2\left(\frac{\sin(\pi\tau)}{\pi\tau}\right)^2$. Determine the dc power and ac power contained in $X(t)$.

4.78 Can $R_X(\tau) = \sin(2\pi\tau)$ be the autocorrelation function of a wide-sense stationary process $X(t)$?

4.79 Give an example of a wide-sense stationary random process that when its samples are taken every 0.4 milliseconds apart, then the reconstructed signal from the sequence of its samples equals the original continuous signal in the mean square sense for all time, and if the samples are taken every 0.5 milliseconds apart, then the reconstructed signal from the sequence of its samples does not equal the original continuous signal in the mean square sense for all time.

4.80 Consider the random process $X(t) = \sin(2\pi f t)$, where the frequency f is a continuous uniform random variable over the frequency range $(0, W)$. Is $X(t)$ a strict-sense stationary random process?

4.81 Suppose the random process $X(t)$ is a Gaussian process, and its mean and the covariance functions are respectively as follows: $E[X(t)] = \sin \pi t$ and $C_X(t_1, t_2) = \exp(-|t_1 - t_2|)$. Determine the joint probability density function at samples $t_1 = 1$ and $t_2 = 1.5$.

4.82 Suppose that a white Gaussian noise of zero-mean and power spectral density $\frac{N_0}{2}$ is applied to an ideal LPF of bandwidth B Hz and passband amplitude response of one. Determine the variance of the output signal and the minimum sampling interval for which the noise samples at the filter output are statistically independent.

4.83 Consider a pair of random processes $Y(t)$ and $Z(t)$ that are respectively related to the wide-sense stationary random process $X(t)$ as follows: $Y(t) = X(t)\cos(t+\theta)$ and $Z(t) = X(t)\sin(t+\theta)$, where the random variable θ is uniformly distributed over the interval $[0, 2\pi]$, and it is also independent of $X(t)$. Show that the random variables obtained by simultaneously sampling the random processes $Y(t)$ and $Z(t)$ at some fixed value of time t are orthogonal to each other.

4.84 Consider a random process $X(t)$ consisting of a sinusoidal component $\cos(2\pi t + \theta)$ and a white noise component $W(t)$ of zero-mean and power spectral density of 1, as represented by $X(t) = \cos(2\pi t + \theta) + W(t)$, where θ is a uniformly distributed random variable over the interval $[0, 2\pi]$. Noting that the sinusoidal and noise components are independent, determine the autocorrelation function of the random process $X(t)$ and identify the values of τ for which $X(t)$ samples are uncorrelated.

4.85 The output of an oscillator is described by $X(t) = A\cos(2\pi ft - \theta)$, where A is a constant amplitude, and the frequency f and the initial phase θ are independent random variables. Note that θ is uniformly distributed over the interval $[0, 2\pi]$. Find the power spectral density of the $X(t)$ in terms of the probability density function of the random variable f.

4.86 Consider a pair of wide-sense stationary random processes $X(t)$ and $Y(t)$, whose autocorrelation functions are $R_x(\tau)$ and $R_y(\tau)$, respectively. Show that the cross-correlation function is bounded as follows: $|R_{XY}(\tau)| \leq \frac{1}{2}|R_x(0) + R_y(0)|$.

4.87 Give an example of two random processes $X(t)$ and $Y(t)$ for which $R_{XY}(t+\tau, t)$ is a function of τ, but $X(t)$ and $Y(t)$ are not stationary random processes.

4.88 Find the power spectral density for which the random process $Z(t) = X + Y$, where X and Y are independent, and X and Y each is uniformly distributed over the interval $[-1, 1]$.

4.89 A zero-mean stationary Gaussian random process $X(t)$ has power spectral density $S_X(f)$. Determine the probability density function of a random variable obtained by observing the process $X(t)$ at some time t_k.

Computer Exercises

4.90 Assume X is a continuous uniform random variable in the interval $[-a, a]$. Suppose we add $n > 1$ such random variables together. Compute 20,000 samples of the sum. Estimate the resulting probability density function through a histogram. Discuss how the normalized version of the histogram can be related to the Gaussian probability density function. Assess the impacts of a and n on the resulting histogram.

4.91 Assume $X(t) = A\cos(2\pi t + \theta)$, where θ is a uniformly distributed random variable in the interval $[0, 2\pi]$. Generate 1000 values of θ to generate 1000 sample functions of the random process $X(t)$. Determine both the time-averaged and ensemble-averaged mean, variance, and autocorrelation functions of the random process $X(t)$.

4.92 Suppose a white noise random process $X(t)$ with unit power spectral density is applied to an ideal low-pass filter whose bandwidth is ρW Hz. Determine and plot the autocorrelation functions of white noise and the filtered white noise, where the inverse FFT algorithm employs 128, 256, or 512 frequency samples, and the bandwidth of the LPF may be 1 Hz, 2 Hz, or 10 Hz. Identify the samples which are uncorrelated.

CHAPTER 5

Analog-to-Digital Conversion

CONTENTS

INTRODUCTION

The focus of this chapter is on analog-to-digital conversion (ADC). We first discuss the sampling process, which transforms a continuous-time, continuous-value signal into a discrete-time, continuous-value signal, along with its theoretical and practical implementation aspects. We then introduce the quantization process, by which a discrete-time, continuous-value signal is converted into a discrete-time, discrete-value signal. Following the quantization process, we describe the digital pulse modulation with a focus on the pulse-code modulation, where discrete values are transformed into short strings of bits. Finally, line codes, which can convert digital data to digital signals for effective transmission, is presented. After studying this chapter and understanding all relevant concepts and examples, students should be able to do the following:

1. Explain the need for sampling.
2. State the sampling theorem.
3. Determine the Nyquist sampling rate and sampling interval.
4. Describe the aliasing effect and the means to mitigate it.
5. Differentiate among the instantaneous, natural, and flat-top sampling techniques.
6. Understand the upsampling and oversampling operations.
7. Apply the sampling process to bandpass signals.
8. Appreciate the role of quantization.
9. Outline the basics of uniform quantization.
10. Analyze how the uniform quantization parameters can impact the performance.
11. Discuss the need for nonuniform quantization.
12. Assess how the widely-used nonuniform quantization techniques operate.
13. Highlight basics of vector quantization.
14. Comprehend all elements involved in the pulse-code modulation (PCM).

Introduction to Digital Communications

15. Portray the differential PCM (DPCM) and adaptive DPCM.
16. Depict the delta modulation (DM) and adaptive DM.
17. Provide the reasons why line codes are used.
18. Identify the selection criteria for line codes.
19. Evaluate the power spectral density of a line code.
20. Connect the concepts of sampling, quantization, digital pulse modulation, and line coding.

5.1 SAMPLING PROCESS

The sampling process is very widely used in digital communications and signal processing and is the first major operation in analog-to-digital conversion. Sampling, as an indispensable operation, provides a bridge between analog signals and their digital representations. Through sampling, a continuous-time, continuous-value signal can be transformed into a discrete-time, continuous-value signal, where samples are usually spaced uniformly in time.

The samples of a signal do not always uniquely determine the corresponding continuous-time signal (i.e., different continuous-time signals can have the same set of samples). For instance, if a sinusoidal signal is sampled at intervals of a period, then the sampled signal appears to be a constant, it is then impossible to determine if the original continuous-time signal was a constant or a sinusoid. It is thus critically important to sample a continuous-time signal at a high enough rate, so the sampled signal can uniquely define only the original continuous-time signal.

The samples do not convey anything about the behavior of the signal in between the times it is sampled. In other words, we do not have (or do not care to have) the values of the continuous-time signal during the time interval between two adjacent samples, nor do we need to assume the values are zero. However, it is required for the signal to make smooth enough transitions from one sample to another so as to be able to completely reconstruct the original continuous-time signal from its discrete version. Noting that the closer two adjacent samples are, the smoother the transition is from one sample to another, the sampling theorem gets to determine the maximum time interval between two adjacent samples to ensure smooth enough transitions.

It is important to note that the rate at which a signal changes in the time domain is directly related to the highest frequency that is present in the signal. It is also obvious that a high sampling rate yields a more accurate version of the original continuous-time signal, but on the other hand, to have a low digital transmission and processing rate, it is important to use a practical sampling rate that is as low as possible. It is thus critical to determine the minimum sampling rate, so the original continuous-time signal can be completely reconstructed and uniquely recovered from its sampled version, and this is the essence of the sampling theorem.

5.1.1 Sampling Theorem

Figure 5.1 shows the ideal ***instantaneous sampling*** process. Figure 5.1a presents a model for instantaneous sampling and signal recovery, where a sequence of impulse functions is used to obtain the ideal samples of the signal. Consider the real-valued, lowpass analog signal $g(t)$ of finite energy, which is specified for all time t, as shown in Figure 5.1b. Let $g(t)$ be strictly band-limited to W Hz (i.e., $G(f)=0$, for $|f|>W$), as shown in Figure 5.1c. Suppose $g(t)$ is sampled at uniform intervals T_s seconds, resulting in the ideal (instantaneously) sampled signal $g_s(t)$, as shown in Figure 5.1d. The time interval T_s is known as the ***sampling period*** and its reciprocal $\frac{1}{T_s}=f_s$ is the ***sampling rate***. The sampling rate of $2W$ samples per second is called the ***Nyquist rate*** and its reciprocal $\frac{1}{2W}$ is the ***Nyquist period***. The ***sampling theorem*** states that $g(t)$ can be completely described by and uniquely recovered from $g_s(t)$ provided that the sampling period is less than the Nyquist period (i.e., $T_s<\frac{1}{2W}$ seconds) or equivalently, the sampling rate is greater than the Nyquist rate (i.e., $f_s>2W$ Hz).

The ***instantaneously sampled signal*** $g_s(t)$ can be viewed as multiplication of $g(t)$ and a periodic impulse train uniformly spaced T_s seconds apart. The ideal sampled signal $g_s(t)$ is therefore an infinite series of delta functions spaced T_s seconds apart and weighted (scaled) by the corresponding instantaneous values of the signal $g(t)$, as mathematically described by:

$$g_s(t)=g(t)\sum_{n=-\infty}^{\infty}\delta(t-nT_s)=\sum_{n=-\infty}^{\infty}g(nT_s)\delta(t-nT_s) \tag{5.1}$$

Since $g_s(t)$ is the product of $g(t)$ and the periodic impulse train, the Fourier transform of $g_s(t)$ is the convolution of the Fourier transforms of $g(t)$ and the periodic impulse train. The Fourier transform of a periodic impulse train is another periodic impulse train where the periods of the two impulse trains are reciprocal to one another and the spectrum is also scaled by its period. The Fourier transform of the sampled signal $g_s(t)$ may be therefore expressed as follows:

$$G_s(f)=G(f)*\left(f_s\sum_{n=-\infty}^{\infty}\delta(f-nf_s)\right) \tag{5.2}$$

where the symbol * denotes the convolution operation and f_s represents the scaling factor. Interchanging the order of summation and convolution and noting that the convolution of the Fourier transform of a function with an impulse function in the frequency domain results in a horizontal shift of the Fourier transform of the function along the frequency axis to where the impulse function is located. Hence, (5.2) may be written as follows:

$$G_s(f)=f_s\sum_{n=-\infty}^{\infty}G(f-nf_s) \tag{5.3}$$

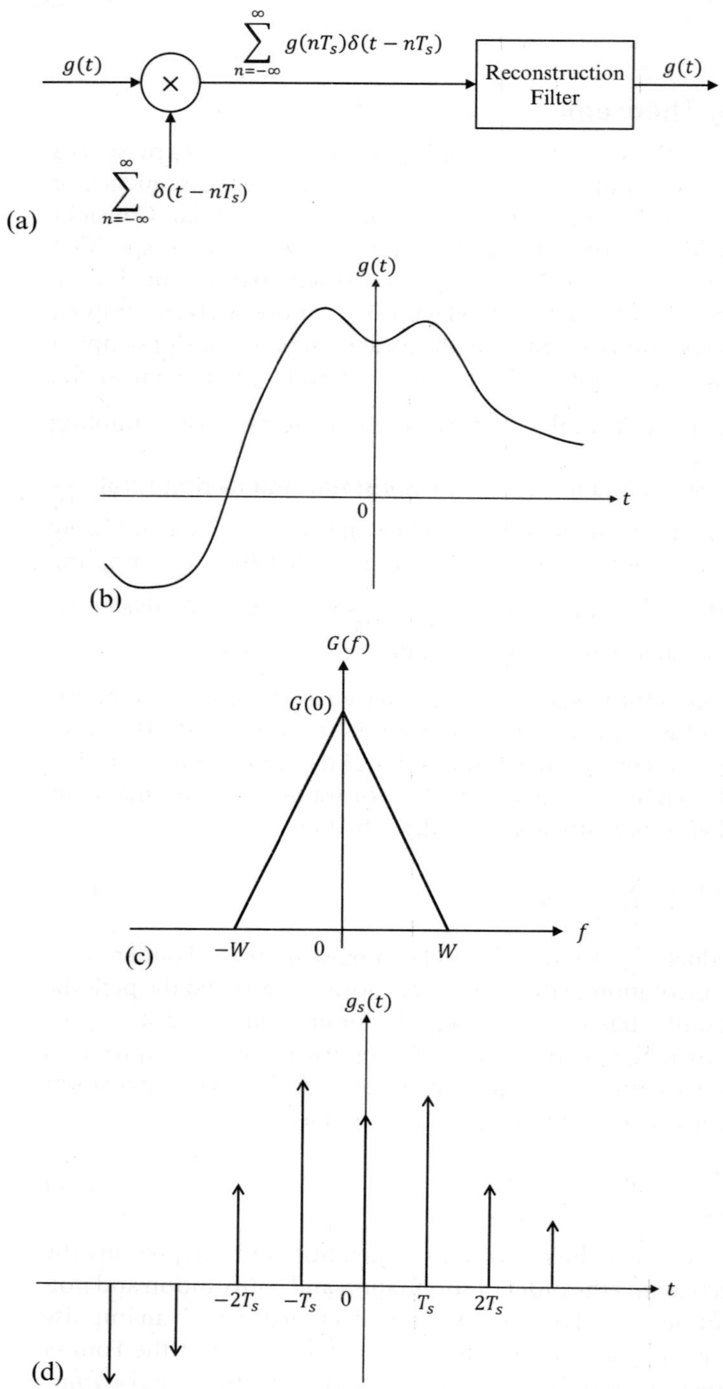

FIGURE 5.1 Ideal sampling process: (a) Instantaneous sampling and signal recovery, (b) analog signal in the time domain, (c) spectrum of the band-limited analog signal, (d) sampled version of the analog signal,

(Continued)

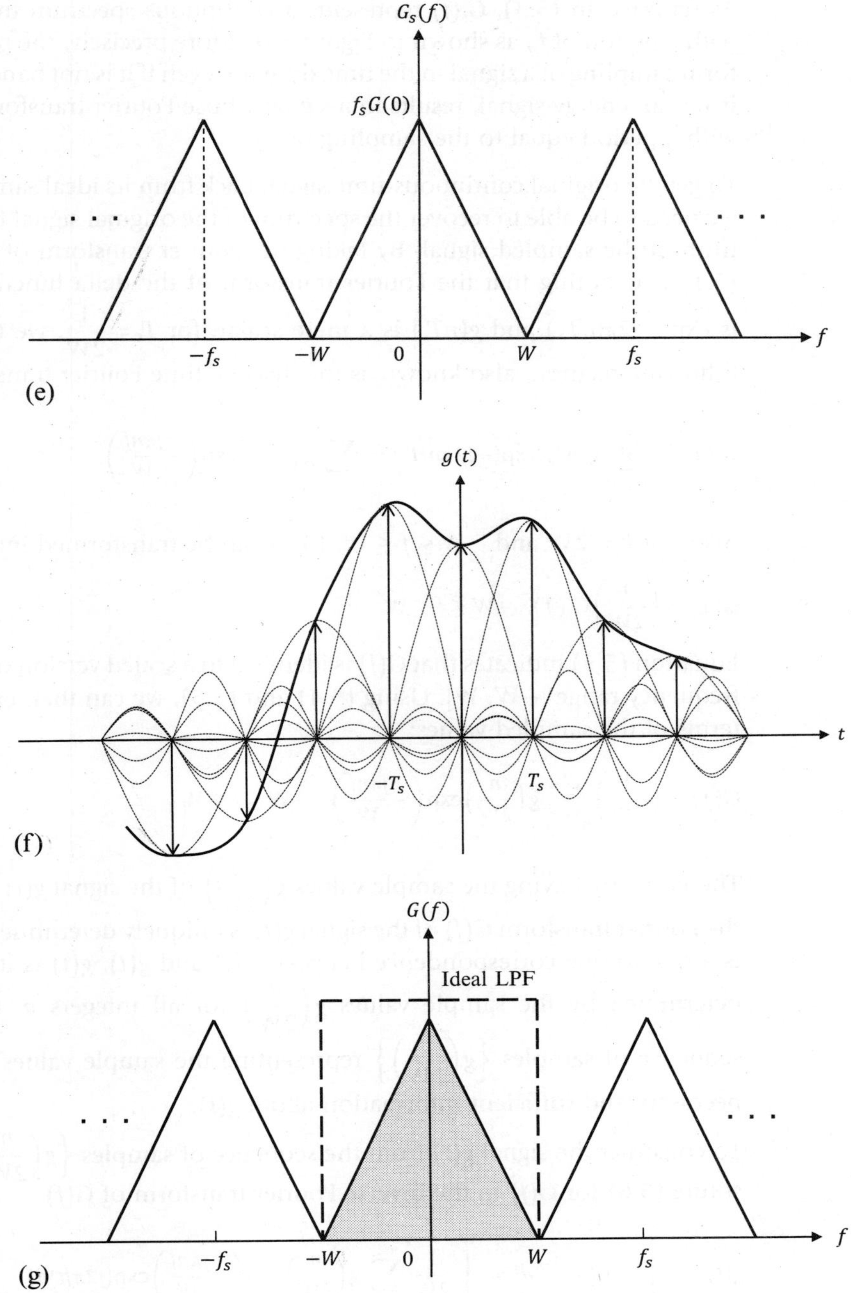

FIGURE 5.1, cont'd (e) spectrum of the sampled signal, (f) ideal interpolation, and (g) ideal lowpass filtering.

As reflected in (5.3), $G_s(f)$ represents a continuous spectrum that is periodic with a period of f_s, as shown in Figure 5.1e. More precisely, the process of uniform sampling of a signal in the time domain, even if it is not band-limited or it is not an energy signal, results in a signal whose Fourier transform is periodic with a period equal to the sampling rate f_s.

To get the original continuous-time signal back from its ideal sampled version, we need to be able to recover the spectrum of the original signal from the spectrum of the sampled signal. By taking the Fourier transform of both sides of (5.1) and noting that the Fourier transform of the delta function $\delta(t-nT_s)$ is $\exp(-j2\pi nfT_S)$ and $g(nT_s)$ is a mere scalar, for $T_s = \frac{1}{2W}$, we thus have the following relation, also known as the discrete-time Fourier transform:

$$G_s(f) = \sum_{n=-\infty}^{\infty} g(nT_s)\exp(-j2\pi nfT_s) = \sum_{n=-\infty}^{\infty} g\left(\frac{n}{2W}\right)\exp\left(-\frac{j\pi nf}{W}\right) \tag{5.4}$$

Also, for $f_s = 2W$ and $-W \leq f \leq W$, (5.3) can be transformed into:

$$G(f) = \left(\frac{1}{2W}\right)G_s(f), \quad -W \leq f \leq W \tag{5.5}$$

Equation (5.5) indicates that $G(f)$ is identical to a scaled version of $G_s(f)$ for the frequency range $[-W, W]$. Using (5.4) and (5.5), we can then express $G(f)$ in terms of the sampled values:

$$G(f) = \left(\frac{1}{2W}\right)\sum_{n=-\infty}^{\infty} g\left(\frac{n}{2W}\right)\exp\left(-\frac{j\pi nf}{W}\right), \quad -W \leq f \leq W \tag{5.6}$$

Therefore, by having the sample values $g\left(\frac{n}{2W}\right)$ of the signal $g(t)$ for all time t, the Fourier transform $G(f)$ of the signal $g(t)$ is uniquely determined. Since there is a one-to-one correspondence between $G(f)$ and $g(t)$, $g(t)$ is itself uniquely determined by the sample values $g\left(\frac{n}{2W}\right)$ for all integers n. In short, the sequence of samples $\left\{g\left(\frac{n}{2W}\right)\right\}$ representing the sample values contains the necessary and sufficient information about $g(t)$.

To construct the signal $g(t)$ from the sequence of samples $\left\{g\left(\frac{n}{2W}\right)\right\}$, we substitute (5.6) for $G(f)$ in the inverse Fourier transform of $G(f)$:

$$g(t) = \int_{n=-\infty}^{\infty} G(f)e^{j2\pi ft}df = \int_{-W}^{W} \frac{1}{2W}\sum_{n=-\infty}^{\infty} g\left(\frac{n}{2W}\right)\exp\left(-\frac{j\pi nf}{W}\right)\exp(j2\pi ft)df \tag{5.7}$$

After interchanging the order of summation and integration, and then evaluating the definite integral term, (5.7) is simplified to the following:

$$g(t)=\sum_{n=-\infty}^{\infty} g\left(\frac{n}{2W}\right)\int_{-W}^{W}\frac{1}{2W}e^{\left(j2\pi f\left(\frac{2Wt-n}{2W}\right)\right)}df=\sum_{n=-\infty}^{\infty} g\left(\frac{n}{2W}\right)\operatorname{sinc}(2Wt-n) \tag{5.8}$$

Equation (5.8) provides an interpolation formula for reconstruction of the original signal $g(t)$ from its sample values $g\left(\frac{n}{2W}\right)$, with the function sinc($2Wt - n$) playing the role of an interpolation function. This points to the fact that each sample is multiplied by the corresponding delayed version of the interpolating function and all the resulting waveforms are added up to obtain the original continuous-time signal $g(t)$, as shown in Figure 5.1f. Noting that the impulse response of an ideal lowpass filter (LPF) of bandwidth W is sinc($2Wt$), (5.8) then represents the response of such a filter when the input signal consists of the sequence of samples $\left\{g\left(\frac{n}{2W}\right)\right\}$. This is a mathematical confirmation that the original signal can be recovered from the sequence of samples $\left\{g\left(\frac{n}{2W}\right)\right\}$ by passing it through an ideal LPF of bandwidth W, as shown in Figure 5.1g. In practice, (5.8) cannot be implemented, since it represents a noncausal system as $g(t)$ depends on the past and future values of the input and also the impact of each sample extends over an infinite length of time as the impulse response has infinite duration.

It is important to note as long as the sampling rate is equal to the Nyquist rate, the original signal can be recovered from the sampled version. However, this is upon the condition that the spectrum of the original signal has no impulse (delta) function at the highest frequency W. If it has an impulse function at the highest frequency, then the sampling rate cannot be equal to the Nyquist rate, as spectrum overlap will occur. We thus require the sampling rate be greater than the Nyquist rate. An example is $g(t)=\sin(2\pi Wt)$, where its samples are taken at $t=\frac{k}{2W}$, with k being an integer. In such a case, $g(t)$ cannot be recovered from its Nyquist samples. For sinusoidal signals, the condition $f_s=2W$ is not sufficient and the condition $f_s>2W$ must thus be satisfied.

EXAMPLE 5.1

Suppose we have $g(t)=A\,\operatorname{sinc}(2Wt)$, where $A\neq 0$ and $W\neq 0$. Determine the condition on the sampling frequency f_s or the sampling period T_s so that $g(t)$ can be uniquely represented by its sampled version.

Solution

The Fourier transform of $g(t)$ is as follows:

$$G(f)=\left(\frac{A}{2W}\right)(u(f+W)-u(f-W))$$

where $u(.)$ is the unit step function. The highest frequency is thus W. Hence, we require that $f_s>2W$ or $T_s<\frac{1}{2W}$.

EXAMPLE 5.2

Suppose the lowpass signal $g(t)$ is band-limited to W (i.e., the Nyquist rate for $g(t)$ is $2W$). Determine the Nyquist rate for each of the following signals derived from $g(t)$:

(a) $y(t)=\frac{d}{dt}g(t)$ (i.e., $y(t)$ is the time derivative of the signal $g(t)$).

(b) $y(t)=g(at),\ a\neq 0$ (i.e., $y(t)$ is the time-scaled version of the signal $g(t)$).

Solution

In this problem, we look into how some signal operations in the time domain may impact the required sampling rate.

(a) From the Fourier transform properties, we have the Fourier transform of $y(t)$ in terms of the Fourier transform of $g(t)$ as follows:

$$Y(f)=j2\pi f\,G(f)$$

Since $G(f)=0$ for $|f|>W$, we also have $Y(f)=0$ for $|f|>W$. Therefore, we can conclude that the Nyquist rate is not changed by the process of differentiation (i.e., the Nyquist rate for $y(t)$ is also $2W$).

(b) From the Fourier transform properties, we have the Fourier transform of $y(t)$ in terms of the Fourier transform of $g(t)$ as follows:

$$Y(f)=\frac{1}{|a|}G\left(\frac{f}{a}\right)$$

In other words, time scaling of the signal $g(t)$ by a factor a results in frequency scaling of the signal $G(f)$ by a factor $\frac{1}{a}$. Consequently, the Nyquist rate for $y(t)$ is $|a|$ times the Nyquist rate for $g(t)$ (i.e., $2|a|W$).

5.1.2 Undersampling and Aliasing Effect

Figure 5.2 shows the impact of sampling rate on the spectrum of the sampled signal. Figure 5.2a shows the spectrum of an analog lowpass band-limited signal whose bandwidth is W. Figure 5.2b shows the spectrum of the sampled signal when the sampling rate is higher than the Nyquist rate $2W$ (i.e., $f_s>2W$). Since one period of $G_s(f)$, apart from a scaling factor, is identical to $G(f)$, such a sampling rate can then allow the spectrum of the original analog signal to be retrieved using a simple, realizable LPF. ***Undersampling*** occurs when a signal is sampled too slowly. In such a case, $G_s(f)$ consists of the frequency-shifted versions of $G(f)$ that overlap (i.e., the higher frequencies in $G(f)$ get reflected into the lower frequencies in $G_s(f)$). As a result, one period of $G_s(f)$ can no longer be identical to $G(f)$. This phenomenon of some of the higher frequencies in the spectrum of the signal $g(t)$ appearing as lower frequencies in the spectrum of its sampled version is called ***aliasing*** or ***frequency overlapping*** or ***fold-over distortion*** or ***spectral folding***. Figure 5.2c shows the spectrum of the sampled signal when the sampling rate is lower than the Nyquist rate $2W$ (i.e., $f_s < 2W$). This frequency overlapping prevents the recovery of the original signal from its sampled version. Undersampling may therefore bring about significant distortion and information is thereby lost. To mitigate the effects of aliasing, the following two pre-emptive measures can be taken:

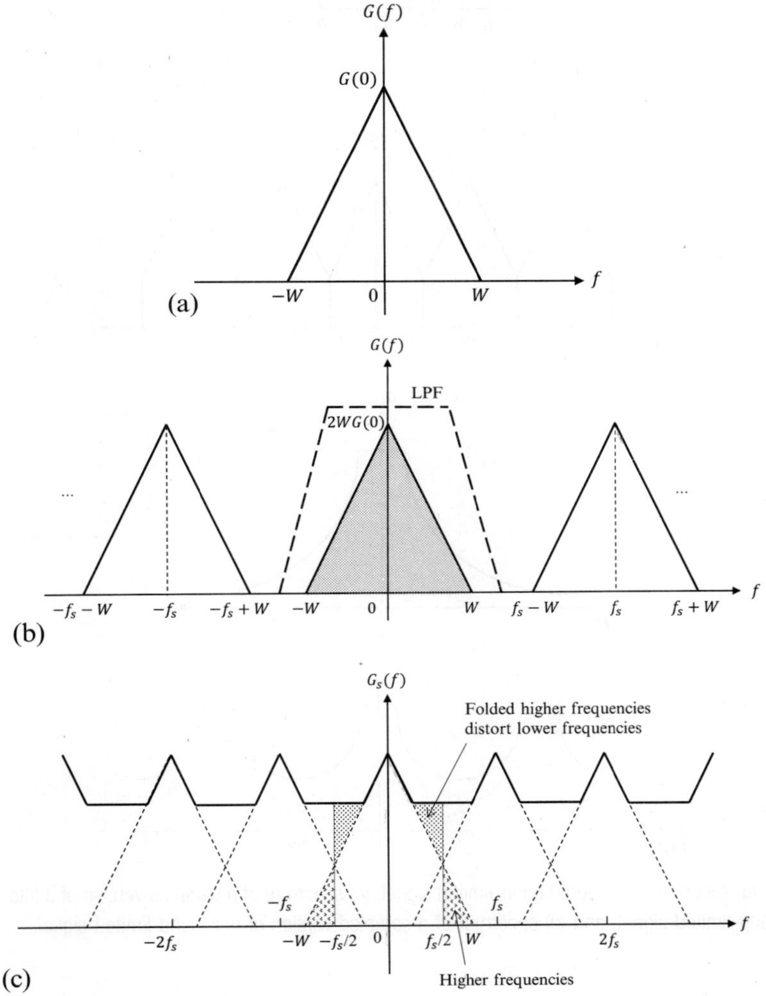

FIGURE 5.2 Impacts of sampling rate on spectrum: (a) Spectrum of a band-limited signal, (b) spectrum of an oversampled version of band-limited signal, (c) spectrum of an undersampled version of band-limited signal,

(Continued)

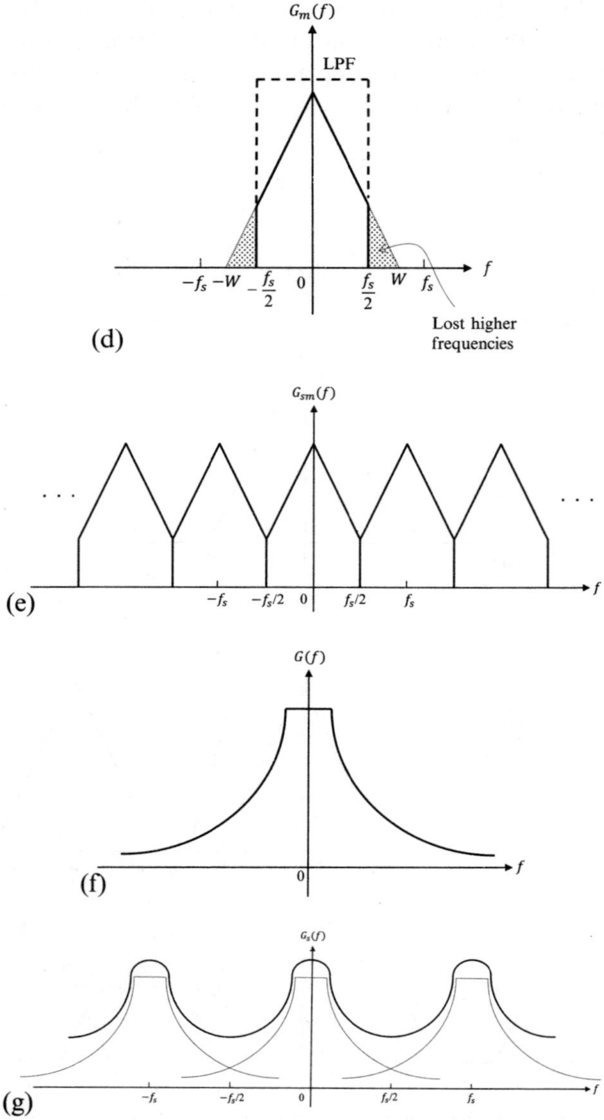

FIGURE 5.2, cont'd (d) spectrum of a filtered band-limited signal, (e) spectrum of a sampled version of a filtered band-limited signal, (f) spectrum of a non-band-limited signal, and (g) spectrum of a sampled version of non-band-limited signal.

i) Employ, prior to sampling, a LPF, known as an ***anti-aliasing filter***. This filter can practically attenuate (or theoretically eliminate) the high frequency components of the signal that are not essential to the information being conveyed by the signal. This prevents the suppressed frequency components from corrupting the components of frequencies below the folding frequency $\frac{f_s}{2}$. However, an anti-aliasing filter always introduces a small, but negligible amount of distortion. Figure 5.2d shows the spectrum of the signal at the output of the anti-aliasing filter and Figure 5.2e shows the spectrum of the sampled version of the filtered signal. An anti-aliasing filter also helps to reduce noise, as noise has a wideband spectrum and without aliasing filter, the aliasing phenomenon itself can cause noise components outside the desired signal band to appear in the signal band.

ii) Sample the filtered signal at a rate slightly higher than the Nyquist rate. This has the beneficial effect of easing the design of the reconstruction filter in the receiver used to recover the original signal. The reconstruction filter can then have a passband up to W, as determined by the aliasing filter in the transmitter, and a transition band from W to $f_s - W$. Filter complexity and cost rise with narrower transition bandwidth, so there is a trade-off between the cost of smaller transition bandwidth and the cost of higher sampling and transmission rate. As a design rule, a transition bandwidth of around 20% of the signal bandwidth is reasonable, and the sampling rate thus needs to be about 2.2 times the bandwidth (i.e., $f_s \cong 2.2W$).

The sampling theorem is based on the assumption that the continuous-time signal is strictly band-limited. But in practice, an information-bearing signal is time-limited, as such it is not band-limited, as shown in Figure 5.2f. Consequently, regardless of how high the sampling rate is, some aliasing is always produced by the sampling process, as shown in Figure 5.2g. However, with an appropriate anti-aliasing filter, the distortion due to the folded lower frequencies can be minimized.

EXAMPLE 5.3

Suppose the minimum sampling rate for a lowpass signal is 8 kHz, and a guard band of 2 kHz is required. Determine the signal bandwidth.

Solution

As shown in Figure 5.2b, we have:

$G = (f_s - W) - W$

i.e., we have:

$$W=\frac{f_s-G}{2}$$

where f_s is the minimum sampling frequency, W is the signal bandwidth, and G is the guard band. We therefore get:

$$W=\frac{f_s-G}{2}=\frac{8-2}{2}=3\,\text{kHz}.$$

EXAMPLE 5.4

Consider the sinusoidal signals $g_1(t)=\cos(2\pi f_1 t)$ and $g_2(t)=\cos(2\pi f_2 t)$, where $f_1<f_2$. Both signals are sampled at f_3, where we have $2f_1<f_3<2f_2$. Determine a relationship among f_1, f_2, and f_3, for which the sampled versions of the two signals can be identical.

Solution – Noting the Fourier transform of a sinusoidal signal is a pair of delta functions, Figure 5.3 shows the spectra of both sinusoidal signals and their sampled versions. Obviously, because of $2f_1<f_3<2f_2$, $g_1(t)$ is sampled higher than the Nyquist rate and $g_2(t)$ is sampled lower than the Nyquist rate. As a result, $g_1(t)$ is being oversampled and it can be recovered back from its sampled version and $g_2(t)$ is being undersampled and it cannot be recovered back from its sampled version. To have the sampled versions of the two signals identical, the spectra of their sampled versions must be identical (i.e., the locations of delta functions in $G_{1s}(f)$ are required to be the same as those in $G_{2s}(f)$). We must then have $f_3-f_2=f_1$ or $f_3-f_1=f_2$ (i.e., $f_3=f_1+f_2$). In other words, if the sampling rate is equal to the sum of the frequencies of the two sinusoidal signals, then the sampled versions of the two signals are the same.

5.1.3 Natural Sampling and Flat-Top Sampling

Although instantaneous sampling is a simple model, a more practical way of sampling is natural sampling. In ***natural sampling***, the continuous-time signal $g(t)$, whose bandwidth is W, is multiplied by a periodic pulse train, where each pulse has width τ and amplitude $\frac{1}{\tau}$, occurring with period T_s. This multiplication can be viewed as the opening and closing of a high-speed switch. This sampling is termed natural sampling, as the top of each pulse in the sequence retains the shape of its corresponding original segment during the pulse interval. Figure 5.4 shows the natural sampling process. The Fourier transform of the sampled signal using a natural sampling method is as follows:

$$G_s(f)=f_s\sum_{n=-\infty}^{\infty}c_nG(f-nf_s) \tag{5.9}$$

where $c_n=\text{sinc}(n\tau f_s)$ are the Fourier series coefficients of the periodic pulse train. As the width of the pulse train approaches zero (i.e., $\tau\rightarrow 0$), the periodic

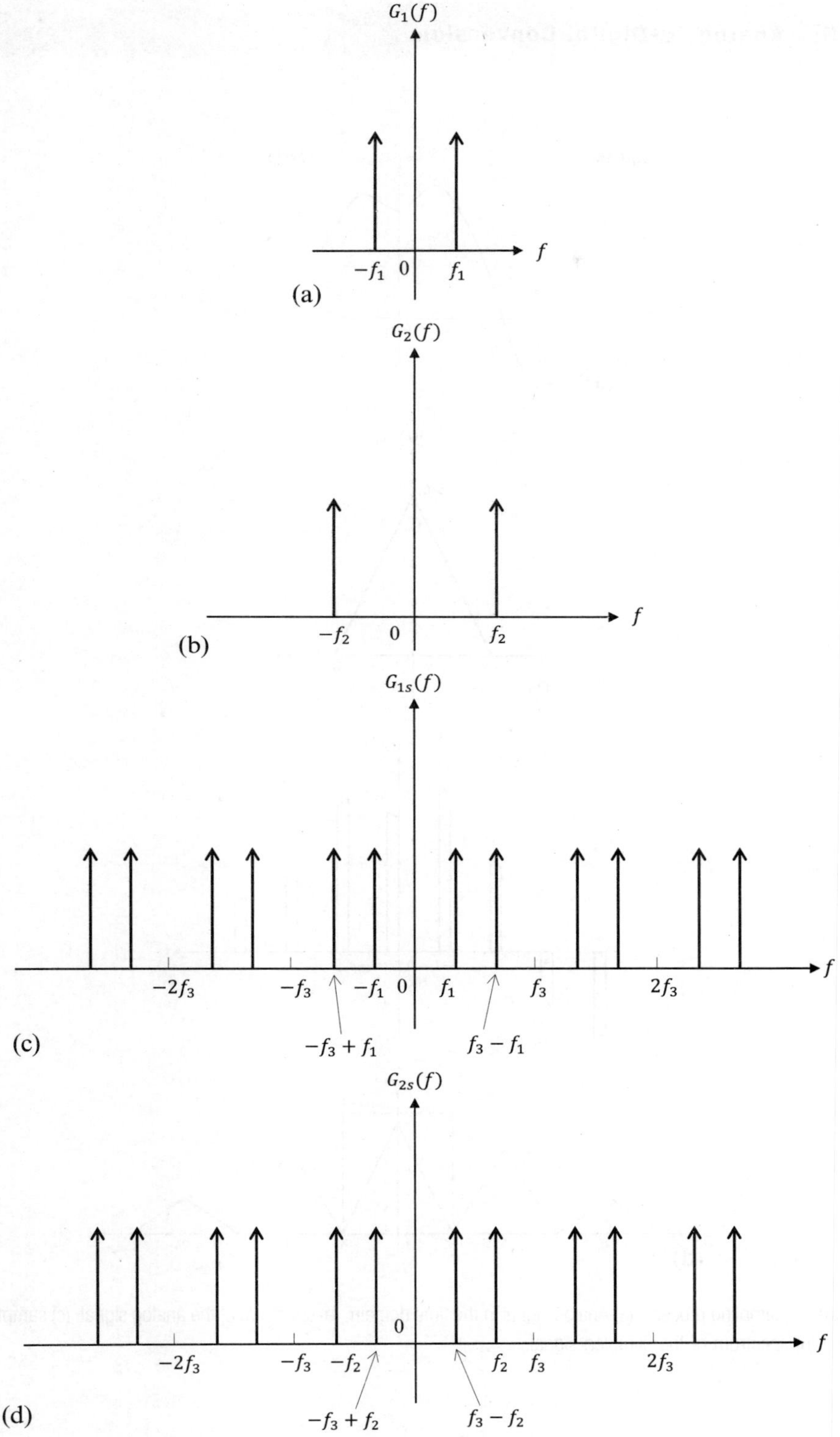

FIGURE 5.3 Example 5.3: (a) Spectrum of $\cos(2\pi f_1 t)$, (b) spectrum of $\cos(2\pi f_2 t)$, (c) spectrum of the oversampled version of $\cos(2\pi f_1 t)$, and (d) spectrum of the undersampled version of $\cos(2\pi f_2 t)$.

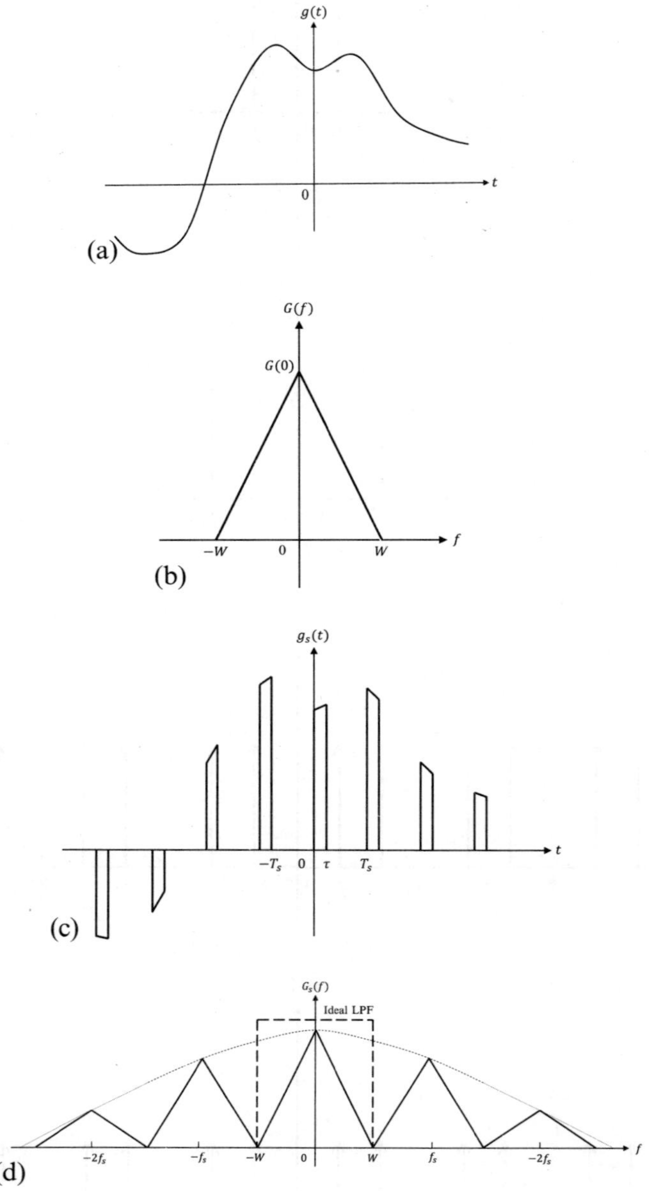

FIGURE 5.4 Natural sampling process: (a) Analog signal in the time domain, (b) spectrum of the analog signal, (c) sampled version of the analog signal, and (d) spectrum of the sampled signal.

pulse train becomes the periodic impulse train, and (5.9) converges to (5.3). Equation (5.9) indicates that $G_s(f)$ consists of numerous copies of $G(f)$, spaced at f_s, but these copies, in contrast to those in (5.3), are not uniformly weighted (scaled), but instead are weighted by the Fourier series coefficients of the periodic pulse train. Despite this difference, the original $g(t)$ can be equally well recovered using a LPF as long as the sampling rate f_s is higher than the Nyquist rate.

Flat-top sampling, also known as pulse amplitude modulation, is the most practical sampling method, in which the ***sample-and-hold operation*** is performed (i.e., the value of each instantaneous sample is maintained for a duration of τ seconds), as shown in Figure 5.5a. The sampled signal using flat-top operation is equivalent to the convolution of an instantaneously sampled signal with a unit-amplitude rectangular pulse $h(t)$ of width τ. The signal $g(t)$ can be recovered as long as the sampling rate f_s is higher than the Nyquist rate. Figure 5.5b shows the flat-top sampling process. The Fourier transform of the sampled signal using sample-and-hold method is as follows:

$$G_s(f) = f_s H(f) \sum_{n=-\infty}^{\infty} G(f - nf_s) \tag{5.10}$$

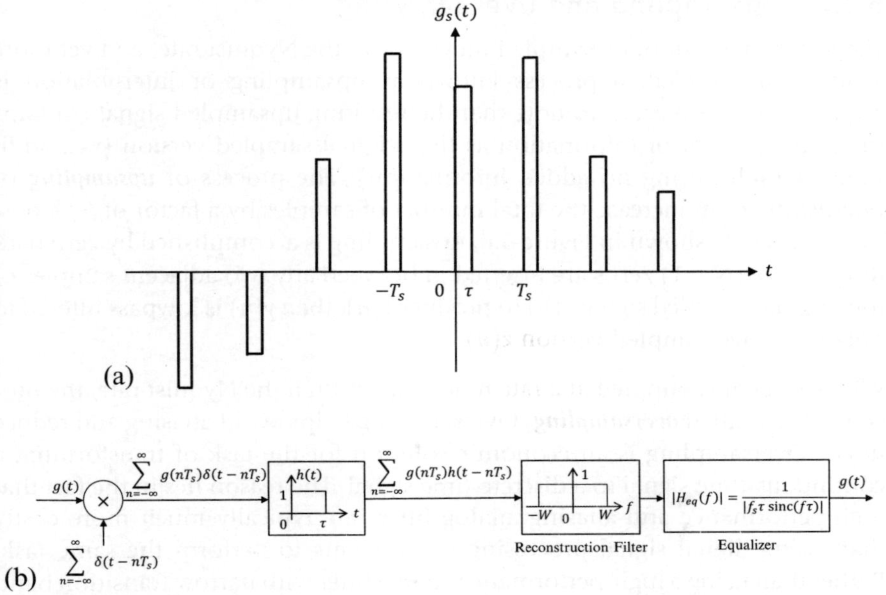

FIGURE 5.5 Flat-top sampling process: (a) Sampled version of the analog signal and (b) block diagram producing the sampled version.

where $H(f) = \tau \operatorname{sinc}(f\tau)$ is the Fourier transform of $h(t)$ the unit-amplitude rectangular pulse of width τ. The Fourier transform $H(f)$ thus plays the role of a LPF, an obvious effect of the hold operation is therefore the significant attenuation of high-frequency spectral components, which is a desired effect. As a first step to recover the original signal $g(t)$, the sampled signal is passed through a lowpass reconstruction filter to attenuate the residual spectral components located at the multiples of the sampling rate. A secondary effect of the sample-and-hold operation is due to the nonconstant $|H(f)| = |\tau \operatorname{sinc}(f\tau)|$ over the bandwidth of interest $\left[-\frac{1}{\tau}, \frac{1}{\tau}\right]$ even when the Nyquist rate sampling is satisfied. This amplitude distortion is referred to as the ***aperture effect*** and can be corrected by an equalizer whose transfer function is $\frac{T_s}{H(f)}$. For very short rectangular pulses, the amount of equalization needed in practice is usually quite small, as the equalizer passband response can be approximated by $\frac{T_s}{\tau}$, for $|f| \leq W$. In fact, with a duty cycle of $\frac{\tau}{T_s} \leq 10\%$, the amplitude distortion can be less than 0.5%, and thus no equalization may be necessary.

5.1.4 Upsampling and Oversampling

When a signal cannot be sampled much above the Nyquist rate, and yet more samples are needed, a process known as upsampling or interpolation is required. It is important to note that the resulting upsampled signal contains the same amount of information as the original sampled version (i.e., additional samples bring no added information). The process of ***upsampling*** or ***interpolation*** can increase the total number of samples by a factor of N, a positive integer. As shown in Figure 5.6, upsampling is accomplished by zero padding, where $(N-1)$ zeros are inserted in between any two adjacent samples of the original sampled signal $x(n)$ to produce $y(n)$, then $y(n)$ is lowpass filtered to obtain the oversampled version $z(n)$.

When a signal is sampled at a rate much higher than the Nyquist rate, the process is then called ***oversampling***. Oversampling helps avoid aliasing and reduce noise. Oversampling is an economic solution for the task of transforming a continuous-time signal to a discrete-time signal. The reason lies in the fact that high-performance anti-aliasing analog filters are typically much more costly than using digital signal processing components to perform the same task. Rather than using a high-performance analog filter with narrow transition band followed by sampling at the Nyquist rate, a low-performance (less-costly) analog filter with wide transition band is employed. The signal is then oversampled at

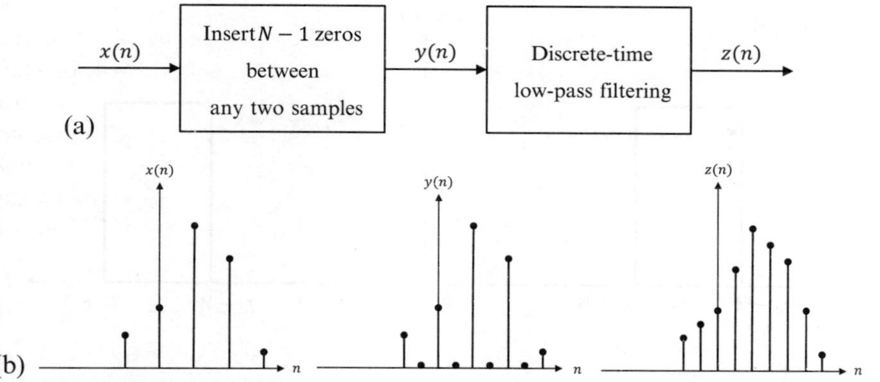

FIGURE 5.6 Upsampling process: (a) Block diagram of an interpolation system and (b) an example for $N = 2$.

several times its Nyquist rate. Once sampled, the signal can be digitally filtered and then, through a process called ***decimation***, the effective rate is reduced to the Nyquist rate or slightly above it. A prime example is the use of oversampling to produce CD-quality audio signal with 20 kHz bandwidth. Rather than sampling an audio signal at 44.1 kHz with a transition bandwidth of 4.1 ($= 44.1 - 20 - 20$) kHz thus requiring a very complex analog filter, oversampling is employed where the sampler operates at 176.4 kHz (i.e., four times the original sampler rate) with a transition bandwidth of 136.4 ($= 176.4 - 20 - 20$) kHz, thus warranting a simple, low-cost analog filter.

5.1.5 Sampling of Bandpass Signals and Random Signals

Bandpass signals can also be represented by their sampled values. Consider a bandpass signal whose Fourier transform occupies the frequency intervals $f_c - W < |f| < f_c + W$, as shown in Figure 5.7a. In other words, the bandpass signal has non-negligible frequency content around f_c with a bandwidth of $2W$. It can be shown that the minimum sampling rate required for such a bandpass signal is $\frac{2(f_c + W)}{m}$, where $f_c + W$ represents the signal's highest frequency component, and m is the largest integer not exceeding the ratio $\frac{f_c + W}{2W}$. Figure 5.7b, in which the shaded regions represent the permissible sampling rates for a bandpass signal, indicates that regardless of passband location, the minimum permissible sampling rate necessary for signal reconstruction always lies between $4W$ and $8W$. Equivalently, the minimum sampling rate is greater than twice the signal bandwidth, but less than four times the signal bandwidth.

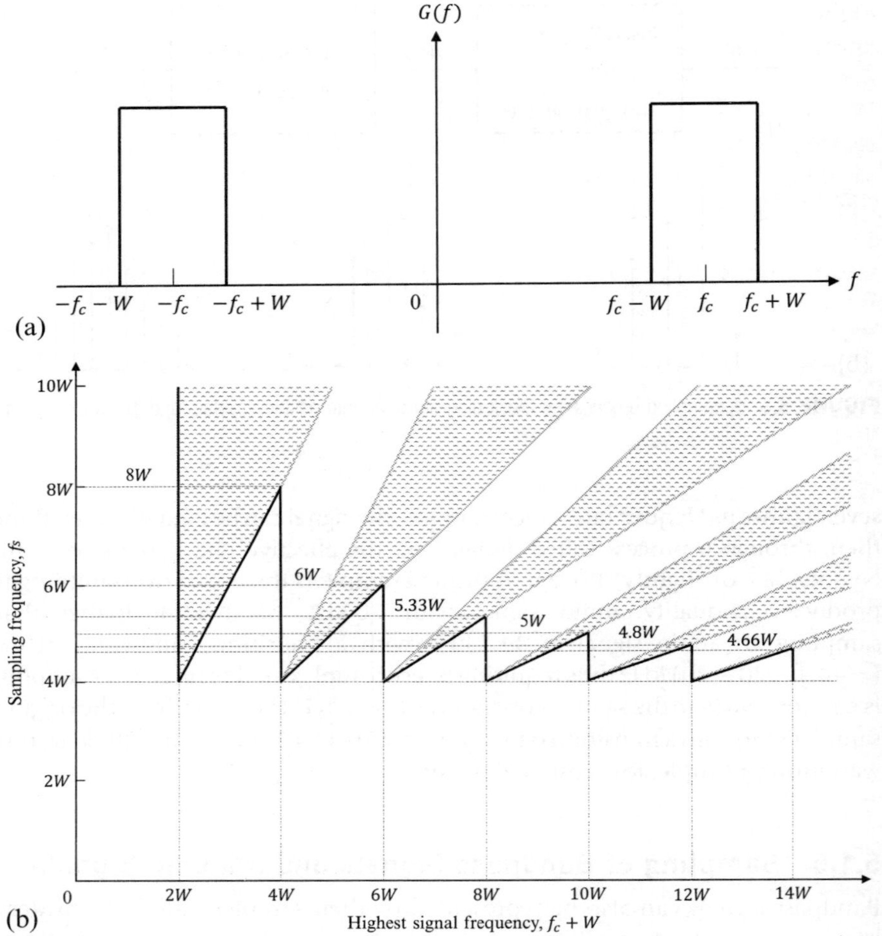

FIGURE 5.7 Sampling of bandpass signals: (a) Spectrum of bandpass signals and (b) minimum sampling rate for bandpass signals.

When we have $f_c \gg W$, the minimum permissible sampling rate then approaches twice the signal bandwidth $2W$. Another way of sampling a bandpass signal of bandwidth $2W$ is to decompose it into two lowpass signals (i.e., the in-phase and quadrature components), each with a bandwidth of W. Each of these may be sampled at a minimum rate of $2W$ samples per second, thus resulting in an overall minimum sampling rate of $4W$ samples per second.

The following examples illustrate how the sampling rates for bandpass signals may be selected. The minimum sampling frequency for a 2-GHz bandpass signal with a bandwidth of 20 MHz is only about 40 MHz, as opposed to twice the highest frequency of 4 GHz. This is a reduction of two orders of magnitude. As another example, suppose a bandpass signal has frequency components between 15 kHz and 25 kHz. We can therefore assume $f_c = 20$ kHz and $W = 5$ kHz. From Figure 5.7b, we see the minimum sampling rate for the highest frequency of 25 ($= 5W$) kHz is $5W$ ($= 25$) kHz, and the allowable ranges of sampling rate are thus $25\,\text{kHz} \leq f_s \leq 30\,\text{kHz}$ and $f_s \geq 50$ kHz. As reflected by this example, for bandpass sampling, exceeding the minimum sampling frequency is necessary but not sufficient, as there is generally a number of frequency intervals where alias-free recovery is possible.

EXAMPLE 5.5

Consider the signal $g(t) = 4\cos(2\pi f_1 t)\cos(2\pi f_2 t)$, where $f_2 = (2k+1)f_1$ and $k \geq 1$ is a positive integer (i.e., f_2 is an odd multiple of f_1).

(a) By treating $g(t)$ as a lowpass signal, determine the lowest permissible sampling rate for this signal.

(b) By treating $g(t)$ as a bandpass signal, determine the lowest permissible sampling rate for this signal.

Solution

Using the trigonometry identity to transform product into summation, we get:

$$g(t) = 2\cos(2\pi(f_1 + f_2)t) + 2\cos(2\pi(f_1 - f_2)t)$$

By taking the Fourier transform of $g(t)$, we get:

$$G(f) = \delta(f + f_1 + f_2) + \delta(f - f_1 - f_2) + \delta(f + f_1 - f_2) + \delta(f - f_1 + f_2)$$

We can therefore conclude the highest frequency component of $G(f)$ is $f_2 + f_1 = 2(k+1)f_1$ and its lowest frequency component is $f_2 - f_1 = 2kf_1$.

(a) Assuming $g(t)$ is a lowpass signal, the lowest permissible sampling rate is twice the highest frequency (i.e., $f_s = 2(f_2 + f_1) = 4(k+1)f_1$).

(b) Assuming $g(t)$ is a bandpass signal, we have $f_c = (2k+1)f_1$ and $W = f_1$. We thus have $m = k$ and the lowest possible permissible sampling rate is $f_s = 4\left(\frac{k+1}{k}\right)f_1$.

For $k \geq 1$, we have $4\left(\frac{k+1}{k}\right)f_1 \leq 4(k+1)f_1$. It is thus better to view $g(t)$ as a bandpass signal, as the required minimum sampling rate could then be lower.

Sampling of random signals was discussed in Chapter 4 in detail, and here we briefly summarize it. Suppose $X(t)$ is a wide-sense stationary random process whose power spectral density is band-limited to W. This random signal can then be reconstructed from the sequence of its samples taken at a minimum rate of twice the highest frequency component (i.e., $2W$) where the sampled version of the process equals the original in the mean-square sense for all time t.

As a final point regarding sampling, it is important to highlight that there is a dual to the time-domain sampling theorem discussed earlier, that is, the frequency-domain sampling theorem. The ***sampling theorem in the frequency domain*** states that if a continuous-time signal is strictly time limited to τ seconds, then the Fourier transform of the signal can be uniquely determined from its samples in the frequency domain provided that the sampling rate in the frequency domain is no greater than $\frac{1}{2\tau}$ Hz. For instance, the Fourier transform of a short pulse with a duration of 2 μs must be sampled at a rate no higher than 250 kHz, so the Fourier transform of the pulse can be uniquely reconstructed from its samples in the frequency domain.

5.2 QUANTIZATION PROCESS

Through ***quantization***, a discrete-time, continuous-value signal can be transformed into a discrete-time, discrete-value signal, where the discrete amplitudes belong to a finite set of possible values. Obviously, if this finite set is chosen such that the spacing between two adjacent levels is sufficiently small, then the approximated (quantized) signal (i.e., the resulting discrete-time, discrete-value signal) can be made virtually identical to (practically indistinguishable from) the original discrete-time, continuous-value signal.

The reason for quantization (i.e., changing a continuous amplitude range with an infinite number of amplitude levels to a discrete amplitude set with a finite number of amplitude levels) is twofold: i) humans, in terms of what they see and hear, cannot always perceive much difference between these two signals, as they can detect only finite intensity differences and that is why quantization is at the core of compression algorithms for audio and visual signals, and ii) digital transmission of a signal whose amplitude can have virtually any value requires an extremely high transmission rate. Quantization is therefore always involved in the rounding of signal values in digital signal processing, transmission, and storage.

Quantization is a nonlinear and lossy process as multiple input values can yield the same output value. Unlike the sampling process, the quantization process is an irreversible process, in that it is not possible to completely recover the original continuous-value signal from the quantized (discrete-value) signal. The degradation due to the quantization and other operations involved in analog-to-digital conversion is in principle either unnoticeable and thus acceptable, such as the quantization of speech signal in the public switched telephone network, or noticeable but still acceptable, such as the quantization and compression of speech signals in low-bandwidth systems involved in search and rescue operations or the quantization and compression of video signals in monitoring of remote and isolated places.

There are two distinct quantization methods: ***scalar quantization***, in which samples are quantized individually (i.e., a scalar (one-dimensional) input value is mapped into a scalar output value), and ***vector quantization***, in which samples are quantized in blocks. Scalar quantization is a memoryless and instantaneous process, which means the quantization of a sample value is not affected by past and future samples, and consists of two distinct types: uniform quantization and nonuniform quantization.

5.2.1 Uniform Quantization

Uniform quantization is not optimum, but is commonly used in practice. This type of quantization is basically a simple rounding process, in which each sample value is rounded to the nearest value from a finite set of possible quantization levels. We assume that the signal amplitude at the input of the quantizer ranges between the maximum value $V > 0$ and the minimum value $-V$, and that the amplitude of the unquantized signal either below $-V$ or above V is simply chopped off. The amplitude range $[-V, V]$ is a limit set by the quantizer, not by the original signal produced by the analog source. The error introduced by this clipping is referred to as ***overload distortion*** or ***clipping distortion***. The amplitude range $[-V, V]$ is divided into L ***quantization levels***. The spacing between two adjacent quantization levels is called the ***step size*** Δ . In a ***uniform quantizer***, the step size is the same between any two adjacent levels. The uniform quantizer has the simplest structure and its target level lies in the middle of the interval. With L as the number of the quantization levels, the step size of a uniform quantizer for a signal with an amplitude range of $2V$ is thus given by

$$\Delta = \frac{2V}{L} \tag{5.11}$$

Within the supported amplitude range, the spacing between the continuous-value and the discrete-value is referred to as its ***granularity***. The error introduced by this spacing is referred to as ***quantization noise*** or ***granular distortion*** or ***rounding error***. In the context of quantization, the terms of noise and distortion are usually used interchangeably. The quantization error is bounded in magnitude and has generally a saw-tooth shape, but overload distortion is unbounded. The quantization noise and overload distortion are functions of the particular quantization process and statistics of the input signal. It is important to have the proper balance between the quantization noise and the overload distortion. For a given number of possible output values, reducing the average quantization noise may involve increasing the average overload distortion, and vice versa.

Each quantization level at the output of quantizer is typically mapped into a codeword with R bits representing a quantized sample value. Using (5.11), the number of quantization levels L is therefore as follows:

$$L = 2^R = \frac{2V}{\Delta} \tag{5.12}$$

The step size Δ and the number of bits R depend on the dynamic range of the signal amplitude and perceptual sensitivity. For toll-quality speech, we have $R = 8$ bits, and for CD-quality music, $R = 16$ bits.

There are two types of uniform quantizers, and both are symmetric. Figure 5.8a and Figure 5.8b show the input-output characteristics of ***mid-tread quantizer*** and ***mid-rise quantizer***, respectively.

Assuming that the input to the quantizer is zero mean and the quantizer is symmetric, the quantizer output and the quantization error will also have zero mean.

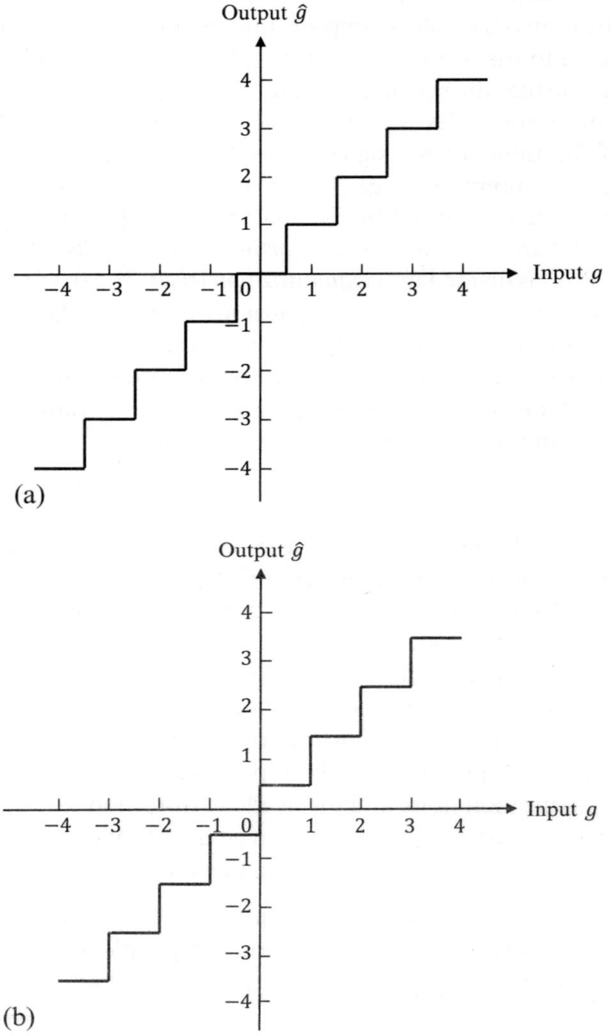

FIGURE 5.8 Types of uniform quantizers: (a) mid-tread quantizer and (b) mid-rise quantizer.

For a uniform quantizer, the quantization error e is a random variable, which is bounded by $-\frac{\Delta}{2} \leq e \leq \frac{\Delta}{2}$. With sufficiently small step size, the quantization error can be assumed to be uniformly distributed and uncorrelated with the quantizer input. Using (5.12) and noting that the quantization error e is zero mean, its variance is the same as the average power and is thus given as follows:

$$\sigma_e^2 = \int_{-\frac{\Delta}{2}}^{\frac{\Delta}{2}} \left(\frac{1}{\Delta}\right) e^2 de = \frac{\Delta^2}{12} = \frac{V^2}{3L^2} = \frac{V^2}{3(2^{2R})} \tag{5.13}$$

From (5.13), it is mathematically evident, and from the basic description of the uniform quantization, it is intuitively obvious that as the number of quantization levels $L \rightarrow \infty$ or the step size $\Delta \rightarrow 0$ or the number of bits per quantized sample $R \rightarrow \infty$, the quantization error $e \rightarrow 0$.

Selecting V so that it corresponds to the maximum value of the signal is not very efficient. Instead, V is commonly selected so that the probability that a sample exceeds V is negligible. To this effect, for a zero-mean random input signal with the standard deviation σ_g, which is a measure of the spread of the signal values about the zero mean, we define the ***loading (crest) factor*** as follows:

$$\alpha = \frac{\text{peak value of the signal}}{\text{rms value of the signal}} = \frac{V}{\sigma_g} \tag{5.14}$$

Noting the signal has a zero mean, the average power of the message signal $g(t)$ is then defined as follows:

$$P = \sigma_g^2 \tag{5.15}$$

By using (5.11) to (5.15), the ***output signal-to-noise ratio*** of a uniform quantizer is as follows:

$$\text{SNR}_\text{o} = \frac{P}{\sigma_e^2} = \left(\frac{3\sigma_g^2}{V^2}\right) 2^{2R} = \left(\frac{3}{\alpha^2}\right) 2^{2R} \tag{5.16}$$

Equation (5.16) indicates that the SNR_o increases exponentially, as the number of bits per sample R is increased. Expressing the SNR_o in dB gives rise to the following:

$$10 \log \text{SNR}_\text{o} = 20 \log \sigma_g + 6R - 20 \log V + 4.77 \cong 6R - 20 \log \alpha + 4.77 \text{ (dB)} \tag{5.17}$$

In practice, a common choice for the loading factor is $\alpha = 4$ (i.e., the total amplitude range of the quantizer is $2V = 8\sigma_g$). Using (5.17), a practical SNR_o in uniform quantization is then as follows:

$$10 \log \text{SNR}_\text{o} = 6R - 7.27 \text{ (dB)} \tag{5.18}$$

It is important to highlight that for each additional bit per level (i.e., R is increased by one bit), an additional 6 dB improvement in the SNR_o can be obtained.

EXAMPLE 5.6

The signal $g(t) = V\sin(2\pi ft)$ is applied to a uniform quantizer. Determine the SNR_o in dB in terms of the number of bits per level. Specify the number of bits per level, the number of quantization levels, and the step size for which the value of SNR_o is about 49.8 dB.

Solution

For $g(t) = V\sin(2\pi ft)$, we have $P = \sigma_g^2 = V^2/2$. The peak-to-peak value is $2V$. Using (5.17), we can get

$$10\log SNR_o = 20\log\left(V/\sqrt{2}\right) + 6R - 20\log V + 4.77 = 1.8 + 6R(\text{dB}).$$

We now set $1.8 + 6R$ equal to 49.8, and thus obtain $R = 8$ bits. By using (5.12), we then get $L = 2^8 = 256$ levels, and by using (5.11), we get $\Delta = \frac{2V}{256} = \frac{V}{128}$.

The uniform quantizer yields the highest (optimal) SNR_o at the output if the signal amplitude has a uniform distribution in the dynamic range $[-V, V]$. However, for a source that does not have a uniform distribution, the optimal quantizer may not be a uniform one. The optimal quantization level in each quantization region must be chosen to be the centroid (conditional expected value) of that region. Since the optimal quantizer requires advance knowledge of both the signal statistics and changes in signal's power level, they do not have many practical applications. For some analog signals, such as speech and music, the loading factor α is large, and, as reflected in (5.17), can significantly reduce the value of SNR_o. To quantize such signals, it is advantageous to have nonuniform spacing, more specifically, smaller spacing near zero and larger spacing at the extremes. Assuming a signal with nonuniform distribution, for a given number of quantization levels, nonuniform quantizers can then outperform uniform quantizers.

5.2.2 Nonuniform Quantization

For a typical voice signal, smaller amplitudes, such as silent periods, low voices, and weak talk, predominate in speech (i.e., there is a higher probability they will occur), whereas larger amplitudes, such as screams and loud voices, are relatively rare. Uniform quantization is thus wasteful for speech signals, as many of the quantizing levels are hardly ever used. An efficient scheme for such signals is to employ a ***nonuniform quantizer*** using a variable step size, where small step sizes are used for small amplitudes, as shown in Figure 5.9a. Figure 5.9b shows how a sampled signal is quantized in a nonuniform fashion. With voice dynamic range of about 40 dB (i.e., the ratio representing the peak of loud voice

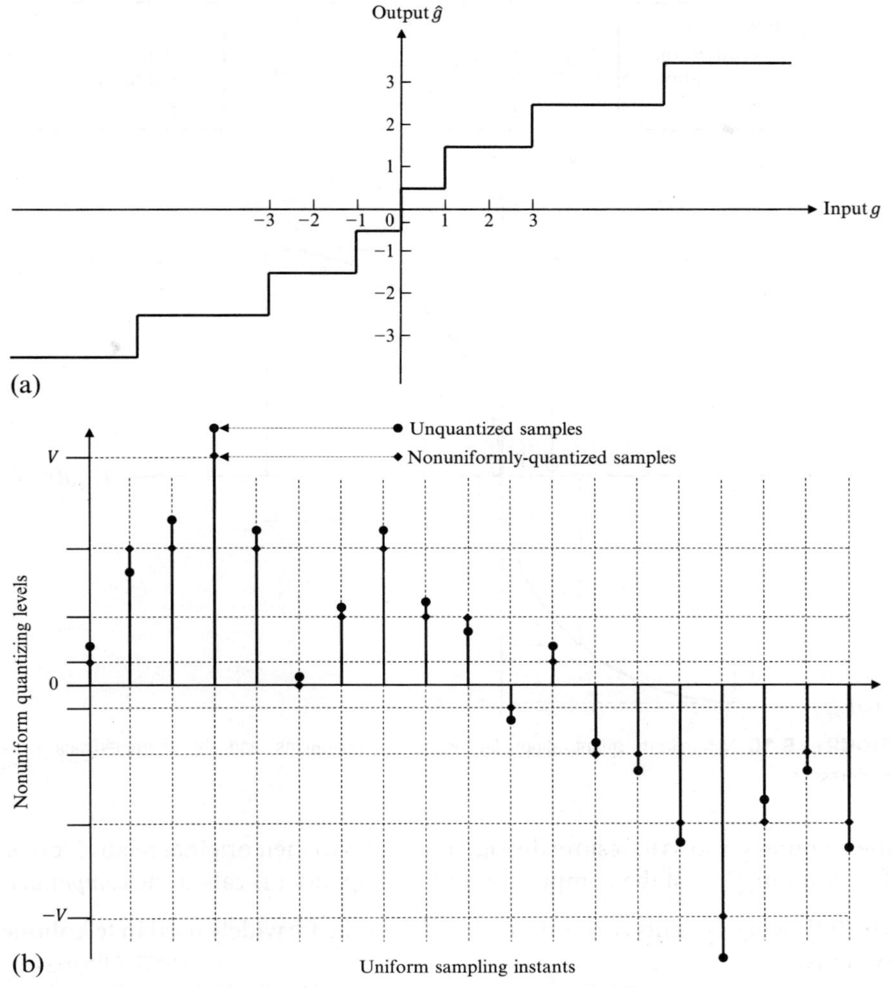

FIGURE 5.9 Nonuniform quantization: (a) a nonuniform quantizer and (b) a nonuniformly quantized signal.

to that of weak voice is in the order of 10,000 to 1), a nonuniform quantizer favors weak signals (by employing small step sizes) that need more protection at the expense of the loud voices. Nonuniform quantization yields a higher SNR_o than the uniform quantizer when the signal distribution is nonuniform.

Equivalently, the signal can be nonlinearly compressed and then passed through a uniform quantizer, as shown in Figure 5.10a. Such a nonlinear compressor, as shown in Figure 5.10b, acts like a variable-gain amplifier. More specifically, it attenuates large amplitudes (i.e., has low gain) and amplifies small amplitudes (i.e., has high gain). At the receiving end, the inverse of compression is carried out by an expander with a characteristic complementary to that of

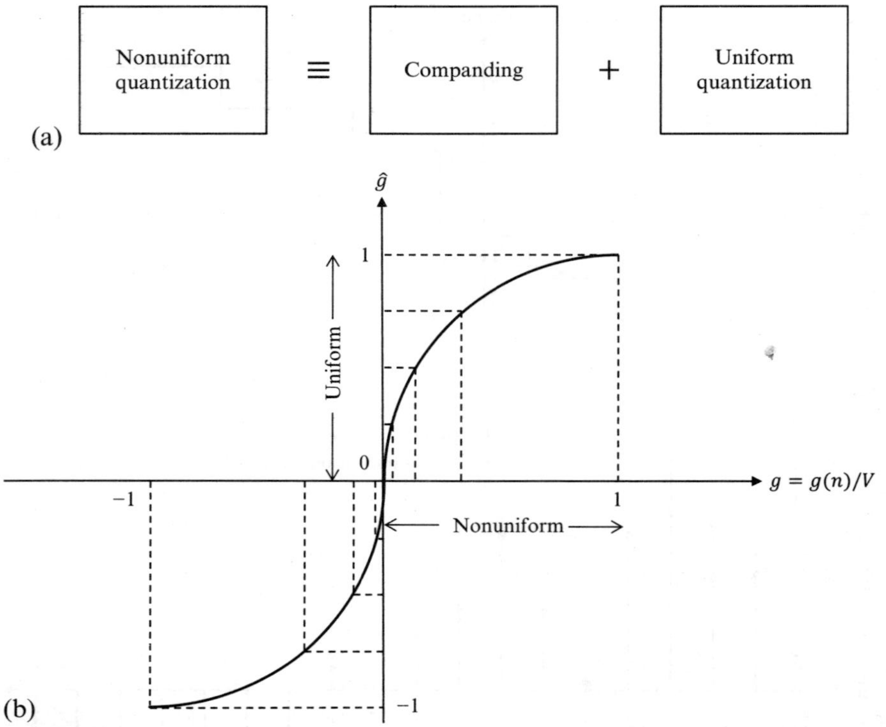

FIGURE 5.10 Nonuniform quantization: (a) equivalent operations and (b) characteristics of a compressor.

the compressor so as to restore the signal samples to their original relative levels. The combination of the compressor and the expander is called the ***compander***.

The following presents two compression laws that are widely used in telephone systems:

$$|\hat{g}| = \frac{\ln(1+\mu|g|)}{\ln(1+\mu)} \tag{5.19a}$$

$$|\hat{g}| = \begin{cases} \dfrac{A|g|}{1+\ln A}, & 0 \le |g| \le \dfrac{1}{A} \\[2ex] \dfrac{1+\ln(A|g|)}{1+\ln A}, & \dfrac{1}{A} \le |g| \le 1 \end{cases} \tag{5.19b}$$

where g and $\hat{g}$ are normalized input and output voltages of the nonuniform quantizer whose peak values range in the interval $[-1, 1]$, and μ and A are both positive constants. Figure 5.11 shows both μ-law and A-law characteristics where they are both odd functions. The ***μ-law*** in (5.19a) is neither strictly linear

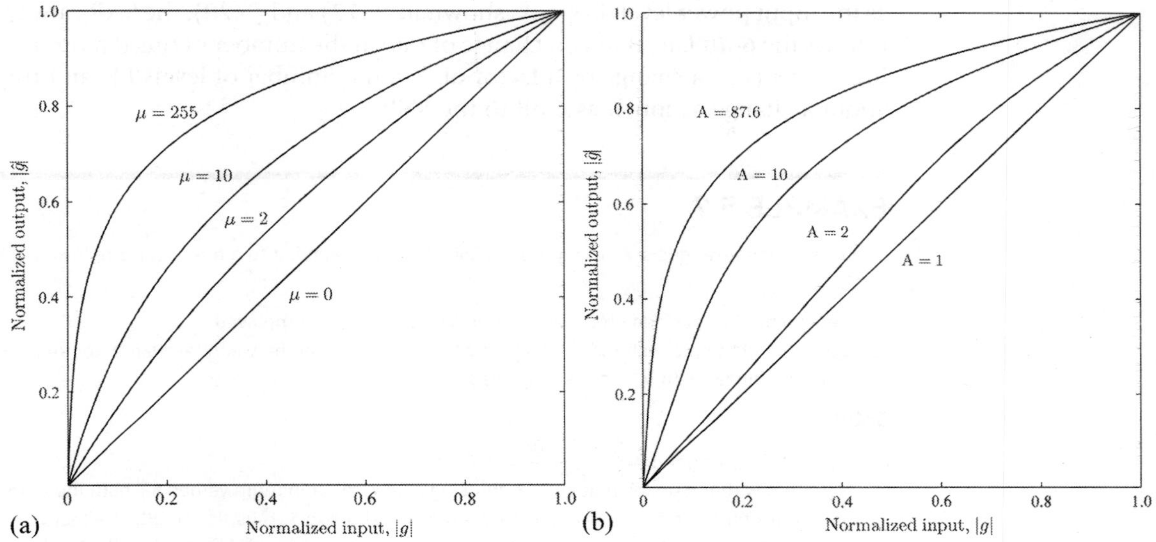

FIGURE 5.11 Compression laws: (a) μ-law and (b) A-law.

nor strictly logarithmic, but it is approximately linear at low input levels and approximately logarithmic at high input levels. The ***A-law*** in (5.19b) is also a combination of linear and logarithmic functions, depending on the input values. Note that for $\mu \to 0$ and $A \to 1$, the nonuniform quantizers in (5.19) become uniform quantizers (i.e., there is no compression involved).

Both 8-bit μ-law and A-law companding quantizers can meet the recommended limits set by ITU-T, but those with 7-bit do not meet the specification requirements. The companding circuitry does not produce an exact replica of the nonlinear compression curve, rather it provides a piecewise linear approximation to the desired curve. By using a large enough number of linear segments, the approximation can approach the true compression very closely. The standard values used for companding in North America and Japan are 8-bit, 15-segment, μ-law compression with $\mu = 255$ and those in Europe are 8-bit, 13-segment, A-law compression with $A = 87.6$. It can be shown that the SNR_o formulas for nonuniform quantization of speech signals for μ-law and A-law, for $\mu \gg 1$ and $A \gg 1$, can be approximated respectively by:

$$10 \log SNR_o \approx 6R + 4.77 - 20 \log(\ln(1+\mu)) \quad (\text{dB}) \tag{5.20a}$$

$$10 \log SNR_o \approx 6R + 4.77 - 20 \log(1 + \ln A) \quad (\text{dB}) \tag{5.20b}$$

For $R = 8$ bits, and either $\mu = 256$ or $A = 87.6$, we have $SNR_o = 38$ dB. This value can give a rather constant SNR_o over an input signal with a dynamic range of about 40 dB, whereas the SNR_o for a uniform quantizer decreases linearly as the input power level drops. As shown in (5.17) and (5.20), the SNR_o always follows the ***6-dB law***, that is, a change of one in the number of bits R representing a level (i.e., a change by a factor of 2 in the number of levels L) can bring about a change as much as 6 dB to the SNR_o.

EXAMPLE 5.7

Suppose a signal ranges over the interval [−50, 50] and is applied to a quantizer employing 128 levels.

(a) Determine the required step size if a uniform quantizer is employed.
(b) Determine the smallest and the largest effective separation between levels if a nonuniform μ-law quantizer with $\mu = 255$ is employed.

Solution

(a) Using (5.11), we get $\Delta = \dfrac{50-(-50)}{128} = 0.78125$.
(b) Note that with nonuniform quantization using μ-law, the minimum values for both input and output are normalized to −1 and their maximum values to 1, thus the smallest effective separation between levels is closest to the origin. It is also assumed that half of the levels are used for positive amplitudes and half for negative amplitudes. Let g_1 be the value of the input corresponding to the output of 1/63, and we thus have:

$$\frac{1}{63} = \frac{\ln(1+255|g_1|)}{\ln(1+255)}.$$

This results in $|g_1| = 0.000361$. The smallest effective separation between levels is thus as follows:

$$\Delta_{min} = 50|g_1| = 50(0.000361) = 0.01805.$$

Let g_{63} be the value of the input corresponding to the output of 62/63. We thus have:

$$\frac{62}{63} = \frac{\ln(1+255|g_{63}|)}{\ln(1+255)}.$$

This gives rise to $|g_{63}| = 0.91541$. The largest effective separation between levels is thus as follows:

$$\Delta_{max} = 50(1-|g_{63}|) = 50(1-0.91541) = 4.243.$$

5.2.3 Vector Quantization

Vector quantization is a lossy compression technique used in speech and image coding. In scalar quantization, a scalar value is selected from a finite list of possible values to represent a sample. In ***vector quantization***, a vector is selected from a finite list of possible vectors to represent an input vector of samples. The key operation in a vector quantization is the quantization of a random vector by encoding it as a binary codeword. Each input vector can be viewed as a point in an n-dimensional space. The vector quantizer is defined by a partition of this space into a set of nonoverlapping n-dimensional regions. The vector is encoded by comparing it with a codebook consisting of a set of stored reference vectors known as ***codevectors***. The optimality criterion is that a quantization region should consist of all vectors that are closer to its codevector than any of the other codevectors, and the codevector should be the average of all vectors that are in the quantization region.

Let k be the number of quantization regions in the n-dimensional space. In other words, since every region has its own codevector, k is the number of codevectors in the codebook, and n represents the number of samples in a codevector. For the number of bits per sample R, we therefore have the following:

$$R = \frac{\log_2 k}{n} \tag{5.21}$$

Figure 5.12 shows an example of a vector quantization with $k = 16$ and $n = 2$ (i.e., $R = 2$ bits per sample). Assuming that the size of the codebook is sufficiently large, it can be shown that the SNR_o for the vector quantizer is given by:

$$SNR_o = 6R + C_n \text{ (dB)} \tag{5.22}$$

where C_n is a constant (expressed in dB) that increases with the dimension n. Note that the SNR_o once again follows the 6-dB law (i.e., it increases approximately 6 dB when there is an increase of one bit in the number of bits per sample). However, the constant term C_n has a higher value than the constant used in scalar quantization. This additional improvement is due to the fact that the vector quantization optimally exploits the correlations among the samples in a vector, but at the expense of increased complexity. Due to the complexity of the codebook search, vector quantization is not quite prevalent.

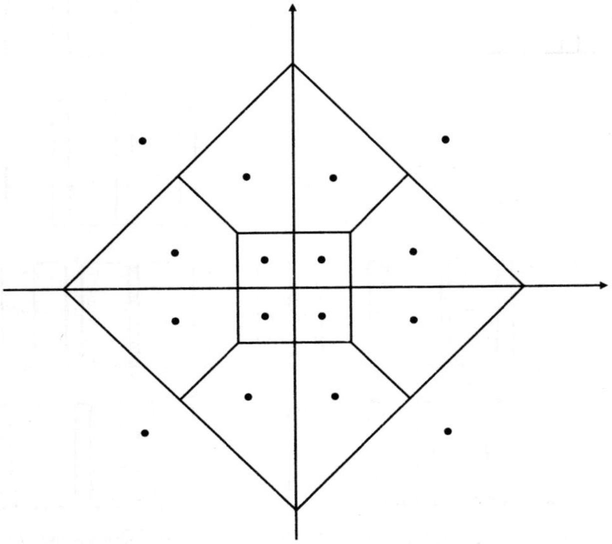

FIGURE 5.12 Vector quantization: two-dimensional decision regions.

5.3 DIGITAL PULSE MODULATION

In pulse modulation, some parameter of a periodic pulse train is varied in accordance with the sample values of a message signal. It can be divided into two groups: analog pulse modulation and digital pulse modulation. In analog pulse modulation, the amplitude, duration (width) or position of pulses is varied in proportion to the sample values of the message signal, thus yielding ***pulse amplitude modulation (PAM)***, ***pulse width modulation (PWM)***, or ***pulse position modulation (PPM)***, as shown in Figure 5.13. In analog pulse modulation, the information is transmitted in analog form, but at discrete times.

Digital pulse modulation allows transmission of the message signal in digital form as a sequence of coded pulses. The process of analog-to-digital conversion is sometimes referred to as digital pulse modulation. At the heart of digital pulse modulation is sampling and quantization, which were discussed in detail earlier. We now discuss pulse-code modulation (PCM), differential pulse-code

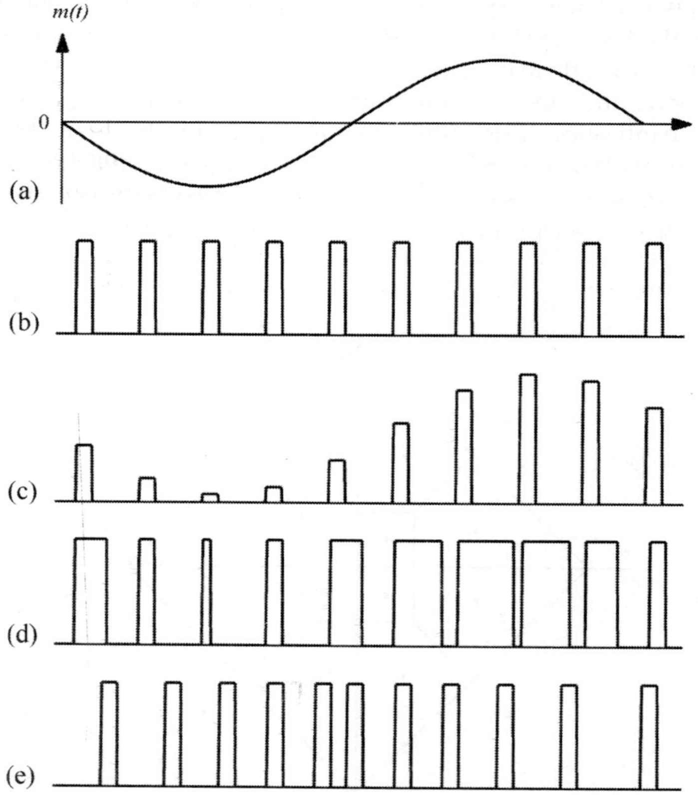

FIGURE 5.13 Analog pulse modulation: (a) modulating signal, (b) pulse carrier, (c) pulse amplitude modulation, (d) pulse width modulation, and (e) pulse position modulation.

modulation (DPCM), and delta modulation (DM). PCM, due to its widespread use, is usually viewed as a benchmark against which other methods of digital pulse modulation are measured in terms of performance and complexity. It is simple, robust, and efficient, but requires increased transmission bandwidth. DPCM reduces the transmission bandwidth at the expense of a significant increase in complexity, and DM is simple, but requires a significant increase in transmission bandwidth.

5.3.1 Pulse-Code Modulation (PCM)

A ***pulse-code modulation*** (PCM) system, as shown in Figure 5.14, is a digital transmission system that provides analog-to-digital conversion in the transmitter and digital-to-analog conversion in the receiver as well as regeneration at intermediate points along the transmission path as necessary. The basic elements of a PCM transmitter are as follows:

Analog source: Producing a continuous-time, continuous-value signal.
Filtering: Using a LPF to attenuate high-frequency components of the original analog signal that are not essential so as to avoid aliasing effect in the sampling process.
Sampling: Providing a discrete-time, continuous-value signal by sampling the band-limited signal using narrow rectangular pulses at a rate at least twice the highest frequency present in the filtered signal.
Quantization: Providing a discrete-time, discrete-value signal by rounding the value of each sample.
Encoding: Translating each of the quantized sample values into a unique binary number (codeword), where any mapping of codewords to levels may be used.

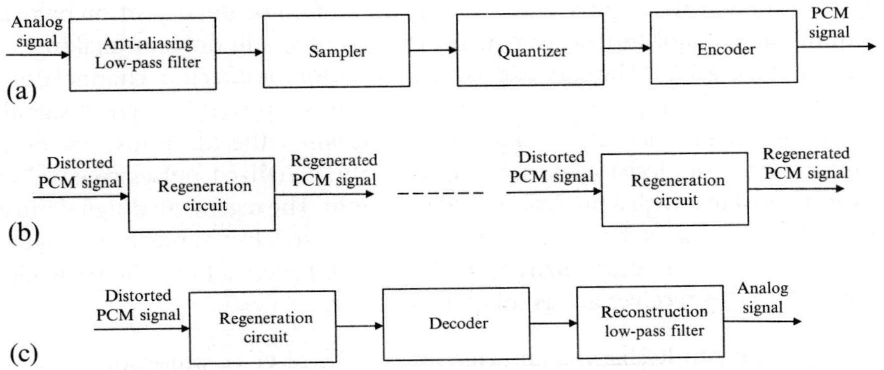

FIGURE 5.14 PCM transmission system: (a) PCM transmitter, (b) PCM transmission path, and (c) PCM receiver.

EXAMPLE 5.8

There are eight levels with numerical values of 3, 2, 1, 0, −1, −2, −3, and −4. As part of encoding, provide various binary codes to establish a one-to-one correspondence between codewords and the corresponding representation levels and numerical values.

Solution

We consider the following three binary codes as presented in the following table:

i) Expressing the ordinal number of the presentation level as a binary number (i.e., changing the decimal system to the binary system). The lowest level is thus mapped into a sequence of all 0s and the highest level is mapped into a sequence of all 1s.
ii) Employing two's complement representation (i.e., the most significant bit is the sign bit). The remaining bits are used to represent the corresponding numerical value.
iii) Applying the Gray code (i.e., there is only one bit change for each step change in the quantized level). Single errors in the received PCM codeword can thus cause minimal errors in the received analog level.

Numerical Values	Ordinal Number of Representation Level	Natural Binary Code	Two's Complement	Gray Code
3	0	000	011	000
2	1	001	010	001
1	2	010	001	011
0	3	011	000	010
−1	4	100	111	110
−2	5	101	110	111
−3	6	110	101	101
−4	7	111	100	100

Regenerative repeaters are used at sufficiently close spacing along the transmission path to provide the ability to control the effects of distortion and noise. A regenerative repeater combats the accumulation of noise and distortion by performing three major functions: equalization, timing, and decision making, as shown in Figure 5.15. The equalizer compensates for the effects of channel nonidealities, mainly amplitude and phase distortions. From the received signal, the timing circuitry determines instants of time where the signal-to-noise ratio is maximum. The decision device compares the equalized pulses received at optimum instants with a predetermined threshold. The regenerated signal must be exactly the same as the signal originally transmitted, but in practice, a regenerative repeater can occasionally introduce few erroneous bits. The basic elements of a PCM receiver are as follows:

Regeneration: Reshaping and cleaning up the received pulses one final time.

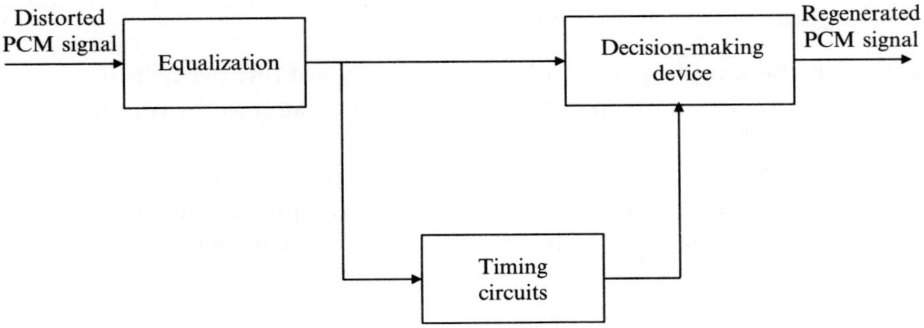

FIGURE 5.15 A regenerative circuit.

Decoding: Generating pulses with amplitudes based on the look-up table used in encoding.
Filtering: Recovering the message signal by passing the decoded output through a lowpass reconstruction filter whose cut-off frequency is equal to the message bandwidth.
Analog sink: Receiving and presenting the original analog signal.

Figure 5.16 presents an example of how PCM is applied to an analog signal to produce binary digits (bits). The PCM bit rate is therefore as follows:

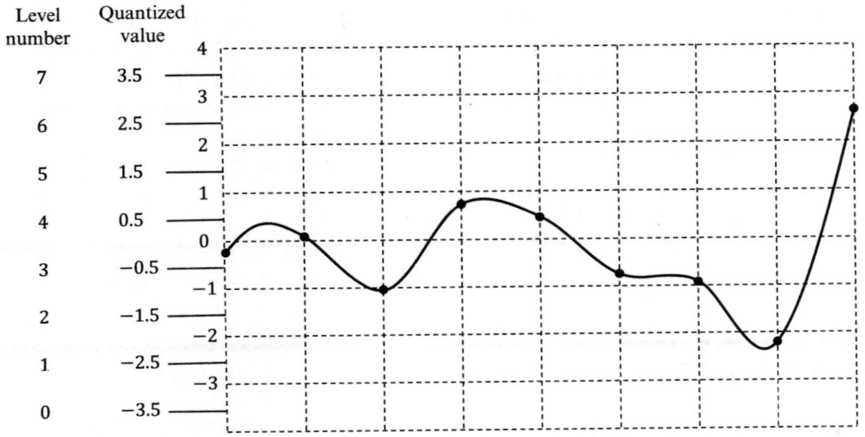

Sampled value	− 0.2	0.1	− 1.1	0.8	0.6	− 0.8	− 0.9	− 2.2	2.6
Quantized value	− 0.5	0.5	− 1.5	0.5	0.5	− 0.5	− 0.5	− 2.5	2.5
Level number	3	4	2	4	4	3	3	1	6
Binary code	011	100	010	100	100	011	011	001	110

FIGURE 5.16 A PCM example.

$$r = f_s R \tag{5.23}$$

where f_s is the sampling rate and R is the number of bits per quantized sample. The required channel bandwidth is directly related to the bit rate and in turn to the number of bits per quantized sample. To this effect, based on (5.18) and (5.23), a salient merit of PCM is that an increase in channel bandwidth can bring about an improvement in signal-to-noise ratio exponentially. Simply put, PCM allows for a trade-off between bandwidth and power.

EXAMPLE 5.9

Discuss how PCM is done for the following cases:

(a) Digital transmission of voice signals in public-switched telephone networks.
(b) Stereo CD-quality music.

Solution

(a) A voice signal is essentially limited to a band from about 100 Hz to 3100 Hz and frequencies outside this band do not impact voice intelligibility. In PCM, the voice signal is often lowpass filtered at 3.1 kHz and then sampled at a rate of 8000 samples per second. This rate is higher than the Nyquist sampling rate of 6200 samples per second, so realizable filters with reasonable guard bands can be applied for signal reconstruction, as the transition band is about 1.8 $(= 8 - 3.1 - 3.1)$ kHz. Each sample is applied to an 8-bit (256-level) nonuniform μ-law quantizer with $\mu = 255$. The standard bit rate for digitized telephone speech signals is therefore 64 kbps (= 8000 samples per second × 8 bits per sample).

(b) The human ear is sensitive to frequencies up to around 20 kHz. Although the Nyquist sampling rate for music should be 40,000, the actual sampling rate, after using oversampling and then decimation, at the input of the quantizer is 44,100 samples per second. High-quality audio requires finer granularity in quantization, and each sample is thus applied to a 16-bit (65,536-level) quantizer. The standard bit rate for a stereo CD-quality of audio signal is therefore 1.4 Mbps (= 44,100 samples per second per channel ×16 bits per sample × 2 channels).

EXAMPLE 5.10

A message signal ranges between 1 and 4 volts, and has an average power of 3W. To transmit this signal by PCM, uniform quantization is adopted. The SNR_o must be at least 45 dB, determine the minimum number of bits per level required for this quantizer and the corresponding SNR_o.

Solution

After substituting $\sigma_g^2 = 3$ and $V = 4 - 1 = 3$ into (5.16), we solve $2^{2R} = 45 \text{ dB} = 10^{4.5}$ for R. We thus obtain $R = 7.47$ bits, however, we need to choose $R = 8$, as the number of bits representing a level must be an integer. For $R = 8$, we get the output $SNR_o = 10\log\left(2^{16}\right) = 48.165$ dB.

EXAMPLE 5.11

Consider the signal $g(t) = A\cos(2\pi Wt)$, where $A \neq 0$ and $W \neq 0$ are the amplitude and frequency of the sinusoidal signal, respectively. This signal is sampled at the Nyquist rate. The sampled signal is uniformly quantized, where the number of bits per sample is R. Suppose the passband channel bandwidth required for transmission is k times the bit rate, where we have $1 \leq k \leq 2$. Determine the required channel bandwidth, and identify the trade-offs between the SNR_o and the required channel bandwidth.

Solution

The signal bandwidth is W, so the Nyquist sampling rate is $2W$. The required channel bandwidth B is then as follows: $B = 2WkR$. Since the signal is sinusoid, we have $\alpha = \sqrt{2}$. Using (5.16), we have $SNR_o = 6R + 1.8$, where R is the number of bits required to represent a level. By replacing $R = B/2Wk$, we have $SNR_o = 3B/kW + 1.8$, where k and W are both constants. Therefore, by increasing the channel bandwidth B, the SNR_o performance can be improved, and that is a very desirable exchange.

EXAMPLE 5.12

A binary channel is available for PCM voice transmission, where the bit rate r is 64 kbps and the signal bandwidth W is 3.4 kHz. Determine the required number of bits per sample R and the resulting sampling rate f_s.

Solution

We require:

$f_s \geq 2W$ and $r \geq f_s R$

We thus have:

$$R \leq \frac{r}{f_s} \leq \frac{64000}{6800} = 9.4$$

Since R must be an integer, we select $R = 9$ and $f_s = \frac{64000}{9} = 7.11$ kHz.

EXAMPLE 5.13

The SNR_o of a 14-bit quantizer is 28 dB, which is assumed to be insufficient. To achieve the desired SNR_o of 40 dB, the number of quantization levels is increased. Determine the fractional increase in the transmission bandwidth required for the increase in the number of levels L, noting that the transmission bandwidth is linearly related to the number of bits per level R.

Solution

Equations (5.17) and (5.21) indicate that by increasing R by one bit, SNR_o is increased by 6 dB. Hence, we need to increase the number of bits R by a factor of 2 (i.e., the number of levels L by a factor of 4) to accommodate the desired SNR_o of 40 dB. Therefore, instead of 14 bits, we need 16 bits, thus an increase of 14.3%, which in turn leads to an increase of 14.3% in the transmission bandwidth.

5.3.2 Differential PCM (DPCM) and Adaptive DPCM (ADPCM)

PCM is a straightforward system, but it is not very efficient as it generates many bits and thus requires so much bandwidth. In a PCM system where the analog signal is sampled at a rate slightly higher than the Nyquist rate, the resulting sample values exhibit a high degree of correlation between adjacent samples (i.e., on average, the signal does not change rapidly from one sample to the next and a sample can thus have some correlation with the next sample). Yet, in a PCM system, every sample is quantized independently and the past samples have no effect on the quantization of the present sample, and thus the resulting encoded signal contains redundant information. Proper exploitation of the redundancy in the Nyquist samples can always lead to fewer encoded bits.

Differential PCM (DPCM) is based on the quantization of the difference between a sample value and the prediction of that sample value using the previous sample values. Since this difference (prediction error) is much smaller than the sample value, fewer bits are required to quantize it. This means that DPCM can achieve performance levels at lower bit rates than PCM. In the case of voice signals sampled at 8 kHz and for a given speech-quality, DPCM may provide a saving of several bits per sample over PCM. Specifically, telephone systems using DPCM can often operate at 32 or even 24 kbps, instead of 64 kbps PCM. At the receiver, we estimate the sample value using the previous sample values and then generate the sample value by adding the received prediction error and the estimate. The samples at the receiver are constructed iteratively. Figure 5.17 shows the DPCM transmitter and receiver. The ***prediction filter***, as shown in Figure 5.18, is a tapped-delay-line (transversal filter) where the predicted value is modeled as a linear combination of past-quantized samples. In the design of the prediction filter, the minimum mean-squared error criterion for best prediction is employed, where the prediction coefficients (tap gains) are determined from the statistical correlation among various samples.

Adaptive DPCM (ADPCM) can improve the efficiency of DPCM by incorporating an adaptive quantizer at the encoder. In that, the step size is small or large depending on whether the prediction error for quantizing is small or large (i.e., the step size is varied automatically so as to match the average power of the input signal). Moreover, the prediction filter is adaptive to accommodate the changing level and spectrum of the input speech signal. The ITU-T standard G.726 specifies an ADPCM speech coder and decoder (codec) for speech signal sampled at 8 kHz. For different quality levels, G.726 specifies four different ADPCM rates at 16, 24, 32, and 40 kbps, which correspond to 2, 3, 4, and 5 bits per sample, respectively.

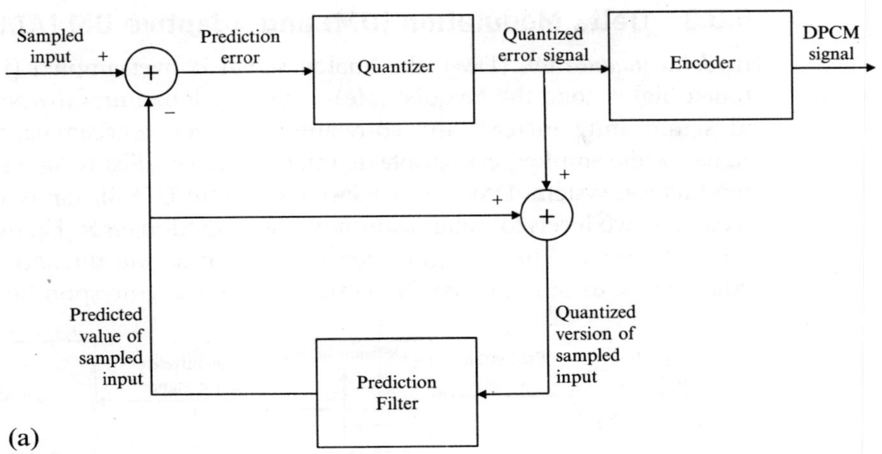

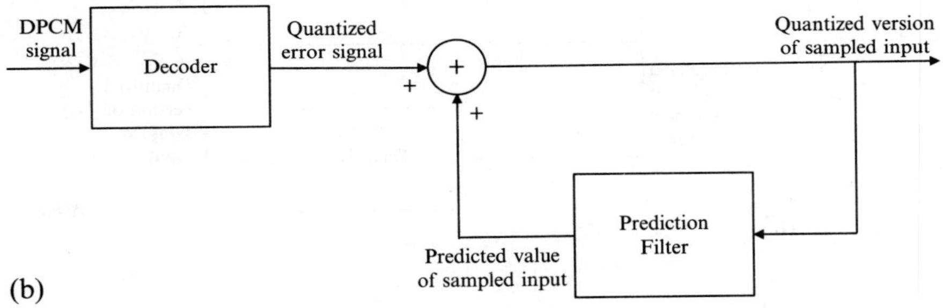

FIGURE 5.17 DPCM Systems: (a) transmitter and (b) receiver.

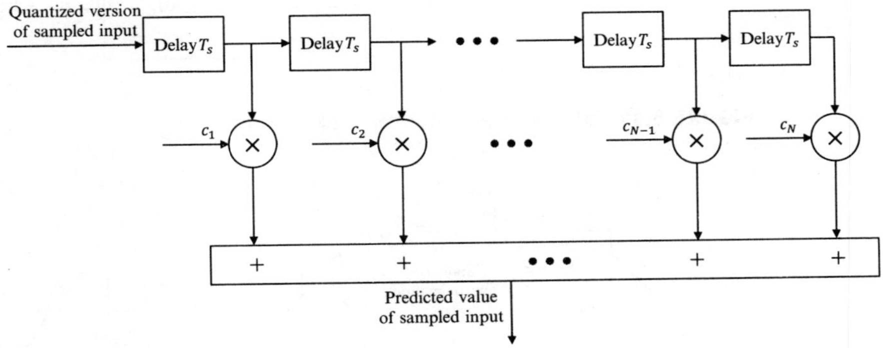

FIGURE 5.18 A predication filter.

5.3.3 Delta Modulation (DM) and Adaptive DM (ADM)

In ***delta modulation*** (DM), the analog signal is oversampled (i.e., at a rate much higher than the Nyquist rate)—typically four times the Nyquist rate—to significantly increase the correlation between adjacent samples of the signal, while employing a simple quantizing strategy. Figure 5.19 shows a delta modulation system. DM can be viewed as a 1-bit DPCM that is a DPCM that uses only two levels for quantization of the prediction error. Figure 5.20 shows how DM works. The difference between the input and the approximation is quantized into only two levels, namely Δ and $-\Delta$, corresponding to positive

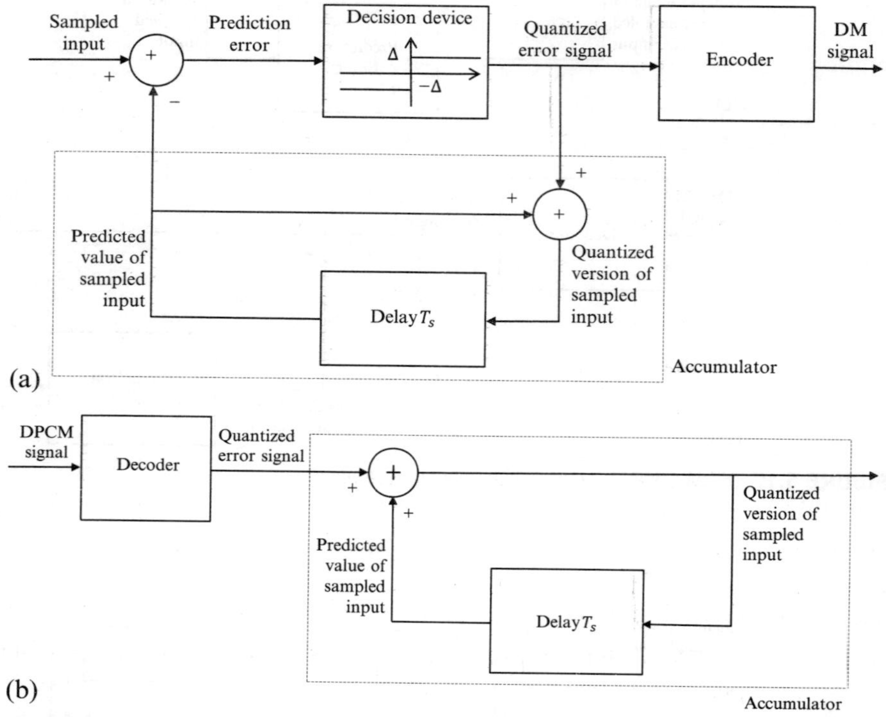

FIGURE 5.19 DM system: (a) Transmitter and (b) receiver.

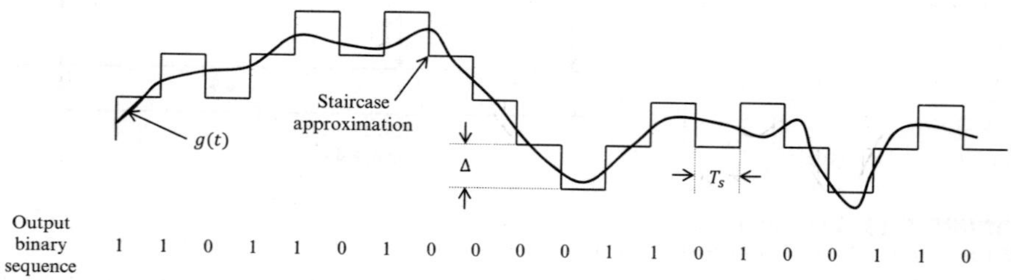

FIGURE 5.20 Signal and bit generation in delta modulation.

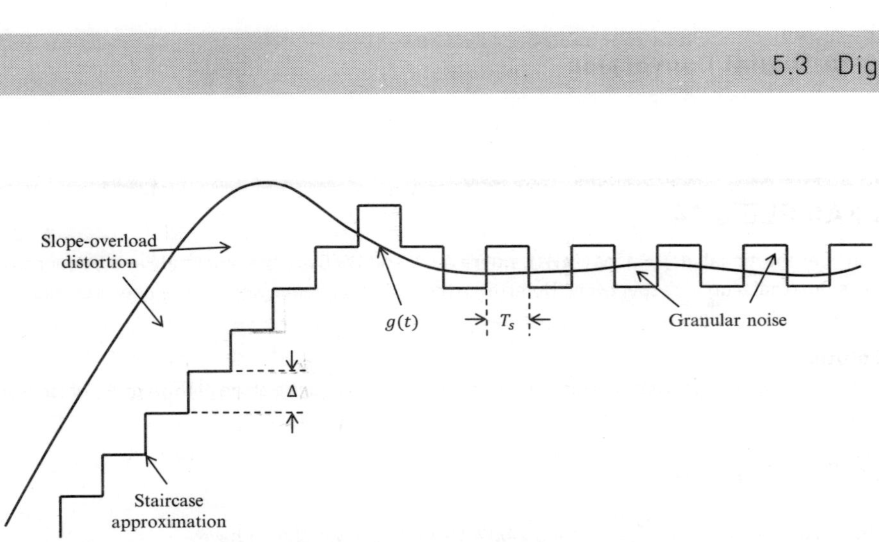

FIGURE 5.21 Types of quantization errors in delta modulation.

and negative differences, respectively. Thus, if the approximation falls below the signal level, it is increased by Δ, and if the approximation lies above the signal, it is diminished by Δ. Obviously, in DM the rate of information transmission is simply equal to the sampling rate.

As shown in Figure 5.21, there are two types of quantization error in DM, slope-overload distortion and granular noise. ***Slope-overload distortion*** occurs when the step size is too small for the staircase approximation to follow a steep segment of the analog signal, with the result that the quantized signal falls behind the original signal. In order to avoid it, we should meet the following condition:

$$\frac{\Delta}{T_s} \geq \max\left|\frac{dg(t)}{dt}\right| \tag{5.24}$$

Equation (5.24) indicates that the maximum slope of the original signal $g(t)$ should be smaller than $\frac{\Delta}{T_s}$. In order to keep up with rapid changes in the analog signal, the bit rate $\frac{1}{T_s}$ and/or the step size Δ should be increased. In contrast, ***granular noise*** occurs when the step size is too large, relative to the small slowly-changing slope of the original signal, thereby causing the staircase approximation to go up and down for a relatively flat segment of the input analog signal. Granular noise is analogous to the quantization noise in a PCM system.

Delta modulation is essentially based on encoding and transmitting the derivative of the analog signal. A drawback of DM is that channel noise can be accumulated to introduce errors in the demodulated signal. To circumvent this problem, an integration operation on the message signal is performed prior to delta modulation. This technique is known as ***delta-sigma modulation***.

Adaptive DM (ADM), also known as ***continuous variable slope DM*** (CVSDM) with a performance superior to that of DM, allows the step size to vary in accordance with the input signal. With adaptive step size, the step size is increased to mitigate the slope-overload distortion, and is decreased to reduce the granular noise.

EXAMPLE 5.14

Consider the signal $g(t) = A\cos(2\pi Wt)$, where $A \neq 0$ and $W \neq 0$ are the amplitude and frequency of the sinusoidal signal, respectively. Determine the condition under which the slope-overload distortion can be avoided.

Solution

In order to avoid slope-overload distortion, we first need to find the slope of the signal, which is as follows:

$$\left|\frac{dg(t)}{dt}\right| = 2\pi AW \sin(2\pi Wt)$$

The maximum slope of $\left|\frac{dg(t)}{dt}\right|$ is then $2A\pi W$. Using (5.24), we should have:

$$\frac{\Delta}{T_s} \geq 2\pi AW$$

or equivalently:

$$\Delta > 2\pi AT_sW$$

5.4 LINE CODES

The output of a quantizer is not in the form best suited for transmission. An encoding process is thus required, through which each of the discrete sequence of sample values is translated into a distinct binary code. ***Line codes***, also known as ***baseband signaling*** or ***baseband modulation***, are then used to convert binary digital data to digital signals for effective transmission or storage. Line coding is a common feature to all types of digital pulse modulation.

5.4.1 Line Coding Schemes and Selection Criteria

There are numerous line codes for an array of applications. However, Figure 5.22 shows few select line codes in the time domain. In the line codes under consideration here, we assume 1s and 0s are equally likely and statistically independent, the bit duration is T_b seconds long, and there may be a maximum of three possible signal values of A, 0, and $-A$ to represent 0s and 1s, according to the line-code format. In a binary code only two of these three values are used, and in a ternary code all three are used. A binary code can withstand a relatively high level of noise and is easy to regenerate, but that is not the case for a ternary code. If a long sequences of A or 0 or $-A$ can be allowed (i.e., there may be no transition of signal value for a long time), timing recovery can become a major problem. If a line code requires a transition in the middle of a bit interval or at the beginning of a bit interval, then that can provide good synchronization capabilities. The line codes with narrow pulses of half-bit duration (half-width pulses), as opposed to the line codes with pulses of

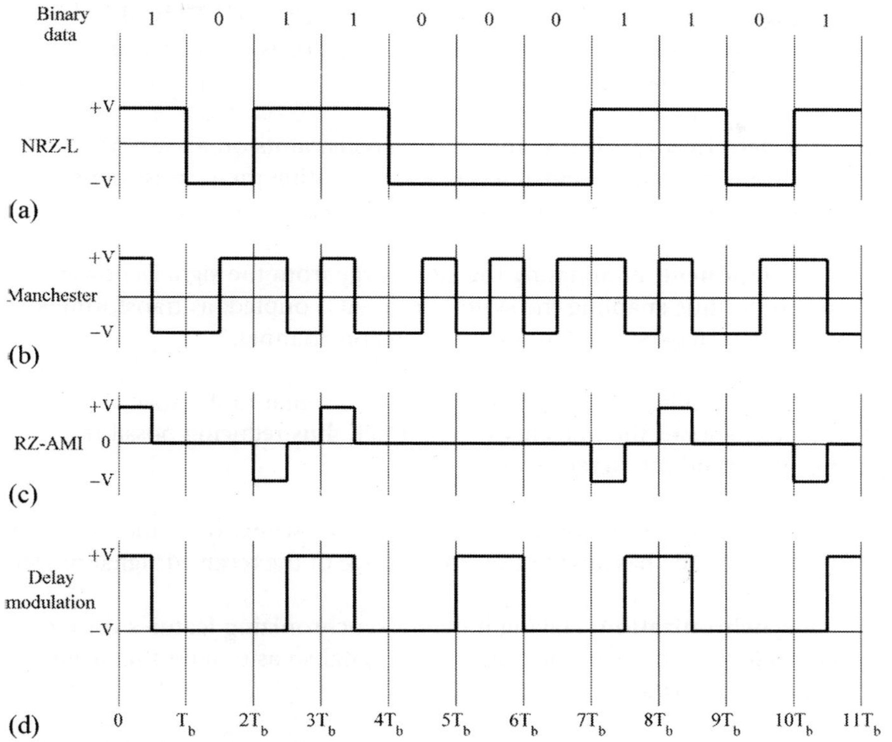

FIGURE 5.22 Various line codes.

bit-long duration (full-width pulses), require twice the bandwidth. Also, a line code is immune to polarity reversals, if the data are encoded by the presence or absence of a transition rather than the presence or absence of a pulse.

In the selection of a line code for a particular application, some criteria, such as transparency and unique decodability, are considered as essential requirements, and most are regarded as desirable features, since they can bring about significant benefits. The selection criteria are briefly as follows:

Transparency: Not imposing any restrictions on the content of the transmitted bit sequence. In other words, any pattern of bits can be encoded into a line code.

Unique decodability: Unambiguously decoding to retrieve the original sequence of inputs, there must thus be a one-to-one mapping between a pattern of bits and a signal representing it.

Noise immunity: Exhibiting superior bit error rate performance in the presence of noise, by having a significant noise margin between levels.

Bandwidth compression: Increasing the efficiency of bandwidth utilization by using multi-level codes, at the expense of a decrease in noise margin or equivalently in bit error rate.

Error detection capability: Introducing constraints on allowable transitions among the signal levels and exploiting these constraints to detect errors and in turn enhance performance.

DC component: Eliminating the DC energy from the signal's power spectrum, thus enabling the system to be AC coupled, as transformers sometimes may be used in the transmission channel.

Spectral shaping: Matching the transmitted signal to the special characteristics of the transmission channel, thus reducing possible distortion and interference levels.

Preventing baseline wandering: Avoiding long strings of 1s and 0s so there is no drift in the baseline (a running average of the received signal power).

Self-synchronization: Having inherent synchronizing features through adequate transitions in the transmitted signal so as to alert the beginning and end of pulses.

Differential encoding: Allowing the polarity of differentially encoded waveforms to be inverted without affecting the data detection, as signals in communication systems experience inversion.

Low complexity: Avoiding complex and thus costly transmitter and receiver implementations.

5.4.2 Power Spectral Density of Line Codes

In order to arrive at physically realizable transmit and receive filters, the spectrum of a line code should be carefully shaped to match the channel characteristics. The ensemble members of a stationary random process, such as a line code, are not energy signals, but have finite average power. Therefore, the straightforward approach of taking the Fourier transform of each time function of the ensemble runs into mathematical difficulties. The approach taken to obtain a frequency-domain characterization of the process is to determine how the average power of the process is distributed in frequency. The power spectral density of the transmitted signal may depend on the signaling pulse and on the statistical properties of sequences of transmitted pulses. Assuming the information bits 1 and 0 are equally likely and they are also statistically independent, the ***power spectral density*** (PSD) of a line code is then given by:

$$S(f) = \frac{|P(f)|^2}{T_b}\left\{R(0) + 2\sum_{k=1}^{\infty} R(k)\cos(2\pi k f T_b)\right\} = \frac{|P(f)|^2}{T_b}C(f) \tag{5.25}$$

where $P(f)$ is the Fourier transform of the pulse, $R(k) = E\left[a_{j+k}\, a_j\right]$ represents the discrete autocorrelation of the symbol sequence $\{a_k\}$, and $C(f)$ thus represents the statistical properties of the transmitted sequence of symbols. The power spectral density for each of the following line codes is given in Figure 5.23.

Non-return-to-zero level (NRZ-L) code: Bit 1 is represented by one voltage level (A) and bit 0 is represented by the opposite voltage level ($-A$) (i.e., the value of the signal level determines the value of the bit). NRZ-L code is widely used in digital logic circuits. The width of the rectangular pulse used in NRZ-L code is assumed to be the same as the bit duration T_b, we therefore have $P(f) = AT_b\text{sinc}(fT_b)$. For the NRZ-L code, there is no correlation between the transmitted symbols, we thus have $C(f) = 1$, and its PSD is as follows:

$$S_{NRZ-L}(f) = (A^2T_b)\,\text{sinc}^2(fT_b) \tag{5.26}$$

Manchester (Bipolar) code: Bit 1 is represented by a transition from a high level (A) to a low level ($-A$) occurring in the middle of the bit interval and bit 0 is represented by a transition from a low level ($-A$) to a high level (A) occurring in the middle of the bit interval (i.e., always two successive half-width $\left(\frac{T_b}{2}\right)$ pulses with opposite polarities are representing a bit).

Therefore, two half-width pulses representing a bit introduce a significant level of correlation. Manchester code is commonly used in the local area

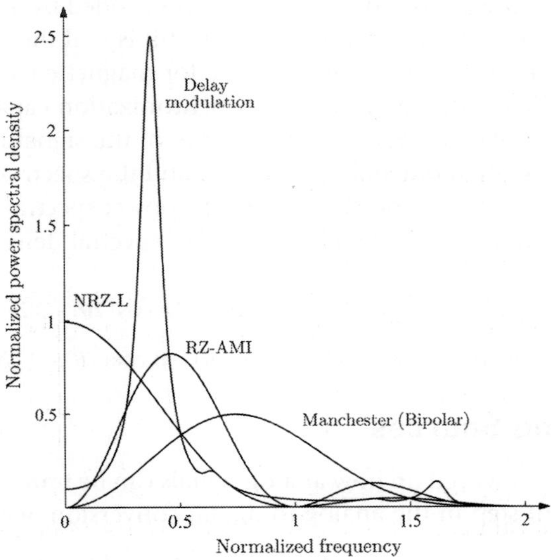

FIGURE 5.23 Power spectral densities of various line codes.

network Ethernet. Due to transition in the middle of every bit, this code is thus known as a self-synchronizing code. This code has no DC component, but requires larger bandwidth, mainly due to shorter rectangular pulses. We therefore have $P(f)=\left(\frac{AT_b}{2}\right)\text{sinc}\left(\frac{fT_b}{2}\right)$. There may be correlation between two adjacent pulses, and it can be shown that in (5.25), $C(f)=2\sin^2\left(\frac{\pi f T_b}{2}\right)$, and the PSD of the Manchester code is thus as follows:

$$S_{bi-phase}(f)=(A^2T_b)\,\text{sinc}^2\left(\frac{fT_b}{2}\right)\sin^2\left(\frac{\pi fT_b}{2}\right) \tag{5.27}$$

Bipolar (Alternate Mark Inversion) code: Bit 0 is represented by no pulse and bit 1 is represented by alternating positive (A) and negative ($-A$) half-width pulses. Bipolar code is widely used in T1 carrier systems. A major benefit of AMI is that it has no DC component. It has a limited error detection capability that allows online performance monitoring at a repeater or a receiver. Bipolar code has a synchronization problem when a long sequence of 0s is present in the data. For a half-width pulse, we have $P(f)=\left(\frac{A^2T_b}{4}\right)\text{sinc}^2\left(\frac{fT_b}{2}\right)$ and using (5.25), we have $C(f)=\sin^2(\pi fT_b)$. The power spectral density of the bipolar code is thus as follows:

$$S_{AMI}(f)=\left(\frac{A^2T_b}{4}\right)\text{sinc}^2\left(\frac{fT_b}{2}\right)\sin^2(\pi fT_b) \tag{5.28}$$

Miller code (Delay modulation): Bit 1 is encoded by a transition in the middle of the bit interval, and depending on the previous bit, the transition may be either upward or downward. Bit 0 is encoded by a transition at the beginning of the bit interval if the previous bit is 0; if the previous bit is 1, then there is no transition. It is attractive for magnetic recording and PSK signaling. Miller code provides good synchronization capabilities and is immune to a polarity reversal. The majority of the signaling energy lies at frequencies less than one half the bit rate, and the spectrum is minimal in the vicinity of $f=0$. For the Miller code, the power spectral density is much more complex, assuming $\theta=\pi fT_b$, its power spectral density is follows:

$$\begin{aligned}S_{Miller}(f)=&\frac{A^2T_b}{2\theta^2(17+8\cos(8\theta))}(23-2\cos(\theta)-22\cos(2\theta)-12\cos(3\theta)\\&+5\cos(4\theta)+12\cos(5\theta)+2\cos(6\theta)-8\cos(7\theta)+2\cos(8\theta))\end{aligned} \tag{5.29}$$

Summary and Sources

In this chapter, we focused on how analog signals can be transformed into bits. As the first salient step in the analog-to-digital conversion, we introduced the sampling process by which a continuous-time signal can be converted into a discrete-time signal. The sampling theorem, as advanced independently by several people, is generally known as the Nyquist-Shannon theorem [1–3]. We then discussed how samples can be quantized in various ways, and zeroed in on multiple digital pulse modulation techniques to produce transmission bits. A detailed treatment of various quantization methods, pulse-code modulation and its variant may be found in [4]. There are also many excellent textbooks that cover major aspects of analog-to-digital conversion [5–12].

[1] H. Nyquist, Certain topics in telegraph transmission theory, *Transactions on AIEE* 47 (Apr. 1928) 617–644 (Reprint as classic paper in: Proc. IEEE, vol. 90, Feb 2002).

[2] C.E. Shannon, Communication in the presence of noise, *Proc. Inst. Radio Eng.* 37 (Jan. 1949) 10–21 (Reprint as classic paper in: Proc. IEEE, vol. 86, Feb 1998).

[3] A.J. Jerri, The Shannon sampling theorem – its various extensions and applications: a tutorial review, *Proc. IEEE* 65 (Nov. 1977) 1565–1596.

[4] N.S. Jayant and P. Noll, *Digital Coding of Waveforms: Principles and Applications to Speech and Video*, Prentice-Hall. ISBN 978-0132119139, (1984).

[5] B.P. Lathi and Z. Ding, *Modern Digital and Analog Communication Systems*, fourth ed., Oxford University Press. ISBN 978-0-19-533145-5, (2009).

[6] S. Haykin, *Digital Communication Systems*, John Wiley & Sons. ISBN 978-0-471-64735-5, (2014).

[7] L.W. Couch II, *Digital and Analog Communication Systems*, eighth ed., Pearson. ISBN 978-0-13-291538-0, (2013).

[8] J.G. Proakis and M. Salehi, *Fundamentals of Communication Systems*, second ed., Pearson. ISBN 978-0-13-335485-0, (2014).

[9] K.S. Shanmugam, *Digital and Analog Communication Systems*, John Wiley & Sons. ISBN 0-471-03090-2, (1979).

[10] R.E. Ziemer and W.H. Tranter, *Principles of Communications*, sixth ed., John Wiley & Sons. ISBN 978-0-470-25254-3, (2009).

[11] A.B. Carlson and P.B. Crilly, *Communication Systems*, fifth ed., McGraw-Hill. ISBN 978-0-07-338040-7, (2002).

[12] H.P. Hsu, *Analog and Digital Communications*, McGraw-Hill. ISBN 0070306362, (1993).

Problems

5.1 Determine the Nyquist rate for each of the following signals:
(a) $g(t) = 5\cos(1000\pi t)\cos(4000\pi t)$
(b) $g(t) = \sin(200\pi t)/(\pi t)$
(c) $g(t) = (-|t| + 1)(u(t+1) - u(t-1))\cos(2\pi t)$

5.2 Consider the signal $g(t) = 2\cos(20\pi t)$ that is sampled at 30 times per second and then filtered by an ideal LPF whose bandwidth is 30 Hz. Determine the LPF output. Determine the LPF output if the sampling rate is 15 times per second.

5.3 Suppose we have $g(t) = A\,\text{sinc}^2(2Wt)$, where $A \neq 0$ and $W \neq 0$. Determine the condition on the sampling rate f_s or the sampling period T_{so} so that $g(t)$ can be uniquely represented by its sampled version.

5.4 Determine the minimum sampling frequency for each of the following bandpass signals:
$G(f) \neq 0$ for 9 kHz $< |f| <$ 12 kHz.
$G(f) \neq 0$ for 18 kHz $< |f| <$ 22 kHz.

5.5 The signal $g(t) = \cos(60\pi t)\cos^2(160\pi t)$ is sampled at the rate of 400 times per second. Determine the range of permissible cut-off frequencies for the ideal reconstruction filter that may be used to recover $g(t)$ from its sampled version.

5.6 In the context of sampling, address the following two questions:

(a) Is it possible that two different real lowpass deterministic signals are ideally sampled in the time domain at two different rates and the Fourier transforms of these two sampled signals turn out to be identical? If so, explain and give an example, if not, why not?

(b) Is it possible that two identical real lowpass deterministic signals are ideally sampled in the time domain both at the same rate and these two sampled signals in the time domain turn out to be different? If so, explain and give an example, if not, why not?

5.7 The signal $g(t) = 4\delta(t) + 2\cos(2\pi t)$ is to be uniformly sampled for digital transmission. Discuss the maximum allowable time interval between sample values that will ensure perfect reconstruction of the signal.

5.8 A seismic signal $g(t) = 10\cos(1000\pi t) + 20\cos(2000\pi t)$ is to be uniformly sampled for digital transmission. Determine the maximum allowable time interval between two adjacent sample values that will ensure perfect signal reproduction.

5.9 Consider a signal $g(t) = 2\cos(200\pi t) + 2\cos(320\pi t)$ is ideally sampled at a rate of 300 Hz. The sampled signal is passed through an ideal lowpass filter (LPF) with a cut-off frequency of 250 Hz. Determine the signal at the output of the LPF, in both time and frequency domains.

5.10 Assuming the signal $x(t) = \cos(200\pi t)(1 + \cos(200\pi t))$ is lowpass filtered, where the cut-off frequency of the LPF is 125 Hz. The output of the LPF is sampled 150 times per second. Then, the output of the sampler is lowpass filtered. The cut-off frequency of this second LPF is 75 Hz. Determine the output of this second LPF in the time domain.

5.11 Design a system, consisting of a sampler and a filter, in such a way that if the input is as follows: $x(t) = \cos(200\pi t)$, the output is then as follows: $y(t) = \cos(150\pi t)$. In other words, determine the sampling rate as well as the type and the bandwidth of the filter, which follows the sampler.

5.12 Determine the Fourier transform of the sampled signal using natural sampling method, i.e., verify (5.9).

5.13 Determine the Fourier transform of the sampled signal using flat-top sampling method, i.e., verify (5.10).

5.14 A binary channel with the bit rate of 36 kbps is available for PCM voice transmission. Find an appropriate value of the sampling rate f_s that yields no aliasing, and determine the number of quantization levels L assuming the bandwidth of the voice signal is 3.2 kHz.

5.15 A TV signal with a bandwidth of 4.2 MHz is digitally transmitted. Assuming the Nyquist sampling rate and noting 9 bits represent each sample, determine the bit rate required to transmit this TV signal.

5.16 A TV signal with a bandwidth of 6 MHz is transmitted using PCM. The number of levels in the quantizer is 4096. Assume the sampling rate is 20% more than the Nyquist rate. Determine the bit rate (i.e., the number of bits per second) required to transmit the binary PCM information.

5.17 Assume the signal $g(t)$ has a Gaussian shape with a standard deviation σ_g, and that the range of the uniform quantizer extends from $-3\sigma_g$ to $3\sigma_g$. Determine the number of bits that are needed if the SNR_o must be at least 90 dB.

5.18 If the signal $g(t) = 10\cos\left(2000\pi t + \frac{\pi}{3}\right) + 20\cos\left(400\pi t + \frac{\pi}{4}\right)$ is uniformly sampled at the Nyquist rate and subsequently quantized using a 64-level quantizer, determine then the number of bytes required for perfect reproduction of one hour of the signal.

5.19 Consider a voice signal whose bandwidth is 3.4 kHz and its maximum value is 8 volts. To transmit this signal, a delta modulation system is used in which the sampling rate is 64 kHz.

(a) Determine the minimum permissible value of the step size to avoid slope-overload distortion.

(b) Determine the average power of granular noise and the required minimum channel bandwidth.

5.20 The signal $g(t) = \cos(100\pi t) + \cos(200\pi t)$ is sampled at four times the Nyquist rate and then passed through a delta modulation system. Determine the bit rate at its output.

5.21 A sinusoidal signal with amplitude 6.5 volts is applied to a uniform quantizer. Sketch the quantized waveform for one complete cycle of the input, if

(a) The quantizer is a mid-tread type whose output takes on the values $0, \pm 1, \pm 2, \pm 3, \pm 4, \pm 5, \pm 6$ volts.

(b) The quantizer is a mid-rise type whose output takes on the values $\pm 0.5, \pm 1.5, \pm 2.5, \pm 3.5, \pm 4.5, \pm 5.5$ volts.

5.22 Consider the signal $g(t) = e^{-2t}\cos(2000\pi t)\,u(t)$. Determine the minimum step size to avoid slope overload.

5.23 The signal $g(t)$ has a bandwidth of 20 kHz, and its amplitude at any time is a random variable whose probability density function is as follows:

$$f_X(x) = (-|t| + 1)(u(x+1) - u(x-1))$$

where $u(.)$ is the step function.

(a) Determine SNR_o, if a uniform quantizer with 256 levels is employed.

(b) Determine the transmission bandwidth increase, if SNR_o must be increased by 30 dB.

5.24 The stationary random signal $g(t)$ has a maximum value of 2, and its autocorrelation function is as follows:

$$R_X(x) = 2e^{-|\tau|}\cos(2\pi\tau)$$

Determine the number of bits required to guarantee an SNR_o of at least 100 dB.

5.25 Suppose a signal that ranges over the interval [−20, 20] is applied to a quantizer employing 256 levels.
Determine the required step size if a uniform quantizer is employed.
Determine the smallest and the largest effective separation between levels if a nonuniform μ-law quantizer with $\mu = 255$ is employed.

5.26 Determine the mean-square quantization error in delta modulation.

5.27 Show step by step how the power spectral density of Manchester code, as expressed in (5.27), can be obtained.

5.28 Show step by step how the power spectral density of AMI code, as expressed in (5.28), can be obtained.

Computer Exercises

5.29 Generate the signal $g(t) = \text{sinc}^2(1000t)$. Using instantaneous sampling, sample it once at 1500 samples per second, once at 2000 samples per second, and once at 2500 samples per second. Using DFT, plot the spectra of all three sampled signals.

5.30 Generate the signal $g(t) = \sin(2\pi t)$. Using a uniform quantizer, quantize it once to 16 levels and once to 32 levels. Plot the original signal and the quantized signals for a period of 2 seconds. Determine the resulting SNR_o for both cases.

5.31 Generate a sequence consisting of 1000 random variables with zero-mean, unit-variance Gaussian distribution. Assuming a μ -law compression with $\mu = 255$, plot the input-output relation for the quantizer, the error, and the SNR_o, where the number of bits per sample is 5, 6, 7, and 8.

CHAPTER 6

Baseband Digital Transmission

INTRODUCTION

In this chapter, we first present the basic elements of a baseband binary transmission system with the intention of introducing the two major channel degradations of intersymbol interference and noise. Detailed discussions on how to eliminate intersymbol interference and minimize the effect of noise are then provided. Next, the transmission of bits using M-ary signaling is introduced, and major trade-offs are identified and assessed. We derive the minimum bit error rate, and the impact of system parameters, such as power and transmission rate, are discussed. Finally, equalizers, which can combat the intersymbol interference due to unknown channel characteristics and imperfect filtering, are presented. After studying this chapter and understanding all relevant concepts and examples, students should be able to do the following:

1. Understand the elements of a baseband pulse amplitude modulation transmission system.
2. Describe intersymbol interference and its root cause.
3. State the Nyquist criterion in both time- and frequency-domain representations.
4. Comprehend the importance of pulse-shaping.
5. Identify the minimum bandwidth requirement.
6. Appreciate the role of the roll-off factor and excess bandwidth.
7. Characterize the raised-cosine pulse spectrum.
8. Examine eye patterns to qualitatively assess digital transmission performance.
9. Construct optimum transmitting and receiving filters to minimize the effect of noise.
10. Derive the expression for the minimum bit error rate.
11. Design baseband transmission systems to meet system requirements.
12. Outline M-ary signaling and why it is used.
13. Highlight the trade-offs in M-ary signaling.
14. Portray the need for equalization.

CONTENTS

Introduction to Digital Communications

15. Grasp the basic operation of Viterbi equalizers.
16. Determine the taps for zero-forcing linear equalizers.
17. Find the taps for minimum mean-square-error equalizers.
18. Explain how decision-feedback equalizers work.
19. Analyze how an adaptive equalizer using the least-mean-square algorithm operates.
20. Connect the concepts of bandwidth, bit rate, bit error rate, power, and complexity.

6.1 BASEBAND BINARY PAM TRANSMISSION SYSTEM MODEL

For the baseband digital transmission, pulse amplitude modulation (PAM) is the most efficient in terms of power and bandwidth utilization. Figure 6.1 shows the basic components of a ***baseband binary*** PAM transmission system. The input sequence $\{b_k\}$ consists of binary digits (***bits***) 1 and 0 with a bit duration of T_b and a bit rate of $r_b = 1/T_b$. The input bits applied to a pulse generator produce the following signal:

$$x(t) = \sum_{k=-\infty}^{\infty} a_k g(t - kT_b) \tag{6.1}$$

where $g(t)$ is the basic shaping pulse with $g(0) = 1$, and the pulse amplitude a_k depends on the input bit b_k such that

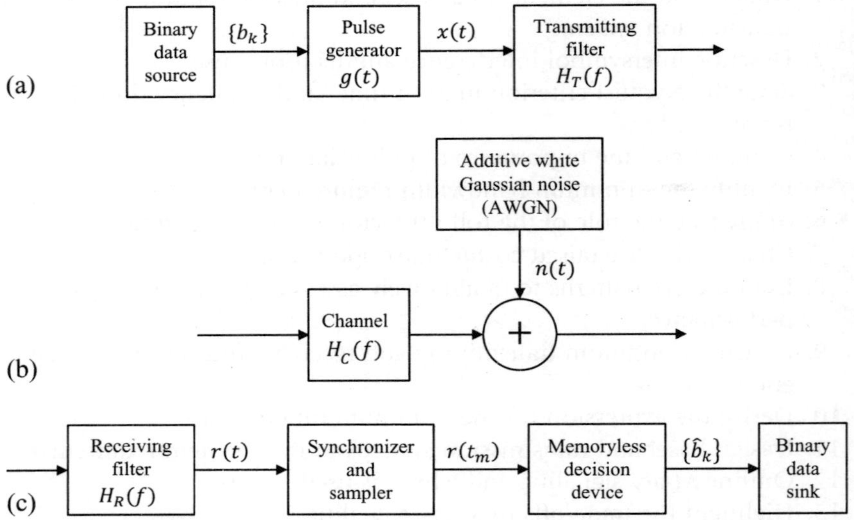

FIGURE 6.1 Baseband binary PAM transmission system: (a) transmitter, (b) channel, and (c) receiver.

$$a_k = \begin{cases} a, & b_k = 1 \\ -a, & b_k = 0 \end{cases} \tag{6.2}$$

where $a > 0$. The PAM signal $x(t)$ is passed through the ***transmitting filter*** $H_T(f)$ to form the transmitted signal. The transmitted signal is affected by the band-limited channel whose transfer function is $H_C(f)$. The channel also adds noise to the signal at the receiver input. Without loss of generality and for convenience, we assume there is no time delay in the system. The noisy signal is then filtered by the ***receiving filter*** $H_R(f)$ whose output is as follows:

$$r(t) = \sum_{k=-\infty}^{\infty} A_k h(t - kT_b) + n(t) \tag{6.3}$$

where $n(t)$ is the filtered noise, $A_k = Ca_k$, $Ch(t)$ is the system response when the input is $g(t)$, and $C > 0$ is a normalizing constant yielding $h(0) = 1$. With $h(t)$ as the inverse Fourier transform of the pulse-shaping filter $H(f)$, we thus have:

$$a_k G(f) H_T(f) H_C(f) H_R(f) = A_k H(f) \tag{6.4}$$

where $G(f)$ is the Fourier transform of the pulse $g(t)$. The received signal $r(t)$ in (6.3) is sampled synchronously at $t_m = mT_b$, where m takes on integer values. The timing signal is usually extracted from the received signal. We thus obtain:

$$r(t_m) = \sum_{k=-\infty}^{\infty} A_k h(mT_b - kT_b) + n(t_m) = A_m + \sum_{\substack{k=-\infty \\ k \neq m}}^{\infty} A_k h((m-k)T_b) + n(t_m) \tag{6.5}$$

The first term of the right-hand side of (6.5) represents the desired m^{th} transmitted bit, and the second term represents the residual effect of all other transmitted bits on the mth bit. This residual effect is called ***intersymbol interference*** (ISI). ISI results when received pulses are smeared into adjacent time intervals. The last term represents the noise sample. In the absence of noise and ISI, the mth bit is correctly decoded into a_m, and in turn, into b_m.

EXAMPLE 6.1

Suppose in a baseband binary PAM system the received pulse $h(t)$ at multiples of the bit duration T_b is defined as follows:

$$h(kT_b) = \begin{cases} 0, & k \leq -3 \\ 0.1, & k = -2 \\ -0.2, & k = -1 \\ 1, & k = 0 \\ -0.3, & k = 1 \\ 0.2, & k = 2 \\ 0, & k \geq 3 \end{cases}$$

Determine the maximum amount of ISI, and identify a sequence for which this maximum can occur.

Solution

The maximum amount of ISI, also known as the peak distortion, is the result of the worst-case transmitted sequence. The maximum value occurs when each term in the summation representing the ISI term in (6.5) is maximum, i.e., when we have

$$\text{ISI}_{\max} = \sum_{\substack{k=-\infty \\ k \neq m}}^{\infty} |h((m-k)T_b)|$$

The peak distortion is then $|0.1| + |-0.2| + |-0.3| + |0.2| = 0.8$. This maximum is obtained when each transmitted bit has the same algebraic sign as the corresponding ISI term. The binary sequence $\{+1, -1, -1, -1, +1\}$ can thus give rise to the peak distortion.

Since both ISI and noise can introduce errors, the major objective is to choose transmitting and receiving filters to ideally eliminate (or practically minimize) ISI and to minimize the effect of noise, thereby delivering the lowest possible bit error rate. In some communication systems, such as the plain old telephone system (POTS), ISI is more dominant than noise, whereas in some other systems, such as a TV broadcast satellite system, noise is more prevalent than ISI.

6.2 INTERSYMBOL INTERFERENCE

ISI is a dominant degradation usually caused by nonideal band-limited channels. As reflected in (6.5), ISI is caused by the nonideal time response of the system $h(t)$ spilling over from one bit into another. A bit is represented by a pulse sent during its interval, and spreading of a pulse beyond its allotted time interval can cause it to interfere with neighboring pulses. ISI, as a manifestation of channel distortion and imperfect filtering, can cause a significant number of errors if it is large enough. In digital transmission, it is thus a primary objective to design pulses to eliminate ISI.

6.2.1 Nyquist Criterion for Distortionless (Zero-ISI) Transmission

The condition for the removal of ISI is known as the ***Nyquist criterion***. A necessary and sufficient condition for the overall received pulse $h(t)$ to satisfy

$$h(mT_b) = \begin{cases} 1, & m = 0 \\ 0, & m \neq 0 \end{cases} \tag{6.6a}$$

is that its Fourier transform $H(f)$ must satisfy

$$\sum_{k=-\infty}^{\infty} H\left(f + \frac{k}{T_b}\right) = T_b, \quad |f| < \frac{1}{2T_b} \tag{6.6b}$$

EXAMPLE 6.2

Prove the Nyquist criterion, i.e., if we have (6.6b), we then have (6.6a).

Solution

Since $h(t)$ and $H(f)$ form a Fourier transform pair, we have:

$$h(t) = \int_{-\infty}^{\infty} H(f)\exp(j2\pi ft)df$$

By dividing the range of the above integration into frequency segments of length $\frac{1}{T_b}$, the received pulse $h(t)$ at sampling instants $t = mT_b$ is then as follows:

$$h(mT_b) = \sum_{k=-\infty}^{\infty} \int_{\frac{2k-1}{2T_b}}^{\frac{2k+1}{2T_b}} H(f)\exp(j2\pi fmT_b)df$$

Making a change of variable, $s = f - \frac{k}{T_b}$ and thus $ds = df$, we can rewrite $h(mT_b)$ as follows:

$$h(mT_b) = \sum_{k=-\infty}^{\infty} \int_{-1/2T_b}^{1/2T_b} H\left(s + \frac{k}{T_b}\right)\exp\left(j2\pi smT_b + j2\pi\left(\frac{k}{T_b}\right)mT_b\right)ds$$

$$= \sum_{k=-\infty}^{\infty} \int_{-1/2T_b}^{1/2T_b} H\left(s + \frac{k}{T_b}\right)\exp(j2\pi smT_b)ds$$

By replacing the variable s by the familiar variable f and also interchanging the order of integration and summation, $h(mT_b)$ can be rewritten as follows:

$$h(mT_b) = \int_{-1/2T_b}^{1/2T_b} \left(\sum_{k=-\infty}^{\infty} H\left(f + \frac{k}{T_b}\right)\right)\exp(j2\pi fmT_b)df$$

By using (6.6b), $h(mT_b)$ then becomes as follows:

$$h(mT_b) = \int_{-1/2T_b}^{1/2T_b} T_b\exp(j2\pi fmT_b)df = \text{sinc}(m).$$

Since we have

$$\text{sinc}(m) = \begin{cases} 1, & m = 0 \\ 0, & m \neq 0 \end{cases}$$

$h(t)$, whose Fourier transform $H(f)$ satisfies (6.6b), produces zero ISI and thus satisfies (6.6a).

The Nyquist criterion in the time domain, as reflected in (6.6a), indicates that the overall received pulse must be zero at all multiples of the bit duration T_b, except at $t = 0$, which has the value of 1. The Nyquist criterion does not uniquely specify $h(t)$ for all values of t. The Nyquist criterion in the frequency domain, as highlighted in (6.6b), states that the Fourier transform of the pulse must have odd symmetry with respect to the frequency $f = \frac{1}{2T_b}$, but the Nyquist criterion does not uniquely specify $H(f)$ for all values of f. This vestigial symmetry implies that the spectrum of the ISI-free pulse is such that if replicated in the frequency domain with spacing of $\frac{1}{T_b}$, the sum of all replicas is the constant T_b. It is of high importance to highlight that although the Nyquist criterion puts a very stringent requirement on the pulse, there are infinitely many pulses that can meet the Nyquist criterion so as to provide a zero-ISI (ISI-free) condition.

EXAMPLE 6.3

Suppose the Fourier transform of a pulse is as follows:

$$H(f)=\begin{cases} T_b, & |f|\le\dfrac{(1-\alpha)}{2T_b} \\ \left(\dfrac{T_b}{\alpha}\right)\left(-T_b|f|+\dfrac{1+\alpha}{2}\right), & \dfrac{(1-\alpha)}{2T_b}<|f|\le\dfrac{(1+\alpha)}{2T_b} \\ 0, & \dfrac{(1+\alpha)}{2T_b}<|f| \end{cases}$$

where $0\le\alpha\le 1$. Show that this pulse in both time and frequency domains satisfies the Nyquist criterion.

Solution

As shown in Figure 6.2a, $H(f)$ satisfies the Nyquist criterion, as there is odd symmetry with respect to the frequency $f=1/2T_b$. In other words, we have:

$$H\left(\frac{1}{2T_b}+x\right)+H\left(\frac{1}{2T_b}-x\right)=T_b$$

where $0\le x\le\frac{1}{2T_b}$. Using the inverse Fourier transform, the pulse in the time domain is then as follows:

$$h(t)=\text{sinc}\left(\frac{t}{T_b}\right)\text{sinc}\left(\frac{\alpha t}{T_b}\right)$$

As shown in Figure 6.2b, $h(t)$ regardless of the value α satisfies the Nyquist criterion, as we have $h(0)=1$ and $h(t)=0$ at all nonzero multiples of T_b.

Depending on the channel bandwidth W and the ***Nyquist bandwidth*** $\frac{1}{2T_b}$, also known as the ***minimum bandwidth***, there can be three distinct cases in a binary transmission system:

1) $W<\frac{1}{2T_b}$: The periodic function of (6.6b), whose period is $\frac{1}{T_b}$, cannot become a constant for all frequencies, since there can be no overlapping replicas of $H(f)$. This clearly points to the fact that we cannot design a digital transmission system with no ISI. In other words, if the bit rate is greater than twice the channel bandwidth $\left(\text{i.e., } 2W<\frac{1}{T_b}\right)$, the channel-induced ISI is unavoidable.

2) $W=\frac{1}{2T_b}$: The periodic function of (6.6b) can become a constant, only if $H(f)$ is an ideal LPF whose bandwidth is $\frac{1}{2T_b}$. Although the ideal lowpass filter with the minimum possible bandwidth $W=\frac{1}{2T_b}$ can theoretically eliminate the

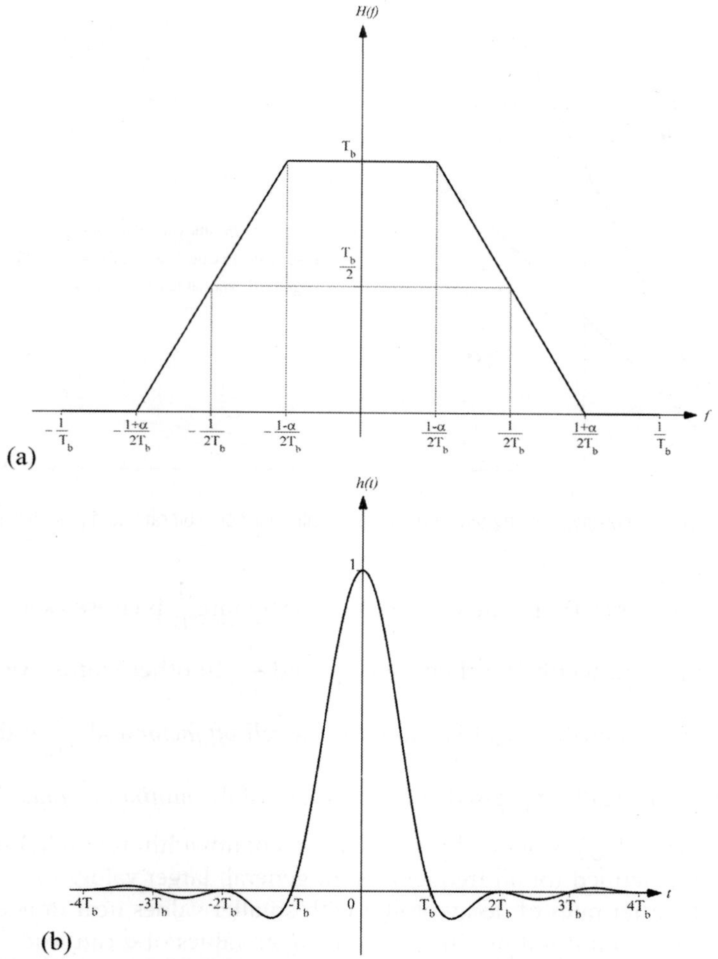

FIGURE 6.2 Pulse in Example 6.3: (a) Fourier transform and (b) impulse response.

problem of ISI, there are two difficulties in the system design: i) an ideal LPF is physically unrealizable because of the abrupt transitions at the band edges $\pm W$, and ii) the rate of convergence of the impulse response $h(t) = \text{sinc}\left(\frac{t}{T_b}\right)$ toward zero is quite slow, in that the tails and precursors of $h(t)$ decay as $\frac{1}{|t|}$, and as a result, a small timing error in sampling can result in an infinite series of ISI components whose sum does not converge.

3) $W > \frac{1}{2T_b}$: The periodic function of (6.6b) can consist of overlapping replicas of $H(f)$ separated by $\frac{1}{T_b}$. This obviously leads to an infinite number

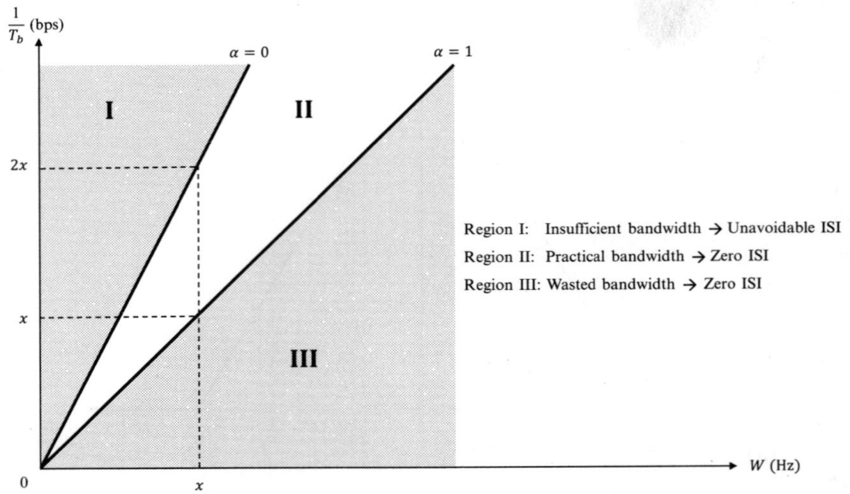

FIGURE 6.3 Relationships among the required bandwidth, allowable bit rate, and potential intersymbol interference.

of choices for $H(f)$. In practical systems, the bit rate $\frac{1}{T_b}$ is chosen such that the available bandwidth W is between $\frac{1}{2T_b}$ and $\frac{1}{T_b}$. In other words, we have $W = \frac{1+\alpha}{2T_b}$, where $0 \leq \alpha \leq 1$ is known as the ***roll-off factor*** and $\frac{\alpha}{2T_b}$ is the ***excess bandwidth*** usually expressed as a percentage of the ***minimum bandwidth*** $\frac{1}{2T_b}$. Note that if $H(f)$ is defined over the excess bandwidth, then $H(f)$ has been uniquely defined for all frequencies. In general, larger values of α can provide faster rates of decay of $h(t)$ with smaller values near nonzero multiples of bit duration. In addition, larger values of α can lead to filters that are easier to realize, as they can have smoother transition bands. However, these benefits are all at the expense of a larger excess bandwidth, as bandwidth is always at a premium.

Figure 6.3 highlights the relationship between the channel bandwidth W, the bit rate $\frac{1}{T_b}$, and the roll-off factor α.

EXAMPLE 6.4

Suppose the roll-off factor is 25% and the bandwidth of a baseband transmission system satisfying the Nyquist criterion is 30 kHz. Determine the bit rate.

Solution

We have $W = \frac{1+\alpha}{2T_b} = 30{,}000$ Hz, where $\alpha = 25\%$. We thus obtain the bit rate $r_b = \frac{1}{T_b} = 48$ kbps.

6.2.2 Raised-Cosine Pulse Spectrum

In the selection of a Nyquist pulse, it is important to consider a pulse that has a fast rate of decay in the time domain and its sample values at nonzero multiples of T_b are small. It is also desirable for the pulse to have a spectrum that can be closely approximated and easily realized. The most commonly used pulse has the raised-cosine spectrum, which consists of a flat amplitude portion up to $(1-\alpha)/2T_b$ and a cosine roll-off portion between $(1-\alpha)/2T_b$ and $(1+\alpha)/2T_b$. The Fourier transform of a ***raised-cosine pulse*** is defined as follows:

$$H(f)=\begin{cases} T_b, & |f|\le\dfrac{(1-\alpha)}{2T_b} \\ T_b\left(\sin\left(\dfrac{\pi T_b}{2\alpha}\left(|f|-\dfrac{1+\alpha}{2T_b}\right)\right)\right)^2, & \dfrac{(1-\alpha)}{2T_b}<|f|\le\dfrac{(1+\alpha)}{2T_b} \\ 0, & \dfrac{(1+\alpha)}{2T_b}<|f| \end{cases} \tag{6.7a}$$

where $0\le\alpha\le 1$. Note that $H(f)$ is real and nonnegative (i.e., its phase spectrum is zero for all frequencies), and the area under this pulse is also unity. The raised-cosine pulse in the time domain is thus as follows:

$$h(t)=\text{sinc}\left(\frac{t}{T_b}\right)\left(\frac{\cos\left(\dfrac{\pi\alpha t}{T_b}\right)}{1-\dfrac{4\alpha^2t^2}{T_b{}^2}}\right) \tag{6.7b}$$

Note that $h(t)$ consists of the product of two terms. The first one is a sinc function through which zero crossings at all nonzero multiples of T_b are guaranteed, and the second one, which is a function of the roll-off factor α, significantly reduces the tails and the predecessors of the pulse.

Figure 6.4 shows (6.7a) and (6.7b). Larger values of α imply that more bandwidth is required for a given bit rate $\frac{1}{T_b}$; however, they can lead to faster decaying pulses. In general, the tails of a raised-cosine pulse $h(t)$ decay as $\frac{1}{t^3}$ for $\alpha>0$. This in turn means that synchronization will be less critical and modest timing errors will not cause large amounts of ISI. Strictly speaking, raised-cosine pulses are noncausal and physically unrealizable; however, a delayed version of these pulses (i.e., $h(t-\tau)$) can be generated by causal filters, if the delay τ is long enough to have $h(t-\tau)\cong 0$ for $t<\tau$.

6.2.3 Eye Diagrams

Eye-pattern generation is straightforward and can provide a great deal of information. The eye diagram or pattern is an effective tool to provide a visual examination of the severity of the ISI, sensitivity to timing errors, and the noise margin.

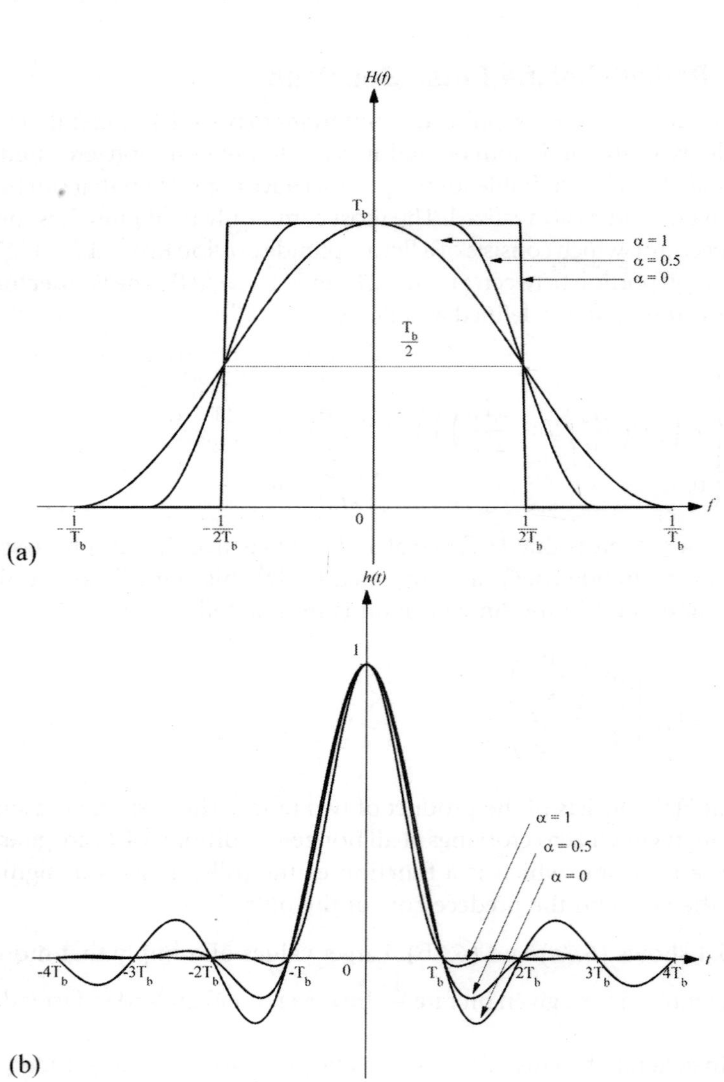

FIGURE 6.4 Raised cosine pulse: (a) pulse in frequency domain and (b) pulse in time domain.

The eye pattern is obtained by displaying the received signal on an oscilloscope. The time base of the scope is triggered at a fraction of the bit rate, and it thus yields a sweep, lasting several bit intervals. The oscilloscope then shows the superposition of many traces of bit intervals from the received signal. The oscilloscope pattern is simply the input signal cut up every couple of bit intervals and then superimposed on top of one another. Figure 6.5 shows various received signals and their corresponding eye patterns. As shown in Figure 6.6, monitoring of an eye pattern can provide a qualitative measure of performance regarding the signal quality, including the following important observations:

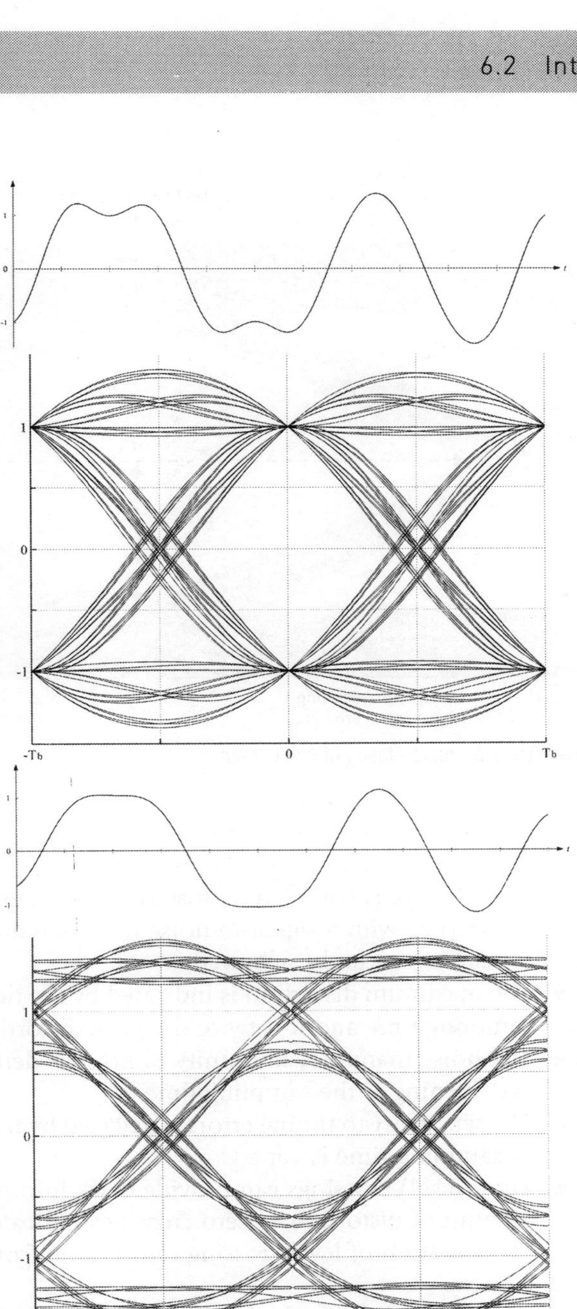

FIGURE 6.5 Various received signals and corresponding eye patterns: (a) ideal signal and (b) distorted signal.

- The width of the eye opening represents the time interval during which the received signal can be sampled without error from ISI.
- The best time to sample the received signal is when the eye is open the widest. When there is no ISI, we have an eye opening of unity, and when there is a significant amount of ISI, we have an eye opening of zero

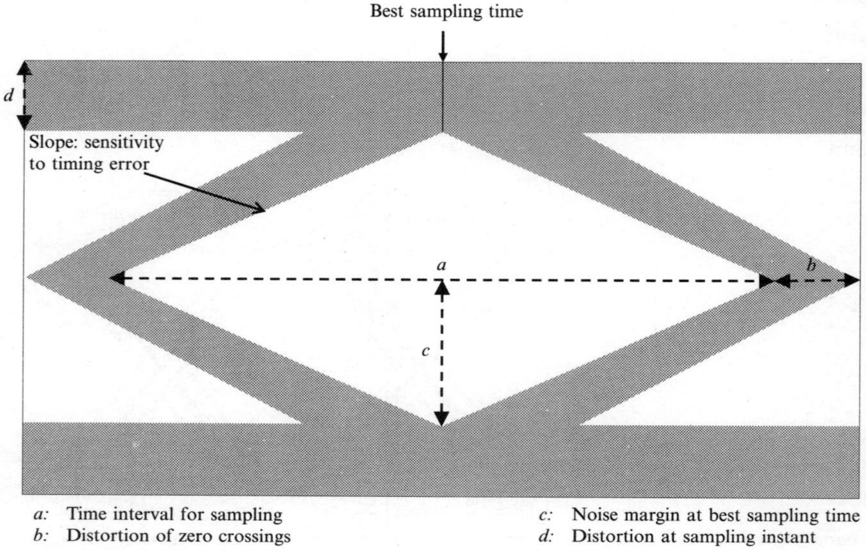

FIGURE 6.6 Interpretation of eye pattern.

(i.e., the eye is completely closed). With an eye opening of 50% or better (i.e., with a signal-to-noise ratio of 6 dB or more), reliable data transmission can be achieved.

- The maximum distortion is indicated by the height of the eye opening at sampling time and it is twice the peak distortion.
- The noise margin or immunity to noise is defined by the height of the eye opening at the sampling time.
- The sensitivity to timing errors is detected by the rate of closure of the eye as sampling time is varied.
- Zero (level) crossings can provide clock information, and the amount of distortion of zero crossings indicates the amount of jitter. The variation of level crossing can be seen from the width of the eye corners.
- In a linear system with truly random data, all the eye openings would be identical.
- Asymmetries in the eye opening generally indicate nonlinearities in the transmission channel.
- When the effect of ISI is quite severe, traces from the upper portion of the eye pattern cross traces from the lower portion, resulting in the eye being completely closed.
- In an M-ary system (as discussed later), the eye pattern contains $(M - 1)$ eye openings stacked up vertically one on the other.

EXAMPLE 6.5

Suppose we have a raised-cosine pulse with 100% roll-off factor. Discuss the properties of this pulse, and sketch its eye pattern.

Solution

A raised-cosine pulse with $\alpha = 100\%$, known as the full-cosine roll-off pulse, has a bandwidth of $\frac{1}{T_b}$. Using (6.7b), the pulse $h(t)$ is then defined as follows:

$$h(t) = \text{sinc}\left(\frac{t}{T_b}\right)\left(\frac{\cos\left(\frac{\pi t}{T_b}\right)}{1-\frac{4t^2}{T_b{}^2}}\right) = \left(\frac{\sin\left(\frac{\pi t}{T_b}\right)}{\frac{\pi t}{T_b}}\right)\left(\frac{\cos\left(\frac{\pi t}{T_b}\right)}{1-\frac{4t^2}{T_b{}^2}}\right) = \frac{\sin\left(\frac{2\pi t}{T_b}\right)}{\frac{2\pi t}{T_b}\left(1-\frac{4t^2}{T_b{}^2}\right)} = \frac{\text{sinc}\left(\frac{2t}{T_b}\right)}{1-\frac{4t^2}{T_b{}^2}}$$

At $t = \pm\frac{T_b}{2}$, we have $h(t) = 0.5$. This in turn means that the pulse width, measured at half amplitude, is exactly equal to the bit duration T_b. Moreover, at other odd multiples of $\pm\frac{T_b}{2}$, there are also zero crossings. These two properties can significantly simplify the extraction of a timing signal from the received signal, a major requirement for most digital transmission systems. However, these benefits are at the expense of requiring a bandwidth as much as $\frac{1}{T_b}$, which is double the minimum bandwidth $\frac{1}{2T_b}$. Figure 6.7 shows the eye pattern for this pulse.

6.3 OPTIMUM SYSTEM DESIGN FOR NOISE IMMUNITY

The major system design objectives are to choose the transmitting filter $H_T(f)$ and receiving filter $H_R(f)$ for the nonideal band-limited channel $H_C(f)$, transmit pulse $G(f)$, and received pulse $H(f)$, in such a way that ISI is eliminated and the

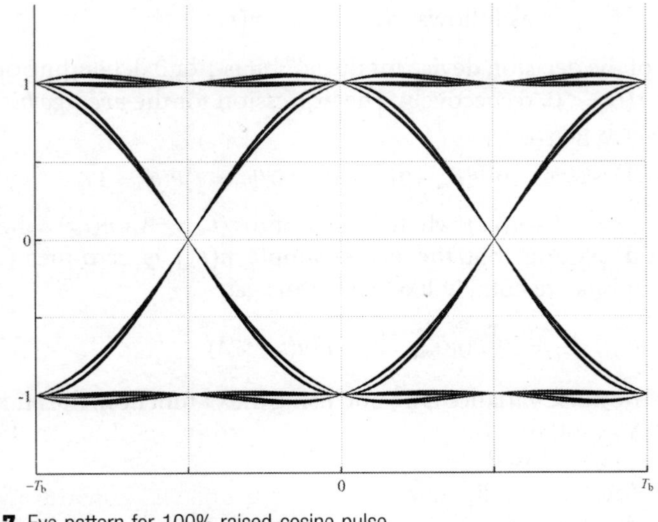

FIGURE 6.7 Eye pattern for 100% raised-cosine pulse.

effect of noise is minimized, thereby delivering the smallest possible bit error rate. The elimination of ISI can be achieved if the received pulse satisfies the Nyquist criterion, and the maximization of noise immunity can be accomplished by maximizing the signal-to-noise ratio (SNR) at the receiver output. As a matter of practical significance, we make the following assumptions:

i) The input bits, applied to a pulse generator to produce the input signal $x(t)$, are statistically independent and equi-probable. The power spectral density of the input signal $x(t)$ is thus as follows:

$$S_X(f) = \frac{a^2|G(f)|^2}{T_b} \quad (6.8)$$

where G(f) is the Fourier transform of the pulse $g(t)$, a narrow rectangular pulse of unit amplitude.

ii) The transmit pulse $g(t)$ is so narrow that its Fourier transform G(f) remains virtually unchanged over the bandwidth of interest. Using (6.4), we thus have:

$$CH(f) = G(f)H_T(f)H_C(f)H_R(f) \cong H_T(f)H_C(f)H_R(f) \quad (6.9)$$

iii) The noise at the input of the receiving filter is an ***additive white Gaussian noise*** (AWGN), with zero mean and power spectral density of $N_0/2$. The noise at the output of the receiving filter is also zero-mean Gaussian, and has the following variance:

$$\sigma_N^2 = \frac{N_0}{2}\int_{-\infty}^{\infty} |H_R(f)|^2 df \quad (6.10)$$

6.3.1 Bit Error Rate Derivation

With the received pulse satisfying the Nyquist criterion (i.e., when there is no ISI), at the mth sampling instant $t_m = mT_b$, the output at the receiving filter, according to (6.5), is as follows: $r(t_m) = A_m + n(t_m)$.

The output of the decision device for the mth bit is 1 or 0 depending on whether $r(t_m) > 0$ or $r(t_m) < 0$, respectively. The expression for the ***average bit error rate*** at the receiver is given by:

$$P_{BER}(e) = P(r(t_m) > 0/b_m = 0)P(b_m = 0) + (r(t_m) < 0/b_m = 1)P(b_m = 1) \quad (6.11a)$$

We have $r(t_m) = -A + n(t_m)$ when $b_m = 0$ and $r(t_m) = A + n(t_m)$ when $b_m = 1$, where $A = Ca$. Noting that the noise sample $n(t_m)$ is zero-mean Gaussian and the input bits are equally likely, we thus get:

$$P_{BER}(e) = \frac{1}{2}P(n(t_m) < -A) + \frac{1}{2}P(n(t_m) > A) = P(n(t_m) > A) \quad (6.11b)$$

Noting that the noise variance is σ_N^2 and using the Q-function, the ***bit error probability*** is then as follows:

$$P_{BER}(e) = Q\left(\frac{A}{\sigma_N}\right) \quad (6.11c)$$

6.3.2 Optimum Transmitting and Receiving Filters

Since the Q-function is a decreasing function, $P_{BER}(e)$ in (6.11c) decreases as $\frac{A}{\sigma_N}$ increases or equivalently as $\frac{A^2}{\sigma_N^2}$ increases. In order to minimize $P_{BER}(e)$, we thus have to maximize $\frac{A^2}{\sigma_N^2}$, which in turn means we need to design the ***optimum transmitting and receiving filters***. Using (6.8), the power spectral density of the transmitted signal is given by:

$$S_T(f) = \frac{a^2|G(f)|^2}{T_b}|H_T(f)|^2$$

Noting we have $A = Ca$, then by using (6.9), we have the ***average transmitted power*** as follows:

$$P_T = \int_{-\infty}^{\infty} S_T(f)df = \int_{-\infty}^{\infty} \frac{a^2|G(f)|^2}{T_b}|H_T(f)|^2 df = \frac{A^2}{T_b}\int_{-\infty}^{\infty} \frac{|H(f)|^2}{|H_C(f)H_R(f)|^2}df$$

Solving for A^2, we get:

$$A^2 = P_T T_b \left[\int_{-\infty}^{\infty} \frac{|H(f)|^2}{|H_C(f)H_R(f)|^2}df\right]^{-1} \qquad (6.12a)$$

Using (6.10) and (6.12a), $\frac{A^2}{\sigma_N^2}$ can then be expressed as follows:

$$\frac{A^2}{\sigma_N^2} = \frac{P_T T_b}{N_0/2}\left[\int_{-\infty}^{\infty} |H_R(f)|^2 df \int_{-\infty}^{\infty} \frac{|H(f)|^2}{|H_C(f)H_R(f)|^2}df\right]^{-1} \qquad (6.12b)$$

In order to minimize the bit error probability in (6.11c), we thus need to minimize the following:

$$\gamma^2 = \int_{-\infty}^{\infty} |H_R(f)|^2 df \int_{-\infty}^{\infty} \frac{|H(f)|^2}{|H_C(f)H_R(f)|^2}df$$

We now use ***Schwartz's inequality***, which is stated as follows: if $U(f)$ and $W(f)$ are complex functions of f, we have:

$$\int_{-\infty}^{\infty} |U(f)|^2 df \int_{-\infty}^{\infty} |W^*(f)|^2 df \geq \int_{-\infty}^{\infty} |U(f)W^*(f)|^2 df$$

The minimum value of the left-hand side of the above relation is obtained when $U(f) = K_1\, W(f)$, where K_1 is a positive constant. In our case, we have:

$$|U(f)| = |H_R(f)|$$

and

$$|W(f)| = \frac{|H(f)|}{|H_C(f)||H_R(f)|}$$

γ^2 is thus minimized when the optimum receiving filter is as follows:

$$|H_R(f)|^2 = \frac{K_1|H(f)|}{|H_C(f)|} \tag{6.13a}$$

Using the above result and (6.9), we have the optimum transmitting filter as follows:

$$|H_T(f)|^2 = \frac{K_2|H(f)|}{|H_C(f)|} \tag{6.13b}$$

where $K_2 = C^2/K_1$. These filters must have either linear phase responses or arbitrary phase responses as long as they compensate one another. From (6.13a) and (6.13b), we can have the following interesting result:

$$|H_R(f)| = K_3|H_T(f)| \tag{6.14}$$

where $K_3 = \frac{K_1}{C}$. It is important to note that with the exception of a gain difference, the transmitting and receiving filters have the same frequency characteristics. This simply means that one design can therefore characterize both filters. Using (6.12b), (6.13a), and (6.13b), the maximum value of $\frac{A^2}{\sigma_N^2}$ is then as follows:

$$\left(\frac{A^2}{\sigma_N^2}\right)_{max} = \frac{P_T T_b}{N_0/2}\left(\int_{-\infty}^{\infty}\frac{|H(f)|}{|H_C(f)|}df\right)^{-2} \tag{6.15a}$$

which in turn gives rise to the following minimum bit error probability:

$$P_{BER}(e)_{min} = Q\left(\frac{A}{\sigma_N}\right)_{max} \tag{6.15b}$$

6.3.3 Design Procedure and Example

The bit error rate under the ideal circumstance of an AWGN channel and zero-ISI system represents the best that can be achieved. Assuming $H_C(f) = 1$ and the Fourier transform of the received pulse $H(f)$ satisfies $\int_{-\infty}^{\infty} |H(f)|df = 1$, the maximum value of the SNR in (6.15a) can be further simplified, and the corresponding minimum bit error probability, as reflected in (6.15b), thus becomes as follows:

$$P_{BER}(e)_{min} = Q\left(\sqrt{\frac{P_T T_b}{N_0/2}}\right) = Q\left(\sqrt{\frac{E_b}{N_0/2}}\right) = Q\left(\sqrt{\frac{P_T}{R_b N_0/2}}\right) \tag{6.16}$$

where $E_b = P_T T_b = \frac{P_T}{R_b}$ is the ***average energy per bit***. As highlighted in (6.16), there are three major parameters that can impact the minimum bit error rate. Since the Q-function is a decreasing function, an increase in the average transmit power P_T or a reduction in the noise power $N_0/2$ or a decrease in the bit rate R_b or a combination of these three changes can reduce the minimum bit error rate.

In the analysis of digital data transmission systems, we cannot assume the bandwidth is unconstrained and unlimited. We cannot thus employ a rectangular pulse at the transmitter to represent a bit, where each pulse has infinite bandwidth, and expect the received pulse to also be a rectangular pulse. We therefore need to design the pulse shapes $g(t)$ and $h(t)$, in addition to the filters $H_T(f)$ and $H_R(f)$, so the smallest possible bit error rate, defined as $P(b_k \neq \hat{b_k})$, can be delivered, while minimizing the system bandwidth for a given bit rate.

In general, there are various inter-related parameters that can impact the system design and the error-rate performance, such as the transmit pulse $g(t)$, received pulse $h(t)$, channel noise power $N_0/2$, channel bandwidth W, average transmit power P_T, bit rate R_b, and of course, system complexity. The design process therefore involves trade-offs among them so as to meet the specified requirements and constraints. In general, we assume the bit rate and the bit error rate are specified, and the channel characteristics, including distortion and noise, are known. More specifically, we assume the channel introduces linear distortion and AWGN. In addition, we also assume the input bit stream is ergodic and bits are independent and equally likely. Since it is a synchronous transmission, a clock signal must be recovered at the receiving end to set the correct sampling rate and sampling times. Synchronization always adds to the system complexity.

EXAMPLE 6.6

Consider a baseband binary PAM system that transmits at 9.6 kbps with a bit error rate less than 10^{-6}. With the bandwidth of 6.4 kHz, the channel response is as follows: $H_C(f) = 10^{-2}$. The channel noise is AWGN with a power spectral density of 10^{-13} watts per Hertz (W/Hz). Design the optimum transmitting and receiving filters and determine the required transmit power.

Solution

We have $\frac{1}{T_b} = 9,600$ bps and $\frac{1+\alpha}{2T_b} = 6,400$ Hz. We can thus assume that the received pulse $H(f)$ is a raised-cosine pulse with the roll-off factor $\alpha = \frac{1}{3}$, as it can satisfy the channel bandwidth constraint. We also assume that the transmit pulse $g(t)$ is a narrow rectangular pulse whose width is much smaller than the bit duration, say 10^{-5} seconds, which is less than 10% of $\frac{1}{9600}$ seconds. We therefore have:

$$|G(f)| = \tau \,\mathrm{sinc}(f\tau)$$

where $\tau = 10^{-5}$. $|G(f)|$ is thus virtually constant over the entire bandwidth of interest. Using (6.13a), (6.13b), and (6.14), we choose to have:

$$|H_R(f)| = |H(f)|^{1/2}$$

and consequently, we have:

$$|H_T(f)| = K_2 |H(f)|^{1/2}$$

where $K_2 = \frac{1}{10^{-5} \times 10^{-2}} = 10^7$ compensates for the scaling factor of $\tau = 10^{-5}$ and the channel attenuation of 10^{-2} so as to ensure $H(f)$ is produced. Based on (6 15b) and the inverse Q-function, to maintain $P_{BER}(e) < 10^{-6}$, we must then have $\frac{A}{\sigma_N} > 4.75$. Using (6.15a), we thus get the required transmit power as follows:

$$P_T = \left(\frac{1}{T_b}\right)\left(\frac{A^2}{\sigma_N^2}\right)\left(\frac{N_0}{2}\right)\left(\int_{-\infty}^{\infty}\frac{|H(f)|}{|H_C(f)|}df\right)^2 =$$

$$(9600)(4.75)^2\left(10^{-13}\right)\left(\frac{1}{10^{-4}}\right) = -36.65\,\text{dB} = -6.65\,\text{dBm}$$

6.4 BASEBAND M-ARY SIGNALING SCHEMES

With binary signaling, each symbol a_k represents one single bit that is transmitted every T_b seconds. For binary transmission, the symbol rate is equivalent to the bit rate $\frac{1}{T_b}$, and according to the Nyquist criterion, the minimum bandwidth requirement is then $\frac{1}{2T_b}$.

With ***M-ary signaling***, instead of transmitting a pulse for each bit, the stream of incoming bits is partitioned into m-bit groups, and the output of the pulse generator takes on one of $M = 2^m$ possible amplitude levels, where m represents a positive integer. Since M is a power of 2, the number of bits transmitted per symbol can be expressed as $m = \log_2 M$. In an M-ary transmission system, for every m bits produced by the source, a symbol, whose duration is T_s seconds long, is transmitted. The ***symbol duration*** is m times longer than the bit duration (i.e., $T_s = mT_b$) or equivalently the ***symbol rate*** is m times smaller than the bit rate $\left(\text{i.e., } \frac{1}{T_s} = \frac{1}{mT_b}\right)$. With M-ary signaling, according to the Nyquist criterion, the minimum bandwidth requirement is then $\frac{1}{2T_s} = \frac{1}{2mT_b} \le \frac{1}{2T_b}$.

6.4.1 Bandwidth and Bit Rate

Spectral efficiency η, measured in bits per second per Hertz (bps/Hz), is defined as the bit transmission rate per unit of occupied bandwidth. For M-ary signaling, a symbol represents m bits, with the symbol transmission rate $\frac{1}{T_s}$, and the bit transmission rate is thus $\frac{m}{T_s}$. For the occupied bandwidth $W = \frac{(1+\alpha)}{2T_s}$, the spectral efficiency η is then as follows:

$$m \le \eta = \frac{\frac{m}{T_s}}{\frac{1+\alpha}{2T_s}} = \frac{2m}{(1+\alpha)} \le 2m \tag{6.17}$$

Note that the lower bound is attained when the excess bandwidth is maximum $(\alpha = 1)$ and the upper bound is reached when the bandwidth is minimum

($\alpha = 0$). For binary signaling, we have $1 \le \eta \le 2$, as $m = 1$. We can thus conclude that in M-ary signaling, the spectral efficiency is enhanced by the factor $m = \log_2 M$. For a given channel bandwidth, the M-ary signaling brings about a bit transmission rate that is faster than the binary signaling and/or for a given bit transmission rate, the M-ary signaling requires a bandwidth that is less than what the binary signaling requires.

EXAMPLE 6.7

Consider an M-ary system with the number of symbols $M = 16$, and the roll-off factor $\alpha = \frac{1}{3}$. Discuss this M-ary system, vis-à-vis the corresponding binary system, for various scenarios.

Solution

With $M = 16$, we have $m = \log_2 M = 4$ (i.e., a pulse represents 4 bits, as a pulse can have one of the 16 different levels). Using (6.17) and noting $\alpha + 1 = \frac{4}{3}$, we then have $\eta = 1.5$ bps/Hz for the binary system and $\eta = 6$ bps/Hz for the M-ary system. Using (6.17), the discussion for three different M-ary scenarios with $\eta = 6$ bps/Hz may be summarized as follows:

(a) To achieve $\eta = 6$, we can increase the bit rate by a factor of 4, as the M-ary pulse represents 4 bits. The bandwidth of the M-ary system then remains the same as that of the binary system, as their pulse durations remain the same.

(b) To achieve $\eta = 6$, we can reduce the bandwidth by a factor of 4, as the M-ary pulse duration is four times longer than the binary pulse duration. The bit rates in both systems remain the same, as the pulse rate in the M-ary system is four times slower, but a pulse represents four bits.

(c) To achieve $\eta = 6$, we can increase the bit rate by a factor of 2 and reduce the bandwidth by a factor of 2, as the M-ary pulse duration is twice as long as the binary pulse duration, and the pulse rate is twice as slower, but a pulse represents 4 bits.

	Binary	Scenario a	Scenario b	Scenario c
Pulse rate	x	x	$x/4$	$x/2$
No. of bits per pulse	1	4	4	4
Bit rate	x	$4x$	x	$2x$
Pulse duration	$1/x$	$1/x$	$4/x$	$2/x$
Pulse bandwidth	$2x/3$	$2x/3$	$x/6$	$x/3$
Spectral efficiency	1.5	6	6	6

6.4.2 Power and Bit Error Rate

Use of M-ary signaling can obviously bring about conservation in transmission bandwidth and/or enhancement in bit transmission rate. However, there is a significant price for such valuable gains. An M-ary system, along with a modest increase in complexity, requires additional power and/or delivers an increase in bit error rate. More specifically, for the same amount of transmission power in both binary and M-ary systems, the interval between two adjacent levels in an M-ary system is less than that in a binary system. In other words, the noise margin in an M-ary system is less than that in a binary system, which in turn results in a higher than average bit error rate. Equivalently, for the same bit error rate in binary and M-ary systems, we thus require the interval between two adjacent levels in an M-ary system to be the same as that in a binary system, that is, we need to increase the average transmit power in an M-ary system, as we have $M > 2$.

In M-ary signaling, a symbol takes on one of the M levels. We assume the symbols can take positive and negative values, the M levels are centered at zero, and the spacing of amplitude levels is uniform. In the binary signaling, we transmit two equally-likely symbols, consisting of $\pm A$. But in the M-ary signaling, the M equally-likely symbols are transmitted by $\pm A \pm 3A, \ldots, \pm(M-1)A$. The average symbol energy E_s is thus as follows:

$$E_s = \frac{2}{M}\left[A^2 + 9A^2 + 25A^2 + \ldots + (M-1)^2 A^2\right] = \left(\frac{M^2-1}{3}\right)A^2 \tag{6.18a}$$

Also, as a single symbol carries $\log_2 M$ bits, its average bit energy E_b is then as follows:

$$E_b = \frac{E_s}{\log_2 M} = \left(\frac{M^2-1}{3\log_2 M}\right)A^2 \tag{6.18b}$$

In the derivation of the symbol error probability, it is important to note that the two symbols at the edges may be erroneously detected by only one neighboring symbol, whereas the other $(M-2)$ can have a higher error probability as they may be erroneously detected by either of the two neighboring symbols. Using (6.18b), and along with the same set of assumptions and line of derivations discussed for the binary system, it can be shown that with optimum filtering, the ***symbol error probability*** is as follows:

$$P_{SER}(e)_{\min} = \frac{2(M-1)}{M} Q\left(\sqrt{\frac{(6\log_2 M)}{(M^2-1)}\left(\frac{E_b}{N_0}\right)}\right) \tag{6.19}$$

If ***Gray code*** is used, two adjacent symbols (amplitude levels) differ in only a single bit. With the high SNR, the most probable errors due to noise result in the erroneous selection of an amplitude level adjacent to the true amplitude level, most symbol errors contain only a single error. Therefore, the ***bit error rate*** can be well approximated as follows:

$$P_{BER}(e)_{\min} \approx \frac{2(M-1)}{M\log_2 M} Q\left(\sqrt{\frac{(6\log_2 M)}{(M^2-1)}\left(\frac{E_b}{N_0}\right)}\right) \tag{6.20}$$

6.4.3 Binary vs. *M*-ary Signaling Schemes

Note that with $M = 2$, both (6.19) and (6.20) turn into (6.16). Figure 6.8 shows (6.20) for various values of M. Assuming both binary and M-ary signaling are delivering the same bit error rate, we can draw the following conclusions:

i) As reflected in (6.20), the transmit power for the M-ary system must be increased by a factor of $\frac{3\log_2 M}{M^2-1}$.

ii) As highlighted in (6.17), the bandwidth requirement for the M-ary system can be reduced by a factor of $\frac{1}{m} = \frac{1}{\log_2 M}$.

iii) The complexity associated with the receiver for the M-ary system is higher than that for the binary system, as it requires $(M-2)$ additional comparators.

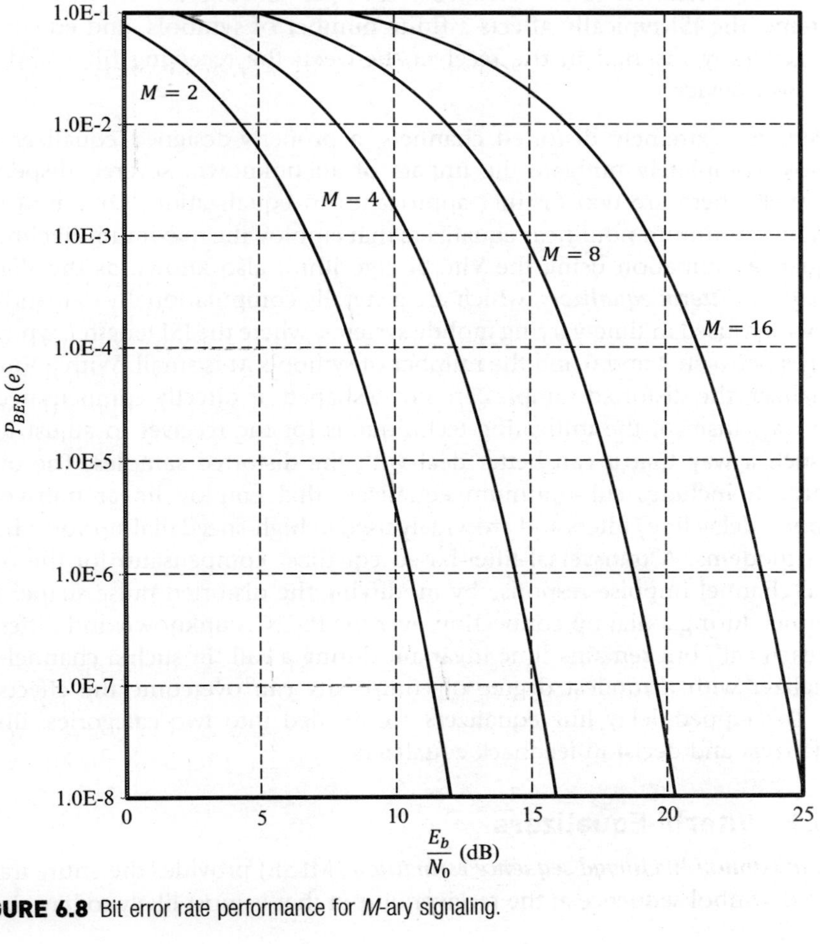

FIGURE 6.8 Bit error rate performance for *M*-ary signaling.

In practice, if the bit rate must be higher than twice the available bandwidth, we then have no choice but to employ M-ary signaling.

6.5 EQUALIZATION

Even with optimum pulses, in practical systems, some amount of residual ISI inevitably occurs. The ISI in almost all real transmission systems is mainly due to imperfect filter design in the transmitter and receiver, incomplete knowledge of channel characteristics, time-varying channel characteristics, and timing errors. Due to the lack of knowledge about the channel-frequency characteristics, we cannot therefore design the optimum transmitting and receiving filters. The resulting ISI may impose a limit on the attainable rate of data transmission that is far below the physical capability of the channel. Hence, corrective measures must be taken to minimize the amount of ISI. ***Equalization*** is an effective technique to combat ISI. In practical systems, the ISI typically affects a finite number of symbols, and equalizers are generally inserted in the receiver, between the receiving filter and the decision device.

Except for extremely distorted channels, a properly-designed equalizer can almost completely mitigate the impact of an unknown, severely-dispersive channel. There are two distinct approaches to equalization. One approach includes optimum nonlinear equalizers that employ the maximum-likelihood sequence estimation using the Viterbi algorithm, also known as the Viterbi equalizer. ***Viterbi equalizers***, which are generally computationally demanding, are widely used in time-varying mobile systems, where the ISI length L typically ranges between 4 and 6 and the number of symbols M is small. With a Viterbi equalizer, the distorted samples are not reshaped or directly compensated in any way; instead, the mitigating technique is for the receiver to adjust itself in such a way that it can better deal with the distorted samples. The other approach includes sub-optimum equalizers that employ linear transversal (tapped-delay line) filters and are widely used in high-speed dial-up voice-band data modems. A transversal-filter-based equalizer compensates for the non-ideal channel impulse response by modifying the distorted pulse shape. The channel during a dial-up connection over the PSTN is unknown and different on each call, but remains time-invariant during a call. In such a channel, an equalizer with a modest degree of complexity can overcome the effects of ISI. The tapped-delay line equalizers are divided into two categories: linear equalizers and decision-feedback equalizers.

6.5.1 Viterbi Equalizers

The ***maximum likelihood sequence estimation*** (MLSE) provides the entire transmitted symbol sequence at the receiver output that is most likely to have been transmitted, on the basis of observing the entire received signal at the receiver input. The crux of MLSE is nonlinear processing, which is most efficiently realized through application of a dynamic programming procedure known as the ***Viterbi algorithm***. The performance criterion is the maximization of the probability that the sequence of decisions is correct.

A brute-force approach to MLSE reflects the fact that there are a total of N transmitted symbols in the sequence, where symbols are independent and each can take one of equally-likely M possible values. There are thus M^N possible transmitted sequences that are all equally likely. The computational complexity is absolutely enormous, as it grows exponentially with N. The salient feature of the Viterbi algorithm is that the ISI length of L allows the application of the recursive principle to reduce the complexity to the order of M^L operations per symbol, for a total of NM^{L+1} operations, which grows linearly as N increases.

We now consider the digital transmission of binary input (i.e., $M=2$) through a nonideal band-limited channel with AWGN, where the channel introduces causal ISI of length L (i.e., the ISI affects the past L bits). The MLSE criterion maximizes the a posteriori probability of a particular transmitted bit sequence $\{a_1, a_2, \ldots, a_N\}$, given observation of the received sample sequence $\{r_1, r_2, \ldots, r_N\}$. It can be shown that this maximization becomes equivalent to the minimum distance decision rule based on the following measure:

$$\sum_{k=1}^{N}\left(r(kT_b)-\sum_{i=0}^{L}h(iT_b)\,a_{k-i}\right)^2 \tag{6.21}$$

where $h(t)$ is the nonideal channel response with causal ISI of length L that the equalizer sees, and it is either known in advance or can be measured at the receiver. The computational complexity of MLSE is massive and includes calculations of 2^N metrics. The Viterbi algorithm can be used to significantly reduce the computational burden by eliminating sequences as a new bit is received. The Viterbi algorithm is a computationally efficient algorithm, as it is based on a sequential trellis search algorithm. Minimizing the above measure is equivalent to maximizing the following measure, which can be recursively calculated:

$$J_k = J_{k-1} + 2\,(r(kT_b))\left(\sum_{i=0}^{L}h(iT_b)a_{k-i}\right)-\left(\sum_{i=0}^{L}h(iT_b)a_{k-i}\right)^2 \tag{6.22}$$

At each node of the trellis, the Viterbi algorithm computes two metrics corresponding to each of the 2^L incoming signal paths. At each stage of the trellis search, there are 2^L surviving sequences with 2^L corresponding Euclidian distance path metrics. The surviving path at each node is then extended to two new paths, which includes one path for each of the two possible input bits, and the search process continues. The Viterbi equalizer can then reduce the computational complexity of the MLSE equalizer to $N2^{L+1}$ metrics; this level of complexity is rather modest even for very large N.

6.5.2 Linear Equalizers

In selection of the parameters of equalizers employing transversal filters, the most meaningful performance measure is the minimization of the average bit error rate. However, the average bit error rate is a highly nonlinear, computationally complex function of the equalizer parameters. Instead, two other criteria have found widespread use in optimizing the parameters associated with transversal-filter-based equalizers: the minimization of the peak distortion and the minimization of the mean-square error.

Because of its versatility and simplicity, the transversal linear equalizer is a common choice for many applications. The ***linear equalizer*** consists of a delay line tapped at T_b second intervals, where each tap is connected through a variable gain device (tap weight coefficient) to a summing device. It is assumed that the linear equalizer has $(2N + 1)$ taps. As shown in Figure 6.9, the past, present, and future values of the received samples are linearly weighted with equalizer coefficients. With an infinite number of taps, it is possible to choose the tap values to eliminate the ISI. However, with the realistic case of having finite number of taps, there is always some residual ISI even when the optimum coefficients are used. There are two methods to optimize the taps: minimization of the peak distortion and minimization of mean-square error.

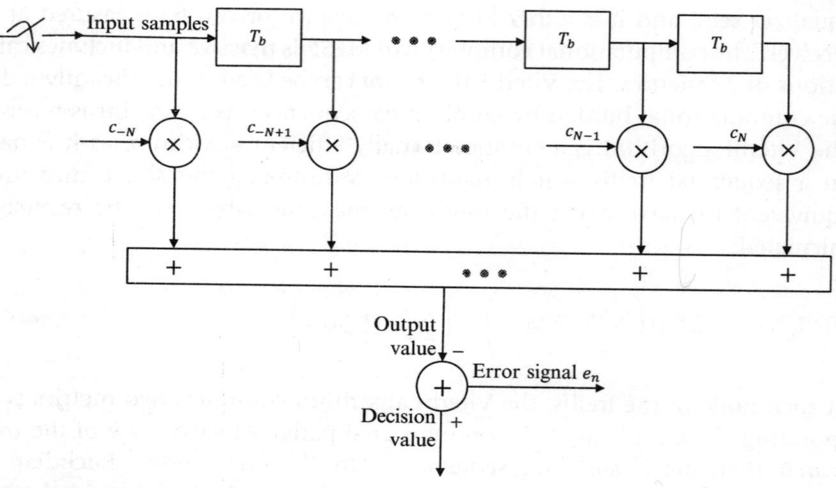

FIGURE 6.9 A linear equalizer.

The zero-forcing equalizer minimizes the peak distortion if the eye is initially open. In ***zero-forcing (ZF) equalization***, the goal is to design a linear equalizer whose frequency response is the inverse of channel frequency response. The ZF equalizer can force the ISI to be zero at the sampling instants. However, the finite impulse response ZF equalizer does not completely eliminate ISI because it has a finite length, it can just minimize it. In ZF equalization, the tap coefficients of the ZF equalizer can be determined by solving the following system of linear equations for the $(2N+1)$ taps of the ZF equalizer:

$$\sum_{n=-N}^{N} c_n h(mT_b - nT_b) = \begin{cases} 1, & m=0 \\ 0, & m=\pm 1, \pm 2, \cdots, \pm N \end{cases} \tag{6.23}$$

where $h(t)$ is the nonideal channel response with causal ISI of length L, $\{c_n\}$ represent the $(2N+1)$ equalizer coefficients, and N is generally chosen sufficiently large so that the equalizer spans the length of the ISI. Under this condition, bit-by-bit detection is considered as optimal, provided that the channel noise is zero. Although the ZF equalizer is relatively easy to design, it is not widely used, since it can lead to overall performance degradation due to noise enhancement. The significant noise enhancement is due to the fact when the channel response is small, the channel equalizer compensates by placing a large gain in that frequency range, thus enhancing noise in that frequency range.

EXAMPLE 6.8

Suppose the samples of the nonideal received pulse are as follows:

$$h(mT_b) = \begin{cases} 0, & m < -1 \\ 0.2, & m = -1 \\ 1, & m = 0 \\ -0.2, & m = 1 \\ 0, & m > 1 \end{cases}$$

Design a three-tap ZF equalizer.

Solution

Using (6.23), we obtain the following system of linear equations:

$$\begin{cases} c_{-1} + 0.2\,c_0 = 0 \\ -0.2\,c_{-1} + c_0 + 0.2\,c_1 = 1 \\ -0.2\,c_0 + c_1 = 0 \end{cases}$$

The tap gains are then as follows: $c_{-1} = -0.185$, $c_0 = 0.926$, and$c_1 = 0.185$.

The ***minimum mean square error (MMSE) equalizer*** selects the channel equalizer taps such that the combined power in the residual ISI and the additive noise at the output of the equalizer are minimized. In the presence of large ISI and noise, an MMSE equalizer is more robust than a ZF equalizer. In fact, for a prescribed computational complexity, an MMSE equalizer performs as well as, and often better than, a ZF equalizer. An MMSE equalizer minimizes the mean-square error of all the ISI terms plus noise; namely, it minimizes the expected value of the squared difference between the desired data symbol and the estimated data symbol. In MMSE equalization for a channel with the causal ISI of length L, the tap coefficients of the equalizer can be determined by solving the following set of linear equations for the $(2N+1)$ taps of the MMSE equalizer:

$$\sum_{n=-N}^{N} c_n \left(\sum_{k=0}^{L} h(kT_b)h(kT_b + mT_b - nT_b) + \sigma^2 \delta_{n-m} \right) = h(-mT_b), \; m = -N, \ldots, N \tag{6.24}$$

where δ_{n-m} is the Kronecker delta and σ^2 is the noise variance. It is important to note that the conditions for the optimum tap gains for MMSE equalizers are similar to those for ZF equalizers, except the autocorrelation function samples are used instead of the samples of the received pulse.

EXAMPLE 6.9

Suppose the samples of the nonideal received pulse are as follows:

$$h(mT_b) = \begin{cases} 0, & m < 0 \\ 0.7, & m = 0 \\ 0.7, & m = 1 \\ 0, & m > 1 \end{cases}$$

and the noise variance is 0.07. Design a three-tap MMSE equalizer.

Solution

Using (6.24), we obtain the following system of linear equations:

$$\begin{cases} 1.05c_{-1} + 0.49\,c_0 = 0.7 \\ 0.49\,c_{-1} + 1.05c_0 + 0.49\,c_1 = 0.7 \\ 0.49\,c_0 + 1.05c_1 = 0 \end{cases}$$

The tap gains are then as follows: $c_{-1} = 0.3727$, $c_0 = 0.6299$, and $c_1 = -0.2939$.

6.5.3 Decision-Feedback Equalizers

Linear equalizers are effective on channels, such as wired-line telephone channels, when the ISI is not severe. However, when the ISI is severe, for instance, when the channel frequency response has nulls, linear equalizers perform poorly. The severity of ISI is not necessarily related to the length of the ISI, but it is rather a function of how significant the contributing ISI components are. In channels with spectral nulls, a linear equalizer will introduce a rather large gain in its frequency response to compensate for the channel null, thus enhancing noise significantly. A ***decision-feedback equalizer*** (DFE) is more effective than a linear equalizer. A DFE is a nonlinear equalizer that uses past symbol decisions to eliminate the ISI caused by previously detected symbols on the current symbol being detected. In effect, the distortion caused by previous pulses on the current pulse is subtracted. Figure 6.10 shows the decision-feedback part of the DFE.

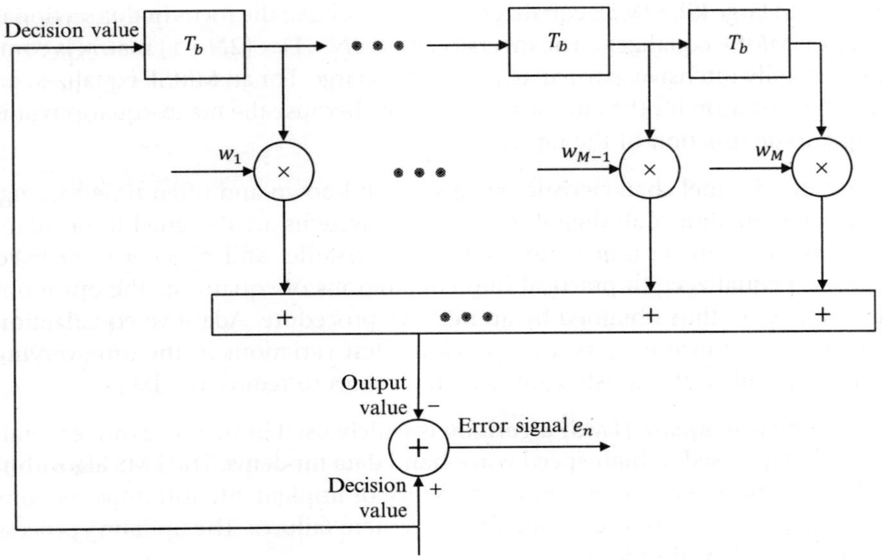

FIGURE 6.10 A decision-feedback part of DFE.

A DFE, as shown in Figure 6.11, has two filters. The first filter is called a feed-forward filter similar to a linear equalizer, and it is generally a fractionally-spaced FIR filter with adjustable tap coefficients, as it is also known as ***fractionally-spaced equalizer*** (FSE). Its input consists of the samples of the received signal. The sampling rate at the input of the FSE, which is a multiple of the bit rate $\frac{1}{T_b}$, can help avoid aliasing, as it is above the Nyquist sampling rate. An FSE, as opposed to an equalizer whose input sampling rate is identical to the bit rate, has the advantage of suppressing time phase sensitivity, while not amplifying the channel noise. In practice, the sampling rate at the input of the FSE is often twice the bit rate.

The second filter is called a feedback filter, and it is a symbol-spaced FIR filter with adjustable coefficients. The nonlinearity of the DFE stems from the nonlinear characteristic of the detector that provides an input to the feedback filter. The erroneous decisions fed to the feedback filter generally result in a modest performance loss of 1 to 2 dB. An important advantage of a DFE is the feedback filter, which is additionally working to remove ISI, operates on noiseless quantized levels, and thus its output is free of channel noise. The MMSE criterion is usually applied to select the taps.

6.5.4 Adaptive Equalization

In order to determine the optimum tap values of the ZF and MMSE linear equalizers, a system of $(2N+1)$ linear equations must be solved. In the presence of noise and large ISI, MMSE equalizers are more robust; the focus in this section is thus on MMSE equalizers. The inversion of a $(2N+1)\times(2N+1)$ matrix is computationally intensive, particularly when N is large. For an MMSE equalizer, an iterative solution for the tap values is possible because the mean-square error is a quadratic function of the tap values.

Since the channel characteristics are always unknown and often time-varying, equalizers in almost all digital transmission systems are designed to be adaptive, as they can be much more effective, versatile, and cheaper than fixed (pre-set) equalizers. In practical implementations of equalizers, the optimum tap values are thus obtained by an iterative procedure. Adaptive equalization also plays a critical role, as it can track modest variations in the time-varying channels and continuously adjusts its tap values to reduce the ISI.

The ***least mean square (LMS) algorithm*** is widely used in many adaptive equalizers that are used in high-speed voice-band data modems. The LMS algorithm exhibits robust performance in the presence of implementation imperfections and simplifications or even some limited system failures. The updating process of the LMS algorithm is as follows:

i) Set all tap values equal to zero.
ii) Compute the output of the equalizer $r(kT_b)$.
iii) Compute the error signal $e(kT_b)=r(kT_b)-d(kT_b)$, the difference signal between the equalizer output $r(kT_b)$ and the ideal (or estimated) output $d(kT_b)$.
iv) Compute the updated values of the taps, for a prescribed step size $\Delta>0$ in accordance with the following relation:

$$c_n(kT_b+T_b)=c_n(kT_b)-2\Delta e(kT_b)r(kT_b) \qquad (6.25)$$

v) Increment the time index k by one, go back to step ii) and repeat the procedure until steady-state conditions are reached.

As shown in Figure 6.11, an adaptive equalizer may have two modes of operation: training (automatic) mode and decision-directed (adaptive) mode. During the training period, a known sequence, such as the pseudo-noise (PN) sequence, is transmitted and a synchronized version of the same sequence is generated in the receiver. The training period of an adaptive equalizer must have a length at least as long as the length of the equalizer. The error signal is the difference between the received samples and the ideal samples. When the training mode is completed the decision-directed mode begins, during which the error signal is the difference between the received samples and the (not necessarily correct) estimates of the transmitted information bits, as carried out by the decision device.

An adaptive linear equalizer employing the LMS algorithm is a feedback system. It can therefore become unstable, as the LMS algorithm can exhibit divergence. The convergence properties of the LMS algorithm are governed by the step

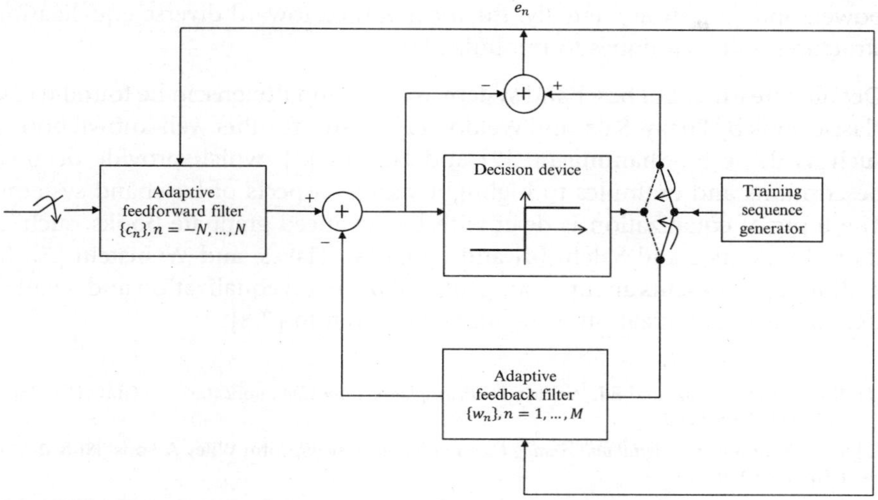

FIGURE 6.11 An adaptive equalizer.

size parameter Δ. If in the adaptive decision-feedback equalizer shown in Figure 6.11, there is no feedback part, then an adaptive linear equalizer results. In an adaptive linear equalizer using LMS algorithm, convergence is guaranteed if the step size parameter Δ is less than the inverse of the largest eigenvalue of the $(2N + 1) \times (2N + 1)$ channel autocorrelation matrix. In fact, the ratio of the largest eigenvalue to the smallest eigenvalue ultimately determines the convergence rate. If the ratio is small, the step size can be selected to achieve rapid convergence. However, if the ratio is large, as it may be the case when the channel frequency response has deep spectral nulls, the convergence rate will be slow. The LMS algorithm gives rise to a steady-state MSE that is more than the minimum MSE (the value that can be achieved when the tap values are at their optimum settings). The larger the step size is, the faster the convergence rate is and the higher the steady-state MSE is. An adjustable step size is attractive where first a rather large step size is selected to have a rapid convergence and then a rather small step size is selected to have a small steady-state MSE.

Summary and Sources

In this chapter, the focus was on the analysis and design of baseband digital transmission systems. A major objective was to discuss intersymbol interference and the criterion by which it can be eliminated. Another objective was to show how the effect of noise can be minimized by designing optimum filters. We also identified the design trade-offs between binary and M-ary signaling schemes, in terms of bandwidth, bit transmission rate, bit error rate, transmit power, and complexity. Finally, the focus turned toward diverse equalization structures and techniques to minimize ISI.

Detailed treatment of baseband system analysis and design can be found in the classic book by Lucky, Salz, and Weldon [1]. There are other well-known books, such as those by Shanmugam [2] and Haykin [3], which provide detailed descriptions and examples to highlight various aspects of baseband systems. The topic of equalization is dealt with by advanced graduate books, such as those by Proakis and Salehi [4] and by Gitlin, Hayes, and Weinstein [5]. In addition, [6] presents an interesting tutorial paper on equalization and detailed treatments of equalization using MLSE are given in [7,8].

[1] R.W. Lucky, J. Salz, and E.J. Weldon Jr., *Principles of Data Communication*, McGraw-Hill, ISBN 007-038960-8.1968.

[2] K.S. Shanmugam, *Digital and Analog Communication Systems*, John Wiley & Sons, ISBN 0-471-03090-2.1979.

[3] S. Haykin, *Communication Systems*, second ed., John Wiley & Sons, ISBN 0-471-09691-1.1983.

[4] J.G. Proakis and M. Salehi, *Digital Communications*, fifth ed., McGraw-Hill, ISBN 978-0-07-295716-7. 2008.

[5] R.D. Gitlin, J.F. Hayes, and S.B. Weinstein, *Data Communications Principles*, Plenum Press, ISBN 0-306-43777-5.1992.

[6] S.U.H. Qureshi, Adaptive equalization, *Proc. IEEE* 73 (Sept. 1985) 1349–1387.

[7] G.D. Forney Jr., Maximum-likelihood sequence estimation of digital sequences in the presence of intersymbol interference, *IEEE Trans Inf Theory* 18 (May 1972) 363–378.

[8] J.F. Hayes, The Viterbi algorithm applied to digital data transmission, *IEEE Comm. Mag.* 13 (March 1975) 5–16.

Problems

6.1 Suppose the three pulses $g(t)$, $k(t)$, and $f(t)$ all satisfy the Nyquist criterion, and also m, n, and p are all positive integers. Determine a relationship among A, B, and C that can make the pulse $v(t) = Ag^m(t) + Bk^n(t) + Cf^p(t)$ satisfy the Nyquist criterion.

6.2 Assuming $h(t) = \sin\left(\frac{2\pi t}{T_b}\right)$ is the overall impulse response of a system and $\frac{1}{T_b}$ is the bit rate, does this system satisfy the Nyquist criterion?

6.3 What is the bandwidth requirement in Hz for baseband binary transmission at 64 kbps, if the roll-off factor is 0.25?

6.4 Assuming $1/T_b$ is the bit rate, determine if each one of the following four binary PAM systems can satisfy the Nyquist criterion, where the spectra of the received pulses are real and even:

(a) $H(f) = T_b\left(u(f) - u\left(f - \frac{1}{4T_b}\right)\right) + \left(2T_b - 4T_b^2 f\right)\left(u\left(f - \frac{1}{4T_b}\right) - u\left(f - \frac{1}{2T_b}\right)\right).$

(b) $H(f) = T_b\left(u(f) - u\left(f - \frac{1}{4T_b}\right)\right) + \left(\frac{3}{2}T_b - 2T_b^2 f\right)\left(u\left(f - \frac{1}{4T_b}\right) - u\left(f - \frac{3}{4T_b}\right)\right).$

(c) $H(f) = T_b\left(u(f) - u\left(f - \frac{1}{4T_b}\right)\right) + \left(\frac{4}{3}T_b - \frac{4}{3}T_b^2 f\right)\left(u\left(f - \frac{1}{4T_b}\right) - u\left(f - \frac{1}{T_b}\right)\right).$

(d) $H(f) = \left(-T_b^2 f + T_b\right)\left(u(f) - u\left(f - \frac{1}{T_b}\right)\right).$

6.5 Determine the magnitude of the optimum transmitting and receiving filter characteristics for a baseband binary system that transmits at a rate of 2400 bps over a channel with the following frequency response:

$$|H_C(f)| = \frac{1}{\sqrt{1 + \left(\frac{f}{W}\right)^2}}, \quad |f| \leq W$$

where $W = 3600$ Hz and the channel noise is assumed to be AWGN.

6.6 In an M-ary PAM system with $M = 4$, determine the required transmit power, if the symbol rate is 5000 symbols per second, the symbol error rate is less than 10^{-4}, and the channel AWGN has a power spectral density of 10^{-12} W/Hz.

6.7 Consider a baseband binary PAM system that transmits at 3600 bps with a bit error rate less than 10^{-4}. The channel introduces no distortion, but attenuates the signal by 20 dB and has a bandwidth of 2.4 kHz. The channel noise is AWGN with a power spectral density of 10^{-14} watts per Hertz (W/Hz). Design the optimum transmitting and receiving filters, and determine the required transmit power.

6.8 Design a baseband binary PAM system that can transmit at a rate of 9.6 kbps with a bit error rate less than 10^{-5}. The channel available is an ideal low-pass channel with a bandwidth of 9.6 kHz and an AWGN power spectral density of 10^{-13} W/Hz. Find the transmit power requirement.

6.9 The sampled values of the received signal in a binary PAM system suffer from ISI such that

$$r(t_m) = \begin{cases} A + I + n(t_m), & b_k = 1 \\ -A - I + n(t_m), & b_k = 0 \end{cases}$$

where I represents the ISI term, and has one of the five values with the following probabilities:

$$P(Q) = \begin{cases} 0.1, & I = 2q \\ 0.2, & I = q \\ 0.4, & I = 0 \\ 0.2, & I = -q \\ 0.1, & I = -2q \\ 0, & \text{elsewhere} \end{cases}$$

Assuming $n(t_m)$ is AWGN with a variance σ^2, derive an expression for the average bit error rate in terms of σ, q, and A.

6.10 In a baseband digital transmission, the bandwidth is 4 kHz, and the bit rate must be at least 38.4 kbps. Assuming M-ary signaling, determine the range of acceptable values of M, and the resulting bit error rate.

6.11 In a baseband three-level binary transmission system, in the absence of noise, there are three values 1, 0, and −1, with probabilities 1/4, 1/2, and 1/4, respectively. Assuming AWGN, determine the optimum threshold settings and the minimum error rate.

6.12 In a baseband digital transmission, the input sequence consists of four equally-likely symbols A, B, C and D. Assuming the channel bandwidth is 4,000 Hz, the noise power spectral density is 10^{-14} W/Hz, the symbol rate is 5000 symbols per second, the symbol error rate is less than 0.0001, and the nonideal channel has the following frequency characteristics:

$$H_c(f) = \frac{5000}{5000 + jf}$$

Design the optimum filters and determine the transmit pulse.

6.13 Consider the duobinary baseband PAM system that utilizes controlled amounts of ISI for transmitting data at a rate twice the minimum bandwidth. A duobinary system is easier than the ideal rectangular filter to accomplish the data transmission at the maximum rate with zero ISI. The duobinary pulse has the following frequency response and impulse response:

$$H(f) = \begin{cases} 2T_b\cos(\pi f T_b), & |f| \leq 1/2T_b \\ 0, & |f| \geq 1/2T_b \end{cases}$$

and

$$h(t) = \frac{4\cos\left(\frac{\pi t}{T_b}\right)}{\pi\left(1 - \frac{4t^2}{T_b^2}\right)}$$

where T_b is the bit duration. Sketch the duobinary pulse in both the time domain and the frequency domain. Determine the probability of bit error for a duobinary system and compare it with that of an ideal binary PAM system.

6.14 Design a three-tap ZF equalizer to reduce the ISI, where the samples of the nonideal received pulse are as follows:

$$r(mT_b) = \begin{cases} 0, & m < -1 \\ 0.1, & m = -1 \\ 1.0, & m = 0 \\ -0.2, & m = 1 \\ 0, & m > 1 \end{cases}$$

Computer Exercises

6.15 Plot the received signal $r(t)$ and determine its values at all integers:

$$r(t) = x(t+9) + x(t+8) - x(t+7) - x(t+6) - x(t+5) + x(t+4) + x(t+3)$$
$$-x(t+2) - x(t+1) + x(t) + x(t-1) + x(t-2) + x(t-3) - x(t-4) - x(t-5),$$
$$-x(t-6) - x(t-7) - x(t-8) - x(t-9)$$

for the following two cases:

(a) $x(t) = \sin(\pi t)\cos(\pi t/2)/\pi t(1-t^2)$.

(b) $x(t) = \sin(\pi t/2)\cos(\pi t/2)/\pi t(1-t^2)$.

6.16 Plot the following class of pulses in both the frequency domain and the time domain for various values of the roll-off α, where $0 \leq \alpha \leq 1$. Note that the Fourier transform of the pulse is real and nonnegative, and has odd symmetry around the frequency $1/2T_b$. The Fourier transform of the pulse is defined as follows:

$$H(f) = \begin{cases} T_b, & |f| \leq (1-\alpha)/2T_b \\ T_b\left(\sin\left(\frac{\pi T_b}{2\alpha}\left(|f| - \frac{1+\alpha}{2T_b}\right)\right)\right)^{2P}, & \frac{(1-\alpha)}{2T_b} < |f| \leq \frac{1}{2T_b} \end{cases}$$

where P is a parameter which has a finite value (i.e., $-\infty < P < \infty$). Note that when $P = 1$, this pulse becomes the well-known raised cosine pulse spectrum.

CHAPTER 7

Passband Digital Transmission

INTRODUCTION

As the performance measure in a digital transmission system is the bit error rate, first the optimum receiver, which is capable of delivering the lowest possible bit error rate, is discussed. In a unified context, the implementation of the optimum receiver and the calculation of the minimum bit error rate in an additive white Gaussian noise channel are presented. The focus then turns towards binary modulation schemes, mainly binary amplitude-shift keying (BASK), binary frequency-shift keying (BFSK), and binary phase-shift keying (BPSK), and a comparison of them, in terms of bit error rate, bandwidth, power, and complexity, is provided. After discussing quaternary signaling schemes, namely quadrature phase-shift keying (QPSK), offset quadrature phase-shift keying (OQPSK), and minimum-shift keying (MSK), major types of *M*-ary modulation techniques, primarily *M*-ary amplitude-shift keying (MASK), *M*-ary phase-shift keying (MPSK), quadrature amplitude modulation (QAM), and *M*-ary frequency-shift keying (MFSK) are provided. After studying this chapter and understanding all relevant concepts and examples, students should be able to achieve the following learning objectives:

1. Define the system model under which the optimum receiver principles are derived.
2. Outline the definition and importance of orthonormal functions.
3. Learn how the Gram-Schmidt orthogonalization procedure works.
4. Provide the geometric representation of signals.
5. Detail the implementations of optimum receivers.
6. Calculate the minimum probability of error.
7. Gain insight into bit error rate, vis-à-vis symbol error rate.
8. Understand the impact of nonwhite noise, vis-à-vis white noise.
9. Differentiate between coherent and noncoherent detection schemes.
10. Describe BASK, BFSK, and BPSK signaling schemes.
11. Identify the trade-offs among binary modulation techniques.
12. Appreciate the need for quaternary signaling schemes.

CONTENTS

13. Comprehend the distinct features of QPSK, OQPSK, and MSK.
14. Grasp the need for M-ary modulation techniques.
15. Perform a comparative analysis of M-ary and binary signaling schemes.
16. Analyze how MASK, QAM, MPSK, and MFSK signaling schemes work.
17. Evaluate the probability of error for various QAM modulation schemes.
18. State why MPSK and QAM are widely-used modulation schemes.
19. Explain the basic principles of OFDM operation.
20. Connect various modulation schemes to the Shannon's channel capacity theorem.

7.1 OPTIMUM RECEIVER PRINCIPLES

Modulation is a process without which digital data cannot be transmitted in bandpass communication systems, as modulation allows modification of the message signal to a form suited to the characteristics of the transmission channel. The majority of practical channels have bandpass characteristics and CW modulation translates the frequency components of the lowpass message signal to the passband range, so the spectrum of the transmitted signal can match the characteristics of the channel.

Before embarking on a discussion on an array of digital modulation schemes and their performances in terms of their error rates, bandwidth and power requirements, and implementation complexities, we need to focus on the optimum receiver principles. Although the study of optimum receivers in digital communications is considered an advanced area, we make an effort in this chapter to highlight the basic principles of the optimum receiver for passband digital transmission systems at a modest level and in a limited scope. This is achieved mostly by avoiding the mathematical derivations as much as possible, and instead focusing on the results and what they mean, which in turn is a reflection of the tone echoed throughout the book.

7.1.1 System Model

Figure 7.1 shows a model of passband digital transmission system. The input to the system is a bit sequence $\{b_i\}$ with a ***bit duration*** of T_b seconds and thus a ***bit rate*** of $r_b = \frac{1}{T_b}$ bits per second (bps). The input bits are statistically independent, and bits 1 and 0 are equally-likely. A symbol, belonging to an alphabet of $M = 2^k$ symbols, where k is a positive integer, is transmitted over a finite time interval

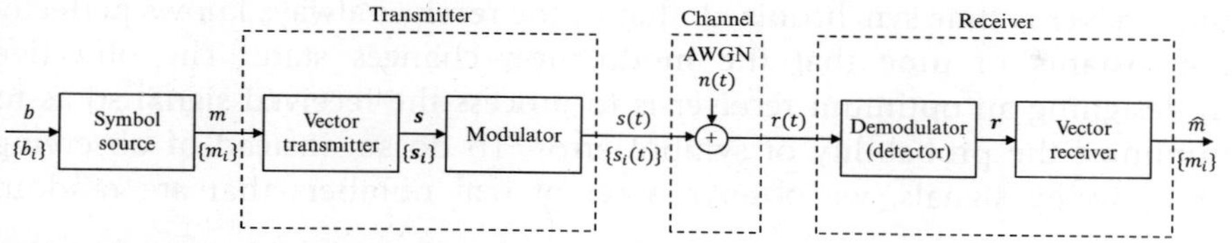

FIGURE 7.1 A model of passband digital communication system.

$T_s = kT_b = T_b \log_2 M$. The ***symbol duration*** T_s is thus $\log_2 M$ times longer than the bit duration T_b, as a symbol conveys k bits. The symbols, which are statistically independent and also equally-likely, are transmitted at the rate of $r_s = \frac{1}{T_s} = \frac{1}{kT_b} = \frac{r_b}{k} = \frac{r_b}{\log_2 M}$ symbols per second (sps). The ***symbol rate*** r_s is thus $\log_2 M$ times slower than the bit rate r_b.

The modulator every T_s seconds maps one of the M symbols into a real-valued continuous signal $s_i(t)$ of duration T_s seconds, where $1 \le i \le M$. It is assumed that all signals in the signal set $\{s_i(t)\}$, $i = 1, 2, \ldots, M$, are equally-likely and the energy of each signal, measured in joules (J), is finite, i.e., we have:

$$E_i = \int_0^{T_S} s_i^2(t)\, dt < \infty, \quad i = 1, 2, \ldots, M \tag{7.1a}$$

With M equally-likely symbols, the ***average energy per symbol*** is thus as follows:

$$E_S = \left(\frac{1}{M}\right) \sum_{i=1}^{M} E_i \tag{7.1b}$$

Noting a symbol represents $\log_2 M$ bits, the ***average energy per bit*** is then as follows:

$$E_b = \frac{E_S}{\log_2 M} \tag{7.1c}$$

The channel is assumed to be ideally of infinite bandwidth, and practically it has a wide-enough bandwidth to accommodate the transmission with no distortion. This essentially means there is no intersymbol interference (ISI). This in a way means our focus is on one-shot transmission, that is, only one single signal representing a single symbol is transmitted. We also assume the channel is an additive white Gaussian noise (AWGN) with a power spectral density of $N_0/2$ watts per Hertz (W/Hz). Moreover, we assume the receiver is time synchronized, that is, the receiver always knows perfectly the instants of time that the modulation changes state. The objective in designing an optimum receiver is to process the received signal so as to minimize the probability of symbol error. To do so, instead of observing time-varying signals, we observe a set of real numbers that are random variables.

7.1.2 Gram-Schmidt Orthogonalization Procedure

The ***Gram-Schmidt orthogonalization procedure*** is a straightforward way by which an appropriate set of orthonormal functions can be obtained from any given signal set. Any set of M finite-energy signals $\{s_i(t)\}$, where $i = 1, 2, \ldots, M$, can be represented by linear combinations of N real-valued orthonormal basis functions $\{\varphi_j(t)\}$, where $j = 1, \ldots, N$, and $N \leq M$, by which we have:

$$\int_0^{T_S} \varphi_i(t)\varphi_k(t)\, dt = \begin{cases} 1, & i = k \\ 0, & i \neq k \end{cases} \tag{7.2a}$$

Equation (7.2a) highlights that each ***orthonormal basis function*** has a unit energy, and is orthogonal with respect to any other one over the interval $[0, T_s]$, hence the term orthonormal. It is important to note that N, known as the dimension of the signal space, can directly impact the complexity of both modulator and demodulator. If the signals are linearly independent (i.e., if and only if no one signal can be expressed as a linear combination of the others), then $N = M$, and if they are not linearly independent, then $N < M$. We can thus have the following representation:

$$s_i(t) = \sum_{k=1}^{N} s_{ik}\varphi_k(t), \quad 0 \leq t \leq T_s, \quad i = 1, 2, \ldots, M \tag{7.2b}$$

where the ***coefficients of the orthonormal basis functions*** for the transmitted signal $s_i(t)$ are defined as follows:

$$s_{ik} = \int_0^{T_S} s_i(t)\varphi_k(t)\, dt, \quad i = 1, 2, \ldots, M, \; k = 1, 2, \ldots, N \tag{7.2c}$$

By using (7.2b) and (7.2c), the energy of the signal $s_i(t)$, i.e., E_i, is then equal to the squared length of the signal vector $s_i = (s_{i1}, \ldots, s_{iN})$, that is, we have:

$$E_i = \int_0^{T_S} s_i^2(t)\, dt = \sum_{k=1}^{N} s_{ik}^2, \quad i = 1, 2, \ldots, M \tag{7.2d}$$

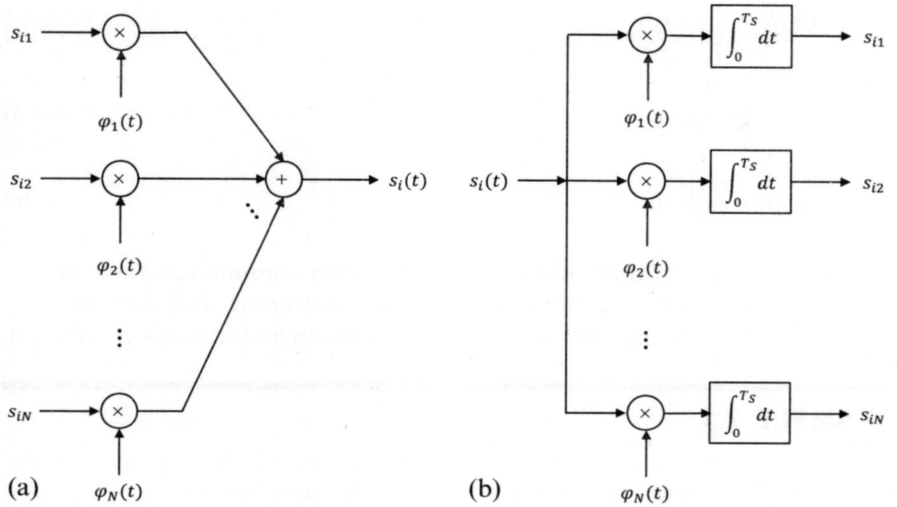

FIGURE 7.2 The Gram-Schmidt orthogonalization procedure: (a) generation of signal from coefficients and (b) extraction of coefficients from signal.

This is a useful relationship between the energy content of a signal and its representation as a vector. Figure 7.2a shows the generation of the signal according to (7.2b), and Figure 7.2b shows the evaluation of the corresponding coefficients according to (7.2c).

It is important to note that for a given set of signals, there are many choices for orthonormal basis functions, but they all yield the same error rate performance. The Gram-Schmidt orthogonalization procedure provides an exact representation (i.e., not an approximation) of each of the M finite-energy signal in terms of N orthonormal basis functions. The procedure is as follows:

i) Set the first orthonormal function as follows:

$$\varphi_1(t) = \frac{s_1(t)}{\sqrt{E_1}} = \frac{s_1(t)}{\sqrt{\int_0^{T_S} s_1^2(t)\,dt}} \tag{7.3a}$$

ii) Construct the subsequent orthonormal functions through the following steps that respectively project, find residual, normalize, and add basis:

$$s_{ik} = \int_0^{T_S} s_i(t)\varphi_k(t)\,dt, \quad i = 2,\ldots,M, \; k = 1,2,\ldots,i-1 \tag{7.3b}$$

$$r_i(t) = s_i(t) - \sum_{k=1}^{i-1} s_{ik}\varphi_k(t) \tag{7.3c}$$

$$V_i = \int_0^{T_S} r_i^2(t)\, dt \tag{7.3d}$$

$$\varphi_i(t) = \frac{r_i(t)}{\sqrt{V_i}}, \quad i = 2, \ldots, N \tag{7.3e}$$

iii) Go to step ii) until all M signals have been examined and $N \leq M$ orthogonal basis functions have been constructed, and stop the process, if at any step $r_i(t) = 0$, as it means there is no new dimension.

EXAMPLE 7.1

Consider the signals $s_1(t)$, $s_2(t)$, $s_3(t)$, and $s_4(t)$ shown in Figure 7.3. Using the Gram-Schmidt orthogonalization procedure, determine a set of orthonormal basis functions.

Solution

Since we have $M = 4$, we have $N \leq 4$. Using (7.3a), we get the first orthonormal function as follows:

$$\varphi_1(t) = \frac{s_1(t)}{\sqrt{\int_0^{T_s} s_1^2(t)\, dt}} = \frac{s_1(t)}{\sqrt{E_s}}$$

Using (7.3b), we get:

$$s_{21} = \int_0^{T_s} s_2(t)\varphi_1(t)\, dt = \int_0^{T_s} s_2(t)\frac{s_1(t)}{\sqrt{E_s}}\, dt = 0$$

Using (7.3c), we then have:

$$r_2(t) = s_2(t) - s_{21}\varphi_1(t) = s_2(t)$$

Using (7.3d), we get:

$$V_2 = \int_0^{T_s} r_2^2(t)\, dt = \int_0^{T_s} s_2^2(t)\, dt = E_s$$

Using (7.3e), we can then get the second orthonormal function:

$$\varphi_2(t) = \frac{r_2(t)}{\sqrt{V_2}} = \frac{s_2(t)}{\sqrt{E_s}}$$

Figure 7.3 also shows the two orthonormal functions $\varphi_1(t)$ and $\varphi_2(t)$. We can therefore express all four signals, as $M = 4$, in terms of only two orthonormal functions, as $N = 2$:

$$s_1(t) = \sqrt{E_s}\varphi_1(t)$$

$$s_2(t) = \sqrt{E_s}\varphi_2(t)$$

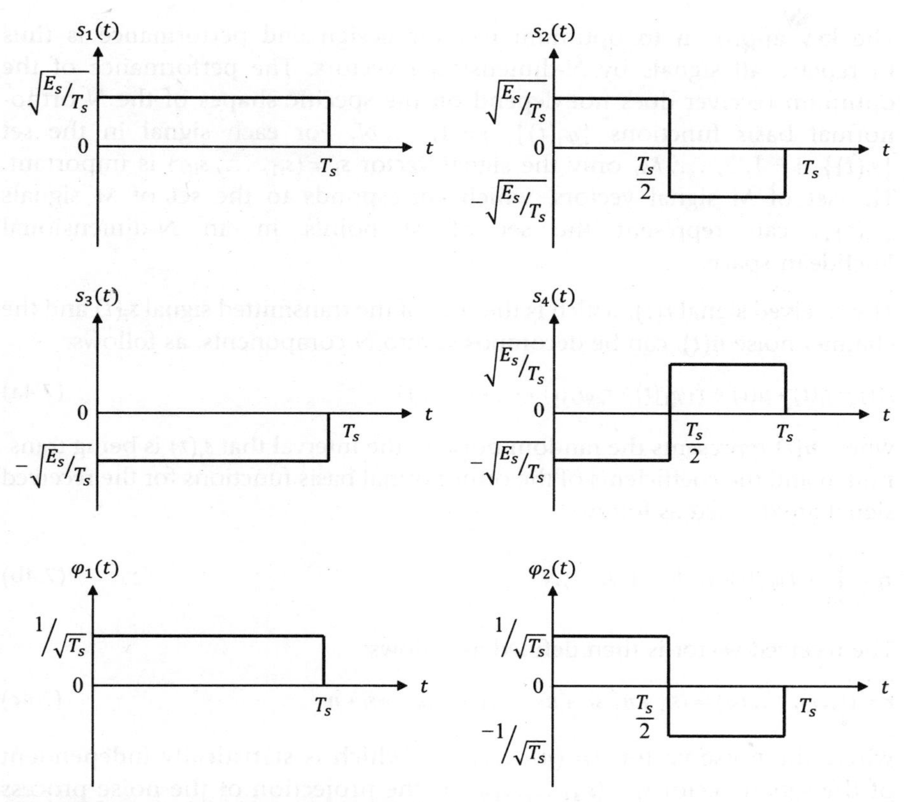

FIGURE 7.3 Set of signals and orthonormal functions for Example 7.1.

$s_3(t) = -\sqrt{E_s}\varphi_1(t)$

$s_4(t) = -\sqrt{E_s}\varphi_2(t)$

7.1.3 Geometric Representation and Interpretation of Signals

As reflected in Figure 7.1, both the transmitter and receiver consist of two parts. The vector transmitter accepts the symbol m_i and correspondingly generates the vector s_i, the modulator then forms $s_i(t)$ from s_i using the orthonormal basis functions. At the receiver, the detector operates on the received signal $r(t)$ to produce the relevant received vector r, and finally the vector receiver, based on the knowledge of r and $\{s_i\}$, determines which message symbol is the most likely one transmitted.

The key approach to optimum receiver design and performance is thus to replace all signals by N-dimensional vectors. The performance of the optimum receiver does not depend on the specific shapes of the N orthonormal basis functions $\{\varphi_j(t)\}$, $j = 1, \ldots, N$. For each signal in the set $\{s_i(t)\}$, $i = 1, 2, \ldots, M$, only the signal vector $\mathbf{s}_i = (s_{i1}, \ldots, s_{iN})$ is important. The set of M signal vectors, which corresponds to the set of M signals $\{s_i(t)\}$, can represent the set of M points in an N-dimensional Euclidean space.

The received signal $r(t)$, which is the sum of the transmitted signal $s_i(t)$ and the channel noise $n(t)$, can be decomposed into N components, as follows:

$$r(t) = s_i(t) + n(t) = r_1\varphi_1(t) + r_2\varphi_2(t) + \cdots + r_N\varphi_N(t) \tag{7.4a}$$

where $n(t)$ represents the random noise in the interval that $s_i(t)$ is being transmitted and the coefficients of the orthonormal basis functions for the received signal are defined as follows:

$$r_k = \int_0^{T_S} r(t)\varphi_k(t)\,dt, \quad k = 1, 2, \ldots, N \tag{7.4b}$$

The received vector is then defined as follows:

$$\mathbf{r} = (r_1, r_2, \ldots, r_N) = (s_{i1} + n_1, s_{i2} + n_2, \ldots, s_{iN} + n_N) = \mathbf{s}_i + \mathbf{n} \tag{7.4c}$$

where the noise vector $\mathbf{n} = (n_1, \ldots, n_N)$, which is statistically independent of the signal vector $\mathbf{s}_i = (s_{i1}, \ldots, s_{iN})$, is the projection of the noise process onto the orthonormal basis functions $\left\{\varphi_j(t)\right\}, j = 1, \ldots, N$. The components of the noise process that do not project into signal space are irrelevant. Figure 7.4 shows the relationship among the noise vector, the signal vector and the received vector for $N = 2$. Since $n(t)$ is a zero-mean white Gaussian noise, the noise vector $(n_1, \ldots, n_N)$ consists of zero-mean, statistically independent Gaussian random variables, and this property is independent of how the orthonormal basis functions $\{\varphi_j(t)\}$, $j = 1, \ldots, N$, are chosen.

7.1.4 Receiver Implementation

The ***optimum receiver*** selects the criterion to minimize the average probability of symbol error $P(\widehat{m} \neq m_i)$, where m_i is the transmitted symbol and $\widehat{m}$ is the estimate produced by the optimum receiver, based on the observation vector $\mathbf{r} = (r_1, \ldots, r_N)$. The optimum receiver, also known as a ***maximum a posteriori probability (MAP) receiver***, thus determines which one of the possible symbols $\{m_i\}$ has maximum a posteriori probability. More precisely, the MAP receiver follows the following decision rule:

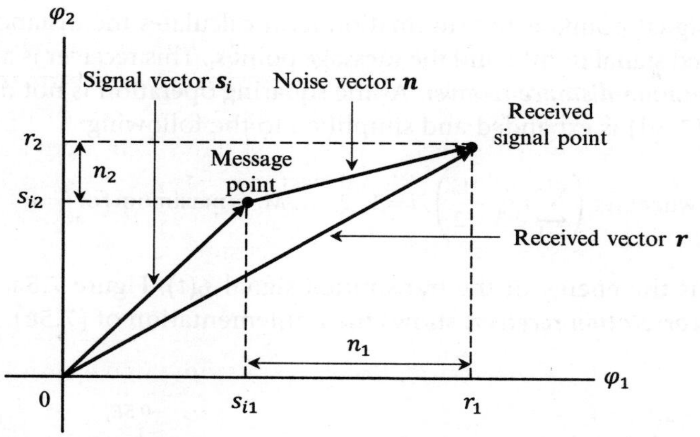

FIGURE 7.4 A geometric representation of transmitted vector, noise vector, and received vector.

Set $\hat{m} = m_k$ whenever $P(m_i/r), i = 1, 2, \ldots, M$, is maximum for $i = k$ (7.5a)

By using the mixed form of Bayes rule, noting all symbols are equally likely and the events represented by m_i and s_i are the same, and highlighting that the natural logarithm of a function is an increasing function, we can simplify (7.5a) to obtain the following decision rule:

Set $\hat{m} = m_k$ whenever $\ln\left(f_{r/s_i}(r/s_i)\right), i = 1, 2, \ldots, M$, is maximum for $i = k$ (7.5b)

The receiver that follows (7.5b) is referred to as the ***maximum-likelihood (ML) receiver***. It is important to highlight that when all symbols are equally likely, both MAP and ML receivers are the same and thus yielding the minimum symbol error rate. Under an AWGN channel with power spectral density $N_0/2$, the likelihood functions are defined as follows:

$$f_{r/s_i}(r/s_i) = (\pi N_0)^{-N/2} \exp\left(-\frac{1}{N_0}\sum_{j=1}^{N}(r_j - s_{ij})^2\right), \quad i = 1, 2, \ldots, M \tag{7.5c}$$

After substituting (7.5c) into (7.5b) and simplifying the result, the decision rule becomes as follows:

Set $\hat{m} = m_k$ whenever $\sum_{j=1}^{N}(r_j - s_{ij})^2, i = 1, 2, \ldots, M$, is minimum for $i = k$ (7.5d)

(7.5d) shows that the maximum likelihood decision rule is simply to choose the message point in an N-dimensional signal space that is closest to the received signal point, as the summation term calculates the distance between the received signal point $\mathbf{r}$ and the message point $\mathbf{s}_i$. This receiver is also known as the ***minimum-distance receiver***. As the squaring operation is not desirable in practice, (7.5d) is expanded and simplified to the following:

$$\text{Set } \hat{m} = m_k \text{ whenever } \left(\sum_{j=1}^{N} r_j s_{ij} - \frac{E_i}{2}\right),\ i = 1, 2, \ldots, M, \text{ is maximum for } i = k \tag{7.5e}$$

where E_i is the energy of the transmitted signal $s_i(t)$. Figure 7.5a, known as ***optimum correlation receiver,*** shows the implementation of (7.5e). Moreover,

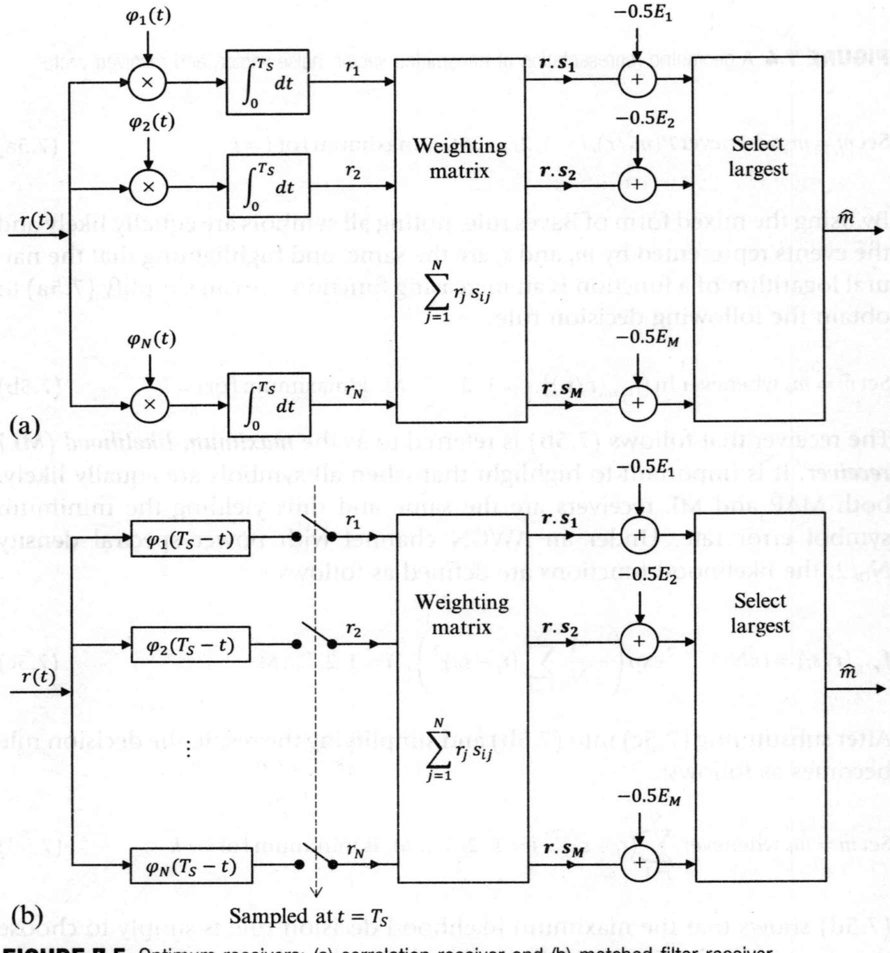

FIGURE 7.5 Optimum receivers: (a) correlation receiver and (b) matched-filter receiver.

the decision rule highlighted in (7.5e) indicates a partitioning of an N-dimensional received signal space into M disjoint N-dimensional decision regions.

It is important to note that regardless of how the optimum receiver is implemented, the bias term E_i in (7.5e), as a prior data, is available to the receiver, since it is independent of the received signal. If all signals have the same energy, then (7.5e) can simply become as follows:

$$\text{Set } \hat{m} = m_k \text{ whenever } \left(\sum_{j=1}^{N} r_j s_{ij} \right), \; i = 1, 2, \ldots, M, \text{ is maximum for } i = k \tag{7.5f}$$

If the orthonormal basis functions are time-limited causal signals (i.e., they are zero outside the interval $0 \le t \le T_s$), analog multipliers and integrators in a correlation receiver can be replaced by linear time-invariant filters, as multipliers are rather difficult to realize physically. The output of a filter whose impulse response is a T_s-delayed, time-reversed version of an orthonormal signal $\varphi_j(t)$ is called matched to $\varphi_j(t)$ and the optimum realization is known as a ***matched-filter receiver***. The impulse response of a matched-filter is thus as follows:

$$h_k(t) = \varphi_k(T_S - t), \; k = 1, 2, \ldots, N \tag{7.6a}$$

The output of a matched filter is then as follows:

$$r_k(t) = \int_{-\infty}^{\infty} r(s) h_k(t - s) ds = \int_{-\infty}^{\infty} r(s) \varphi_k(T_s - t + s) ds, \quad k = 1, 2, \ldots, N \tag{7.6b}$$

The output of this matched filter sampled at $t = T_s$ is the same as the output of a correlator, as reflected below:

$$r_k = r_k(T_s) = \int_{-\infty}^{\infty} r(s) \varphi_k(T_s - T_s + s) ds = \int_{0}^{T_s} r(t) \varphi_k(t) dt, \quad k = 1, 2, \ldots, N \tag{7.6c}$$

The right-hand side of (7.6c) is the same as the output produced in a correlation receiver, as reflected in (7.4b). The requirement that the orthonormal signal vanishes for $t > T_s$ is necessary in order that the matched filter may be physically realizable, that is the impulse response of the filter is zero for $t < 0$. The output signal-to-noise ratio of a matched filter depends only on the ratio of the signal energy to the power spectral density of the white noise at the filter input. The optimum receiver that employs matched filters is referred to as the matched-filter receiver. Figure 7.5b shows the implementation of (7.6c), known as ***optimum matched-filter receiver***.

7.1.5 Probability of Error

It is important to note that the symbol error rate due to a signal set is completely independent of the shapes of the chosen orthonormal basis functions, as only the signal coefficients and the noise power spectral density can impact the minimum attainable symbol error rate. Also, the probability of symbol error is not affected by the signal space translation, for the signal and noise are independent, nor is it impacted by the signal space rotation, as noise is spherically symmetric.

The N-dimensional space is partitioned into M disjoint regions $\mathbf{I}_1, \ldots, \mathbf{I}_M$, and an error occurs whenever the received signal point does not fall in the region $\mathbf{I}_k$ associated with the message point m_k. The ***average probability of symbol error***, also known as the ***average symbol error rate*** (SER), when symbols are equally-likely, is as follows:

$$\begin{aligned} P_{\text{SER}} &= \sum_{i=1}^{M} P(m_i)P(e/m_i) = \sum_{i=1}^{M} P(m_i)P(\mathbf{r} \notin \mathbf{I}_i/m_i) = 1 - \sum_{i=1}^{M} P(m_i)P(\mathbf{r} \in \mathbf{I}_i/m_i) \\ &= 1 - \frac{1}{M}\sum_{i=1}^{M} P(\mathbf{r} \in \mathbf{I}_i/m_i) = 1 - \frac{1}{M}\sum_{i=1}^{M} \int_{\mathbf{I}_i} f_{\mathbf{r}/\mathbf{s}_i}(\mathbf{r}/\mathbf{s}_i)d\mathbf{r} \end{aligned} \tag{7.7a}$$

where the integral is N-dimensional, and in general, the N-dimensional integration cannot be analytically done, and instead it should be numerically calculated. In calculating the average symbol error rate with no closed form formula, numerical computation of the integral may be very difficult. To circumvent this problem, we resort to bounds, which can provide good approximations, and for low error probabilities, tight upper bounds can be developed.

The union bound can provide an approximation to the average probability of symbol error for a set of M equally-likely symbols in an AWGN channel. The union bound is based on the fact that the probability of a finite union of events is bounded by the sum of the probabilities of the constituent events. It can be shown that the average probability of symbol error is upper bounded as follows:

$$P_{\text{SER}} \leq \sum_{\substack{k=1 \\ k \neq i}}^{M} Q\left(\frac{d_{ik}}{\sqrt{2N_0}}\right) \tag{7.7b}$$

where the Q-function represents the pairwise error probability when in a system there is only a pair of equally-likely vector signals $\mathbf{s}_i$ and $\mathbf{s}_k$, and d_{ik} represents the Euclidean distance between $\mathbf{s}_i$ and $\mathbf{s}_k$, and is defined as:

$$d_{ik}^2 = \sum_{j=1}^{N} (s_{ij} - s_{kj})^2 = \int_{-\infty}^{\infty} (s_i(t) - s_k(t))^2 dt \tag{7.7c}$$

EXAMPLE 7.2

Consider the two equally-likely signals $s_1(t)$ and $s_2(t)$ that are transmitted, over an AWGN channel with the noise power spectral density of $N_0/2$, to represent bits 1 and 0, where we have:

$s_1(t) = -s_2(t) = \sqrt{2}\exp(-2t)u(t)$

The receiver makes its decision solely based on observation of the received signal over a restricted interval of interest. Determine the average bit error rate in terms of Q-function, assuming the interval is [0, 3]. Contrast numerically with the performance of an optimum receiver that observes all the received signal, i.e., the interval of interest is $(-\infty, \infty)$.

Solution

Using (7.7c), we determine the Euclidean distance d between $s_1(t)$ and $s_2(t)$, first when the observation interval is unlimited:

$$d^2 = \int_{-\infty}^{\infty} (s_1(t) - s_2(t))^2 dt = \int_0^{\infty} \left(2\sqrt{2}\exp(-2t)\right)^2 dt = 2$$

and then for the restricted interval [0, 3]:

$$d^2 = \int_0^3 (s_1(t) - s_2(t))^2 dt = \int_0^3 \left(2\sqrt{2}\exp(-2t)\right)^2 dt = 2 - 2e^{-12}$$

When $\mathbf{s}_2$ is transmitted, an error occurs if and only if the AWGN noise component n_2, which is zero-mean Gaussian with variance $N_0/2$, exceeds $d/2$, i.e., we have:

$$P(e/m_2) = \int_{d/2}^{\infty} \frac{1}{\sqrt{\pi N_0}} \exp\left(-\frac{\alpha^2}{N_0}\right) d\alpha = Q\left(\frac{d}{\sqrt{2N_0}}\right)$$

Since, by symmetry, the conditional probability of error is the same for either signal, using (7.7a), we get the following:

$$P_{\text{SER}} = 1 - \frac{1}{2} \times 2\left(1 - Q\left(\frac{d}{\sqrt{2N_0}}\right)\right) = Q\left(\frac{d}{\sqrt{2N_0}}\right)$$

The bit error rate is the same as the symbol error rate for binary transmission (i.e., we have $P_{\text{SER}} = P_{\text{BER}}$). We see that different observation intervals, i.e., different values of d, bring about different values of bit error rates. However, the Euclidean distances in these two cases are extremely close to one another, as such, the loss in performance due to restricted observation interval is absolutely negligible, especially when N_0 is large.

Suppose there are M equally-likely, equal-energy signals and all symbol errors are equally-likely, that is, each signal vector is equidistant from all others. The bit error rate P_{BER} and the symbol error rate P_{SER} for such a case (e.g., MFSK signaling scheme as described later) is related as follows:

$$\frac{1}{2} \leq \frac{P_{\text{BER}}}{P_{\text{SER}}} = \frac{2^{k-1}}{2^k - 1} = \frac{M}{2(M-1)} \leq 1$$

where k represents the number of bits per symbol. Note that the lower bound is approached when $k \to \infty$ and the upper bound is attained when $k = 1$ (i.e., $M = 2$).

Suppose there are M equally-likely, equal-energy signals and all symbol errors are not equally-likely. Moreover, we assume the probability of taking one symbol instead of adjacent symbols in the signal space is much greater than any other kind of symbol error, that is, each signal vector is not equidistant from all others. We further assume Gray code is employed. The ***Gray code*** provides a binary to M-ary mapping in which the binary sequences corresponding to adjacent symbols in the signal space differ in only one bit position and the Gray code brings this benefit without incurring any additional circuitry and cost. Therefore, when an M-ary symbol error occurs, it is more likely that only one of the k bits will be in error. The bit error rate P_{BER} and the symbol error rate P_{SER} for such a case (e.g., MPSK signaling scheme, as described later) is related as follows:

$$\frac{1}{\log_2 M} \le \frac{P_{\text{BER}}}{P_{\text{SER}}} \le 1 \tag{7.8b}$$

Note that the lower bound is approached when the symbol error probability is low and the upper bound is attained when $k=1$ (i.e., $M=2$).

EXAMPLE 7.3

Consider the equally-likely signals $s_1(t)$, $s_2(t)$, $s_3(t)$, and $s_4(t)$, as shown in Figure 7.6a. Determine the orthonormal functions and the impulse responses of the matched-filter receivers. Assuming the signals are transmitted over an AWGN channel with the noise power spectral density of $N_0/2$, determine the average bit error rate P_{BER}.

Solution

By inspection, we can easily find the orthonormal functions $\varphi_1(t)$ and $\varphi_2(t)$, as shown in Figure 7.6b. By using (7.6a), we can get the corresponding impulse responses of the matched filters, as shown in Figure 7.6c. Figure 7.6d shows the optimum decision region is rectangular, and it is symmetrical with respect to both axes, i.e., we have the following identical probability of correct decisions for all four signals:

$$P(\mathbf{r}\in I_1/m_1) = P(\mathbf{r}\in I_2/m_2) = P(\mathbf{r}\in I_3/m_3) = P(\mathbf{r}\in I_4/m_4)$$

Using (7.7a) for $M=4$ and noting all four integrands and integration limits are identical as shown in Figure 7.6d, we then have the following:

$$P_{\text{SER}} = 1 - \frac{1}{4}\sum_{i=1}^{4}\int_{I_i} f_{\mathbf{r}/\mathbf{s}_i}(^{\mathbf{r}}/_{\mathbf{s}_i})d\mathbf{r} = 1 - \frac{1}{4}\times 4 \times \left(\int_{-\infty}^{d/2} f_n(\alpha)d\alpha\right)^2$$

$$= 1 - \left(1 - Q\left(\frac{d}{\sqrt{2N_0}}\right)\right)^2 = 2Q\left(\frac{d}{\sqrt{2N_0}}\right) - Q^2\left(\frac{d}{\sqrt{2N_0}}\right)$$

where $f_n(\alpha)$ is the probability density function of a zero-mean Gaussian random variable with variance $N_0/2$. Using (7.7c), we get $d=\sqrt{2E_s}$, and thus have:

$$P_{\text{SER}} = 2Q\left(\sqrt{\frac{E_s}{N_0}}\right) - Q^2\left(\sqrt{\frac{E_s}{N_0}}\right) \le 2Q\left(\sqrt{\frac{E_s}{N_0}}\right)$$

With $\frac{E_s}{N_0} \gg 1$, the quadratic term is negligible and we thus have the following approximation:

$$P_{\text{SER}} \approx 2Q\left(\sqrt{\frac{E_s}{N_0}}\right)$$

Noting that there are two bits per symbol, the average transmitted signal energy per symbol is twice the average signal energy per bit (i.e., $E_s = 2E_b$) and also assuming the Gray code is employed, i.e., only one bit in a symbol representing two bits is in error, the above symbol error rate then gives rise to the following bit error rate:

$$P_{\text{BER}} = Q\left(\sqrt{\frac{2E_b}{N_0}}\right).$$

As discussed later, this result is identical to the bit error rate for the widely-used QPSK modulation scheme.

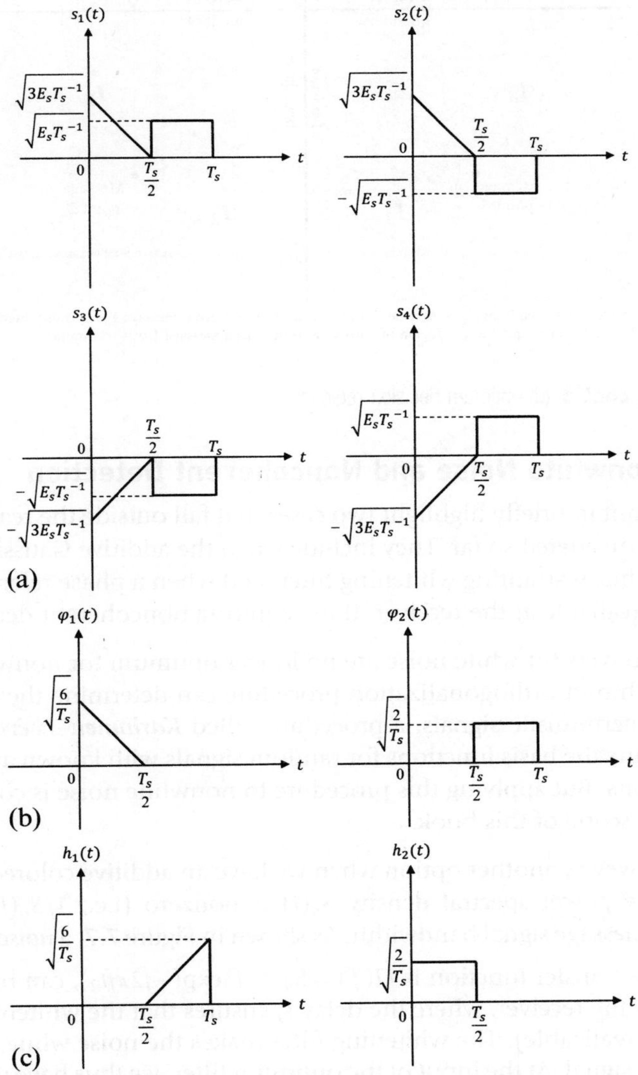

FIGURE 7.6 Example 7.3: (a) signal set, (b) orthonormal functions, (c) matched filters, and

(Continued)

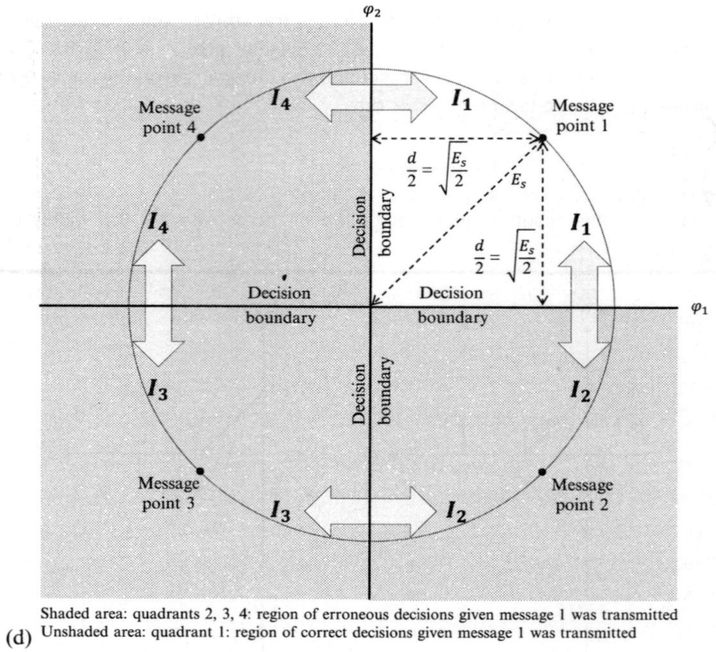

FIGURE 7.6, cont'd (d) optimum decision regions.

7.1.6 Nonwhite Noise and Noncoherent Detection

It is important to briefly highlight two cases that fall outside the realm of what have been considered so far. They include when the additive Gaussian noise is not white, thus warranting whitening filter, and when a phase reference signal cannot be available at the receiver, thus requiring noncoherent detection.

Optimal receivers for white noise are no longer optimum for nonwhite noise. As Gram-Schmidt orthogonalization procedure can determine the basis functions for deterministic signals, a procedure called ***Karhunen–Loève expansion*** can determine the basis functions for random signals with known autocorrelation functions. But applying this procedure to nonwhite noise is complex and beyond the scope of this book.

There is, however, another option when we have an additive colored Gaussian noise whose power spectral density $S_n(f)$ is nonzero (i.e., $1/S_n(f)$ is finite) within the message signal bandwidth. As shown in Figure 7.7, a ***noise-whitening filter***, whose transfer function is $H(f) = S_n^{-\frac{1}{2}}(f)\exp(-j2\pi f t_d)$, can be placed at the input of the receiver, where the delay t_d ensures that the whitening filter is causal (i.e., realizable). The whitening filter makes the noise white, and alters the received signal. At the input of the optimum filter, we thus have white noise

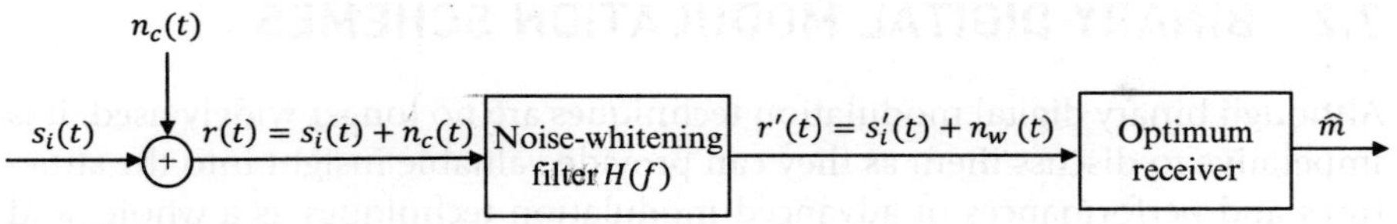

FIGURE 7.7 Optimum receiver for nonwhite noise.

and a filtered-version of the received signal, for which the bit error rate can be determined. However, it is important to note that the whitening filter can spread the received signals beyond the symbol duration. This results in two types of degradation; one is that the signal energy spread beyond the interval under consideration is not used by the matched filter, and the other is that signals can spread out and introduce intersymbol interference.

The development of the optimum receiver principles, discussed earlier, is under the assumption that the carrier is known at the receiver. However, the phase of a digitally-modulated transmitted signal is not exactly known at the receiver. The phase typically is not only unknown, but may also change over time. One reason of this phase uncertainty is the slow drift in the receiver's local oscillator, and another is possible changes in the propagation time between the transmitter and receiver. Optimum receivers using ***coherent detection*** schemes require a reference signal at the receiver that is matched in phase to the transmitted signal, i.e., the receiver's local oscillator has the same phase as the transmitter's local oscillator. The carrier recovery will be discussed in the next chapter. However, when a phase reference cannot be maintained or phase control is uneconomical, we can no longer use coherent detection methods. Noncoherent receivers do not require knowledge of the carrier phase, but do require knowledge of bit-timing information.

Noncoherent detection is based on the presence or absence of the signal envelope. It can be shown that when the unknown phase is uniformly distributed over the interval $[0, 2\pi]$, the optimum detector employing a noncoherent detection scheme is then a filter matched to the received signal followed by an envelope detector, a symbol-rate sampler, and a comparator to make the decision, as shown in Figure 7.8. The simplest form of envelope detection is a rectifier in series with a lowpass filter. The mathematical analysis of noise for noncoherent detection is more complicated than that in coherent detection. The advantage of noncoherent over coherent systems is reduced complexity, and the price paid is a deterioration of error rate at the receiver and/or an increase in transmit power.

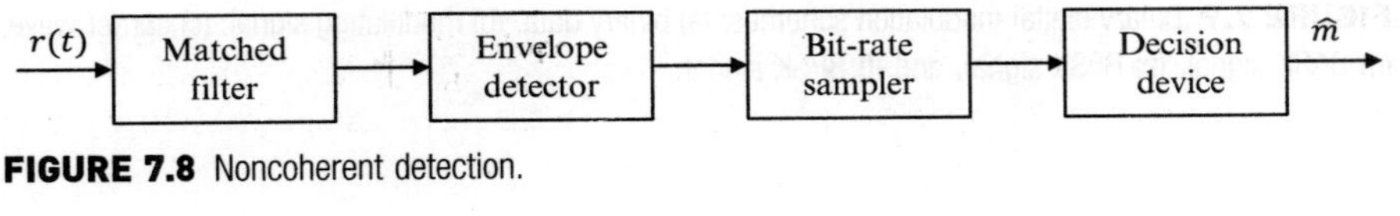

FIGURE 7.8 Noncoherent detection.

7.2 BINARY DIGITAL MODULATION SCHEMES

Although binary digital modulation techniques are no longer widely used, it is imperative to discuss them as they can provide valuable insight into the structures and performances of advanced modulation techniques as a whole, and help pave the way to understand today's widely-employed M-ary digital modulation techniques. In binary modulation, we have $M = 2$, the symbol error rate is thus the same as the bit error rate.

In a binary digital modulation technique, during every single bit interval, a sinusoidal signal is transmitted. The amplitude, frequency, or phase of the sinusoidal carrier is modified according to the input bits to produce the modulated signal. There are therefore three types of binary digital modulation techniques: binary amplitude-shift keying (BASK), binary frequency-shift keying (BFSK), and binary phase-shift keying (BPSK). Assuming the average energy per bit is the same for these modulation schemes, the bit error rates are determined. Figure 7.9 shows the sinusoidal carrier and the modulated BASK, BFSK, and BPSK signals for a bit stream.

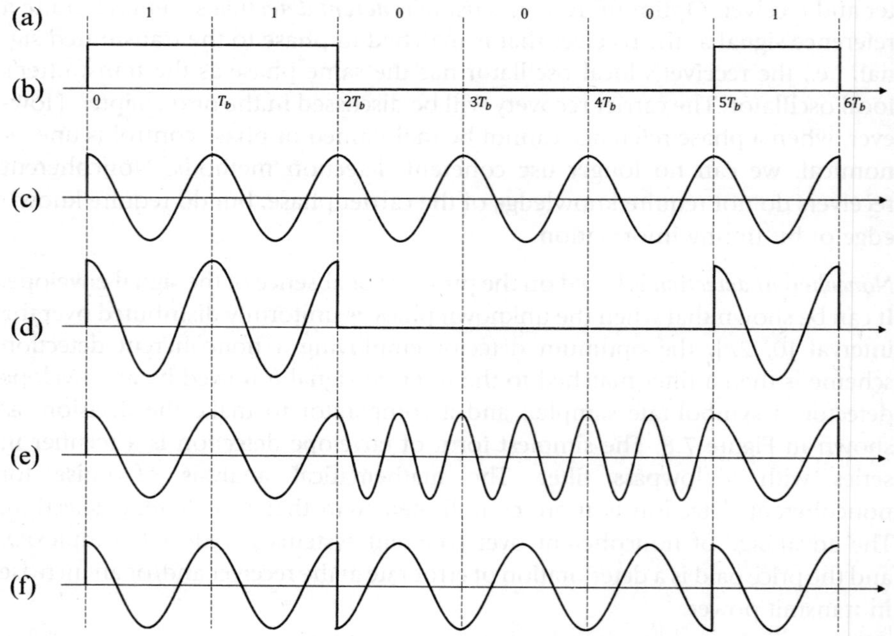

FIGURE 7.9 Binary digital modulation schemes: (a) binary data, (b) modulating signal, (c) carrier wave, (d) BASK signal, (e) BFSK signal, and (f) BPSK signal.

7.2.1 Binary Amplitude-Shift Keying

The ***binary amplitude-shift keying*** (BASK) is a very simple modulation technique. It was used in wireless (radio) telegraphy about a century ago, but it is now used in fiber optic communications, where the light source is turned on when the bit is a 1 and turned off when the bit is a 0. The carrier wave is turned on and off every T_b seconds to represent a 1 or a 0, respectively, it is thus also known as ***on-off keying*** (OOK). The BASK signal set can be analytically described as:

$$s_{\text{BASK}}(t) = \begin{cases} s_1(t) = 0\cos(2\pi f_c t) = 0, & \text{bit} = 0 \\ s_2(t) = 2\sqrt{\dfrac{E_b}{T_b}}\cos(2\pi f_c t), & \text{bit} = 1 \end{cases} \tag{7.9a}$$

where the carrier frequency and phase are both remain unchanged and only the amplitude varies. Figure 7.9d shows a transmitted BASK signal for a stream of bits. Using (7.1a), the BASK signal energy is then as follows:

$$E_{\text{BASK}} = \begin{cases} E_1 = \displaystyle\int_0^{T_b} s_1^2(t)\,dt = 0, & \text{bit} = 0 \\ E_2 = \displaystyle\int_0^{T_b} s_2^2(t)\,dt = 2E_b, & \text{bit} = 1 \end{cases} \tag{7.9b}$$

Since bits 1 and 0 are equally-likely, according to (7.1b), the average energy per bit is E_b. We need a set of only one orthonormal basis function to represent the BASK signal set, as given by:

$$\varphi_1(t) = \frac{s_2(t)}{\sqrt{2E_b}} = \sqrt{\frac{2}{T_b}}\cos(2\pi f_c t) \tag{7.9c}$$

A coherent BASK can thus be characterized by a one-dimensional signal space and two message points. Figure 7.10a shows a BASK transmitter, Figure 7.10b shows the signal space and optimum decision regions, and Figure 7.10c shows the optimum receiver using coherent detection. Using (7.7a), the average bit error rate is then as follows:

$$P_{\text{BER-BASK(coherent)}} = Q\left(\sqrt{\frac{E_b}{N_0}}\right) \tag{7.9d}$$

For noncoherent detection of BASK signals, as shown in Figure 7.10d, the received signal is passed through a filter matched to the BASK signal $s_2(t)$. The envelope will be close to maximum at the sampling instant. The filtered signal is thus passed through an envelope detector consisting of a rectifier followed by a lowpass filter. The resulting output is then sampled at integer multiples of the bit rate, and sent to a decision device. It can be shown that

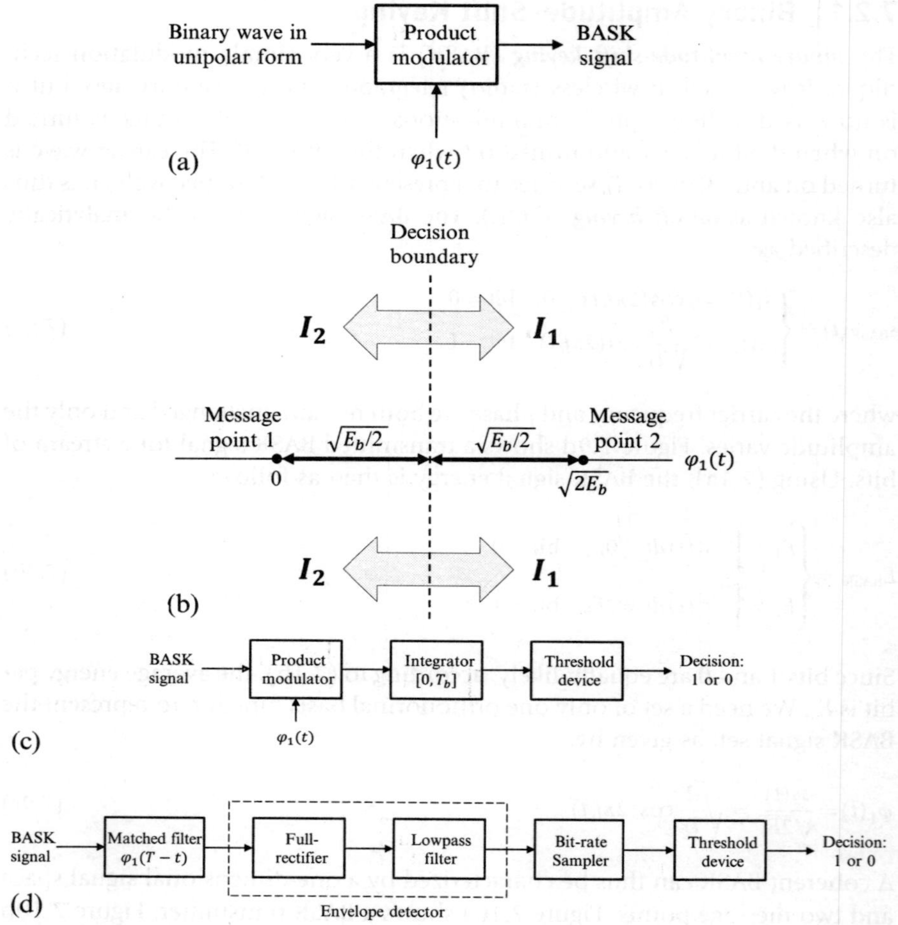

FIGURE 7.10 BASK modulation: (a) transmitter, (b) signal space and optimum decision regions, (c) coherent detection, and (d) noncoherent detection.

when we have $\frac{E_b}{N_0} \gg 1$, the average bit error rate for noncoherent BASK can be closely approximated as follows:

$$P_{\text{BER-BASK(noncoherent)}} \approx 0.5e^{-\frac{E_b}{2N_0}} \tag{7.9e}$$

In order to maintain optimum performance, the threshold value at the receiver should be adjusted as the signal level changes. Assuming a rectangular pulse is used, the power spectral density of the BASK signal is as follows:

$$S_{\text{BASK}}(f) = \left(\frac{E_b}{4T_b}\right)\left((\delta(f+f_c)+\delta(f-f_c)) + T_b\left(\text{sinc}^2(T_b(f+f_c)) + \text{sinc}^2(T_b(f-f_c))\right)\right) \tag{7.9f}$$

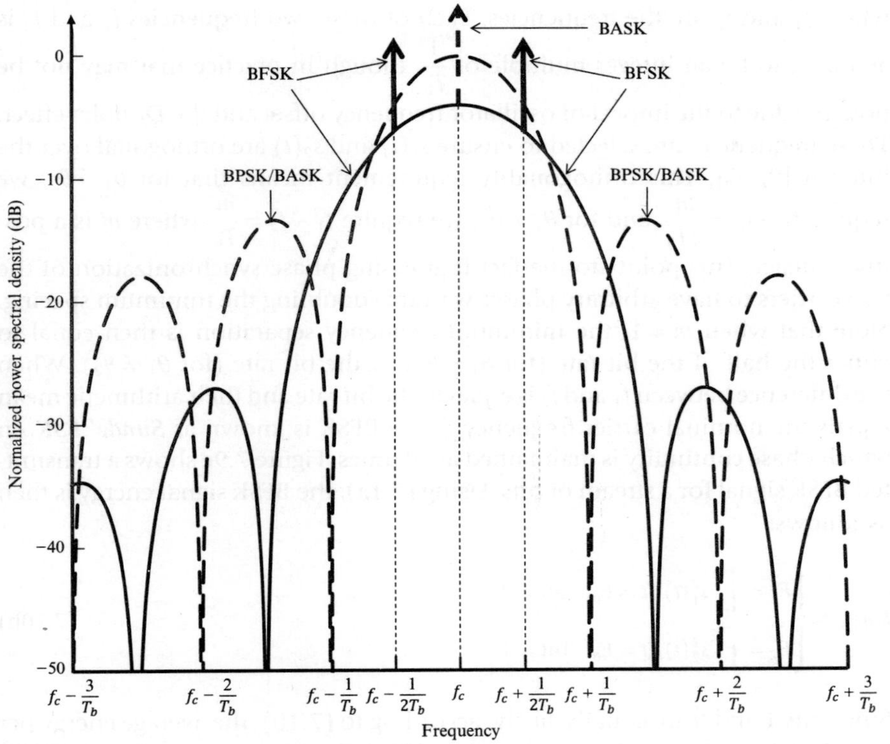

FIGURE 7.11 Power spectral density functions for BASK, BFSK, and BPSK modulation schemes.

As shown in Figure 7.11, the power spectral density function is not band-limited, and falls off as the inverse square power of frequency, also the null-to-null bandwidth is $\frac{2}{T_b}$. The discrete frequency components can help synchronizing the receiver with the transmitter.

7.2.2 Binary Frequency-Shift Keying

The ***binary frequency-shift keying*** (BFSK) is a simple nonlinear modulation technique. It was used, mainly due to hardware advantages, in low-speed data modems over wired telephone lines decades ago, but it is now used in caller ID and remote sensing applications. The BFSK signal set can be analytically described as:

$$s_{BFSK}(t) = \begin{cases} s_1(t) = \sqrt{\dfrac{2E_b}{T_b}}\cos(2\pi f_1 t + \theta_1), & \text{bit} = 0 \\ s_2(t) = \sqrt{\dfrac{2E_b}{T_b}}\cos(2\pi f_2 t + \theta_2), & \text{bit} = 1 \end{cases} \tag{7.10a}$$

where f_1 and f_2 are the frequencies. Each of these two frequencies f_1 and f_2 is assumed to be an integer multiple of $\frac{1}{T_b}$, though in practice that may not be possible due to the impact of oscillator frequency offset and the Doppler effect. These frequencies are selected to ensure $s_1(t)$ and $s_2(t)$ are orthogonal over the interval $[0,\ T_b]$. This orthogonality requirement means that for $\theta_1 = \theta_2$, we require $f_1 - f_2 = \frac{m}{2T_b}$, and for $\theta_1 \neq \theta_2$, we require $f_1 - f_2 = \frac{m}{T_b}$, where m is a positive integer. This points to the fact that easing phase synchronization of the two carriers to have arbitrary phases warrants doubling the minimum spacing. Note that when $m = 1$, the minimum frequency separation is then equal to either the half of the bit rate (for $\theta_1 = \theta_2$) or the bit rate (for $\theta_1 \neq \theta_2$). When the difference between f_1 and f_2 is equal to the bit rate and their arithmetic mean equals the nominal carrier frequency f_c, the BFSK is known as ***Sunde' FSK***, in which phase continuity is maintained at all times. Figure 7.9e shows a transmitted BFSK signal for a stream of bits. Using (7.1a), the BFSK signal energy is then as follows:

$$E_{BFSK} = \begin{cases} E_1 = \int_0^{T_b} s_1^2(t)\,dt = E_b, & \text{bit} = 0 \\ E_2 = \int_0^{T_b} s_2^2(t)\,dt = E_b, & \text{bit} = 1 \end{cases} \tag{7.10b}$$

Since bits 1 and 0 are equally-likely, according to (7.1b), the average energy per bit is E_b. We need a set of two orthonormal basis functions to represent the BFSK signal set, as given by:

$$\varphi_1(t) = \frac{s_1(t)}{\sqrt{E_b}} = \sqrt{\frac{2}{T_b}}\cos(2\pi f_1 t + \theta_1) \tag{7.10c}$$

$$\varphi_2(t) = \frac{s_2(t)}{\sqrt{E_b}} = \sqrt{\frac{2}{T_b}}\cos(2\pi f_2 t + \theta_2)$$

A coherent BFSK can thus be characterized by a two-dimensional signal space and two message points. Figure 7.12a shows a BFSK transmitter, Figure 7.12b shows the signal space and optimum decision regions, and Figure 7.12c shows the optimum receiver using coherent detection. In BFSK, where the transmitted bit is represented by one of the two possible signals, it is always possible by a proper choice of the orthonormal basis to reduce the two correlators or matched filters to only one correlator or matched filter, as only the difference between the two signals is important in making the optimum decision at the receiver. Using (7.7a), the average bit error rate is then as follows:

$$P_{\text{BER-BFSK(coherent)}} = Q\left(\sqrt{\frac{E_b}{N_0}}\right) \tag{7.10d}$$

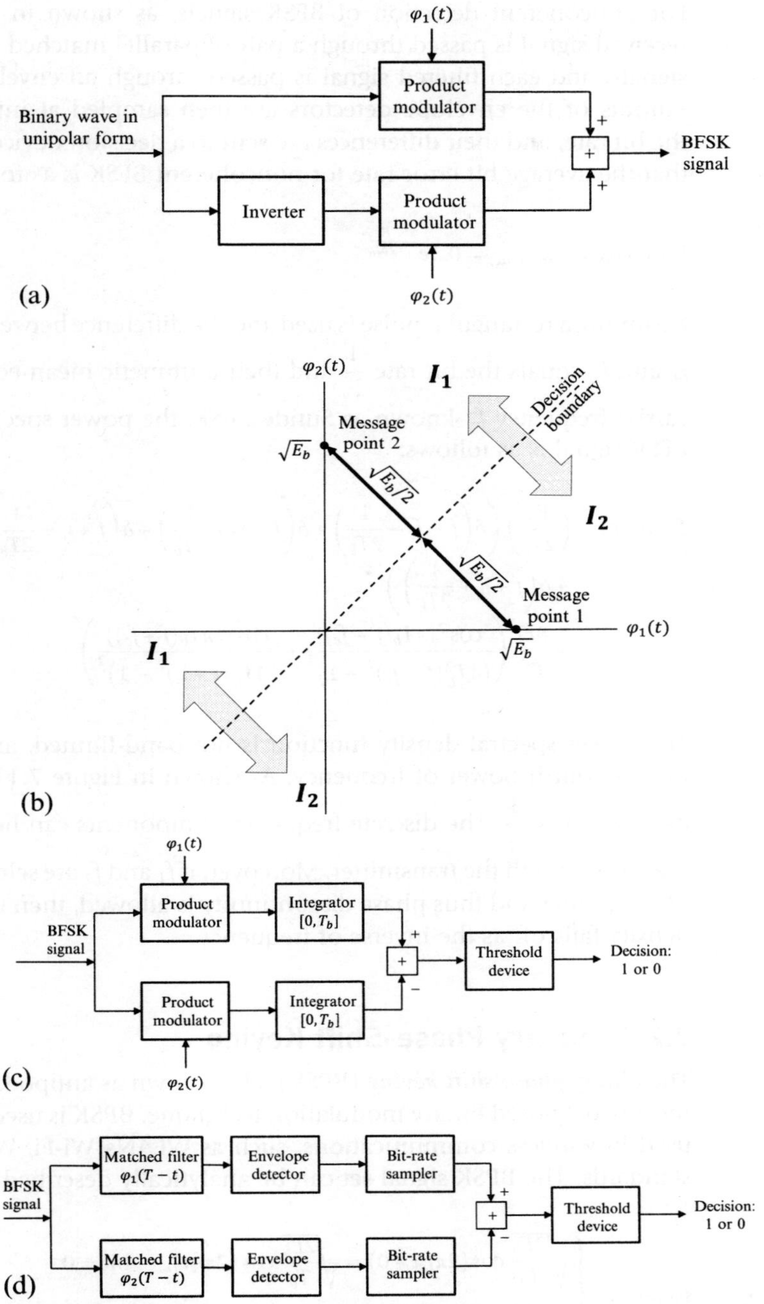

FIGURE 7.12 BFSK modulation: (a) transmitter, (b) signal space and optimum decision regions, (c) coherent detection, and (d) noncoherent detection.

For noncoherent detection of BFSK signals, as shown in Figure 7.12d, the received signal is passed through a pair of parallel matched filters to the BFSK signals, and each filtered signal is passed through an envelope detector. The outputs of the envelope detectors are then sampled at integer multiples of the bit rate, and their differences are sent to a decision device. It can be shown that the average bit error rate for noncoherent BFSK is as follows:

$$P_{\mathrm{BER-BFSK(noncoherent)}} = 0.5e^{-\frac{E_b}{2N_0}} \tag{7.10e}$$

Assuming a rectangular pulse is used and the difference between the frequencies f_1 and f_2 equals the bit rate $\frac{1}{T_b}$ and their arithmetic mean equals the nominal carrier frequency f_c, known as Sunde's FSK, the power spectral density of the BFSK signal is as follows:

$$\begin{aligned} S_{BFSK}(f) = &\left(\frac{E_b}{2T_b}\right)\left(\delta\left(f - f_c - \frac{1}{2T_b}\right) + \delta\left(f - f_c + \frac{1}{2T_b}\right) + \delta\left(f + f_c - \frac{1}{2T_b}\right)\right. \\ &\left.+\,\delta\left(f + f_c + \frac{1}{2T_b}\right)\right) \\ &+ \frac{8E_b}{\pi^2}\left(\frac{\cos^2(\pi T_b(f - f_c))}{\left(4T_b^2(f - f_c)^2 - 1\right)^2} + \frac{\cos^2(\pi T_b(f + f_c))}{\left(4T_b^2(f + f_c)^2 - 1\right)^2}\right) \end{aligned} \tag{7.10f}$$

The power spectral density function is not band-limited, and falls off as the inverse fourth power of frequency. As shown in Figure 7.11, the null-to-null bandwidth is $\frac{3}{T_b}$. The discrete frequency components can help synchronizing the receiver with the transmitter. Moreover, if f_1 and f_2 are selected independent of each other and thus phase discontinuity is allowed, then the power spectral density falls off as the inverse of frequency.

7.2.3 Binary Phase-Shift Keying

The ***binary phase-shift keying*** (BPSK), also known as antipodal signaling, is the most widely-used binary modulation technique. BPSK is used in GPS. It is also used in wireless communications, such as WLANs/Wi-Fi, WiMAX, and RFID standards. The BPSK signal set can be analytically described as:

$$s_{BPSK}(t) = \begin{cases} \sqrt{\frac{2E_b}{T_b}}\cos(2\pi f_c t + 0) = \sqrt{\frac{2E_b}{T_b}}\cos(2\pi f_c t), & \text{bit} = 0 \\ \sqrt{\frac{2E_b}{T_b}}\cos(2\pi f_c t + \pi) = -\sqrt{\frac{2E_b}{T_b}}\cos(2\pi f_c t), & \text{bit} = 1 \end{cases} \tag{7.11a}$$

Figure 7.9f shows a transmitted BPSK waveform for a stream of bits. Using (7.1a), the BPSK signal energy is then as follows:

$$E_{\text{BPSK}} = \begin{cases} E_1 = \int_0^{T_b} s_1^2(t)\,dt = E_b, & \text{bit} = 0 \\ E_2 = \int_0^{T_b} s_2^2(t)\,dt = E_b, & \text{bit} = 1 \end{cases} \qquad (7.11b)$$

Since bits 1 and 0 are equally-likely, according to (7.1b), the average energy per bit is E_b. We need only one orthonormal basis function to represent the BPSK signal set, as given by:

$$\varphi_1(t) = \frac{s_1(t)}{\sqrt{E_b}} = -\frac{s_2(t)}{\sqrt{E_b}} = \sqrt{\frac{2}{T_b}}\cos(2\pi f_c t) \qquad (7.11c)$$

A coherent BPSK can thus be characterized by a one-dimensional signal space and two message points. Figure 7.13a shows a BPSK transmitter, Figure 7.13b shows the signal space and optimum decision regions, and Figure 7.13c shows the optimum receiver using coherent detection. Using (7.7a), the average bit error rate is then as follows:

$$P_{\text{BER}-\text{BPSK(coherent)}} = Q\left(\sqrt{\frac{2E_b}{N_0}}\right) \qquad (7.11d)$$

The noncoherent detection using envelope detection cannot be effective for BPSK, for unlike BASK, it has a constant envelope, and unlike BFSK, it has only one carrier frequency. To circumvent this, an interesting approach, known as differential encoding, can be employed, which is primarily based on the premises that phase uncertainty remains almost unchanged over time or changes very slowly with time. In other words, the phase reference is derived from the phase of the carrier during the preceding bit interval, and the receiver decodes the received information based on the differential phase.

In ***differential encoding***, the bits are encoded in terms of signal transition. For instance, bit 0 may represent a transition (i.e., a phase change) and bit 1 may represent no transition (i.e., no phase change). A signaling technique that combines differential encoding and BPSK is known as ***differential BPSK*** (DBPSK). The differentially encoded sequence thus needs to have an extra initial bit to provide a reference in the receiver.

The differential encoding operation by the modulator at the transmitter generates the encoded bit d_k using the following logical equation:

$$d_k = d_{k-1} b_k \oplus \bar{d}_{k-1} \bar{b}_k \qquad (7.11e)$$

where b_k is the input bit, $\bar{b}_k$ is the logical inversion of the input bit, d_{k-1} is the previous encoded bit, $\bar{d}_{k-1}$ is the logical inversion of the previous encoded bit,

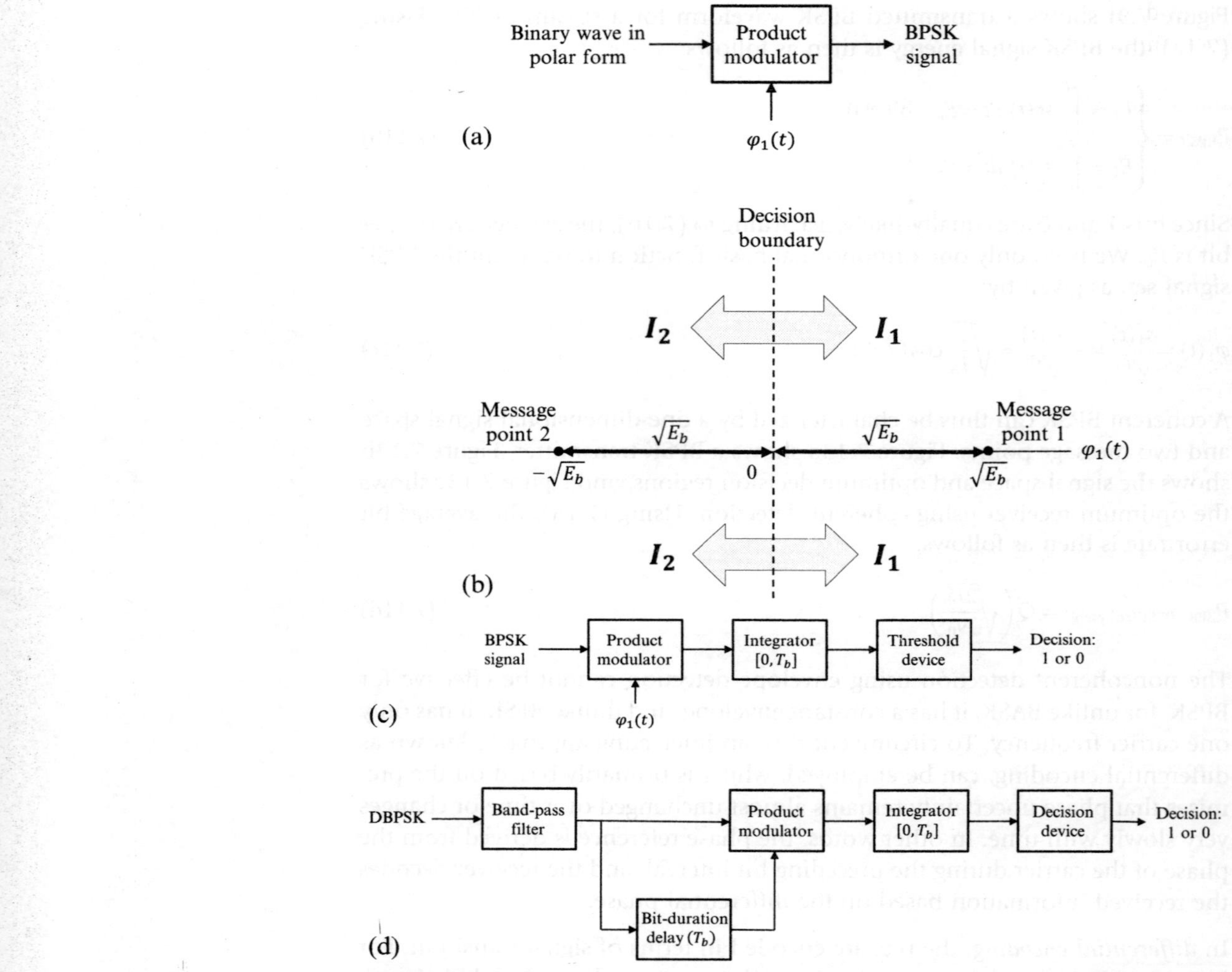

FIGURE 7.13 BPSK modulation: (a) transmitter, (b) signal space and optimum decision regions, (c) coherent detection, and (d) differential detection.

and $\oplus$ denotes modulo-two addition. Although phase reference in DBPSK is corrupted by noise, the error propagation is not catastrophic, and thus the degradation in performance is not significant. Figure 7.13d shows DBPSK demodulator. It can be shown that the average bit error rate for DBPSK is as follows:

$$P_{\text{BER-BPSK(noncoherent)}} = 0.5e^{-\frac{E_b}{N_0}} \tag{7.11f}$$

The average bit error rate for DBPSK receiver is higher than that for coherent one. DBPSK receiver may require about 1 dB more power than the coherent one to deliver the same average bit error rate. However, DBPSK detection is much simpler than the coherent one.

EXAMPLE 7.4

An input bit sequence consisting of 100111000 is applied to a DBPSK system. Determine the corresponding transmitted bits, and show how the phase comparison can be used to determine the output sequence.

Solution

A 1 as an arbitrary reference bit is assumed for the initial bit of the encoded sequence. For each bit of the encoded sequence, the present bit is used as a reference for the following bit in the sequence. Using (7.11e), a 0 in the input sequence is encoded as a transition from the state of the reference bit to the opposite state in the encoded sequence, and a 1 is encoded as no change of state. Since the first bit in the input sequence is a 1, no change in state is made in the encoded sequence, and a 1 appears as the next bit. This serves as the reference for the next bit to be encoded. Since the second bit appearing in the input sequence is a 0, the next encoded bit is a 0, as it reflects a transition from the past encoded bit, which was a 1. Since the third bit appearing in the input sequence is a 0, the next encoded bit is a 1, as it reflects no transition from the past encoded bit, which was a 0. Since the fourth bit appearing in the input sequence is a 1, the next encoded bit is a 1, as it reflects no transition from the past encoded bit, which was a 1. This process continues until all input bits are differentially encoded one by one. The encoded sequence then phase-shift keys a carrier with the phases 0 and π as shown below:

Bit number k	1	2	3	4	5	6	7	8	9	
Input sequence b_k		1	0	0	1	1	1	0	0	0
Encoded sequence d_k	1	1	0	1	1	1	1	0	1	0
Transmitted phase	0	0	π	0	0	0	0	π	0	π
Phase comparison output	+	+	−	−	+	+	+	−	−	−
Output sequence $\hat{b}_k$		1	0	0	1	1	1	0	0	0

The phase comparison, which provides information about the phase change, gives rise to the output sequence.

Assuming a rectangular pulse is used, the power spectral density of the BPSK signal is as follows:

$$S_{\text{BPSK}}(f) = \left(\frac{E_b}{2}\right)\left(\text{sinc}^2(T_b(f-f_c)) + \text{sinc}^2(T_b(f+f_c))\right) \tag{7.11g}$$

As shown in Figure 7.11, the shapes of the PSD of the BPSK and BASK signals are similar, and the only distinction is that BPSK spectrum does not have an impulse at the carrier frequency. Note that the power spectral density of BPSK falls off as the inverse second power of frequency.

7.2.4 Comparison of Binary Digital Modulation Schemes

In order to make a fair comparison of binary digital modulation schemes in terms of their error rate performances, we assume they all have the same average energy per bit E_b, bit rate $1/T_b$, and noise environment (i.e., AWGN with the same noise power spectral density $N_0/2$). The bit error rate performance of binary digital modulation schemes for both the coherent and noncoherent detection methods are shown in Figure 7.14. The following general observations about binary digital modulation schemes can be made:

- The performance curves, which show the average bit error rate P_{BER} expressed as a nonlinear function of the average bit energy to noise power $\frac{E_b}{N_0}$, are all monotonically decreasing and have water-fall like shapes when both axes are in the logarithmic scale.

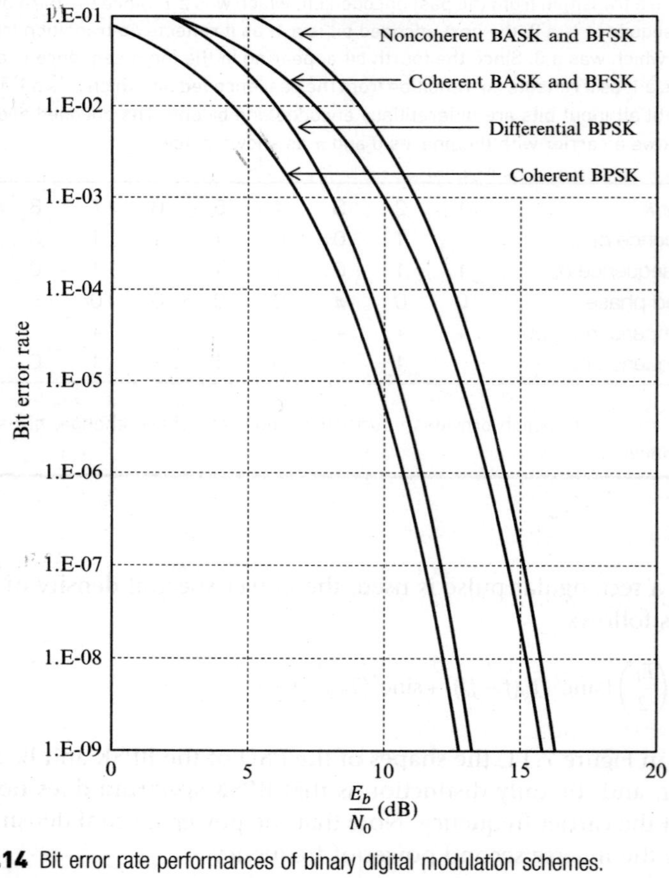

FIGURE 7.14 Bit error rate performances of binary digital modulation schemes.

- For a modulation scheme, coherent detection outperforms noncoherent detection. In other words, for a given $\frac{E_b}{N_0}$, the resulting P_{BER} for coherent detection is lower than that for noncoherent detection, and for a fixed P_{BER}, the required $\frac{E_b}{N_0}$ for coherent detection is less than that for noncoherent detection. As $\frac{E_b}{N_0}$ increases (i.e., P_{BER} decreases), the asymptotic performances of coherent detection and noncoherent detection are equivalent.
- BASK and BFSK have the same performance, and BPSK has a 3-dB power advantage over both BASK and BFSK for both coherent and noncoherent detection schemes.
- For a very low P_{BER}, the best scheme (coherent BPSK) requires an average power that is about 4 dB less than what is required for the poorest scheme (noncoherent BFSK or BASK).
- There is little difference in the complexity of the transmit equipment for all schemes. Receiver design simplification due to noncoherent detection is at the expense of performance degradation. Among the noncoherent schemes, DBPSK and noncoherent BFSK are more complex than noncoherent BASK.
- Since the cost of transmitting and receiving equipment is generally a function of the peak power requirement rather than the average power requirement, BASK falls short. The power margin over noncoherent BFSK at low bit error rates is inconsequential. Because of the comparable performance and the added simplicity of noncoherent BFSK, it is almost exclusively employed instead of coherent FSK.
- BASK is more sensitive to variations in received signal level due to variations in channel characteristics, such as amplitude nonlinearities and fading, as BFSK and BPSK are both constant amplitude signals.
- Assuming a rectangular pulse, the power spectral density for each of these schemes decays as $\frac{1}{f^2}$ for frequencies away from the carrier frequency. Except the discrete components, BASK and BPSK have the same power spectral density, and thus the same bandwidth requirements. BFSK has lower side-lobes than BPSK and BASK. In general, the bandwidth of BFSK signal is greater than the bandwidth of the BASK and BPSK signals.
- With a smoother pulse than the rectangular pulse, the power spectral density for a modulation scheme can become more compact. This valuable reduction in bandwidth is of course at the expense of a modest increase in complexity of the pulse shaping.
- Overall, BPSK scheme, in terms of both power and bandwidth utilization, is more efficient than BASK and BFSK schemes.

7.3 COHERENT QUATERNARY SIGNALING SCHEMES

Binary digital modulation techniques are quite simple, but they are not spectrally efficient. To increase the spectral efficiency (i.e., to increase the transmission bit rate without increasing the bandwidth requirement or to reduce the bandwidth requirement while not reducing the transmission bit rate), quaternary signaling schemes, which may include quadrature phase-shift keying (QPSK), offset QPSK (OQPSK), and minimum-shift keying (MSK), are attractive choices. Quaternary signaling schemes are all examples of quadrature-carrier multiplexing system, as they combine two independent signals to occupy the same transmission bandwidth, and yet it allows for the separation of the two signals at the receiver. In quaternary signaling schemes, the information is embedded in the carrier phase, while the carrier amplitude and frequency remain unchanged. They all encode two bits into one symbol (i.e., $M = 4$), and have a bit error rate performance that is the same as that of the BPSK scheme.

In addition to the spectral efficiency requirement, it is desirable for a digital modulation scheme to have constant envelope. Constant envelope can prevent amplitude fluctuations when the signal passes first through a bandpass filter to reduce its side-lobes to conform to the required out-of-band emission, and when it goes through a highly nonlinear amplifier in the transmitter. The envelope of the QPSK signal is ideally constant. However, a QPSK signal may have occasional ± 180 degrees phase shifts at multiples of symbol duration, which can cause the envelope to go to zero at instants of time. The nonlinear amplification of a filtered QPSK signal can bring back the unwanted side-lobes. This in turn requires linear amplifiers that usually have low efficiency.

The OQPSK scheme, on the other hand, allows staggered in-phase and quadrature components which do not change states simultaneously, and the phase changes are thus limited to only 0 and ± 90 degrees at multiples of a bit duration. In order to eliminate instantaneous phase changes (i.e., rapid jumps at the transitions), MSK is an attractive modulation scheme, as it can provide continuous phase at all times. The MSK does not produce as much interference outside the signal band of interest as the QPSK and OQPSK schemes. Band-limiting the MSK signal to meet the out-of-band power requirements does not make the envelope to pass through zero, for there are no discontinuities at the bit transitions in the MSK signal.

7.3.1 Quadrature Phase-Shift Keying

The QPSK scheme is the most-widely used digital modulation technique, as it is used in wireless communications, such as WLANs/Wi-Fi and WiMAX standards, as well as many digital cellular mobile systems and TV broadcast satellite systems. In the ***quadrature phase-shift keying*** (QPSK) scheme, two bits are grouped at a time, and mapped into one of the four possible signals. As with BPSK ($M=2$), the information in QPSK ($M=4$) is contained in the carrier phase (i.e., the phase of the carrier takes on one of four equally-spaced values). The QPSK signal set can thus be analytically described as:

$$s_i(t)=\sqrt{\frac{2E_s}{T_s}}\cos\left(2\pi f_c t+\frac{\pi(2i-1)}{4}\right),\quad 0\le t\le T_s,\quad i=1,2,3,4 \tag{7.12a}$$

where the carrier frequency f_c is an integer multiple of the symbol rate $1/T_s$. Using (7.1a), the following shows that the energy of each signal is the same as the average energy per symbol E_s:

$$E_i=\int_0^{T_b} s_i^2(t)\,dt=E_s,\quad i=1,2,3,4 \tag{7.12b}$$

After using a well-known trigonometric identity to expand $s_i(t)$ in (7.12a), it is easy to see that the following two orthonormal basis functions can represent the QPSK signal set:

$$\begin{aligned}\varphi_1(t)&=\sqrt{\frac{2}{T_s}}\cos(2\pi f_c t),\quad 0\le t\le T_s\\ \varphi_2(t)&=\sqrt{\frac{2}{T_s}}\sin(2\pi f_c t),\quad 0\le t\le T_s\end{aligned} \tag{7.12c}$$

Using (7.12c), the QPSK signal set in (7.12a) can thus be characterized as follows:

$$\begin{aligned}s_i(t)=&\sqrt{E_s}\cos\left(\frac{\pi(2i-1)}{4}\right)\varphi_1(t)-\\ &\sqrt{E_s}\sin\left(\frac{\pi(2i-1)}{4}\right)\varphi_2(t),\quad 0\le t\le T_s,\quad i=1,2,3,4\end{aligned} \tag{7.12d}$$

Figure 7.15a shows the input binary signal $m(t)$ in polar form for a stream of bits. Figure 7.15b shows the decomposition of $m(t)$ into two independent signals $m_I(t)$ and $m_Q(t)$, consisting of the odd-numbered and even-numbered input bits, respectively, and Figure 7.15c shows the corresponding transmitted QPSK signal. Figure 7.15d and Figure 7.15e show the QPSK transmitter and receiver, respectively. The QPSK signal space is thus two-dimensional, and represents four signal points. Figure 7.15f shows the signal space and the corresponding optimum (minimum-distance) decision regions. The signal points lie on a circle of radius $\sqrt{E_s}$, and are spaced every $\pi/2$ radians.

Assuming $\frac{E_s}{N_0}$ is so high that only the two nearest message points can be potential candidates for error, employing the Gray code, and using (7.7a), the

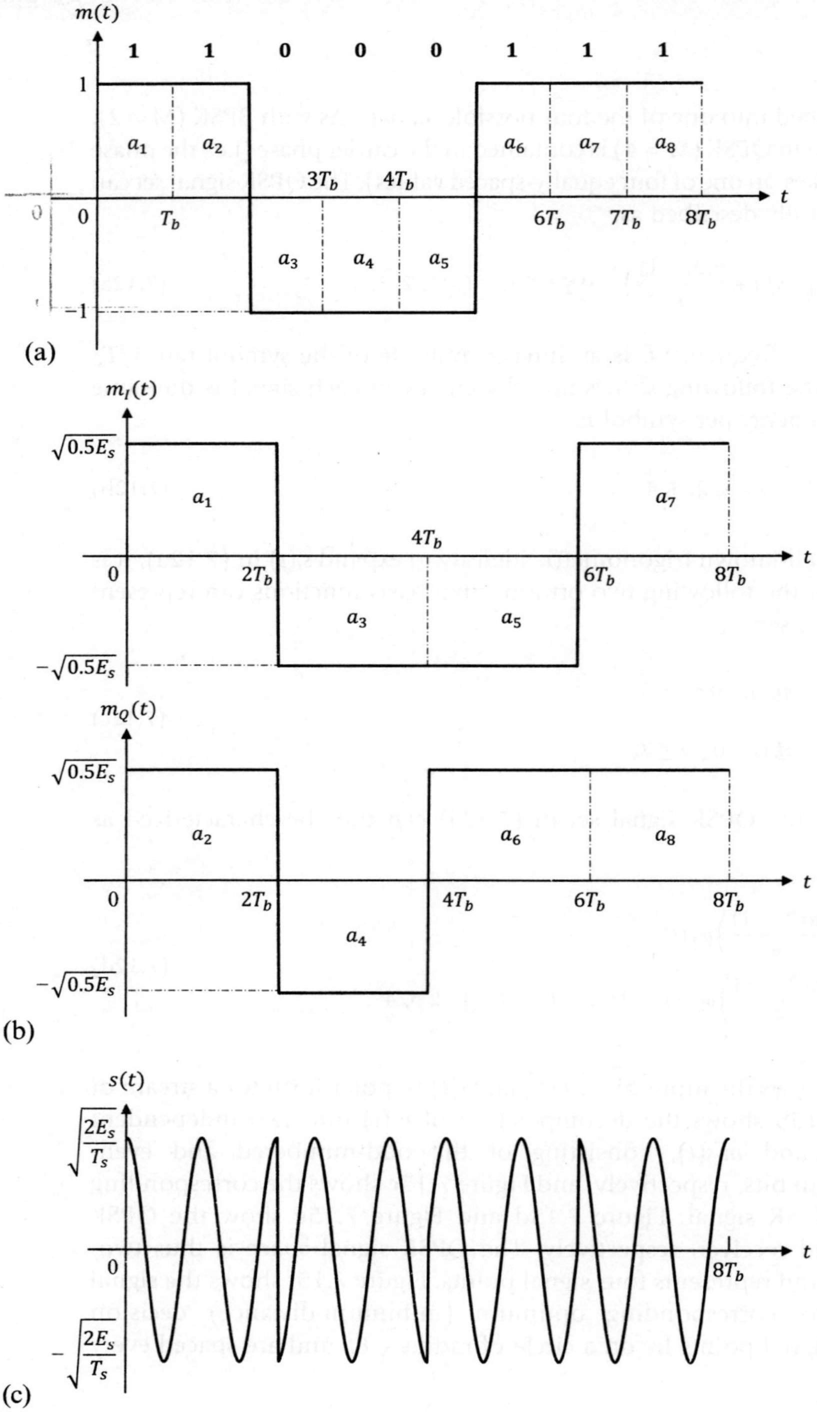

FIGURE 7.15 QPSK modulation: (a) input binary signal in polar form, (b) signal decomposition into two independent signals, (c) transmitted signal,

(Continued)

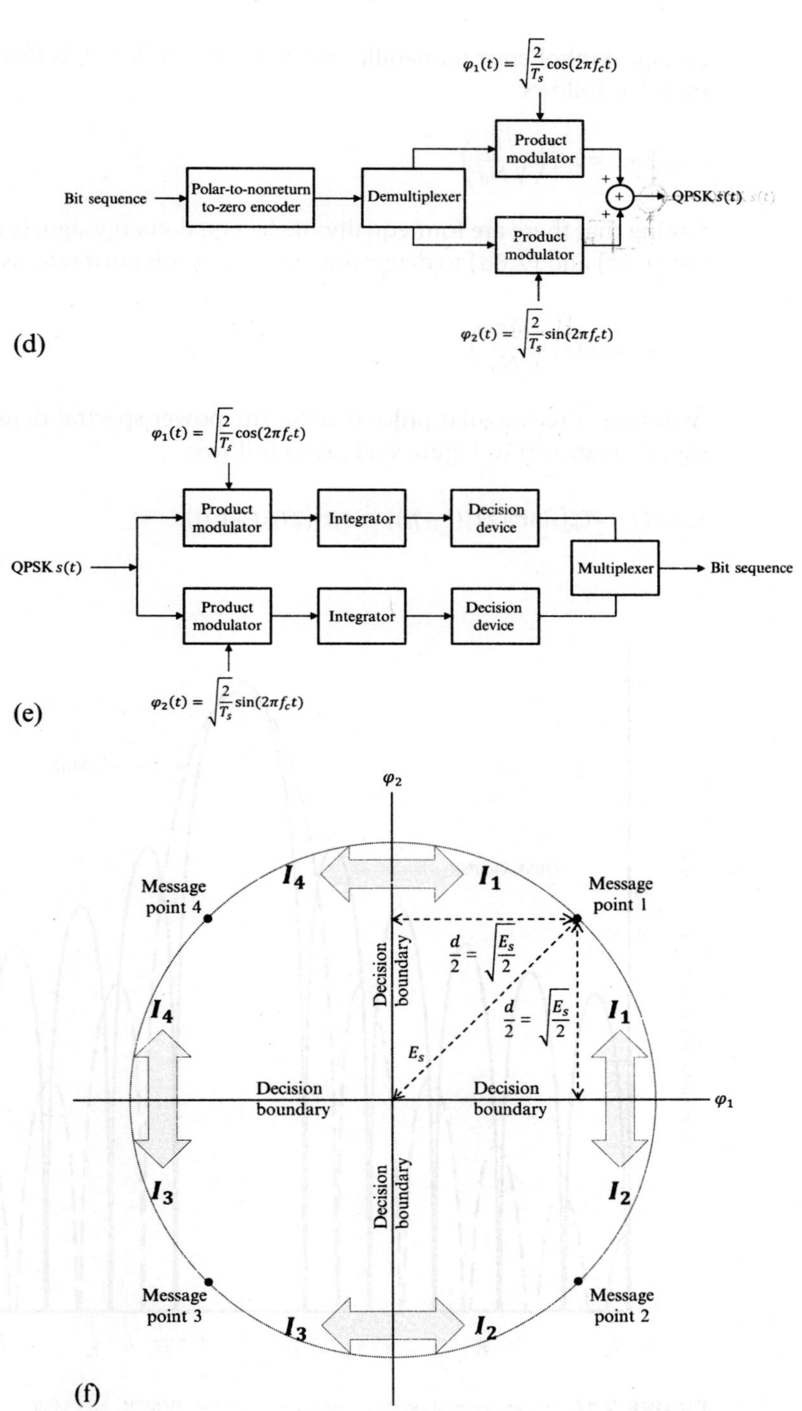

FIGURE 7.15, cont'd (d) transmitter, (e) receiver, and (f) signal space and optimum decision regions.

average symbol error probability, similar to Example 7.3, is then tightly approximated as follows:

$$P_{\text{SER-QPSK}} \approx 2\,Q\left(\sqrt{\frac{E_s}{N_0}}\right) \tag{7.12e}$$

Noting that there are four equally-likely, equal-energy signals in QPSK, we can use (7.1c) and (7.8b) to determine the average bit error rate, as reflected below:

$$P_{\text{BER-QPSK}} = Q\left(\sqrt{\frac{2E_b}{N_0}}\right) \tag{7.12f}$$

Assuming a rectangular pulse is used, the power spectral density of the QPSK signal, as shown in Figure 7.16, is as follows:

$$S_{\text{QPSK}}(f) = E_b\left(\text{sinc}^2(2T_b(f-f_c)) + \text{sinc}^2(2T_b(f+f_c))\right) \tag{7.12g}$$

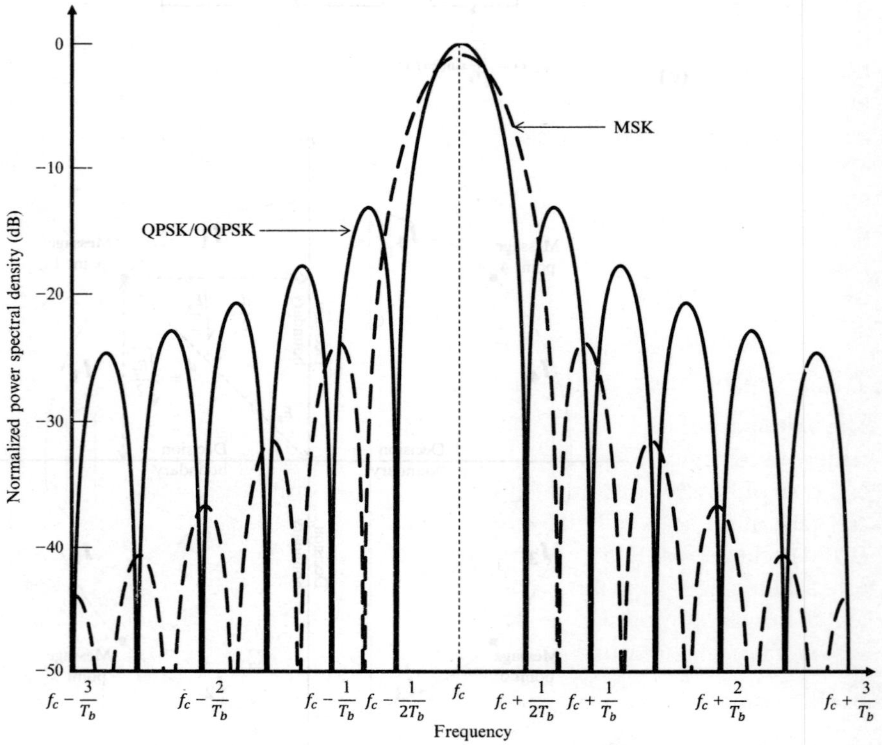

FIGURE 7.16 Power spectral density functions for QPSK, OQPSK, and MSK.

A comparison of (7.11g) and (7.12g) reveals that the power spectral density of the QPSK signal is thus twice the power spectral density of the BPSK signal, with $2T_b$ substituted for T_b. In other words, QPSK, vis-à-vis BPSK, halves the bandwidth required for given bit rate.

7.3.2 Offset Quadrature Phase-Shift Keying

There is a variation of QPSK, known as ***offset QPSK*** (OQPSK), in which the in-phase and quadrature components are offset by one bit interval T_b. Figure 7.17a shows the input binary signal $m(t)$ in polar form for a stream of bits. Figure 7.17b shows the decomposition of $m(t)$ into two independent signals $m_I(t)$ and $m_Q(t)$, consisting of the odd-numbered and even-numbered input bits, respectively. In OQPSK, also known as ***staggered QPSK*** (SQPSK), the timing of the signals $m_I(t)$ and $m_Q(t)$ is shifted such that the alignment of the two signals is offset by T_b. Figure 7.17c shows the corresponding transmitted OQPSK signal. The resulting modulated signal cannot thus have a phase change of 180.

The optimum receiver for OQPSK is almost identical to that of QPSK, the only difference is that the time shift of T_b must be taken into account by the correlator and sampler. The symbol error rate and the corresponding bit error rate for OQPSK are thus the same as those for QPSK. Both QPSK and OQPSK signals in the time domain can have discontinuities, for QPSK at multiples of symbol duration and for OQPSK at multiples of bit duration. The power spectral densities of OQPSK and QPSK are identical, as the power spectral density of signal does not depend on the phase. To eliminate these possible discontinuities (rapid transitions), thus reducing the large bandwidth associated with their power spectral density, MSK is an attractive modulation scheme.

7.3.3 Minimum-Shift Keying

The ***minimum-shift keying*** (MSK) scheme is used in GSM, a pioneer and a widely-used digital cellular mobile system. MSK can be viewed as either a special case of binary continuous-phase frequency-shift keying (CPFSK) or a special case of OQPSK. When MSK is viewed as a continuous phase modulation (CPM) scheme, MSK is a binary modulation with interval T_b, but as a quadrature scheme, it is a quaternary modulation over a double interval $2T_b$. Regardless of how MSK modulation is viewed, not only it has a constant envelope, but it also has a continuous phase.

In expressing MSK as a special case of CPFSK, the change in carrier frequency occurring every bit duration is equal to one half the bit rate, which is the minimum separation possible for the two sinusoidal carriers to be coherently

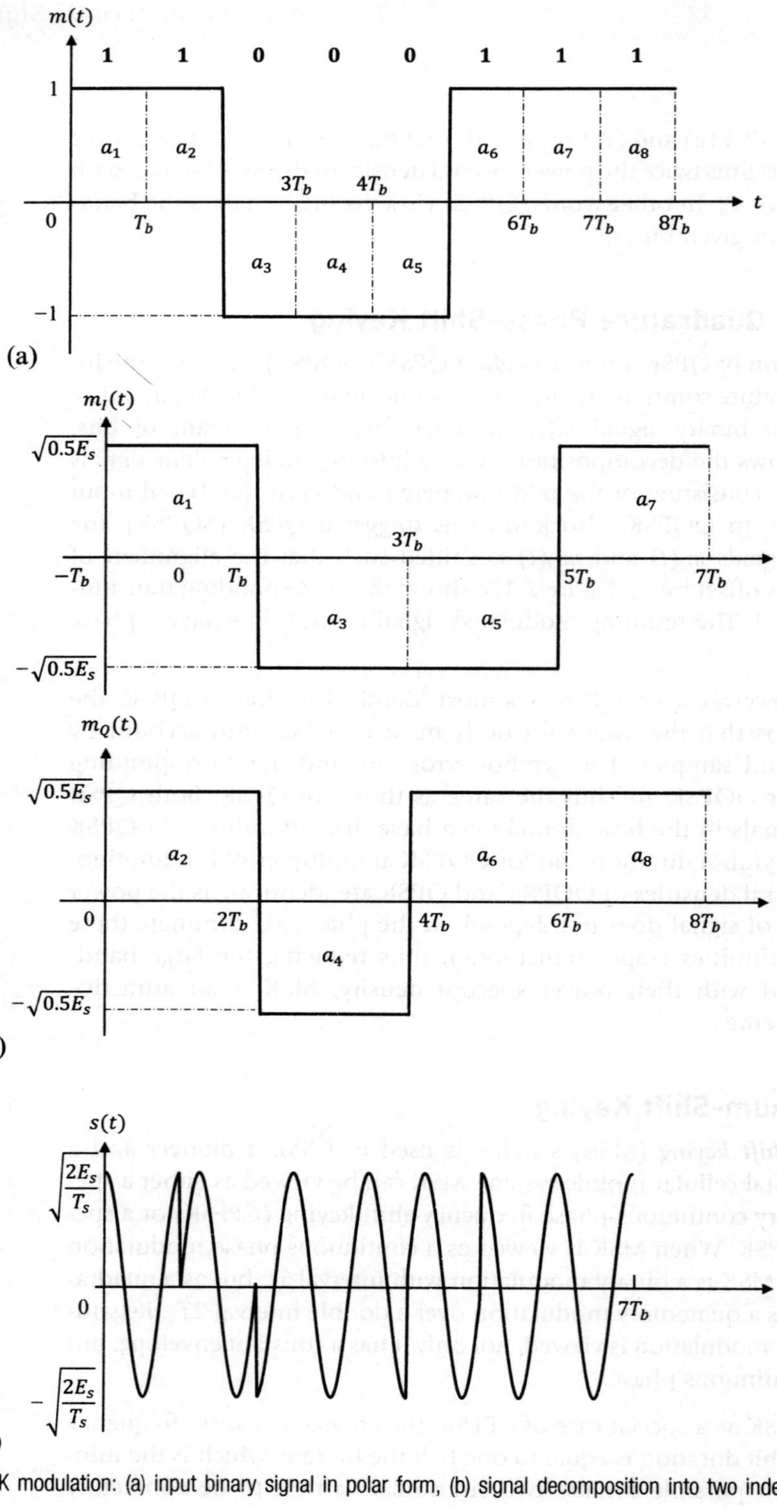

FIGURE 7.17 OQPSK modulation: (a) input binary signal in polar form, (b) signal decomposition into two independent signals, and (c) transmitted signal.

orthogonal. In expressing MSK as a special case of OQPSK, the MSK signal can be expressed as follows:

$$s(t) = a_I(t)\sqrt{\frac{2E_s}{T_s}}\cos(2\pi f_c t)\cos\left(\frac{\pi t}{2T_b}\right) - a_Q(t)\sqrt{\frac{2E_s}{T_s}}\sin(2\pi f_c t)\sin\left(\frac{\pi t}{2T_b}\right) \quad (7.13a)$$

where $a_I(t)$ and $a_Q(t)$ represent the odd-numbered and even-numbered input bits, respectively. This shows that the two carriers are weighted by sinusoids of frequency $\frac{1}{4T_b}$. The two weighted carriers are orthogonal over the interval of two-bit duration, and have the same energy. MSK can thus be viewed as a special case of OQPSK with sinusoidal pulse shaping used in place of rectangular pulses. Figure 7.18 shows how an MSK signal can be formed.

In QPSK, the phase-shift $\theta(t)$ assumes one of the four constant values for every two input bits (i.e., the entire duration of a symbol), depending on the two consecutive bits being transmitted. In MSK, on the other hand, the phase-shift $\theta(t)$ is a function of time, and for the duration of a bit, it varies linearly with time with the slope of $\frac{\pi}{4T_b}$ or $-\frac{\pi}{4T_b}$, and depending on the two consecutive bits being transmitted, a 0 is represented by a linear increase in phase and a 1 by a linear decrease in phase. Assuming Gray code is employed, Figure 7.19 provides insight into the carrier phase for QPSK scheme and the carrier phase for MSK scheme with the initial condition $\theta(0) = 0$.

The bit error rate of MSK is the same as those of QPSK and OQPSK, and the power spectral density of MSK, as shown in Figure 7.16, is as follows:

$$S_{MSK}(f) = \frac{8E_b}{\pi^2}\left(\left(\frac{\cos(2\pi T_b(f - f_c))}{16T_b^2(f - f_c)^2 - 1}\right)^2 + \left(\frac{\cos(2\pi T_b(f + f_c))}{16T_b^2(f + f_c)^2 - 1}\right)^2\right) \quad (7.13b)$$

The MSK spectrum rolls off at a rate proportional to the inverse fourth power of frequency, whereas in the case of the QPSK signal, the spectrum falls off as the inverse square of the frequency. The MSK decay reflects the fact that there are no discontinuities in the transmitted signal.

For MSK, the transmission bandwidth, which contains 99% of the total power, is less 20% higher than the bit rate $\left(< \frac{1.2}{T_b}\right)$, while QPSK/OQPSK has a bandwidth that is a bit more than eight times the bit rate $\left(> \frac{8}{T_b}\right)$. However, for the null-to-null bandwidth, QPSK and OQPSK are more spectrally efficient than MSK.

The quaternary signaling schemes have superior performance to their binary counterparts. For instance, the bandwidth requirements for MSK and

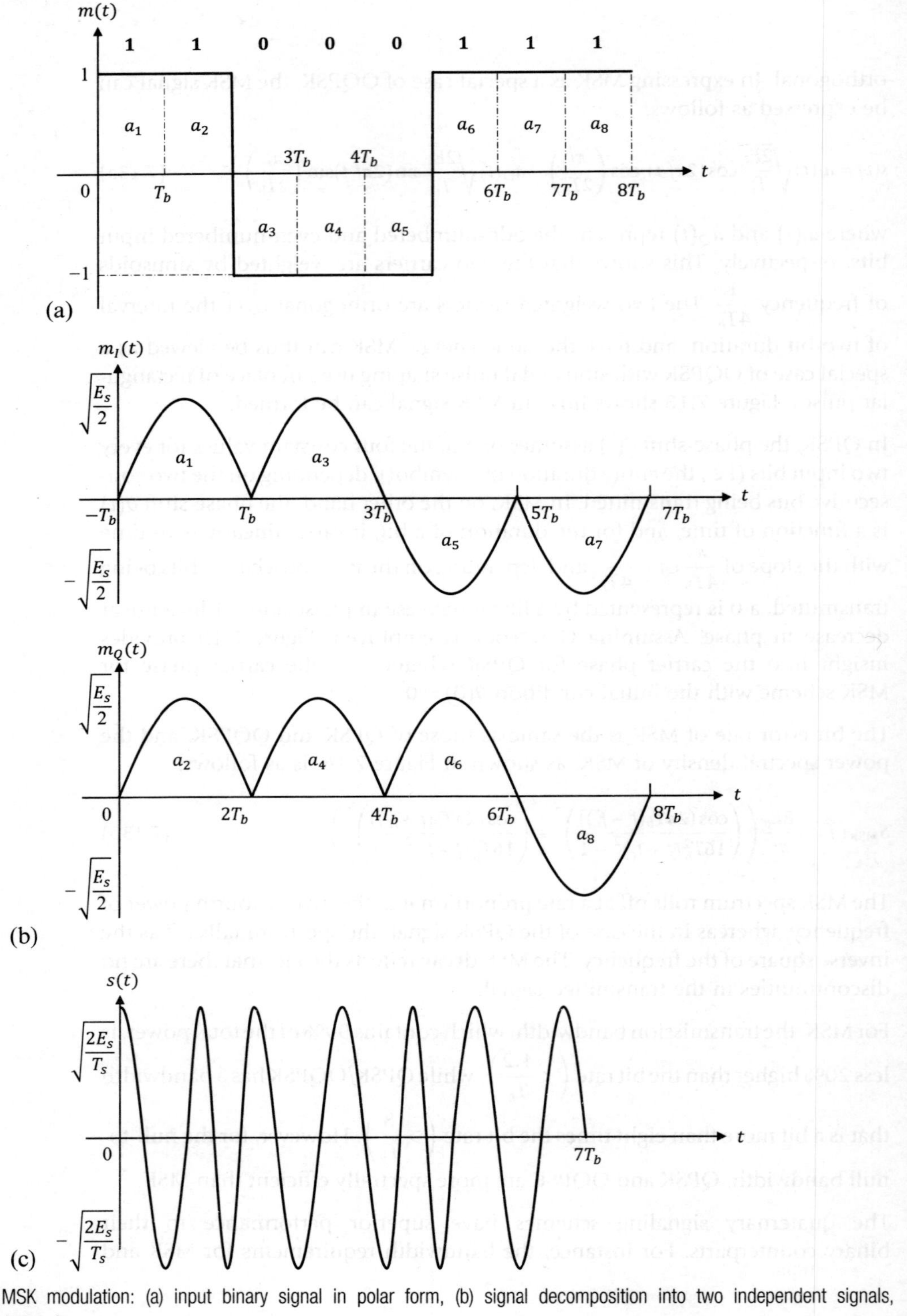

FIGURE 7.18 MSK modulation: (a) input binary signal in polar form, (b) signal decomposition into two independent signals, and (c) transmitted signal.

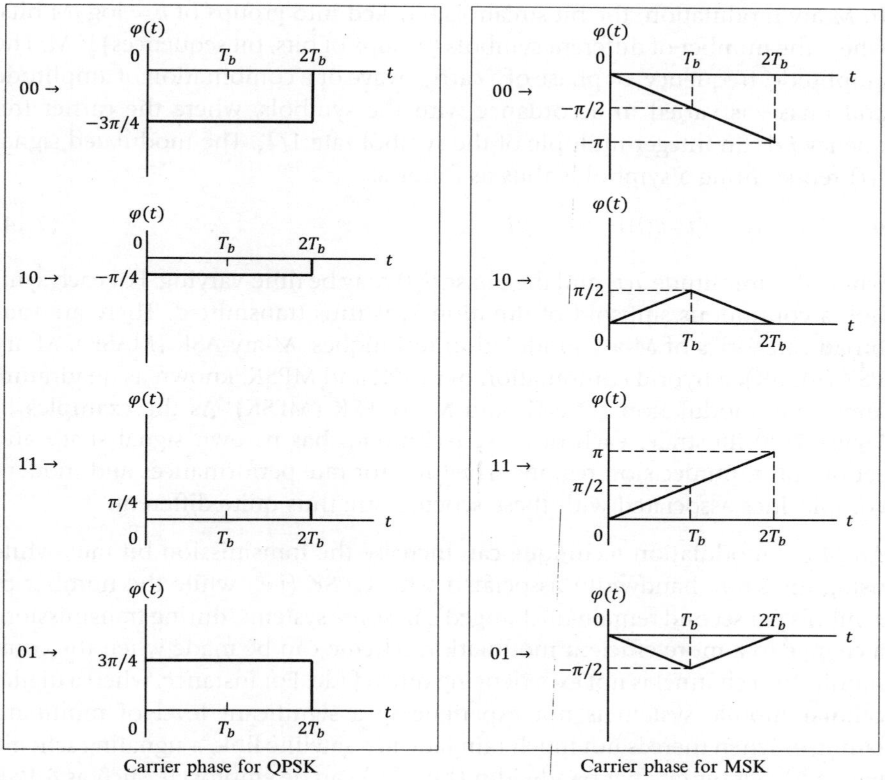

FIGURE 7.19 Carrier phases for QPSK and MSK schemes.

QPSK/OQPSK are half as much as those for BFSK and BPSK, respectively, while their bit error rates are no greater than their binary counterparts.

7.4 *M*-ARY COHERENT MODULATION TECHNIQUES

The bandwidth scarcity dictates the necessity of modulation techniques with significant spectral efficiency. For instance, using high-speed voice-band data modems, the upstream data transmission over the PSTN (i.e., the digital data from the user's premises to the central office over the twisted-pair telephone line) is carried out at 33.6 kbps over a bandwidth of 4 kHz set by the channel filter at the central office. This in turn requires a spectral efficiency of 8.4 bits per second per Hertz (bps/Hz), and *M*-ary modulation is thus required. *M*-ary modulation techniques are widely used in bandwidth-limited channels, as they can help conserve bandwidth quite significantly, but of course at the expense of an increase in bit error rate and modem complexity.

In M-ary modulation, the bit stream is blocked into groups of $k = \log_2 M$ bits, where the number of different symbols (groups of bits, bit sequences) is M. The amplitude, frequency, or phase of a carrier wave or a combination of amplitude and phase, is varied in accordance with the symbols, where the carrier frequency f_c is an integer multiple of the symbol rate $1/T_s$. The modulated signal $s(t)$ representing a symbol is thus as follows:

$$s(t) = a(t)\cos(2\pi f_c t + \theta(t)), \quad 0 \le t \le T_s \tag{7.14}$$

where the amplitude $a(t)$ and the phase $\theta(t)$ may be time-varying. For each symbol, a continuous sinusoid of duration T_s is thus transmitted. There are four broad categories of M-ary modulation techniques: M-ary ASK (MASK), M-ary PSK (MPSK), a hybrid combination of MASK and MPSK, known as quadrature amplitude modulation (QAM), and M-ary FSK (MFSK). As the examples in Figure 7.20 illustrate, each of these techniques has its own signal space and set of optimum decision regions. The bit error rate performances and modem complexities associated with these schemes are thus quite different.

An M-ary modulation technique can increase the transmission bit rate, while using the same bandwidth associated with QPSK (i.e., while the number of symbols per second remain unchanged). In some systems, during transmission, a change to a more efficient modulation scheme can be made when the communication channel is not experiencing much fade. For instance, when a digital cellular mobile system is not experiencing a significant level of multipath fading or when there is not much rain fade in a satellite link, a signaling scheme with a higher bit rate per bandwidth (bps/Hz) can be employed, such as 8-PSK or 16-QAM instead of QPSK. ***Adaptive modulation*** can thus enhance the link throughput and system capacity, but at the expense of an increase in modem complexity and/or a modest degradation in performance.

7.4.1 *M*-ary Amplitude-Shift Keying

M-ary amplitude-shift keying (MASK) is not a widely-used modulation scheme. However, a vestigial sideband (VSB) version of 8-ASK signaling scheme is employed in the HDTV standard in the US. MASK employs a set of M nonequal energy signals to represent M equally-likely symbols. In MASK, the amplitude of the carrier takes on one of M possible values $\sqrt{\frac{2E_i}{T_s}}$, where $i = 1, 2, \ldots, M$. The MASK signal set is thus analytically given by:

$$s_i(t) = \sqrt{\frac{2E_i}{T_s}}\cos(2\pi f_c t), \quad 0 \le t \le T_s, \quad i = 1, 2, \ldots, M \tag{7.15a}$$

where the frequency and phase both remain constant and only the carrier amplitude varies. We assume a uniform spacing of amplitude levels, where

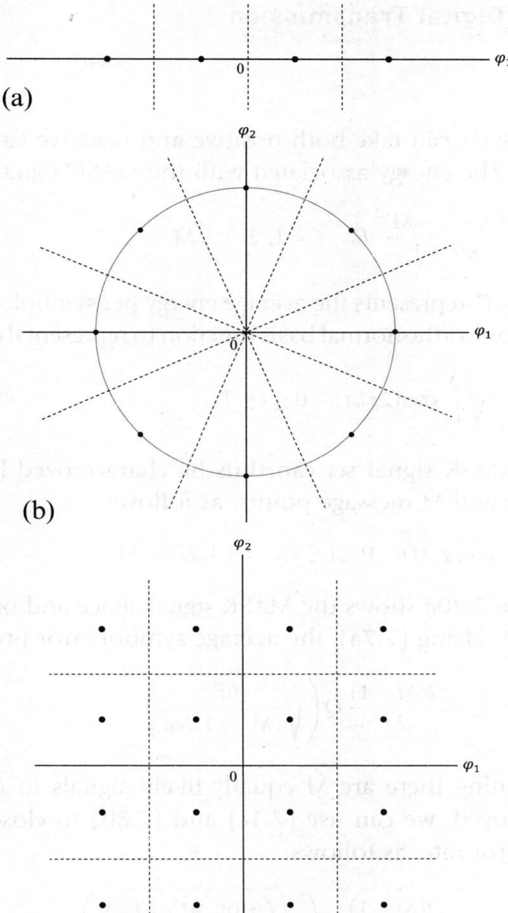

FIGURE 7.20 Signal space and optimum decision regions for M-ary modulation schemes: (a) MASK ($M = 4$), (b) MPSK ($M = 8$), (c) QAM ($M = 16$), and (d) MFSK ($M = 3$).

the levels can take both positive and negative values and their mean value is zero. The energy associated with the MASK signal set is as follows:

$$E_i = \frac{3(2i-1-M)^2}{M^2-1} E_s, \quad i = 1, 2, \ldots, M \tag{7.15b}$$

where E_s represents the average energy per symbol, as defined in (7.1b). We need only one orthonormal basis function to represent the MASK signal set, as given by:

$$\varphi_1(t) = \sqrt{\frac{2}{T_s}} \cos(2\pi f_c t), \quad 0 \le t \le T_s \tag{7.15c}$$

The MASK signal set can thus be characterized by a one-dimensional signal space and M message points, as follows:

$$s_i(t) = \sqrt{E_i}\, \varphi_1(t), \quad 0 \le t \le T_s, \quad i = 1, 2, \ldots, M \tag{7.15d}$$

Figure 7.20a shows the MASK signal space and optimum decision regions for $M = 4$. Using (7.7a), the average symbol error probability is as follows:

$$P_{\text{SER-MASK}} = \frac{2(M-1)}{M} Q\left(\sqrt{\frac{6E_s}{(M^2-1)N_0}}\right) \tag{7.15e}$$

Assuming there are M equally-likely signals in MASK and Gray mapping is employed, we can use (7.1c) and (7.8b) to closely approximate the average bit error rate, as follows:

$$P_{\text{BER-MASK}} \approx \frac{2(M-1)}{M \log_2 M} Q\left(\sqrt{\left(\frac{6 \log_2 M}{M^2-1}\right)\left(\frac{E_b}{N_0}\right)}\right) \tag{7.15f}$$

Figure 7.21 shows the MASK bit error rate performance in terms of signal-to-noise ratio per bit $\frac{E_b}{N_0}$.

7.4.2 *M*-ary Phase-Shift Keying

M-ary phase-shift keying (MPSK) is employed in some of the digital cellular standards and communication geostationary satellite systems. MPSK employs a set of M equal-energy signals to represent M equiprobable symbols. This constant energy restriction (i.e., the constant envelope constraint) warrants a circular constellation for the signal points. In MPSK, the phase of the carrier takes on one of M possible values $\frac{2\pi(i-1)}{M}$, where $i = 1, 2, \ldots, M$. The MPSK signal set is thus analytically given by:

$$s_i(t) = \sqrt{\frac{2E_i}{T_s}} \cos\left(2\pi f_c t - \frac{2\pi(i-1)}{M}\right), \quad 0 \le t \le T_s, \quad i = 1, 2, \ldots, M \tag{7.16a}$$

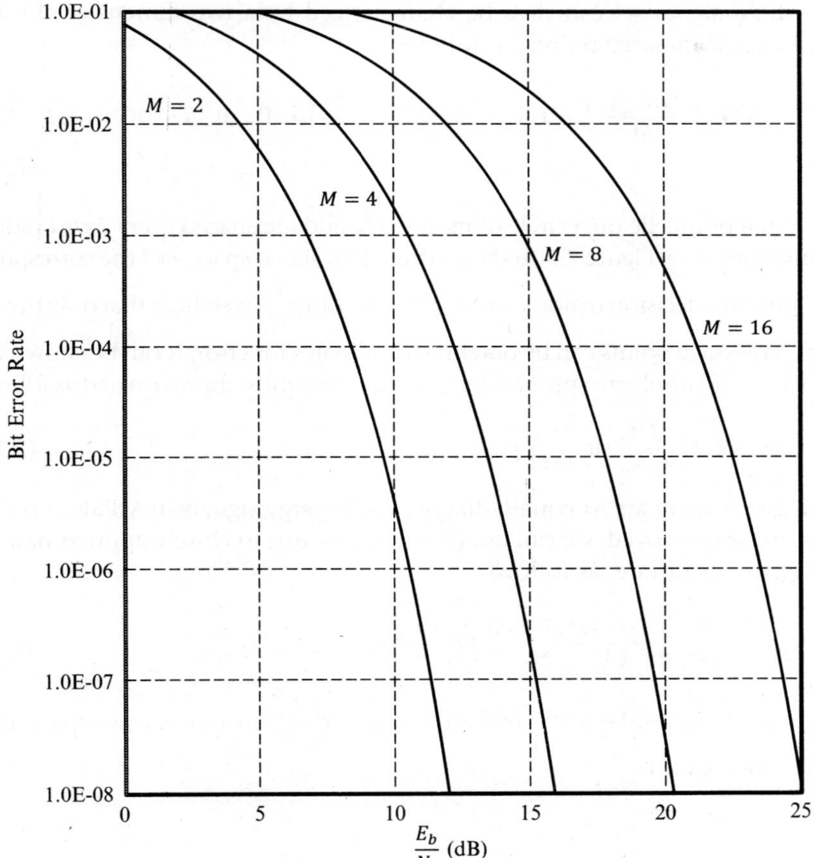

FIGURE 7.21 MASK bit error rate performance.

We assume a uniform spacing of phase values, i.e., the phase separation between any two adjacent signal points is constant. The energy associated with the MPSK signal set is as follows:

$$E_i = E_s, \quad i = 1, 2, \ldots, M \tag{7.16b}$$

where E_s represents the average energy per symbol, as defined in (7.1b). After using a trigonometric identity to expand $s_i(t)$ in (7.16a), it is easy to see that the following two orthonormal basis functions can represent the MPSK signal set:

$$\begin{aligned} \varphi_1(t) &= \sqrt{\frac{2}{T_s}} \cos(2\pi f_c t), \quad 0 \le t \le T_s \\ \varphi_2(t) &= \sqrt{\frac{2}{T_s}} \sin(2\pi f_c t), \quad 0 \le t \le T_s \end{aligned} \tag{7.16c}$$

The MPSK signal set can thus be characterized by a two-dimensional signal space and M message points, as follows:

$$s_i(t) = \sqrt{E_i}\,\cos\left(\frac{2\pi(i-1)}{M}\right)\varphi_1(t) + \sqrt{E_i}\,\sin\left(\frac{2\pi(i-1)}{M}\right)\varphi_2(t), \quad 0 \le t \le T_s, \quad i = 1, 2, \ldots, M \tag{7.16d}$$

The signal points lie on a circle of radius $\sqrt{E_s}$ and are spaced every $2\pi/M$ radians around the circle. Figure 7.20b shows the MPSK signal space and the corresponding optimum decision regions for $M = 8$. Assuming $\frac{E_s}{N_0}$ is so high that only the two nearest message points can be potential candidates for error, it can be shown that the average symbol error probability can then be tightly approximated as follows:

$$P_{\text{SER}-\text{MPSK}} \approx 2\,Q\left(\sqrt{\frac{2E_s}{N_0}}\,\sin\left(\frac{\pi}{M}\right)\right) \tag{7.16e}$$

Noting that there are M equally-likely equal-energy signals in MPSK and Gray mapping is employed, we can use (7.1c) and (7.8b) to closely approximate the average bit error rate, as follows:

$$P_{\text{BER}-\text{MPSK}} \approx \frac{2}{\log_2 M}\,Q\left(\sqrt{\frac{2E_b \log_2 M}{N_0}}\,\sin\left(\frac{\pi}{M}\right)\right) \tag{7.16f}$$

Figure 7.22 shows the MPSK bit error rate performance in terms of signal-to-noise ratio per bit $\frac{E_b}{N_0}$.

7.4.3 *M*-ary Quadrature Amplitude Modulation

***M*-ary quadrature amplitude modulation** (MQAM), simply known as QAM, is employed in many digital communication systems, including 16-QAM, 64-QAM, and 256-QAM in DOCSIS, an international telecommunications standard to provide high-speed Internet access over cable TV. Other applications of QAM lie in broadband digital cellular standards, such as LTE, WiMAX, as well as public safety standards, such as TETRA, and TV white spaces, such as cognitive WRAN.

QAM employs a set of M nonequal energy signals to represent M equally-likely symbols. Since QAM is a hybrid form of amplitude modulation and phase modulation, the amplitude and phase of the carrier takes on one of the possible values $\sqrt{\frac{2E_i}{T_s}}$ and θ_i, respectively, where $i = 1, 2, \ldots, M$. The in-phase and quadrature components are independent, and the envelope is no longer constrained to remain constant. The QAM signal set is thus analytically given by:

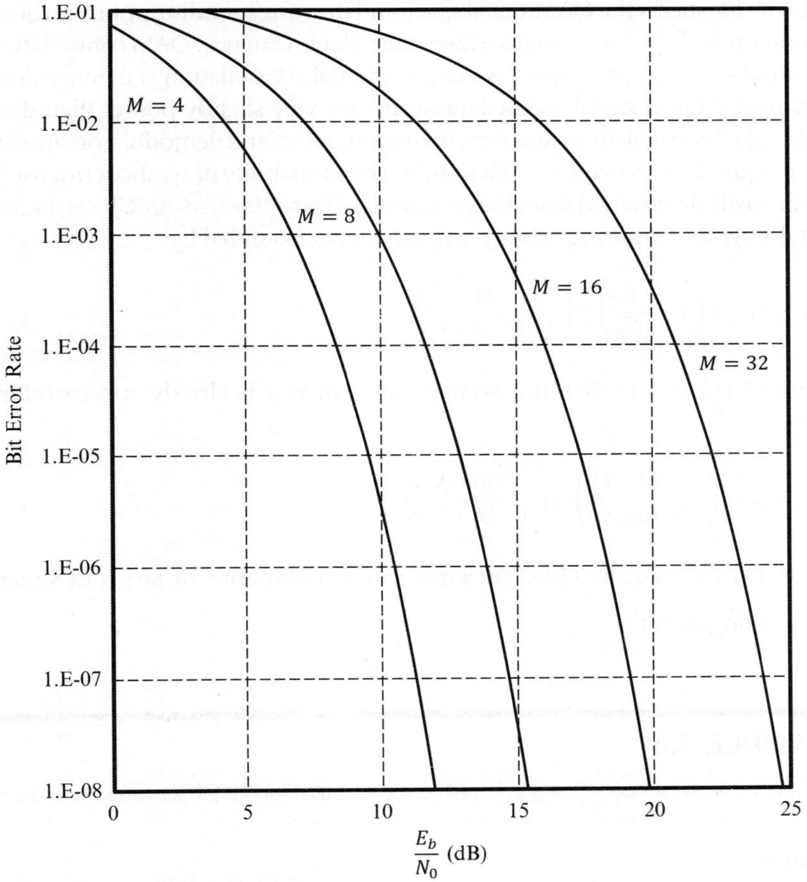

FIGURE 7.22 MPSK bit error rate performance.

$$s_i(t) = \sqrt{\frac{2E_i}{T_s}} \cos(2\pi f_c t - \theta_i), \quad 0 \le t \le T_s, \quad i = 1, 2, \ldots, M \tag{7.17a}$$

By expanding $s_i(t)$ in (7.17a), it is easy to identify the following two orthonormal basis functions:

$$\begin{aligned} \varphi_1(t) &= \sqrt{\frac{2}{T_s}} \cos(2\pi f_c t), \quad 0 \le t \le T_s \\ \varphi_2(t) &= \sqrt{\frac{2}{T_s}} \sin(2\pi f_c t), \quad 0 \le t \le T_s \end{aligned} \tag{7.17b}$$

The QAM signal set can thus be characterized by a two-dimensional signal space and M message points, as follows:

$$s_i(t) = \sqrt{E_i} \cos(\theta_i) \varphi_1(t) + \sqrt{E_i} \sin(\theta_i) \varphi_2(t), \quad 0 \le t \le T_s, \quad i = 1, 2, \ldots, M \tag{7.17c}$$

Figure 7.20c shows the QAM signal space and the corresponding optimum decision regions for $M = 16$. For a given M, there exist a large variety of QAM constellations. If the number of bits per symbol is even, the signal constellation is then rectangular. Rectangular QAM signal constellations are just very slightly poorer than the best QAM signal constellation, however, their modulators and demodulators are simple, as it is equivalent to two $\sqrt{M}$-ASK signals. The probability of symbol error for QAM can be easily determined from the probability of error for $\sqrt{M}$-ASK. It can be shown that the symbol error probability is tightly upper bounded by:

$$P_{\text{SER-QAM}} \leq 4\left(1 - \frac{1}{\sqrt{M}}\right) Q\left(\sqrt{\frac{3E_s}{(M-1)N_0}}\right) \tag{7.17d}$$

Using (7.1c) and (7.8b), the average bit error rate is closely approximated as follows:

$$P_{\text{BER-QAM}} \approx \left(\frac{4(\sqrt{M}-1)}{\sqrt{M}\log_2 M}\right) Q\left(\sqrt{\frac{3\log_2 M}{M-1}\frac{E_b}{N_0}}\right) \tag{7.17e}$$

Figure 7.23 shows the QAM bit error rate performance in terms of signal-to-noise ratio per bit $\frac{E_b}{N_0}$.

EXAMPLE 7.5

Assuming the signal size M is a power of 4, compare MPSK and QAM schemes, in terms of the average signal-to-noise ratio per bit for a low bit error rate.

Solutions

Since the bit error rate is dominated almost exclusively by the argument of the Q-function, especially for a low bit error rate, the factors in (7.16f) and (7.17e), by which Q-functions are multiplied, can be disregarded. The ratio of the two arguments in the Q-functions in dB is then as follows:

$$D = 1.76 - 10\log(M-1) - 20\log\left(\sin\frac{\pi}{M}\right) \text{ (dB)}$$

The parameter D, which represents the additional $\frac{E_b}{N_0}$ required by MPSK to deliver the same low bit error rate that QAM delivers, is reflected below:

M	D (dB)
4	0
16	4.20
64	9.95
256	15.92
1024	21.93

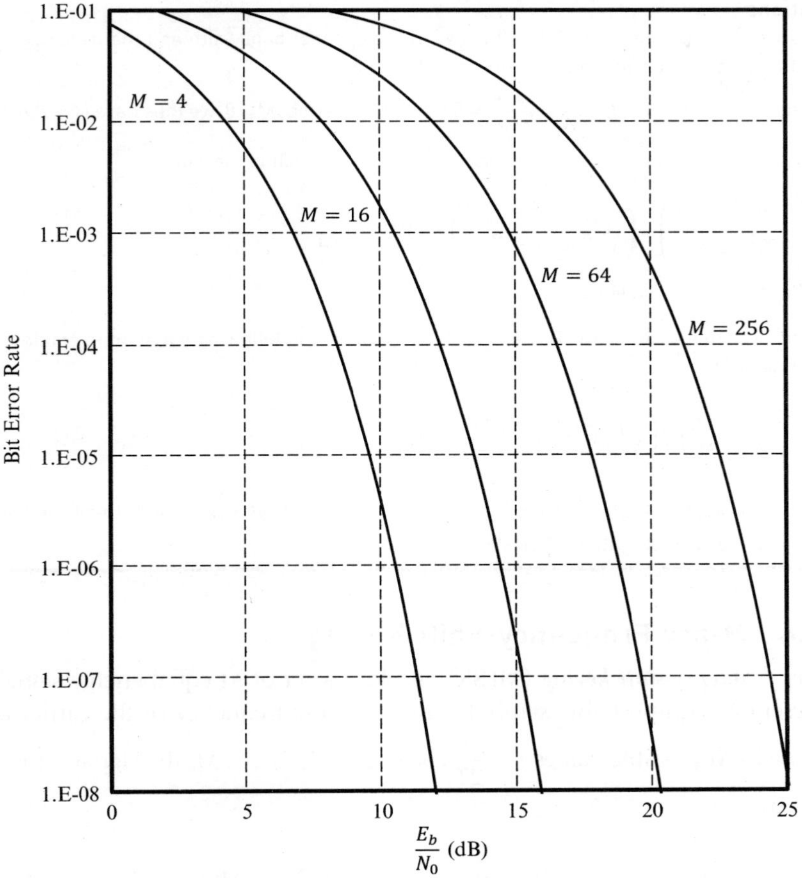

FIGURE 7.23 QAM bit error rate performance.

It is evident that for rather large M by doubling the number of signal points M, a gain advantage of QAM over MPSK is about 3 dB. The gain advantage is at the expense of increased sensitivity to amplitude and phase degradation in the transmission. Since QAM is not a constant amplitude modulation, it is important to ensure that the power amplifier at the transmitter operates in the linear region.

EXAMPLE 7.6

Suppose the transmission bit rate over a bandpass channel is 51.84 Mbps, QAM modulation with Nyquist filtering is employed, and the average bit error rate is 10^{-7}.

(a) Suppose the available channel bandwidth is 6.48 MHz, determine the required $\frac{E_b}{N_0}$.

(b) Suppose the available $\frac{E_b}{N_0}$ is 15.18 dB, determine the required channel bandwidth.

Solutions

This example highlights the trade-off between the channel bandwidth and the transmit power. Note that Nyquist filtering implies zero roll-off factor.

(a) The spectral efficiency is $\frac{r_b}{W} = \frac{51.84}{6.48} = 8$ bps/Hz. Since $\log_2 M = 8$, we thus have $M = 256$. Using (7.17e), we solve the following equation to obtain x, which is the value of $\frac{E_b}{N_0}$:

$$\left(\frac{4\left(\sqrt{256}-1\right)}{\sqrt{256}\log_2 256}\right) Q\left(\sqrt{\frac{3\log_2 256}{256-1}10^{x/10}}\right) = 10^{-7}$$

We thus get $x = 24.34$ dB.

(b) The available $\frac{E_b}{N_0}$ is 15.18 dB. Using (7.17e), we solve the following equation to obtain the value of M:

$$\left(\frac{4\left(\sqrt{M}-1\right)}{\sqrt{M}\log_2 M}\right) Q\left(\sqrt{\frac{3\log_2 M}{M-1}10^{15.18/10}}\right) = 10^{-7}$$

We thus get $M = 16$. Since we have $\frac{r_b}{W} = \log_2 M$, we can find W from $\frac{51.84}{W} = \log_2 16 = 4$ bps/Hz. The required bandwidth W is thus 12.96 MHz.

7.4.4 *M*-ary Frequency-Shift Keying

M-ary frequency-shift keying (MFSK) employs a set of M equal-energy signals to represent M equiprobable symbols. In MFSK, the frequency of the carrier takes on one of M possible values $f_c + \frac{i}{2T_s}$, where $i = 1, 2, \ldots, M$, the signal set is thus given by:

$$s_i(t) = \sqrt{\frac{2E_s}{T_s}}\cos\left(2\pi\left(f_c + \frac{i}{2T_s}\right)t\right), \quad 0 \le t \le T_s, \quad i = 1, 2, \ldots, M \tag{7.18a}$$

where f_c, the frequency of the unmodulated carrier, is an integer multiple of the symbol rate $\frac{1}{T_s}$. Since the individual frequencies are separated by $\frac{1}{2T_s}$ Hz, the signals are orthogonal. There are therefore M orthonormal basis functions to represent the MFSK signal set, as follows:

$$\varphi_i(t) = \sqrt{\frac{2}{T_s}}\cos\left(2\pi\left(f_c + \frac{i}{2T_s}\right)t\right), \quad 0 \le t \le T_s, \quad i = 1, 2, \ldots, M \tag{7.18b}$$

The MFSK signal set can thus be characterized by an M-dimensional signal space and M message points, as follows:

$$s_i(t) = \sqrt{E_s}\varphi_i(t), \quad 0 \le t \le T_s, \quad i = 1, 2, \ldots, M \tag{7.18c}$$

Figure 7.20d shows the MFSK signal space and the corresponding optimum decision regions for $M = 3$. As it is very difficult to derive the symbol error rate, union bound is employed. It can be shown that as $\frac{E_S}{N_0}$ increases the symbol error rate for MFSK using coherent detection is tightly upper bounded, as follows:

$$P_{SER-MFSK} \leq (M-1)Q\left(\sqrt{\frac{E_S}{N_0}}\right) \tag{7.18d}$$

Using (7.1c) and (7.8a), the bit error rate for MFSK is bounded as follows:

$$P_{BER-MFSK} \leq \left(\frac{M}{2}\right)Q\left(\sqrt{\frac{E_b \log_2 M}{N_0}}\right) \tag{7.18e}$$

Note that for $M=2$, the bound becomes an equality. Figure 7.24 shows the MFSK bit error rate performance in terms of signal-to-noise ratio per bit $\frac{E_b}{N_0}$. An increase in M brings about a reduction in the bit error rate.

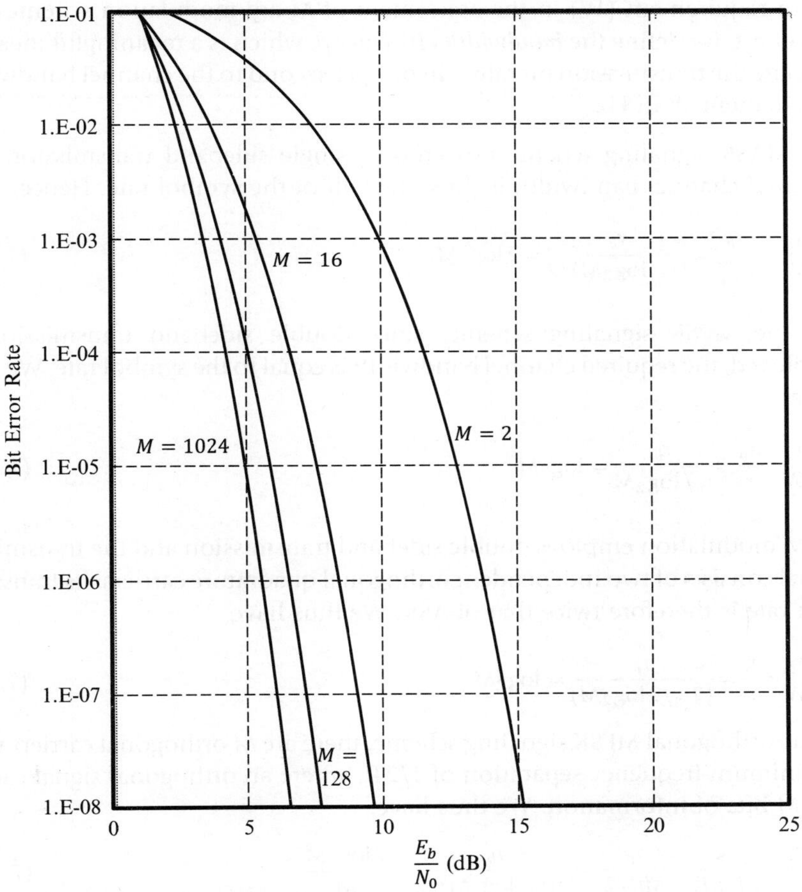

FIGURE 7.24 MFSK bit error rate performance.

7.4.5 Comparison of *M*-ary Modulation Schemes

MFSK and MPSK signals have constant envelope (i.e., the amplitude of the carrier remains constant). This feature allows them to be more robust to amplitude nonlinearities, which exist in high-frequency radio communications, such as satellite channels. QAM can be generated by the MPSK transmitter; the only difference is that the symbol mapping for QAM generates nonconstant symbol amplitudes.

The bit error rate performance for all M-ary modulation schemes can be improved at the expense of an increase in signal-to-noise ratio per bit $\frac{E_b}{N_0}$. M-ary modulation schemes can thus be compared in terms of the required $\frac{E_b}{N_0}$ to achieve a certain bit error rate. It is, however, important to include the impact of the ***modulation efficiency*** (M), transmission bit rate (r_b), and bandwidth requirement (W) in the assessment of M-ary modulation schemes. To this effect, we define the ***bandwidth efficiency*** ρ, which is a meaningful measure to relate the transmission bit rate r_b in bits per second to the channel bandwidth requirement W in Hz.

The MASK signaling scheme can employ single sideband transmission, the required channel bandwidth is thus one half of the symbol rate. Hence,

$$\rho=\frac{r_b}{W}=\frac{r_b}{r_s/2}=\frac{r_b}{(r_b/\log_2 M)/2}=2\log_2 M \tag{7.19a}$$

For the MPSK signaling scheme, since double sideband transmission is employed, the required channel bandwidth is equal to the symbol rate. We thus have:

$$\rho=\frac{r_b}{W}=\frac{r_b}{r_s}=\frac{r_b}{r_b/\log_2 M}=\log_2 M \tag{7.19b}$$

QAM modulation employs double sideband transmission and the transmitted signal consists of two independent orthogonal quadrature carriers, its transmission rate is therefore twice that of ASK. We thus have:

$$\rho=\frac{r_b}{W}=\frac{r_b}{r_s}=\frac{r_b}{(2r_b/2\log_2 M)}=\log_2 M \tag{7.19c}$$

In the orthogonal MFSK signaling scheme, there are M orthogonal carriers with a minimum frequency separation of $1/2T_s$, where an orthogonal signal carries $\log_2 M$ bits of information. We thus have:

$$\rho=\frac{r_b}{W}=\frac{r_b}{M/2T_s}=\frac{r_b}{Mr_s/2}=\frac{r_b}{M(r_b/\log_2 M)/2}=\frac{2\log_2 M}{M} \tag{7.19d}$$

For MASK, MPSK, and QAM modulation schemes, the bandwidth efficiency ρ is an increasing function of M (i.e., for a fixed bit rate r_b, as M increases, the channel bandwidth W decreases logarithmically). Therefore, they are attractive modulation candidates for bandwidth-limited channels. In fact, QAM and MPSK are widely used in wire-line telephone channels employing high-speed voice-band modems and in digital cellular wireless channels providing broadband multimedia communications.

For MFSK, the bandwidth efficiency ρ is a decreasing function of M, and we always have $\rho \leq 1$. As such, for a fixed bit rate r_b, as M increases, the channel bandwidth W for MFSK increases. To this effect, MFSK is most suited for power-limited channels. Using (7.18e) and noting $Q(x) < \exp\left(-\frac{x^2}{2}\right)$, the following upper bound on the bit error rate for MFSK can be obtained:

$$P_{BER}(e) \leq \exp - \left(\frac{\ln(0.5M)}{\ln 4} \left(\frac{E_b}{N_0} - \ln 4 \right) \right) \tag{7.20}$$

Equation (7.20) shows that as long as $\left(\frac{E_b}{N_0} - \ln 4\right) > 0$, i.e., $\frac{E_b}{N_0} > 1.42$ dB, the bit error rate for MSK is a decreasing function of M. For the MFSK, as $M \to \infty$, the bit error rate can be thus made as small as possible, provided that we have $\frac{E_b}{N_0} > 1.42$ dB, but of course the bandwidth required for such a transmission is then infinite.

It is also meaningful to compare M-ary modulation schemes in terms of signal space, as we can divide them in two distinct groups. For MASK, MPSK, and QAM, the dimensionality of the signal space remains unchanged as more signals (i.e., larger values of M) are included. In other words, signal points are packed closer together as the number of signal points is increased. This in turn yields degradation of the symbol error rate, while the required bandwidth, regardless of the value of M, remains essentially constant. As the number of signal points (states) in MASK, MPSK, and QAM is increased, the bandwidth efficiency can thus be improved, but at the expense of an increase in the bit error rate performance. Although MPSK and QAM have identical bandwidth efficiencies, for a fixed peak transmitted power, the average bit error rate performance for QAM is better than that for MPSK (i.e., QAM has a better power efficiency than MPSK). This improved performance can be achieved if the channel is linear and the transmit amplifier can operate in linear region. However, for MFSK, an increase in M brings about a direct increase in the dimensionality, and in turn a significant increase in modem complexity. With increasing dimensionality as more signals are added, the signal points do not need to be crowded closer together. In MFSK, as M increases, the power efficiency increases. In fact, as M increases, the Shannon limit can be achieved. MFSK can thus be used in the deep space communications, where there is a huge bandwidth available in EHF band.

7.5 ORTHOGONAL FREQUENCY-DIVISION MULTIPLEXING

Orthogonal frequency-division multiplexing (OFDM) is a multicarrier modulation technique used in European digital audio broadcasting (DAB) and digital video broadcasting (DVB), digital subscriber line (DSL), wireless local area networks (WLAN), widely known as Wi-Fi (IEEE 802.11) connectivity, and mobile Wi-MAX (IEEE 802.16) networks. OFDM is effective when the magnitude response of the bandpass channel is not flat in the frequency domain over the bandwidth of interest. However, over a very small portion of the channel bandwidth, the magnitude response is approximately constant. The primary reason to employ OFDM is its resilience to the multipath distortion in mobile channels and the linear distortion in the telephone local loop. The alternative to OFDM in a channel with severe distortion is to employ single-carrier transmission with an equalizer with a very high degree of complexity. With multicarrier transmission, the spectrum of the individual carriers is relatively undistorted except for possible gain change and phase rotation.

It is important to highlight that FDM, as discussed later, is a multiplexing technique for analog signals and OFDM is a modulation technique to combat the nonideality of the bandpass channel. The major differences between them lie in the fact that OFDM uses multiple sub-carriers that are mutually orthogonal to one another, and the sub-carriers are overlapping to maximize spectral efficiency, while not causing adjacent channel interference. In addition, OFDM, vis-à-vis FDM, lends itself to digital transmission, and requires strict frequency synchronization, but with relaxed bandpass filter requirements.

The basic idea of OFDM is to transmit blocks of symbols in parallel by employing a large number of orthogonal sub-carriers. With block transmission, the source symbols are converted into a block of parallel modulated symbols each with period that is much larger than the length of the channel ISI. Since the symbol rate on each sub-carrier is much less than the source rate (i.e., the symbol period on each sub-carrier is much greater than the source symbol period), the effects of ISI are greatly reduced.

In OFDM, the available channel bandwidth W is sub-divided into a number of equal-bandwidth sub-channels K, where the bandwidth of a sub-channel Δf is small enough so the frequency response characteristic of the sub-channel can be considered almost ideal. With each sub-channel, we have the following sub-carrier:

$$c_k(t) = \cos(2\pi f_k t), \quad k = 1, 2, \ldots, K \tag{7.21}$$

where the sub-carrier frequency $f_k = (2k-1)W/2K, k = 1, 2, \ldots, K$, is the mid-frequency in the k-th sub-channel. The sub-carrier spacing is thus as follows:

$$\Delta f = f_{k+1} - f_k = \frac{W}{K} \tag{7.22}$$

Suppose the symbol rate on each of the sub-channels is selected to be equal to the sub-carrier spacing, i.e., we have:

$$\frac{1}{T} = \Delta f \tag{7.23}$$

Using (7.21) to (7.23), the modulated sub-carriers are then mutually orthogonal over the symbol period T, independently of their initial phases, i.e., we have:

$$\int_0^T \cos(2\pi f_k t)\cos(2\pi f_j t)\,dt = 0, \tag{7.24}$$

where $f_k - f_j = \frac{n}{T}$, for $n = 1, 2, \ldots$. As (7.24) expresses an orthogonality property, we now have OFDM. In short, instead of sending serial symbols at a rate K/T over a channel with bandwidth W, K symbols in parallel, each at the rate of $1/T$, are sent over a sub-channel with bandwidth W/K. With OFDM, the symbol duration becomes K times longer and the effects of ISI and multipath can be thus reduced. To minimize ISI caused by multipath for a given channel bandwidth W, we select K so that T is significantly greater than the duration of the channel time-dispersion. The ISI can be made arbitrarily small through appropriate selection of K, that is, with large enough K, we can ensure that the frequency response of each sub-channel is constant. OFDM thus provides multiple flat fading channels.

Figure 7.25 shows the block diagrams for an OFDM transmitter and receiver. The IDFT at the transmitter transforms the frequency-domain data at the modulator output into time-domain output and the DFT at the receiver performs the inverse operation. For efficient implementation of DFT and IDFT, the FFT algorithm is employed.

There are two methods to further reduce ISI. One method is to insert a time guard between the transmissions of successive data blocks; this allows the channel response to die out before the next block of K symbols is transmitted. The other method is to insert cyclic prefix, that is, to append the last samples of a symbol to the beginning of the symbol (i.e., repetition of the end). In order for the cyclic prefix to be effective, the length of the cyclic prefix must be at least equal to the length of the channel impulse response.

In OFDM, when the signals in the K sub-channels add constructively in phase, large signal peaks occur and may thus saturate the power amplifier. This can in turn cause intermodulation interference. This is known as the ***peak-to-average ratio*** (PAR) problem. This problem can, however, be reduced by power backoff

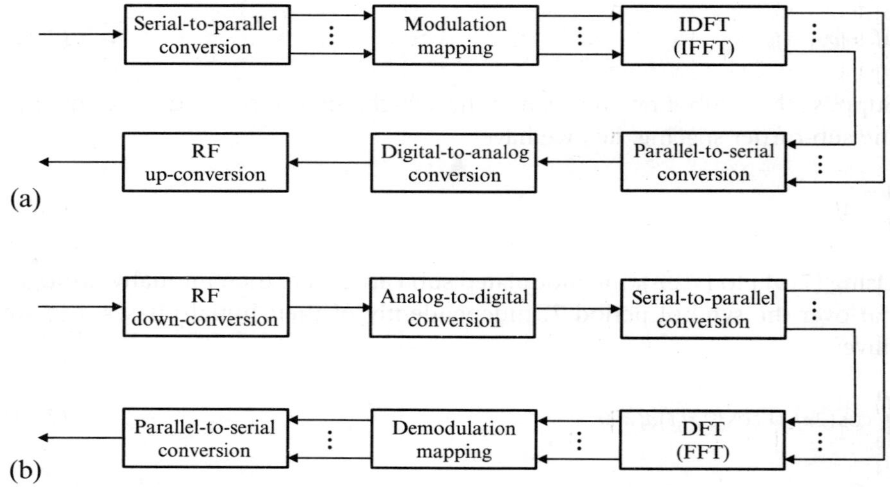

FIGURE 7.25 Block diagram of an orthogonal frequency-division multiplexing: (a) transmitter and (b) receiver.

at the expense of inefficient operation of the OFDM, or by phase adjustments where sub-carriers have pseudo-randomly phase shifts, or by peak clipping at the expense of some signal distortion, to name just few. There is no single best technique to address PAR-reduction problem.

Summary and Sources

Modulation is a salient requirement for all passband channels, including all wireless communication systems. The primary motivation for the widely-used M-ary modulation schemes, such as MPSK and QAM, is bandwidth conservation, but at the expense of an increase in transmit power and/or an increase in bit error rate. On the other hand, MFSK with its significant expansion of bandwidth allows a reduction in transmit power and/or a decrease in bit error rate.

A classic presentation of optimum receivers can be found in [1]. There are also several books at the graduate level that provide a detailed treatment of digital modulation techniques [2–7]. A nice treatment of OFDM in practical systems can be found in [8] and a detailed review of all major aspects of OFDM in [9]. There are a number of pertinent references which cover various aspects of passband digital transmission [10–18].

[1] J.M. Wozencraft and I.M. Jacobs, *Principles of Communication Engineering*, John Wiley & Sons, ISBN: 0-471-96240-6, 1965.

[2] T.T. Ha, *Theory and Design of Digital Communication Systems*, Cambridge University Press, ISBN: 978-0-521-76174-1, 2011.

[3] R.G. Gallager, *Principles of Digital Communication*, Cambridge University Press, ISBN: 9780521879071, 2008.

[4] R.D. Gitlin, J.F. Hayes, and S.B. Weinstein, *Data Communications Principles*, Plenum Press, ISBN: 0-306-43777-5, 1992.

[5] B. Sklar, *Digital Communications*, second ed., Prentice-Hall, ISBN: 0-13-084788-7, 2001.

[6] J.G. Proakis and M. Salehi, *Digital Communications*, fifth ed., McGraw-Hill, ISBN: 978-0-07-295716-7, 2008.

[7] H. Nguyen and E. Shwedyk, *A First Course in Digital Communications*, ISBN: 978-0-521-87613-1, 2009, Cambridge.

[8] J.A.C. Bingham, Multicarrier modulation for data transmission: an idea whose time has come, *IEEE Comm. Mag.* 28 (May 1990) 5–14.

[9] A.F. Molisch, *Wireless Communications*, second ed., Wiley-IEEE. ISBN: 978-0-470-74186-3, 2011.

[10] T. Jiang and Y. Wu, An overview: peak-to-average power ratio reduction techniques for OFDM signals, *IEEE Trans. Broadcast.* 54 (June 2008) 257–268.

[11] S. Pasupathy, Minimum shift keying: a spectrally efficient modulation, *IEEE Comm. Mag.* 17 (April 1979) 14–22.

[12] J.D. Gibson, *The Communications Handbook*, second ed., CRC Press, ISBN: 0-8493-0967-0, 2002.

[13] D.R. Smith, *Digital Transmission Systems*, third ed., Kluwer, ISBN: 1-4020-7587-1, 2004.

[14] I.A. Glover and P.M. Grant, *Digital Communications*, third ed., Pearson, ISBN: 978-0-273-71830-7, 2010.

[15] J.G. Proakis and M. Salehi, *Fundamentals of Communication Systems*, second ed., Pearson, ISBN: 978-0-13-335485-0, 2014.

[16] B.P. Lathi and Z. Ding, *Modern Digital and Analog Communication Systems*, fourth ed., Oxford University Press, ISBN: 978-0-19-533145-5, 2009.

[17] S. Haykin, *Digital Communication Systems*, John Wiley & Sons, ISBN: 978-0-471-64735-5, 2014.

[18] K.S. Shanmugam, *Digital and Analog Communication Systems*, John Wiley & Sons, ISBN: 0-471-03090-2, 1979.

Problems

7.1 The split-phase (Manchester) code is used for the transmission of equally-likely symbols 1 and 0. Assuming AWGN, draw the optimum matched filter and find the average symbol error rate.

7.2 The bit rate in a passband digital transmission system is 5 kbps. Assuming the power spectral density of the AWGN is 10^{-11} W/Hz and the carrier amplitude is 1 mV, determine the average bit error rate if coherent BPSK signaling scheme is employed.

7.3 The bit stream 000110010101001011 is to be transmitted using the differential 8-PSK signaling scheme. Determine the transmitted phase sequence, and show that the phase comparison scheme can be used for demodulation of the signal.

7.4 The bit rate in a passband digital transmission system is 1 Mbps. Assuming the power spectral density of the AWGN is 10^{-10} W/Hz and the bit error rate must be less than 10^{-4}, determine the values of $\frac{E_b}{N_0}$ for coherent BPSK and differential BPSK detection schemes.

7.5 The bit rate in a passband digital data transmission system is 3 Mbps. Assuming the power spectral density of the AWGN is 10^{-12} W/Hz and the bit error requirement is 10^{-8}, determine the bandwidth and power requirements for QPSK and 16-FSK schemes.

7.6 One of the nine equally-likely messages is transmitted over an AWGN channel. A signal point is represented by (a, b). in a two-dimensional signal constellation, where a. and b each could have values of d, 0, and $-d$. Determine the average symbol error in terms of d.

7.7 There are two alternate designs, corresponding to two different sets of signaling waveforms. Assume in each design, there are six equally-likely signal points. In one design, all six signal points are equally-spaced on a circle with radius d_1, and in the other design, a signal point is represented by (a, b) in a two dimensional signal constellation, where a could have values of d_2, 0, and $-d_2$ and b could have values $d_2/2$ and $-d_2/2$. Assuming that the average power is the same for both signal sets, compare the robustness against the additive white Gaussian noise channel.

7.8 The following signal set is usedo communicate one of four equally-likely messages over a channel disturbed by AWGN: $s_1(t) = -u\left(t - \frac{T_s}{2}\right) + u(t - T_s)$, $s_2(t) = u(t) - u(t - T_s)$, $s_3(t) = u\left(t - \frac{T_s}{2}\right) - u(t - T_s)$, $s_4(t) = -u(t) + u(t - T_s)$, where T_s is the symbol duration. Draw the block diagram of the optimum receiver.

7.9 A correlation receiver for a BPSK system uses a carrier reference $\sin(2\pi f_c t)$ for detecting two equally-likely signals $s_1(t) = \sin(2\pi f_c t + \Delta\theta)$ and $s_2(t) = \cos(2\pi f_c t + \Delta\theta)$. Assuming an AWGN channel, determine the average bit error rate in terms of $\Delta\theta$.

7.10 Suppose one of the following eight equally-likely messages is communicated over an AWGN channel: $s_1(t) = u(t) - u(t-1)$, $s_2(t) = u(t-1) - u(t-2)$, $s_3(t) = u(t) - u(t-2)$, $s_4(t) = u(t-2) - u(t-3)$, $s_5(t) = u(t) - u(t-1) + u(t-2) - u(t-3)$, $s_6(t) = 0$, $s_7(t) = u(t-1) - u(t-3)$, and $s_8(t) = u(t) - u(t-3)$. Determine the average symbol error rate.

7.11 The MPSK signaling scheme is employed over an AWGN channel to transmit one of $M > 2$ equally-likely messages. Use geometric arguments to show that the minimum attainable symbol error rate is bounded by p and $2p$, where $p = Q\left(\sqrt{\frac{2E_s}{N_0}} \sin\left(\frac{\pi}{M}\right)\right)$.

7.12 Show that the following three functions are pairwise orthogonal over the interval $(-2, 2)$:

$f_1(t) = A(-u(t+2) + 2u(t+1) - 2u(t-1) + u(t-2))$,
$f_2(t) = A(-u(t+2) + 2u(t) - u(t-2))$, and
$f_3(t) = A(-u(t+2) + u(t-2))$.
Determine the value of A that makes the set of functions an orthonormal set. Assuming $x(t) = u(t) - u(t-2)$, express $x(t)$ in terms of these orthonormal functions.

7.13 Derive the average bit error rate for noncoherent BASK.

7.14 Determine which of the following schemes over an AWGN channel yields a lower bit error rate: BFSK signaling scheme with $\frac{E_b}{N_0} = 12$ dB using coherent detection or BFSK signaling scheme with $\frac{E_b}{N_0} = 14$ dB using noncoherent detection.

7.15 Derive the average symbol error rate for a 16-QAM with rectangular signal constellation.

Computer Exercises

7.16 Generate a long sequence of pseudorandom bits. Apply it to a 16-QAM modulation scheme with a rectangular signal constellation. Assume the carrier frequency is 100 times the bit rate. Add white Gaussian noise to the transmitted signal. Assuming we have perfect synchronization, count the number of errors, when signal-to-noise ratio per bit ranges between 0 and 20 dB.

7.17 Consider MPSK and QAM modulation schemes. Simulate these systems so as to determine the value of $\frac{E_b}{N_0}$ for each of the following nine cases, where $M = 4$, 16, and 64, and the bit error rate is 10^{-3}, 10^{-5}, and 10^{-7}.

CHAPTER 8

Synchronization

CONTENTS

INTRODUCTION

In this chapter, we first present various levels of synchronization before focusing on carrier recovery and symbol synchronization. After providing the rationale behind scrambling, two types of scramblers are introduced. The discussion turns toward the phase-locked loop, which can lock onto the frequency of a received sinusoid and estimate the phase offset. In an overview fashion, we then introduce the carrier-recovery mechanisms for suppressed-carrier modulation techniques, and finally discuss two timing-recovery schemes. After studying this chapter and understanding all relevant concepts and examples, students should be able to do the following:

1. Comprehend the need for synchronization.
2. Identify various levels of synchronization.
3. Compare data-directed and non-data-directed synchronization approaches.
4. Understand why scramblers are sometimes needed.
5. Grasp the idea behind the maximum-length shift register and pseudorandom sequences.
6. Describe the operation of a pseudorandom scrambler.
7. Outline the operation of a self-synchronizing scrambler.
8. Highlight the function of a phase-locked loop (PLL).
9. Characterize the basic operation of a PLL.
10. Illustrate why and how a PLL is linearized.
11. Discuss the impact of the first-order PLL on performance.
12. Assess the impact of the second-order PLL on performance.
13. Evaluate the impact of the third-order PLL on performance.
14. State the objective of carrier recovery.
15. Portray the principles of the Mth-power loop scheme.
16. Explain the fundamentals of the Costas loop scheme.
17. Detail the objective of timing recovery.

18. List the three general approaches to symbol synchronization.
19. Summarize the essentials of the nonlinear filter symbol synchronization.
20. Present the details of the early-late gate symbol synchronization.

8.1 SYNCHRONIZATION LEVELS

Synchronization broadly refers to the process of coordinating events to occur at the same time and operate in a timely fashion. Synchronization is an indispensable component in all digital communication systems, and requires a high degree of complexity in both acquisition (start-up) and tracking (steady-state) modes. Synchronization may be required at several levels, including frame synchronization, network synchronization, symbol timing, and carrier frequency and phase recovery. Frequency, phase, symbol, and frame synchronization are done at the receiver, but network synchronization involves the transmitter as well. Carrier frequency, phase recovery, and symbol synchronization are done at the physical layer, but network synchronization is done at the network layer and frame synchronization is done either at the physical layer or the network layer.

Network synchronization is required when transmitters need to be synchronized by varying the timing and frequency of their transmissions to correspond to the expectations of the receiver to ensure satisfactory operation of the receiver. Examples include transmitting base stations to a mobile receiver crossing the cell boundaries in a mobile cellular system or satellite dishes uplinking signals toward a single satellite receiver. In most cases, the transmitter relies on a return path from the receiver to determine the accuracy of its synchronization.

Frame synchronization is required after the transmitted bit sequence has been detected at the receiver as the sequence may need to be segmented into blocks (groups of bits), such as eight-bit words representing voice samples, codewords used in forward error correction, and time slots in a time-shared channel. To know the location of boundaries between received blocks of bits, a signal at the frame rate must be generated, with the zero crossings coincident with the transitions from each frame to the next or a framing bit is inserted.

Carrier synchronization is the generation of a reference sinusoidal (carrier) signal with a frequency and phase closely matching those of the transmitted (modulated) signal. This reference carrier is used to perform a coherent demodulation operation to reconstruct the original baseband (modulating) signal. Note that in a noncoherent demodulation, carrier synchronization is obviously of no concern.

Symbol synchronization is the generation of a timing reference to find the correct sampling instants at the receiver. This clock is used to extract the input sequence of symbols. Symbol synchronization and phase synchronization are rather similar, as they both need to provide in the receiver a replica of a portion of the transmitted signal. However, symbol synchronization, vis-à-vis phase synchronization, is viewed as coarser, since the carrier frequency is much higher than the symbol rate.

Synchronization can be generally classified into data-directed synchronization and non-data-directed synchronization. In ***data-directed synchronization,*** a preamble is transmitted with the information bits in a time-multiplexed format on a regular (periodic) basis. The preamble bits can provide information regarding synchronization and that information is extracted at the receiver. The obvious advantage of data-directed synchronization is to minimize the time required to synchronize and enhance synchronization accuracy. However, reduced throughput efficiency and power efficiency are its disadvantages, as the preamble transmits a sequence of non-information bearing bits and requires some transmit power to do it. In ***non-data-directed synchronization,*** synchronization is performed by processing the degraded signal at the receiver to extract all relevant information. The clear benefits are improved throughput and power efficiency, but at the expense of a longer synchronization time and more complexity. Our focus in this chapter is on non-data-directed forms of carrier synchronization (carrier recovery) and symbol synchronization (timing recovery).

8.2 SCRAMBLING

The statistics of the input bits can sometimes bring about degradation in a digital transmission system. For instance, a long sequence of 1s or 0s may cause the bit synchronizer to lose synchronization momentarily and thereby causing a long burst of erroneous bits. Another example is when a sequence of periodic patterns of 1s and 0s creates discrete spectral lines and that in turn may cause difficulty in bit synchronization, as the bit synchronizer may lock falsely to one of them. ***Scrambling*** is a method of achieving dc balance, increasing the period of a periodic input, and eliminating long sequences of 1s and 0s to ensure timing recovery.

Although line coding is a safer method of achieving these objectives, scrambling is attractive and often used on channels with extreme bandwidth constraints as scrambling requires no bandwidth overhead. A prime example of such channels is low-bandwidth twisted-pair telephone lines; to this effect, all the ITU-T standardized voice-band data modems incorporate scrambling. In fact, full-duplex modems using echo cancellation employ different scramblers in different directions of transmission to ensure the scrambled bits in the two directions are uncorrelated. A scrambler at the transmitter manipulates the input stream, and is usually placed before the channel encoder. The descrambler at the receiver unscrambles so as to preserve the overall bit sequence transparency. Scrambling is quite simple and generally effective; however, it is possible, but not likely, that a scrambler fails to prevent the occurrence of all undesirable sequences.

Scramblers use ***maximum-length shift register*** on the input bit stream to randomize or whiten the data by producing bits that appear to be independent and equi-probable. There are two classes of scramblers: pseudorandom scramblers and self-synchronizing scramblers. In the following discussion, the focus is on applications of scramblers to binary transmission using modulo-2 addition, but the techniques can be generalized to M-ary transmission using modulo-M addition, if need be.

Although the sequences generated by the maximum-length shift register are periodic, they are called ***pseudorandom sequences***, since they can be predicted from the knowledge of the shift register length and feedback taps. A pseudorandom sequence generated by an n-bit shift register is a binary sequence with period $r = 2^n - 1$. The output of an n-bit shift register $x(k)$ is obtained by

$$x(k) = h(1)x(k-1) \oplus h(2)x(k-2) \oplus \ldots \oplus h(n)x(k-n) \quad (8.1)$$

where $h(1), \ldots, h(n)$ are feedback taps, and each may be a zero (i.e., no feedback connection) or a one (i.e., direct connection of the shift register output to modulo-2 summation), and the operation $\oplus$ denotes modulo-2 addition. The number of 1s generated in one cycle of the output sequence is one greater than the number of 0s. The autocorrelation of the pseudorandom sequence has a peak equal to the sequence length $2^n - 1$ at multiples of the sequence length. At all other shifts, the autocorrelation is -1. The correlation property of a pseudorandom sequence results in a flat power spectral density as the sequence length increases (i.e., by increasing the sequence length, the output bits become less correlated).

8.2.1 Pseudorandom Scrambler

As shown in Figure 8.1, a ***pseudorandom scrambler*** at the transmitter scrambles via modulo-2 addition of a pseudorandom bit sequence with the input bit sequence and a ***pseudorandom descrambler*** at the receive end descrambles via modulo-2 addition of the same pseudorandom bit sequence with the received bit sequence to recover the original input bit sequence. The scrambler output

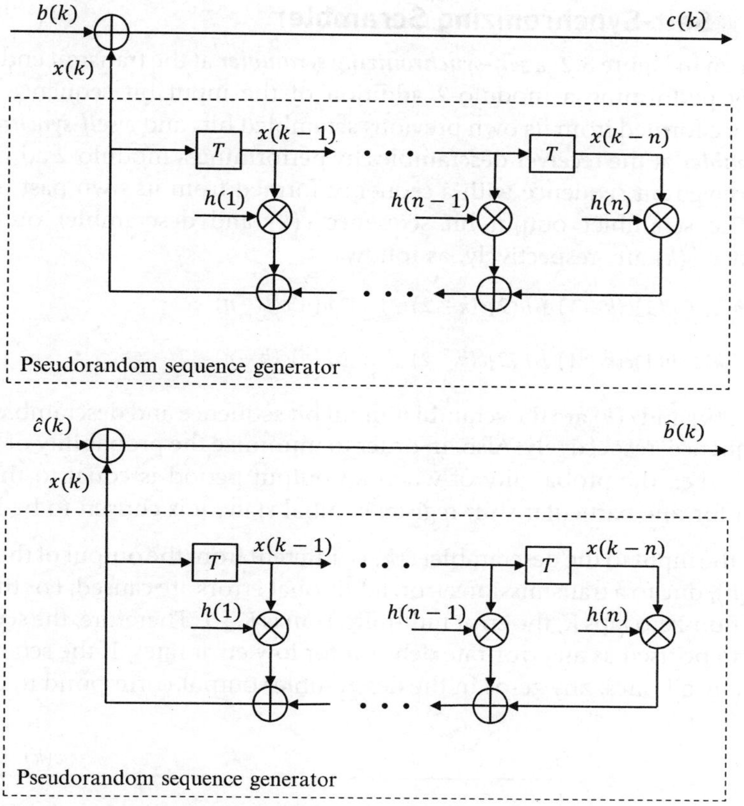

FIGURE 8.1 (a) A pseudorandom scrambler and (b) a pseudorandom descrambler.

bit sequence $c(k)$ and descrambler output bit sequence $\hat{b}(k)$ are, respectively, as follows:

$$
\begin{aligned}
c(k) &= b(k) \oplus x(k) \\
\hat{b}(k) &= \hat{c}(k) \oplus x(k)
\end{aligned}
\tag{8.2}
$$

where $b(k)$ and $\hat{c}(k)$ are the scrambler input bit sequence and descrambler input bit sequence, respectively. Note that the correct operation depends on the alignment in time of the two maximal-length sequences of period r in the scrambler and descrambler. The scrambler must be reset by the frame synchronization; if this fails, a complete frame is left descrambled and significant error propagation thus results. Pseudorandom scrambling is used in a high burst-rate time-division-multiple-access based satellite system, which includes a frame alignment signal to enable such synchronization to take place.

8.2.2 Self-Synchronizing Scrambler

As shown in Figure 8.2, a ***self-synchronizing scrambler*** at the transmit end scrambles by performing a modulo-2 addition of the input bit sequence with a sequence formed from its own previous scrambled bits and a ***self-synchronizing descrambler*** at the receiver descrambles by performing a modulo-2 addition of the received bit sequence with a sequence formed from its own past received bits. The scrambler output bit sequence $c(k)$ and descrambler output bit sequence $\hat{b}(k)$ are, respectively, as follows:

$$
\begin{aligned}
c(k) &= b(k) \oplus h(1)c(k-1) \oplus h(2)c(k-2) \oplus \ldots \oplus h(n)c(k-n) \\
\hat{b}(k) &= \hat{c}(k) \oplus h(1)\hat{c}(k-1) \oplus h(2)\hat{c}(k-2) \oplus \ldots \oplus h(n)\hat{c}(k-n)
\end{aligned}
\tag{8.3}
$$

where $b(k)$ and $\hat{c}(k)$ are the scrambler input bit sequence and descrambler input bit sequence, respectively. Also, in order to minimize the probability of lock up $(=2^{-n})$, i.e., the probability of when an output period is equal to the input period for one particular shift register's initial state, n is chosen to be large.

When the input to the descrambler $\hat{c}(k)$ is different from the output of the scrambler $c(k)$, due to a transmission error, additional errors are caused. For the number of non-zero taps K, the error multiplication is $K+1$. Therefore, the scrambler can also be used as an error-rate detector for low error rates. If the scrambler is driven by all ones, any zeros in the descrambler output correspond to channel

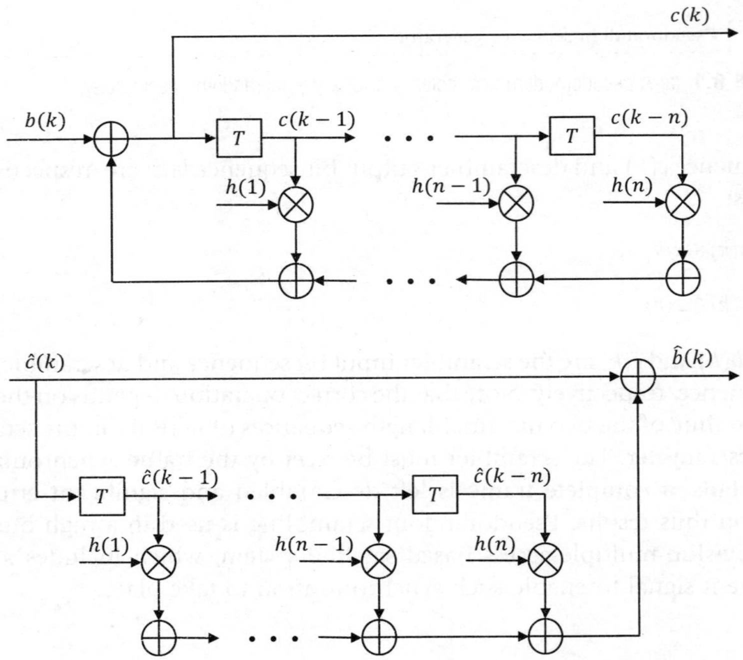

FIGURE 8.2 (a) A self-synchronizing scrambler and (b) a self-synchronizing descrambler.

errors. Since a single channel error results in $K+1$ output errors, one only needs to count the number of zeros in the descrambler output and divide by $K+1$ to determine the error rate. In practice, we usually have $2 \le K \le 4$, as such the additional degradation due to error propagation is usually considered negligible. Error propagation stops when the descrambler has full of correct bits.

EXAMPLE 8.1

Consider a simple three-stage self-synchronizing scrambler, where its output and input are related as follows:

$$c(k) = b(k) \oplus c(k-1) \oplus c(k-3)$$

(a) Assuming error free-transmission, show that the descrambled data is identical to the original data sequence.

(b) Assuming an initial state (111), determine the scrambler output for an all zero input.

Solution

Using (8.3), the output of the scrambler can be determined.

(a) For this scrambler, the output of the descrambler is then as follows:

$$\hat{b}(k) = \hat{c}(k) \oplus \hat{c}(k-1) \oplus \hat{c}(k-3)$$

With no errors in transmission, we have $\hat{c}(k) = c(k)$, and accordingly we have $\hat{b}(k) = b(k)$, as reflected below:

$$\hat{b}(k) = b(k) \oplus c(k-1) \oplus c(k-3) \oplus c(k-1) \oplus c(k-3) = b(k)$$

(b) The following table presents the output sequence:

Time	Input	Output	State		
k	$b(k)$	$c(k)$	$c(K-1)$	$c(K-2)$	$c(K-3)$
1	0	1	1	1	0
2	0	0	1	1	1
3	0	1	0	1	1
4	0	0	1	0	1
5	0	0	0	1	0
6	0	1	0	0	1
7	0	1	1	0	0
8	0	1	1	1	0

The scrambler output has period $7\left(=2^3-1\right)$. Note that should there be an error in transmission, the error multiplication factor is 3, since we have $K=2$.

8.3 PHASE-LOCKED LOOP (PLL)

At the core of most synchronization circuits is a phase-locked loop. The ***phase-locked loop (PLL)*** is a closed-loop negative feedback system whose function is to track the frequency and phase of a received sinusoid. The PLL is thus a circuit in which a signal is generated to lock onto the frequency and estimate the phase of an incoming sinusoid. Even with slowly time-varying frequency and phase, the feedback circuit can generally adjust in a dynamic fashion. However, a PLL can track the incoming frequency only over a finite range of frequency shift, and if the input and output frequencies are not close enough initially, the loop may not acquire lock. The PLL circuits can also be found in FM demodulators, frequency synthesizers, frequency multipliers and dividers, and multiplexers. PLL circuits with various degrees of complexity and performance are all implemented by digital signal processing and are readily available as relatively inexpensive integrated circuit (IC) chips.

8.3.1 Basic Operation

As shown in Figure 8.3, a generic PLL consists of three major components: a ***phase detector***, a ***loop filter***, and a ***voltage-controlled oscillator (VCO)***. Because of the multiplier, the circuit is nonlinear and thus difficult to analyze, as the Fourier transform cannot be easily employed. Hence, the analysis is in the time domain. The VCO is a sinusoidal oscillator whose frequency is linearly controlled by a voltage applied to it from an external source (the PLL output); in a way, any analog frequency modulator can function as a VCO. The multiplier simply produces a measure of the difference in phase between an incoming sinusoidal signal and the local replica produced by the VCO. As the received signal and the local replica change with respect to each other, the phase difference (or error) becomes a time-varying signal that is sent into the loop filter. The loop filter, which is a low-pass filter, removes high-frequency components and governs the PLL's response to variations in the error signal.

The goal is to generate a VCO output whose frequency is the same as the frequency of the received signal and phase is different from the phase of the received signal by 90 degrees. Phase lock is achieved by feeding a filtered version of a signal, which consists of the phase difference between the received

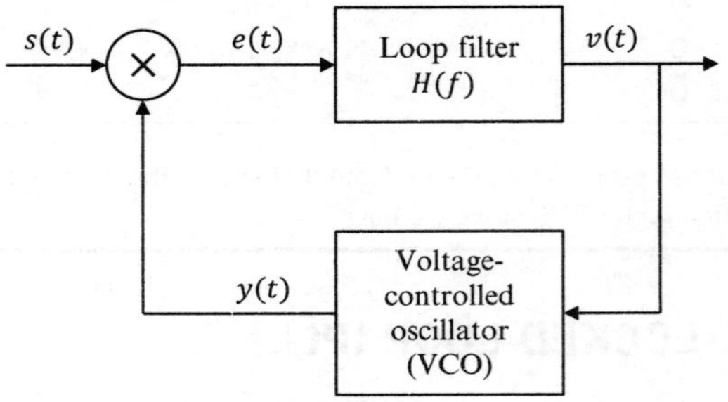

FIGURE 8.3 Basic components of a phase-locked loop.

signal and the VCO output, back to the input of the VCO. The VCO adjusts its own frequency such that its frequency and phase can track those of the PLL input signal. The received sinusoidal signal (i.e., the PLL input) is defined as follows:

$$s(t) = A_i \sin(2\pi f_c t + \theta_i(t)) \tag{8.4}$$

where A_i and f_c represent the amplitude and frequency, respectively, and $\theta_i(t)$ is a slowly-varying phase. The PLL output provides the control voltage for the VCO. The output of the VCO is defined by

$$y(t) = A_o \cos(2\pi f_c t + \theta_o(t)) \tag{8.5}$$

where A_o and f_c are the amplitude and frequency, respectively, and $\theta_o(t)$ represents the estimate of $\theta_i(t)$. The phase error is thus defined as follows:

$$\theta_e(t) = \theta_i(t) - \theta_o(t) = \theta_i(t) - 2\pi k \int_0^t v(s)ds \tag{8.6}$$

where $v(t)$ is the VCO input (i.e., PLL output) and k is a constant representing the frequency sensitivity of the VCO. With $s(t)$ and $y(t)$ as the inputs to the multiplier with a gain of m, the output of the multiplier is then as follows:

$$ms(t)y(t) = m(A_i \sin(2\pi f_c t + \theta_i(t)))(A_o \cos(2\pi f_c t + \theta_o(t))) \tag{8.7}$$

After using a trigonometric identity to transform the product of two sinusoids into the sum of two sinusoids, it becomes obvious that the output of the multiplier has a high-frequency component and a low-frequency component, as follows:

$$ms(t)y(t) = \left(\frac{mA_iA_o}{2}\right)(\sin(4\pi f_c t + \theta_i(t) + \theta_o(t)) + \sin(\theta_i(t) - \theta_o(t))) \tag{8.8}$$

Since the high-frequency term is suppressed by the loop filter, we could assume the effective input to the loop filter is in fact the low-frequency term. The error signal $e(t)$, which is the input to the loop filter, is then considered as follows:

$$e(t) = \left(\frac{mA_iA_o}{2}\right)\sin(\theta_e(t)) \tag{8.9}$$

The error signal is solely a function of the difference of the phase of the PLL input and the phase of the VCO output. With $h(t)$ as the impulse response of the loop filter, the output of the PLL $v(t)$ is then defined by the following convolution:

$$v(t) = e(t) * h(t) = \left(\frac{mA_iA_o}{2}\right) \int_{-\infty}^{t} \sin(\theta_e(\tau))h(t-\tau)\,d\tau \tag{8.10}$$

where * denotes the convolution operation. If we substitute (8.10) into (8.6), we then end up with a double integral. To avoid the complexity of a double integral, we first differentiate (8.6) and then use (8.10) to obtain the following nonlinear integro-differential equation describing the dynamic PLL behavior:

$$\frac{d\theta_e(t)}{dt} = \frac{d\theta_i(t)}{dt} - 2\pi C \int_{-\infty}^{t} \sin(\theta_e(\tau))h(t-\tau)\,d\tau \tag{8.11}$$

where $C = mA_iA_ok/2$ is the loop-gain parameter.

8.3.2 Linear Model of PLL

It is difficult to analyze the behavior of the nonlinear model of a PLL, and we thus linearize the model to simplify the analysis. When the phase error is very small at all times (i.e., when the PLL is near-phase lock), we have the following close approximation:

$$\sin(\theta_e(t)) \approx \theta_e(t) \tag{8.12}$$

This is accurate to within about 2% when the phase error is less than 0.1 radians ($< 6^\circ$) or within about 4% when the phase error is less than 0.5 radians ($< 30^\circ$). This small-error PLL analysis reduces the nonlinear system to the linear time-invariant (LTI) system shown in Figure 8.4. By taking the Fourier transform of (8.11) and exploiting the Fourier transform property of the differentiation in the time domain, as well as using the approximation in (8.12) and solving for the Fourier transform of $\theta_e(t)$, we get the following:

$$\Theta_e(f) = \frac{jf}{jf + CH(f)}\Theta_i(f) = \frac{1}{1+G(f)}\Theta_i(f) \tag{8.13}$$

where $\Theta_e(f)$ and $\Theta_i(f)$ are the Fourier transforms of $\theta_e(t)$ and $\theta_i(t)$, respectively, and $H(f)$ and $G(f)$ are the transfer function of the loop filter and the open-loop transfer function of PLL, respectively. Assuming for all frequencies of interest, we have $|G(f)| \gg 1$, and (8.13) suggests that $\Theta_e(f)$ converges to zero. In other

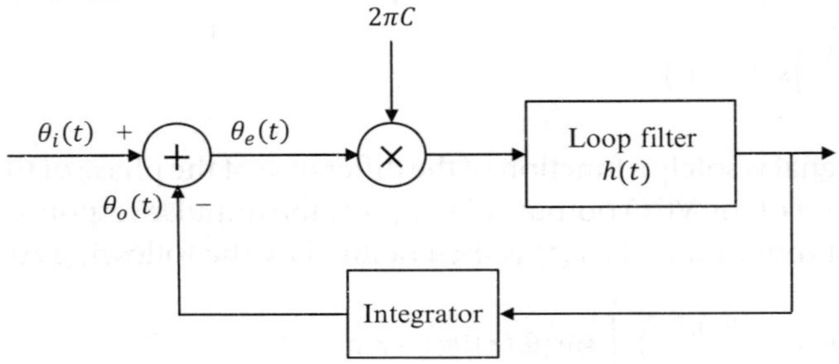

FIGURE 8.4 Linearized model of a phased-locked loop.

words, the phase of VCO $\theta_o(t)$ becomes asymptotically equal to the phase of the incoming signal $\theta_i(t)$ (i.e., the phase error $\theta_e(t)$ goes to zero).

The complexity of a PLL is determined by the transfer function of its loop filter $H(f)$. Higher-order loops can track a wide range of inputs, but are harder to stabilize. Loop filters can enable the PLL to capture and track input signals with different types of frequency variations, whereas the loop gain C controls the loop bandwidth and the range of the trackable frequency variations. If the bandwidth of the loop is sufficiently wide enough to track any time variations in the phase of the received sinusoid, then more noise is being allowed to pass into the loop. Table 8.1 shows the steady-state phase errors for various phase-locked loops by considering the following three different cases:

Case-I: The incoming sinusoidal signal has a constant phase shift of K_1 radians and zero-frequency offset, as compared with the initial VCO output. A PLL of any order can track and the steady-state phase error becomes zero.

Case-II: The incoming sinusoidal signal has a constant frequency offset of K_2 radians per second, vis-à-vis the initial VCO output. A first-order PLL fails to track as its steady-state phase error converges to a non-zero constant. However, a higher-order PLL can track and the steady-state phase error becomes zero.

Case-III: The incoming sinusoidal signal has a frequency offset, which linearly changes with time at a rate of K_3 radians per second per second, in relation to the initial VCO output. A first-order PLL fails to track the steady-state phase error as it is continually changing. A second-order PLL fails to track, as its steady-state phase error converges to a non-zero constant. However, a higher-order PLL can track and the steady state error becomes zero.

Table 8.1 Performances of various phase-locked loops

	Time-varying phase of sinusoidal at PLL input	First-order PLL	Second-order PLL	Third-order PLL
		$H(f)=1$	$H(f)=1+\frac{a}{jf}$	$H(f)=1+\frac{a}{jf}+\frac{b}{(jf)^2}$
Case-I	$\Theta_i(f)=\frac{K_1}{jf}$	Zero	Zero	Zero
Case-II	$\Theta_i(f)=\frac{K_2}{(jf)^2}$	Constant	Zero	Zero
Case-III	$\Theta_i(f)=\frac{K_3}{(jf)^3}$	Changing	Constant	Zero

Note: K_1, K_2, K_3, *a* and *b* are all non-zero constants.

8.4 CARRIER RECOVERY

Since the local oscillators, employed at the transmitter and receiver, cannot be phase locked, a carrier recovery mechanism at the receiver is required. The phase-locked loop lies at the core of carrier recovery, and the operation of the PLL, as highlighted earlier, depends entirely on a simple unmodulated sinusoidal signal that has a spectral component at the carrier frequency. A digital modulation is generally a suppressed-carrier modulation, as the transmission of a spectral component represents a waste of power. It is thus important to acquire such a discrete spectral component from the received modulated signal by which the PLL can then estimate the carrier phase.

With a focus on MPSK modulation, we provide a qualitative discussion of two methods for carrier recovery using a PLL at the receiver: the Costas loop and the Mth-power loop. Since the noise components at the input of the PLL for both methods are the same, with identical loop filters, the probability density function of the phase error of the two loops is identical. Although their block diagrams are quite different, their theoretical performances can thus be shown to be the same. Moreover, in both methods, phase ambiguity, which is a multiple of $M/2\pi$, results. To overcome the phase ambiguity, differential encoding before modulation at the transmitter and differentially decoding after demodulation at the receiver can be employed. However, this method, which is called coherent detection of differentially encoded MPSK, yields a very small degradation in performance.

8.4.1 The Mth-Power Loop

The Mth-power loop can perform carrier recovery for MPSK modulation, as shown in Figure 8.5. To lock onto the frequency and estimate the phase of an incoming sinusoid, the effects of the modulation need to be eliminated (i.e., removing the modulating signal from the modulated signal and thus obtaining the unmodulated carrier). At the heart of this technique lies the fact that an Mth-power of a sinusoidal function can be converted into a linear combination of sinusoidal functions of multiple angles (i.e., using the

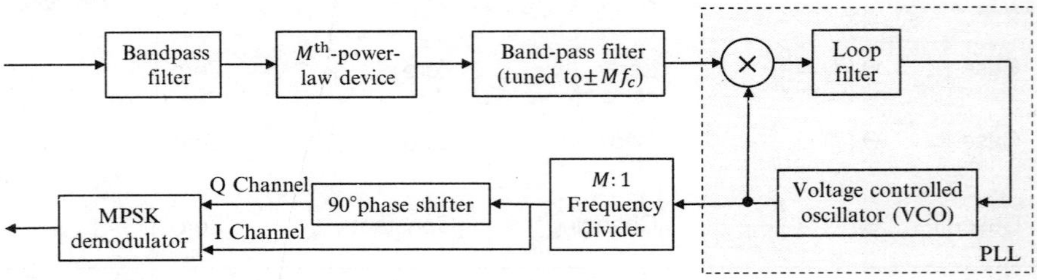

FIGURE 8.5 M^{th} power loop for carrier recovery for MPSK.

trigonometric identity $\cos^M(\varphi) = \sum_{i=0}^{M} a_i \cos(i\varphi)$, where, a_0, a_1, ..., a_M are some real constants.).

The received (modulated) signal is initially passed through a bandpass filter (BPF) to remove the noise outside the band required for the signal itself. The Mth-power-law device then raises the received signal to the Mth power to produce a spectral component at Mf_c for the PLL circuit. Since at the output of the device there are many spectral components, one of which is a sinusoid of frequency Mf_c, a narrowband BPF tuned to Mf_c is used to isolate the sinusoid at frequency Mf_c and to remove more of the noise. The BPF also completely suppresses the components whose spectrum is centered at zero frequency, and its output, which has some residual unwanted components, then drives the PLL.

The PLL input thus consists of a carrier whose phase angle has been increased by a factor of M as well as some noise, which can interfere with loop operation. The phase noise has also been increased by a factor M and the phase-error variance has been increased by M^2. Assuming the bandwidth of the loop is significantly smaller than the bandwidth of the BPF, the total noise spectrum may be approximated by a constant within the loop bandwidth. By using a frequency divider, more specifically a divide-by-M circuit, the VCO output is divided by a factor of M to generate the desired carrier signal for demodulating the received signal.

8.4.2 The Costas Loop

The Costas loop is a method to perform carrier recovery (i.e., carrier-phase estimation) for coherent demodulation of the received signal when MPSK modulation techniques are employed. It is a practical method when M is small (i.e., $M = 2$ or 4), as squaring or fourth-power devices required in the Mth power-law carrier recovery are difficult to implement, especially at high frequencies. On the other hand, when M is rather large, due to a larger number of filters and multipliers required for the implementation, the circuitry complexity of the Costas loop becomes quite significant. Figure 8.6 shows the block diagram of the Costas loop for carrier recovery for QPSK modulation scheme.

After the received QPSK modulated signal is multiplied in the in-phase and quadrature channels, the signals are filtered out to remove higher frequency components. The group delay and impulse response of each of these filters must be equal to prevent possible carrier recovery problems. The hard-limiters (signum functions) in each of the I and Q arms are used to maintain a balance between the in-phase and quadrature channels and a crossover processing between the inputs and outputs of these nonlinearities forms the error signal. This error signal drives the VCO to make the phase error as small as possible.

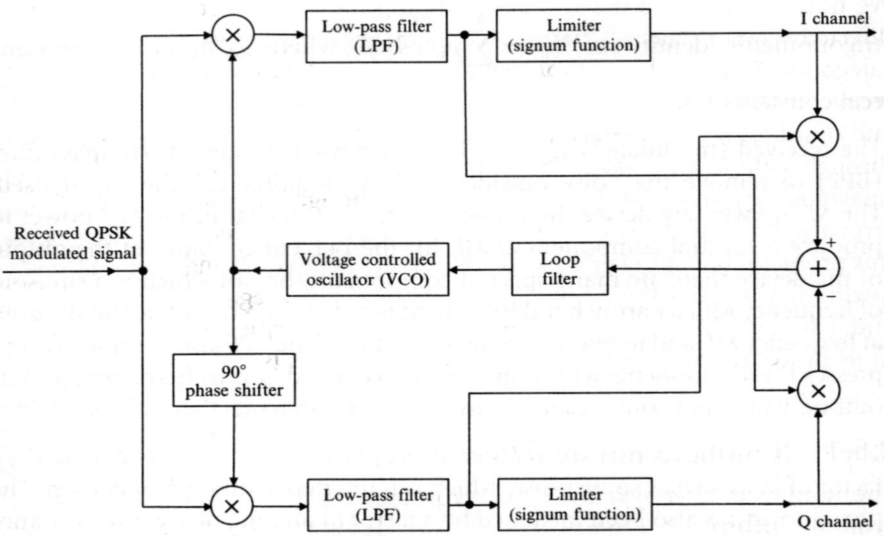

FIGURE 8.6 Costas loop for carrier recovery for QPSK.

8.5 SYMBOL SYNCHRONIZATION

To achieve optimum demodulation in a digital communication system, symbol synchronization is required at the receiver. Symbol synchronization is the generation of a timing reference to find the precise sampling instants (i.e., to determine both the correct symbol rate and the timing phase within the symbol duration). In a practical communication system, the receiver clock must be continuously adjusted for the sampling rate and the sampling phase. There are three general approaches to perform symbol synchronization:

1. Extraction of the timing information from a master clock is an approach in which the transmitter and receiver are both synchronized (slaved) to a master clock that provides a precise timing reference. Due to its high cost, this method is suited for large high-speed radio communication systems, where precise clock signals are sent from a master radio transmitter.

2. Transmission of a synchronizing signal along with the message signal is an approach in which the transmitter simultaneously sends a clock pilot at a multiple of symbol rate along with the information data, and the receiver then employs a very narrow BPF tuned to the clock frequency. This method is quite simple and reliable, and is used in large telephone systems, but at the expense of wasting transmit power.

3. Derivation of the clock signal from the received signal itself is an approach in which the receiver performs self-synchronization. This is an efficient approach that can be achieved by various symbol timing recovery circuits.

We now focus on the self-synchronization approach and consider non-data-directed symbol synchronization for binary baseband systems. There are two categories of symbol synchronizers, namely, ***open-loop synchronizers***, which recover a replica of the transmitter clock directly from the received waveform, and ***closed-loop synchronizers***, which lock a local clock to the received waveform through comparative measurements. An open-loop synchronizer yields an unavoidable non-zero-mean tracking error. Though small for large SNR, the error always exists. A closed-loop synchronizer, due to its feedback, can resolve this problem, but at the expense of additional complexity and cost. In the following two symbol synchronization schemes, we disregard noise for clarity, and assume NRZ signaling scheme, where it has no spectral-line component in its power spectral density at the symbol rate or its harmonic frequencies.

8.5.1 Nonlinear-Filter Synchronizer

The nonlinear filter synchronizer is a popular open-loop non-data-directed symbol synchronizer. There are various methods to implement it, as shown in Figure 8.7. The different implementations are all based on a cascade of a linear filter, to reduce the noise level and highlight the symbol transitions, and an instantaneous (memoryless) nonlinear device, to produce a spectral line at the symbol rate. The difference between these methods lies in the way the signal with spectral line is produced. In all three implementations, the spectral line is then isolated by a BPF and shaped with an ideal saturating amplifier to produce a sine wave at the clock rate (zero crossings at the symbol-transition times). A PLL can also be used to extract a sinusoidal signal.

In Figure 8.7a, the received signal is first sent to a matched filter, which can eliminate some of the noise and can also be approximated by a simple lowpass filter, and then to a device with even-law nonlinearity, such as a square-law device and a full-wave rectifier. The resulting output has positive amplitudes

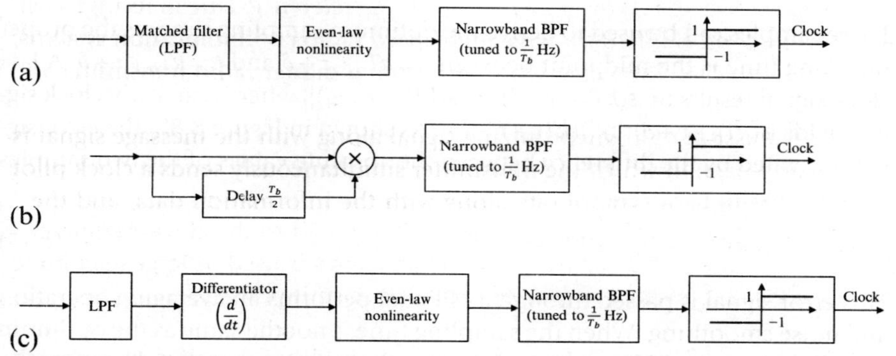

FIGURE 8.7 Nonlinear filter symbol synchronizer: (a) even-law-based, (b) correlation-based, and (c) differentiation-based.

(peaks) highlighting input symbol transitions, thus producing a spectral component at the symbol rate. In Figure 8.7b, the received signal is multiplied by a signal that is a delayed version of the received signal, a delay of one half of a symbol period. The product can thus provide the strongest spectral components, as the signal is always positive in the second half of every symbol period, but can be negative in the first half if two successive symbols are different. In Figure 8.7c, before the differentiation process, the received signal is sent to a LPF, as a differentiator is generally sensitive to wideband noise. The differentiator produces a sequence of positive and negative spikes at symbol transitions, which goes to a square-law device or a rectifier to produce positive spikes with a spectral component at the symbol rate.

A drawback of an open-loop synchronizer is an unavoidable non-zero average tracking error. To circumvent this problem, especially for small SNR, a closed-loop symbol synchronizer, such as early-late gate synchronizer, is employed.

8.5.2 Early-Late Gate Synchronizer

The early-late gate synchronizer is a widely-used closed-loop non-data-aided symbol synchronizer, with simple implementation. This technique is independent of the zero crossings of the received NRZ signal. It utilizes the property that the signal at the output of the matched filter has a peak at the optimum sampling instant and is reasonably symmetric on either side (i.e., the pulse shape is symmetrical about the optimum sampling time), as shown in Figure 8.8a. Due to noise, the detection of the peak at the output of the matched filter is difficult. However, the absolute value of the early samples at $t = kT_b + \tau - \delta$, i.e., $|s(kT_b + \tau - \delta)|$, and the absolute value of the late samples at $t = kT_b + \tau + \delta$, i.e., $|s(kT_b + \tau + \delta)|$, on average, are smaller than the peak value $|s(kT_b + \tau)|$, where τ is the optimum sampling time and $0 < \delta < T_b/2$ is the relative sampling phase. Due to symmetry, we thus have:

$$|s(kT_b + \tau + \delta)| = |s(kT_b + \tau - \delta)| < |s(kT_b + \tau)| \tag{8.14}$$

These samples can be used to derive the optimum sampling time, as the proper sampling time is the midpoint between $t = kT_b + \tau - \delta$ and $t = kT_b + \tau + \delta$. A late clock signal results in $|s(kT_b + \tau + \delta)| < |s(kT_b + \tau - \delta)|$, whereas an early clock signal yields $|s(kT_b + \tau + \delta)| > |s(kT_b + \tau - \delta)|$. As shown in Figure 8.8b, the error signal generated by the difference between the absolute values of the two samples is as follows:

$$e(kT_b + \tau) = |s(kT_b + \tau + \delta)| - |s(kT_b + \tau - \delta)| \tag{8.15}$$

This error signal is passed through a LPF that performs an averaging operation and noise smoothing. When the sampling time is not the same as the optimum sampling time, the LPF output representing the average error signal is non-zero.

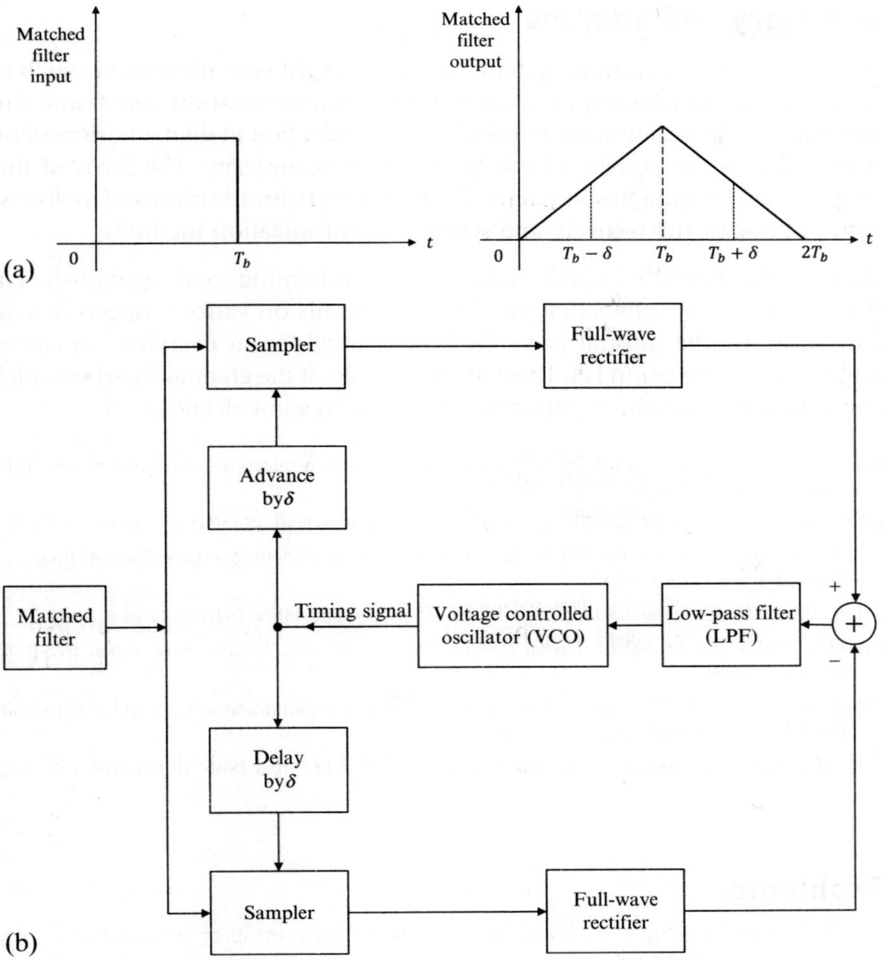

FIGURE 8.8 Early-late gate symbol synchronizer: (a) matched-filter input and output and (b) block diagram.

This non-zero error signal drives a VCO that produces a clock signal. A positive error signal increases the frequency of the VCO and a negative error signal decreases it. A late clock signal speeds up the clock, and conversely, an early clock signal slows down the VCO. By advancing or delaying the frequency of the clock in an iterative fashion, symbol synchronization can thus be established. It is worth noting that instead of using a matched filter and a sampler advanced by δ in the upper branch, an integrator over the interval $[\delta, T_b]$ can be used, and similarly in the lower branch, an integrator over the interval $[0, T_b - \delta]$ can be employed.

Summary and Sources

In a digital communication system, various levels of synchronization, such as carrier phase and frequency recovery, symbol synchronization, and frame and network synchronization are required. Synchronization in digital transmission is provided at the expense of a high degree of complexity. The focus of this chapter was to highlight some general aspects of synchronization and to discuss some ad hoc carrier recovery and symbol synchronization methods.

There are excellent books in the area of carrier and timing recovery published in the 1970s and the 1980s that provide great details on various aspects of synchronization. The tutorial paper by Franks provides an overview on carrier and bit synchronization [1]. There are also books at the graduate level in which some aspects of synchronization are discussed in some detail [2–7].

[1] L.E. Franks, Carrier and bit synchronization in data communication—a tutorial review, *IEEE Trans. Comm. 28 (August 1980) 1107–1121.*

[2] J.J. Spilker Jr., *Digital Communications by Satellite*, Prentice-Hall, ISBN: 0-13-214155-8. 1977.

[3] R.D. Gitlin, J.F. Hayes, and S.B. Weinstein, *Data Communications Principles*, Plenum Press. ISBN: 0-306-43777-5. 1992.

[4] B. Sklar, *Digital Communications*, second ed., Prentice-Hall. ISBN: 0-13-084788-7. 2001.

[5] J.G. Proakis and M. Salehi, *Digital Communications*, fifth ed., McGraw-Hill. ISBN: 978-0-07-295716-7. 2008.

[6] H. Nguyen and E. Shwedyk, *A First Course in Digital Communications*, Cambridge University Press. ISBN: 978-0-521-87613-1. 2009.

[7] J.D. Gibson, *The Communications Handbook*, second ed., CRC Press. ISBN: 0-8493-0967-0. 2002.

Problems

8.1 Consider a simple six-stage self-synchronizing scrambler, where its output and input are related as follows:

$$c(k) = b(k) \oplus c(k-5) \oplus c(k-6)$$

Assuming error free-transmission, show that the descrambled data is identical to the original data sequence. Assuming an initial state (110101), determine the descrambler output for an all zero input.

8.2 With reference to Table 8.1, confirm the performance of the first-order PLL for all three different incoming inputs.

8.3 With reference to Table 8.1, confirm the performance of the second-order PLL for all three different incoming inputs.

8.4 With reference to Table 8.1, confirm the performance of the third-order PLL for all three different incoming inputs.

Computer Exercises

8.5 Consider a PLL, where the transfer function of the loop filter is known, and assume all relevant constants in the PLL model are known. Assuming it is a first-order PLL, determine the response of the PLL if the input has a phase error of $\pi/10$.

8.6 Consider a baseband binary communication system with the transmission rate of 38.4 kbps and a raised-cosine pulse with a roll off-factor 0.25. Simulate the operation of an early-late gate.

CHAPTER 9

Information Theory

INTRODUCTION

In this chapter, we first present what information is and how it can be measured, and then focus on the importance of average information. Discrete sources, in the form of being memoryless or having memory, are identified. Source codes from various perspectives are classified, and lossless data compression techniques are highlighted in detail. All Shannon's three theorems, which form the cornerstone of information theory and establish basic theoretical bounds for the performances of digital communication systems, are briefly discussed. After studying this chapter and understanding all relevant concepts and examples, students should be able to achieve the following learning objectives:

1. Define the message information content.
2. Understand the role of the probability of a message in the message information content.
3. Describe the function measuring information content.
4. Appreciate the importance of average information content.
5. Analyze the importance of the source entropy and how it can be evaluated.
6. Characterize the discrete memoryless source.
7. Recognize the impact of sources with or without memory on entropy.
8. Explain fixed-length and variable-length codes.
9. Differentiate between instantaneous and uniquely-decodable codes.
10. State the Kraft inequality and its impact on instantaneous codes.
11. Gain insight into the Shannon's source coding theorem.
12. Determine how extension codes can be implemented.
13. Outline the entropy (probability-based) and universal (adaptive) coding techniques.
14. Provide a step-by-step process how to employ the Huffman coding.
15. Know how to apply Lempel-Ziv coding.

CONTENTS

Introduction to Digital Communications

16. Derive the expression for mutual information.
17. Evaluate the capacity of the discrete memoryless channel.
18. Understand Shannon's information-capacity theorem.
19. Comprehend Shannon's channel coding theorem.
20. Connect Shannon's theorems to performance bounds on communication systems.

9.1 MEASURE OF INFORMATION

On an intuitive basis, the amount of information received from the knowledge of occurrence of an event is related to the probability of occurrence of that event. For instance, if we say that during the next winter it will snow in a European country, we are then providing an extremely small amount of information, as it is almost a certain event to occur. However, if we say that during the next summer there will be heavy snowfalls in all African countries, we are then giving an extremely large amount of information, as it is almost an impossible event to occur. The amount of information in a message depends only on the uncertainty of the underlying event rather than its actual content, and is inversely related to the probability of occurrence of that event. The message associated with an event least likely to occur contains the most information.

9.1.1 Information Content

To provide a quantitative measure of information, we assume the source is a discrete source. This is a reasonable assumption, as continuous sources can be turned into discrete sources using analog-to-digital conversion techniques. A discrete information source has only a finite set of output symbols. Information sources can be classified as having memory or being memoryless. A source with memory is one for which the current output symbol depends on some of the previous output symbols. A memoryless source is one for which the current symbol is independent of all previous output symbols. A ***discrete memoryless source*** (DMS), also known as a ***zero-memory source***, generates a sequence of independent, identically distributed (iid) random variables that take values in a discrete set. In other words, a DMS produces symbols from the alphabet consisting of K statistically independent symbols $m_1, m_2, \ldots, m_K$, whose probabilities of occurrence are $p_1, p_2, \ldots, p_K$, respectively. We thus have:

$$p_1 + p_2 + \cdots + p_K = 1 \tag{9.1}$$

It is intuitively obvious that a meaningful measure of information for symbols produced by a DMS requires to be a monotonically decreasing function of the probability of the source symbol (i.e., high probability of occurrence conveys relatively little information) as well as a continuous function of the probability of the source symbol (i.e., a slight change in the probability of a certain symbol should bring about a slight change in the information delivered by that symbol). It is thus a continuous function related to the inverse of the probability of occurrence of the event.

The measure of information should also be a function that when an event is almost certain to occur, that is the event occurs with probability close to one, zero information is almost conveyed, and when an event is almost impossible to occur, that is the probability of occurrence is approximately zero, an infinite amount of information is almost conveyed. It should also be a function that gives non-negative information for any event, regardless of its probability of occurrence. Lastly, the function should reflect the fact that the total information received from two statistically independent events is the same as the sum of the information contained in each of the two events. Assuming the information content of a symbol m_i is denoted by $I(m_i)$, the function that defines the ***information content*** must then meet the following essential requirements:

$$\begin{aligned} &I(m_i) > I(m_j) \text{ if } p_i < p_j \\ &I(m_i) \to 0 \text{ as } p_i \to 1 \\ &I(m_i) \to \infty \text{ as } p_i \to 0 \\ &I(m_i) \geq 0 \text{ for } 0 \leq p_i \leq 1 \\ &I(m_k) = I(m_i) + I(m_j) \text{ if } p_k = p_i\, p_j \end{aligned} \tag{9.2}$$

The only function that satisfies all these requirements is the logarithmic function, as defined below:

$$I(m_i) = \log_2\left(\frac{1}{p_i}\right) = -\log_2 p_i \text{ (bits)} \tag{9.3}$$

The base of the logarithm in (9.3) is assumed to be 2, and the information is thus expressed in bits per symbol. Note that in order to determine the information content using (9.3), we can use the relation $\log_2 x = \frac{\log_{10} x}{\log_{10} 2}$ to find a logarithm in base 2. Figure 9.1 shows (9.3) as how the information content of an event and the probability of the event are related. Using the familiar bit as the unit of information is based on the fact that if two possible binary symbols occur with equal probabilities (i.e., $p_1 = p_2 = \frac{1}{2}$), the correct amount of information carried by each binary symbol is then $I(m_1) = I(m_2) = -\log_2\left(\frac{1}{2}\right) = 1$ bit. That is, one ***bit*** is the amount of information that can be gained when one of two possible and equally-likely events occurs.

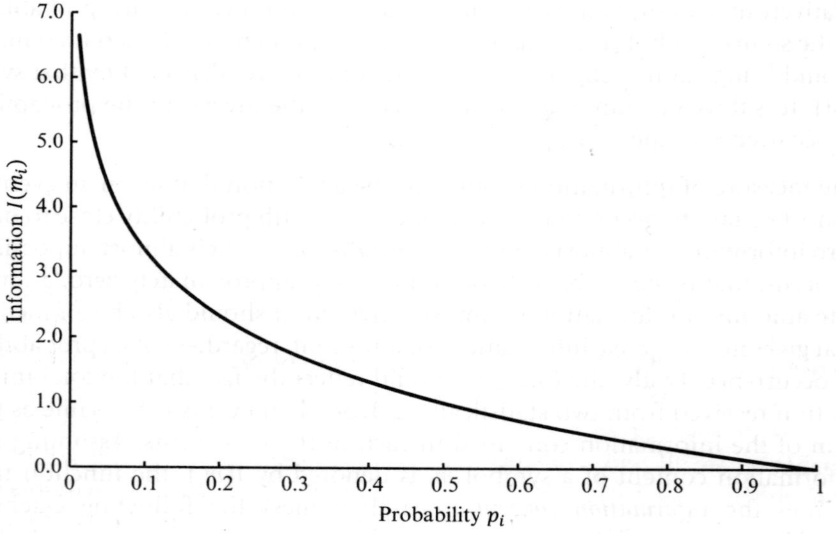

FIGURE 9.1 Information content of an event in terms of the probability of the event.

EXAMPLE 9.1

In a random experiment that constitutes rolling a typical (six-sided) fair die, determine the information content associated with each outcome.

Solution

Since the die is fair, all six outcomes are equally likely, that is the probability of each outcome is $\frac{1}{6}$. Using (9.3), we therefore have $I(m_i) = \log_2\left(\frac{1}{\frac{1}{6}}\right) = \log_2 6 \cong 2.585$ bits, where $i = 1, 2, \ldots, 6$. The information content for each outcome is greater than one bit, for the probability of each outcome is less than one half.

9.1.2 Average Information Content

The instantaneous flow of information generated by a source may fluctuate widely due to the randomness involved in the symbols that the source selects. Thus, we are more interested in the average information content that a source produces than the information content of a single symbol. The average information content per symbol is called the ***entropy*** (or equivalently uncertainty) of the discrete memoryless source X with K symbols, and is given by:

$$H(X) = E[I(m_i)] = \sum_{i=1}^{K} p_i\, I(m_i) = -\sum_{i=1}^{K} p_i \log_2 p_i \tag{9.4}$$

where $E[\ ]$ denotes the expectation operator and for $x \to 0$, we have $x \log_2 x \to 0$. The source entropy $H(X)$ can be considered as the average amount of uncertainty within source X. A simple interpretation of the source entropy is that, on the average, we can expect to get $H(X)$ bits of information per symbol in long messages from the information source X, even though we cannot say in advance what symbol sequence will occur in these messages. In other words, the source entropy is the measure of the lack of knowledge before the source symbol is revealed. The entropy $H(X)$ of a DMS is bounded as follows:

$$0 \le H(X) \le \log_2 K \tag{9.5}$$

where K is the number of distinct symbols that can be produced by a DMS. The lower-bound on the entropy in (9.5) corresponds to no uncertainty (i.e., $H(X)=0$) if and only if $p_i=1$ for some i and the other probabilities in the alphabet set are all zero. The upper-bound on the entropy in (9.5) is achieved if and only if $p_i=\frac{1}{K}$, for all $i=1, 2, \ldots, K$. In other words, when all symbols in the alphabet set are equally likely (equiprobable) to occur, the maximum uncertainty results.

EXAMPLE 9.2

A binary source produces a symbol 1 with probability p and a symbol 0 with probability $1-p$. Derive and plot the source entropy in terms of p, and comment on the result.

Solution

Using (9.4), we thus have:

$$H(X) = -p \log_2 p - (1-p) \log_2 (1-p).$$

We first take the derivative of $H(X)$ with respect to p, and then set it to zero to obtain the maximum value of the entropy. As shown in Figure 9.2, the maximum value of the entropy $H(X)$ is 1 bit. The maximum entropy occurs when $p=0.5$ (i.e., when the uncertainty is maximum or equivalently when the binary symbol is the least predictable). However, if $p=0$ or $p=1$, then the binary source symbols are all zeros or ones. When all the symbols are zeros or ones, the uncertainty is thus zero, i.e., $H(X)=0$, as the source symbol is totally predictable and we know exactly which symbol will certainly occur, in short, the source provides no information at all.

If the source emits r symbols per second, the ***average source information rate*** R is then as follows:

$$R = r H(X) \tag{9.6}$$

where R is measured in bits per second (bps), r in symbols per second, and $H(X)$ in bits per symbol.

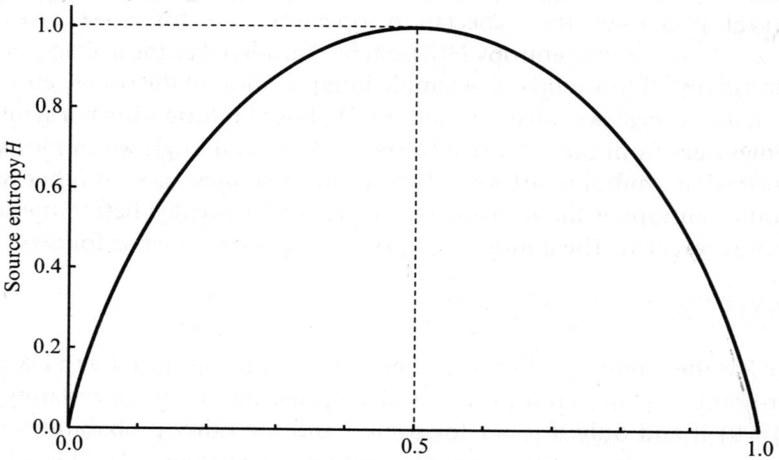

FIGURE 9.2 Entropy of a binary memoryless source in terms of symbol probability.

EXAMPLE 9.3

A memoryless source can generate one of the four symbols A, B, C, and D with probabilities $P(A)=0.5$, $P(B)=0.25$, $P(C)=0.125$, and $P(D)=0.125$. Assuming the source emits at the rate of 8 million symbols per second, determine the average source information rate.

Solution

Using (9.4), we have the source entropy as follows:

$$H(X)=-\frac{1}{2}\log_2\left(\frac{1}{2}\right)-\frac{1}{4}\log_2\left(\frac{1}{4}\right)-\frac{1}{8}\log_2\left(\frac{1}{8}\right)-\frac{1}{8}\log_2\left(\frac{1}{8}\right)=1.75$$

Using (9.6), the average source entropy information rate is thus as follows:

$$R=8,000,000\times 1.75=14\times 10^6 \text{ bits per second}=14 \text{ Mbps}$$

9.1.3 Extended DMS

For a DMS, blocks of symbols rather than individual symbols, where each block may consist of n successive source symbols, may be considered. With K as the number of distinct symbols produced by the source, there are then K^n distinct blocks in an extended source. In the case of a DMS, the probability of each of these blocks of n symbols is equal to the product of the probabilities of the n source symbols. The ***entropy of an extended DMS*** is thus equal to n times the entropy of the original (non-extended) source.

$$H(X^n)=nH(X) \tag{9.7}$$

EXAMPLE 9.4

A DMS can generate one of the three symbols x_1, x_2, and x_3 with probabilities $P(x_1) = 0.5$, $P(x_2) = 0.25$, and $P(x_3) = 0.25$. Determine the entropy $H(X^n)$ for $n = 1$ and $n = 2$ (second extension).

Solution

Using (9.4), we have the source entropy as follows:

$$H(X) = -\frac{1}{2}\log_2\left(\frac{1}{2}\right) - \frac{1}{4}\log_2\left(\frac{1}{4}\right) - \frac{1}{4}\log_2\left(\frac{1}{4}\right) = \frac{3}{2}$$

Since the source has three distinct symbols, the second-order extension of the source has nine distinct blocks of two symbols with the following probabilities:

$$P(x_1x_1) = \frac{1}{4},$$

$$P(x_2x_2) = P(x_2x_3) = P(x_3x_2) = P(x_3x_3) = \frac{1}{16}, \text{ and}$$

$$P(x_1x_2) = P(x_2x_1) = P(x_3x_1) = P(x_1x_3) = \frac{1}{8}.$$

Using (9.4), we thus have the entropy of the extended source as follows:

$$H(X^2) = \left(-\frac{1}{4}\log_2\left(\frac{1}{4}\right)\right) + 4\left(-\frac{1}{16}\log_2\left(\frac{1}{16}\right)\right) + 4\left(-\frac{1}{8}\log_2\left(\frac{1}{8}\right)\right) = 3$$

Since we have $H(X^2) = 2H(X) = 2(\frac{3}{2}) = 3$ bits, (9.7) is satisfied.

It is important to note that in a DMS, symbols are generated in a statistically independent fashion, but most practical sources produce symbols that are statistically dependent, and statistical dependence lowers the amount of information. The average information content per symbol emitting dependent symbols decreases as the message length increases (i.e., the average number of bits per symbol needed to represent a message decreases as the message length increases). Messages that are highly structured usually convey less information per symbol, hence the decrease in its entropy.

A prime example of a source producing non-independent symbols is the English language, which like any natural language has a statistical structure, as a letter in a multi-letter word may depend upon a number of preceding letters. Such a source producing dependent symbols from a set of 27 symbols, the 26 letters and a space, is considered ergodic, for if observed for a very long time, will (with probability 1) produce a sequence of source symbols that is typical.

In a long typical English text, the letter *E* occurs more frequently than any other letter, the letter *Z* is the least frequently letter, the letter *Q* is almost always followed by the letter *U*, the letter *T* occurs more frequently than any other consonant, and occurrence of a consonant generally implies that the following letter will be more likely to be a vowel than another consonant. The number of letters in a word on average is about 4.4, and some English two-letter words, such as "of," "to" "in," "it," "is," "be," "as" and "at," and three-letter words, such as "the," "and," "for," "are," "but," "not" and "you," and "all," are more likely to occur than most two-letter and three-letter words.

Suppose all 27 symbols (26 letters and a space) in the English language are independent of one another. This simplistic and invalid assumption in turn allows us to view it as a DMS. If we assume all symbols are equally probable, its entropy is then 4.75 bits per symbol, and if the actual probability of occurrence of each of the 27 symbols is taken into consideration, its entropy is then 4.03 bits per symbol. However, if we take into account the dependencies among letters forming words, as adjacent letters in English text highly depend on one another, the entropy of English text is then between 0.6 and 1.3 bits per symbol. Thus in principle the dependencies among source symbols imply a reduction in the information content of a source.

9.2 CLASSIFICATION OF SOURCE CODES

Efficient transmission requires a binary encoding process that takes into consideration the variable amount of information per symbol. In order to discuss the connection between source coding and the information measure, it is first necessary to define certain codes along with their properties.

9.2.1 Block Codes

A ***block code*** is a code that maps each of the symbols of the source onto a fixed sequence of bits. These fixed sequences of bits are called ***codewords***. The codewords defining a block code may or may not have equal number of bits.

9.2.2 Fixed-Length Codes

Using a ***fixed-length code*** is the simplest method to encode each symbol of a discrete source into a block of bits, where each block consists of the same number of m bits. There are thus 2^m different blocks for a block of m bits. Assuming the number of symbols in the source alphabet is K and $K \leq 2^m$, then a different binary m-tuple may be assigned to each symbol. Assuming the decoder in the receiver knows the beginning of the encoded sequence is, the decoder can segment the received bits into m-bit blocks and then decode each block into the corresponding source symbol. The encoder in the transmitter and the decoder in the receiver must both obviously employ the same look-up table. Each source symbol thus requires $m = [\log_2 K]^+$ bits—where $[w]^+$ denotes the smallest positive integer greater than or equal to the positive number w—we thus have $\log_2 K \leq m \leq \log_2 K + 1$, where the lower-bound can be achieved if and only if K is an integer power of 2, i.e., $K = 2^m$, with m being a positive integer.

9.2.3 Variable-Length Codes

The ***variable-length code*** is one whose codeword length is not the same for all source symbols. The genesis of variable-length encoding is based on the intuition that efficient data compression can be achieved by mapping more probable symbols into shorter bit sequences and less likely symbols into longer bit sequences. Morse code of old telegraphy is the first application of the variable-length encoding, where for example, E is represented by a single dot, but Q is represented by dash-dash-dot-dash. Successive codewords of a variable length code are assumed to be transmitted as a continuing sequence of bits, with no demarcation of codeword boundaries, the decoder, given an original starting point, must determine where the codeword boundaries are. Synchronization in general, and initial synchronization in particular, as well as bit error rate performance and buffer overflow are all critical issues in variable-length encoding.

9.2.4 Distinct Codes

A code is ***distinct***, also known as ***non-singular***, if each codeword is distinguishable from other codewords. It is however possible that all the codewords be distinct, yet the decoding turns to be ambiguous. We therefore need to define an even more restrictive condition than non-singularity if we are to obtain practical codes.

9.2.5 Prefix-Free (Instantaneous) Codes

Any sequence consisting of the initial part of the codeword is called a prefix of the codeword. In a ***prefix-free code***, no codeword is a prefix of another codeword. The decoding of a prefix-free code can be accomplished as soon as the codeword representing a source symbol is fully received. Prefix-free codes are also called ***instantaneous codes***. Note that in the construction of an instantaneous code, the shorter some of the codewords are, the longer some others will be.

9.2.6 Uniquely Decodable Codes

A distinct code must be ***uniquely decodable***, in that for each sequence of source symbols, there is a corresponding codeword that is different from a codeword corresponding to any other sequence of source symbols. Decoding the output from a uniquely decodable code, and even determining whether it is uniquely decodable, can be complicated. A sufficient condition, but not a necessary one, for a code to be uniquely decodable is to be prefix-free. In other words, all prefix-free codes are uniquely decodable, but the converse is not true. Figure 9.3 presents the classification of codes leading to instantaneous codes.

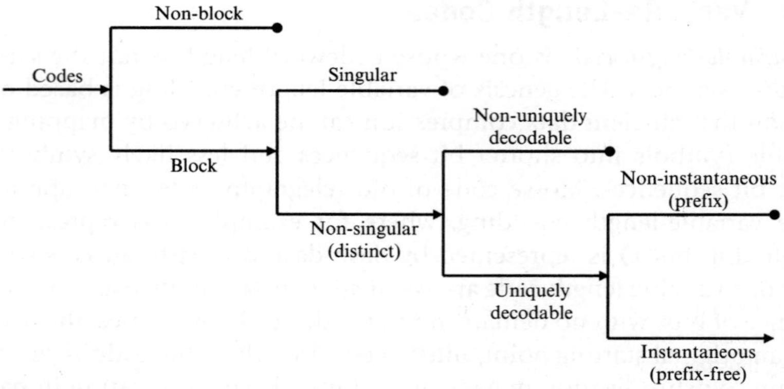

FIGURE 9.3 Classification of codes.

9.2.7 Kraft Inequality

Consider a DMS and assume the binary codeword assigned to symbol m_i, with the probability p_i, has length l_i bits, and the number of source symbols is K. A necessary and sufficient condition for the existence of an instantaneous (prefix-free) binary code is as follows:

$$\sum_{i=1}^{K} 2^{-l_i} \leq 1 \tag{9.8}$$

which is known as the ***Kraft inequality***. Note that satisfying the inequality does not mean the code is automatically uniquely decodable. The inequality is merely a condition on the codeword lengths of the code and not on the codewords themselves. The inequality does not show how these codewords can be obtained.

EXAMPLE 9.5

Consider the following three codes:

Symbol	Code 1	Code 2	Code 3
x_1	0	0	0
x_2	100	100	10
x_3	110	110	110
x_4	111	11	11

Determine whether or not each of these three codes satisfies the Kraft inequality, and if a code does, determine whether or not the code is instantaneous.

Solution

We first calculate the left-hand side of (9.8) for each code, and then compare it to 1 to determine if the Kraft inequality holds. As reflected below, Code 1 satisfies the inequality:

$$\sum_{i=1}^{4} 2^{-l_i} = \frac{1}{2} + \frac{1}{8} + \frac{1}{8} + \frac{1}{8} = \frac{7}{8} \leq 1$$

The codeword lengths of this code are thus acceptable as codeword lengths of an instantaneous code. From the inspection of the codewords themselves, we see that the code is actually instantaneous and thus uniquely decodable. As reflected below, Code 2 satisfies the inequality:

$$\sum_{i=1}^{4} 2^{-l_i} = \frac{1}{2} + \frac{1}{8} + \frac{1}{8} + \frac{1}{4} = 1$$

The codeword lengths of this code are thus acceptable as codeword lengths of an instantaneous code. The inspection of the codewords themselves reveals the fact that a codeword is a prefix of another, thus the code is not instantaneous, nor is it uniquely decodable. As reflected below, Code 3 does not satisfy the inequality:

$$\sum_{i=1}^{4} 2^{-l_i} = \frac{1}{2} + \frac{1}{4} + \frac{1}{8} + \frac{1}{4} = \frac{9}{8} \geq 1$$

As no inspection of the codewords is required, we easily conclude that Code 3 cannot possibly be an instantaneous code. The code is not uniquely decodable either. The results for all three codes are summarized as follows:

	Code 1	Code 2	Code 3
Is the Kraft inequality satisfied?	Yes	Yes	No
Is the code instantaneous?	Yes	No	No

9.2.8 Extension Codes

To achieve a more efficient code, ***extension codes*** can be employed, where rather than encoding individual source symbols, successive blocks of n symbols are encoded at a time. In other words, the K^n n-tuples are regarded as the elements of a larger alphabet. Each n-tuple can be encoded into $L_n = [\log_2 K^n]^+$ bits—where $[w]^+$ denotes the smallest positive integer greater than or equal to the positive number w. We thus have $\log_2 K^n \leq L_n \leq \log_2 K^n + 1$ or equivalently we have the following:

$$\log_2 K \leq \frac{L_n}{n} \leq \log_2 K + \frac{1}{n} \tag{9.9}$$

In other words, the average number of bits per original source symbol $\frac{L_n}{n}$ is lower-bounded by $\log_2 K$ and upper-bounded by $\log_2 K + \frac{1}{n}$. Note that by increasing n, the lower-bound and the upper-bound become closer to one another, and the average number of bits per symbol can thus be made arbitrarily close to $\log_2 K$, regardless of whether K is an integer power of 2. This increase in code efficiency is of course at the expense of additional encoding/decoding complexity and modest delay.

EXAMPLE 9.6

A source can generate four symbols x_1, x_2, x_3, and x_4. Provide classification of the codes illustrated in the following table:

Symbol	Code 1	Code 2	Code 3	Code 4	Code 5	Code 6
x_1	00	00	0	0	0	1
x_2	01	01	1	10	01	01
x_3	00	10	00	110	011	001
x_4	11	11	11	111	0111	0001

Solution

All six codes are block codes, but none of them are extension codes. Codes 1 and 2 are fixed-length codes and the others are variable-length codes. Except Code 1, all others are distinct codes. Only codes 2, 4, and 6 are prefix-free (instantaneous) codes, and obviously they are also uniquely decodable. Code 5 does not satisfy the prefix condition, and yet it is uniquely decodable since the bit 0 indicates the beginning of each codeword. Codes 1 and 3 are not uniquely decodable. Code 6 provides a demarcation of codeword boundaries, as the last bit of a codeword is a 1.

9.3 SOURCE CODING THEOREM

Source coding, as shown in Figure 9.4, is a process by which the output of a DMS is converted into a sequence of bits, while meeting the requirement of being uniquely decodable. The objective is to minimize the average number of bits per source symbol by reducing the redundancy of the information source. Assuming the binary codeword assigned to the symbol m_i, with the probability p_i, has length l_i bits, and the number of source symbols is K, the ***average codeword length*** of the source encoder is then defined as follows:

$$\bar{L} = \sum_{i=1}^{K} p_i\, l_i \qquad (9.10)$$

Let $L_{\min}$ denote the minimum possible value of the average codeword length $\bar{L}$. We then define the ***code efficiency*** η of the source encoder as follows:

$$\eta = \frac{L_{\min}}{\bar{L}} \leq 1 \qquad (9.11)$$

For a very efficient code, we have $\eta \rightarrow 1$. The fundamental question is how to determine $L_{\min}$. ***Shannon's source coding theorem*** can provide the answer to this question. This theorem may be stated as follows: For a DMS of entropy $H(X)$,

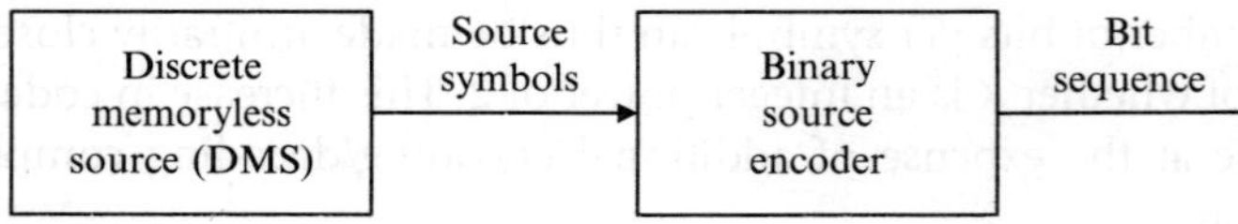

FIGURE 9.4 Source encoding.

the average codeword length $\bar{L}$ for any distortionless source encoding is bounded as follows:

$$H(X) \le \bar{L} \tag{9.12}$$

Accordingly, the entropy $H(X)$ of a DMS provides a fundamental limit on the average number of bits per source symbol, furthermore $\bar{L}$ can be made as close to $H(X)$ as desired for some suitably chosen code. This theorem only gives the necessary and sufficient condition for the existence of source codes. However, it fails to provide an algorithm for the design of source codes that can realize the performance predicted by this theorem. Note that with $L_{min} = H(X)$, we may write the code efficiency as follows:

$$\eta = \frac{H(X)}{\bar{L}} \le 1 \tag{9.13}$$

The source entropy provides a limit at which the source output can be compressed, where above the source entropy, it is possible to design such a source code, and below it, no source code can exist. Given a DMS of entropy $H(X)$, the average codeword length $\bar{L}$ of a prefix-free code is bounded as follows:

$$H(X) \le \bar{L} < H(X) + 1 \tag{9.14}$$

Furthermore, the equality is satisfied if and only if each symbol probability is an integer power of $\frac{1}{2}$. If blocks of n bits are encoded, that is we employ n^{th}-order extension codes, the average codeword length of the extended code $\bar{L}_n$ is then as follows:

$$H(X) \le \bar{L}_n < H(X) + \frac{1}{n} \tag{9.15}$$

For $n = 1$, (9.15) becomes (9.14). It is important to highlight the fact that when $n \to \infty$, we get $\bar{L}_n \to H(X)$, as desired. In other words, in a DMS, by increasing the encoding/decoding complexity caused by the large number of source symbols in the extension code, the average codeword length can be reduced to approach the source entropy.

EXAMPLE 9.7

A source emits five equally-likely symbols x_1, x_2, x_3, x_4, and x_5, that is we have $P(x_1) = P(x_2) = P(x_3) = P(x_4) = P(x_5) = 0.2$. Find the source entropy $H(x)$. Find fixed-length codes when $n = 1$, $n = 2$, and $n = 3$. Determine the average number of bits for each case, and comment on the results.

Solution

Figure 9.5 shows the codewords for all three codes. Using (9.4), we calculate the source entropy, we thus have $H(X) = 5(-0.2 \log_2(0.2)) \cong 2.322$ bits.

For $n = 1$, each codeword has three bits and there are five codewords, each with a probability of $0.2\left(= (0.2)^1\right)$. The average codeword length when $n = 1$ is thus as follows: $\bar{L}_1 = 3 \times 5 \times 0.2 = 3$ bits.

(a)

Symbol	Probability	Codeword
x_1	0.2	000
x_2	0.2	001
x_3	0.2	010
x_4	0.2	011
x_5	0.2	100

(b)

Symbol	Probability	Codeword
x_1x_1	0.04	00000
x_1x_2	0.04	00001
x_1x_3	0.04	00010
x_1x_4	0.04	00011
x_1x_5	0.04	00100
x_2x_1	0.04	00101
x_2x_2	0.04	00110
x_2x_3	0.04	00111
x_2x_4	0.04	01000
x_2x_5	0.04	01001
x_3x_1	0.04	01010
x_3x_2	0.04	01011
x_3x_3	0.04	01100
x_3x_4	0.04	01101
x_3x_5	0.04	01110
x_4x_1	0.04	01111
x_4x_2	0.04	10000
x_4x_3	0.04	10001
x_4x_4	0.04	10010
x_4x_5	0.04	10011
x_5x_1	0.04	10100
x_5x_2	0.04	10101
x_5x_3	0.04	10110
x_5x_4	0.04	10111
x_5x_5	0.04	11000

(c)

Symbol	Probability	Codeword
$x_1x_1x_1$	0.008	0000000
$x_1x_1x_2$	0.008	0000001
$x_1x_1x_3$	0.008	0000010
$x_1x_1x_4$	0.008	0000011
$x_1x_1x_5$	0.008	0000100
$x_1x_2x_1$	0.008	0000101
$x_1x_2x_2$	0.008	0000110
.	.	.
.	.	.
.	.	.
$x_5x_4x_4$	0.008	1110110
$x_5x_4x_5$	0.008	1110111
$x_5x_5x_1$	0.008	1111000
$x_5x_5x_2$	0.008	1111001
$x_5x_5x_3$	0.008	1111010
$x_5x_5x_4$	0.008	1111011
$x_5x_5x_5$	0.008	1111100

FIGURE 9.5 Extension codes for Example 9.7: (a) $n=1$ and 5 codewords, (b) $n=2$ and 25 codewords, and (c) $n=3$ and 125 codewords.

For $n=2$, each codeword has five bits and there are 25 codewords, each with a probability of 0.04 $\left(=(0.2)^2\right)$. The average codeword length when $n=2$ is thus as follows: $\bar{L}_2 = 5 \times 25 \times 0.04 =$ 5 bits. However, for $n=2$, each 5-bit codeword represents two symbols, we therefore have on average 2.5 $\left(=\frac{5}{2}\right)$ bits representing a symbol.

For $n=3$, each codeword has seven bits, there are 125 codewords and each with a probability of 0.008 $\left(=(0.2)^3\right)$. The average codeword length when $n=3$ is thus as follows: $\bar{L}_3 = 7 \times 125 \times 0.008 = 7$ bits. However, for $n=3$, each 7-bit codeword represents three symbols, we therefore have on average 2.333 $\left(\cong\frac{7}{3}\right)$ bits representing a symbol.

We can thus conclude, as the source coding theorem indicates, that as n increases, the average codeword length approaches the source entropy, as reflected below:

$$\bar{L}_1 = 3 > \bar{L}_2 = 2.5 > \bar{L}_3 = 2.333 > H(x) = 2.322$$

For $n=3$, the average codeword length is already almost equal to the source entropy. Thus, there is no need to employ an extension code with $n=4$, especially as n is increased, the code complexity is significantly increased.

9.4 LOSSLESS DATA COMPRESSION

Symbols generated by physical sources generally contain a significant amount of information that is redundant (i.e., most messages are longer than they need to be to convey the information they contain). For efficient signal transmission, the redundancy should be removed from the signal prior to transmission; otherwise, primary communication resources, such as power and bandwidth, are partially wasted. The process to remove redundancy is called ***compression***, and is transparent to end users. Removal of redundancy from the data, with the condition that the original digital information can be exactly recovered from encoded binary stream, is known as ***lossless data compression***. There are two distinct lossless data compression mechanisms:

i) A compression mechanism that requires advanced knowledge of the message statistics, this leads to the class of ***entropy (probability-based) source coding***, such as Huffman coding.
ii) A compression mechanism that does not require prior knowledge of the message statistics, this leads to the class of ***universal (adaptive) source coding***, such as the Lempel-Ziv algorithm.

9.4.1 Huffman Source Coding Algorithm

In ***Huffman coding***, fixed-length blocks of the source symbols are mapped onto variable-length binary blocks. Huffman code is a prefix-free code, which can thus be decoded instantaneously and uniquely. Huffman codes are formulated to be an optimal code, i.e., they achieve the shortest average code length (minimum average codeword length), which may still be greater than or equal to the entropy of source. The average length of a Huffman code is the same as the entropy (i.e., maximum efficiency), if the probability of every symbol produced by the source is an integer power of $\frac{1}{2}$.

Modified versions of Huffman coding are employed in fax machines and scanners as well as in the assignments of area and country codes for long-distance telephone calls in most parts of the world. Of course, Huffman code has its own drawbacks, such as the statistics must be known in advance and it performs poorly, if the actual statistics of the message differ from the assumed statistics. There is a mismatch of source and channel rates, as a source produces symbols at a constant rate that are then encoded into variable-length codewords. Another shortcoming associated with Huffman coding is that in order to increase its efficiency, we need to design the code for blocks of two or more symbols; this exponentially increases the complexity of the algorithm. For certain high-speed applications, the complexity and speed of Huffman coding can then become a bottleneck.

The task of assigning shorter codewords to the more frequent source symbols and longer codewords to the less frequent source symbols lies at the heart of Huffman coding. The Huffman coding algorithm may be summarized by the following steps:

i) Sort source symbols in decreasing order of their probabilities that is the symbol with the highest probability is on the top of the list and the symbol with the lowest probability is at the bottom of the list. If there are two symbols or more with equal probabilities, choose any of the various possibilities.
ii) Combine the bottom two entries (i.e., the two symbols with the lowest probabilities) to form a new entry with a probability that is the sum of the two probabilities. If necessary, reorder the list so that probabilities, including the newly formed one, are all still in decreasing order. This step reduces the list of symbols by one.
iii) Continue combining in pairs, i.e., repeat step ii), until only two entries remain. In other words, if there are K source symbols, then step ii) needs to be repeated $K-2$ times.
iv) Assign arbitrarily 0 and 1 as codewords for the two remaining symbols.
v) Append the current codeword with a 0 and a 1 to obtain the codeword for the preceding symbol, should a symbol be the result of the merger of two symbols in a preceding step (i.e., a 0 or a 1 forms a prefix for all the prior symbols).
vi) Continue step v) until no symbol is preceded by another symbol, and then stop.

It is important to note that the Huffman code is not unique, as it is arbitrary how to assign a 0 or a 1 to the two remaining source symbols. Another difference occurs when the combined probabilities of two symbols become equal to the probability of a symbol already in the list. In such a case, where to place the probability of the new entry in the list can impact the lengths of the codewords and thus the variance over the ensemble of source symbols; nevertheless, the average codeword length remains the same.

EXAMPLE 9.8

The alphabet set of a DMS consists of five symbols A, B, C, D, and E whose probabilities are 0.7, 0.1, 0.1, 0.05, and 0.05, respectively. Assuming symbols are encoded one at a time (individually), design two different Huffman codes with different variances, and show that both codes have the same average number of bits per symbol.

Solution

Figure 9.6 shows two different Huffman trees, and tabulates, for each Huffman tree, the codewords. The means of the two Huffman codes are as follows:

$$\overline{L}_{\text{code\_1}} = 0.7 \times 1 + 0.1 \times 2 + 0.1 \times 3 + 2 \times 0.05 \times 4 = 1.6 \text{ (bits)}$$

and

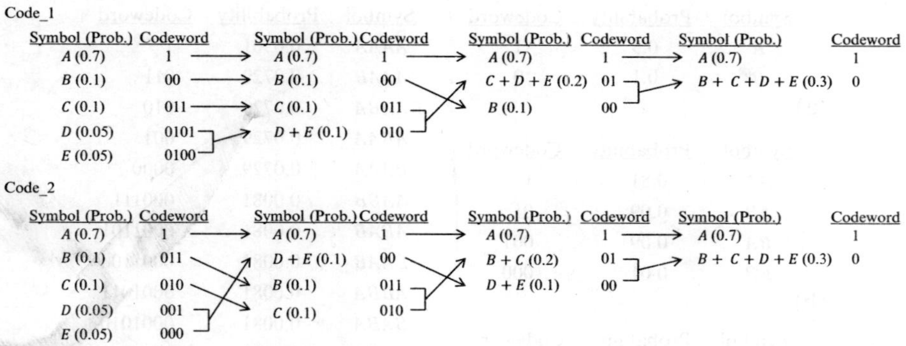

FIGURE 9.6 Huffman codes for Example 9.8.

$$\overline{L}_{\text{code\_2}} = 0.7 \times 1 + (0.1 + 0.1 + 0.05 + 0.05) \times 3 = 1.6 \text{ (bits)}$$

As expected, both Huffman codes have the same average codeword lengths. However, their variances are different as follows:

$$\sigma^2_{\text{code\_1}} = 0.7(1-1.6)^2 + 0.1(2-1.6)^2 + 0.1(3-1.6)^2 + 2 \times 0.05(4-1.6)^2 = 1.04$$

and

$$\sigma^2_{\text{code\_2}} = 0.7(1-1.6)^2 + (0.1 + 0.1 + 0.05 + 0.05)(3-1.6)^2 = 0.84$$

The standard deviation of code-1 is thus 1.02 bits and that of code-2 is 0.92 bits. It is important to note that once a combined symbol, due to its probability, is moved on the list as high as possible, a Huffman code with the smallest possible variance, a desirable feature in a code, results.

The Huffman coding can be effectively employed to create extension codes, in which blocks of symbols are encoded at a time.

EXAMPLE 9.9

The alphabet of a DMS consists of two symbols A and B whose probabilities are 0.9 and 0.1, respectively. Find the entropy of this source. Design a Huffman code for this source and determine the average number of bits per symbol if symbols are encoded a) one at a time (individually), b) two at a time (pair-wise), c) three at a time, and d) four at a time. Compare the average number of bits for each of these four cases with the source entropy, and comment on the results.

Solution

Using (9.4), the source entropy, which provides a lower-bound for the average code length, is calculated as follows: $H(X) = -0.1 \log_2 0.1 - 0.9 \log_2 0.9 \cong 0.469$ bits per symbol. We employ n^{th}-order extension codes, for $n = 1$, 2, 3, and 4. Figure 9.7 shows the Huffman codewords for each of the four cases, after arranging them in decreasing order.

(a) When symbols are encoded one at a time (i.e., $n = 1$), the average number of bits per symbol is as follows: $\overline{L}_1 = 1 \times 0.9 + 1 \times 0.1 = 1$ bit per symbol.

(b) When symbols are encoded two at a time (i.e., $n = 2$), the average number of bits per symbol is as follows: $\overline{L}_2 = 1 \times 0.81 + 2 \times 0.09 + 3 \times 0.09 + 3 \times 0.01 = 1.29$ bits per two symbols or equivalently 0.645 bits per symbol.

Symbol	Probability	Codeword
A	0.9	1
B	0.1	0

(a)

Symbol	Probability	Codeword
AA	0.81	1
AB	0.09	01
BA	0.09	001
BB	0.01	000

(b)

Symbol	Probability	Codeword
AAA	0.729	1
AAB	0.081	001
BAA	0.081	000
ABA	0.081	011
BBA	0.009	01011
BAB	0.009	01010
ABB	0.009	01001
BBB	0.001	01000

(c)

Symbol	Probability	Codeword
$AAAA$	0.6561	1
$AAAB$	0.0729	011
$AABA$	0.0729	010
$ABAA$	0.0729	001
$BAAA$	0.0729	0000
$AABB$	0.0081	000111
$ABAB$	0.0081	0001101
$BAAB$	0.0081	0001100
$ABBA$	0.0081	0001011
$BABA$	0.0081	0001010
$BBAA$	0.0081	0001001
$ABBB$	0.0009	000100011
$BABB$	0.0009	000100010
$BBAB$	0.0009	000100001
$BBBA$	0.0009	0001000001
$BBBB$	0.0001	0001000000

(d)

FIGURE 9.7 Huffman coding using extension codes for Example 9.9.

(c) When symbols are encoded three at a time (i.e., $n = 3$), the average number of bits per symbol is as follows: $\overline{L}_3 = 1 \times 0.729 + 3 \times 3 \times 0.081 + 3 \times 5 \times 0.009 + 5 \times 0.001 = 1.598$ bits per three symbols or equivalently 0.533 bits per symbol.

(d) When symbols are encoded four at a time (i.e., $n = 4$), the average number of bits per symbol is as follows: $\overline{L}_4 = 1 \times 0.6561 + 3 \times 3 \times 0.0729 + 4 \times 0.0729 + 1 \times 6 \times 0.0081 + 5 \times 7 \times 0.0081 + 3 \times 9 \times 0.0009 + 10 \times 0.0009 + 10 \times 0.0001 = 1.9702$ bits per four symbols or equivalently 0.493 bits per symbol.

In all four cases, (9.15) is satisfied. By encoding longer strings of symbols, the average number of bits per source symbol can get closer to the uncertainty of the source (i.e., source entropy). We can therefore expect $\overline{L}_n \to H(X)$ as $n \to \infty$. As expected, by considering higher extension codes, the code efficiency $\eta_n = \dfrac{H(X)}{\overline{L}_n}$ is improved, as reflected below:

	$n = 1$	$n = 2$	$n = 3$	$n = 4$
Average number of bits per n symbols	1	1.29	1.598	1.9702
Average number of bits per symbol	1	0.645	0.533	0.493
Source entropy	0.469	0.469	0.469	0.469
Code efficiency	46.9%	72.7%	88%	95.3%

An increase in n, which brings about an increase in the complexity of the encoding/decoding process, results in an improvement in the code efficiency; however, the rate of improvement decreases.

9.4.2 Lempel-Ziv Source Coding Algorithm

In ***Lempel-Ziv coding***, variable-length blocks of the source symbols are mapped onto fixed-length binary blocks. In other words, any sequence of source symbols is uniquely parsed into phrases of varying length and these phrases are encoded using codewords of equal length. This coding is based on the realization that any stream of data with some measure of redundancy consists of repetitions of typical sequences for that data set. Lempel-Ziv coding realizes optimum compression in the limit for very large data set, and it is intrinsically adaptive and can encode frequently occurring groups of source symbols, when symbol and pattern probabilities are unknown.

Most compression programs use a variation of the Lempel-Ziv adaptive dictionary-based algorithm. Text and programming files are very redundant; a reduction of 50% or more is typical. In general, the longer the file is, the higher the rate of reduction is. For a stationary source, as the length of the original sequence, which needs to be parsed, is increased, the compression role of Lempel-Ziv coding becomes more apparent, and as the length of the sequence increases, the number of bits in the compressed sequence approaches $nH(X)$. When the Lempel-Ziv algorithm is applied to a typical English text, it achieves a compaction of approximately 55%, vis-à-vis 43% achieved with Huffman coding. The reason lies in the fact that Huffman coding does not take advantage of the inter-character redundancies. Lempel-Ziv coding, in contrast to Huffman coding, is suitable for synchronous transmission. The size of the dictionary can theoretically grow infinitely large. However, in practice, fixed blocks of 12 bits long or a couple of bits longer are used, which implies a codebook of at least 4096 entries. Lempel-Ziv, in one version or another, is the standard algorithm for file compression.

The task of parsing the source symbol stream into segments that are the shortest sequences of symbols not seen previously lies at the heart of the Lempel-Ziv algorithm. As soon as the new output sequence is different from the previous output sequences, it is recognized as a new phrase and encoded. It is very important to highlight that the new phrase is the concatenation of a previous phrase, already compiled in a codebook, and a single new source symbol. The basis for Lempel-Ziv coding universal coding is the idea that we can achieve compression of a string (an arbitrary sequence of bits) by always coding a series of zeros and ones as some previous string (the prefix string) plus one new bit (a 0 or a 1). Then, the new string formed by adding the new bit to the previously used prefix string becomes a potential string for future strings. Compression results from reusing frequently occurring strings. It is important to note that the codebook (dictionary), along with codewords, are transmitted and the decomposition of the encoded sequence is straightforward, as the decoder knows exactly where to lock and find the matching string.

EXAMPLE 9.10

Illustrate the Lempel-Ziv algorithm by parsing and encoding on the following 42-bit sequence: 010000011110000111000110010101010000000011.

Solution

Figure 9.8 summarizes the codewords along with the dictionary locations and contents. We first assume bit 0 and bit 1 are in 0001 (the first) and 0010 (the second) addresses in the codebook (dictionary). We parse the sequence into the shortest possible phrases not in the dictionary, which each consists of a previous phrase already in the dictionary and a single new source symbol of 0 or 1. The sequence is therefore parsed into the following phrases: 0, 1, 00, 000, 11, 110, 0001, 1100, 01, 10, 010, 101, 010, 0000, 00011.

After 0 and 1, the next phrase is 00. The phrase 00 consists of two parts, a 0 which is already stored in the first address (0001) in the dictionary and a 0, as such 00 is encoded into 00010, and 00 forms the content of the third address (0011) in the dictionary. After 00, the next new phrase is 000. The phrase 000 consists of two parts, a 00 which is already stored in the third address (0011) in the dictionary and a 0, as such 000 is encoded into 00110, and 000 forms the content of the fourth address (0100) in the dictionary. After 000, the next new phrase is 11. The phrase 11 consists of two parts, a 1 which is already stored in the second address (0010) in the dictionary and a 1, as such 11 is encoded into 00101, and 11 forms the content of the fifth address (0101) in the dictionary.

The encoding process continues until all 15 phrases can be represented by four bit-addresses in the dictionary. Therefore, each phrase requires five bits, the four-bit address plus an extra bit to represent the new source symbol. For each phrase we thus require five bits, for a total of 75 bits. This example highlights how Lempel-Ziv coding works, as 75 bits is not a compressed version of the original 42 bits. In principle, the longer the uncompressed original data file is, the more effective Lempel-Ziv coding can be.

Dictionary Locations		Dictionary Contents	Codewords
1	0001	0	0000 0
2	0010	1	0000 1
3	0011	00	0001 0
4	0100	000	0011 0
5	0101	11	0010 1
6	0110	110	0101 0
7	0111	0001	0100 1
8	1000	1100	0110 0
9	1001	01	0001 1
10	1010	10	0010 0
11	1011	010	1001 1
12	1100	101	1010 1
13	1101	010	1001 0
14	1110	0000	0100 0
15	1111	00011	0111 1

FIGURE 9.8 Lempel-Ziv coding algorithm for Example 9.10.

9.5 DISCRETE MEMORYLESS CHANNELS

The focus in this section is on information transmission through a discrete memoryless channel rather than on information generation through a DMS. A discrete channel is a statistical model with an input X and an output Y. During each signaling interval (symbol period), the channel accepts an input symbol from X, and in response, it generates an output symbol from Y, generally a noisy version of X. The channel is discrete when the alphabets of X and Y are both finite. X and Y in all practical channels are random variables. In a ***discrete memoryless channel*** (DMC), the current output symbol depends only on the current input symbol and not on any of the previous input symbols.

9.5.1 Channel Transition Probabilities

The input X consists of input symbols $x_1, x_2, \ldots, x_J$ and the a priori probabilities of these source symbols are $p(x_1), p(x_2), \ldots, p(x_J)$, respectively, and are all assumed to be known. The output Y consists of output symbols $y_1, y_2, \ldots, y_M$, and the ***transition probabilities*** $p(y_m/x_j)$, for $m = 1, 2, \ldots, M$ and $j = 1, 2, \ldots, J$, are all assumed to be known as they describe a DMC. In short, a DMC is completely defined by the $J \times M$ channel matrix consisting of all transition probabilities. Since each input to the channel results in some output, we always have the following:

$$\sum_{m=1}^{M} p(y_m/x_j) = 1, \quad j = 1, 2, \ldots, J \tag{9.16}$$

The joint probability distribution of the random variables X and Y, i.e., the joint probability of transmitting x_j and receiving y_m for all cases, are also given by:

$$p(x_j, y_m) = p(y_m/x_j)p(x_j), \; j = 1, 2, \ldots, J; \quad m = 1, 2, \ldots, M \tag{9.17}$$

The marginal probability distribution of the output random variable is thus as follows:

$$p(y_m) = \sum_{j=1}^{J} p(y_m/x_j)p(x_j), \; m = 1, 2, \ldots, M \tag{9.18}$$

EXAMPLE 9.11

The transition probability diagram of a binary symmetric channel (BSC) is shown in Figure 9.9. Explain why it is called a BSC and identify the transition probabilities.

Solution

The channel has two input symbols ($x_1 = 0$, $x_2 = 1$) and two output symbols ($y_1 = 0$, $y_2 = 1$). This binary channel is symmetric as the probability of receiving a 1 if a 0 is transmitted, i.e., p, is the same as the probability of receiving a 0 if a 1 is transmitted. The transitional probabilities are as follows:

$$p(y_1/x_1) = p(y_2/x_2) = 1 - p$$

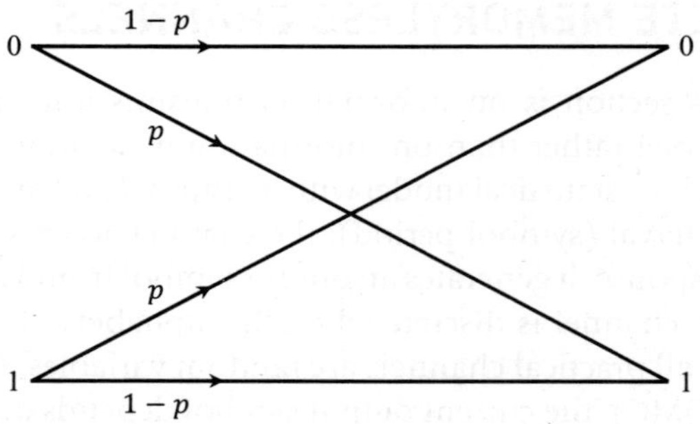

FIGURE 9.9 Binary symmetric channel (BSC).

and

$p(y_1/x_2)=p(y_2/x_1)=p$

Note that if $p=0$, then the BSC channel is called noiseless.

9.5.2 Mutual Information

The entropy $H(X)$ is a measure of the prior uncertainty about the channel input X (i.e., before observing the channel output Y) and is given by:

$$H(X) = -\sum_{j=1}^{J} p(x_j)\,\log_2 p(x_j) \tag{9.19}$$

and the ***conditional entropy*** $H(X/Y)$ representing the amount of uncertainty remaining about the channel input after the channel output has been observed is given by:

$$H(X/Y) = \sum_{m=1}^{M} H(X/y=y_m)p(y_m) = -\sum_{m=1}^{M}\sum_{j=1}^{J} p(x_j, y_m)\,\log_2(p(x_j/y_m)) \tag{9.20}$$

The entropy $H(X)$ represents the uncertainty about the channel input before observing the channel output, and the conditional entropy $H(X/Y)$ represents the uncertainty about the channel input after observing the channel output. Their difference, $I(X;Y)=H(X) - H(X/Y)$, also known as ***mutual information***, thus represents our uncertainty about the channel input that is resolved by observing the channel output. We therefore have:

$$I(X;Y) = H(X) - H(X/Y) = \sum_{j=1}^{J}\sum_{m=1}^{M} P(x_j, y_m)\,\log_2\left(\frac{p(x_j/y_m)}{p(x_j)}\right) \tag{9.21}$$

Mutual information is symmetric and non-negative, i.e., $I(X;Y)=I(Y;X)>0$. As shown in Figure 9.10, we have the following useful relationships:

$$I(X;Y)=I(Y;X)=H(X)-H(X/Y)=H(Y)-H(Y/X)=H(X)+H(Y)-H(X,Y) \tag{9.22}$$

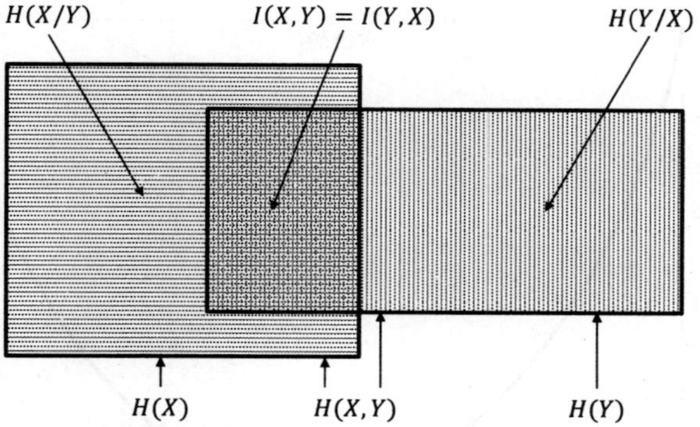

FIGURE 9.10 Entropy, conditional entropy, and mutual information.

The mutual information of a channel therefore depends not only on the channel, but also on how the channel is utilized.

9.5.3 Capacity of Discrete Memory Channel

Noting that the input probability distribution is independent of the channel, the ***capacity of a DMC,*** as defined by Shannon, is as follows:

$$C = \max_{\{P(x_j)\}} I(X;Y) \tag{9.23}$$

where the maximization is over all possible input probability distributions $\{p(x_j)\}$ on X and the capacity is measured in bits per symbol. The channel capacity is a function of only the channel transition probabilities $p(x_j/y_m)$ that define the channel. The maximization is over J input variables $p(x_1), p(x_2), \ldots, p(x_J)$, subject to two obvious constraints that each input probability is non-negative and the sum of all input probabilities is 1.

EXAMPLE 9.12

Determine the capacity of a BSC, where the probabilities of the input symbols 0 and 1 are α and $1-\alpha$, respectively, and the probability of error is represented by p.

Solution

Using (9.17) and noting $p(x_1)=\alpha$ and $p(x_2)=1-\alpha$, the joint probabilities are as follows:

$p(x_1, y_1)=\alpha(1-p)$,
$p(x_2, y_1)=(1-\alpha)p$,
$p(x_1, y_2)=\alpha p$ and
$p(x_2, y_2)=(1-\alpha)(1-p)$.

Using (9.18), the marginal probabilities are as follows:

$p(y_1)=p(x_1, y_1)+p(x_2, y_1)=\alpha(1-p)+(1-\alpha)p=\alpha+p-2\alpha p$

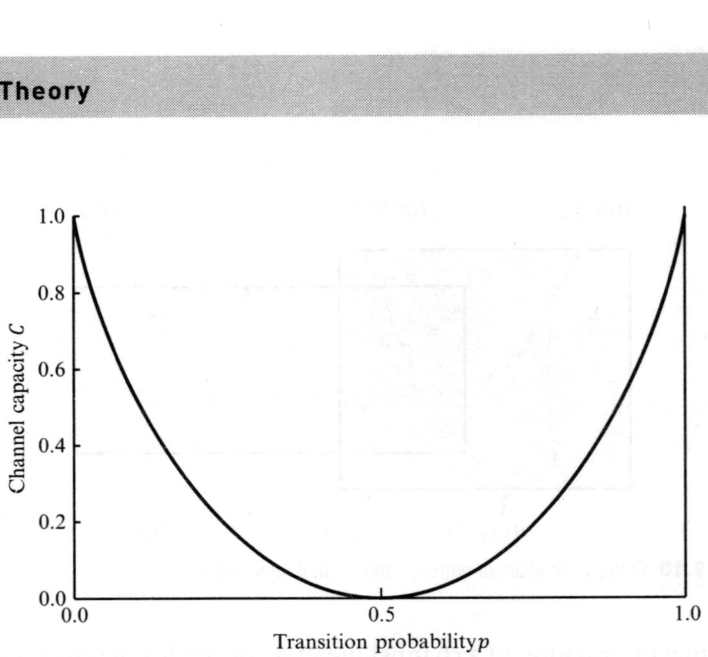

FIGURE 9.11 Channel capacity of a BSC.

and

$p(y_2) = p(x_1, y_2) + p(x_2, y_2) = \alpha p + (1-\alpha)(1-p) = 1 - \alpha - p + 2\alpha p.$

Using (9.22), we have:

$$\begin{aligned} I(Y;X) &= H(Y) - H(Y/X) \\ &= (-(\alpha + p - 2\alpha p)\log_2(\alpha + p - 2\alpha p) - (1 - \alpha - p + 2\alpha p)\log_2(1 - \alpha - p + 2\alpha p)) \\ &\quad - (-\alpha(1-p)\log_2(1-p) - \alpha p \log_2 p - (1-\alpha)p\log_2 p - (1-\alpha)(1-p)\log_2(1-p)) \\ &= H(Y) - (-p\log_2 p - (1-p)\log_2(1-p)) \end{aligned}$$

Note that $H(Y/X)$ is not a function of α and only $H(Y)$ is a function of α. In order to find the channel capacity, we need to differentiate $I(Y;X)$ with respect to α and set it equal to zero. We find that for $\alpha = 0.5$, C is then maximum. We therefore have $C = 1 + p\log_2 p + (1-p)\log_2(1-p)$. Figure 9.11 shows how channel capacity varies with the transition probability p. We note that if $p \to 0$ or $p \to 1$, then $C \to 1$, which is the maximum value of the channel capacity. It is important to note that if $p \to \frac{1}{2}$, then $C \to 0$, which is the minimum value, that is no information is being transmitted at all and in fact the channel is said to be useless, as an equally acceptable decision could be easily made by flipping a coin at the receiver.

9.6 CHANNEL CODING THEOREM

The essence of communications is randomness, for the receiver has no prior knowledge of the information bits transmitted across the channel. The inevitable presence of noise in a channel causes errors between the output and input bit sequences in a digital communication system. Errors occur when the original bit is a 1 and it becomes a 0 or when a 0 becomes a 1. Channel coding refers to mapping the input bit sequence into a channel input bit sequence by the channel encoder in the transmitter and inverse mapping the channel output bit sequence into an output bit sequence by the channel decoder in the receiver, with the objective to better withstand the effects of various channel impairments (i.e., to improve digital communication system performance by reducing the bit error rate). The channel encoder introduces controlled redundancy, called parity bits, and the channel decoder exploits the redundancy to facilitate the detection and correction of bit errors and thus determine the actual transmitted input bit sequence.

The ***channel coding theorem*** states that for a DMS with entropy $H(X)$ bits per symbol and emitting at $1/T_s$ symbols per second (called source average information rate) and a DMC with channel capacity C/T_s bits per symbol (called the critical rate), there exists a coding scheme for which the source output can be transmitted over the channel with an arbitrarily small probability of error, if $H(X)/T_s \leq C/T_s$. Conversely, if $H(X)/T_s > C/T_s$, it is not possible to transmit information over the channel with an arbitrarily small probability of error.

This theorem specifies the channel capacity as a fundamental limit on the rate at which the transmission of reliable error-free messages can go through a DMC. It is important to highlight the fact that the channel coding theorem only asserts the existence of codes, not how they can be constructed.

9.7 GAUSSIAN CHANNEL CAPACITY THEOREM

It is assumed that the channel input is a zero-mean stationary random process that is band-limited to W Hertz and has an average transmitted power of S Watts. The channel output is perturbed by additive white Gaussian noise (AWGN) of zero-mean and power spectral density $N_0/2$ Watts/Hertz. Assuming the Nyquist rate sampling (i.e., taking $2W$ samples per second), the noise sample is Gaussian with zero-mean and variance $N = N_0 W$ Watts and the samples of the received signal are statistically independent. It can be shown that by using the average mutual information between the channel input samples and the channel output samples, the information capacity of band-limited, power-limited Gaussian channels can be defined. The result is known as the ***Shannon's Gaussian channel capacity theorem***:

$$C = W \log_2\left(1 + \frac{S}{N}\right) = W \log_2\left(1 + \left(\frac{E_b}{N_0}\right)\left(\frac{R}{W}\right)\right) \tag{9.24}$$

Note that the capacity C is in bits per second (bps), the bandwidth W is in Hz, the signal-to-noise ratio S/N is in a linear (not logarithmic) scale, and the logarithm is to the base 2. We also have $S = RE_b$, where R is the bit rate in bps and E_b is the bit energy in Joules. The bit error rate can be made arbitrarily small only if the transmission rate R is less than channel capacity C. However, Shannon's information-capacity theorem does not say how to design the system. The larger the ratio R/C is, the more efficient the system is.

EXAMPLE 9.13

Determine the capacity of a wired dial-up voice-grade telephone line, in which the noise is assumed to be additive white Gaussian with a signal-to-noise ratio of 35 dB and a usable bandwidth of 3.2 kHz.

Solution

Noting we have $W = 3200$ Hz and $\frac{S}{N} = 10^{\frac{35}{10}} = 3162$, we can then apply (9.24) to find the channel capacity as follows:

$C = (3200)\log_2(1 + 3162) = 37.2$ kbps

Using (9.24), Figure 9.12 shows the bandwidth-efficiency diagram for $R = C$ (i.e., when the transmission rate R is as high as the channel capacity C). Note that the axis R/W represents bits per second per Hertz (bps/Hz) in logarithmic scale and the axis E_b/N_0 represents energy per bit per noise density in dB. The curve represents a boundary that separates a region for which a system can be practically realized from a region for which no system is theoretically possible. When the system operates at a rate greater than the information capacity (i.e., $R > C$), it is forced to have a high probability of error, regardless of the choice of signal set used for transmission or the receiver used for processing the received signal. Moreover, for a given R, the formula provides a basis for the tradeoff between the channel bandwidth W and the received S/N. In short, S/N and W set a limit on transmission rate, not on bit error rate. There exists a limiting value of $E_b/N_0 = -1.59$ dB, known as the ***Shannon's limit***, below which there can be no error free communication at any information rate. This theoretical limit is reached when $W \to \infty$.

To reach the Shannon limit, the bandwidth availability and the implementation complexity must increase without bound. Any practical system will thus perform worse than the ideal system described by Shannon's limit. The goal of digital communication system designers is to find practical codes that approach the performance of Shannon's ideal (yet unknown) code. Today, most of that promised improvement is realizable by combining coding and modulation using high-performance turbo codes and trellis-coded modulation.

Due to the central limit theorem, the Gaussian noise model is a very reasonable assumption. It is also important to highlight that results obtained for the Gaussian channel often provide a lower-bound on the performance of a system operating over a non-Gaussian channel. In other words, if a particular coding scheme yields a certain bit error rate over the Gaussian channel, another coding scheme can be designed for a non-Gaussian channel to yield a smaller bit error rate. The Gaussian channel model is thus a conservative model in the study of digital communications.

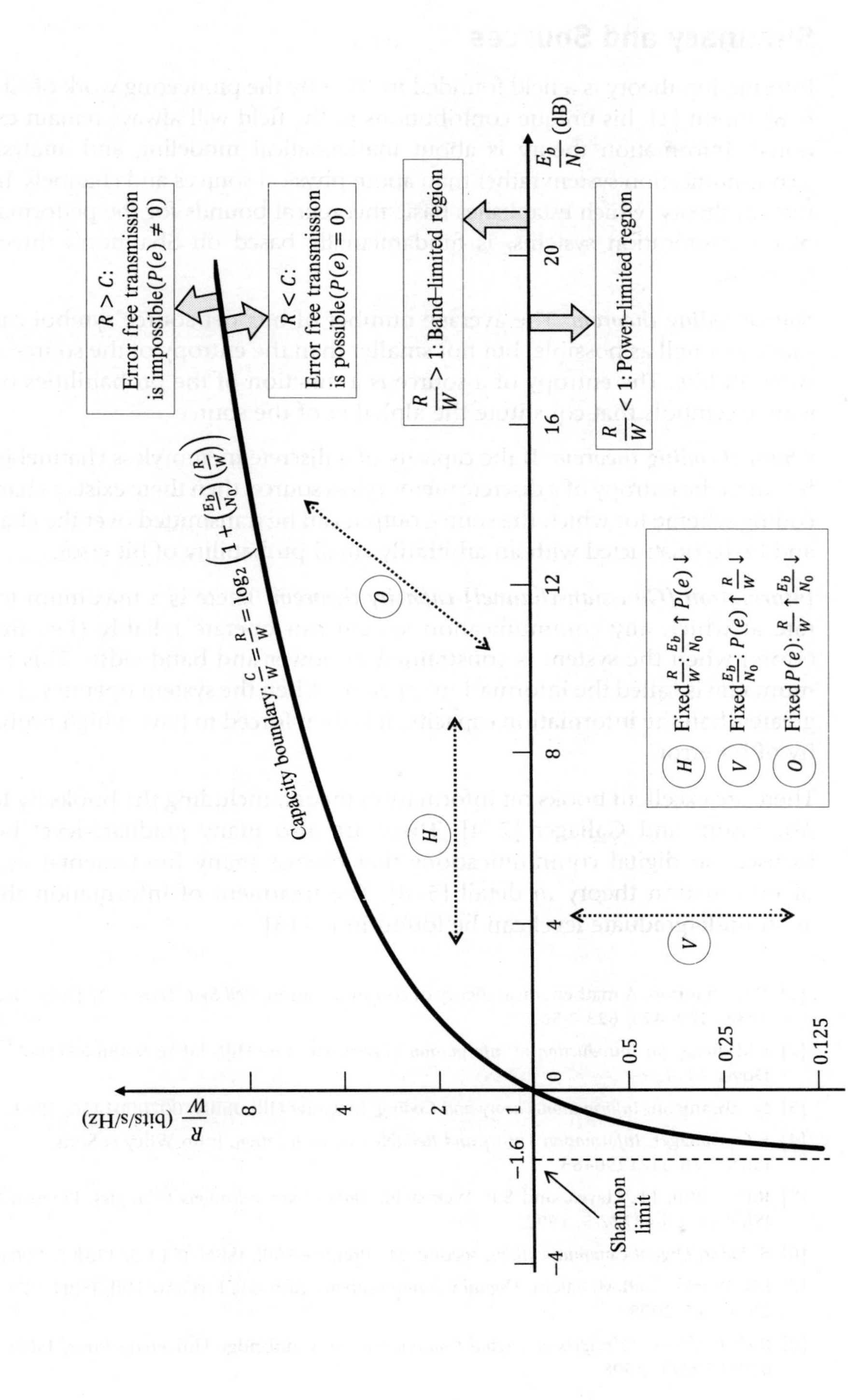

FIGURE 9.12 Bandwidth efficiency diagram.

Summary and Sources

Information theory is a field founded in 1948 by the pioneering work of Claude E. Shannon [1]; his unique contributions to the field will always remain exceptional. Information theory is about mathematical modeling and analysis of a communication system rather than about physical sources and channels. Information theory, which establishes basic theoretical bounds for the performances of communication systems, is fundamentally based on Shannon's three key theorems.

Source coding theorem: The average number of bits per source symbol can be made as small as possible, but not smaller than the entropy of the source measured in bits. The entropy of a source is a function of the probabilities of the source symbols that constitute the alphabet of the source.

Channel coding theorem: If the capacity of a discrete memoryless channel is not less than the entropy of a discrete memoryless source, then there exists a channel-coding scheme for which the source output can be transmitted over the channel and be reconstructed with an arbitrarily small probability of bit error.

Information (Gaussian-channel) capacity theorem: There is a maximum to the rate at which any communication system can operate reliably (i.e., free of errors) when the system is constrained in power and bandwidth. This maximum rate is called the information capacity. When the system operates at a rate greater than the information capacity, it is then forced to have a high probability of bit error.

There are excellent books on information theory, including the books by Reza, Abramson, and Gallager [2–4]. There are also many graduate-level books focused on digital communications that discuss many fundamental aspects of information theory in detail [5–8]. The treatment of information theory at an undergraduate level can be found in [9–13].

[1] C.E. Shannon, A mathematical theory of communication, *Bell Syst. Tech. J.* 27 (July, October, 1948) 379–423, 623–656.

[2] F.M. Reza, *An Introduction to Information Theory*, McGraw-Hill, ISBN: 0-486-68210-2, 1961, Dover 1994.

[3] N. Abramson, *Information Theory and Coding*, McGraw-Hill, ISBN: 0070001456, 1963.

[4] R.G. Gallager, *Information Theory and Reliable Communication*, John Wiley & Sons, ISBN: 978-0471290483.

[5] R.D. Gitlin, J.F. Hayes, and S.B. Weinstein, *Data Communications Principles*, Plenum Press, ISBN: 0-306-43777-5, 1992.

[6] B. Sklar, *Digital Communications*, second ed., Prentice-Hall, ISBN: 0-13-084788-7, 2001.

[7] J.G. Proakis, and M. Salehi, *Digital Communications*, fifth ed., McGraw-Hill, ISBN: 978-0-07-295716-7, 2008.

[8] R.G. Gallager, *Principles of Digital Communication*, Cambridge University Press, ISBN: 978-0521879071, 2008.

[9] S. Haykin, *Digital Communication Systems*, John Wiley & Sons, ISBN: 978-0-471-64735-5, 2014.

[10] B.P. Lathi and Z. Ding, *Modern Digital and Analog Communication Systems*, fourth ed., Oxford University Press, ISBN: 978-0-19-533145-5, 2009.

[11] R.E. Ziemer and W.H. Tranter, *Principles of Communications*, sixth ed., John Wiley & Sons, ISBN: 978-0-470-25254-3, 2009.

[12] K.S. Shanmugam, *Digital and Analog Communication Systems*, John Wiley & Sons, ISBN: 0-471-03090-2, 1979.

[13] H.P. Hsu, *Analog and Digital Communications*, McGraw-Hill, ISBN: 0070306362, 1993.

Problems

9.1 A card is drawn from a deck of playing cards; determine how much information in bits is received in each of the following cases:
(a) The card is a spade.
(b) The card is an ace.
(c) The card is an ace of spades.

9.2 A pair of fair dice is thrown; determine the amount of information in each of the following cases:
(a) The outcome is double 6, i.e., (6, 6).
(b) The outcome is (1, 2).

9.3 A computer monitor is composed of 1920×1080 pixels. Each pixel can have 256 different brightness levels. Determine the information content of a computer frame in bits.

9.4 A source emits a sequence of independent symbols from an alphabet consisting of only four symbols A, B, C, and D. We know that the symbol probabilities for A and B are equal and the symbol probabilities for C and D are also equal. Determine the symbol probabilities for which the source entropy is maximum.

9.5 The following table lists four different codes for a source emitting A, B, C, and D. Determine the source entropy, the average codeword length for each code, and if each code satisfies the Kraft inequality. Comment on each code.

9.6 A source emits an independent sequence of symbols from an alphabet consisting four symbols A, B, C, and D. The symbol probabilities of A and B are equal to α and β, respectively, where $\alpha \geq 0.5$ and $\beta \geq 0.25$. Assuming the symbols are encoded individually using Huffman code, determine the lower- and higher-bounds on the average codeword length.

Symbol (probability)	Code I	Code II	Code III	Code IV
A (0.5)	00	0	0	0
B (0.25)	01	1	01	10
C (0.125)	10	10	011	110
D (0.125)	11	11	0111	111

9.7 A source can independently emit three equally-likely symbols A, B, and C and Huffman code is employed to encode symbols.

(a) Assuming the symbols are encoded one at a time (i.e., individually), determine the average number of bits per symbol.

(b) Assuming the symbols are encoded two at a time (i.e., pair wise), determine the average number of bits per symbol.

9.8 Assuming the symbol rate is 1, X and Y are the channel input and output, respectively, and $P(X=0)=P(X=3)=P$ and $P(X=1)=P(X=2)=Q$, calculate the capacity of the discrete channel with the following transition probabilities: $P(Y=0/X=0)=P(Y=3/X=3)=1$, $P(Y=1/X=1)=P(Y=2/X=2)=p$, and $P(Y=1/X=2)=P(Y=2/X=1)=1-p$.

9.9 Determine the maximum (theoretical) rate at which data can be transmitted from source to sink without errors, provided that there are 256 equally-likely source symbols, the usable channel bandwidth is 200 kHz, and the output signal-to-noise ratio is 30 dB.

9.10 In Shannon-Fano encoding, the source outputs are first ranked in order of non-increasing probability of occurrence. The set is then partitioned into two sets that are as close to equiprobable as possible, and 0s are assigned to the upper set and 1s to the lower set. This process is continued, each time partitioning the sets with as nearly equal probabilities as possible and assigning 0s and 1s to the upper and lower sets, until further partitioning is not possible. Assuming a source can emit eight symbols with the following probabilities: $P(x_1)=P(x_2)=0.27$, $P(x_3)=P(x_4)=P(x_5)=0.13$, and $P(x_1)=0.07$, apply Shannon-Fano encoding and determine the average codeword length.

9.11 Find the channel capacity of the noiseless discrete channel, where $P(Y=0/X=0)=1$ and $P(Y=1/X=1)=1$.

9.12 Consider an AWGN channel with 4-kHz bandwidth and the noise power spectral density 10^{-12} W/Hz. The signal power required at the receiver is 0.1 mW. Calculate the capacity of this channel.

9.13 Show that $H(X/Y)=H(X)$ when X and Y are statistically independent, and $H(X/Y)=0$ when $X=Y$.

9.14 How long will it take to transmit one million 8-bit ASCII characters over a Gaussian channel with a bandwidth of 1 MHz and signal-to-noise ratio of 30 dB?

9.15 In a binary erasure channel, the data in error is erased. Hence, there is an erasure probability p, but the error probability is zero. Determine $H(X)$, $H(X/Y)$ and $I(X; Y)$ assuming the two transmitted messages are equiprobable.

9.16 Use the Lempel-Ziv algorithm to encode the following sequence: 010110111011110111110010011001110011110011111000100011000111000111110 00111.

9.17 A DMS produces seven symbols A, B, C, D, E, F, and G whose probabilities of occurrence are as follows: $P(A)=P(B)=0.05$, $P(C)=P(D)=0.1$, $P(E)=P(F)=0.2$, and $P(G)=0.3$. Find two Huffman codes for this source, one with the lowest possible variance and the other with the highest possible variance.

9.18 A DMS produces three symbols A, B, and C whose probabilities of occurrence are as follows: $P(A)=\alpha$, $P(B)=\beta$, and $P(C)=\gamma$. When a Huffman code is applied to this source, the average codeword length is 1.6 bits per symbol. Determine a relation among α, β, and γ.

9.19 Through a voice-grade telephone channel whose bandwidth is 3.3 kHz and output signal-to-noise ratio of 28 dB, 256 equally-likely statistically-independent symbols are transmitted. Calculate the information capacity of the channel and the maximum symbol rate for which error-free transmission over the channel is possible.

9.20 Show that for a lossless channel, $H(X/Y)=0$, $I(X;Y)=H(X)$, and determine the channel capacity per symbol.

9.21 Show that for a noiseless channel, $I(X;Y)=H(X)=H(Y)$, and determine the channel capacity per symbol.

9.22 In a binary source, we have $P(X=0)=0.4$ and $P(Y=0)=0.6$. Suppose the transition probabilities are as follows: $P(Y=0/X=0)=0.8$, $P(Y=1/X=0)=0.2$, $P(Y=0/X=1)=0.7$ and $P(Y=1/X=1)=0.3$. Find $H(X)$, $H(Y)$, $H(Y/X)$, and $I(X;Y)$.

9.23 Show that the channel capacity of an ideal AWGN channel with infinite bandwidth is given by 1.44 S/N_0 bps, where S is the average signal power and $N_0/2$ is the power spectral density of the additive white Gaussian noise.

9.24 An analog signal having 4-kHz bandwidth is sampled at 1.5 times the Nyquist rate, and each sample is quantized into one of 256 equally-likely levels. Assume that the successive samples are statistically independent.

(a) Determine the information rate of this source.

(b) Can the output of this source be transmitted without error over an AWGN channel with a bandwidth of 10 kHz and a signal-to-noise ratio of 20 dB?

(c) Find the signal-to-noise ratio required for error-free transmission for part (b).

Computer Exercises

9.25 Two identical BSC with $0 \leq p \leq 1$ are connected in cascade. Determine the transition probabilities for the resultant equivalent channel diagram and plot its channel capacity in terms of p.

9.26 Determine the source entropy and use Huffman coding to find the average number of bits for the English alphabet, if the following provides the probabilities of occurrence of all letters of the English alphabet and that of space:

Space:	0.1859	I:	0.0575	R:	0.0484
A:	0.0642	J:	0.0008	S:	0.0514
B:	0.0127	K:	0.0049	T:	0.0796
C:	0.0218	L:	0.0321	U:	0.0228
D:	0.0317	M:	0.0198	V:	0.0083
E:	0.1031	N:	0.0574	W:	0.0175
F:	0.0208	O:	0.0632	X:	0.0013
G:	0.0152	P:	0.0152	Y:	0.0164
H:	0.0467	Q:	0.0008	Z:	0.0005

CHAPTER 10

Error-Control Coding

CONTENTS

INTRODUCTION

We first briefly discuss the sources and types of errors and the classes of codes and decoding methods. We then introduce several error-detection schemes used in automatic repeat request (ARQ) systems, and present various ARQ techniques along with their performances. The focus then turns toward the linear block and convolutional codes. Fundamental characteristics of block codes along with some well-known block codes as well as major features of convolutional codes along with their applications in trellis-coded modulation are briefly discussed. We finally expand on compound codes by describing the interleaving process and the high-performance turbo codes. After studying this chapter and understanding all relevant concepts and examples, students should be able to achieve the following learning objectives:

1. Define error and acceptable bit error rates.
2. Categorize types of errors.
3. Identify methods of controlling errors.
4. Understand hard-decision and soft-decision decoding schemes.
5. Describe parity-check codes.
6. Introduce the details of checksum.
7. Explain how cyclic redundancy check works.
8. Outline stop-and-wait, go-back-*N* and selective-repeat ARQ techniques.
9. Discuss ARQ error rate and throughput performances.
10. Characterize linear block codes and their error-detecting and correcting capabilities.
11. Analyze syndrome-based decoding of linear block codes.
12. Know the features of Hamming and Reed-Solomon codes.
13. State representations and properties of convolutional codes.
14. Detail how the maximum-likelihood decoding using the Viterbi algorithm works.

Introduction to Digital Communications

15. Appreciate the idea behind the trellis-coded modulation.
16. Grasp the underlying structures of block and convolutional interleaving.
17. Apply interleaving to introduce combining codes.
18. Differentiate between classical algebraic codes and probabilistic compound codes.
19. Expand on the underlying features and structure of turbo codes.
20. Portray the error-control coding performance-complexity trade-offs.

10.1 ERRORS

When bits in a digital transmission system are corrupted, errors have occurred. An ***error*** occurs when a transmitted bit is a 1 and its corresponding received bit becomes a 0 or a 0 becomes a 1. Virtually all digital transmission systems introduce errors, even after they have been optimally designed. Faced with this problem, the only viable remedy to reduce the bit error rate is the application of error-control coding through the calculated use of redundancy. The entire field of error-control coding is devoted to the development of techniques to achieve the performance that Shannon's channel coding theorem promised possible.

The acceptability of a given bit error rate primarily depends on the application requirement and the transmission medium performance. From the application standpoint, for instance, speech and video applications can tolerate some errors, whereas certain applications, such as electronic funds transfer, transmission and storage of critical raw digital data, and high-resolution medical imaging, require essentially error-free transmission. On the other hand, various transmission media have a wide range of performances in terms of their bit error rates. For instance, bit error rates may be roughly as high as 10^{-3} in cellular systems, in the order of 10^{-6} in copper wires, and as high as 10^{-9} in fiber optics. In order to improve the error rate performance required for an application in a digital communication system with an unacceptable bit error rate, error-control coding needs to be employed, but generally at the expense of an increase in bandwidth requirements.

10.1.1 Types of Errors

Many factors can alter one or more information (message) bits during digital transmission and storage. Sources of errors may include white noise (e.g., a hissing noise on the phone), impulse noise (e.g., a scratch on CD/DVD), crosstalk (e.g., hearing another phone conversion), echo (e.g., hearing talker's or listener's voice again), interference (e.g., unwanted signals due to frequency reuse in cellular systems), multipath fading (e.g., due to reflected, refracted paths in mobile systems), and thermal and shot noise (e.g., due to the transmitting and receiving equipment), to name just a few. The combined objective of the channel encoder at the transmitter and the channel decoder at the receiver is to minimize the effect of the channel noise, where the performance of a channel code is often assessed over a Gaussian channel.

There are two types of errors: random (single-bit) errors and burst (multiple-bit) errors. In ***random errors***, the bit errors occur independently of each other, and usually when one bit has changed, its neighbouring bits remain correct (unchanged). Examples causing random errors may include shot noise in the transmitting and receiving equipment as well as thermal noise in free-space communication channel. The transmission errors due to additive white Gaussian noise (AWGN) are generally referred as random errors, though it is possible that the AWGN channel, due to imperfect filtering and timing operations at the receiver, introduces errors that are localized in a short interval.

In ***burst errors***, two or more bits in a row have usually changed, in that periods of low-error rate transmission are interspersed with periods in which clusters of errors occur. The burst errors are not independent and tend to be spatially concentrated. The length of the burst is measured from the first corrupted bit to the last corrupted bit; some bits in between may not have been corrupted. Examples of the sources of burst errors may include magnetic recording channels (tape or disk), impulse noise due to lightening and switching transients in radio channels, and mobile fading channels where the signal power can wax and wane in time.

A burst error is more common to occur than a random error. It is important to highlight that through the interleaving process the burst errors can be dispersed so as to form single errors, and single errors are then handled by codes capable of handling single errors. Interleaving does not affect actual data loss, but affects the perceived loss.

10.1.2 Methods of Controlling Errors

The central concept in detecting and/or correcting errors is redundancy in that the number of bits transmitted is intentionally over and above the required information bits. The transmitter sends the information bits along with some extra (also known as parity) bits. The receiver uses the redundant bits to detect or correct corrupted bits, and then removes the redundant bits. The crux of error control coding is the introduction of redundant bits, however, memory through which correlations among the transmitted bits are created plays a critical role.

In ***error detection***, which is simpler than error correction, we are simply interested only to find out if errors have occurred. We are not even interested in the number of errors, let alone to determine which bits are in error. Error detection may result in data rejection. However, every error-detection technique will fail to detect some errors. Error detection in a received data unit (bit stream) is the prerequisite to the retransmission request. A digital communication system, which requires a data unit to be retransmitted as necessary until it is correctly received, is called an automatic repeat request (ARQ) system.

In ***error correction***, we need to find out which bits are in error, i.e., to determine their locations in the received bit stream. In other words, the initial part of error correction is inherently error detection. The techniques that introduce redundancy to allow for correction of errors are collectively known as ***forward error correction*** (FEC) coding techniques. FEC codes are commonly used in digital storage systems, deep-space and satellite communication systems, cellular mobile systems, and digital video broadcasting systems. Error-correcting codes are thus more complex than error-detecting codes, and require more redundancy (parity) bits. Error correction generally yields a lower bit error rate, but at the expense of significantly higher transmission bandwidth and more decoding complexity. It is important to note that in theory it is possible to correct all errors, but the price in bandwidth may be too high as too many extra (redundant) bits are then required.

10.1.3 Classes of Codes

The codes described here are binary codes, for which the alphabet consists of only binary symbols 0 and 1. In the selection of a code, the ratio of the redundancy (also known as extra or parity or check) bits to the information bits, the level of the encoding/decoding complexity, and the error-detecting and/or correcting capabilities are all critical factors.

Error control codes are usually divided into two broad classes: block codes and convolutional codes. Of course, there are also codes, such as ***concatenated codes***, that employ both block codes and convolutional codes in tandem so as to considerably improve the bit error rate performance. Block and convolutional codes are different not only in their structures and thus complexities, but in their performances and applications. The comparison between these two categories of codes may not be simple, as each has its own merits and drawbacks.

In ***block codes***, a block of k information bits is followed by $r(=n-k)$ check bits that are exclusively derived from the block of information bits. The check bits of an (n, k) block code can be used at the receiver to detect or correct erroneous bits, as there is a one-to-one correspondence between each k-tuple information message and each n-tuple codeword.

In ***convolutional codes***, check bits are continuously interleaved with information bits to verify the information bits not only in the block immediately preceding them, but also in the previous $K-1$ blocks, as they have memory. In other words, the n-tuple codeword emitted by the convolutional encoding procedure is not only a function of an input k-tuple information message, but it is also a function of the previous $K-1$ input k-tuples, as K represents the constraint length of the code.

10.1.4 Decoding Methods

Decoding of a code at the receiver involves either hard decisions or soft decisions on the demodulator output values. In ***hard decisions***, demodulation outputs only a symbol value for each received symbol, whereas in ***soft decisions***, demodulation outputs an estimate of the received symbol value along with an indication of the reliability of this value using multi-level quantization.

When the decoder operates on data that takes on a fixed set of two possible values (i.e., single-bit quantization) it is called ***hard-decision decoding***. A binary symmetric channel can represent hard-decisions. If the transmitted bits are independent of one another, the performance of the receiver is optimum. However, error-correcting or detecting codes (as well as some physical channels) introduce correlations among the transmitted bits, and hard-decision decoding is not optimum even in white noise. Each bit interval thus contains information about adjacent bit intervals. When hard decisions are made, this information is lost. However, when the decoder operates on data that takes on a whole range of values (i.e., multi-bit quantization) it is called ***soft-decision decoding***. In soft-decision decoding, the number of quantization levels can impact the confidence in the estimate, however, in practice, there is little to be gained by using many soft-decision quantization levels. A Gaussian channel can represent soft decisions. For an ideal soft-decision decoding (i.e., infinite-bit quantization), the demodulator output values are directly used in the channel decoder. A soft-decision decoder typically performs better in the presence of corrupted data than its hard-decision counterpart. In other words, when the bits are correlated, processing several received samples collectively at the same time rather than individually at different times can provide significant performance improvement. Hard-decision decoding, which has limited resolution, discards the information about other bits, whereas soft-decision decoding with the needed resolution utilizes the information about all bits useful to the overall decoding process.

In order to make decisions, hard-decision decoders employ minimum ***Hamming distance*** (the number of bits in which n-bit codewords differ) and soft-decision decoders utilize minimum ***Euclidean distance*** (the distance between the received and transmitted signals in n-dimensional Euclidean space). For block codes, soft-decision decoders are substantially more complex than hard-decision decoders; therefore, block codes are relatively easily implemented with hard-decision decoders, especially when n and k are large. On the other hand, for convolutional codes, both hard-decision and soft-decision implementations can be employed. In fact, a convolutional decoder using the Viterbi algorithm can make soft decisions in a natural manner. In general, soft-decision decoding, roughly possesses an advantage of 1 to 2 dBs over hard-decision decoding. As 1 dB increase in power translates roughly into one order of magnitude reduction in the bit error rate, this advantage is obviously considered significant. However, in order to deploy soft-decision decoding, a major increase in processing complexity becomes a requirement and sometime an impediment.

10.2 ERROR-DETECTION METHODS

There are three distinct widely-used error-detection methods: i) parity-check codes, ii) checksum, and iii) cyclic redundancy check (CRC). These techniques, which can be concurrently employed, require different levels of complexities and have different performances.

10.2.1 Parity-Check Codes

Parity checking can be one-dimensional or two dimensional. In a ***single parity-check code***, an extra bit is added to every data unit (e.g., byte, character, block, segment, frame, cell, and packet). The objective of adding the parity bit (a 0 or a 1) is to make the total number of 1s in the data unit (including the parity bit) to become even. Some systems may use odd-parity checking, where the total number of 1s should then be odd. Even parity is typically used for synchronous transmission and odd parity for asynchronous transmission. The single parity-check code is used in ASCII where characters are represented by seven bits and the eighth bit is a parity bit. Simple parity-check codes can detect all single-bit errors. It can also detect multiple errors only if the total number of errors in a data unit is odd. A single parity-check code has a remarkable error-detecting capability, as the addition of a single parity bit can bring about half of all possible error patterns detectable.

The single parity-check code takes k information bits and appends a single check bit using modulo-2 arithmetic to form a codeword length of

$n(=k+1)$, thus yielding a $(k+1, k)$ block code with $\frac{k}{k+1}$ code rate. The parity bit b_{k+1} is determined as the modulo-2 sum of the information bits:

$$b_n = b_{k+1} = b_1 + b_2 + \cdots + b_k \tag{10.1}$$

Note that in ***modulo-2 arithmetic***, we have $0+0=0$, $0+1=1$, $1+0=1$, and $1+1=0$. Many transmission channels introduce bit errors at random, independent of each other, and with low probability of p, where p is assumed to be the probability of an error in a single-bit transmission. Some error patterns are more probable than others. For instance, with the extremely reasonable assumption of $p<0.5$, error pattern with a given number of bit errors is more likely than an error pattern with even a larger number of bit errors. In other words, it follows that patterns with no error is more likely than patterns with one error and that in turn is more likely than patterns with two errors, so on and so forth. The single parity-check code fails if the error pattern has an even number of 1s. The probability of error-detection failure (i.e., the probability of undetectable error pattern or equivalently error patterns with even number of 1s) is as follows:

$$P_{Failure} = \binom{n}{2} p^2 (1-p)^{n-2} + \binom{n}{4} p^4 (1-p)^{n-4} + \cdots + \binom{n}{m} p^m (1-p)^{n-m} \tag{10.2}$$

where n represents the total number of k information bits and one parity-check bit (i.e., $n=k+1$, and $m \le n$ is the largest possible even number). In today's digital communication systems, we always have $p \ll 1$, and the probability of detection failure can thus be closely approximated as follows:

$$P_{Failure} \cong \binom{n}{2} p^2 (1-p)^{n-2} \cong \binom{n}{2} p^2 \cong \frac{n(n-1)}{2} p^2 = \frac{k(k+1)}{2} p^2 \tag{10.3}$$

As (10.3) indicates, for a given probability of error $p \ll 1$, the probability of error-detection failure exhibits quadratic growth, as the number of information bits $k(=n-1)$ increases.

EXAMPLE 10.1

Consider a (15, 14) single parity-check code. Compute the probability of an undetected message error, assuming that all bit errors are independent and the probability of bit error is $p=10^{-6}$.

Solution

Using (10.3) and noting that $k=14$, we have the probability of error-detection failure $P_{Failure} \cong 10^{-10}$. This points to the fact that with a very high code rate of $\frac{14}{15}$, with a redundancy of only 6.7%, an impressive error rate reduction of nearly four orders of magnitude can be easily achieved.

In a ***two-dimensional parity-check code***, the information bits are organized in a matrix consisting of rows and columns. For each row and each column, one parity-check bit is calculated. As a result, the last column consists of check bits for all rows and the bottom row consists of check bits for all columns. In other words, the resulting encoded matrix of bits satisfies the pattern that all rows have even parity and all columns also have even parity. Assuming there are M information bits in each row and N information bits in each column, the code rate is then as follows:

$$\frac{k}{n}=\frac{MN}{(M+1)(N+1)} \tag{10.4}$$

The two-dimensional parity checks can detect and correct all single errors and detect two and three errors that occur anywhere in the matrix. However, only some patterns with four or more errors can be detected. Figure 10.1 shows examples of detectable and undetectable error patterns, for $M=5$, $N=6$, and thus $\frac{k}{n}=\frac{5}{7}$. A two-dimensional parity check increases the likelihood of detecting burst errors, but on the other hand, requires more check bits. We will later expand on this in the context of interleaving to combat burst errors.

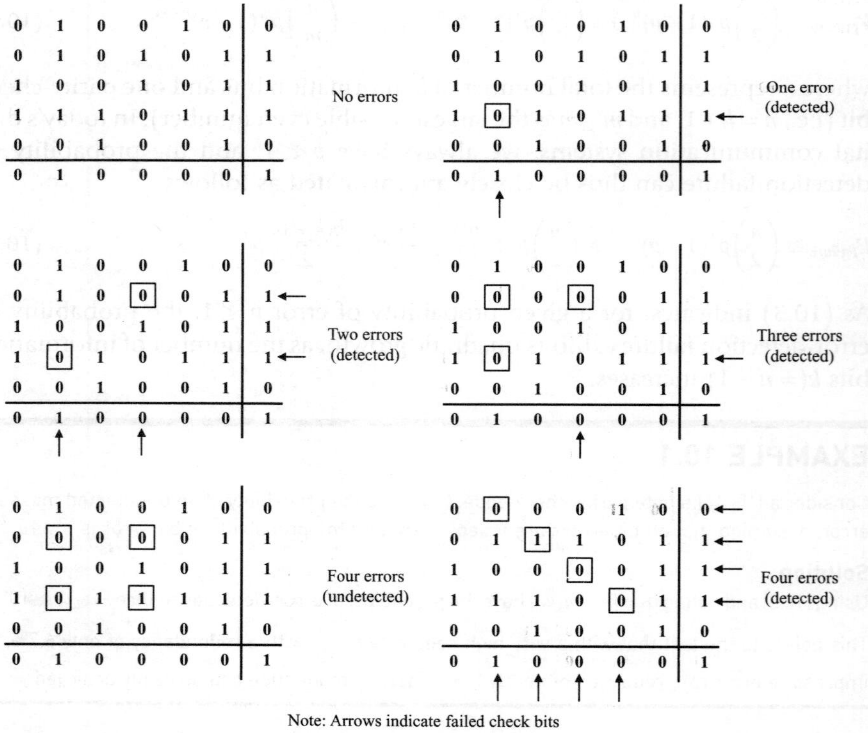

FIGURE 10.1 Examples of detectable and undetectable error patterns for two-dimensional parity-check code.

10.2.2 Checksum

The checksum is an effective method to detect errors, and is used in the Internet at the network and transport layers, such as IP, TCP, UDP, rather than the data-link layer. Checksum is employed in every router; the algorithm for the checksum is thus selected for ease of implementation in software rather than the effectiveness in terms of its error-detecting capability.

Checksum is calculated using ***one's complement arithmetic,*** i.e., if there is a carry in the most significant bit, we swing the carry bit back to the least significant bit. More specifically, in this arithmetic, unsigned numbers between 0 and $2^m - 1$ can be represented by using only m bits; when a number has more than m bits, the extra leftmost bits need to be added to the m rightmost bits (wrapping).

At the transmitter, the checksum is calculated and sent with the message, not necessarily at the end of the message, as it can be inserted in the middle of the message as well. At the destination, a new checksum, based on the received message and checksum, is calculated. If the new checksum is all 0s, the message is accepted, as it indicates with a high probability the message was not altered during the transmission; otherwise, the message is discarded. Table 10.1 shows the steps followed by the transmitter and the receiver.

EXAMPLE 10.2

Assuming the information bit sequence 010011111100111011001101111101101 is divided into 8-bit segments, determine the checksum sent along with data, and show how the checksum checker operates on the received bit stream.

Solution

As shown in Figure 10.2, the checksum at the transmitter is 00100110, and the new checksum at the receiver is 00000000, and the message is thus accepted.

Table 10.1 Procedure to determine the checksum

Steps	Checksum generator at the transmit end	Checksum checker at the receive end
1	The information bits are divided into q sections of L bits each; in the Internet checksum, L is selected to be 16.	The received bits—consisting of all $q + 1$ sections of L bits each, including the received checksum—is divided into L-bit sections.
2	All q sections are added using one's complement to get the sum.	All $q + 1$ sections are added using one's complement.
3	The sum is complemented (i.e., all bits are inverted) to form the checksum.	The sum is complemented (i.e., all bits are inverted) to form a new checksum.
4	The checksum, consisting of L bits, is sent along with the information bits.	If the value of new checksum is 0, the message is accepted; otherwise, it is rejected.

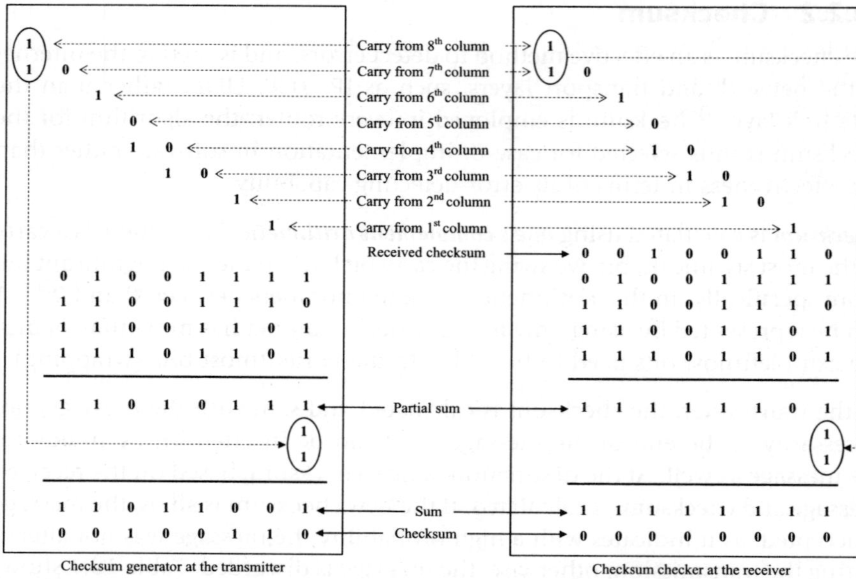

FIGURE 10.2 An example illustrating how checksum generator and checker work.

The checksum detects all errors involving an odd number of bits as well as most errors involving an even number of bits. However, any time a bit inversion (i.e., a bit in error) is balanced by an opposite bit inversion (i.e., another bit in error) in the corresponding position of another data segment, the error is invisible (undetected). In fact, if the value of an L-bit word is incremented and the value of another L-bit word is decremented by the same amount, the two errors cannot be detected because the checksums remain the same. Checksum requires an overhead of L bits, regardless of the data-unit size qL, where q is a positive integer. The code rate is therefore $\frac{qL}{qL+L}=\frac{q}{q+1}$. Checksum is not as powerful as CRC (as will be discussed in the next section). For instance, checksum cannot detect when the sections are not in correct order. The tendency in the designing of new protocols in the Internet is to replace checksum with CRC.

10.2.3 Cyclic Redundancy Check

Cyclic redundancy check (CRC) is a powerful error-detection technique, which is widely used in digital networks, such as LANs and WANs, as well as in some storage devices. CRC, which is simple to implement, is used to detect data units, such as packets, especially with burst errors, and sometimes after error correction.

CRC is based on modulo-2 division, in that addition is performed by exclusive-OR operation (i.e., the subtraction operation is identical to the addition operation, meaning $1+1=0$). In CRC, a sequence of redundant bits (called the CRC remainder) is appended to the end of a data unit, thus the resulting data unit becomes exactly divisible by a pre-determined binary number (divisor). At its destination, the incoming data unit, which includes the information bits and parity bits, is divided by the same binary number (divisor). If there is no remainder, that is the remainder is zero, the data unit is assumed to be intact and thus accepted, while a non-zero remainder indicates that data must be rejected and a retransmission of the data unit be requested. The CRC checker at the transmitter and the CRC generator at the receiver function exactly the same.

The divisor in the CRC generator is most often represented not as a string of 1s and 0s, but as an algebraic polynomial. The polynomial format is used for it is short and it can be used to prove the concept mathematically. A string of 0s and 1s can be represented as a polynomial with coefficients of 0 and 1, where the power of each term in the polynomial indicates the position of the bit and the corresponding coefficient reflects the value of the bit (0 or 1). A polynomial is represented by removing all terms with zero coefficients. The calculation of CRC bits is as follows:

1. The k information bits ($i_{k-1}, i_{k-2}, \ldots, i_1, i_0$) are used to form the **information polynomial** $i(x)$ of degree $k - 1$:

$$i(x) = i_{k-1}x^{k-1} + i_{k-2}x^{k-2} + \cdots + i_1x + i_0 \tag{10.5}$$

2. The string of information bits are shifted to the left (i.e., adding extra 0s as rightmost bits). Shifting to the left to produce $p(x)$ with n terms is accomplished by multiplying each term of the polynomial $i(x)$ by x^m, where $m = n - k$ is the number of shifted bits, i.e., m represents the number of parity-check bits:

$$p(x) = x^{n-k}i(x) = i_{k-1}x^{n-1} + i_{k-2}x^{n-2} + \cdots + i_1x^{n-k+1} + i_0x^{n-k} \tag{10.6}$$

3. A ***generator polynomial*** $g(x)$, which specifies the CRC of interest, is selected. $g(x)$ with the degree $n - k$ has the form:

$$g(x) = x^{n-k} + g_{n-k-1}x^{n-k-1} + \cdots + g_1x + 1 \tag{10.7}$$

where $g_{n-k-1}, g_{n-k-2}, \ldots, g_1$ are binary numbers, i.e., each may be a 0 or a 1.

4. The polynomial $p(x)$ is divided by the polynomial $g(x)$ to obtain the ***remainder polynomial*** $r(x)$, which can have maximum degree $n - k - 1$ or lower with the following form:

$$r(x) = r_{n-k-1}x^{n-k-1} + \cdots + r_1x + r_0 \tag{10.8}$$

As expected, the remainder polynomial has a degree lower than the generator polynomial. It is quite important to note that in the calculation of CRC, the resulting quotient $q(x)$ plays no role, it is thus discarded.

5. The remainder $r(x)$, which may rarely consist of all zeros, is added to $p(x)$ to form the ***codeword polynomial*** $b(x) = p(x) + r(x) = x^{n-k}i(x) + r(x)$, we thus have

$$b(x) = i_{k-1}x^{n-1} + \cdots + i_1x^{n-k+1} + i_0x^{n-k} + r_{n-k-1}x^{n-k-1} + \cdots + r_1x + r_0 \quad (10.9)$$

6. Note that $b(x)$ is a binary polynomial in which the k higher-order terms are based on the information bits and the $n-k$ lower-order terms provide the CRC bits. The codeword polynomial $b(x)$ is divisible by $g(x)$ because we have:

$$b(x) = p(x) + r(x) = x^{n-k}\, i(x) + r(x) = g(x)\, q(x) + r(x) + r(x) = g(x)q(x) \quad (10.10)$$

where in modulo-2 arithmetic, we have $r(x) + r(x) = 0$. Since, as reflected above, all codewords $b(x)$ are multiples of the generator polynomial $g(x)$, at the destination, the received polynomial is divided by $g(x)$. If the remainder is non-zero, then an error in the received data unit, consisting of one or more bits, has been detected. If the remainder is zero, either no bit is corrupted or some bits are corrupted, but the decoder fails to detect them.

EXAMPLE 10.3

Assuming the information bits are 1100 and the generator polynomial is $x^3 + x + 1$, determine the transmitted bit sequence consisting of the information bits and the CRC bits. If the middle bit in the transmitted bit sequence is corrupted, show how the detector at the receiver can determine the received bit sequence is in error.

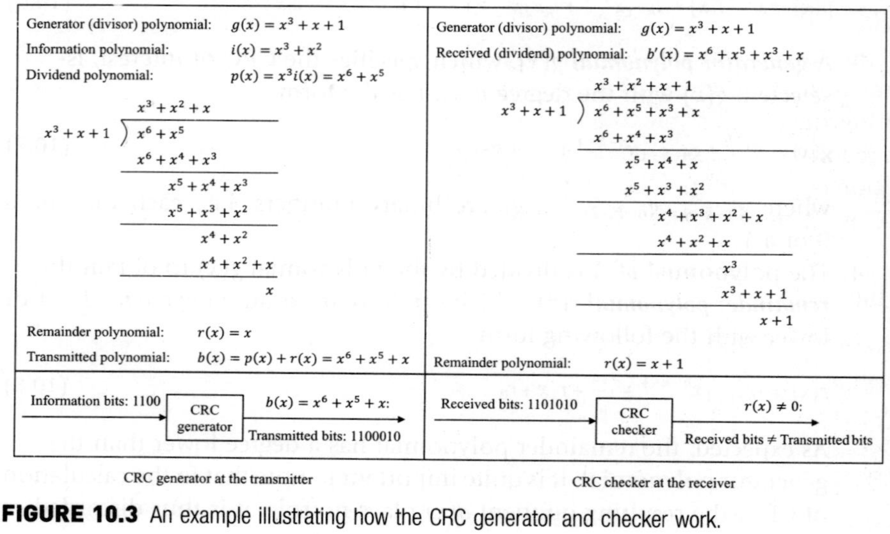

FIGURE 10.3 An example illustrating how the CRC generator and checker work.

Solution

For the information bits 1100, we have the information polynomial $i(x)=x^3+x^2$. As shown in Figure 10.3, the encoding process involves dividing $i(x)x^3=x^6+x^5$ by $g(x)=x^3+x+1$. With the remainder $r(x)=x$, we have the transmitted polynomial $b(x)=x^6+x^5+x$, and in turn the transmitted sequence is thus as follows: 1100010.

The received sequence is, however, 1101010. The received polynomial is thus $b'(x)=x^6+x^5+x^3+x$. As shown in Figure 10.3, the decoding process involves dividing $b'(x)$ by $g(x)$, which in turn yields a non-zero remainder (i.e., $r(x)=x+1\neq 0$) thus implying the received sequence is in error.

Table 10.2 shows some of the standard polynomials. The design criterion to select a generator polynomial is a function of what types of errors need to be caught. In fact, it can be shown that certain properties associated with generator polynomials can provide certain capabilities, as reflected below:

- If the generator polynomial $g(x)$ has at least two non-zero terms, then all single-bit errors can be detected.
- If the generator polynomial $g(x)$ cannot divide x^t+1 $(0\leq t\leq n-1)$, then all isolated double errors can be detected.
- If the generator polynomial $g(x)$ has a factor $x+1$, then all odd-numbered errors can be detected.
- The generator polynomial $g(x)$ can detect any burst of error for which the length of the burst is less than or equal to $n-k$.

10.3 AUTOMATIC REPEAT REQUEST (ARQ)

Automatic repeat request (ARQ) combines error detection and retransmission of data units to ensure, to the extent possible, a sequence of data units, such as packets, is delivered in order and without errors or duplications despite possible transmission errors. Since ARQ requires error detection, rather than error correction, the number of parity-check bits is quite modest and the decoding complexity is rather low. ARQ is generally employed when very low error rates are required, transmission does not involve delay-sensitive applications, information occurs naturally in data units, and the round-trip delay is not very long. ARQ is adaptive as it only retransmits when errors occur. In other words, when

Table 10.2 CRC standard polynomials

Name	Generator polynomial	CRC bits	Application
CRC-8	x^8+x^2+x+1	8	ATM header
CRC-12	$x^{12}+x^{11}+x^3+x^2+x+1$	12	IBM Bisync
CRC-16	$x^{16}+x^{15}+x^2+1$	16	HDLC
CRC-32	$x^{32}+x^{26}+x^{23}+x^{22}+x^{16}+x^{12}+x^{11}+x^{10}+x^8+x^7+x^5+x^4+x^2+x+1$	32	LANs, V.42 modem

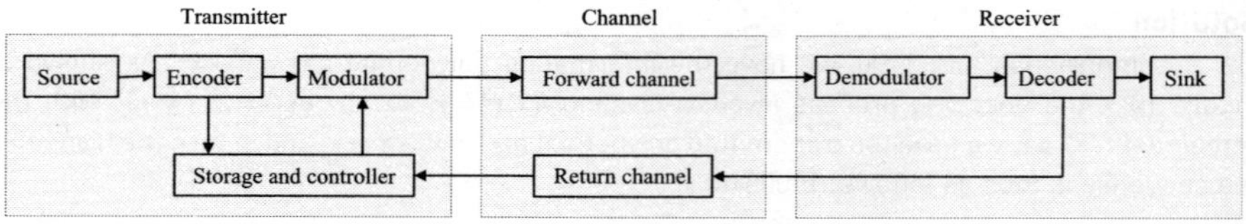

FIGURE 10.4 Block diagram for an ARQ system.

the channel is quite noisy, ARQ adapts to the poor capability of the channel, and when the channel is rather ideal, ARQ operates with very high efficiency. ARQ is thus relatively robust to the channel conditions, without prior detailed knowledge of the channel characteristics. ARQ is used in computer communication systems over telephone lines and is also employed to provide reliable data transmission over the Internet or VSAT applications over the satellite.

The block diagram for an ARQ system is shown in Figure 10.4. The crux of ARQ systems is the presence of a feedback channel from the receiver to the transmitter. Over this channel, the receiver transmits a ***positive acknowledgement*** (ACK) signal or a ***negative acknowledgement*** (NAK) signal regarding the condition of the received data unit. An ACK indicates the received data unit had no erroneous bits and a NAK reflects the opposite. The transmitter responds to a NAK (i.e., an unsuccessful transmission) by retransmitting the data unit. Each data unit is stored at the transmitter and retransmitted upon request until it has been successfully received, as indicated by an ACK from the receiver. The data units as well as ACK and NAK signals may be lost during transmission. An ARQ technique is thus implemented using a set of timers to allow the transmitter to retransmit those unacknowledged data units, for which it cannot receive a response from the receiver in a certain time interval.

10.3.1 Stop-and-Wait, Go-Back-*N*, and Selective-Repeat ARQ Techniques

As shown in Figure 10.5, there are three ARQ techniques: stop-and-wait ARQ, go-back-*N* ARQ, and selective-repeat ARQ. The stop-and-wait ARQ technique requires half-duplex operation (i.e., two-way transmission, but one at a time), whereas the other two require full-duplex operation (i.e., two-way transmission, at all times).

In the ***stop-and-wait ARQ***, the transmitter sends a data unit of information (e.g., a packet of data) to the receiver. The receiver processes the received data unit to determine if there are any errors in it. If the receiver detects no error, it then sends back to the transmitter an ACK signal. Upon receipt of the ACK signal, the transmitter sends the next data unit. If the receiver does detect an error, it returns to the transmitter a NAK signal. If either a NAK is received or a fixed timeout interval has elapsed, the data unit is retransmitted. The transmitter then waits again for an ACK or a NAK response before undertaking further

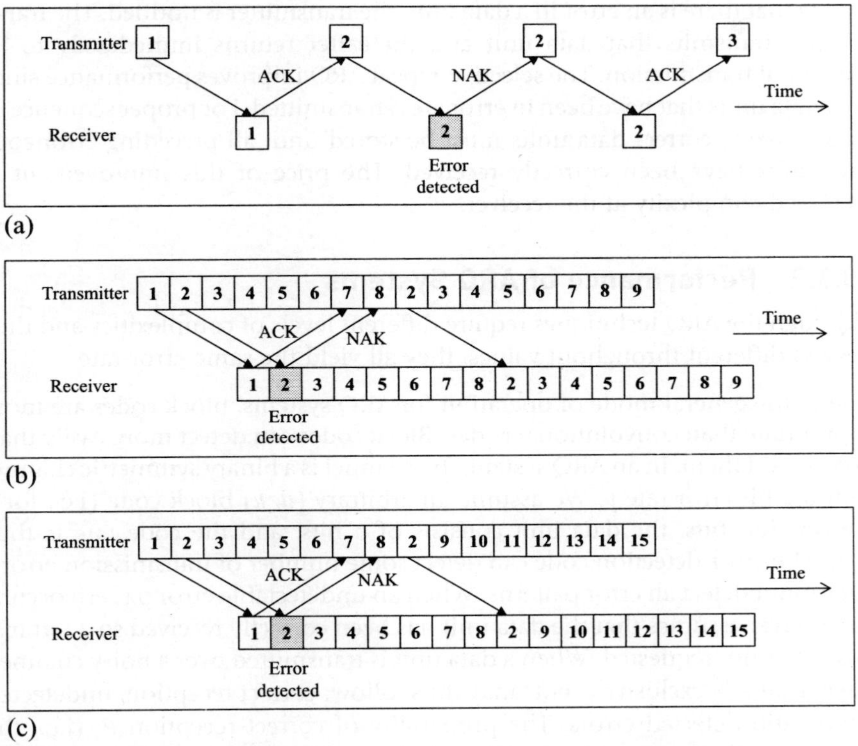

FIGURE 10.5 ARQ techniques: (a) stop-and-wait ARQ, (b) go-back-*N* ARQ, and (c) selective-repeat ARQ.

transmission. Clearly, the limitation of this type of ARQ is that it must stand by idly without transmission while waiting for an ACK or a NAK; nevertheless, it has the virtue of simplicity.

In the ***go-back-N ARQ***, *N* represents the window size (the number of data units outstanding without acknowledgement). The transmitter is in continuous operation, and saves again all unacknowledged data units. The transmitter sends data units, one after another, without delay, and does not wait for an ACK signal. When, however, the receiver detects an error in a data unit, a NAK signal is sent to the transmitter. In response to the NAK, the transmitter returns that data unit and starts all over again at that data unit (i.e., that data unit along with all subsequent data units are retransmitted). The receiver discards the $W(=N-1)$ intervening data units, correct or not, in order to preserve proper sequence. The transmitter and the receiver both have a modest increase in complexity. The obvious penalty is the repeated transmission of some correct data units and the resulting unnecessary delay.

In the ***selective-repeat ARQ***, the transmitter sends data units of information in succession, again without waiting for an ACK after each data unit. If the receiver detects that there is an error in a data unit, the transmitter is notified. The transmitter retransmits that data unit and thereafter returns immediately to its sequential transmission. The selective-repeat ARQ improves performance since only data units that have been in error are retransmitted. For proper sequence of data delivery, correct data units must be stored until all preceding erroneous data units have been correctly received. The price of this improvement is increased complexity at the receiver.

10.3.2 Performance of ARQ Systems

Although the ARQ techniques require different levels of complexities and thus possess different throughput values, they all yield the same error rate.

Due to the general mode of operation for ARQ systems, block codes are more appropriate than convolutional codes. Block codes can detect more easily than they correct them. In an ARQ system, the channel is a binary symmetric channel with the bit error rate p. We assume an arbitrary (n, k) block code (i.e., for k information bits, the data unit consists of n bits, and the code rate is thus k/n). The error-detection code can detect some number of transmission errors, but cannot detect all error patterns. When an undetectable error pattern occurs, the receiver assumes that the data unit has been correctly received so a retransmission is not requested. When a data unit is transmitted over a noisy channel, three mutually exclusive events may thus follow: correct reception, undetected errors, and detected errors. The probability of correct reception P_c (i.e., the probability that no errors occur) is as follows:

$$P_c = (1-p)^n \tag{10.11}$$

The probability of an undetected error P_u corresponds to a pattern of errors that match a codeword, and the probability of a detected error P_d on each transmission can thus be determined by:

$$P_d = 1 - P_c - P_u \tag{10.12}$$

Since ACK and NAK signals are short, hence easily protected, it is reasonable to assume that no errors are made in the feedback channel. The transmission of a data unit terminates when no error is detected. With P_d as the probability of retransmitting a data unit, the total probability of receiving a data unit in error, denoted as P_b, is the sum of the probabilities of error on the first, second, third, and all other transmissions. We thus have:

$$P_b = P_u + P_d P_u + P_d^2 P_u + P_d^3 P_u + \cdots = \frac{P_u}{1-P_d} = \frac{P_u}{P_c + P_u} \tag{10.13}$$

As reflected in (10.13), the ***data-unit error rate*** P_b is a function of the error-detection capabilities of the code, but not a function of the specific ARQ technique. To achieve a low P_b, the block code (n, k) code must be chosen to have a low undetectable error probability P_u, as P_c is a function of n and the bit error rate p.

The ARQ system ***throughput*** (also known as transmission efficiency or utilization factor) η is defined as the ratio of the average number of information bits accepted at the receiver per unit of time to the number of information bits that would be accepted per unit of time if ARQ were not used. While all ARQ systems yield the same data-unit error rate, their throughput efficiencies are different. It can be shown that with the transmission bit rate R, the processing and transmission time T, delay-bandwidth product $D(=2RT)$, and the transmission pipe size in multiples of data units $W(=D/n)$, the throughputs of ARQ techniques can be approximated, as summarized in Table 10.3.

The three ARQ systems differ rather significantly in both implementation complexity and transmission efficiency performance. A close examination of their efficiency expressions indicates that they are linearly related to the probability of retransmitting a data unit. In addition, the efficiency of the selective repeat ARQ is superior to that of the go-back-N ARQ, and that in turn is better than that of the stop-and-wait ARQ. It is important to highlight that when $P_d \rightarrow 0$, the performance of the go-back-N ARQ is then about the same as that of the selective repeat ARQ, and when $P_d \rightarrow 1$, the performance of the go-back-N ARQ is then about the same as that of the stop-and-wait ARQ.

There is also the possibility of hybrid techniques that combine error detection and error correction. Hybrid techniques have proved useful in systems having long delay. In one approach, known as ***Type I hybrid ARQ***, when the noise level is constant with time, a code is used to correct the great majority of the errors, and detect certain unlikely error patterns. To this effect, all the necessary parity bits for error detection and error correction are sent with each data unit. If such error patterns occur, retransmission is requested, and the receiver attempts to correct the errors in the retransmitted data units. The process is repeated until no error is detected in a retransmitted data unit. In another approach, known as the ***Type II hybrid ARQ***, no attempt is made to correct errors on the first transmission; however, when an error is detected in the first transmission, the retransmission contains extra parity bits for error correction. The first transmission is saved so that it along with the second and subsequent retransmissions can be used to retrieve the information bits. Error correction significantly reduces the number of data units that must be retransmitted, thereby increasing the throughput.

Table 10.3 ARQ throughput performance

Stop-and-Wait ARQ	Go-Back-*N* ARQ	Selective-Repeat ARQ
$\eta_{SW} = \dfrac{\left(\frac{k}{n}\right)(1-P_d)}{1+W}$	$\eta_{GB} = \dfrac{\left(\frac{k}{n}\right)(1-P_d)}{1+WP_d}$	$\eta_{SR} = \left(\frac{k}{n}\right)(1-P_d)$

10.4 BLOCK CODES

In ***block codes***, a block of k information bits is encoded into a block of $n > k$ bits by adding $n - k$ check (extra, redundant) bits derived from the k message bits. The code is then referred to as an (n, k) block code with the ***code rate*** $R = \frac{k}{n} < 1$. The n-bit block of the channel encoder output is called a codeword (also known as a codevector). The total number of possible n–bit codewords is 2^n while the total number of possible k-bit messages is 2^k. There are therefore $2^n - 2^k$ possible n-bit codewords that do not represent possible messages. In a ***linear block code***, the sum of any two codewords, in modulo-2 arithmetic, is a codeword in the code. A code in which the information bits appear unaltered at the beginning of a codeword is called a ***systematic code***. The focus here is on systematic linear block codes.

The basic goals in choosing a particular code are to have a high code rate and the codewords to be as far apart from one another as possible. The encoding operation of a systematic linear block code consists of first partitioning the stream of information bits into groups of k successive information bits and then transforming each k-bit group into a larger block of n bits according to the set of rules associated with a particular block code. The additional $n - k$ bits are generated from a linear combination of the k information bits. The encoding and decoding operations can be described using matrices and vectors.

10.4.1 Description and Capabilities of Linear Block Codes

The message M is denoted as a row vector or k-tuple $M = (m_1, m_2, \ldots, m_k)$, where each information bit can be a 0 or a 1. A codeword C of length n bits is represented by a row vector or n-tuple $C = (c_1, c_2, \ldots, c_n)$. In a systematic linear block code, the first k bits of the codeword are the information bits, i.e., we have:

$$c_i = m_i, \quad i = 1, 2, \ldots, k \tag{10.14}$$

and the last $n - k$ bits of the codeword are the parity-check bits, and can be represented by $B = (b_1, b_2, \ldots, b_{n-k})$. The $n - k$ check bits are linear sums of the k information bits, i.e., we have:

$$c_i = b_{i-k} = \sum_{j=1}^{k} p_{j,i-k} m_j, \quad i = k+1, k+2, \ldots, n \tag{10.15}$$

where the coefficients $p_{j,i-k}$ are 0s and 1s and the addition operations are performed in modulo-2 arithmetic so every bit in the codeword C is a 0 or a 1.

In order to determine the error-detecting and correcting capabilities of linear block codes, we first need to introduce the Hamming weight of a codeword, the Hamming distance between two codewords, and the minimum distance $d_{\min}$ of a block code. The ***Hamming weight*** of a codeword C is defined as the number of non-zero elements (i.e., 1s) in the codeword. The ***Hamming distance*** between two codewords is defined as the number of elements in which they differ. The ***minimum distance*** $d_{\min}$ of a linear block code is the smallest Hamming distance between any two different codewords, and is equal to the minimum Hamming weight of the non-zero codewords in the code.

EXAMPLE 10.4

Consider a linear block code whose codewords are as follows: (000000), (001011), (010101), (011110), (100110), (101101), (110011), and (111000). Determine the minimum weights and the mininum distance of the code.

Solution

As reflected in the following table, the minimum Hamming weight for this linear block code is 3 and hence the minimum distance of the code is 3.

Codewords	Weight
000000	0
001011	3
010101	3
011110	4
100110	3
101101	4
110011	4
111000	3

It can be shown that a linear block code of minimum distance $d_{\min}$ can detect up to t errors if and only if $d_{\min} \geq t+1$ and correct up to t errors if and only if $d_{\min} \geq 2t+1$. Obviously, for a given n and k, the design objective is to design an (n,k) code with the largest possible minimum distance $d_{\min}$. However, there is no systematic way to achieve it in all cases.

We now combine (10.14) and (10.15) and write them in in the following matrix form as:

$$(c_1, c_2, \cdots, c_n) = (m_1, m_2, \cdots, m_k) \begin{pmatrix} 1000\cdots0 & p_{11} & p_{12} & \cdots & p_{1,n-k} \\ 0100\cdots0 & p_{21} & p_{22} & \cdots & p_{2,n-k} \\ \vdots & \vdots & \vdots & & \vdots \\ 0000\cdots1 & p_{k1} & p_{12} & \cdots & p_{k,n-k} \end{pmatrix}$$

or equivalently:

$$C = MG \tag{10.16}$$

where the $k \times n$ matrix G is called the ***generator matrix*** of the code and it has the following form:

$$G = [I_k \mid P] \tag{10.17}$$

where the matrix I_k is the identity matrix of order k and the $k \times (n-k)$ matrix P is known as the ***coefficient matrix***. All k rows of the generator matrix G are linearly independent, that is, no row of the matrix can be expressed in terms of the other rows. In other words, the generator matrix G must have rank k. When P is specified, it defines the (n, k) block code completely. Each of the elements in P may be a 0 or a 1, and are chosen in such a way that the rows of the generator matrix P are linearly independent. Note that we have:

$$C = [M \mid B] \tag{10.18}$$

where $B = (b_1, b_2, \cdots, b_{n-k})$ represents the vector consisting of the parity-check bits. Using (10.16) to (10.18) gives rise to the following:

$$B = MP \tag{10.19}$$

(10.19) clearly points to the fact that the matrix P determines the parity-check vector B for a given message vector M.

EXAMPLE 10.5

Determine all codewords for a (6, 3) systematic linear block code whose generator matrix is as follows:

$$G = \begin{pmatrix} 1 & 0 & 0 & | & 1 & 1 & 0 \\ 0 & 1 & 0 & | & 1 & 0 & 1 \\ 0 & 0 & 1 & | & 0 & 1 & 1 \end{pmatrix}$$

Solution
Since we have $k = 3$, there are eight possible message blocks: (000), (001), (010), (011), (100), (101), (110), and (111). Using (10.16), the following table provides the assignment of codewords to messages:

Messages (*M*)	Codewords (C)
000	000000
001	001011
010	010101
011	011110
100	100110
101	101101
110	110011
111	111000

The encoder essentially has to store the generator matrix G or the coefficient matrix P of the code and perform binary arithmetic operation to generate the check bits. The encoder complexity increases as k increases and/or n increases.

The message bits and parity-check bits of a systematic linear block code are related by the parity-check matrix H, which is defined as follows:

$$H = \begin{pmatrix} p_{11} & p_{21} & \cdots & p_{k1} & 1 & 0 & 0 & 0 & \ldots & 0 \\ p_{12} & p_{22} & \cdots & p_{k2} & 0 & 1 & 0 & 0 & \ldots & 0 \\ \vdots & \vdots & & \vdots & \vdots & & & & & \vdots \\ p_{1,n-k} & p_{2,n-k} & \cdots & p_{k,n-k} & 0 & 0 & 0 & 0 & \cdots & 1 \end{pmatrix} = [P^T | I_{n-k}]$$

where P^T is an $(n-k) \times n$ matrix representing the transpose of the coefficient matrix P and I_{n-k} is an identity matrix of order $(n-k)$. The parity-check matrix H can be used to verify whether a codeword C is generated by the generator matrix G. More specifically, C is a codeword if and only if we have:

$$CH^T = 0 \tag{10.20}$$

where H^T is the transpose of the parity-check matrix H. The rank of H is $n-k$ and the rows of H are linearly independent. The minimum distance $d_{\min}$ of a linear block code is closely related to the structure of the parity-check matrix H.

As the generator matrix G is used in the encoding operation, the parity-check matrix H is used in the decoding operation. Let the received vector R be the sum of the transmitted codeword C and the noise vector E, that is

$$R = C + E \tag{10.21}$$

where R and E are both $1 \times n$ vectors as well. An element of E equals 0 if the corresponding element of R is the same as that of C. An element of E equals 1 if the corresponding element of R is different from that of C, in which case an error is said to have occurred in that location. The decoder does not know C and E, and its function is to decode C from R, and determine the message block M from C. The decoder performs the decoding operation by determining the $(n-k)$ ***syndrome*** vector S, defined as follows:

$$S = RH^T \tag{10.22}$$

Using (10.20) and (10.21), (10.22) becomes as follows:

$$S = EH^T \tag{10.23}$$

The syndrome S depends only on the error pattern and not on the transmitted codeword. For a linear block code, the syndrome S is equal to the sum of those rows of H^T where errors have occurred. The syndrome of a received vector is zero if R is a valid codeword. If errors occur, then the syndrome S is non-zero. Since the syndrome S is related to the error vector E, the decoder uses the syndrome S to detect and correct errors.

EXAMPLE 10.6

Consider a (6, 3) systematic linear block code whose parity-check matrix is as follows:

$$H=\begin{pmatrix} 1 & 1 & 0 & | & 1 & 0 & 0 \\ 1 & 0 & 1 & | & 0 & 1 & 0 \\ 0 & 1 & 1 & | & 0 & 0 & 1 \end{pmatrix}$$

Determine the syndrome S when (a) $R=(111000)$ and (b) $R=(111111)$.

Solution

Using (10.22), we have the following:

(a) $S=RH^T=(000)$, as S is a zero vector, (111000) is a valid codeword.

(b) $S=RH^T=(111)$, as S is a non-zero vector, (111111) is not a valid vector and an error has occurred.

10.4.2 Syndrome-Based Decoding

For an (n, k) linear block code, $C_1, C_2, \cdots, C_{2^k}$ are the 2^k different codewords of C. However, the received vector R can be any one of the 2^n different n-tuples. The task of the decoder is to associate the received vector R with one of the 2^k n-tuples that are valid codewords. The decoder thus partitions the 2^n n-tuples into 2^k disjoint sets such that each set contains only one codeword C_i for $1 \le i \le 2^k$. The received vector R is decoded into C_i if it is in the ith set. Correct decoding results, if the error vector E is such that $R=C_i+E$ belongs to the ith set, and incorrect decoding results, if $R=C_i+E$ does not belong to the ith set.

The 2^k codewords constitute a ***standard array*** of the linear block codes, as shown in Table 10.4. The array consists of 2^k columns that are disjoint. All codewords are placed in the first row, with the codeword of all zeros in the leftmost position. The first element in the second row E_2 is any one of the $(2^n - 2^k)$ n-tuples not appearing in the first row. E_2 is then added to the codewords to form the second row. An unused n-tuple E_3 is chosen to begin the third row, and E_3 is then added to the codewords to form the third row. The process continues until all of 2^n n-tuples are used in the array. Each column now has 2^{n-k} n-tuples with the top most n-tuple as a codeword.

Table 10.4 A standard array for an (n, k) linear block code

C_1	C_2	C_3	$\cdots$	C_{2^k}
E_2	C_2+E_2	C_3+E_2	$\cdots$	$C_{2^k}+E_2$
E_3	C_2+E_3	C_3+E_3	$\cdots$	$C_{2^k}+E_3$
$\vdots$	$\vdots$	$\vdots$	$\vdots$	$\vdots$
$E_{2^{n-k}}$	$C_2+E_{2^{n-k}}$	$C_3+E_{2^{n-k}}$	$\cdots$	$C_{2^k}+E_{2^{n-k}}$

The rows of the array are called ***co-sets*** and the first element in each row is called a ***co-set leader***. If the error pattern caused by the channel coincides with a co-set leader, then the received vector is correctly decoded. On the other hand, if the error pattern is not a co-set leader, then an incorrect decoding will result. For a given channel, the probability of decoding error is minimized when the most likely error patterns are chosen as the co-set leaders. Hence, the co-set leader should be chosen as the vector with a minimum Hamming weight from the remaining available vectors.

It can be shown that all the 2^k n-tuples of a co-set have the same syndrome and the syndromes of different co-sets are different. The one-to-one correspondence between a co-set leader (correctable error pattern) and a syndrome leads to the following procedure known as syndrome-based decoding:

1. Compute $\boldsymbol{S} = \boldsymbol{R}\boldsymbol{H}^T$ for the received vector $\boldsymbol{R}$.
2. Locate the co-set leader $\boldsymbol{E}_i$ that has the same syndrome $\boldsymbol{S}$, as $\boldsymbol{E}_i$ can then be assumed to be the error pattern caused by the channel.
3. Obtain the codeword $\boldsymbol{C}$ from $\boldsymbol{R}$ by $\boldsymbol{C} = \boldsymbol{R} + \boldsymbol{E}_i$. Since the most probable error patterns have been chosen as the co-set leaders, this scheme will correct the 2^{n-k} most likely error patterns introduced by the channel.

We thus require storing the 2^{n-k} syndrome vectors of length $n-k$ bits and the 2^{n-k} n-bit error patterns corresponding to these syndromes. Thus, the storage required is of the order of $2^{n-k}(2n-k)$. Since the encoding operations for linear block codes are moderately complex and their syndrome-based decoding schemes are rather impractical, binary cyclic codes, which form a sub-class of linear block codes, are of importance.

They have algebraic properties that allow them to be easily encoded and decoded by efficient schemes using simple shift registers. In a ***cyclic code***, any cyclic shift of a codeword results in another codeword and the sum of any two codewords is also a codeword.

If $g(x)$ is a polynomial of degree $n-k$ and is a factor of $x^n + 1$ (modulo-2), then $g(x)$ is a generator polynomial that generates an (n, k) linear cyclic block code. With the message polynomial $m(x)$, the code polynomial $c(x)$ can be found in two different ways:

i) $c(x) = m(x)g(x)$, resulting in codewords that are not in the systematic form, and
ii) $c(x) = x^{n-k}m(x) + r(x)$, where the parity-check polynomial $r(x)$ is the remainder from dividing $x^{n-k}m(x)$ by $g(x)$, yielding systematic codewords (as already discussed earlier in the context of CRC).

EXAMPLE 10.7

Show $g(x)=x^3+x+1$ can be a generator polynomial for a (7, 4) cyclic code, and determine the message polynomial for the message 1100. Determine the corresponding codeword for both cases of systematic and non-systematic cyclic codes.

Solution

With $n=7$ and $k=4$, the generator polynomial $g(x)=x^3+x+1$ is of the order of $n-k=3$. Also, $g(x)$ divides x^7+1, as we have $x^7+1=(x^3+x+1)(x^4+x^2+x+1)$. $g(x)=x^3+x+1$ can therefore be a generator polynomial for a (7, 4) cyclic code. With the message 1100, we have the message polynomial $m(x)=x^3+x^2$.

For the non-systematic cyclic code, we have $c(x)=m(x)g(x)=(x^3+x^2)(x^3+x+1)=x^6+x^5+x^4+x^2$, which in turn means the codeword is 1110100. For the systematic cyclic code, we first divide $x^3(x^3+x^2)$ by x^3+x+1 to obtain the remainder polynomial $r(x)$, we therefore have $r(x)=x$. The code polynomial is thus given by $c(x)=x^{n-k}m(x)+r(x)=x^3(x^3+x^2)+x=x^6+x^5+x$, which in turn means the codeword is 1100010, similar to what was discussed in CRC.

For an (n,k) systematic cyclic code, the encoding and decoding processes, as shown in Figure 10.6, are simple and straightforward.

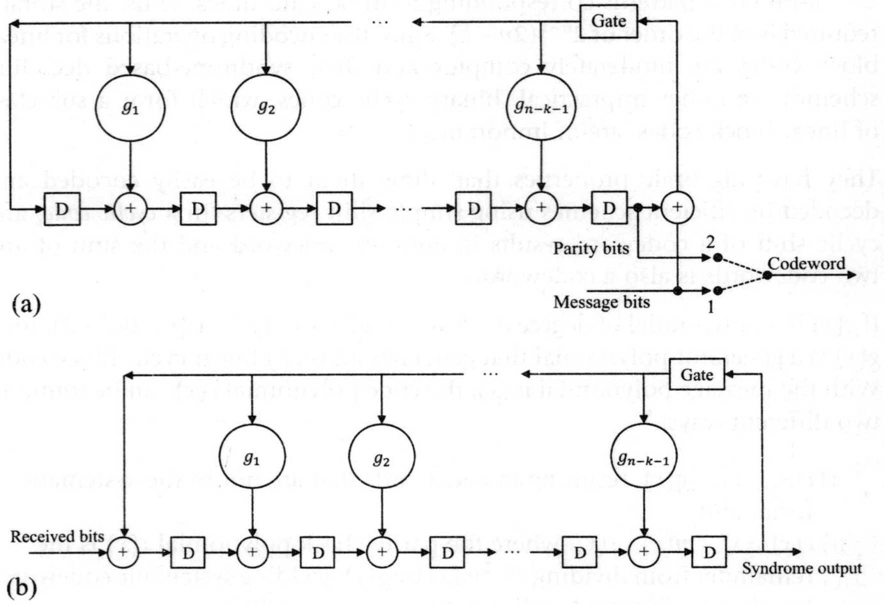

FIGURE 10.6 Encoder and decoder for an (n, k) cyclic code: (a) encoder and (b) syndrome calculator.

10.4.3 Well-Known Codes

There are many important linear block codes, including $(k+1, k)$ single parity-check bit codes and CRC codes, which cannot correct errors and were discussed earlier as effective error-detection schemes. Noting there are many well-known codes with error-correcting capability, we first describe repetition (repeated) codes and then briefly discuss BCH codes, which form a large class of cyclic linear block codes.

Repetition codes are the simplest type of linear block codes with error-correcting capability. A bit is encoded into a block of n identical bits, resulting in an $(n, 1)$ block code. Assuming the code has error-correcting capability t, a bit is encoded as a sequence of $2t+1$ identical bits, thus yielding $(2t+1, 1)$ linear block codes. In the case of hard-decision decoding, a majority logic decision needs to be made, i.e., if the number of 0s exceeds the number of 1s, the decoder decides in favor of a 0, otherwise, it decides in favor of a 1. The soft-decision decoding can be easily implemented to enhance the error rate performance at a modest level of complexity and the performance improvement due to soft-decision decoding can be significant. There are thus only two codewords in the code: all-zero codeword and all-one codeword. This code requires the use of significant bandwidth as it has a very low code rate $\frac{1}{2t+1} \leq \frac{1}{3}$, and therefore such codes are inefficient. However, repetition codes are attractive for deep-space communications, as there exists huge bandwidth at extremely high frequency band.

Bose-Chaudhuri-Hocquenghem (BCH) codes offer flexibility in the selection of the block length and code rate, and can be designed for correction of any given number of errors. A fast decoding algorithm can be employed for hard-decision decoding of the BCH codes. For any integer $m \geq 3$ and $0 < t < 2^{m-1}$, there exists a t-error-correcting BCH (n, k) code with $n = 2^m - 1$ and $n - k \leq mt$, whose minimum distance $d_{\min}$ is bounded as follows: $2t+1 \leq d_{\min} \leq 2t+2$. BCH codes can be defined in the binary field, such as the Hamming codes, and in the non-binary (symbol) field, such as the Reed-Solomon codes.

For single error-correcting codes, if the total number of bits in a transmitted codeword is n, then $m = n - k$ check bits must be able to indicate at least $n+1$ different states. Of these, one state means no error, and n states indicate the location of an error in each of the n positions, where it is also possible to have an error in the redundancy bits themselves. So $n+1$ states must be discoverable by $n-k$ bits, and $n-k$ bits can indicate 2^{n-k} different states. Therefore, we must have $2^{n-k} \geq n+1$ or equivalently $2^m - 1 \geq n$, for an (n, k) code with single error-correcting capability.

Hamming codes have $d_{\min} = 3$, and thus $t = 1$, i.e., a single error can be corrected regardless of the number of parity-check bits. An (n, k) Hamming code has $m = n - k$ parity-check bits, where $n = 2^m - 1$ and $k = 2^m - 1 - m$, for $m \geq 3$.

The parity-check matrix H of a Hamming code has m rows and n columns, and the last $n-k$ columns must be chosen such that it forms an identity matrix. No column consists of all zeros; each column is unique and has m elements. In view of this, the syndrome of all single errors will be distinct and single errors can be detected. By increasing the number of parity check bits k, the error-correcting capability remains unchanged (i.e., $t=1$), but the code rate $\frac{k}{n}$ improves, of course at the expense of additional encoding and decoding complexity.

EXAMPLE 10.8

Find the parity-check matrix, the generator matrix, and all the 16 codewords for a (7, 4) Hamming code. Determine the syndrome, if the received codeword is a) 0001111 and b) 0111111.

Solution

The parity-check matrix ***H*** matrix consists of all binary columns except the all zero sequence, we thus have it in the following form:

$$H = \begin{pmatrix} 1 & 1 & 0 & 1 & | & 1 & 0 & 0 \\ 1 & 0 & 1 & 1 & | & 0 & 1 & 0 \\ 0 & 1 & 1 & 1 & | & 0 & 0 & 1 \end{pmatrix}$$

and the corresponding generator matrix ***G*** is as follows:

$$G = \begin{pmatrix} 1 & 0 & 0 & 0 & | & 1 & 1 & 0 \\ 0 & 1 & 0 & 0 & | & 1 & 0 & 1 \\ 0 & 0 & 1 & 0 & | & 0 & 1 & 1 \\ 0 & 0 & 0 & 1 & | & 1 & 1 & 1 \end{pmatrix}$$

The resulting codewords are all listed in the following table:

Message (*M*)	Codeword (*C*)
0000	0000000
0001	0001111
0010	0010011
0011	0011100
0100	0100101
0101	0101010
0110	0110110
0111	0111001
1000	1000110
1001	1001001
1010	1010101
1011	1011010
1100	1100011
1101	1101100
1110	1110000
1111	1111111

(a) $S = RH^T = 000$. Since the syndrome is a zero vector, there are no errors in the codeword.
(b) $S = RH^T = 110$. Since the syndrome corresponds to the first row of column of H, the first bit of the received codeword is in error (i.e., the transmitted codeword was 1111111).

Reed-Solomon (RS) codes are non-binary cyclic codes with symbols each made up of m-bits, where $m \geq 1$. A Reed-Solomon (n, k) code is used to encode k symbols into blocks of $n = 2^m - 1$ symbols by adding $n - k$ parity symbols, where each symbol consists of m bits. A Reed-Solomon code with the symbol-error-correcting capability t has $n - k = 2t$ parity-check symbols and a minimum distance $d_{min} = 2t + 1$.

Reed-Solomon codes achieve the largest possible minimum distance for any linear block code with the same encoder input and output block lengths, as they can make highly-efficient use of redundancy. Block lengths and symbol sizes can be quite easily adjusted to meet various input message sizes. A unique and valuable merit of Reed-Solomon codes is their capability to correct burst errors. With efficient decoding techniques, Reed-Solomon codes have wide applications. In fact, they have applications in deep-space communications, wireless communications, such as WiMAX, storage devices, such as CDs, DVDs, Blu-ray discs, and digital video broadcasting systems, in the form of concatenated codes.

EXAMPLE 10.9

Determine the parameters of an 8-bit RS code whose error-correcting capability is 16 symbols.

Solution

With $m = 8$, as the number of bits in a symbol, we thus have $n = 2^8 - 1 = 255$ symbols in a codeword. With $n = 255$ and $t = 16$, we have $k = n - 2t = 255 - 32 = 223$ symbols in a codeword. We therefore have the code rate $R = \frac{k}{n} = \frac{223}{255} \cong 0.875$. The total number of bits in a codeword is $255 \times 8 = 2040$ bits. Since this code can correct 16 symbols, it can thus correct $16 \times 8 = 128$ consecutive bits. This 8-bit Reed-Solomon code is thus extremely powerful for correcting bursts of errors. However, if the errors are at random, and there is, at most, one error per symbol, then this code can correct only 16 bit errors in 2040 bits, hence not an efficient code for correcting random errors.

10.5 CONVOLUTIONAL CODES

A convolutional code is described by three integers, n, k, and K. K is a parameter known as the constraint length. In practice, n and k are small integers and K, also a small integer, is varied to control the level of redundancy and the resulting correlations. An increase in K can result in an increase in coding gain,

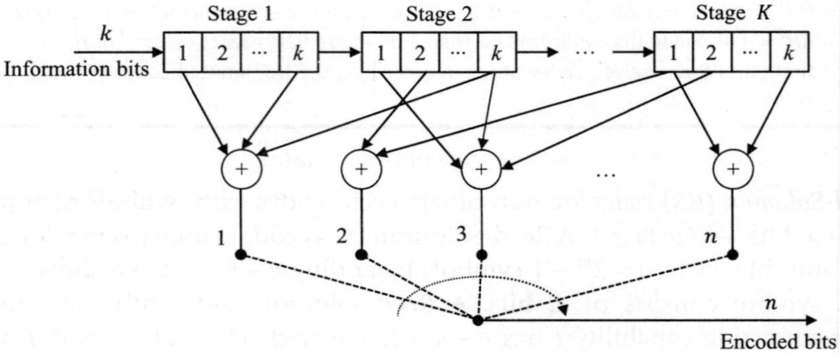

FIGURE 10.7 A block diagram of an (n, k, K) convolutional encoder.

but at the expense of higher decoding complexity. An important characteristic of convolutional codes, and a differentiating factor from block codes, is that the encoder has significant memory. Each encoded n-bit output depends not only on the corresponding k-bit input, but also on the previous $(K-1)$ k-bit inputs.

A general encoder for an (n, k, K) convolutional code, as shown in Figure 10.7, has a k K-stage shift register and n modulo-2 adders. At each unit of time, k bits are shifted into the first k stages of the register and all bits in the register are shifted k stages to the right. The outputs of the n adders, which form the n-linear combination of the contents of the shift register, yield the encoded bits. In order to clear or flush the encoding shift register of the input bits, $k(K-1)$ zero bits are appended to the end of the input message sequence and the corresponding n outputs are transmitted over the channel. This in turn provides the convolutional encoder with the all-zero state. The effective code rate is less than the ratio $\frac{k}{n}$. The reason for the disparity is that the final message bit into the encoder needs to be shifted through the encoder, as all the encoded bits are needed in the decoding process. Assuming the message sequence consists of L bits, then the encoded sequence consists of $n(L+K-1)$ bits, i.e., the effective rate is $\frac{L}{n(L+K-1)}$. Noting that in practice, we have $L \gg K-1$, the effective code rate thus simplifies to $\frac{1}{n}$.

10.5.1 Representations of Convolutional Codes

A binary convolutional code is a finite-state machine with $2^{k(K-1)}$ states. In a finite state machine, a state consists of the smallest amount of information that together with the knowledge of the input can determine the output. There are several methods for representing a convolutional encoder in graphical form; they include the state transition diagram, the tree diagram, and the trellis diagram. As a convention, in the state transition and trellis diagrams, a solid line represents an input 1, whereas a dashed line represents an input 0.

In a ***state transition diagram***, transitions between states are shown by paths connecting the states. There are 2^k paths coming from each state, corresponding to the k possible input bits. The number of paths going to a state is also 2^k. In a state transition diagram, it is not possible in a single transition to move from a given state to any arbitrary state. The state transition diagram completely characterizes the encoder, but falls short in tracking the transitions as a function of time.

The ***tree diagram*** adds the dimension of time, which in turn allows dynamically describing an encoder as a function of a particular input sequence. The encoding process is traced from left to right in accordance with the input bits. When an input bit is a 0, we move to the next rightmost branch in the upward direction and if the input is a 1, we move to the rightmost direction in the downward position. The drawback of the tree diagram is that the number of branches increases exponentially.

The ***trellis diagram***, by exploiting the repetitive structure, provides a more manageable encoder description. The nodes of the trellis characterize the encoder states. There is a one-to-one correspondence between the states of the transition state diagram, those of the trellis diagram and the nodes of the tree diagram. The trellis diagram is obtained by specifying all states on a vertical axis. Transition between two states is denoted by a path on two adjacent vertical axes. There are 2^k branches of the trellis leaving each state and 2^k branches arriving at each state.

A convolutional encoder can be represented by a set of n generator polynomials, one for each of the n modulo-2 adders. Each polynomial is of degree $K-1$ or less and describes the connection of the encoding shift register to that modulo-2 adder, where the coefficient of each term is either a 1 or a 0, depending on whether a connection exists or does not exist between the shift register and the adder. The product of each of these n generator polynomials and the input polynomial gives rise to the corresponding output polynomial, from which the corresponding encoded output can be formed.

EXAMPLE 10.10

A convolutional encoder, with $k=1$, $n=2$, and $K=3$, is shown in Figure 10.8a.

(a) Determine the number of states, and present the state transition, tree, and trellis diagrams.

(b) Determine the generator polynomial to identify the encoded bits if the message sequence is 11011, and determine the effective code rate.

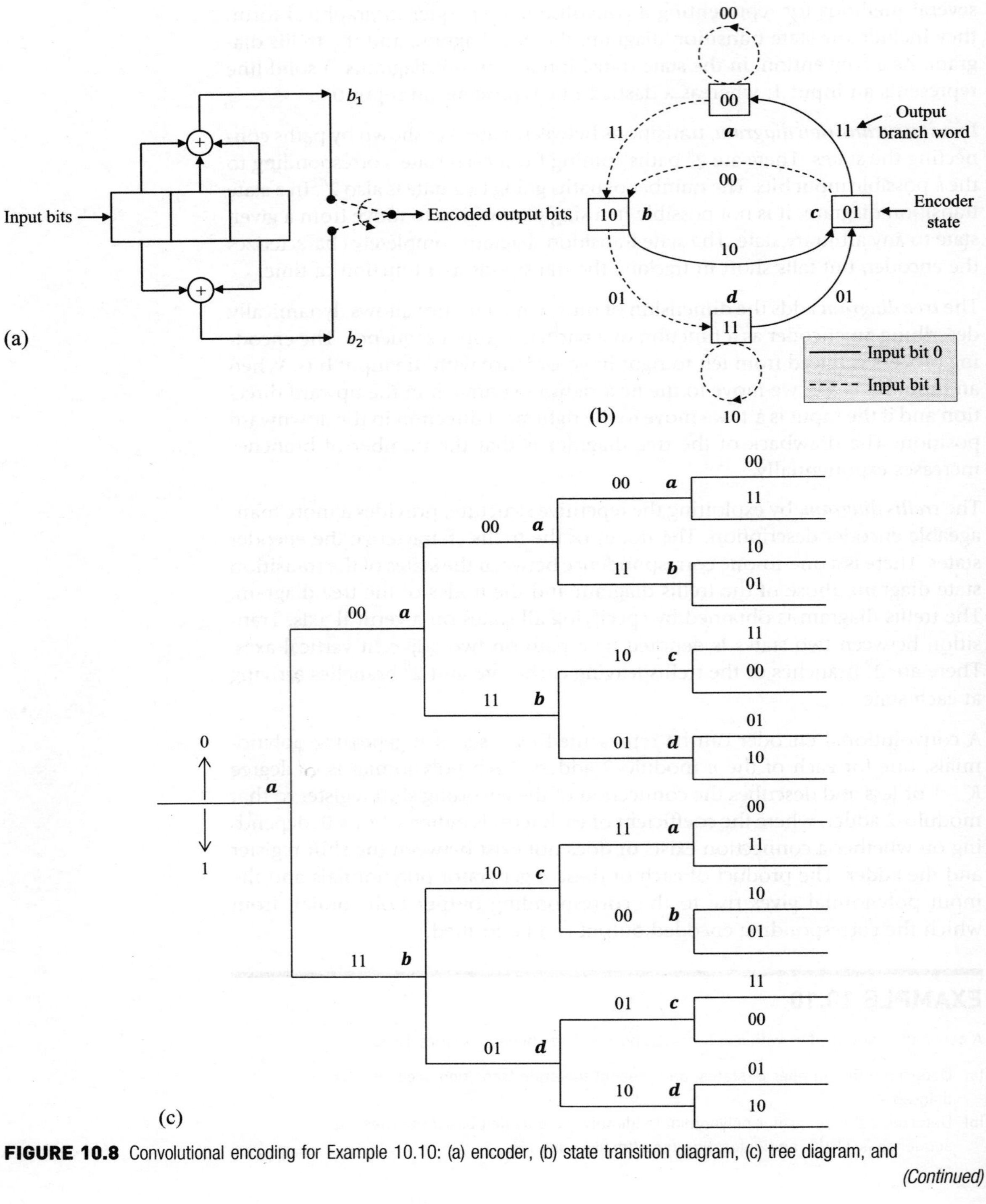

FIGURE 10.8 Convolutional encoding for Example 10.10: (a) encoder, (b) state transition diagram, (c) tree diagram, and

(Continued)

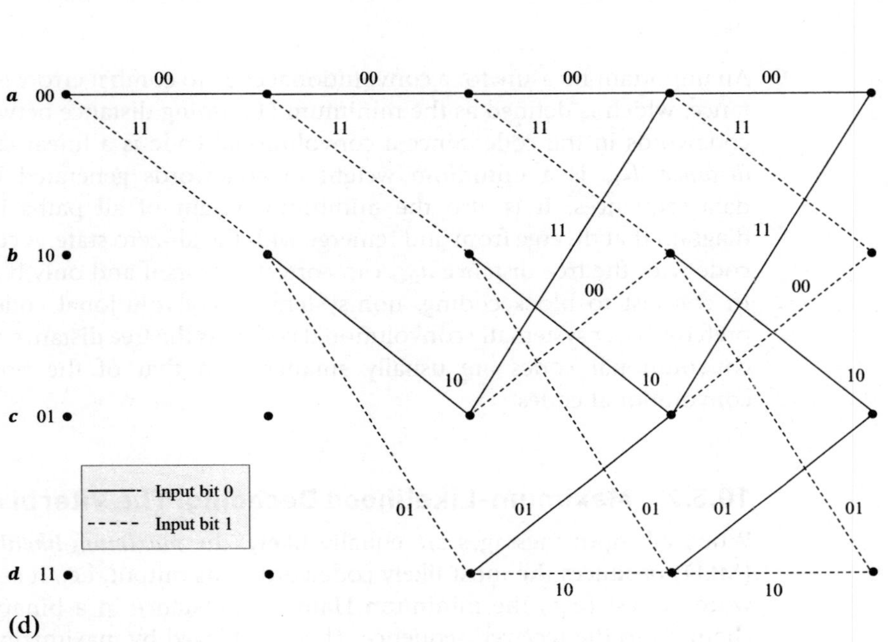

FIGURE 10.8, cont'd (d) trellis diagram.

Solution

(a) The number of states is $2^{(K-1)k} = 2^{(3-1)} = 4$. All three diagrams are all shown in Figure 10.8.

(b) The generator polynomial for the upper connection is $g_1(x) = 1 + x + x^2$ and that for the lower connection is $g_2(x) = 1 + x^2$. The polynomial corresponding to the input sequence 11011 is $m(x) = 1 + x + x^3 + x^4$. The polynomial corresponding to the output sequence for the upper path is given by $m(x)g_1(x) = 1 + x^6$ and thus its output sequence is 1000001. The polynomial corresponding to the output sequence for the lower path is given by $m(x)g_2(x) = 1 + x + x^2 + x^4 + x^5 + x^6$ and thus its output sequence is 1110111. By multiplexing the output sequences of both paths, we obtain the encoded sequence {11 01 01 00 01 01 11}. The effective code rate is thus $\frac{5}{2(5+3-1)} = \frac{5}{14}$.

Any change in the choice of connections results in a different code. The connections are, of course, not chosen arbitrarily. The problem of choosing connections to yield good distance properties is rather complicated. When a convolutional code that maps information bits that are far apart into codewords that are not far apart is not a good code, as the codewords can then be mistaken and the result would be a significant number of erroneous bits. Codes that allow such error propagation are called ***catastrophic codes***.

An important measure for a convolutional code to combat errors is the free distance, which is defined as the minimum Hamming distance between any two codewords in the code. Since a convolutional code is a linear code, the ***free distance*** d_{free} is a minimum weight of codewords generated by non-zero data sequences. It is also the minimum weight of all paths in the trellis diagram that diverge from and remerge with the all-zero state. A convolutional code with the free distance d_{free} can correct t errors if and only if $d_{\text{free}} \geq 2t + 1$. In contrast to block coding, non-systematic convolutional codes is usually preferred over systematic convolutional codes, as the free distance of systematic convolutional codes are usually smaller than that of the non-systematic convolutional codes.

10.5.2 Maximum-Likelihood Decoding: The Viterbi Algorithm

When all input messages are equally likely, the ***maximum-likelihood decoder*** (MLD) produces the most likely codeword as its output, i.e., it selects a codeword closest (e.g., the minimum Hamming distance in a binary symmetric channel) to the received sequence. This is achieved by maximizing the conditional probabilities, also known as likelihood functions, of received sequence over all possible transmitted sequences.

An MLD involves searching the entire code space, thus requiring a very high degree of computation. This brute-force approach can lead to a computational complexity that is an exponential function of the number of bits in the transmitted sequence. Maximization of the conditional probability can be performed recursively and efficiently using the Viterbi algorithm. The complexity associated with the Viterbi algorithm is a linear function of the number of bits in the transmitted sequence, but an exponential function of the constraint length.

For a received sequence, the ***Viterbi algorithm*** chooses a path in the trellis diagram such that the code sequence corresponding to the chosen path is at minimum distance from the received sequence. In other words, the algorithm involves calculating a measure of similarity between the received sequence, at a given time, and all the trellis paths entering each state at that time. It reduces the computational load by exploiting the structure in the code trellis, as it removes from consideration those trellis paths that could not possibly be candidates for the maximum likelihood choice. When two paths enter the same state, the one with the best minimum distance is chosen. The retained path is called the surviving path at that state. This selection of surviving paths is performed for all the states. The decoder assigns to each branch of each surviving path a distance (metric). Summing the branch metric yields the path metric. The decoder continues in this way to advance deeper into the trellis, making decisions by eliminating the least likely paths. The sequence is finally decoded as the surviving path with the smallest metric.

The Viterbi algorithm is a form of dynamic programming algorithm for finding the optimum path, in one case it may be the most likely path in another the shortest path. Dynamic programming is based on the principle that any portion (sub-path) of the overall optimum path must be the optimum path between the end points of that portion (sub-path). This is obvious, since if it were not true the portion (sub-path) could be replaced to yield a lower overall path length, a contradiction. The operation of Viterbi's algorithm can be best stated by means of a trellis diagram.

EXAMPLE 10.11

Using the Viterbi algorithm, determine the shortest path between the nodes *a* and *h* in the trellis diagram shown in Figure 10.9a, where a number next to a dashed line represents the distance between two adjacent nodes.

Solution

The shortest path between *a* and *h* must go through either *b* or *c*. If it goes through *b*, then the distance up to *b* is 1 and up to *c* is 2, where the metrics at *b* and *c* are then 1 and 2, respectively, as shown in Figure 10.9b.

If the shortest path between *a* and *h* must go through *d*, then it must go through either *b* or *c* to get to *d*. The distance from *a* to *d* via *b* is 4(= 1 + 3) and that via *c* is 7(= 2 + 5). It is then obvious that the path from *a* to *d*, via *c*, is not part of the overall optimum path between *a* and *h*, and will therefore not be included in subsequent calculations, and the surviving path is from *a* to *b* to *d*. If the shortest path between *a* and *h* must go through *e*, then it must go through either *b* or *c* to get to *e*. The distance

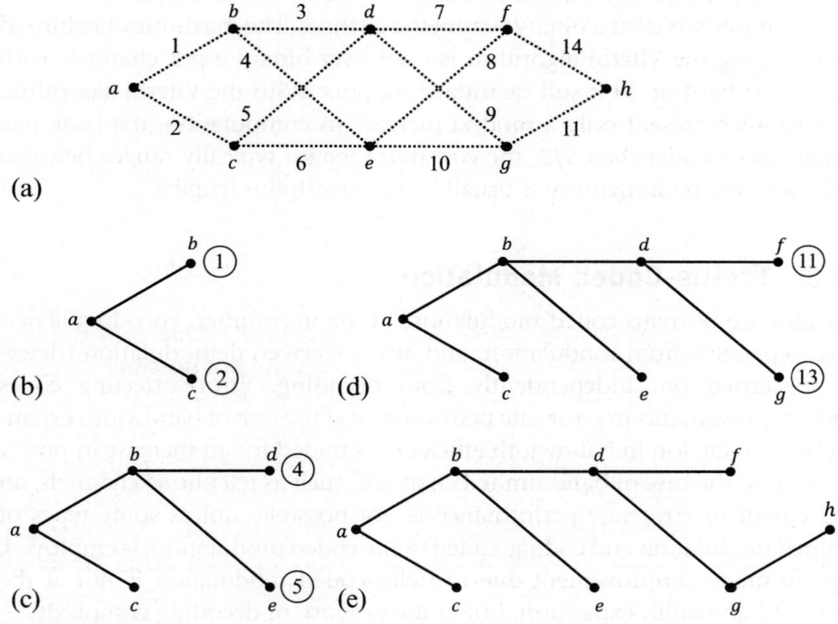

FIGURE 10.9 Illustrating step in the Viterbi algorithm for Example 10.11.

from a to e via b is $5(=1+4)$ and that via c is $8(=2+6)$. It is then obvious that the path from a to e, via c, is not part of the overall optimum path between a and h, and will therefore not be included in subsequent calculations, and the surviving path is from a to b to e. It is already evident that the shortest distance between a and h, whether it goes through d or e, will not include the path going through c. In other words, we already know that the path from a to b is part of the optimum path between a and h, where the metrics at d and e are 4 and 5, respectively, as shown in Figure 10.9c.

If the shortest path between a and h must go through f, then it must go through either d or e to get to f. The distance from a to f via d is $11(=4+7)$ and that via e is $13(=5+8)$. It is then obvious that the path from a to f, via e, is not part of the overall optimum path between a and h, and will therefore not be included in subsequent calculations, and the surviving path is from a to b to d to f. If the shortest path between a and h must go through g, then it must go through either d or e to get to g. The distance from a to g via d is $13(=4+9)$ and that via e is $15(=5+10)$. It is then obvious that the path from a to g, via e, is not part of the overall optimum path between a and h, and will therefore not be included in subsequent calculations, and the surviving path is from a to b to d to g. It is already evident that the shortest distance between a and h, whether it goes through f or g, will not include the path going through e. In other words, we already know that the path from a to b to d is part of the optimum path between a and h, where the metrics at f and g are 11 and 13, respectively, as shown in Figure 10.9d.

The distance from a to h via f is $25(=11+14)$ and that via g is $24(=13+11)$. It is then obvious that the path from a to h, via f, is not part of the overall optimum path between a and h and the overall optimum path is thus from a to b to d to g to h, as shown in Figure 10.9e. The Viterbi algorithm yields linear complexity, whereas the brute-force algorithm, which compares all possible path combinations to find the shortest path, gives rise to exponential complexity.

The Viterbi algorithm is a maximum-likelihood decoder that is optimum for an AWGN channel as well as a binary symmetric channel. The maximum-likelihood decoding using the Viterbi algorithm is used over binary input channels with either (1-bit) hard or 3-bit soft quantized outputs. With the Viterbi algorithm, soft-decisions represent only a modest increase in computation, the code rate is usually not smaller than 1/3, the constraint length typically ranges between 3 and 9 and the path memory is usually a few constraint lengths.

10.5.3 Trellis-Coded Modulation

In the absence of trellis-coded modulation, at the transmitter, encoding is performed separately from modulation, and at the receiver, demodulation (detection) is carried out independently from decoding. Error-correcting codes provide improvements in error-rate performance at the cost of bandwidth expansion (i.e., a reduction in bandwidth efficiency is traded for an increase in power efficiency). In the case of band-limited channels, such as telephone channels, an improvement in error rate performance is not possible, unless some types of combined modulation and coding, called trellis-coded modulation, is employed. The performance improvement due to trellis-coded modulation is not at the expense of bandwidth expansion, but at the expense of decoding complexity.

A limitation to the performance of error-control codes is the modulation technique, as selection of a code must go hand-in-hand with the choice of modulation technique for the channel. ***Trellis-coded modulation*** (TCM) combines an amplitude and/or phase modulation signaling set with a trellis-coding scheme, such as convolutional codes. The number of signal points in the constellation using TCM is larger than what is required when coding is not employed. This additional signal points, at a constant power level, can decrease the minimum Euclidean distance within the constellation. However this reduction in minimum Euclidean distance can be well compensated by an increase in the distance due to channel coding such that the error rate significantly improves only at the expense of the bandwidth conserved due to the use of a larger set of signal points.

The trellis-coding scheme, such as a convolutional code that has memory, allows only certain sequences of signal points for transmission. In the design of the trellis-codes, the emphasis is on maximizing the Euclidean distance between codewords rather than maximizing their Hamming distance. Using optimal soft-decision decoding algorithm for convolutional codes, such as the Viterbi algorithm, the possible sequence of signals is modeled as a trellis structure. Assuming an AWGN channel, maximum-likelihood decoding of a trellis code consists of finding that particular path through the trellis with minimum Euclidean distance to the received sequence.

The key concept in the construction of efficient TCM schemes is set partitioning. The approach is to partition an M-ary constellation successively into $2i$ sub-sets with size $M/2i$ signal points, where i is a positive integer, with the goal to further increasing minimum Euclidean distance between their respective signal points. A set is partitioned into two sub-sets that are congruent and ensure the signal points within each partition are maximally apart. The process continues as far as the code allows.

Figure 10.10 shows the block diagram of a TCM scheme. The incoming block of k information bits consists of two streams of k_1 bits and k_2 bits (i.e., $k = k_1 + k_2$). The first k_1 bits are the input to an (n_1, k_1) encoder, and the output thus consists of n_1 bits. The signal points in the constellation are partitioned into 2^{n_1} sub-sets. The remaining k_2 information bits determine a signal point in a given sub-set (i.e., in each sub-set there are 2^{k_2} signal points). In other words, the constellation should contain $2^{n_1 + k_2}$ points. This also leads to the number of steps required in partitioning of the constellation.

The objective of trellis-coded modulation is to increase the minimum distance between the signals that are the most likely to be confused, without increasing the average signal power. Even though the increase in signal set reduces the minimum distance between symbols, the Euclidean distance between trellis-coded sequences more than compensates for the signal points bring jammed together.

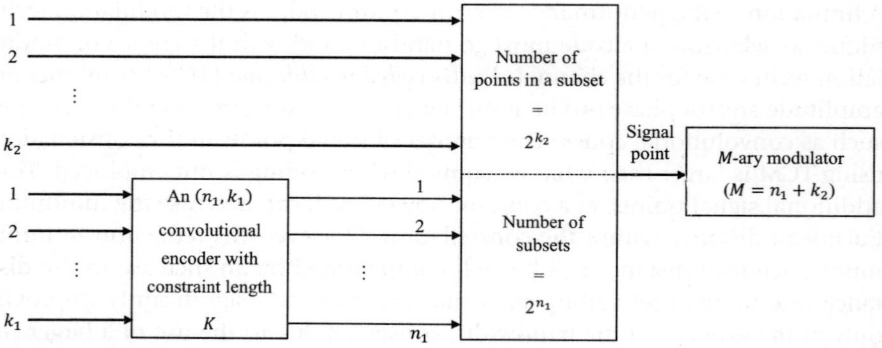

FIGURE 10.10 Block diagram of a TCM scheme.

The Viterbi algorithm is employed in the decoding of TCM, as the modulator has memory and maximum likelihood sequence detection must thus be performed. First, the most likely signal point in each partition is determined, i.e., we find the signal point in each sub-set that has the smallest Euclidean distance from the received signal. This Euclidean distance is then used to find a path through the trellis diagram whose total Euclidean distance from the received sequence is minimum.

EXAMPLE 10.12

Provide an example of set portioning for a coded 8-PSK signal set, where two information bits per point are transmitted and compare the result with an uncoded QPSK signal set.

Solution

Figure 10.11 shows the partitioning of an 8-PSK constellation. If the minimum Euclidean distance of an uncoded QPSK is $d_1 = \sqrt{2}$, the minimum distance of a coded 8-PSK is then $d_2 = 2$, as it represents the Euclidean distance between the antipodal signal points of the same sub-set. This can thus yield an asymptomatic gain of $20\log\left(2/\sqrt{2}\right) = 3$ dB.

10.6 COMPOUND CODES

The computational complexity increases exponentially by increasing the length of a linear block code or the constraint length of a convolutional code. In order to approach the Shannon limit, the required computational complexity of the decoder must then be enormous. To circumvent this problem, traditional algebraic linear and convolutional codes can be combined through interleaving to improve the performance at the expense of a modest degree of complexity.

Another approach of high importance is to have probabilistic compound codes, such as turbo codes and low-density parity-check codes. These codes

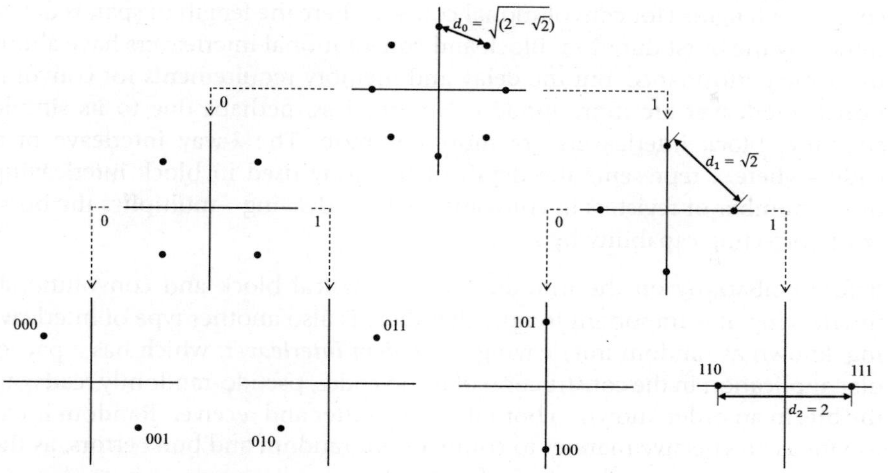

FIGURE 10.11 Partitioning of 8-PSK constellation for Example 10.12.

can approach the Shannon limit at a similar degree of computational complexity through use of sufficiently long codeword.

10.6.1 Interleavering

There are a number of channel degradations, which can give rise to burst errors. In contrast to AWGN channels that can generally cause statistically independent random errors, impulse noise, produced by lightning and switching transients, can cause burst errors. Also, errors in wireless channels characterized by multipath fading, in particular fast fading, are in burst, as signal fading due to time-varying multipath propagation often causes the signal to fall below the noise level. Another source of burst errors are magnetic recording channels in which defects in the recording tape or disk may result in clusters of errors.

An effective technique, which only requires knowledge of the duration or span of the channel memory, i.e., the burst length, and not its exact statistical characterization, is interleaving. Interleaving before transmission and de-interleaving after reception can cause channel-induced burst errors to be spread out in time and thus could be handled as if they were random errors. Separating the bits in time effectively transforms a channel with memory to a memoryless channel, and thus enabling random-error-correcting codes to combat burst errors.

There are several interleaving types, but only the block interleavers (better matched with block codes) and convolutional interleavers (more suited to convolutional codes) are briefly discussed. In short, ***interleaving*** shuffles the encoded data over a span of several block lengths (for block codes) or several constraint lengths (for convolutional codes), where the length of span is determined by the burst duration. Block and convolutional interleavers have about the same performance, but the delay and memory requirements for convolutional interleaver are more modest. Nevertheless, perhaps due to its simple structure, block interleavers are more common. The λ-way interleave of a code—where λ represents the depth of the array used in block interleaving or the number of registers in convolutional interleaving—multiplies the burst error-correcting capability by λ.

Before embarking on the introduction of classical block and convolutional interleaving, it is important to note that there is also another type of interleaving, known as random interleaving. A ***random interleaver***, which has a particular application in the construction of turbo codes, pseudo-randomly reads out the bits in an order known to both the transmitter and receiver. Random interleaving is an effective manner to combat both random and burst errors, as the output bits are not produced in a fixed order.

Figure 10.12 shows the block diagram for block interleaving. The ***block interleaver*** is an array that is filled row by row. A row has n columns corresponding

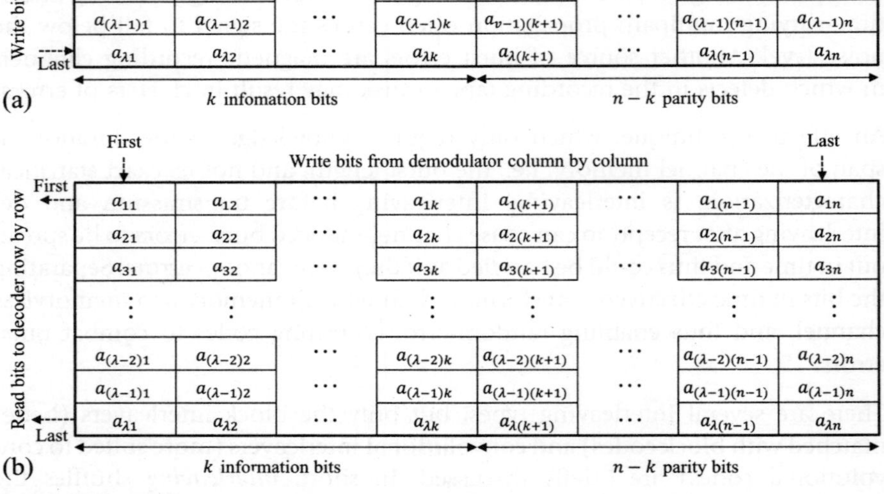

FIGURE 10.12 Block interleaving: (a) interleaver and (b) deinterleaver.

with the n bits in a codeword, where the first k bits in each row are the information bits and the remaining $n - k$ bits are the parity bits. The choice of n, the number of columns, is dependent on the block-coding scheme. The array has λ rows, which corresponds either to the expected burst length or the worst burst length. The parameter λ is called the ***interleaver degree or depth***. These λ codewords of n bits are then transmitted column by column until the interleaver is emptied. Then the interleaver is loaded again and the cycle repeats. At the receiver, the inverse operation is performed; the bits are entered into the deinterleaver array by columns, and removed by rows. Any burst of less than λ errors results in isolated errors at the deinterleaver output that are separated from each other by n bits.

If the code has single error-correcting capability, then the process of block interleaving permits the correction of a burst of λ bits. The interleaver/deinterleaver end-to-end delay is approximately $2n\lambda$ bits. Since the $n \times \lambda$ array needs to be filled before it can be read out, a memory of $2n\lambda$ bits is generally implemented at each location to allow the emptying of one array while the other is being filled, and vice versa.

Figure 10.13 shows the block diagram for convolutional interleaving. In a ***convolutional interleaving***, the bits are sequentially shifted into the bank of λ registers. Each successive register provides M bits more storage than did the preceding one. The first register provides no storage (the bit is transmitted immediately). The four switches operate in step and move from line-to-line at the bit rate of the input bit stream. Thus, each switch makes contact with line 1 at the same time, and then moves to line 2 together, etc., returning to line 1 after line λ. With each new bit, the commutator switches to a new register, and the new bit is shifted in while the oldest bit in that register is shifted out to the transmitter. The deinterleaver performs the inverse operation. The input and output commutators for both interleaving and deinterleaving must be synchronized.

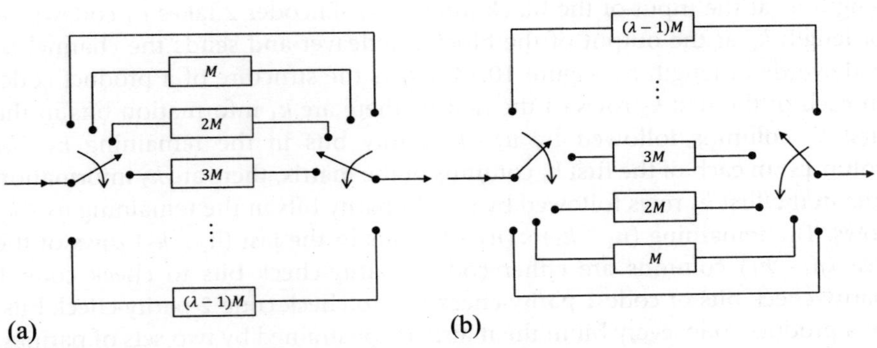

FIGURE 10.13 Convolutional interleaving: (a) interleaver and (b) deinterleaver.

With convolutional interleaving, the end-to-end delay is $M(\lambda-1)$ bits and the memory is $M(\lambda-1)/2$ at both ends of the channel, which in turn are one half of the corresponding values in a block interleaving for a similar level of interleaving. The convolutional interleaving structure can be changed easily and conveniently by changing the number of lines λ and the incremental number of elements per line M.

10.6.2 Simple Combining Codes

Simple combining codes, such as product codes and concatenated codes, allow the creation of codes which are quite powerful, yet have relatively low complexity. These codes are used when a single code cannot correct all types of errors encountered on the channel.

Codes with higher block length can offer higher error correction capability, and in turn increase the decoding complexity. One approach to design block codes with long block lengths and rather low complexity is to begin with two or more simple codes with short block lengths. These codes, in combination, can give rise to codes with longer block lengths and improved capabilities.

A two-dimensional parity-check code discussed earlier as an error-detection scheme with very limited capabilities is an extremely simple case of powerful product codes. A ***product code*** combines two block codes into a single more powerful code. A product code can be formed from two systematic linear block codes (n_1, k_1) and (n_2, k_2) with minimum distances of d_{min_1} and d_{min_2}, respectively. The resulting product code is an $(n_1 n_2, k_1 k_2)$ linear block code, whose bits are arranged in an $n_2 \times n_1$ matrix, with the minimum distance $d_{min}{=}d_{min\_1}\, d_{min\_2}$. The product code has thus the error-correcting capability of t, where t is is the largest integer no greater than $\left(\frac{d_{min}-1}{2}\right)$.

Encoder 1 takes k_2 message blocks of k_1 bits and provides k_2 codewords of length n_1 at the input of the block interleaver. Encoder 2 takes n_1 codewords of length k_2 at the output of the block interleaver and sends the channel n_1 codewords of length n_2. Figure 10.14 shows the structure of a product code. In each of the first k_2 rows of the matrix, there are k_1 information bits in the first k_1 columns followed by n_1-k_1 parity bits in the remaining n_1-k_1 columns. In each of the first k_1 columns of the matrix, there are k_2 information bits in the first k_2 rows followed by n_2-k_2 parity bits in the remaining n_2-k_2 rows. The remaining $(n_1-k_1)\times(n_2-k_2)$ bits in the last (n_2-k_2) rows of the last (n_1-k_1) columns are either code 2 parity-check bits to check code 1 parity-check bits or code 1 parity-check bits to check code 2 parity-check bits. In a product code, every bit in the matrix is constrained by two sets of parities, one from each of the two codes.

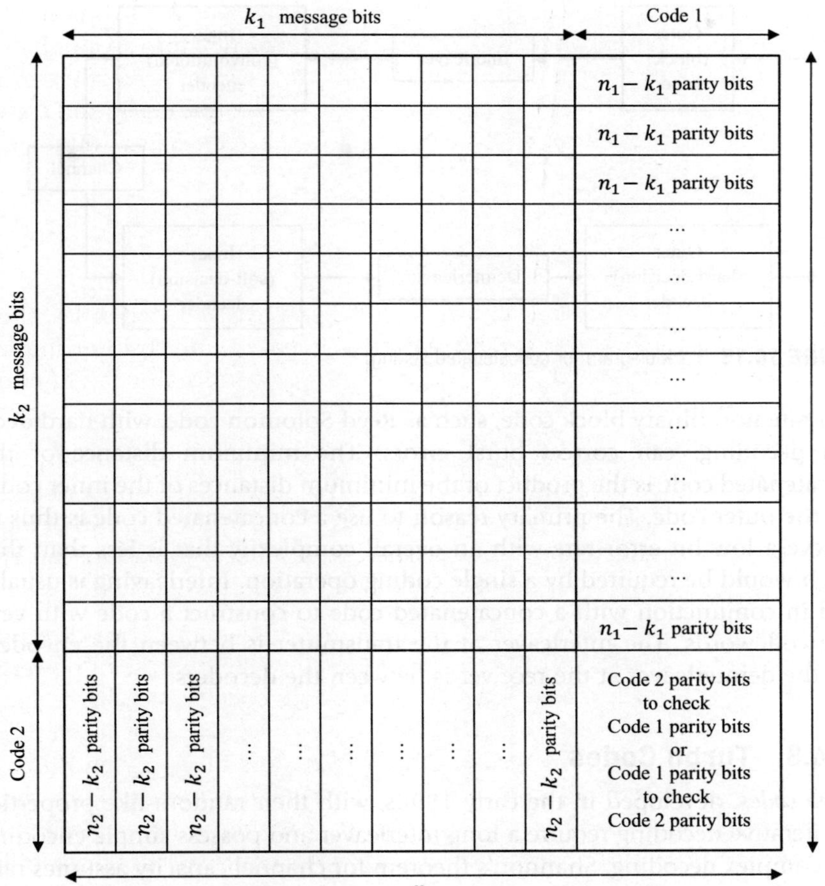

FIGURE 10.14 Structure of a product code.

As the old adage suggests that the whole is greater than the sum of its parts, simple codes can be combined to provide a high-performance low-rate code to combat channel errors, especially of burst types. A ***concatenated code*** is one that uses two levels of coding to achieve the desired error performance, where the codes are in series. The additional decoding complexity associated with a concatenated code is justified for poor communication channels, such as fading channels, and power-limited communication channels, such as satellite channels.

Figure 10.15 shows the block diagram for concatenated coding. In a concatenated code, the two codes are as follows: i) an inner code, which is usually a low-rate binary convolutional code with soft-decision decoding, can correct most of the random errors, and ii) an outer code, which is usually a

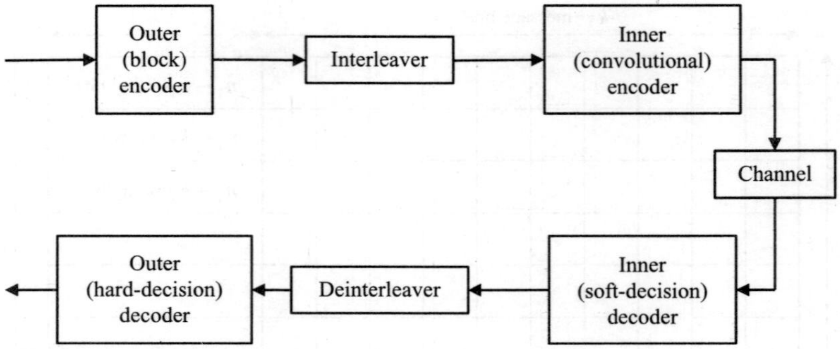

FIGURE 10.15 Block diagram for concatenated coding.

high-rate non-binary block code, such as Reed-Solomon code, with hard decision decoding, can correct burst errors. The minimum distance of the concatenated code is the product of the minimum distances of the inner coder and the outer code. The primary reason to use a concatenated code is thus to achieve a low bit error rate with an overall complexity that is less than that which would be required by a single coding operation. Interleaving is usually used in conjunction with a concatenated code to construct a code with very long codewords. The interleaver at the transmitter is between the encoders and the deinterleaver at the receiver is between the decoders.

10.6.3 Turbo Codes

Turbo codes, developed in the early 1990s, with their random-like properties and iterative decoding require a long interleaver and possess simple encoding and complex decoding. Shannon's theorem for channel capacity assumes random coding with the bit error rate approaching zero as the code's block or constraint length approaches infinity. Since increases in block or constraint length require exponential increases in decoding complexity, it is not possible to decode a truly random code. Turbo codes can be made sufficiently random to approach the Shannon limit and, by using iterative techniques, they can be efficiently decoded in a computationally feasible manner. The mechanism that made turbo codes possible is its simplified decoder, as the term turbo in turbo codes is more about the decoding process rather than the encoding process. Figure 10.16 shows the block diagrams of a turbo encoder and decoder. Turbo codes can be viewed as linear block codes, where the block size being determined by the size of the interleaver. Turbo codes are employed in UMTS, cdma2000 and IEEE802.16 WiMAX wireless systems.

A ***turbo encoder*** employs two generally identical recursive systematic short constraint-length linear convolutional encoders in parallel, where one of the encoders is preceded by a large-size pseudo-random interleaver. In a recursive

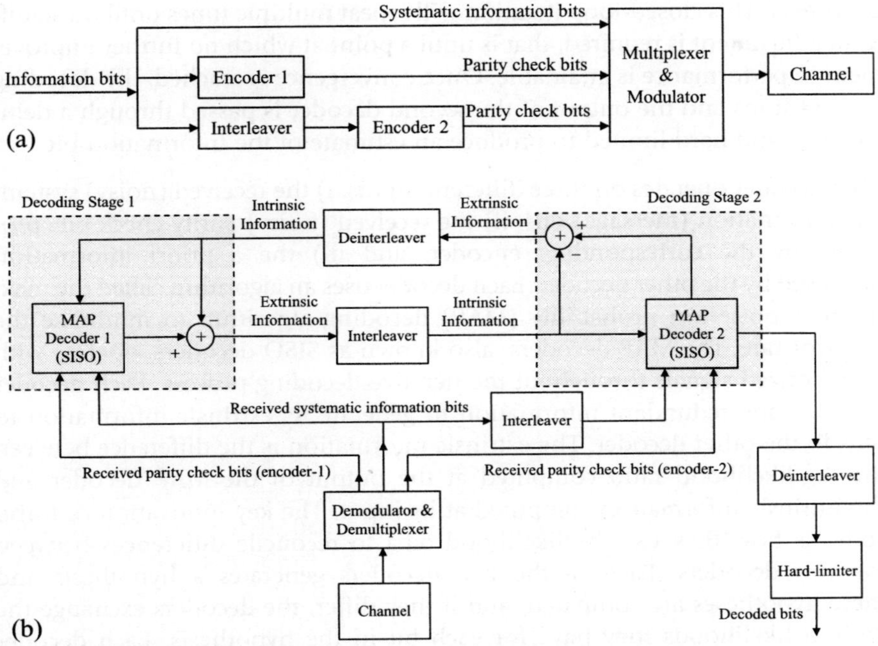

FIGURE 10.16 Block diagram for turbo coding: (a) encoder and (b) decoder.

systematic convolutional encoder, the information bits appear directly as part of the encoded bits and the parity-check bits by each encoder are generated by a recursive feedback shift register. The output of the turbo encoder contains the information bits and two sets of parity-check bits. The pseudo-random interleaver has a large size in the order of tens of thousands of bits. The pseudo-random interleaver takes the information bits at the input and produces bits at the output in a different temporal manner. The interleaver can provide a robust performance regardless of the channel statistics, while tying channel errors together to improve performance.

The optimal decoding of turbo codes is an impossible task, for the number of states in the code trellis is quite large. However, the sub-optimal iterative turbo decoding algorithm can provide excellent performance. The unique feature of turbo codes lies in iterative decoding, that is the concept of allowing the two decoders with low-complexity to exchange information iteratively. The ***turbo decoder*** forms a closed-loop feedback system. The use of feedback in a turbo decoder highlights the fact some information from one decoder to the next is sent in an iterative manner, where decoders have soft-input and soft-output (SISO) values. In other words, each decoder uses a soft-decoding algorithm (i.e., a decoder accepts soft input values and generates soft output values for the other). This closed-loop iteration will repeat multiple times until no significant adjustment is required, that is until a point at which no further improvement in performance is attainable. Once convergence is reached, the decoding process stops and the output of the second decoder is passed through a deinterleaver and hard-limited to produce an estimate of the information bit.

Each decoder operates on three different inputs: i) the received (noisy) systematic information (message) bits, ii) the received (noisy) parity-check bits produced by the corresponding encoder, and iii) the a priori information produced by the other decoder. Each decoder uses an algorithm called the maximum a posteriori probability (MAP) decoding algorithm to minimize the bit error rate. The MAP decoders, also known as SISO decoders, operate with unquantized signals throughout the iterative decoding process. Each decoder removes any redundant information to generate its extrinsic information to pass to the other decoder. The extrinsic information is the difference between the log-likelihood ratio computed at the output of the MAP decoder and the intrinsic information computed at its input. The key innovation of turbo codes is how they use the likelihood data to reconcile differences between the two decoders. Each of the two decoders generates a hypothesis and these hypotheses are compared, and if they differ, the decoders exchange the derived likelihoods they have for each bit in the hypothesis. Each decoder incorporates the derived likelihood estimates from the other decoder to generate a new hypothesis for the bits. Then, they compare these new hypotheses. This iterative process continues until the two decoders come up with the same hypothesis. The following general observations regarding the performance of turbo codes can be made:

- To achieve high performance, the length of the interleaver should be very large, and the performance improves as the length of the interleaver increases.
- The performance significantly improves as the number of iterations increases, but the rate of increase diminishes.
- An increase in the number of iterations results in an increase in the decoder latency.
- A change in the constraint length of either of the two convolutional codes can impact the performance, and consequently the decoder complexity.
- At low very E_b/N_0, the BER for the turbo-coded transmission is even higher than that for uncoded transmission.
- The BER for turbo-coded transmission falls quite rapidly (i.e., its negative slope is quite significant) as soon as certain threshold for E_b/N_0 has been reached.
- At a BER of about 10^{-5}, the turbo code is only about 0.5 dB from the Shannon's theoretical limit.

- There exists an error floor, in the sense that once it is reached, an increase in E_b/N_0—when it is in the range of medium to large values—does not bring any substantial improvement in BER. The error floor is affected by the choice of interleaver.

10.6.4 Low-Density Parity-Check Codes

Low-density parity-check (LDPC) codes, developed in the early sixties and revived in the nineties, are linear non-cyclic block codes and characterized by a sparse parity-check matrix, require a long codeword, and possess rather complex encoding and simple decoding. LDPC codes can perform as well as turbo codes with comparable code lengths, code rates, and decoding complexity. An LDPC code is characterized by a sparse parity-check matrix consisting mostly of 0s and very few 1s, where the number of 1s in a row or in a column are both much smaller than the code length. When all rows have the same number of 1s and all columns have the same number of 0s, the LDPC code is called regular; otherwise, it is irregular. Regular codes are easier to generate, but the irregular codes, with its inherent flexible structure, can have a performance well within a fraction of dB from the Shannon's channel capacity. There are two decoding schemes for decoding LDPC codes: the hard-decision bit-flipping scheme with low-complexity and the soft-decision sum-product scheme with high-complexity.

Summary and Sources

Although error-control coding is an advanced area in digital communications, it was presented at a level consistent with how other major areas in digital communications are covered in this book. Error-detection schemes and ARQ techniques were discussed in detail. We provided also basic fundamentals of classical block and convolutional codes, as well as brief discussions about modern and high performance coding techniques, such as trellis-coded modulation and turbo coding.

Shannon showed that error free transmission could be achieved if in an AWGN environment with infinite bandwidth, the signal-to-noise ratio per bit exceeds the Shannon limit of −1.6 dB [1]. He did not, however, indicate how this could be achieved. This thus led to a significant amount of research, over many decades, to develop a number of techniques that introduce redundancy to allow for correction of errors.

There are a number of excellent sources on error-control coding including the book by Lin and Costello [2]. The topic of error-control coding is also discussed extensively in some graduate textbooks [3–6]. There are also papers by which high-performance coding schemes have been introduced, such as the trellis-coded modulation by Ungerboeck [7,8], turbo coding by Berrou, *et al.* [9], and LDPC developed by Gallager [10] and revived by Mackay and Neal [11]. An excellent survey on channel coding has been captured in [12].

[1] C.E. Shannon, A mathematical theory of communication, *Bell Syst. Tech. J.* 27 (July, October, 1948) 379–423, 623–656.

[2] S. Lin and D.J. Costello Jr., *Error Control Coding,* second ed., Prentice Hall, ISBN: 978-0130426727, 2004.

[3] R.D. Gitlin, J.F. Hayes and S.B. Weinstein, *Data Communications Principles,* Plenum Press, ISBN: 0-306-43777-5, 1992.

[4] B. Sklar, *Digital Communications,* second ed., Prentice-Hall, ISBN: 0-13-084788-7, 2001.

[5] J.G. Proakis and M. Salehi, *Digital Communications,* fifth ed., McGraw-Hill, ISBN: 978-0-07-295716-7, 2008.

[6] Leon-Garcia and I. Widjaja, *Communication Networks - Fundamental Concepts and Key Architectures,* second ed., McGraw-Hill, ISBN: 0-07-119848-2, 2004.

[7] G. Ungerboeck, Channel coding with multi-level/phase signals, *IEEE Trans. Inf. Theory* (January 1982) 55–67.

[8] G. Ungerboeck, Trellis-coded modulation with redundant signal sets, Parts 1 and 2", *IEEE Comm. Mag.* (January 1987) 5–21.

[9] C. Berrou, A. Glavieux and P. Thitmajshima, Near Shannon limit error-correction coding and decoding: turbo codes, in: *Proceedings of IEEE International Conference on Communications,* Geneva, May 1993.

[10] R.G. Gallager, Low-density parity-check codes, *IRE Trans. Inf. Theory* (January 1962) 21–28.

[11] D.J.C. MacKay and R.M. Neal, Near Shannon limit performance of low density parity check codes, *Electron. Lett.* 33 (March 1997) 457–458.

[12] D.J. Costello and G.D. Forney, Channel coding: the road to channel capacity, *Proc. IEEE* 95 (June 2007) 1150–1177.

Problems

10.1 Determine the probability of error for a repetition code, where for decoding, a majority rule is employed and the bit error rate is p and a bit is repeated $n = 2t + 1$ times, where t is the error-correcting capability.

10.2 In a single parity-check code, compute the probability of an undetected bit error if a single parity-check bit is appended to a block of seven bits.

10.3 Show that the code consisting of 000, 111, and 101 codewords is not linear.

10.4 Consider a rate of $\frac{1}{3}$ convolutional encoder, where the three generator polynomials are as follows: $1 + x + x^2$, 1, and $1 + x$. Assuming the input sequence is 101001, determine the encoded sequence, present the state transition, tree, and trellis diagrams, and employ the Viterbi algorithm to decode the received sequence.

10.5 Consider a (2, 1, 2) convolutional encoder whose two generator polynomials are as follows: $1 + x + x^2$ and $1 + x^2$. Assuming the message sequence to the convolutional encoder is 110111001000, determine the encoded sequence.

10.6 Consider $g(x) = x^3 + x + 1$, with 1001 as the information sequence. Determine the transmitted codeword. With the first received bit in error, how the error checking is done at the receiver?

10.7 A repetition code is an $(n, 1)$ code in which the $n-1$ parity bits are repetitions of the information bit. Is the repetition code a linear code? What is the minimum distance of the code?

10.8 Consider a (5, 1) repetition code. Determine the syndrome for all 10 possible double-error patterns.

10.9 An error-detecting code takes k information bits and generates a codeword with $n = 2k + 1$ encoded bits whose first k bits and second k bits are identical to the k information bits and the last bit of the codeword is the exclusive-or (XOR) of the first k bits. Determine the parity-check matrix and the minimum distance of this code.

10.10 Find the set of all codewords for a (6, 3) linear systematic code whose check bits are as follows: $c_4 = c_1 + c_2$, $c_5 = c_1 + c_3$ and $c_6 = c_2 + c_3$.

10.11 Assuming the information bits are 111000101 and the generator polynomial is $x^8 + x^2 + x + 1$, determine the transmitted bit sequence consisting of the information bits and the CRC bits.

10.12 Consider the input bit sequence is as follows:

01001001110110011011111011011001110110011 01101101.

Assuming the bit sequence is divided into 16-bit segments, determine the checksum sent along with data, and show how the checksum checker operates on the received bit stream.

10.13 The generator polynomial for a (15, 7) cyclic code is $g(x) = 1 + x^4 + x^6 + x^7 + x^8$. Find the codeword (in the systematic form) for the message polynomial $m(x) = x^2 + x^3 + x^4$. Assuming the first and the last bits of the codeword are in error, determine the corresponding syndrome.

10.14 Show that in a (7, 4) Hamming code with generator matrix G and the parity-check matrix H, we have $HG^T = 0$.

10.15 The parity-check bits of a (8, 4) linear systematic code are generated by $c_5 = c_1 + c_2 + c_4$, $c_6 = c_1 + c_2 + c_3$, $c_7 = c_1 + c_3 + c_4$, and $c_8 = c_2 + c_3 + c_4$. Determine the generator matrix and the parity-check matrix for this code, as well as its minimum weight and error detecting and correcting capabilities.

Computer Exercises

10.16 Determine all the codewords of a (15, 11) Hamming code and verify the minimum distance is 3. Show how a hard-decision syndrome-based decoding works.

10.17 In a (7, 4) Hamming code with a generator polynomial $g(x) = x^3 + x + 1$, determine the generator matrix. Noting the received codeword is (1 0 1 0 1 1 1), determine the corrected codeword.

10.6 Consider $g(x) = x^3 + x + 1$ with 1001 as the information sequence. Determine the transmitted codeword. With the [illegible] received bit in error, show how the error checking is done at the receiver.

10.7 A repetition code is an $(n, 1)$ code in which the $n - 1$ parity bits are repetitions of the information bit. Is the repetition code a linear code? What is the minimum distance of the code?

10.8 Consider a (15, 11) Hamming code. Determine the syndrome for all [illegible] possible double-error patterns.

10.9 An error-detecting code takes k information bits and generates a codeword with $2k + 1$ encoded bits where the first k bits and second k bits are identical to the k information bits and the last bit of the codeword is the exclusive-or (XOR) of the k [illegible] bits. Determine the parity-check matrix and the minimum distance of this code.

10.10 Find the set of all codewords for a (6, 3) linear systematic code where the check bits are as follows: [illegible]

10.11 Assuming the information bits are [illegible] and the generator polynomial is [illegible], determine the transmitted bit sequence consisting of the information bits and the CRC bits.

10.12 Consider the input bit sequence is as follows:

[illegible]

Assuming the bit sequence is divided into [illegible]-bit segments, determine the checksum sent along with data, and show how the checksum checker operates on the received bit stream.

10.13 The generator polynomial for a (15, 7) cyclic code is $g(x) =$ [illegible]. Find the codeword in the systematic form for the message polynomial [illegible]. Assuming the first and the last bits of the codeword are in error, determine the corresponding syndrome.

10.14 Show that in a (7, 4) Hamming code with generator matrix G and the parity-check matrix H, we have $HG^T = 0$.

10.15 The parity-check bits of a (8, 4) linear systematic code are generated by [illegible]. Determine the generator matrix and the parity-check matrix for the code, as well as its minimum weight and error detecting and correcting capabilities.

Computer Exercises

10.16 Enumerate all the codewords of a (7, 4) Hamming code and verify the minimum distance is 3. Show how hard decision syndrome based decoding works.

10.17 In a (7, 4) Hamming code with a generator polynomial $g(x) =$ [illegible], determine the generator matrix. Noting the received codeword is [illegible], determine the corrected codeword.

CHAPTER 11

Communication Networks

INTRODUCTION

We first expand on multiplexing, duplexing, and multiple access schemes along with their merits, drawbacks and applications. Various random-access and controlled-access schemes are briefly discussed. The focus then turns mainly towards some aspects of wired communication networks, such as circuit-switched and packet-switched networks, and telephone and cable networks. We then briefly introduce cryptography and network security, mainly the fundamentals of private-key and public-key cryptography and digital signature. After studying this chapter and understanding all relevant concepts, students should be able to achieve the following learning objectives:

1. Define multiplexing and characterize its applications.
2. Identify differentiating aspects of FDM and TDM techniques.
3. Distinguish the difference between synchronous TDM and asynchronous TDM.
4. Understand communication modes.
5. Know the difference between the duplexing methods FDD and TDD methods.
6. Elaborate on the need for multiple access schemes.
7. Assess FDMA, TDMA, and CDMA schemes and compare them.
8. Analyze unslotted and slotted ALOHA random-access methods.
9. Detail the differences among various CSMA schemes.
10. Portray how controlled-access methods work.
11. Provide basic descriptions of circuit-switched and packet-switched networks.
12. Expand on various forms of network topologies.
13. Discuss routing and flow-control functions.
14. Appreciate the evolution and current status of wired LANs.
15. Grasp how digital data transmission over telephone networks operates.
16. Explain how digital data transmission over cable networks works.

CONTENTS

17. List the network security requirements.
18. Differentiate between private-key cryptography and public-key cryptography.
19. Understand the need for digital signatures and how they work.
20. Connect various aspects of multiuser communications.

11.1 MULTIPLEXING

Multiplexing is a technique in the physical layer, whereby the simultaneous transmission of several independent signals from different sources is carried out. With multiplexing, there generally exists a priori resource allocation, and the resource sharing is usually done within the confines of a local site, but over a single common communication channel. Multiplexing is done when the bandwidth of the channel is higher than those of individual sources. At the transmitter, signals are combined (multiplexed) together, while keeping them apart enough to avoid interference, so at the receiver, they can be separated (demultiplexed). Multiplexing is thus done by a multiplexer in the transmitter and a demultiplexer in the receiver. There are three common types of multiplexing, namely, frequency-division multiplexing, time-division multiplexing, and wavelength-division multiplexing.

11.1.1 Frequency-Division Multiplexing

Frequency-division multiplexing (FDM) is a multiplexing technique that combines many signals into a single, high-bandwidth signal. In FDM, the bandwidth of a link is greater than the combined bandwidths of the signals to be transmitted, and the available transmission channel bandwidth is thus divided into a number of nonoverlapping frequency bands. In FDM, signals from all sources are transmitted simultaneously, but each occupying a different frequency band. FDM has generally been viewed as an analog multiplexing technique. FM stereo broadcasting represents a typical application of FDM. However, in principle, a digital system can employ FDM as well, such as cable telephony, data upstream and downstream, and TV channels over co-axial cable, and DSL telephony and data upstream and downstream over twisted-wire pair. A block diagram of a typical FDM system is shown in Figure 11.1a.

In FDM, the incoming lowpass signals all filtered to make them frequency limited. The removed high-frequency components do not significantly contribute to signal representation, but they are capable of interfering with other signals. The band-limited signals individually modulate carriers to shift their frequency ranges to occupy mutually exclusive frequency bands and guard bands separate

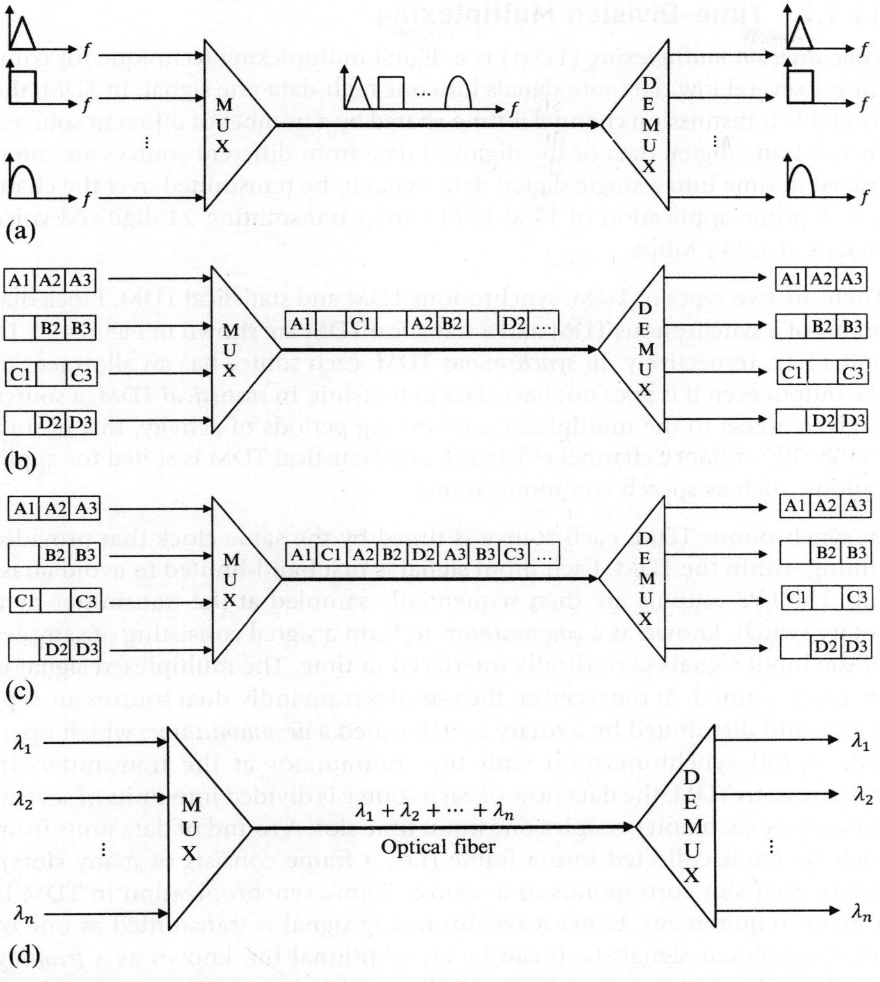

FIGURE 11.1 Multiplexing: (a) frequency-division multiplexing, (b) synchronous time-division multiplexing, (c) asynchronous time-division multiplexing, and d) wavelength-division multiplexing.

adjacent channels. The larger the guard band, the easier it is to design the filters to separate the signals, but the price being paid is the reduction in the number of channels. The SSB modulation is a good choice for FDM. The modulated signals are bandpass filtered to restrict the modulated signals to prescribed range. The resulting signals are combined to produce a composite multiplexed signal to be transmitted over the channel. At the receiver, a bank of bandpass filters separates the individual modulated signals. Individual demodulators recover the original baseband signals.

11.1.2 Time-Division Multiplexing

Time-division multiplexing (TDM) is a digital multiplexing technique for combining several low-data-rate signals into one high-data-rate signal. In TDM, the available transmission channel is time-shared by a number of different sources. In TDM, the digital data or the digitized data from different sources are interleaved in time into a single digital data signal to be transmitted over the channel. A prime application of TDM is T1 carrier transmitting 24 digitized voice signals at 1.544 Mbps.

There are two types of TDM: synchronous TDM and statistical TDM. Block diagrams of a synchronous TDM and a statistical TDM are shown in Figures 11.1b and 11.1c, respectively. In ***synchronous TDM***, each source has an allotment in the output even if it does not have data to transmit. In ***statistical TDM***, a source is given access to the multiplexer only during periods of activity, this in turn can greatly enhance channel efficiency, and statistical TDM is suited for applications, such as speech communications.

In synchronous TDM, each source is timed by the same clock that provides timing within the TDM. Each input signal is first band-limited to avoid aliasing. The LPF outputs are then sequentially sampled at the transmitter by a rotary switch, known as a ***commutator***, to form a signal consisting of samples of the input signals periodically interlaced in time. The multiplexed signal is then transmitted. At the receiver, the samples from individual sources are separated and distributed by a rotary switch called a ***decommutator***, which operates in full synchronization with the commutator at the transmitter. In synchronous TDM, the data flow of each source is divided into units of several bits, where each unit occupies one input time slot. A round of data units from each source is collected into a frame (i.e., a frame consists of many slots), where each slot corresponds to a source. Frame synchronization in TDM is a major requirement. Either a synchronizing signal is transmitted as one of the multiplexed signals or it can be an additional bit, known as a ***framing bit***, through which synchronization is done. In the case of T1 carrier, we have a frame consisting of a framing bit and 192 information bits ($=24$ slots $\times$ 8 bits per slot) and a transmission rate of 1.544 Mbps ($=193$ bits per frame $\times$ 8000 frames per second).

11.1.3 Wavelength-Division Multiplexing

Wavelength-division multiplexing (WDM) is a multiplexing technique to combine optical signals. In WDM, the available fiber-optic transmission channel is shared by a number of different light sources. WDM is conceptually quite similar to FDM. The advantage of WDM is to exploit the full capacity of the fiber-optic cable by allowing multiple beams of light at different frequencies to be transmitted on the same fiber-optic cable. A prime application of WDM is the SONET (Synchronous Optical Network) standard developed in North America. A block diagram of a synchronous WDM system is shown in Figure 11.1d.

Optical signals at different optical wavelengths (colors) are combined by the multiplexer at the transmitter to form a single light to be transmitted through the high-speed fiber-optic cable, and the splitting of the light sources is done by demultiplexer at the receiver. The combining and splitting of light sources are done by various optical devices, such as prism and diffraction gratings. The channel spacing in WDM systems must be large enough to prevent interference between adjacent channels. Most WDM systems use 50-GHz channel spacing, such as ITU-G.692 that accommodates 80 channels over 4 THz.

11.2 DUPLEXING

Before we introduce the duplexing methods, it is important to highlight various communication modes. Communication modes can be categories into three distinct types: simplex, half-duplex, and full-duplex (also known as duplex), as shown in Figure 11.2.

In *simplex mode*, transmission is unidirectional (i.e., transmission always occurs only in one direction). The simplex mode uses the entire capacity of the channel to send data in one direction. Examples of simplex communication are baby monitoring, public address, and commercial broadcasting.

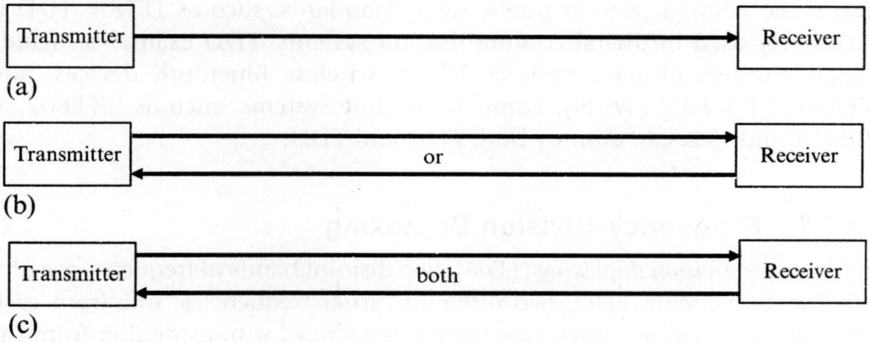

FIGURE 11.2 Communication modes: (a) simplex communication, (b) half-duplex communication, and (c) full-duplex communication.

In ***half-duplex mode***, transmission is bi-directional, but only in one direction at a time. The end devices can both transmit and receive, but not at the same time. In half-duplex mode, the entire capacity of the channel is taken over by whichever of the two devices is transmitting at the time. Examples of half-duplex communication are walkie-talkies and CB radios as well as dial-up fax machines.

In ***full-duplex mode***, transmission is simultaneously bi-directional. The end devices can transmit and receive simultaneously. A prime example of full-duplex communications is the PSTN that provides two-way communications. ITU-T voice-band dial-up data modems can also provide full-duplex communications in one of the following three ways:

- Using four telephone wires, with a pair for each direction, such as V.26 modem.
- Dividing up the bandpass spectrum of a telephone channel into two disjoint frequency bands, with an exclusive band for each direction, such as V.22 bis modem.
- Employing echo cancellation (i.e., subtraction of the echo of its own transmission from the incoming signal to recover the signal sent by the other side), while allocating the entire spectrum to both ends, such as V.32 modem.

The means to provide two independent channels for two-way communications is called ***duplexing***. A duplexing scheme is a crucial element of a wireless communication system, and thus needs to be carefully defined from outset in a system design. There are two distinct methods to achieve duplexing: frequency-division duplexing (FDD) and time-division duplexing (TDD), where each has its own merits. FDD is a legacy method, and has been used in both analog and digital communication systems. FDD examples include all communication satellite systems, many cellular mobile systems, such as AMPS and GSM, as well as public safety standards, such as TETRA. TDD is exclusively used in digital communication systems. TDD examples include digital cordless phones, such as DECT, wireless Bluetooth devices, and IEEE802.11 WLAN (Wi-Fi). Some 4G mobile systems, such as IEEE802.16 WiMAX and LTE, can employ both FDD and TDD.

11.2.1 Frequency-Division Duplexing

In ***frequency-division duplexing*** (FDD), two disjoint bands of frequency are provided to users. With FDD, two different carrier frequencies, one from each band, are assigned to a user; one carrier frequency for transmission from the user (also known as upstream, return link, or uplink) and one carrier frequency for reception by the user (also known as downstream, forward link, or downlink), as shown in Figure 11.3a. A guard band is required between the two

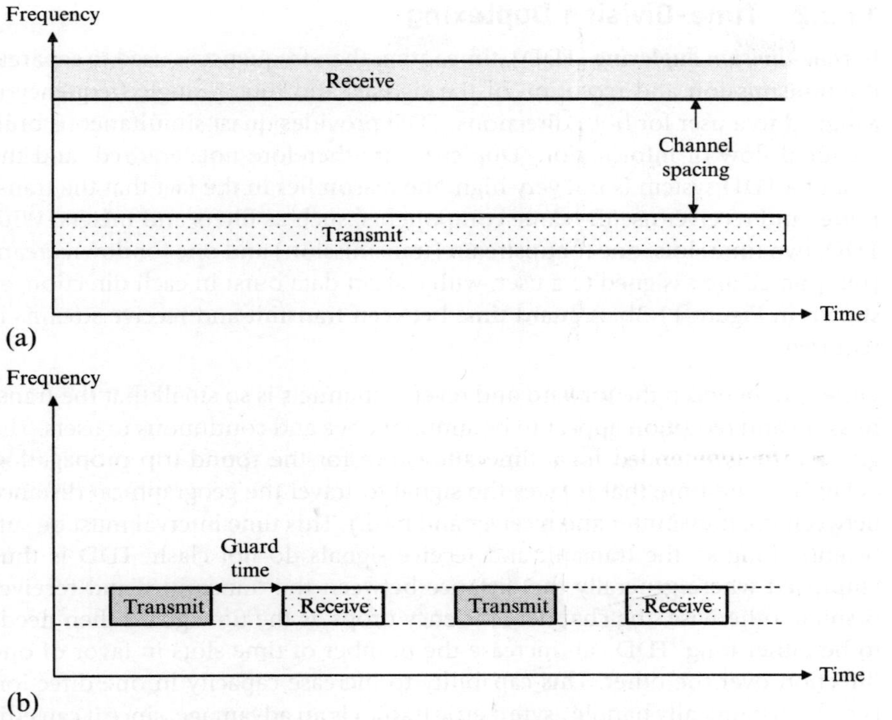

FIGURE 11.3 Duplexing: (a) frequency-division duplexing and (b) time-division duplexing.

bands. The difference between the two assigned frequencies, also known as the ***frequency split***, remains constant, and must be large enough to allow the use of low-cost techniques to separate the two signals; otherwise, the transmit and receive signals may be adversely affected by one another.

Since the same antenna is generally employed for both transmission and reception, a ***duplexer*** is needed to separate the transmitted and received signals. This additional hardware complexity in the handheld transceivers can be a cost-driving factor. The frequency plan for FDD, as set by a regulatory body or limited by the functionality of the available equipment, warrants fixed equal bandwidths, simply because it is not normally possible to reallocate spectrum from one direction to another. This thus makes it ideal for symmetric communications, such as voice applications, with almost identical information flows in both directions. Although FDD provides true simultaneous transmission and reception, it is not always spectrally efficient, since the traffic may be asymmetric.

11.2.2 Time-Division Duplexing

In *time-division duplexing* (TDD), time rather than frequency is used to separate the transmission and reception of the signals, and thus a single frequency is assigned to a user for both directions. TDD provides quasi-simultaneous bidirectional flow of information. Duplexers are therefore not required, and the cost of a TDD system is not very high, the reason lies in the fact that the transmitter and receiver use the same components, such as filters and mixers. With TDD, two time slots, one for upstream (transmission) and one for downstream (reception), are assigned to a user, with a short data burst in each direction, as shown in Figure 11.3b. A guard time between transmit and receive streams is required.

Time split between the forward and reverse channels is so small that the transmission and reception appear to be simultaneous and continuous to users. The guard time is intended for a time allowance for the round-trip propagation delay (i.e., the time that it takes the signal to travel the geographical distance between the transmitter and receiver and back). This time interval must be sufficiently long so the transmit and receive signals do not clash. TDD is thus employed where generally the distance between the transmitter and receiver is small; otherwise, the channel efficiency drops as the time guard then needs to be rather long. TDD can increase the number of time slots in favor of one direction over the other. This capability to increase capacity in one direction (i.e., to dynamically handle asymmetric traffic) is an advantage, since it can efficiently accommodate the Internet applications.

11.3 MULTIPLE ACCESS

Multiple access, also known as *channelization*, allows remote sharing of a common transmission medium by many users, in which the medium is partitioned into separate communication channels and then dedicated to particular users upon their requests. Multiple access techniques can be classified into three broad categories: frequency-division multiple access (FDMA), time-division multiple access (TDMA), and code-division multiple access (CDMA). These major access techniques are used to share the available bandwidth in a wireless communication system. In general, channelization techniques are not suitable for the transmission of bursty data traffic, and instead lend themselves to continuous, steady traffic data flow. Since a fixed assignment strategy would be wasteful of resources and degradation to capacity, access channels are not assigned on a permanent basis. Initial channel assignment is generally done by a random-access channel. FDMA, TDMA, and CDMA are access methods in the data-link layer.

11.3.1 Frequency-Division Multiple Access

Frequency-division multiple access is the oldest of all multiple access schemes, and was used in the first demand assignment system for satellites (i.e., single channel per carrier (SCPC)) and the first-generation of cellular mobile systems (i.e., the advanced mobile phone system (AMPS)). In ***frequency-division multiple access*** (FDMA), the available channel bandwidth is divided into many nonoverlapping frequency bands, where each band is dynamically assigned to a specific user to transmit data. In an FDMA system, signals, while occupying their assigned frequency bands, can be transmitted simultaneously and continuously without interfering with eachother. In FDMA, there is a central controller that allocates the frequency band to users, solely based on their needs. This is usually done during the call set up. Once a band is allocated to a user, it then belongs to the user exclusively for the continuous flow of information during the call. To prevent interference, the allocated bands are separated from one another by small guard bands. In other words, FDMA allows the users to transmit simultaneously, but over disjoint frequency bands, a user exploits a fixed portion of the band all the time, as shown in Figure 11.4a. FDMA is best suited for connection-oriented applications; it is, however, inefficient in terms of utilization of power and bandwidth. If an FDMA channel is not in use by the user, then it sits idle and cannot be used by other users. It has poor spectral efficiency, since guard bands must be employed to avoid overlapping of the adjacent channels, and this in turn reduces the channel capacity.

Bandpass filters are used to confine the transmitted energy within the assigned band and tight RF filtering is required to minimize adjacent channel interference. Duplexers must be employed since both the transmitter and receiver operate at the same time. FDMA is a low-cost technology to implement, and has low transmission overhead. Synchronization in FDMA is simple, once it is established during the call set up, it can be easily maintained, as transmission occurs continuously. At the hub or base station, due to the significant susceptibility to nonlinear effects of power amplifiers, such as signal spreading and intermodulation, either each FDMA channel must employ its own amplifier or a highly-linear amplifier with a significant back-off power is required for the transmission of the composite signal. FDMA is generally used in combination with other multiple access schemes, where the spectrum is divided into large sub-bands. Each sub-band serves a large group of users, where within a group, another multiple access method can be employed. Examples include employing FDMA/TDMA in the GSM cellular mobile systems or in satellite systems offering VSAT applications.

11.3.2 Time-Division Multiple Access

Time-division multiple access is a multiple access scheme, which is widely used in VSAT and broadband satellite systems and the GSM cellular mobile systems.

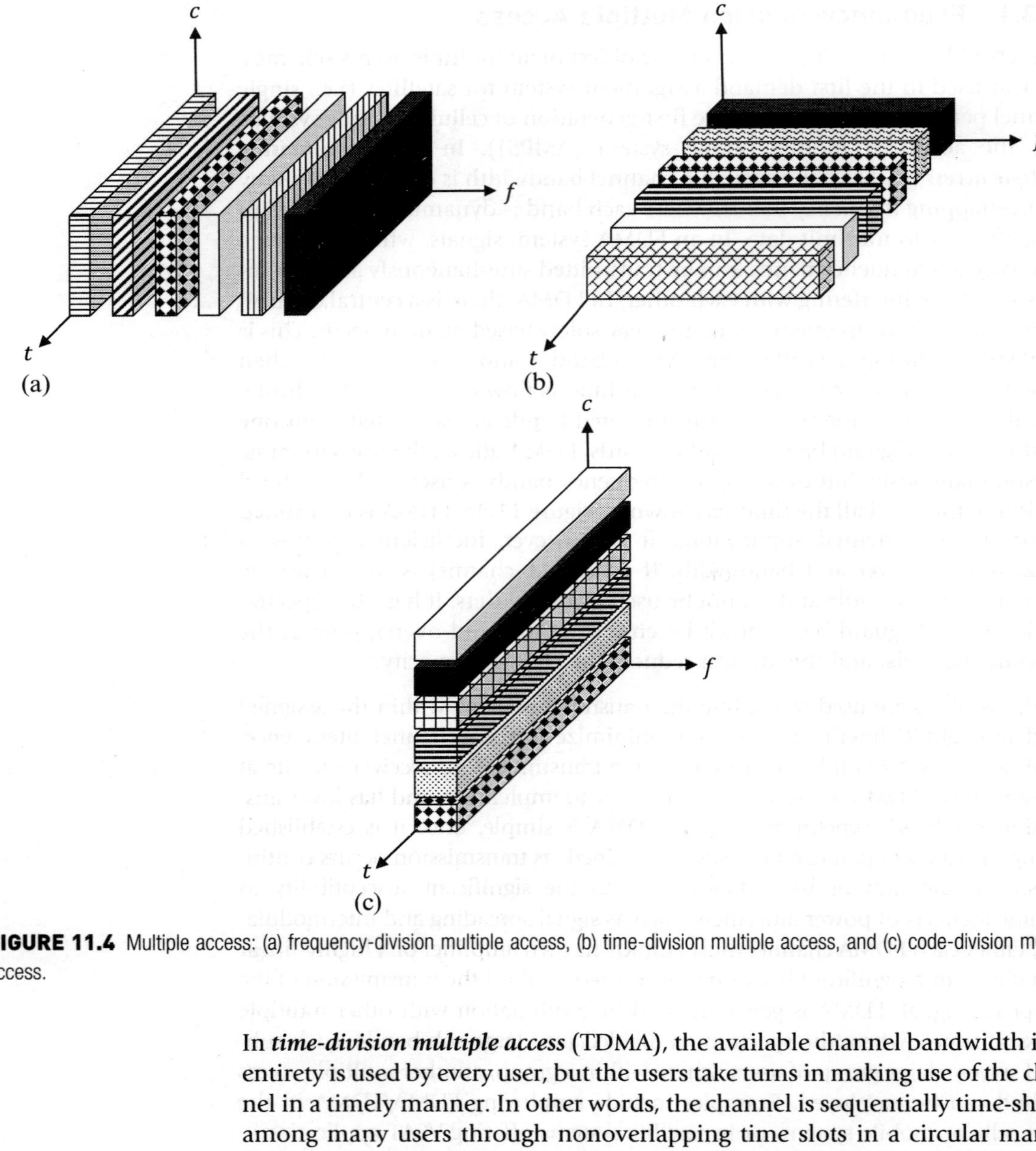

FIGURE 11.4 Multiple access: (a) frequency-division multiple access, (b) time-division multiple access, and (c) code-division multiple access.

In ***time-division multiple access*** (TDMA), the available channel bandwidth in its entirety is used by every user, but the users take turns in making use of the channel in a timely manner. In other words, the channel is sequentially time-shared among many users through nonoverlapping time slots in a circular manner (i.e., one after the other). A user is allowed to transmit in a buffer-and-burst mode only in its allocated time slot. The transmission for any user is thus noncontinuous, and that in turn requires transmission to be in digital form. The noncontinuous transmission also results in low battery consumption, since the transmitter can be turned off when not in use, which is most of the time. All users employ the same frequency band to transmit their signals, as shown in Figure 11.4b. In TDMA/FDD systems, the frame structure for forward transmission is the same as that for reverse transmission. However, in TDMA/FDD systems, such as GSM, for a given user, there are several time slots of delay between the forward and reverse time slots, a duplexer is thus not needed in a transceiver.

Synchronization in TDMA is a critical requirement. To accomplish synchronization for geographically-dispersed users with different propagation delays, guard times are required to ensure transmissions do not overlap. Another source of overhead is a preamble consisting of pre-determined bits to allow the receiver to synchronize to the transmitted bit stream. In TDMA, a central controller sends a certain bit stream to all users with which all transmitters synchronize their clocks. Because of the higher data rate and subsequently the shorter symbol duration, adaptive equalization is usually required. In TDMA, it is possible to allocate different numbers of time slots per frame to different users for their different traffic patterns (i.e., the bandwidth-on-demand feature can be accommodated). In a mobile environment, TDMA yields a lower level of co-channel interference, as only a small percentage of users are transmitting, and the hand-off process is more efficient, since the transmission is not continuous. Since the burst transmission rate is quite high, a frequency band with a large bandwidth is required. In general, the spectrum is divided into many disjoint bands (i.e., FDMA) and then in a given band, TDMA is employed. A prime example of FDMA/TDMA is the GSM cellular mobile system, in which a frequency band of 200 kHz is allocated to eight TDMA users, where the burst rate is about 271 kbps.

11.3.3 Code-Division Multiple Access

Spread spectrum is a multiple access through which a transmission bandwidth several orders of magnitude greater than the minimum required RF bandwidth is used. This is achieved by using a pseudorandom noise-like spreading code in the transmitter to spread the bandwidth (i.e., to make it into a wideband signal), and employing the same code in the receiver to despread the received signal so as to recover the original message signal. Spread spectrum is not very efficient when used by a single user, but when there are many users sharing the same bandwidth without interfering with one another, spread spectrum systems become bandwidth efficient. Spread spectrum provides a high degree of immunity to multipath interference. Two forms of spread spectrum are used: ***frequency-hopping spread spectrum*** (FHSS) and ***direct-sequence spread spectrum*** (DSSS), also known as ***code-division multiple access*** (CDMA). In FHSS, the spectrum is widened by changing the carrier frequency in a pseudorandom manner. FHSS is used in Bluetooth wireless devices. Frequency hopping does not cover the entire spread spectrum at any time, as such we can select the rates at which hopping can occur. In the ***slow-frequency hopping***, the symbol rate is an integer multiple of the hop rate, whereas in the ***fast-frequency hopping***, the hop rate is an integer multiple of the symbol rate. An FHSS system provides a level of security.

In DDSS, the baseband modulated signal is created by multiplying the modulating signal, which consists of information bits, by a pseudorandom sequence, whose bandwidth is much larger than that of the signal itself, thereby spreading the bandwidth. In CDMA, all users employ the same frequency band to simultaneously transmit (i.e., there is no clear separation in time or frequency). In CDMA, each user is assigned a unique randomized code sequence, which is different from and orthogonal to (i.e., uncorrelated with) all other codes. A code is used to generate the randomized noise-like high-bit-rate signal that is mixed with the information signal to spread the spectrum and the receiver uses the code to recover the desired signal. As shown in Figure 11.4c, users transmit over the entire frequency band at the same time, while using their own distinct codes. Because of bandwidth re-use, CDMA is bandwidth efficient, and delivers gradual degradation in performance as the number of users is increased. In a CDMA system, there is a ***near-far problem*** that occurs when the received power levels from different users do not appear to be equal. It is thus a critical requirement to provide a precise automatic power control mechanism. Power control is implemented by rapidly sampling the radio signal strength indicator levels and then sending a power change command over the forward link. As channel data rates are very high, the symbol (chip) duration is very short and much less than the channel delay spread. The reception can be improved by collecting the time-delayed versions of the signal. CDMA is employed in cellular mobile systems, such as CDMA-2000.

11.4 RANDOM ACCESS

Random access involves dynamic sharing of the transmission medium among many users so as to better match bursty data traffic. Transmission is random among users and since there is no scheduled time, access to the medium is based on contention. Users access the channel when they have one packet or more to transmit. Simultaneous transmissions from multiple users result in collision. The resulting conflict must thus be resolved by some channel protocol for retransmission of the packets. The random-access schemes are simple to implement and under light traffic can provide low-delay packet transfer. Under heavy traffic, the throughput and packet delays both can suffer.

11.4.1 ALOHA

The unslotted ALOHA protocol, also called pure ALOHA or original ALOHA, is a simple random-access scheme, which was designed for a radio (wireless) LAN in the early seventies. In *unslotted ALOHA* scheme, whenever a user has a packet, it is transmitted. However, because there is only one communication channel, there is the possibility of collision among packets from different users. When the data from two or more users collide, they become garbled and are lost to the system. The unslotted ALOHA scheme relies on acknowledgments, if the acknowledgement does not arrive after a time-out period, the user then assumes that the packet or the acknowledgement has been destroyed and retransmits the packet. When the time-out period passes, each transmitter waits a random amount of time before resending its packet. In other words, the unslotted ALOHA scheme requires the transmitter to use a ***back-off algorithm***, which chooses a random number in a certain retransmission time interval. The randomness can help spread out the transmissions and thus reduce the likelihood of additional collision among transmitters. In principle, when traffic is very light, the probability of collision is very small and retransmissions are thus hardly required.

In an unslotted ALOHA, there are two distinct modes. In one mode, collision occurs occasionally, this occurs when the traffic load is light. In the other mode, when the traffic is heavy, there is a surge of collisions and this in turn results in a snowball effect (i.e., the increased number of backlogged transmitters increases the likelihood of additional collisions). As shown in Figure 11.5a, the vulnerable

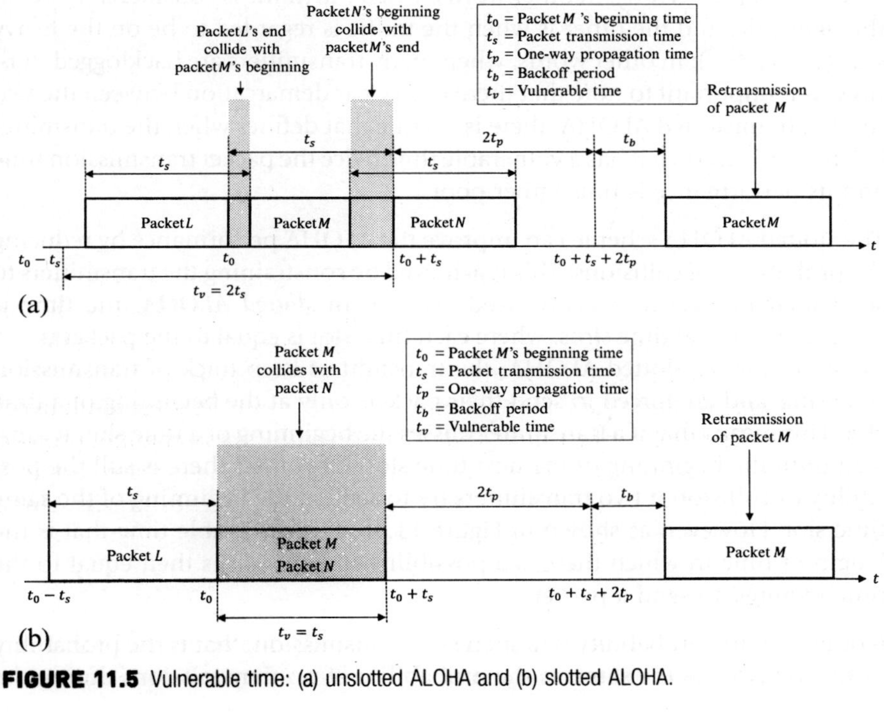

FIGURE 11.5 Vulnerable time: (a) unslotted ALOHA and (b) slotted ALOHA.

time that is the length of time in which there is a possibility of collision is twice as long as the time required for the transmission of a packet. In other words, for a transmitter to send its packet collision free, no other transmitter should transmit less than half of the vulnerable time before this transmitter starts transmission and no transmitter should start sending during half of the vulnerable time after this transmitter has sent its packet.

Noting that the probability of a successful transmission (i.e., the probability of no collision) is the same as the probability of no transmissions during the vulnerable time, the ***throughput*** S (i.e., the average number of successfully transmitted packets) is as follows:

$$S = Ge^{-2G} \tag{11.1}$$

where G is the average number of packets generated during one packet transmission time. The maximum value of the throughput S is $\frac{1}{2e} \cong 18.4\%$ that occurs at $G = 0.5$ and corresponds to a total arrival rate of exactly one packet per vulnerable period. This is a reflection of the fact that two or more arrivals in a vulnerable period result in a collision.

For a given value of the throughput S, there are two different values of the load G corresponding to the two possible modes. One mode is when the arrival rate G is modest (i.e., $G \approx S$); in other words, when the traffic is considered to be on the light side, and the other is when the traffic is regarded to be on the heavy side (i.e., $G \gg S$); in other words, when many transmitters are backlogged. It is, however, important to note that there is no clear demarcation between the two modes. In unslotted ALOHA, there is no rule that defines when the transmitter can transmit, as such it has a vulnerable time twice the packet transmission time and its performance is thus rather poor.

The slotted ALOHA scheme can improve the ALOHA performance by reducing the probability of collisions. This is achieved by constraining the transmitters to send their packets in synchronized fashion. In ***slotted ALOHA***, the time is divided into equal time slots, where each time slot is equal to the packet transmission time. In slotted ALOHA, the transmitters keep track of transmission time slots and are forced to send their packets only at the beginning of a time slot. This means that if a transmitter misses the beginning of a time slot, it must wait until the beginning of the next time slot. Of course, there is still the possibility of collision if two transmitters try to send at the beginning of the same time slot. However, as shown in Figure 11.5b, the vulnerable time that is the length of time in which there is a possibility of collision is then equal to the time required to send a packet.

Noting that the probability of a successful transmission, that is the probability of no collision, is the same as the probability of no transmissions during the vulnerable time, the throughput S (i.e., the average number of successfully transmitted packets) is as follows:

$$S = Ge^{-G} \tag{11.2}$$

where G is the average number of packets generated during one packet transmission time. The slotted ALOHA scheme, similar to the unslotted ALOHA scheme, may display a bimodal behavior. The maximum value of the throughput S is $\frac{1}{e} \cong 36.8\%$ that occurs at $G = 1$ and corresponds to a total arrival rate of exactly one packet per vulnerable period. This is a reflection of the fact that two or more arrivals in a vulnerable period result in a collision and if one packet is generated during one packet transmission time, then 36.8% of these packets reach their destination successfully.

11.4.2 CSMA

An ALOHA scheme with an essentially uncoordinated access to transmission medium has a low maximum throughput, which is primarily due to packet collisions. In ***carrier sense multiple access*** (CSMA), the chance of collision is minimized by sensing the medium for the presence of a carrier signal from other transmitters. CSMA is based on the principle of sense before transmit, that is, each transmitter in the network must first check the state of the medium (i.e., determine whether there is an ongoing transmission) before sending a packet. However, because of the propagation delay (i.e., the time needed for a signal to go from one end of the medium to the other), it is still possible for a collision to occur. When a transmitter sends a packet, it takes time to reach every other transmitter and for every transmitter to sense it. A transmitter may sense the medium and find it idle, only because the packet sent by another transmitter has not yet been received. Thus, the vulnerable period consists of one propagation delay, and if no other transmitter sends a packet during this period, the transmitter will in effect have the channel for its transmission simply because no other transmitter will transmit thereafter.

As shown in Figure 11.6, when a transmitter finds the channel busy in CSMA, there are three different methods that it can employ to portray its behavior: 1-persisitent method, nonpersistent method, and p-persistent method. All three approaches are sensitive to the end-to-end propagation delay of the medium.

In ***1-persistent CSMA***, if the channel is busy, the transmitter with a packet to send continuously senses the channel until the channel becomes idle. As soon as the channel is sensed idle, the transmitter sends its packet (with probability 1). This method has the highest chance of collision, for two or more transmitters with ready packets may find the channel idle and send their packets immediately. Transmitters that are involved in a collision perform the back-off algorithm to

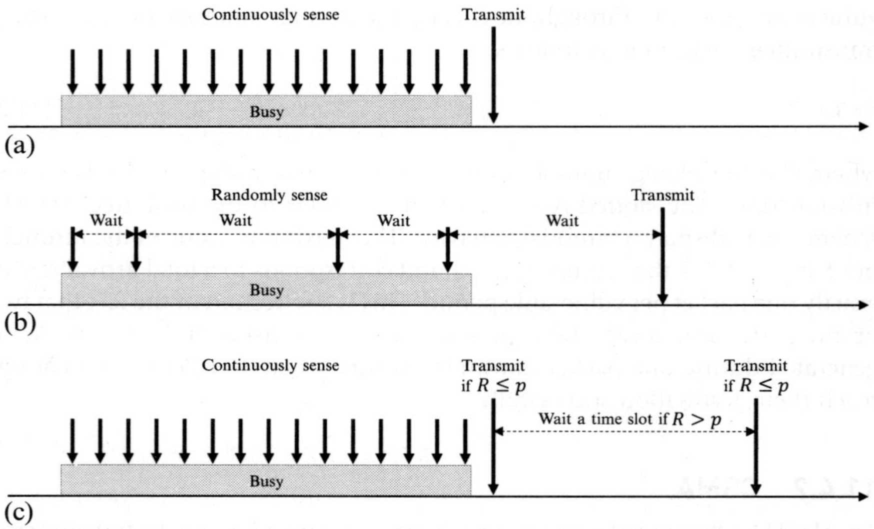

FIGURE 11.6 Behavior of persistence methods: (a) 1-persistent, (b) nonpersistent, and (c) p-persistent.

schedule a future time to resense the channel. Since the transmitters behave in a greedy fashion, 1-persistent CSMA has a relatively high collision rate.

In ***nonpersistent CSMA***, if the channel is busy, the transmitter with a packet to send immediately runs the back-off algorithm, and reschedules a future resensing time. By immediately rescheduling a resensing time and not persisting, the chance of collision is reduced relative to 1-persistent CSMA. This is due to the fact that it is unlikely that two or more transmitters will wait the same amount of time and retry to send immediately. This method, vis-à-vis 1-persientent CSMA, yields a longer delay and lower network efficiency. The reason lies in the fact that the channel may remain idle when there may be transmitters with packets to send.

Suppose the channel has time slots with a slot duration equal to the round-trip propagation time. In ***p-persistent CSMA***, a transmitter with a packet to send senses the channel, if the channel is busy, it persists with sensing until the channel becomes idle, if the channel is idle, with probability p, the transmitter sends its packet, and with probability of $1 - p$, it decides to wait for the beginning of the next time slot and senses the channel again. If the channel is then idle, with probability p, it transmits, and if the channel is busy, the transmitter waits for a random period of time (i.e., a back-off period) as if a collision has occurred. This approach combines the advantages of the other two methods. This method spreads out the transmission attempts by the transmitters that have been waiting for transmission to be completed and hence to increase the likelihood that a transmitter with a packet successfully seizes the channel.

In CSMA, if two transmitters with packets to send begin sending at the same time, each will transmit its complete packet, even though they collide. In the ***carrier sense multiple access with collision detection*** (CSMA/CD) scheme, the amount of wasted bandwidth can be reduced by terminating its transmission as soon as a collision is detected and the transmitter then attempts to transmit later after waiting for a random amount of time. CSMA/CD, which is commonly used in wired LANs, such as Ethernet, yields a throughput that is greater than those of the ALOHA schemes.

In a wireless environment, either transmission or sensing is done, that is both simultaneous transmission and sensing is not possible and the collision detection time is twice the end-to-end propagation delay. CSMA/CD cannot be used in a wireless environment of a shared channel. In wireless networks, the collision detection of CSMA/CD is unreliable due to the ***hidden-node problem,*** i.e., when a node is visible from a wireless access point, but not from other nodes communicating with that access point. In ***carrier-sense multiple access collision avoidance*** (CSMA/CA), before a transmitter sends its packet, it has to broadcast a signal onto the network in order to listen for collision scenarios and to tell other devices not to broadcast. Collisions are avoided by forcing transmitters to send reservation messages when they find the channel is idle. When a packet is transmitted, it is then done in its entirety.

11.5 CONTROLLED ACCESS

To achieve high throughputs in medium access control, some form of coordination is required. In ***controlled access***, sharing a transmission medium is based on scheduling, i.e., a transmitter cannot send unless it has been authorized to do so. The systems employing controlled-access schemes are sensitive to the reaction time in the form of propagation delay and network latency.

11.5.1 Reservation

In a ***reservation*** system, a transmitter needs to make a reservation before sending data. Time is divided into cycles that can be variable in length. Each cycle consists first of a reservation interval and then an interval during which the transmitters with reservations send data. The number of mini-slots in a reservation interval corresponds to the number of transmitters in the system. Transmitters use their corresponding mini-slots in the reservation interval to broadcast that they have a packet to transmit in a corresponding cycle. By listening to the reservation interval, the transmitters can determine the order of transmissions in the corresponding cycle.

If the number of transmitters in a network is very large, then the overhead associated with the reservation interval becomes significant. To alleviate this problem, a mini-slot is not allocated to each transmitter. Instead, transmitters contend for a reservation mini-slot by using a random-access technique, such as slotted ALOHA. In fact, this is the way packet service is provided over GSM cellular telephone networks.

11.5.2 Polling

In ***polling***, transmitters take turns accessing the medium. At any given time, only one transmitter can send data, after it is done, the right to transmit is passed to another transmitter. There are various methods for passing the right to transmit from one transmitter to another. In one method, a central controller periodically polls the transmitters to determine their service request. The central controller polls the transmitters sequentially in a circular fashion or another polling order. Polling can also be implemented in a distributed fashion on networks with a ring topology, which is known as token passing method. A token goes around the ring; once a transmitter has it, then the transmitter has the right to access channel and send its packet data. In a way, receiving a token corresponds to receiving a polling message. When the transmitter has no more data to send, it releases the token, thus passing it to the next transmitter in the ring.

If the numbers of transmitters is very large and the traffic is bursty, the time required to poll all transmitters in the network can be an excessive overhead burden. One efficient way for rapidly polling a large number of transmitters with light traffic is called ***probing*** or ***tree search***. In that, rather than polling individual transmitters, groups of transmitters are polled. A group polling message is broadcast to all transmitters in a group, all transmitters in the group that have packets to send then respond, if multiple transmitters respond, a collision will occur. Subsequently, that group is sub-divided into two sub-groups, the process of probing will then proceed, until the transmitter with a packet is isolated, and then it transmits its packet.

11.6 WIRED COMMUNICATION NETWORKS

A ***network*** is a set of devices connected by a number of communication links to provide information transfer among users located at different places. In assessing data-communication networks, there are a number of measures to consider. Performance is an important measure that can be evaluated by several networking metrics, including:

- ***Throughput***: The actual rate at which information, in the form of bits and packets, is successfully transmitted over the network.

- *Delay*: It consists of processing, buffer, transmission, and propagation delays associated with transfer of data packets.
- *Jitter*: It represents the delay variation experienced by received data packets.
- *Accuracy*: It is primarily measured by bit error rates and packet-loss rates.

There are of course other measures of high importance, such as network reliability, availability, and security, to name just few.

11.6.1 Circuit-Switched and Packet-Switched Networks

A ***switched network*** consists of a series of interlinked nodes by which temporary connections among nodes, including the intermediate switches and the end devices, can be made. There are two distinct methods of switching. One is circuit switching that occurs at the physical layer. The other one is packet switching, which in turn is divided into two sub-categories. One is the virtual-circuit packet switching that is normally done at the data link layer, and the other one is the datagram packet switching that normally occurs at the network layer. It is not necessary for the layers to operate in the same switching method.

A ***circuit-switched network*** is made of a set of switches connected by physical links, in which each link is divided into multiple channels. Communication via circuit switching involves three phases: setup phase, data transfer phase, and teardown phase. In circuit switching, the resources need to be reserved during the setup phase, and the resources remain dedicated, without interruption, for the entire duration of data transfer until the teardown phase.

Since the link is exclusively dedicated to the communicating pair, even during intervals when the communication path happens to be idle, circuit switching is not efficient. Despite its low efficiency, a circuit-switched network has minimal delay, as during data transfer the data are not delayed at each switch. Also, in a circuit-switched network, data rate is guaranteed. The PSTN is a prominent application of circuit switching, as it can provide interconnection for voice signal exchange between telephones, data transfer between dial-up modems, and image transfer between fax machines.

In a ***packet-switched network***, there is no resource reservation and resources are allocated on demand. The allocation is done on a first-come, first-served basis. Packet switching is a method of transmitting data in which long messages are sub-divided into packets. The size of the packet is determined by the network and the governing protocol. Each packet is passed from source to destination through intermediate nodes. When a switch receives a packet, the packet must wait (i.e., be stored) if there are other packets being processed. There are two categories of packet-switching; one is ***datagram***, also known as ***connectionless packet switching***, and the other is the ***virtual-circuit packet switching***, also known as ***connection-oriented packet switching***.

In a ***datagram network***, each packet, referred to as a datagram, is routed independently of all others. It is normally done at the network layer. In a datagram network, the destination address in the header of a packet remains the same during the entire transmission of the packet, and a switch uses a routing table that is based on the destination address to route each packet. Although call setup time is avoided, which is an advantage for short messages, each packet may experience a wait at a switch before it is forwarded. Since not all packets in a message necessarily travel through the same switches (i.e., the same path) the delay is not uniform for the packets of a message. The packets may arrive out of order and resequencing may be required at the destination. By sharing the transmission line among multiple packets, a high utilization, at the expense of queuing delays, can be achieved. The Internet Protocol (IP) and the User Datagram Protocol (UDP), which are the core members of the Internet protocol suite, both employ connectionless packet switching.

A ***virtual-circuit packet-switched network*** is a cross between a circuit-switched network and a datagram network. On the one hand, as in a circuit-switched network, there are call setup and teardown phases in addition to the data transfer phase, and on the other hand, as in a datagram network, data are packetized. However, the address in a header defines what the next switch should be and not the final destination. In a virtual-circuit packet switched network, all packets follow the same path established during the connection, and arrive in sequence. Due to not requiring routing decisions for each packet, packet transmission and delivery may take less time. For sustained packet flows, such as long file transfers, the Internet downloads, audio and video streaming, virtual-circuit packet switching is appropriate. Transmission Control Protocol (TCP), used in the Internet protocol suite, provides reliable connection-oriented packet switching.

11.6.2 Topology

In the context of communication networks, ***topology*** refers to the way in which a network is physically laid out, that is, how the end-point devices, also known as network nodes, attached to the network are inter-linked. Topologies can be broadly categorized as follows: star, mesh, bus, ring, and tree. As each of them possesses its own merits and drawbacks, a hybrid topology may be implemented in a communication network, such as star clusters used with both ring and bus topologies to create the star-ring and the star-bus hybrid topologies. The focus of topologies discussed here is on wired networks, as it is easy to implement any type of topology in a wireless network.

In a ***star topology***, network nodes are directly connected by point-to-point links to a central node, usually called a hub, as shown in Figure 11.7a. Typically, each node requires two links to connect to a central hub, one for transmission and

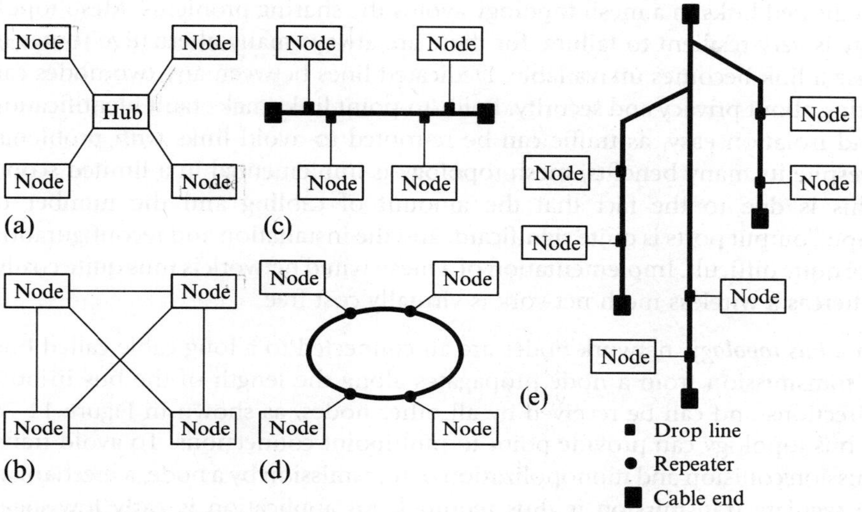

FIGURE 11.7 Topology: (a) star, (b) mesh, (c) bus, (d) ring, and (e) tree.

one for reception. In a star topology, there is no direct link between the nodes. In case of node-to-node communications requirement, a node must send the data to the hub, which then relays to another node, hence double-hub communications. Applications of the star topology may include the local loops in the PSTN, satellite VSAT networks, and 1-Gbps Ethernet LANs.

A star topology has the benefit of easy installation and reconfiguration of access nodes. This reduces the overall network costs and makes network management much easier. It also has the advantage of being robust, when one link fails, all other links remain active, which in turn brings about easy fault identification and isolation. In a star topology, a variety of network media can be used, making it easier to merge legacy and new networks. In a star topology, transmissions are virtually collision free. The huge drawback of star is its vulnerability to the hub failure that can cause a complete suspension of network operation. To enhance reliability, hub redundancy is an important consideration for this topology. Also, in a wired network environment, cable costs can be higher than they would be in some other topologies.

In a ***mesh topology***, network nodes are all connected by dedicated point-to-point links to one another. In a mesh network of n nodes, $n(n-1)/2$ two-way connections are required, as shown in Figure 11.7b. Each device must have $n-1$ input/output ports. Applications of the mesh topology may include the connection of regional offices in the PSTN, satellite telephone networks using SCPC to provide telephony in remote and isolated areas, and connecting main computers of a hybrid network consisting of other topologies.

Dedicated links in a mesh topology avoids the sharing problems. Mesh topology is very resilient to failure, for there are always many alternative routes in case a link becomes unavailable. Dedicated lines between any two nodes can bring about privacy and security. Point-to-point links make fault identification and isolation easy, as traffic can be re-routed to avoid links with problems. Despite its many benefits, mesh topology is implemented in a limited scope. This is due to the fact that the amount of cabling and the number of input/output ports is quite significant, and the installation and reconfiguration are quite difficult. Implementation of a mesh wired network is thus quite costly, whereas a wireless mesh network is virtually cost free.

In a ***bus topology***, network nodes are all connected to a long cable called bus. A transmission from a node propagates along the length of the bus in both directions and can be received by all other nodes, as shown in Figure 11.7c. A bus topology can provide point-to-multipoint connections. To avoid transmission collision and monopolization of transmission by a node, a mechanism to regulate transmission is thus required. An application is early low-speed Ethernet LANs.

As the signal travels along the backbone bus, it becomes weaker, and that can limit the number of nodes and appropriate hardware interfacing. In a bus topology, the problem of ringing (i.e., signal reflection from the cable ends) needs to be resolved, for they can cause degradation in signal quality. In a bus topology, installation is easy with modest cabling. Additional nodes, which can be easily added by more taps to the network backbone, can slow the network for all nodes. Moreover, a fault in the bus cable stops all transmission, and reconfiguration is difficult, simply because new nodes may require modification of the backbone bus. Privacy and security is poor, for the signal from a node is broadcast to all.

In a ***ring topology***, each node is allowed to have dedicated point-to-point connections with only two neighboring nodes in a closed loop, as shown in Figure 11.7d. The links are unidirectional (i.e., the data is passed along the ring in one direction, from one node to another, until it reaches its destination). When a node receives a signal from a neighboring node that is intended for another node, it regenerates the bits and passes them along the ring. The IBM Token Ring local area network employs ring topology.

In a ring topology, a single node cannot monopolize the network and its resources. Since in a ring topology, adding or removing a node requires changing only two connections, installation reconfiguration, and fault isolation are all easy. In fault isolation, an alarm is issued once a signal is not received by a node within a specified period. A break in the ring, such as a disabled node, can bring the network down. This is viewed as a significant drawback, and a dual ring may thus be used. Also, adding nodes to the ring can disrupt the entire ring.

Tree topology is a general form of bus topology. The tree layout begins at a point known as the head-end. Each cable starting at the head-end may have branches, and branches in turn may have branches, as shown in Figure 11.7e. The structure is hierarchical, and the nodes at higher levels are thus more important. Applications may include cable television network and some lightly-loaded LANs.

A tree topology is not robust to failure, because there is only one path between any pair of nodes. A transmission from a node is broadcast to all, i.e., it is received by all other nodes; it is therefore not very secure. To resolve this issue and also prevent a node to transmit continuously, nodes must transmit data in blocks, known as frames, where each frame has its own destination address and control information.

11.6.3 Routing and Flow Control

Routing is concerned with the paths travelled by packets through the network. The objective is to determine the best paths in a network for packets to follow from a source to a destination. ***Flow control*** is concerned with the timing and rate of packet transmissions, and its objective is to ensure that the source does not overwhelm the destination with packets. We briefly outline some aspects of routing and flow control from a high-level perspective, and the details of various algorithms implementing these two major network functions are beyond the scope of this chapter.

The criteria to find the best path connecting a source and a destination may include the minimum number of links (hops), the minimum overall end-to-end delay, the highest user or network throughput, the lowest overall cost, the highest overall reliability, the lowest packet loss rate, the minimum buffer requirements, the maximum number of users that can be supported, and network fairness (i.e., users are receiving a fair share of system resources). However, minimum-delay routing is often used and routers thus exchange information to get a picture of the delays throughout the network. This in turn helps to balance loads, thus decreasing local congestion.

In order to identify the set of links that lead to the best path, a routing algorithm with global knowledge about the state of the network is required. Overall, an effective routing algorithm is to accommodate as many goals as possible. They may include rapid and accurate delivery of packets, adaptability to node or link failure as well as to varying traffic loads, ability to avoid congested links, and low overhead.

Flow control in datagram and virtual-circuit packet networks is done differently. In connectionless networks, sources do not interact with the network prior to the transmission of data. It is thus possible that sources overload the network, causing buffer overload and packet loss. The sources with packet loss retransmit the lost packets, and that in turn will cause more buffers to overflow and require further retransmissions. This leads to a decrease in the network throughput to an unacceptable level. There are various techniques for flow control, and we briefly describe the one implemented in the Internet. The network nodes that experience congestion, that is, buffer overflow, send the network nodes causing the congestion special control packets requesting the transmit nodes to decrease the rate at which packets are injected into the network. However, for this scheme, there is no standard to specify under what conditions control packets should be sent and how the receiving nodes must react to control packets.

Flow control in connection-oriented networks may be done at two levels. The first level is when a connection request is made, and the network responds whether it has the required resources to provide the connection. The second level is when a connection is made, in that the packet rate and the burstiness of sources are controlled by the network.

11.6.4 Local Area Networks

A ***local area network*** (LAN) links a number of telecommunications equipment, while spanning a relatively small area. LANs are capable of transmitting at very high rates with limited distances. Wired LANs of various types have been in operation for the past several decades. Today's wired LANs are several orders of magnitude faster than the earlier ones. Today, a LAN not only connects computers and smart phones and allows sharing of resources in a small geographical area, but more importantly, a wired LAN is now connected to the Internet.

Of all wired LANs, which existed over many years, the only survival is ***Ethernet***. As such, our discussion of wired LANs is limited to Ethernet. The IEEE 802.3 standard, known as Ethernet, comprises four generations of Ethernet: i) standard (traditional) Ethernet at 10 Mbps, ii) fast Ethernet at 100 Mbps, iii) 1-Gigabit Ethernet at 1 Gbps, and iv) 10-Gigabit Ethernet at 10 Gbps.

All IEEE LANs sub-divide the data link layer, i.e., the second layer of the communication network protocol, into two sub-layers: logical link control (LLC) and medium access control (MAC). The ***MAC sub-layer***, the lower portion of the data-link layer which interfaces with the physical layer and performs part of framing function, defines the specific access method for each type of LAN. For instance, it defines CSMA/CD for Ethernet LANs and the token-passing for Token Ring LANs. The ***LLC sub-layer***, the upper part of the data-link layer which interfaces with the network layer, handles flow control and error control and part of framing tasks. This allows interconnectivity between different LANs, as it makes the MAC sub-layer transparent.

Table 11.1 presents some of the main characteristics associated with various Ethernet LANs. All Ethernet LANs employ baseband signaling, in that, the bits employ a line code to send the digital signal on the line. In 10-Mbps and 100-Mbps Ethernet LANs, the control access method to the sharing medium is CSMA/CD with 1-persistent method. 1-Gbps and 10-Gbps Ethernet LANs, however, operate in a switched full-duplex mode, in that there is no need for CSMA/CD method, as each node is connected to the switch via two separate links and there is no need for collision detection.

Table 11.1 Ethernet LANs

LAN types	Transmission medium	Maximum length	LAN topology	Line coding
10-Mbps Ethernet LAN				
10Base5	Thick coaxial	500 m	Bus	Manchester
10Base2	Thin coaxial	185 m	Bus	Manchester
10Base-T	Twisted pair	100 m	Star	Manchester
10Base-F	Optical fiber	2 km	Point-to-point	Manchester
100-Mbps Ethernet LAN				
100Base-TX	Two unshielded twisted pairs	100 m	Star	4B5B + MLT-3
100Base-FX	Two optical fiber multimode	2 km	Star	4B5B + NRZ-I
100Base-T4	Four unshielded twisted pairs	100 m	Star	Two 8B-6 T
1-Gbps Ethernet LAN				
1000BaseSX	Two optical fiber multimode	550 m	Star	8B-10B + NRZ
1000BaseLX	Two optical fiber single-mode	5 km	Star	8B-10B + NRZ
1000BaseCX	Two shielded twisted pairs	25 m	Star	8B-10B + NRZ
1000BaseT	Four unshielded twisted pairs	100 m	Star	4D-PAM5
10-Gbps Ethernet LAN				
10GBase-SR	Two optical fibers multimode at 850 nm	300 m	Point-to-point	64B-66B
10GBase-LR	Two optical fibers single-mode at 1310 nm	10 km	Point-to-point	64B-66B
10GBase-EW	Two optical fibers single-mode at 1550 nm	40 km	Point-to-point	SONET
10Gbase-X4	Two optical fibers multimode at 1310 nm	0.3 - 10 km	Point-to-point	8B-10B

11.6.5 Telephone and Cable Networks

Plain Old Telephone Service (POTS), developed over a century ago, is the voice-grade telephone service that is based on analog signal transmission over a pair of twisted-wire connecting the user's telephone set and the central office. In the PSTN, the communication link between the customer's premises and the central office is known as the ***last mile*** or the ***local loop*** providing access to the end user. During the past half century, the PSTN has also been used, at a growing rate, for the transmission and reception of digital data, such as e-mail, fax, and data file transfer. The device that performs the conversion between the digital signal and a standard form suitable for transmission over a telephone channel in the PSTN is known as a ***voice-band dial-up modem***. The fundamental role of such a modem is to transmit digital data over the telephone network in a transparent fashion, as the PSTN treats the transmitted digital data like the analog voice.

A large array of voice-band dial-up modems, including the ITU-T V-series modems over the telephone network, was developed between the early sixties and the late nineties. There are still millions of them being used in rural and remote areas to provide connectivity to the Internet. The ITU-T V-series recommendations on data communication over the telephone network specify the protocols that govern approved modem communication standards and interfaces. These standard modems were designed to have different capabilities, such as half-duplex and full-duplex communications, symmetric and asymmetric configurations, as well as adaptive bit rates. Their evolution started with the introduction of V.21 modem standard employing binary FSK operating at 300 bps and ended up with the development of V.34 modem standard employing 240-QAM with trellis-coding operating at 33.6 kbps, over a hundred times faster than the first generation of dial-up modems.

As discussed in Chapter 2, Shannon stated that the channel capacity for a band-limited, power-limited channel with additive white Gaussian noise (AWGN) is given by the following formula:

$$C = W \log_2\left(1 + \frac{S}{N}\right) \tag{11.3}$$

Note that the channel bandwidth W is measured in Hz and the signal-to-noise ratio at the receiver input in linear scale (not in dB). In a typical telephone line, the bandwidth W is roughly 3.4 kHz and the line signal-to-noise ratio is about 30 dB. Using (11.3), the capacity of a typical telephone network then turns out to be around 34 kbps. It is thus fair to say that V.34 modem approached the capacity that Shannon promises for a typical telephone channel.

In response to providing faster modems over the PSTN, the V.90 ***modem standard*** was developed in the late nineties. V.90 modem, also known as

56 K modem, may be used only if the other end is using digital signaling, such as the digital modem at the Internet service provider (ISP). This higher data rate is due to the higher SNR, which in turn is due to no quantization noise, for there is no sampling involved in downlink. To arrive at the 56-kbps figure, there are 8000 samples per second and 8 bits per sample; however, one of the bits in each sample is used for control purposes, hence 56 kbps. The analog modem at the user's end for uplink is a V.34 modem standard. V.90 was anticipated to be the last standard for modems operating near the channel capacity of POTS lines to be developed. V.90 is generally used in concert with the V.42bis compression standard.

Digital subscriber line (DSL) refers to a group of digital technologies that can provide high-speed digital signal transmission over the existing twisted-wire pair in local loops. The term DSL is primarily a set of standards that define the central office interface. Through the central office, the user is connected directly to the broadband backbone network. The twisted-wire pair used in the local loop, originally designed for voice analog signals, is intentionally loaded, at regular intervals across the local loop, with coils. The extra inductance makes the frequency response fairly flat across the effective voice band. This helps to improve the voice quality, but at the expense of significant attenuation beyond 3.4 kHz. DSL uses an adaptive technology, in that it uses a bit rate based on the condition of the local loop. Factors such as the distance between the user location and the switching office, the size of the wire, the signaling type, the level of crosstalk interference from other lines, and the level of signal-to-noise ratio can all affect the available bandwidth.

DSL, which includes the family of ADSL, VDSL, HDSL, and SDSL, is often referred to as *x*DSL. A widely-used DSL technology offered by a number of service providers is the ADSL. **ADSL** stands for ***asymmetric DSL***, in that, the speed in the downstream direction is higher than the speed in the upstream direction. The twisted-wire pair in the local loop potentially has a bandwidth of about 1.1 MHz, but the filter used at the end office where each local loop terminates limits the bandwidth to 4 kHz. Once the filter is removed, the entire 1.1 MHz bandwidth can be utilized for data transmission and voice communications. ADSL allows the subscriber to use voice and high-speed data at the same time, as shown in Figure 11.8a. This is achieved by using frequency division multiplexing to divide the bandwidth into a voice channel, an upstream channel (25–138 kHz), and a downstream channel (138–1104 kHz). The lowest part of the band up to 25 kHz is reserved for POTS, which nominally requires a bandwidth of 4 kHz. The ADSL bandwidth is separated by a LPF for voice and a HPF for data, where both have cutoff frequencies of 25 kHz.

The ADSL uses ***discrete multitone (DMT) modulation***, similar to OFDM. In that, multiple carrier signals at different frequencies are employed. The available bandwidth is divided into 256 parallel DMT channels, each consisting of

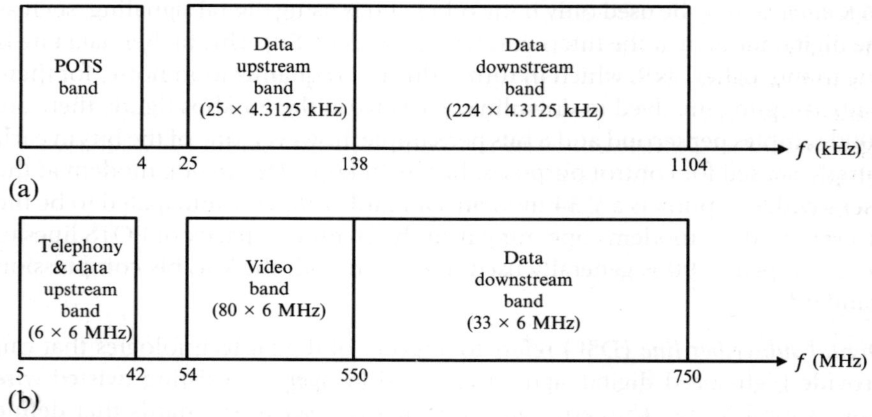

FIGURE 11.8 Spectrum allocation: (a) ADSL and (b) CATV.

4.3125 kHz and capable of carrying about 60 kbps. It would be possible to have an upstream data rate of 1.44 Mbps and a downstream data rate of 13.4 Mbps. In practice, however, transmission impairments prevent attainment of these data rates. Current implementations of ADSL operate at from 1.5 to 9 Mbps downstream and at from 16 to 640 kbps downstream in a bandwidth of up to 1.1 MHz and over a distance of 2.7 to 5.5 km. VDSL does even better, as it can support data rates of 13 to 52 Mbps downstream and 1.5 to 2.3 Mbps upstream in an aggregate bandwidth up to 30 MHz and over a distance of 0.3 to 1.5 km.

Many decades ago, cable TV started to distribute broadcast TV signals to locations where reception was poor, and it was called Community Antenna Television (CATV). CATV used coaxial cable and due to signal attenuation and thus use of dozens of amplifiers, the cable network was unidirectional. During the past couple of decades, the second generation of cable network, called a hybrid fiber-coaxial (HFC) network, was developed. The use of fiber-optic cable reduces the need for amplifiers down to very few. This move from traditional to hybrid infrastructure made the cable network bi-directional. Yet, the last part of the HFC network, from the fiber node to the subscriber is still a coaxial cable.

As shown in Figure 11.8b, the coaxial cable part of HFC has a bandwidth ranging from 5 MHz to 750 MHz, consisting of 6-MHz channels. To provide bidirectional connectivity, the bandwidth is divided into three bands: video, upstream data and cable telephony, and downstream data. The video band occupies frequencies from 54 MHz to 550 MHz, thus accommodating more than 80 channels. The downstream-data band occupies the upper band from 550 MHz to 750 MHz, consisting of 33 channels. The upstream-data band occupies the lower band from 5 to 42 MHz, comprising 6 channels.

Both upstream and downstream bands are time shared by many subscribers. The channels are shared, statically or dynamically, by a group of subscribers. In short, a subscriber with data must contend for the channel with others. The same situation exists for downstream, the channel must be shared among a group of users using multicasting concept. The throughput per 6-MHz channel is about 10 to 30 Mbps for the upstream and about 42 Mbps for the downstream.

11.7 NETWORK SECURITY AND CRYPTOGRAPHY

Private, dedicated communication links among users are quite rare; instead, there are always public communication networks shared by many users. The security threats that can arise in public networks are numerous, the array of attacks is constantly widening, and network security is continually becoming more challenging. Cryptography is an effective means of combating network threats, especially in e-commerce and m-commerce applications. Although the area of cryptography is very mathematical, only a very brief and simple introduction to this topic is made here.

To make a network secure, there are network security requirements that must be met. They include:

- *Confidentiality*, i.e., ensuring the transmitted message is hidden from unauthorized parties.
- *Authentication*, i.e., verifying the communicating parties are those they claim to be.
- *Integrity*, i.e., confirming that the message content has not been tampered with.
- *Nonrepudiation*, i.e., not being able to deny the transmission between the two parties has taken place.

Cryptography is the science of making secret communication to make messages secure. By ***encryption***, an original message, called ***plaintext***, is transformed into a coded message, called ***ciphertext***. The reverse process is called ***decryption***. The algorithm used for encryption and decryption is often called a ***cipher*** and the process of encryption and decryption requires a ***secret key***, without which the unauthorized parties must not be able to recover the original message.

A key is a number (value) that the cipher operates on. To encrypt a message, an encryption algorithm, an encryption key, and the plaintext are needed and to decrypt it, a decryption algorithm, a decryption key, and the ciphertext are required. The encryption and decryption algorithms are public, that is, anyone can access them, but the keys are secret and thus need to be protected.

There are two broad categories of cryptography: ***private-key cryptography***, also known as ***secret-key cryptography*** and ***symmetric-key cryptography***, and ***public-key cryptography***, also referred to as ***asymmetric-key cryptography***.

It is important to emphasize that there is a fundamental question as how secret keys in symmetric-key cryptography and public keys in asymmetric-key cryptography are efficiently and securely distributed and maintained. As the two widely used ways to distribute keys, we will briefly discuss the key distribution center (KDC) for symmetric-key cryptography and a certification authority (CA) for asymmetric-key cryptography. It is important to note that it is also possible to create a session key between two users without using a KDC or a CA. One such method is Diffie-Hellman key agreement, through which the two users create a secret shared key by using a series of exchanges over a public network.

11.7.1 Private-Key Cryptography

The private-key cryptography uses the same key for both the encryption at the transmitter and the decryption at the receiver, as shown in Figure 11.9a. In secret-key cryptography, decryption algorithm is the inverse of encryption algorithm, and the number of symmetric keys for N users to communicate is $\frac{N(N-1)}{2}$, as each pair must have a unique symmetric key. The number of keys grows quadratically, thus making these systems unfeasible for larger-scale use. The

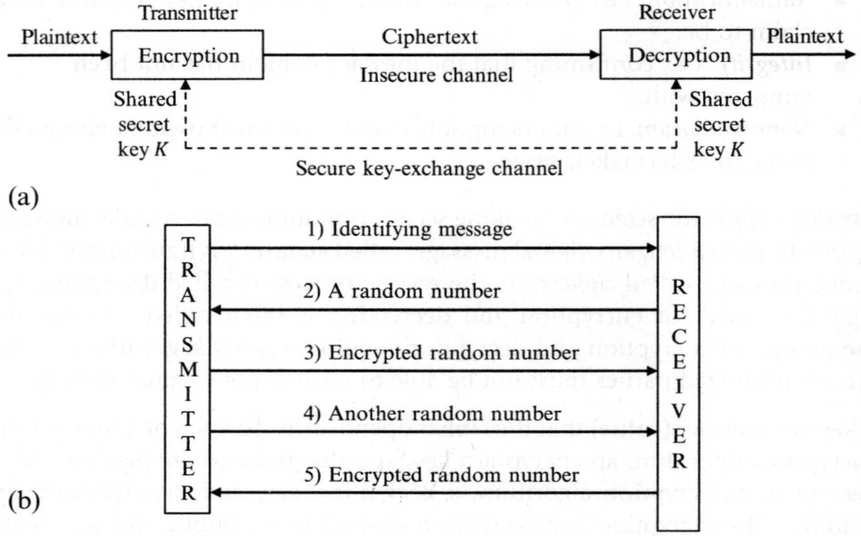

FIGURE 11.9 Private-key: (a) cryptography and (b) authentication.

symmetric-key cryptography is more efficient and widely practiced than asymmetric-key cryptography, and they are often used for long messages, for they also require less time to encrypt. An example of asymmetric-key cryptography is the Data Encryption Standard (DES). At the transmitter, a 64-bit plaintext is created into a 64-bit ciphertext, and at the receiver, a 64-bit ciphertext is converted back to a 64-bit plaintext, noting that in DES, the same 56-bit key is used for both encryption and decryption.

Figure 11.9b shows a secret-key authentication. The transmitter first sends a message identifying itself, the receiver, as a challenge, then sends back a message containing a random number. The transmitter then sends, as a response, an encrypted version of the random number. The receiver decrypts it by using the shared key. If the encrypted number is the same random number as the one sent earlier, then the receiver has authenticated the given transmitter. Similarly, the transmitter can then authenticate the receiver, of course, using another random number.

In symmetric-key distribution, a trusted third party, referred to as a ***key distribution center*** (KDC), is used. In symmetric-key cryptography, each user establishes a shared secret key with the KDC. The secret keys, created by the KDC, are used exclusively between the KDC and the users, and not among the users themselves. When a user wants to transmit secretly with another one, the transmitter then asks the KDC for a session (temporary) secret key to be used between the two users. A session symmetric key between two parties is used only once.

11.7.2 Public-Key Cryptography

The public-key cryptography is based on personal secrecy rather than sharing secrecy. In public-key cryptography, as shown in Figure 11.10a, two different keys, a public key and a private key are used. It is a salient requirement that it must not be possible to determine the private key from the public key. In general, the public key is small and the private key is large. A pair of keys can be used many times. The number of keys for N users to communicate is $2N$. The algorithm is complex and more efficient for short messages.

Figure 11.10b shows a public-key authentication. The transmitter first sends a message identifying itself. The receiver, as a challenge, then sends back a message containing a random number that has been encrypted by using the transmitter's public key. The transmitter then uses its own private key to determine the random number, and then responds by sending that random number. To develop a public-key cryptographic system is a complex task. A widely-used public cryptographic system is RSA (named after its inventors, Rivert, Shamir, and Adleman). The RSA algorithm is a block cipher based on modular arithmetic and factorization of a number that is the product of two large prime numbers.

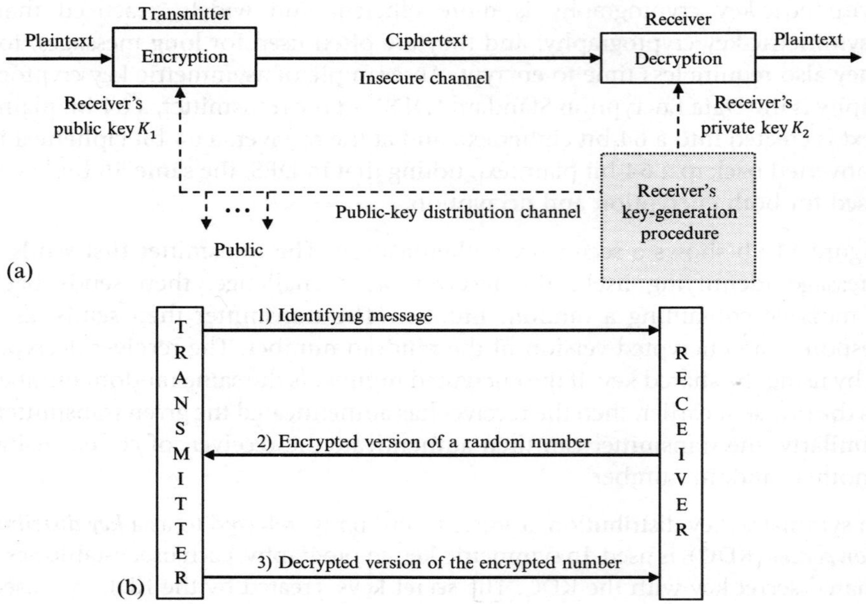

FIGURE 11.10 Public-key: (a) cryptography and (b) authentication.

In asymmetric-key distribution, a federal or state organization, known as a ***certification authority*** (CA), is used. In asymmetric-key cryptography, public keys, like secret keys, need to be distributed securely; the process can otherwise be subject to forgery. The CA first checks the identification of a user, asks the user's public key and writes it on the certificate. To prevent the certificate itself from being forged, the CA signs the certificate with its own private key, which is difficult to be forged. The user uploads the signed certificate. Anyone who wants a user's public key downloads the user's signed certificate and then uses the CA's public key tc obtain the user's public key.

11.7.3 Digital Signatures

Message authentication protects two communicating parties from any third party; it does not, however, protect the two parties against each other. In situations where something more than authentication is needed, the digital signature is the most attractive solution, in addition, it can also prevent denial and forgery. Digital-signature signing and verification processes are shown in Figure 11.11. Public-key cryptography can be used to provide nonrepudiation by producing a digital signature. A ***digital signature*** uses a pair of private-public keys belonging to the sender to provide message integrity and message authentication.

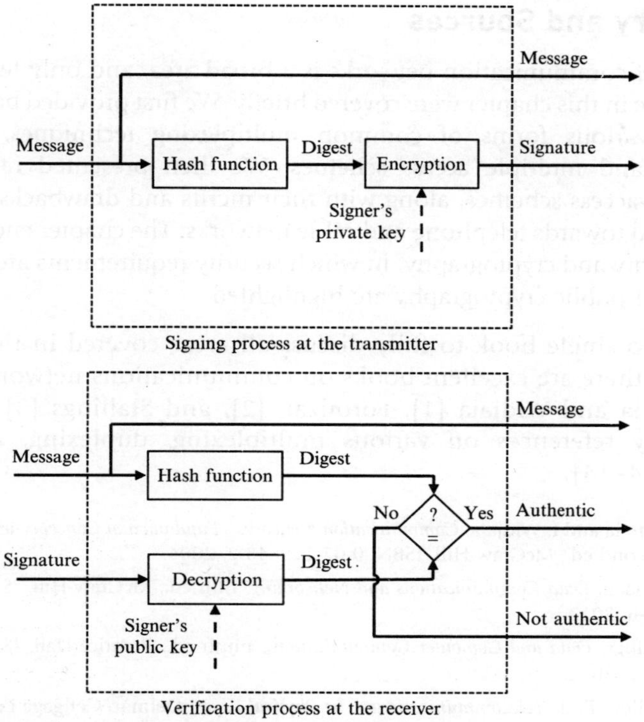

FIGURE 11.11 Digital-signature signing and verification processes.

In a digital-signature system, on the one hand the messages are normally long, but on the other hand we must use asymmetric-key cryptography systems that are very inefficient when dealing with long messages. The solution is to create a ***digest*** of a message through a hashing function (e.g., a checksum is produced that is much smaller than the message). Therefore, the transmitter first produces a digest, then encrypts it using its own private key to produce the signature, and then sends the signature along with the message to the receiver. At the receiver, the signer's public key is applied to the signature to get the transmitted digest, and the digest is also directly determined from the message. If both digests are the same, then only the given transmitter could have issued the message and the message has maintained its integrity.

It is important to highlight the distinction between how private and public keys are used in digital signatures, vis-à-vis in public-key cryptography, for confidentiality. In a digital signature, the signer (transmitter) signs the message digest with the signer's private key and the verifier (receiver) verifies with the signer's public key. In contrast, in cryptography, the public and private keys of the receiver are used in the process.

Summary and Sources

The area of communication networks is a broad area, and only few topics of importance in this chapter were covered briefly. We first provided brief descriptions of various forms of common multiplexing techniques, duplexing methods, and multiple access schemes. We then presented random and controlled-access schemes, along with their merits and drawbacks. The focus then turned towards telephone and cable networks. The chapter ends with network security and cryptography, in which security requirements are noted and private and public cryptography are highlighted.

There is no single book to fully discuss all areas covered in this chapter. However, there are excellent books on communications networks, such as Leon-Garcia and Widjaja [1], Forouzan [2], and Stallings [3]. There are also many references on various multiplexing, duplexing, and access methods [4–14].

[1] Leon-Garcia and I. Widjaja, *Communication Networks - Fundamental Concepts and Key Architectures*, second ed., McGraw-Hill, ISBN: 0-07-119848-2, 2004.

[2] A. Forouzan, *Data Communications and Networking*, fifth ed., McGraw-Hill, ISBN: 978-0-07-337622-6, 2013.

[3] W. Stallings, *Data and Computer Communications*, ninth ed., Prentice-Hall, ISBN: 978-0-13-139205-2, 2011.

[4] G.J. Mullett, *Basic Telecommunications: The Physical Layer*, Delmar, Cengage Learning, ISBN: 978-1-4018-4339-7, 2003.

[5] Gitlin, J.F. Hayes and S.B. Weinstein, *Data Communications Principles*, Plenum Press, ISBN: 0-306-43777-5, 1992.

[6] Sklar, *Digital Communications*, second ed., Prentice-Hall, ISBN: 0-13-084788-7, 2001.

[7] J.D. Gibson, *The Communications Handbook*, second ed., CRC Press, ISBN: 0-8493-0967-0, 2002.

[8] P.M. Shankar, *Introduction to Wireless Systems*, John Wiley and Sons, 2002. ISBN: 0-471-32167-2.

[9] J.F. Hayes, *Modeling and Analysis of Computer Communications Networks*, Perseus Publishing, 1984. ISBN: 0306417820.

[10] D.P. Agrawal and Q. Zeng, *Introduction to Wireless and Mobile Systems*, third ed., Delmar, Cengage Learning, 2011. ISBN: 978-1-4390-6205-0.

[11] R.L. Freeman, *Fundamentals of Telecommunications*, second ed., IEEE-Wiley, 2005. ISBN: 0-471-71045-8.

[12] International Telecommunications Union, *Handbook on Satellite Communications*, third ed., John Wiley & Sons, 2002. ISBN: 978-0-471-22189-0.

[13] T.S. Rappaport, *Wireless Communications*, second ed., Prentice-Hall, 2002. ISBN: 0-13-042232-0.

[14] J.J. Spilker Jr., *Digital Communications by Satellites*, Prentice-Hall, 1977. ISBN: 0-13-214155-8.

Problems

11.1 Suppose 1000-bit packets are transmitted on a shared channel of 10 Mbps. Determine the throughput for the following two cases:

(a) The system is an unslotted ALOHA system with a packet rate of 1000 packets per second.

(b) The system is a slotted ALOHA system with a packet rate of 2000 packets per second.

11.2 Propose a strategy to improve the performance of probing algorithm.

11.3 Describe all major aspects of the TDMA used in GSM.

11.4 Describe all major aspects of the CDMA used in IS-95.

11.5 Describe all major aspects of the FDMA in AMPS.

11.6 Show bit rate equivalence of FDMA and TDMA.

11.7 Compare the message delay in FDMA and TDMA.

CHAPTER 12

Wireless Communications

INTRODUCTION

We first discuss various sources of noise, loss, and interference, and then focus on major aspects of radio-communications link. The frequency-reuse and the cell concepts are presented. We highlight radio-propagation mechanisms, and describe various forms of channel fading. The descriptions of all forms of diversity schemes along with the diversity-combining methods are provided. Finally, our focus turns toward the next generation of wireless communications systems. After studying this chapter and understanding all relevant concepts, students should be able to achieve the following learning objectives:

1. Categorize various sources of loss and interference.
2. Know how to make a link budget for a radio-link analysis.
3. Explain how the EIRP is calculated.
4. Calculate the receive figure of merit.
5. Determine the carrier-to-noise ratio.
6. Explain the role of the link budget, margin, and threshold.
7. Understand the need for the frequency-reuse and cell concepts.
8. Describe the reuse distance and reuse factor in spatial separation.
9. Discuss the cell-splitting and cell-sectoring concepts.
10. Explain radio-propagation mechanisms.
11. Define the Doppler effect.
12. Understand the role of delay spread and coherence bandwidth.
13. Appreciate the role of Doppler spread and coherence time.
14. Provide the definitions of slow fading and fast fading.
15. Give the definitions of flat fading and frequency-selective fading.
16. Describe various methods of diversity.
17. List diversity-combing methods.
18. Detail TV white spaces and emerging applications.
19. Classify 0G, 1G, 2G, 3G, and 4G systems.
20. Expand on LTE-Advanced and its enabling technologies.

CONTENTS

Introduction to Digital Communications

12.1 RADIO-LINK ANALYSIS

In the design of a radio communication system, the link analysis, with its output, the link budget, or more precisely, the link power budget, is a must. The link comprises the entire communications path from the information source to the information sink. The ***link budget*** is a balance sheet of all gains and losses incurred in a radio communication link. The link budget outlines the allocation of transmit and receive resources, sources and levels of interference and noise, sources and amounts of losses, and effects of processes throughout the link. The link budget is an estimation technique to assess the performance of a radio link, such as the link availability, information rate, and bit error rate, and is thus a basic tool to provide an overall system insight, as it is a score sheet in considering system design trade-offs and configuration changes.

12.1.1 Sources of Interference, Loss, and Noise

There are quite many sources of interference, loss, and noise, and these sources and their contributions in one radio communication system may be different from those in another system. For instance, in satellite broadcasting systems, the link is generally noise-limited, and in cellular mobile systems, the interference is usually more dominant than noise.

Interference is an unwanted signal, and there are various sources of interference. In an ideal system, the interfering signals, if not eliminated, must be significantly minimized. Not all sources of interference exist in all systems, but what matters in a system is the aggregate interference level. We now briefly identify four types of interference. ***Co-channel interference*** arises in a system employing the frequency reuse concept. It occurs when the wanted signal from within the cell arrives at the receiver along with the unwanted signals from other cells, while all employing the same carrier frequency. ***Adjacent carrier interference*** is caused by power from signals in adjacent carriers in the system. It occurs in multi-carrier channels with modest carrier spacing and inadequate filtering in the transmitter and receiver. ***Adjacent system interference*** is produced by signals belonging to another system using the same frequency as the wanted signal. This type of interference exists between two geostationary satellites operating in two adjacent orbital slots while using the same frequency band and having the same footprints or between a satellite and terrestrial system sharing the same frequency band while covering the same geographical area. ***Intermodulation interference*** is primarily due to the processing of the signal by a nonlinear device at or close to saturation. It is of high importance to point out that intersymbol interference, however, is not included in the link budget simply because a change in signal power cannot alter the degradation that intersymbol interference causes.

Loss represents signal attenuation, and there are various sources of loss, including ***path loss*** (a decrease in the signal strength of an electromagnetic wave as a nonlinear function of both distance and frequency), ***implementation loss*** (due to imperfect equipment components and system operation), ***pointing loss*** (due to imperfect pointing of transmit and receive antennas), ***atmospheric loss*** (primarily due to rainfall), ***antenna loss*** (due to low antenna efficiency and increase in antenna temperature), ***backoff-power loss*** (to ensure amplification in the linear region), ***cross-polarization loss*** (as no antenna is perfectly polarized in a single polarization mode), and ***depolarization loss*** (loss of polarization in high-frequency antennas). It is important to note that fading and its impact on the transmitted signal is included in the link budget by providing additional link margin to account for it.

Noise is an unwanted, uncontrollable, ever-present random signal and there are diverse sources of noise, including ***thermal noise*** (due to the random motion of electrons in a conductor) and ***shot noise*** (due to the discrete nature of current flow in electronic devices). However, phase noise due to phase jitter in the local oscillator is not included in the link budget because a change in signal power cannot alter the degradation that phase noise causes.

12.1.2 Received Signal Power and Path Loss

A gain of an antenna reflects its directivity, and an isotropic (omni-directional) antenna has thus unity (zero-dB) gain. A transmit antenna with a gain G_T has directivity in a particular direction, and is assumed to be pointed in the direction of the receive antenna with a gain G_R. When the transmit antenna radiates at a power level P_T watts, then the product of the transmitting power and the gain of the transmitting antenna (i.e., $P_T G_T$) is called ***effective isotropically radiated power*** (EIRP), which is the radiated power relative to an isotropic (omni-directional) antenna.

Assuming the distance between the transmit antenna and the receive antenna is d meters, the signal power density at the receive antenna is thus $P_T G_T/4\pi d^2$ W/m^2, where $4\pi d^2$ represents the surface area of a sphere with a radius of d meters. The radiated power captured by the receive antenna is proportional to its effective area A. From the basic electromagnetic theory, we have $A = G_R c^2/4\pi f^2$, where c represents the speed of light in meters per second and f is the frequency of the transmitted signal in Hertz. The received signal power P_R is thus as follows:

$$P_R = \left(\frac{P_T G_T}{4\pi d^2}\right) A = \left(\frac{P_T G_T}{4\pi d^2}\right)\left(\frac{G_R c^2}{4\pi f^2}\right) = \frac{P_T G_T G_R}{(4\pi d f/c)^2} = \frac{P_T G_T G_R}{L_s} \quad (12.1a)$$

where L_s is called the ***free-space path loss*** (absolute units), and is proportional to the square of both distance and frequency. Equation (12.1a), known as ***Friis transmission formula***, relates the received power to the transmitted power. The received signal power in dB is thus as follows:

$$P_R = P_T + G_T + G_R - L_s = \text{EIRP} + G_R - L_s \quad \text{(dB)} \quad (12.1b)$$

Note that other losses, such as absorption, pointing, and implementation losses, can further reduce the received signal power dB for dB. The path loss for a non-free-space wireless environment, such as a path with obstructions, is difficult to model. For a free-space path, the path loss varies as the square of the distance (i.e., $n = 2$), but because of the propagation characteristics of mobile radio propagation, we have $n > 2$. Some rough values for the path-loss exponent n is given in Table 12.1.

12.1.3 Noise Temperature and Receive Figure of Merit

The received signal power is important when compared to the noise present in the system. The noise consists mainly of thermal noise. The available power from a thermal noise source is dependent on the noise temperature of the source, and ***noise power*** is given by:

$$N = kT_s B = N_0 B \quad (12.2)$$

Table 12.1 Path-loss exponents for different environments

Environment	n
Free space	2
Obstructed in a large closed-space	2.5
Flat rural	3
Hilly rural	3.5
Suburban	4
Downtown	4.5
Obstructed in building	5

where N is measured in watts, $k = 1.38 \times 10^{-23}$ joules/Kelvin is the Boltzmann's constant, T_s is the ***system noise temperature*** in Kelvin, B is the noise bandwidth in Hertz, and N_0 is the noise power spectral density in watts/Hertz. The system noise temperature in turn is composed of several factors, such as antenna noise temperature and receiver noise temperature.

The ratio of the receiving antenna gain G_R to the system noise temperature T_s (i.e., G_R/T_s) is called the ***receive figure of merit,*** where it is given in dBi/K and thus expressed in $G_R/T_s = G_R - 10\log T_s$. For instance, when the receive antenna gain is 30 dBi and the system-noise temperature is 100 degrees K, the figure of merit is 10 ($= 30 - 10\log 100$) dBi/K.

Using (12.1a) and (12.2), the ratio of the received signal power to the noise power over the bandwidth of interest, widely known as the ***carrier-to-noise ratio*** $\left(\frac{C}{N}\right)$, is as follows:

$$\frac{C}{N} = \frac{P_R}{kT_sB} = \frac{P_T G_T G_R}{L_s k T_s B} \tag{12.3a}$$

The carrier-to-noise ratio in dB is thus as follows:

$$\frac{C}{N} = \text{EIRP} + \frac{G_R}{T_s} - L_s - 228.6 - 10\log B \ \text{(dB)} \tag{12.3b}$$

Note that $-228.6\ (= 10\log(1.38 \times 10^{-23}))$ reflects the Boltzmann's constant in dB.

12.1.4 Link Margin and Link Threshold

As discussed earlier, in digital communications, E_b/N_0, which is a normalized version of average signal power to average noise power ratio, is the measure of performance, as it can determine the average bit error rate for a given modulation technique and channel coding scheme. Since E_b/N_0 measures the bit energy to the noise power spectral density, using (12.2), we have the following at the detector input:

$$\frac{E_b}{N_0} = \frac{C/R_b}{N/B} = \left(\frac{C}{N}\right)\left(\frac{B}{R_b}\right) \tag{12.4a}$$

where R_b is the bit rate. The value of $\frac{E_b}{N_0}$ in dB is thus as follows:

$$\frac{E_b}{N_0} = \frac{C}{N} + 10\log B - 10\log R_b \ \text{(dB)} \tag{12.4b}$$

Using (12.3b), (12.4b) can be expresses as follows:

$$\frac{E_b}{N_0} = \text{EIRP} + \frac{G_R}{T_s} - L_s - 228.6 - 10\log R_b \text{ (dB)} \tag{12.4c}$$

The value of $\frac{E_b}{N_0}$ in (12.4c) reflects the required value to yield the target bit error rate. However, due to fade and the randomness associated with it, a link is always designed to have a link margin. In other words, a link is designed so the received $\frac{E_b}{N_0}$ is always several dBs more than the required $\frac{E_b}{N_0}$, and the difference between these two values is known as the ***link margin***. The link margin is set based on the link-propagation characteristics and the target-link availability.

Another point of high importance is that in a radio link, the impact of various types of interference must be included and the aggregate interference is then taken into account. More specifically, we need to include $C/(N+I)$ in the link budget. To do that, the aggregate interference, in absolute unit (i.e., not in dB), is added to the noise level in absolute unit (i.e., not in dB). Then the $C/(N+I)$ in dB is used in place of C/N in dB to determine the link margin. As an example, suppose there are two types of interferences, one at 20 dB and the other at 18.2 dB, and the noise level is at 17.1 dB, all with respect to the carrier (signal) level. The aggregate level of interference is thus 16 $\left(=10\log\left(10^{-\frac{20}{10}}+10^{-\frac{18.2}{10}}\right)\right)$ dB, which in turn reduces the received signal power to 13.5 $\left(=10\log\left(10^{-\frac{17.1}{10}}+10^{-\frac{16}{10}}\right)\right)$ dB.

In a link budget, after including the impacts of noise, aggregate interference, and combined losses, the link resources must be enough to help close the link and deliver the following ***link threshold***:

$$\text{Link threshold} = \frac{E_b}{N_0} + 10\log R_b + \text{Link margin (dB)} \tag{12.5}$$

12.2 FREQUENCY REUSE

Radio spectrum is the scarcest resource in radio communications. Efficient use of spectrum is of paramount importance, as it can bring about an increase in system capacity, an improvement in system performance, and a reduction in transmit power. It is thus imperative to employ any which method possible to save spectrum, including bandwidth-efficient trellis-coded and adaptive modulation schemes, efficient source coding and compression techniques, high-performance channel coding schemes with modest coding rates, and diversity techniques. These techniques, along with some others employed in wireless communications, can save the amount of spectrum used, but of course at the expense of complexity. However, in parallel with saving spectrum, we can also increase the amount of spectrum by reusing the allocated raw spectrum. This can be achieved through dual polarization and spatial separation.

12.2.1 Dual Polarization

An antenna is a transducer that converts a radio-frequency electric current to an electromagnetic wave that is then radiated into space. ***Polarization*** of electromagnetic-wave propagation is the direction of its electric-field vector in relationship to the surface of the earth. Dual polarization exploits orthogonality, and thus allows frequency reuse.

There are two distinct types of polarization, linear polarization and circular polarization, and each type can have dual polarization. A linear polarized antenna radiates energy wholly in one plane containing the direction of propagation, but a circular polarized antenna radiates energy in both the horizontal and vertical planes and all planes in between. The polarization of the receive antenna must be the same as that of the transmitted radio wave for best reception and the choice of polarization is sometimes dictated by the method of propagation and the operating frequency band.

In ***linear polarization***, the electric-field vector does not change its orientation (i.e., it remains the same) with respect to an observer. Linear polarization (LP), in turn, is of two types, horizontal and vertical. In ***horizontal polarization*** (HP), the electric-field vector is parallel to the surface of the earth. Off-the-air TV transmissions in the United States use HP. Man-made radio noise is predominantly vertically polarized and the use of HP would provide some discrimination against interference from noise. In ***vertical polarization*** (VP), the electric-field vector is perpendicular to the surface of the earth. Ground-wave propagation requires VP, as such AM radio broadcast towers and the whip antennas on cars have vertical antennas. Mobile communication systems usually use VP, as it is desirable to radiate a radio signal in all directions. Linear polarization is also used in FSS C-band (6/4 GHz) and FSS Ku-band (14/12 GHz) satellite communication systems providing fixed-satellite services. For instance, due to dual polarization, the 500-MHz raw spectrum allocated to fixed satellite services (FSS) in either C-band or Ku-band is reused to make it into 1 GHz spectrum.

Circular polarization (CP), in turn, is of two types, right-hand and left-hand. In ***right-hand circular polarization*** (RHCP), the electric wave rotates in a clockwise direction as it travels, and in ***left-hand circular polarization*** (LHCP), it rotates in a counter-clockwise direction. FM radio broadcasting commonly uses circular polarization, producing a signal that can be received by either horizontal or vertical antennas. Circular polarization is also used in satellite communications, especially in TV broadcast satellites operating at BSS Ku-band (17/12 GHz) and high-capacity broadband satellites operating at Ka-band (30/20 GHz). The reason lies in the fact that circular polarization can keep the satellite signal constant regardless of anomalies, such as Faraday rotation in the ionosphere or geometric differences as the satellite may appear to move with respect to the satellite dishes.

It is important that for the line-of-sight communications the polarization be the same at the two ends of a communication link, as any polarization mismatch brings about a loss. A linearly polarized transmit antenna can work with a circularly polarized receive antenna and vice versa, and there can be about a 3-dB loss in signal strength. If the transmit antenna has one form of linear polarization and the receive antenna has the other linear form or if the transmit antenna is circularly polarized with one sense and the receive antenna is circularly polarized with the other sense, a loss of about 20 dB can then be incurred.

Dual polarization is an effective technique in satellite communications to double the amount of spectrum allocated to a geostationary satellite operating in an orbital slot at a given frequency band. In fact, almost all geostationary communication and broadcast satellites employ dual polarization, whether that be linear (HP and VP) or circular (RHCP and LHCP). To this effect, onboard the satellite, there are separate antennas, each with different polarization and followed by separate receivers, all allowing simultaneous access of the satellite from the same region of the earth. This in turn requires that each dish antenna be polarized in the same way as its counterpart antenna onboard the satellite. In dual polarization, cross polarization is a consideration. It happens when unwanted radiation is present from a polarization that is different from the polarization in which the antenna was intended to radiate. For example, an antenna with vertical polarization may radiate signal energy in horizontal polarization, and vice versa.

12.2.2 Spatial Separation

Spatial separation can allow frequency reuse and the frequency-reuse principle forms the basis for cellular mobile communications and high-capacity multi-spot-beam satellite systems. When the wide service coverage, either provided by a cellular wireless network or a satellite system, is divided into a number of small geographical areas, it is possible to use the same frequency band in more than one area, provided that the areas are sufficiently distanced apart. In the context of cellular networks, such an area is called a cell where mobile devices are in communications with a cell's base station, and in the context of satellite communications, it is called a spot beam where satellite dishes are in communications with an onboard transceiver dedicated to the spot beam. In short, the same frequency band in a cell (beam) can be reused in another cell (beam) as long as the cells (beams) are far apart and the signals in cells (beams) using the same frequency do not interfere with one another.

The most natural shape for a cell to take on is a circle, as it can provide constant power at the cell boundary. However, circles cannot fill a plane without either gaps or overlaps. Hexagons, on the other hand, have shapes similar to circles, and can fill up a plane, while avoiding overlaps. Hexagons are thus considered the basic cell shape in cellular networks, especially for theoretical considerations. In practice, however, due to propagation irregularities, cells do not happen to be hexagonal.

The key characteristic of a cellular network is the ability to re-use frequencies to increase both service coverage and system capacity. In a cellular system, adjacent cells do not use the same frequency band. A group of contiguous cells where the frequency band in each cell is different is called a ***cluster of cells***. Therefore, there can be no co-channel interference within a cluster of cells. The number of cells in a cluster is called the ***cluster size*** *N*. The total service coverage is divided into such clusters. Since we have $N = i^2 + j^2 + ij$, where i and j take on nonnegative integer values, N can be 1, 3, 4, 7, 9, 12, 13, 16, 19, etc. We have $N=1$ in the CDMA system (3G), $N=7$ in the AMPS system (1G), and $N=12$ in the GSM system (2G). Figure 12.1 shows clusters of three cells and seven cells. Maximization of system capacity requires minimization of cluster size, and that can increase the interference level.

Cells with the same frequency band must have a minimum distance from each other, known as the ***reuse distance*** *D*:

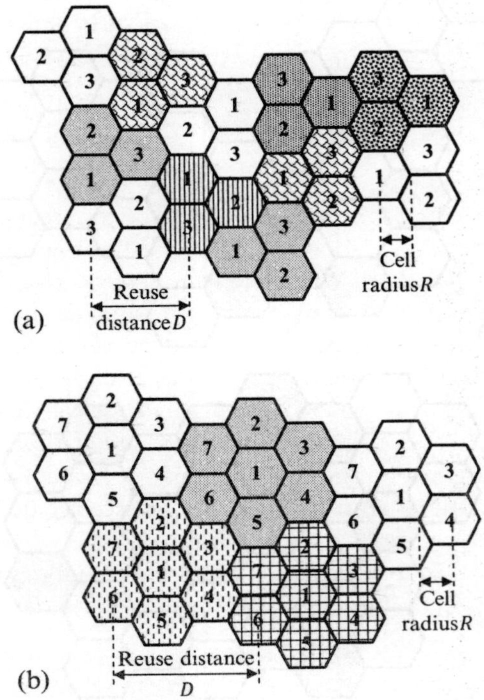

FIGURE 12.1 Frequency reuse pattern of hexagonal cells: (a) three-cell clusters and (b) seven-cell clusters.

$$D=\sqrt{3NR} \tag{12.6}$$

where R is the distance between the center of hexagon and one of its vertices, the so-called ***cell radius***. Therefore, the ***reuse factor*** q, which is the reuse distance normalized to the radius of a cell, is as follows:

$$q=\frac{D}{R}=\sqrt{3N} \tag{12.7}$$

The signal power is proportional to R^{-n}, while the co-channel interference power is proportional to D^{-n}, where $n \geq 2$ is the ***loss exponent*** or ***loss factor***, which can typically range between 2 and 5. Due to the fact that the power (either from the wanted signal or the interfering signal) decreases faster than an inverse square law, the cellular concept could work. Comparison of figures in Figure 12.2 clearly shows that irrespective of the number of cells in a cluster, the number of first-tier (closest) interfering hexagonal cells is six, and the second-tier (second closest) interfering hexagonal cells, which are at two

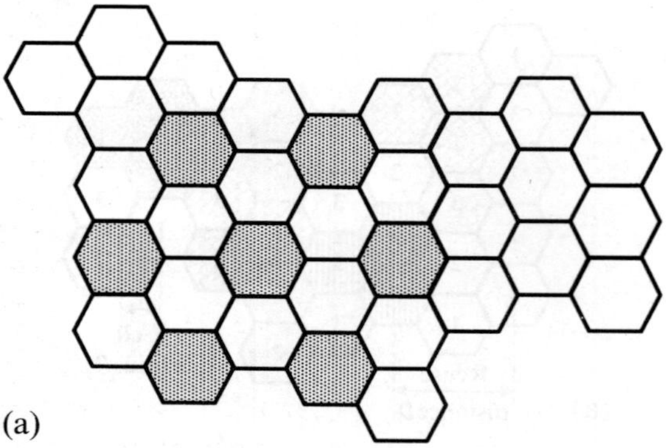

(a)

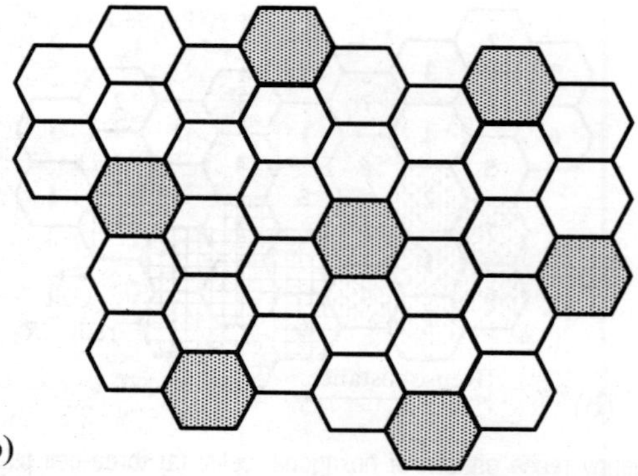

(b)

FIGURE 12.2 Interfering cells: (a) three-cell clusters and (b) seven-cell clusters.

times the reuse distance apart, do not have much bearing on the aggregate co-channel interference. Assuming all six interfering signals are at the same distance and using (12.7), the ***carrier-to-cochannel-interference ratio*** is expressed as follows:

$$\frac{C}{I}=\frac{1}{6}q^{n}=\frac{1}{6}\left(\frac{D}{R}\right)^{n}=\frac{1}{6}(3N)^{n/2} \qquad (12.8)$$

The co-channel interference from other clusters is a decreasing function of the frequency reuse factor and the cluster size. To reduce co-channel interference, cell splitting and cell sectoring can be employed, as shown in Figure 12.3.

If required, cell splitting is accomplished on an as-needed basis in some cells, either to reduce the co-channel interference or to enhance the system capacity or both. In ***cell splitting***, a cell is split into several smaller cells and thus requiring more base stations and in turn more handovers. As the coverage area of new split cells is smaller, the transmitting power levels are lower, this is mainly due to the fact that it is necessary to maintain an acceptable carrier-to-interference ratio, and this in turn helps in reducing co-channel interference. For instance, when the radius of a cell is reduced by a factor of m, the transmitted power from the antenna of the new smaller cell needs to be reduced so as to maintain the same co-channel interference level. In other words, the power required at the

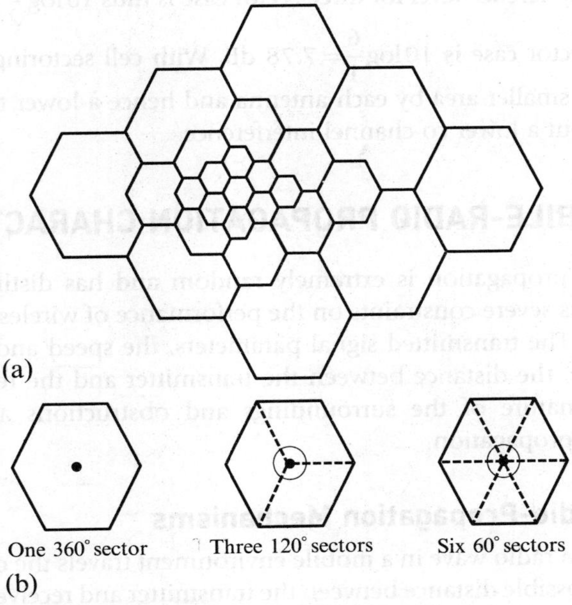

FIGURE 12.3 Hexagonal cells: (a) cell splitting and (b) cell sectoring.

cell boundary must remain unchanged before and after cell splitting, i.e., we should have the following:

$$P_O R^{-n} = P_N \left(\frac{R}{m}\right)^{-n} \tag{12.9a}$$

where P_O is the transmitted power from the antenna in the old (larger) cell and P_N is the transmitted power from the antenna in the new (smaller) cell. Using (12.9a), the reduction in the transmitted power is then as follows:

$$10 \log \left(\frac{P_O}{P_N}\right) = (10n) \log m \tag{12.9b}$$

For instance, when the cell radius is reduced by a factor of 4 (i.e., $m=4$) and the loss exponent is 4 (i.e., $n=4$), the new transmitted power is reduced by about 24.1 dB.

In ***cell sectoring***, rather than one single omni-directional antenna at the center of a cell, several directional antennas are placed on a single tower at the center of the cell to cover the whole 360 degrees of the cell, such as three antennas each covering 120 degrees or six antennas each covering 60 degrees. In the case of using three sectors, the first-tier interfering signals are from two cells, and in the case of six sectors, there is only a single first-tier interfering signal. Since there are six first-tier interfering signals with an omni-directional antenna, the reduction in the interference level for three-sector case is thus $10 \log \frac{6}{2} = 4.77$ dB, and that for six-sector case is $10 \log \frac{6}{1} = 7.78$ dB. With cell sectoring, the resulting coverage of a smaller area by each antenna and hence a lower transmit power can bring about a lower co-channel interference.

12.3 MOBILE-RADIO PROPAGATION CHARACTERISTICS

Mobile-radio propagation is extremely random and has distinguishing features, as it puts severe constraints on the performance of wireless communication systems. The transmitted signal parameters, the speed and the direction of the mobile, the distance between the transmitter and the receiver, terrain profile, and nature of the surroundings and obstructions all impact the mobile-radio propagation.

12.3.1 Radio-Propagation Mechanisms

It is ideal that a radio wave in a mobile environment travels the direct line, i.e., the shortest possible distance between the transmitter and receiver, also known as the ***line-of-sight propagation***. Whether there is a line-of-sight transmission

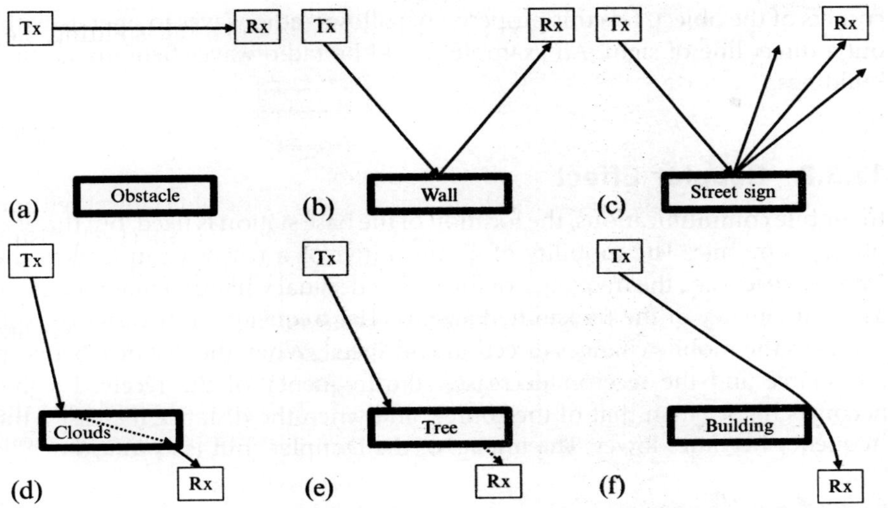

FIGURE 12.4 Radio-wave-propagation mechanisms: (a) line-of-sight transmission, (b) reflection, (c) scattering, (d) refraction, (e) absorption, and (f) diffraction.

or not, an electromagnetic wave in mobile-radio communications can meet objects. Radio waves exhibit certain characteristics when coming into contact with obstacles. The radio-propagation mechanisms, as shown in Figure 12.4, are diverse, and reflection, diffraction, and scattering are generally more dominant.

Reflection occurs when a radio wave impinges on an object that is larger than the wavelength of the radio signal. The radio wave is then reflected off the surface. An example would be radio waves bouncing off walls.

Scattering results when a radio wave hits an object of irregular shape, usually an object with a rough surface area that is smaller than the wavelength. The radio wave bounces off in multiple directions. Examples would be radio waves hitting street signs, lamp posts, and foliage.

Refraction arises when a radio wave meets an object with a density different from its current medium. The radio wave now travels at a different angle. An example would be radio waves propagating through clouds.

Absorption ensues when a radio wave passes through an object and a portion of the strength is absorbed as heat, so the signal strength will be weaker if it comes out the other side. An example would be radio waves going through trees.

Diffraction follows when a radio wave is blocked by objects with sharp irregular edges standing in its path. The radio wave is broken up and bends around the corners of the object. It is this property that allows radio waves to operate without a direct line of sight. An example would be radio waves bending around buildings.

12.3.2 Doppler Effect

In mobile communications, the location of the base station is fixed, but the user phone is mobile. The mobility of a transmitter or a receiver can lead to the ***Doppler effect*** (i.e., the frequency of the received signal will not remain the same as the frequency of the transmitted signal). The frequency shift varies considerably as the mobile changes direction and speed. When the distance between the source and the receiver decreases, the frequency of the received signal becomes higher than that of the source, and when the distance increases, the frequency becomes lower. The impact of the Doppler shift is as follows:

$$f_r = f_t - f_d = f_t - \frac{f_t}{c}(v\cos\theta) \qquad (12.10)$$

where f_r is the frequency of the received signal, f_t is the frequency of the transmitted signal, f_d is the ***Doppler frequency*** or ***Doppler shift***, c is the speed of light, v is the moving speed, and $v \cos \theta$ represents the speed of movement in the direction of wave propagation (i.e., the velocity component of the receiver in the direction of the transmitter), as θ represents the angle between the propagation direction and moving direction, as shown in Figure 12.5.

It is important to note that when the transmitter or the receiver is moving directly toward the other one (i.e., $\theta = 180^\circ$) we have $f_r = f_t(1 + \frac{v}{c})$, and when one is directly moving away from the other one (i.e., $\theta = 0^\circ$) we have $f_r = f_t(1 - \frac{v}{c})$. For instance, when the source carrier frequency is 900 MHz and the speed of a mobile user, while driving on a highway, is 120 kilometers

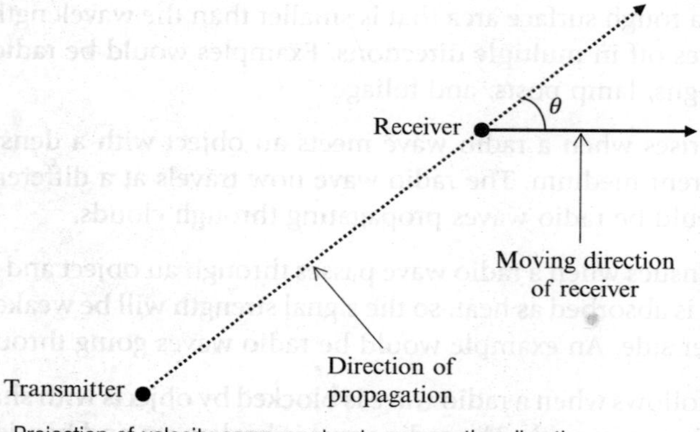

FIGURE 12.5 Projection of velocity component onto propagation direction.

per hour, the maximum Doppler shift is 100 Hz, and when the source carrier frequency is 1.8 GHz and the speed of a mobile user, while walking in a park, is 3 kilometers per hour, the maximum Doppler shift is 5 Hz. In fact, the maximum Doppler shift almost always is below 1 kHz.

Since the Doppler shifts are small, the effect on radio-link performance would be negligible, if all component waves were shifted by the same amount, as the local oscillator could easily compensate for such a shift. However, different paths have different Doppler shifts and the superposition of Doppler-shifted waves creates the sequence of dips. For instance, component waves arriving from ahead of the mobile experience a positive Doppler shift, whereas those arriving from behind the mobile have a negative Doppler shift. Doppler frequency is thus a measure for the rate of change of the mobile channel and the superposition of many slightly Doppler-shifted signals leads to phase shifts of the total received signal that can impair the reception of angle-modulated signals.

12.3.3 Delay Spread and Coherent Bandwidth

Multipath propagation, an inherent feature of a mobile communications channel, results in a received signal that is dispersed in time. Each path has its own delay and the time dispersion leads to a form of intersymbol interference. ***Delay spread*** is a measure of the multipath profile of a mobile communications channel. It is generally defined as the difference between the time of arrival of the earliest component (e.g., the line-of-sight wave if there exists) and the time of arrival of the latest multipath component. Delay spread is a random variable, and the standard deviation is a common metric to measure it. This measure is widely known as the ***root-mean-square delay spread*** σ_τ.

Coherence bandwidth B_c is a statistical measure of the range of frequencies over which the channel can be considered flat (i.e., it passes all spectral components with approximately equal gain and linear phase). All frequency components of the transmitted signal within the coherence bandwidth will fade simultaneously. The coherence bandwidth is inversely proportional to the delay spread, and we thus have the following:

$$B_c = \frac{1}{\sigma_\tau} \tag{12.11}$$

Delay spread σ_τ and coherent bandwidth B_c are parameters that describe the time dispersion nature of the mobile channel, and their values with respect to the transmitted signal bandwidth B_s and the symbol duration T_s can help determine if the channel is experiencing flat fading or frequency-selective fading.

The difference between path lengths is rarely greater than a few kilometers, so the delay spread σ_τ is rarely more than several micro-seconds. The coherence bandwidth B_c is thus typically greater than 100 kHz. If a channel is faded at one frequency, the frequency must be very roughly changed by the coherence bandwidth B_c to find an unfaded frequency.

12.3.4 Doppler Spread and Coherence Time

Doppler spread B_d is a measure of spectral broadening caused by the time rate of change of the mobile radio channel and is defined as the range of frequencies over which the received Doppler spectrum is essentially nonzero. When the bandwidth of the transmitted signal is much larger than the Doppler spread, the effects of the Doppler spread are negligible at the receiver.

Coherence time T_c is a statistical measure of the time duration over which the channel impulse response essentially remains unchanged (i.e., highly correlated). If the time interval between the signal transmissions is much greater than the coherence time, the channel will likely affect the two signal transmissions differently; otherwise, they will be affected similarly. The Doppler spread is inversely proportional to the coherence time, and we thus have the following:

$$B_d = \frac{1}{T_c} \tag{12.12}$$

Doppler spread and coherence time are parameters that describe the frequency-dispersion nature of the mobile channel, and their values with respect to the transmitted signal bandwidth B_s and the symbol duration (period) T_s can help determine if the channel is experiencing fast fading or slow fading.

The coherence time T_c is fundamentally interpreted as the order-of-magnitude duration of a fade at a given frequency. The Doppler shift and Doppler spread are both linear functions of the signal frequency. The variation of Doppler spread with frequency is important when the operating frequency bands are different. For instance, a system operating at 2 GHz has a Doppler spread twice that of a 1 GHz system, and thus resulting in a coherence time half as large. This gives rise to fading faster, with shorter fade duration, and channel measurements that become outdated twice as fast.

12.3.5 Large-Scale Fading and Small-Scale Fading

Fading can be broadly grouped into two types: large-scale fading and small-scale fading. ***Large scale-fading*** represents the average signal-power attenuation or path loss due to motion over large areas and it is impacted by terrain configuration between the transmitter and receiver, and over a very long distance (several hundreds or thousands of meters), there is a steady decrease in power. Examination of the power over such a distance reveals that the power fluctuates around a mean value and these fluctuations have a rather long period. The statistics of large-scale fading, described in terms of a mean-path loss (n^{th} -power law) and a log-normally distributed variation about the mean, can lead to an estimate of path loss as a function of distance.

Small-scale fading refers to the rapid changes of the amplitude and phase of a radio signal over a short period of time (on the order of seconds) or a short distance (a few wavelengths). In small-scale fading, the instantaneous received signal power may vary as much as 30 to 40 dB when the receiver is moved by only a fraction of a wavelength. In a mobile-radio environment, each path has its own Doppler shift, time delay, and path attenuation, and multipath propagation results in a time-varying signal as the mobile moves position. Such a channel is linear, but time-varying. Small-scale fading is also called Rayleigh fading because when the number of versions of the transmitted signal which arrive at slightly different times is large, the envelope of the received signal is statistically described by a Rayleigh distribution if there is no line-of-sight component. If there is a line-of-sight component, it is then described by a Rician distribution.

Small-scale fading depends on the nature of the transmitted signal with respect to the characteristics of the channel. Depending on the relation between the signal parameters, such as the bandwidth and the symbol period, on the one hand, and the channel parameters, such as the coherence time, Doppler spread, coherence bandwidth and delay spread, on the other hand, different transmitted signals will experience different types of fading. Delay spread leads to time dispersion and frequency-selective fading. Doppler spread leads to frequency dispersion and time-selective fading. Time dispersion and frequency dispersion are caused by independent propagation mechanisms.

12.3.6 Fast Fading and Slow Fading

Fast fading and slow fading are considered as small-scale fading. Frequency dispersion due to Doppler spreading causes the transmitted signal to undergo either fast fading or slow fading, where the high Doppler spread gives rise to fast fading and the low Doppler spread brings about slow fading. Depending on how rapidly the transmitted baseband signal changes as compared to the rate of change of the channel, a channel may be classified either as a fast-fading or slow-fading channel.

Fast fading may be caused when the channel impulse response changes rapidly within the symbol duration. This implies that the coherence time of the channel is smaller than the symbol period. Signal distortion due to fast fading increases with increasing Doppler spread relative to the signal bandwidth. A signal thus undergoes fast fading, if we have the following:

$$T_s > T_c, \; B_s < B_d \tag{12.13}$$

Slow fading may be caused when the channel impulse response changes at a rate much slower than the transmitted signal. A signal thus undergoes slow fading, if we have the following:

$$T_s < T_c, \; B_s > B_d \tag{12.14}$$

In general, when the coherence time is about less than hundreds of symbol periods, fast fading occurs, and when the coherence time is roughly in thousands of symbol periods, slow fading is expected. In practice, fast fading only occurs for very low data rates.

12.3.7 Flat Fading and Frequency-Selective Fading

Flat fading and frequency-selective fading are considered as small-scale fading. Time dispersion due to multipath causes the transmitted signal to undergo either flat fading or frequency-selective fading, where the small delay spread gives rise to flat fading and the large delay spread brings about frequency-selective fading.

All frequency components of the transmitted signal that fall within the coherence bandwidth will fade simultaneously. In other words, if the bandwidth of the transmitted signal is smaller than the coherent bandwidth, only the gain and phase of the signal are changed, and this is called ***flat fading***. Suppose the multipath delays are all so much smaller than the symbol period that they are assumed to be almost zero. In such a case, the only distortion in the received signal is a time-varying gain. Such channels do not introduce ISI, and thus require no equalization. Instead, these channels have time-varying outputs, when the signal is strong, error-free transmission periods are expected, and when the signal is weak, periods with error bursts are expected. To combat burst errors, interleaving and burst error-correcting codes are employed. A signal thus undergoes flat fading, if we have the following:

$$T_s > \sigma_\tau, \; B_s < B_c \tag{12.15}$$

Assuming the multipath delays have a large spread, such a channel is called a ***frequency-selective channel*** and results in ISI. When there is no mobility in a frequency-selective channel, the Doppler shift is zero, and the channel is thus time-invariant. An equalizer with modest complexity can minimize the impact of ISI. When there is mobility in a frequency-selective channel, the Doppler shift is nonzero, and the channel is thus time-varying. The time-varying gain of the channel output is also frequency dependent. When channels are time-varying and also dependent on frequency, they are called ***frequency-selective fading*** channels. Such channels are characterized by time-varying ISI, and thus require complex equalization. If the bandwidth of the signal is greater than the coherence bandwidth, the frequencies of the signal separated by an amount larger than the coherence bandwidth will be affected differently by the channel (i.e., fade independently). Since some frequency components in the transmitted signal may fade, whereas other frequency components may not, the signal is said to experience frequency-selective fading. A signal thus undergoes frequency-selective fading, if we have the following:

$$T_s < \sigma_\tau, \ B_s > B_C \tag{12.16}$$

The delay spread usually takes a value of about 2 to 3 microseconds in urban areas and about 5 to 10 microseconds in rural and hilly areas. If the symbol period is less than about four times the root-mean-square delay spread, then the multipath induced ISI generally needs to be corrected so as to ensure the system with acceptable performance. As a rule of thumb, a channel is flat fading if $T_s \geq 10\sigma_\tau$ and a channel is frequency-selective fading if $T_s \leq 10\sigma_\tau$, though this depends on the modulation type used.

12.4 DIVERSITY

In the context of radio communications, ***diversity*** refers to the transmission and reception of various versions of the message signal to combat signal fading and improve the message reliability at relatively low cost. Diversity plays an important role in reducing the effects of fade and possibly other degradations. The rationale behind diversity is that the probability of receiving several replica of the same message signal, where each transmission is impacted statistically independent of the others, is quite low. In fact, diversity techniques can be effective, even if there may exist some correlation among the received signals of the same message signal.

Diversity is now a critical part of wireless communications. In mobile communications, diversity allows the transmit power on the reverse link, which is limited by the battery capacity and is required to protect the link during the short intervals of deep fading, to be reduced. Also, low-signal outage improves voice quality and handoff performance. In addition, in mobile cellular communications which is mostly interference limited, diversity helps reduce the variability of carrier-to-interference ratio, thus improving the frequency-reuse factor and system capacity.

Large-scale fading is caused by shadowing, which is due to variations in the terrain profile and the nature of the surroundings. In deeply shadowed conditions, the received signal strength at a mobile can be much less than that of free space. Large-scale fading is a log-normal distribution. To combat large-scale fading, that is, to significantly improve the average signal-to-noise ratio (SNR), ***macro-diversity*** can be employed. Since shadowing is almost independent of transmit frequency and polarization, frequency and polarization diversity are not effective. The simplest method for macro-diversity is the use of ***on-frequency repeaters*** that receive the signal and retransmit an amplified version of it, but at the cost of additional delay. Another viable method is ***simulcast***, by which the same signal is transmitted simultaneously from different sites, but at the cost of further synchronization.

Small-scale fading is characterized by deep and rapid amplitude fluctuations that occur as the mobile moves over distances of just a few wavelengths. Small-scale fading has a Rayleigh distribution. To combat small-scale fading (i.e., to prevent deep fades from occurring) ***micro-diversity*** can be employed. For instance, with two antennas, one may receive a null while the other receives a strong signal.

There are many ways to achieve diversity, including time diversity, space diversity, site diversity, frequency diversity, polarization diversity, angle diversity, and path diversity, or some combination of these techniques. Most of these techniques are suitable for micro-diversity, except site diversity, which is best suited for macro-diversity. The overall diversity performance is due to the combination of different diversity techniques and how signals are combined.

12.4.1 Time Diversity

In mobile communications, time selective fading of the signal with Rayleigh fading statistics for the signal envelope occurs. ***Time or temporal diversity*** is when the message signal is transmitted multiple times at different time instants separated by intervals longer than the underlying fade duration, so the transmitted copies of the message signal are then likely subjected to independent fading. Time diversity is effective when the time separation between transmissions exceeds the coherence time of the channel (i.e., it is greater than the time between peaks or valleys in the fading signal). The coherence time depends on the Doppler spread of the signal, which in turn is a function of the mobile speed and the carrier frequency. If the channel is static, for instance, when neither the transmit end nor the receive end is on the move, time diversity is not very effective, as the coherence can be quite long. Time diversity is not suitable for delay-sensitive applications, such as voice communications. Time diversity requires storage, additional processing, such as interleaving, additional bandwidth for FEC coding, and additional power for repeated transmissions using ARQ techniques.

12.4.2 Space Diversity

Space diversity, due to its ease of implementation, is widely used in mobile-radio base stations. Space diversity takes advantage of random nature of propagation in different directions. ***Space or spatial diversity*** exploits propagation environment characteristics by employing multiple antennas at the transmitter and/or receiver to create spatial channels, for it is not very likely that all the channels will fade simultaneously. Depending on the physical separation between the two antennas, also known as coherence distance, in a site, signals arriving at the two antennas may be independent or at least uncorrelated. The required spacing depends on the degree of multipath angle spread. In principle, the smaller the angle of arrival between the two signals, the farther the distance between the two antennas must be. For instance, in the cellular telephony, to achieve effective diversity for decorrelation of received signals, a separation on the order of 10 to 20 times the wavelength is required at the base station, whereas the separation on the order of 1 to 3 times the quarter of the wavelength is needed at the mobile.

12.4.3 Site Diversity

Site diversity, as an effective macro-diversity, is a form of space diversity, where different transmit or receive antennas are located in geographically-dispersed sites. Site diversity can thus by definition be applied to base stations in cellular networks or gateway (hub) stations in satellite networks. In satellite networks, site diversity is employed in broadcast satellite systems, as the feeder-link (the link between the hub and the satellite) availability, which is susceptible to rain fade attenuation, is of paramount importance.

12.4.4 Frequency Diversity

Frequency diversity allows the transmission of the same message signal at different carrier frequencies. In order for the received signals to be statistically independent or at least uncorrelated, the carrier frequencies must have a separation that is greater than the coherence bandwidth of the radio channel. The coherence bandwidth depends on the multipath delay spread of the channel. One limitation of this technique is the ability of the receiver to pick up all these signals (i.e., the need for multiple receivers to tune to these frequencies). It is not common to actually repeat the same message signal at two different frequencies, as this would greatly decrease spectral efficiency. Instead, the signal is spread over a large bandwidth, so parts of the signal are conveyed by different frequency components. This spreading can be done by different ways, including multicarrier modulation using an inverse DFT and frequency hopping using widely-separated frequencies from burst to burst.

12.4.5 Polarization Diversity

In mobile radio communications, signals transmitted on orthogonal polarizations experience uncorrelated fading or low fade correlation, as the reflection and diffraction processes depend on polarization. Since the fading of signals with different polarizations is statistically independent, receiving both polarizations using a dual-polarized antenna and processing the received signals independently, known as ***polarization diversity***, offers potential for diversity combining. The cross-polarized antennas do not need large physical separation as needed in space diversity antennas. The only limitation of this technique is the inability to generate more than two diverse signals. There are two ways to achieve polarization diversity. One is that the transmit antenna transmits on both polarizations, thus power for each polarization will be 3 dB lower than if single polarization is used. The other one is due to the fact that the scattering medium can depolarize the polarized transmitted signal. The depolarized signal received at the antenna can be split into two polarizations, producing two independently fading signals. In other words, the transmission is a single polarization and reception is on both polarizations; however, the average received signal strength in the two diversity branches is not identical. In mobile communications, polarization diversity cannot be effective for mobile devices, but can be effective for base stations. As the mobile phone is held at random orientations during a call, the resulting depolarization of the transmitted signal on the reverse link and use of cross-polarized antennas at the base station can make polarization diversity attractive.

12.4.6 Angle Diversity

Angle or angular diversity, also known as pattern diversity, makes use of directional antennas with different patterns that can be pointed in different directions to provide uncorrelated replicas of the transmitted signal, even when mounted close to each other at the receiver site. Angular diversity is usually used in conjunction with space diversity. Antennas with different patterns can see differently-weighted multipaths, even if they are identical antennas and mounted close to each other. Although space diversity is implemented at the base station, angle diversity may be implemented at the base station or at the mobile unit. The different patterns are more pronounced when the antennas are located on different parts of the casing.

12.4.7 Path Diversity

Multipath signals are all time shifted with respect to one another, as they travel different paths. Although multipath is usually detrimental, it can be sometimes beneficial. In ***path or multipath diversity***, the multipath components when they are resolvable and nonoverlapping can be effectively utilized. This implicit diversity is available if the signal bandwidth is much larger than the channel coherence bandwidth. When the time duration of the pulses is very small, such as more than one chip period in CDMA systems or more than one symbol period in high-burst-rate TDMA systems, the multipath signals can be nonoverlapping and uncorrelated.

12.5 DIVERSITY-COMBINING METHODS

Through a ***diversity-combining method***, the multiple versions of the diversity signals at the receiver are combined to provide improved system performance, in terms of reducing the SNR required to deliver an acceptable level of bit error rate. The methods of combining the diversity signals are primarily selection combining, maximal-ratio combining, and equal-gain combining, which can all employ linear receivers. Overall, maximal-ratio combining is the most complex, and has the best performance. On the other hand, selection combing is the least complex, and has the poorest performance.

In describing diversity combining methods, the fading signals in the diversity branches are assumed to be all uncorrelated. In implementation of diversity techniques, however, the signals from the different branches can be correlated. It is important to note that the degradation in performance will not be significant and the performance of the diversity system is still better than that of a system with no diversity. In fact, the performance improvement in SNR due to diversity can go down roughly by a factor of $\sqrt{1-\rho^2}$, where ρ is the correlation coefficient.

Suppose there are M diversity branches and all M Rayleigh fading signals in the diversity branches are statistically independent with equal mean power, and the noise levels are the same on all diversity branches. Suppose γ_n represents the ***instantaneous SNR*** in branch n, where $n = 1, 2, \ldots, M$, and $\bar{\gamma}_n$ represents the ***mean SNR*** of branch n (when no diversity is used). Moreover, we assume each branch has the same average SNR (i.e., $\bar{\gamma} = \bar{\gamma}_n$, for $n = 1, 2, \ldots, M$).

12.5.1 Selection Combining

Selection combining is a very simple technique that is based on the premise that not all signals coming out of diversity branches have low signal values at the same time. As a result, the diversity branch with the highest SNR is selected as the primary received signal and all other signals are discarded. With γ_S representing the ***mean SNR of the selection combiner output***, it can be shown that we can have the following:

$$\gamma_S = \bar{\gamma}\sum_{k=1}^{M}\frac{1}{k} \tag{12.17}$$

Note that by increasing the number of diversity signals M, the performance improves; however, the rate of improvement rapidly decreases. For instance, with four branches, i.e., $M=4$, the mean SNR of the selected branch (γ_S) is 2.08 times (or equivalently 3.2 dB) better than the mean SNR in any one branch ($\bar{\gamma}$).

As it is required, the selection of the largest instantaneous SNR must be made continuously. This requirement is, however, unwieldy. To circumvent this practical difficulty, we may resort to a scanning version of this method, while maintaining almost the same performance. In that, the procedure starts with the strongest output signal, as soon as the SNR of the branch goes below a preset threshold, a new receiver that offers the strongest output signal is selected, and the process continues.

12.5.2 Maximal-Ratio Combining

Maximal-ratio combining is a simple technique that creates a signal that is a linear combination of all available diversity signals with co-phasing and appropriate weighting. The weight of each diversity signal is proportional to the SNR of the diversity signal. Due to fading, the diversity signal levels fluctuate and these weights thus continuously change. With γ_R representing the ***mean SNR of the maximal-ratio combiner output***, it can be shown that we can have the following:

$$\gamma_R=\bar{\gamma}M \tag{12.18}$$

This confirms the intuitive notion that the mean SNR of the output should provide gain linearly proportional to the number of diversity branches. Maximal ratio combining is optimal, as it yields the best statistical reduction of fading of any linear diversity combiner. Its performance is superior to the selection combining, as it takes advantage of multiple signals. However, the price paid is increased complexity. For instance, with four branches, i.e., $M=4$, the mean SNR of the combined signal (γ_R) is 4 times (or equivalently 6 dB) better than the mean SNR in any one branch ($\bar{\gamma}$).

12.5.3 Equal-Gain Combining

Equal-gain combining is a simpler version of maximal-ratio combining, where the diversity signals are added, all with equal weighting, after co-phasing. With γ_E representing the ***mean SNR of the equal-gain combiner output***, it can be shown that we can have the following:

$$\gamma_E=\bar{\gamma}\left(1+\frac{\pi}{4}(M-1)\right) \tag{12.19}$$

Similar to the maximal-ratio combining, the mean SNR for equal-gain combining increases linearly with the number of diversity branches M. For instance, with four branches, i.e., $M = 4$, the mean SNR of the combined signal (γ_E) is 3.36 times (or equivalently 5.2 dB) better than the mean SNR in any one branch ($\bar{\gamma}$). As M increases, the difference between equal-gain combing and maximal-ratio combining becomes much smaller. In fact, it is only one decibel poorer than the maximal-ratio combining even when the number of branches becomes extremely large (i.e., $M \rightarrow \infty$).

12.6 EMERGING WIRELESS COMMUNICATION SYSTEMS

Before embarking on a brief discussion of some of the emerging wireless communication systems, we glance at their evolution.

12.6.1 Evolution of Wireless Communication Systems

The cellular mobile system introduced in the early 1980s was preceded by the pre-cellular mobile telephony technology, also known as **0G *system***. These expensive mobile telephones, available from the 1940s to the 1970s, were usually mounted in cars or carried in briefcases, and there could be only very few mobile users in a given service area, as spectrum could not be reused and thus shared.

The AMPS system, also known as **1G *system***, was the first generation of cellular mobile phones in North America. The system was analog, employing FM modulation and the FDMA access scheme. It was based on dividing the entire service area into smaller areas called cells, and the frequency spectrum divided among a cluster of cells was reused again and again to serve a great number of users in the service area.

In the early 1990s, several digital cellular mobile systems, also known as **2G *systems***, such as the GSM system using FDMA/TDMA access scheme and IS-95 using CDMA access scheme, were introduced. The goal was to enhance system capacity and allow roaming capability. Based on GSM, other systems, such as GPRS, EDGE, came along, and allowed implementation of packet-switching to easily access the Internet and provide higher transmission rates. These systems are known as 2.5G, an informal term, unlike 2G or 3G officially defined by the International Telecommunication Union Radio sector (ITU-R).

The success of 2G, especially GSM, motivated the development of its successor system (i.e., 3G system). The **3G *systems*** were based on a set of standards used for mobile devices, services and networks that comply with the International Mobile Telecommunications-2000 **(IMT-2000)** specifications set by the ITU-R. The IMT-2000 goals were:

- Better spectral efficiency
- Higher peak data rates, namely, up to 2 Mbps indoor and 384 kbps outdoor, with a channel bandwidth of 5 MHz

- Supporting multimedia applications, requiring increased flexibility in the choice of data rates
- Backward compatibility to 2G systems

The following were identified as being IMT-2000 compatible and thus represent 3G systems:

- IMT Direct Spread (IMT-DS, also known as UMTS/UTRA-FDD)
- IMT Multicarrier (IMT-MC, also known as CDMA2000)
- IMT Time Code (IMT-TC, also known as UMTS/UTRA-TDD, TD-CDMA, TD-SCDMA)
- IMT Single Carrier (IMT-SC, also known as UWC-136 or EDGE)
- IMT Frequency Time (IMT-FT, also known as DECT)
- IMT OFDMA TDD WMAN (also known as mobile WiMAX)

Another category of wireless systems is ***wireless local area networks*** (WLANs), which have become quite popular during the past decade or so. WLANs, also known as Wi-Fi, are now standard equipment on all computers and mobile phones. As a cordless phone, such as DECT, provides connectivity to the wired PSTN, Wi-Fi provides high-speed data connectivity to the Internet, where the distance between the phone/computer and the access point connected to the wired digital network is rather short. IEEE 802.11 is involved in the standardization of Wi-Fi. There is a plethora of IEEE 802.11 standards, each with a letter suffix. Of these the standards that are most widely known are the network bearer standards, 802.11a, 802.11b, 802.11g, and now 802.11n. All the 802.11 Wi-Fi standards operate within the 2.4 or 5 GHz ISM frequency bands, while providing peak rates at 54 Mbps over 20-MHz channel for the a, b, and g standards, and 600 Mbps over 20 and 40 MHz channels for the n standard.

12.6.2 4G Systems

The set of high-level requirements of the International Telecommunication Union Radio sector (ITU-R) for the fourth-generation (4G) radio communication standard is known as the International Mobile Telecommunications-Advanced (IMT-Advanced) set of standards. An ***IMT-Advanced*** cellular system, representing the next-generation wireless technology, must fulfill the following high-level requirements:

- A high degree of commonality of functionality worldwide while retaining the flexibility to support a wide range of services and applications in a cost-efficient manner
- Compatibility of services within IMT and with fixed networks
- Capability of interworking with other radio-access systems
- High-quality mobile services
- User equipment suitable for worldwide use

- User-friendly applications, services, and equipment
- Worldwide roaming capability
- Enhanced peak data rates to support advanced services and applications (100 Mbps for high and 1 Gbps for low mobility)

The above general requirements have led to the following specific requirements for ***4G systems***:

- A 4G network must achieve 1 Gbps downlink speed while stationary and 100 Mbps while mobile
- An all-IP packet switched network
- Peak data rates of up to approximately 100 Mbps for high mobility such as travel on trains or cars, and up to approximately 1 Gbps for low mobility such as local wireless access
- Dynamically share and use the network resources to support more simultaneous users per cell
- Scalable channel bandwidth 5 to 20 MHz, optionally up to 40 MHz
- Peak link spectral efficiency of 15 bps/Hz in the downlink, and 6.75 bps/Hz in the uplink (meaning that 1 Gbps in the downlink should be possible over less than 67 MHz bandwidth)
- System spectral efficiency of up to 3 bps/Hz/cell in the downlink and 2.25 bps/Hz/cell for indoor usage
- Seamless connectivity and global roaming across multiple heterogeneous networks with smooth handovers
- Ability to offer high-quality service for next-generation multimedia support
- Interoperability with existing wireless standards

The LTE (Long Term Evolution) and WiMAX (Worldwide Interoperability for Microwave Access) systems are often referred to as 4G systems, though they do not fully comply with the ITU's requirements. The ***LTE*** and ***WiMAX*** are predecessors to ***LTE-Advanced***, standardized by the 3rd Generation Partnership Project (3GPP), and ***Mobile WiMAX 2.0***, standardized by the IEEE 802.16 m, respectively. Table 12.2 highlights major features of LTE-Advanced and Mobile WiMAX 2.0, which both meet IMT-Advanced set of requirements set by the ITU-R.

Before expanding on LTE-Advanced, it is important to note the differences between WiMAX (IEEE 802.16e) and Mobile WiMAX 2.0 (IEEE 802.16 m). The baseline MIMO antenna configuration for mobile WiMAX 2.0 is 2×2, rather than 1×1, which is for WiMAX. Another difference is that mobile WiMAX 2.0 employs carrier aggregation (as discussed in the context of LTE-Advanced) to achieve bandwidths up to 100 MHz.

LTE-Advanced is meant to enhance LTE, and the two standards are thus mutually compatible (i.e., the emerging LTE-Advanced phones will work on LTE

Table 12.2 Major system parameters of 4G and 4G-like systems

	WiMAX (IEEE 802.16e)	4G: Mobile WiMAX 2.0 (IEEE 802.16m)	LTE	4G: LTE-Advanced
Modulation type	BPSK, QPSK, 16-QAM, 64-QAM	BPSK, QPSK, 16-QAM, 64-QAM	QPSK, 16-QAM, 64-QAM	QPSK, 16-QAM, 64-QAM
Access scheme	SOFDMA (128, 256, 512, 1024, 2048)	SOFDMA (128, 256, 512, 1024, 2048), OFDM (256)	OFDMA (downlink) SC-FDMA (uplink)	OFDMA (downlink) SC-FDMA (uplink)
Duplex method	TDD, FDD	TDD, FDD	FDD, TDD	FDD, TDD
Channel bandwidth	5 to 20 MHz, optionally to 40 MHz	5 MHz, 7 MHz, 8.75 MHz, 10 MHz	Scalable to 20 MHz	Scalable to 100 MHz
Peak data rate (downlink)	128 Mbps (20 MHz, 2 × 2 MIMO)	300 Mbps (20 MHz, 4 × 4 MIMO)	300 Mbps (20 MHz, 4 × 4 MIMO)	3 Gbps (100 MHz, 8 × 8 MIMO)
Peak data rate (uplink)	56 Mbps (20 MHz, 2 × 2 MIMO)	135 Mbps (20 MHz, 2 × 4 MIMO)	75 Mbps (20 MHz, 64 QAM)	1.5 Gbps (100 MHz, 4 × 4 MIMO)
Standardization forum	www.ieee802.org/16	www.ieee802.org/16	www.3gpp.org	www.3gpp.org

OFDMA: Orthogonal FDMA, SOFDMA: Scalable OFDMA, SC-FDMA: Single-Carrier FDMA

networks and the current LTE phone will work on LTE-Advanced networks). We now briefly discuss the key enabling technologies that highly distinguish LTE-Advanced from its predecessor LTE.

Carrier aggregation, through which up to five LTE frequency channels or carriers, each as wide as 20 MHz residing in different parts of radio spectrum, can be combined to provide wider bandwidth up to 100 MHz, and in turn achieve higher bit rate, as shown in Figure 12.6. To an LTE device, each component carrier appears as an LTE carrier, while an LTE-Advanced device can exploit the total aggregated bandwidth. There are a number of ways in which LTE carriers can be aggregated: i) intra-band carrier aggregation with contiguous component carriers, in which the aggregated channel can be considered as a single enlarged channel from the RF viewpoint, as such only one transceiver is required, ii) intra-band carrier aggregation with noncontiguous component carriers, in which the multi-carrier signal cannot be treated as a single signal and therefore two transceivers are required, thus adding significant complexity, and iii) inter-band carrier aggregation, in which multiple transceivers with the usual impact on cost, performance and power are required with additional complexities resulting from the requirements to reduce intermodulation.

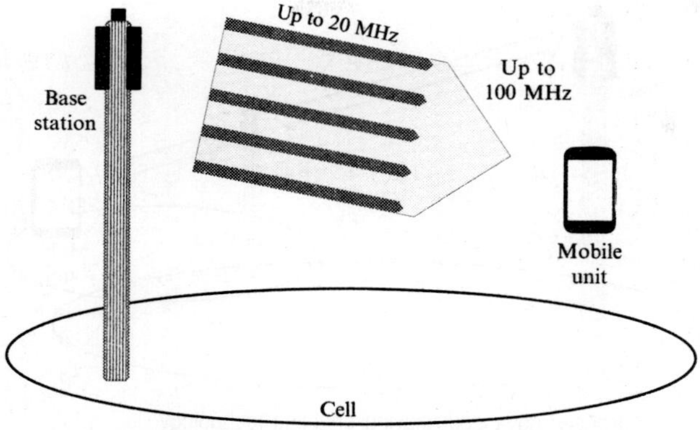

FIGURE 12.6 LTE-Advanced carrier aggregation-enabling technology.

Multiple-input, multiple-output, which allows base stations and mobile units to send and receive data using multiple antennas, as shown in Figure 12.7. LTE-Advanced allows for up to eight antenna pairs for the downlink and up to four pairs for the uplink. When signals are weak and noise is dominant, such as at the edge of a cell or inside a moving vehicle, the multiple transmitters and receivers can help focus the radio signals in one particular direction to boost the strength of the received signal without an increase in transmit power. If signals are strong and noise is low, such as when stationary users are close to a base station, the multiple transmitters and receivers can help increase data rates for a given amount of spectrum. The technique, called ***spatial multiplexing,*** permits a base station with eight transmitters to send eight streams simultaneously to a mobile device with eight receivers. As a rule of thumb, spatial multiplexing, under the best case circumstances, can increase data rates roughly eightfold.

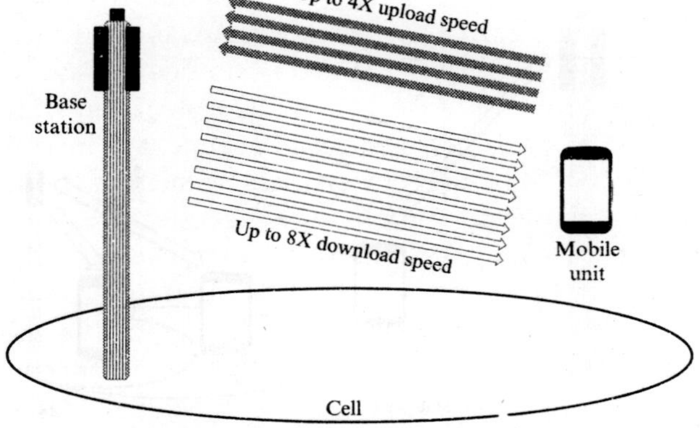

FIGURE 12.7 LTE-Advanced multiple-input multiple-output enabling technology.

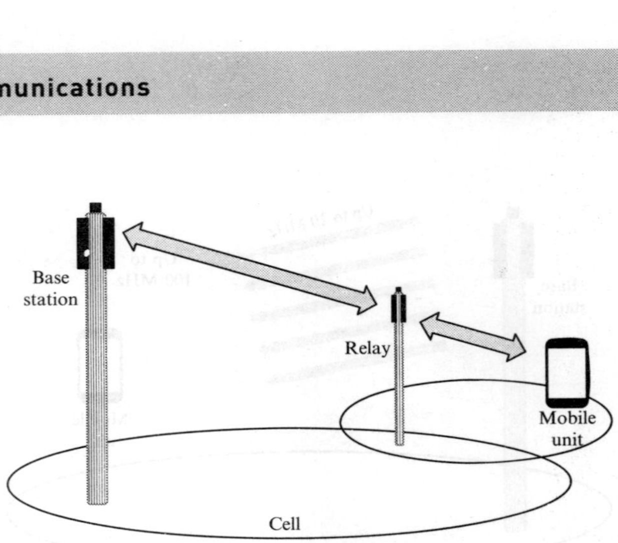

FIGURE 12.8 LTE-Advanced advanced relaying-enabling technology.

Advanced relaying through which capacity and coverage can be enhanced. Relay is effective in mitigating the problem of reduced data rates at the cell edge where signal levels are lower and interference levels are typically higher, as shown in Figure 12.8. Relaying in LTE-Advanced is basically receiving, demodulating and decoding the data, and then re-transmitting a new signal. In this way, the signal quality is enhanced with an LTE relay, rather than suffering degradation from a reduced signal-to-noise ratio when just amplifying and retransmission. The relay, which requires no backhaul connection, avoids interfering with the base station by scheduling its transmissions during certain times when the base station is silent. The merits of LTE-Advanced relaying include increased network capacity, network coverage, and rapid network roll-out.

Enhanced inter-cell interference coordination (eICIC) helps mitigate the interference when small low-power cells overlay high-power larger cells. The two cells coordinate their spectrum use in a dynamic fashion so as to expand the transmission range in the smaller cell, as shown in Figure 12.9. The LTE-Advanced

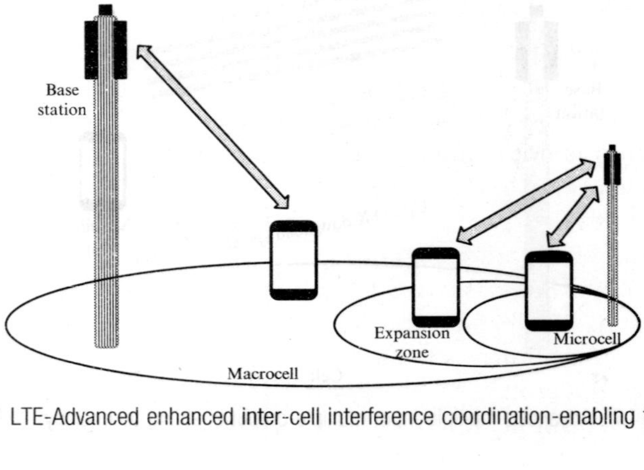

FIGURE 12.9 LTE-Advanced enhanced inter-cell interference coordination-enabling technology.

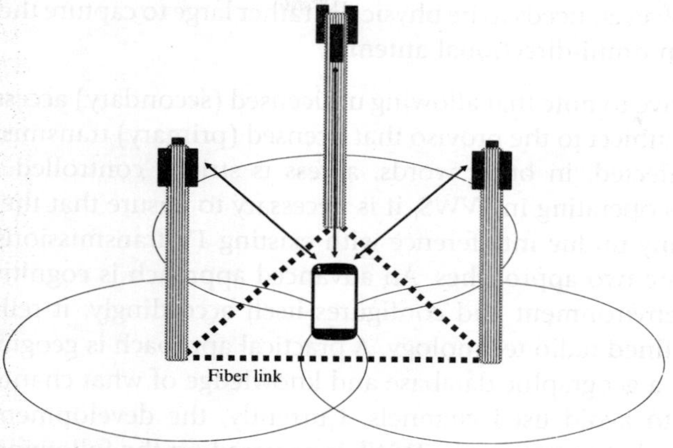

FIGURE 12.10 LTE-Advanced coordinated multipoint-enabling technology.

has developed eICIC techniques, which can be classified into three categories: time-domain techniques, such as scheduling, frequency-domain techniques, such as orthogonal signaling, and power-control techniques.

Coordinated multipoint (CoMP) is a set of complex tools to improve overall quality and increase data rates at a cell's edge by enabling the dynamic coordination of transmission and reception over a variety of different base stations, as shown in Figure 12.10. CoMP can thus bring about many benefits, such as making better utilization of network, providing enhanced reception performance, including a reduction in the number of dropped calls, an increase in received power at the hand set due to multiple site reception, and an interference reduction by utilizing the interference constructively rather than destructively.

12.6.3 TV White Spaces

The term ***white space*** refers to parts of the licensed radio spectrum that licensees do not use all the time or in all geographical locations. ***TV white spaces*** (TVWS) are portions of radio spectrum made available for unlicensed use at locations where spectrum is not being used by licensed services, as also referred to as ***interleaved spectrum***. TVWS are referred to as those currently unoccupied portions of spectrum in the terrestrial TV frequency bands, where the amount and exact frequency of unused spectrum varies from location to location. This spectrum in the United States is located in the VHF (54–216 MHz) and UHF (470–698 MHz) bands. This band has characteristics that make it highly desirable for wireless communications, as radio signals at these frequencies can travel long distances over and around hills and through buildings (i.e., excellent outdoor and indoor coverage and non-line-of-sight propagation properties). The receive antenna, however, needs to be physically rather large to capture the signal transmitted by an omni-directional antenna.

It is imperative to note that allowing unlicensed (secondary) access to these frequencies is subject to the proviso that licensed (primary) transmissions are not adversely affected, in other words, access is strictly controlled. For wireless applications operating in TVWS, it is necessary to ensure that the system does not create any undue interference with existing TV transmissions. To achieve this, there are two approaches. An advanced approach is cognitive radio that senses the environment and configures itself accordingly; it relies highly on software-defined radio technology. A practical approach is geographic sensing that utilizes a geographic database and knowledge of what channels are available so as to avoid used channels. Currently, the development of wireless devices intended to operate in TVWS is centered on the following three applications: machine-to-machine communications, wireless regional area networks, and wireless local area networks.

Machine-to-machine communications (M2M) allows exchanging data between a base station and thousands of machines around it using TVWS with high levels of security. It consists of very low-power radio transmitters used for low-data rate industrial and commercial applications, such as monitoring, tracking, metering and control, giving rise to the concept of smart machines.

Wireless regional area network (WRAN) is intended to operate primarily in a low-population density area in order to provide broadband access to data networks. ***IEEE 802.22*** is the standard for WRAN using TVWS spectrum between 54 and 862 MHz. Its key strength is incorporation of multiple cognitive radio functionalities, and its potential challenges are implementation complexity and cost-effectiveness. A WRAN system is envisaged to be point to multipoint, in that a fixed base station provides high-speed Internet service for up to 512 fixed or portable user devices. A typical operating range may be between 10 to 30 km from the base station with no special scheduling and up to maximum 100 km with proper scheduling, depending on its EIRP and antenna height. While employing OFDM technology and TDD method with asymmetric traffic, adaptive modulation schemes over a channel bandwidth of 6, 7, or 8 MHz can be employed. With a peak data rate of about 23 Mbps, modulation schemes are 64-QAM up to about 15 km, 16-QAM in the range of 15 to 20 km, and QPSK between 20 and 30 km. The downstream medium access is TDM, while the upstream is managed by using an OFDMA system.

Wireless local area network can be employed in TVWS spectrum. ***IEEE 802.11af***, also referred to as ***White-Fi***, is a wireless standard in the IEEE 802 Wi-Fi that allows WLAN operation in TVWS spectrum. Its key strength is utilization of 802.11 standards user experience, and its potential challenge is the uncertainty of the performance of conventional GHz-band WLAN physical layer design in the TV band. Using 6 MHz channels, an array of modulation schemes, which include BPSK, QPSK, 16-QAM, 64-QAM, and 256-QAM, can be employed. With OFDM technology, TDD method, and 4 × 4 MIMO technology, the peak data rate can be as high as about 570 Mbps.

Summary and Sources

The topic of wireless communications is quite broad and an entire book can thus be easily dedicated to it. In here, we just covered some of the major aspects of wireless communications, descriptively. Sklar provides characterization of the Rayleigh fading channels, their degradation effects, and means to mitigate them [1,2]. Diversity techniques and combining methods are described in detail in [3–6]. Reports by ITU provides basic requirements for 4G systems [7,8]. There are many good introductory and advanced books and numerous great papers on wireless communications [9–18]. There are also a number of valuable recommendation, position and white papers by ITU, standardization forums and mobile product manufacturers [19–42].

[1] B. Sklar, Rayleigh fading channels in mobile digital communication systems, Part I: characterization, *IEEE Comm. Mag.* 23 (July 1997) 90–100.

[2] B. Sklar, Rayleigh fading channels in mobile digital communication systems, Part II: mitigation, *IEEE Comm. Mag.* 23 (July 1997) 102–109.

[3] W.C. Jake, A comparison of specific space diversity techniques for the reduction of the fast fading in UHF mobile radio systems, *IEEE Trans. Veh. Tech.* 20 (1971) 81–92.

[4] A.F. Molisch, *Wireless Communications*, second ed., Wiley-IEEE, ISBN: 978-0-470-74186-3, 2011.

[5] T.S. Rappaport, *Wireless Communications*, second ed., Prentice-Hall, ISBN: 0-13-042232-0, 2002.

[6] P.M. Shankar, *Introduction to Wireless Systems*, John Wiley and Sons, ISBN: 0-471-32167-2, 2002.

[7] ITU, *Next Generation Mobile and Wireless Networks Module 3:* 4G Mobile Networks: LTE-Advanced.

[8] ITU, *Next Generation Mobile and Wireless Networks Module 4:* Mobile WiMAX 2.0 (IEEE 802.16 m).

[9] G.D. Gordon and W.L. Morgan, *Principles of Communications Satellites*, Wiley, ISBN: 0-471-55796-X, 1993.

[10] J.D. Gibson, *The Communications Handbook*, second ed., CRC Press, ISBN: 0-8493-0967-0, 2002.

[11] B. Sklar, *Digital Communications*, second ed., Prentice-Hall, ISBN: 0-13-084788-7, 2001.

[12] D.P. Agrawal and Q. Zeng, *Introduction to Wireless and Mobile Systems*, third ed., Delmar, Cengage Learning, ISBN: 978-1-4390-6205-0, 2011.

[13] R.L. Freeman, *Fundamentals of Telecommunications*, second ed., IEEE-Wiley, ISBN: 0-471-71045-8, 2005.

[14] R. Blake, *Electronic Communication Systems*, second ed., Delmar, Cengage Learning, ISBN: 978-0-7668-2684-7, 2002.

[15] R. Price, *Fundamentals of Wireless Networking,* McGraw-Hill, ISBN: 978-0-07-225668-0, 2007.

[16] T. Tran, Y. Shin and O. Shin, Overview of enabling technologies for 3GPP LTE-advanced, *EURASIP J. Wirel. Comm. Netw.* (Springer, 2012).

[17] A.B. Flores, R.E. Guerra, E.W. Knightly, P. Ecclesine and S. Pandey, IEEE 802.11af: a standard for TV white space spectrum sharing, *IEEE Comm. Mag.* 51 (October 2013) 92–100.

[18] C. Sum, G.P. Villardi, M.A. Rahman, T. Baykas, H.N. Transm, Z. Lan, C. Sun, Y. Alemseged, J. Wang, C. Song, C. Pyo, S. Filin and H. Harada, Cognitive communication in TV white spaces: an overview of regulations, standards, and technology, *IEEE Comm. Mag.* 51 (July 2013) 138–145.

[19] S. Bleicher, LTE-advanced is the real 4G, *IEEE Spectr.* (December 2013).

[20] Rohde & Schwarz, *Wireless Communications Standards,* (2013).

[21] ITU, Requirements related to technical performance for IMT-Advanced radio interfaces, Report ITU-R M.2134.

[22] ITU, TV White Spaces: managing spaces or better managing inefficiencies? GSR13 TVWS Discussion paper.

[23] Agilent Technologies, Inc., *Introducing LTE-Advanced,* 2011.

[24] Rohde & Schwarz, *LTE-Advanced Technology Introduction,* White Paper.

[25] Motorola, *TV White Space,* position paper, 2011.

[26] Rohde & Schwarz, *IEEE 802.16 m Technology Introduction,* White Paper.

[27] www.itu.int.

[28] www.ieee.org/16.

[29] www.ieee.org/11.

[30] www.ieee.org/22.

[31] www.ieee.org/15.

[32] www.bluetooth.org.

[33] www.zigbee.org.

[34] www.etsi.org.

[35] www.iso.org.

[36] www.3gpp.org.

[37] www.3gpp2.org.

[38] www.dect.org.

[39] www.wimaxforum.org.

[40] www.weightless.org.

[41] www.wi-fi.org.

[42] www.electronics-radio.com.

Problems

12.1 Consider an antenna transmitting a power of 20 W at 1 GHz. Calculate the received power in dBm at a distance of 10 km if the propagation is taking place in free space and if the loss parameter is 3.5.

12.2 Determine the equation for the distance between any two cells for hexagonal cells.

12.3 In a cellular system using seven cell reuse pattern, the received power at the mobile is −100 dBm, the thermal noise power is −130 dBm, and the co-channel interference from each interfering cell is −115 dBm, calculate the signal-to-noise-plus-interference ratio.

12.4 Consider a mobile phone operating at a distance of 10 km from its own station. A single interfering station is operating at a distance of 20 km from the mobile unit. If the loss factor is 4, calculate the signal-to-interference ratio.

12.5 The transmit power of a base station is 10 W. Suppose the coverage area is to be split in four so the mini-cells of the quarter size can be created to accommodate additional users in the region. Assuming the loss factor is 3.5, determine the transmit power of the base station of this mini-cell to keep the level of interference at the same level as that of the undivided cell.

12.6 Plot the signal-to-noise ratio improvement for various diversity-combining methods in terms of number of branches.

12.7 A typical impulse of a wireless channel is 1 at 1 μs delay, 2 at 2 μs, 3 at 3 μs, and 4 at 4 μs. If the data rate is 1 Mbps, classify the channel as frequency selective or flat.

12.8 Consider an antenna transmitting at 2 GHz. The mobile receive is traveling at a speed of 60 km/h toward the transmitter, while transmitting data at 1 Mbps. Examine whether the channel fading is slow or fast.

12.9 A receiver with 60-dB gain and an effective noise temperature of 1000 K is connected to an antenna that has a noise temperature of 500 K. Determine the noise power that is available from the source over a 40 MHz band.

12.10 In a wireless system, there are three types of interference and the interference levels are 23 dB, 20 dB, and 17 dB, and the noise level is 14 dB. Determine the ratio reflecting the signal to the noise plus interference levels.

Analog Continuous-Wave Modulation

INTRODUCTION

We first discuss analog continuous-wave modulation in a unified context, under which both amplitude modulation (AM) and frequency modulation (FM). For all modulation schemes, we identify the bandwidth and power requirements and present the block diagrams to show how modulators and demodulators are implemented. We then assess the impact of amplitude nonlinearity and noise on AM and FM systems in an overview fashion. The focus then turns toward commercial radio broadcasting. We finally feature some of the trade-offs among various modulation schemes. After studying this appendix and understanding all relevant concepts and examples, students should be able to achieve the following learning objectives:

1. Categorize analog continuous-wave (CW) modulation.
2. Define instantaneous amplitude, phase and frequency in the context of CW modulation.
3. Understand why modulation is a time-varying and/or nonlinear process.
4. Describe DSB, SSB, and VSB amplitude modulation schemes.
5. Appreciate the trade-offs between suppressed-carrier and plus-carrier modulation schemes.
6. Identify power and bandwidth requirements of various amplitude modulation schemes.
7. Explain how AM modulators and demodulators operate.
8. Outline the basic definition of frequency modulation.
9. Distinguish the difference between narrowband and wideband FM.
10. Analyze spectrum of an FM signal.
11. Provide an overview of FM modulators and demodulators.
12. Assess the impact of nonlinearity on AM and FM signals.
13. Express the performance metric for received AM and FM signals.
14. Measure the effect of noise on AM and FM signals.
15. Grasp the role of pre-emphasis and de-emphasis filters in FM.
16. Detail how a superheterodyne receiver operates.

17. Explain the concept behind image interference.
18. List the fundamental aspects of AM and FM radio broadcasting.
19. Show the structure of FM stereo broadcasting.
20. Compare various modulation schemes.

A.1 ANALOG CONTINUOUS-WAVE (CW) MODULATION

There are two basic types of analog modulation: continuous-wave modulation and pulse modulation. In ***analog pulse modulation***, as briefly introduced in Chapter 5, the message signal is uniformly sampled at discrete time intervals, and the amplitude, width, or position of a pulse is varied in one-to-one correspondence with the values of the samples. The focus of this appendix is exclusively on analog continuous-wave (CW) modulation.

In ***analog continuous-wave modulation***, a parameter of a high-frequency sinusoidal ***carrier wave*** $c(t)$ is varied proportionally to the analog ***modulating signal*** $m(t)$ so as to produce the ***modulated signal*** $s(t)$. The ***unmodulated carrier wave*** in analog CW modulation is defined as follows:

$$c(t) = A_c \cos(2\pi f_c t) \tag{A.1}$$

where f_c and A_c are the carrier frequency and carrier amplitude, respectively, and with no loss of generality, the initial phase of the carrier wave is assumed to be zero. A ***modulated carrier wave***, i.e., the modulated signal, can thus be represented as follows:

$$s(t) = A(t)\cos(2\pi f_c t + \varphi(t)) \tag{A.2}$$

where $A(t)$ and $\varphi(t)$ are called the ***instantaneous amplitude*** and ***instantaneous phase deviation***, respectively. When the instantaneous amplitude $A(t)$ is linearly related to the modulating signal $m(t)$, the result is ***amplitude modulation*** (AM). When the instantaneous phase deviation $\varphi(t)$ or its time derivative, known as the ***instantaneous frequency deviation***, is linearly related to the modulating signal $m(t)$, the result is ***phase modulation*** (PM) or ***frequency modulation*** (FM).

AM is referred to as ***linear modulation***, for the instantaneous amplitude is linearly related to the modulating signal. The spectrum of an AM signal is essentially the translated message spectrum and the bandwidth of an AM signal never exceeds twice the message bandwidth. However, FM and PM, collectively referred to as ***angle modulation***, are considered nonlinear modulation, as the superposition principle does not apply. The spectrum of an FM or a PM signal is not related in a simple manner to that of the modulating signal. In addition, the bandwidth of an FM signal or a PM signal theoretically is infinite, and practically is much greater than twice the message bandwidth.

FM and PM are closely related in that properties of one can be derived from those of the other. In this appendix, we will concentrate solely on FM, since FM, unlike PM, is widely used; a prime example is FM radio broadcasting. FM, due to its inherent nonlinearity, is more difficult than AM to analyze and more complex to implement. FM, vis-à-vis AM, offers a high degree of immunity toward noise and robustness toward amplitude nonlinearity, while requiring a significant increase in modem complexity and channel bandwidth.

Figures A.1 and A.2 each show a modulating signal, a carrier wave, and the corresponding AM, PM, and FM signals. In principle, CW modulation allows a slowly time-varying modulating signal $m(t)$, whose spectrum contains lower frequency components, to turn into a rapidly time-varying modulated signal $s(t)$, whose spectrum possesses higher frequency components.

The modulated signal $s(t)$ contains new frequency components that the modulating signal $m(t)$ does not possess. A modulator must therefore be a time-varying and/or nonlinear system, i.e., a modulator cannot be modeled as a linear time-invariant system. The modulation process, however, preserves the main characteristics of the message signal, so that the demodulation process can retrieve the modulating signal $m(t)$ from the modulated signal $s(t)$.

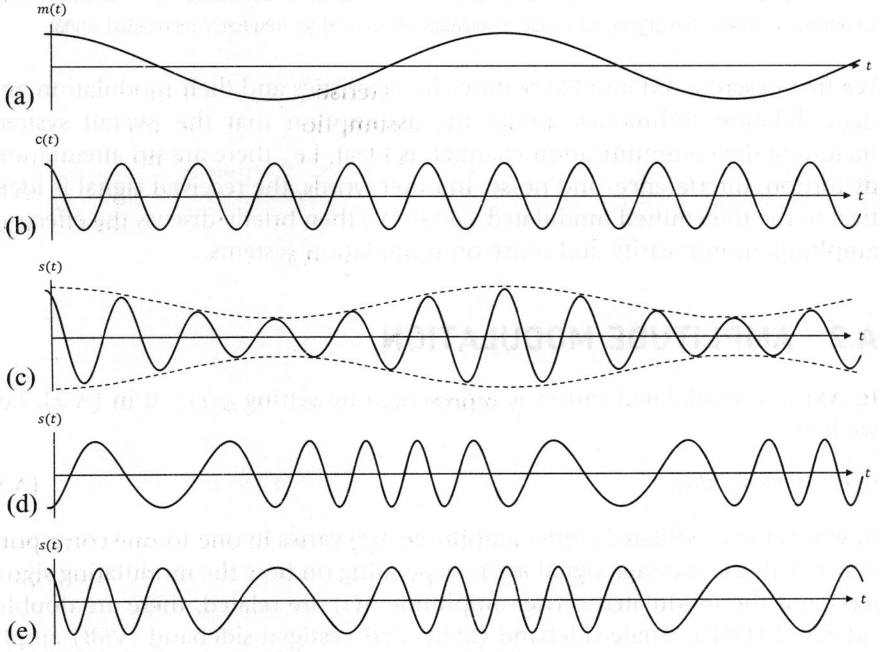

FIGURE A.1 CW modulation for a single tone: (a) sinusoidal modulating signal, (b) carrier wave, (c) amplitude modulated signal, (d) phase modulated signal, and (e) frequency modulated signal.

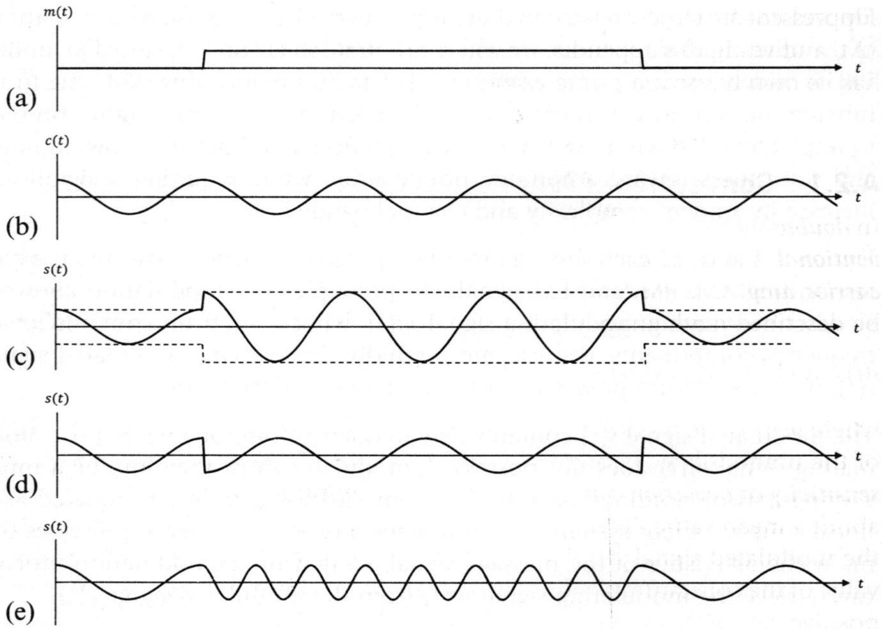

FIGURE A.2 CW modulation for a rectangular pulse: (a) rectangular modulating signal, (b) carrier wave, (c) amplitude modulated signal, (d) phase modulated signal, and (e) frequency modulated signal.

We first describe AM and FM feature characteristics and their modulation and demodulation techniques, under the assumption that the overall system, including the communication channel, is ideal, i.e., there are no attenuation, distortion, interference, and noise. In other words, the received signal is identical to the transmitted modulated signal. We then briefly discuss the effects of amplitude nonlinearity and noise on modulation systems.

A.2 AMPLITUDE MODULATION

In AM, the modulated carrier is represented by setting $\varphi(t) = 0$ in (A.2), i.e., we have:

$$s(t) = A(t)\cos(2\pi f_c t) \tag{A.3}$$

in which the modulated carrier amplitude $A(t)$ varies in one-to-one correspondence with the message signal $m(t)$. Depending on how the modulating signal $m(t)$ and the modulated carrier amplitude $A(t)$ are related, there are double-sideband (DSB), single-sideband (SSB), and vestigial-sideband (VSB) amplitude modulation schemes, each with suppressed-carrier (SC) transmission or plus-carrier (PC) transmission. Our focus here is on the widely known AM techniques, namely, double-sideband plus-carrier (DSB-PC) AM, double-sideband suppressed-carrier (DSB-SC) AM, single-sideband suppressed-carrier (SSB-SC) AM, and vestigial-sideband suppressed-carrier (VSB-SC) AM. Each AM scheme has its own advantages, disadvantages, and applications.

A.2.1 Conventional Amplitude Modulation

In ***double-sideband amplitude modulation*** (DSB AM), also widely known as ***conventional AM*** or ***commercial AM***, or more accurately as ***double-sideband plus-carrier amplitude modulation*** (DSB-PC AM), the modulated signal $s(t)$ may be described mathematically as follows:

$$s(t) = A_c(1 + km(t))\cos(2\pi f_c t) \tag{A.4}$$

where $m(t)$ is the modulating signal, A_c and f_c are the amplitude and frequency of the unmodulated carrier wave $c(t)$, respectively, and $k > 0$ is the ***amplitude sensitivity*** or ***deviation constant***. In a way, the amplitude of the carrier is varied, about a mean value, linearly with the modulating signal $m(t)$ so as to produce the modulated signal $s(t)$. Figure A.3(a) shows a modulating signal $m(t)$. The value of the constant k is chosen in such a way that the envelope of $s(t)$ is always positive, i.e., $|s(t)| > 0$, $\forall t$, as shown in Figure A.3(b). Figure A.3(c) shows when the envelope of $s(t)$ is negative for some range of t.

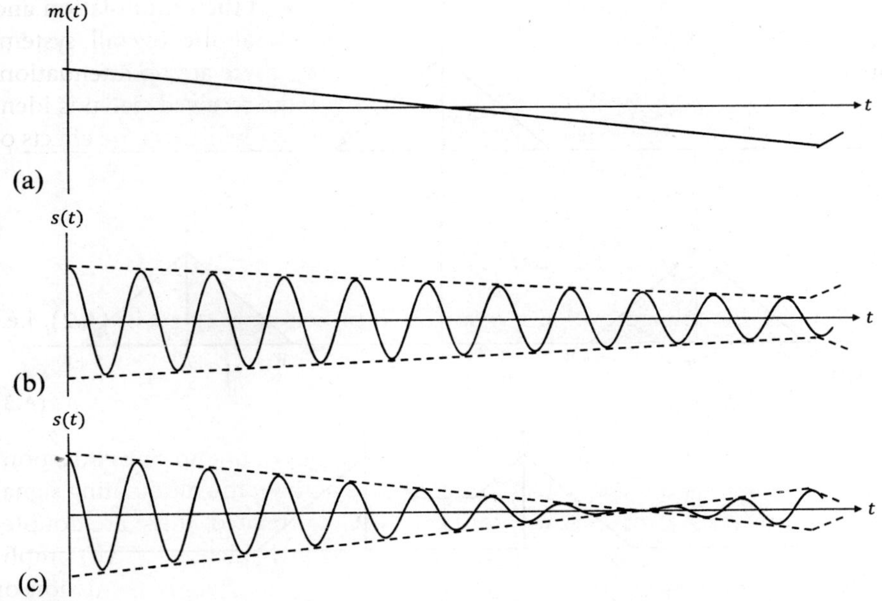

FIGURE A.3 DSB-PC-AM envelope: (a) modulating signal, (b) envelope is always positive, and (c) envelope is not always positive.

Assuming $M(f)$ is the Fourier transform of the message signal $m(t)$, the Fourier transform of the DSB-PC-AM signal $s(t)$ is then given by:

$$S(f) = \frac{A_c}{2}(\delta(f - f_c) + \delta(f + f_c)) + \frac{kA_c}{2}(M(f - f_c) + M(f + f_c)) \tag{A.5}$$

We assume that the spectrum of the modulating signal $M(f)$, as shown in Figure A.4(a), is band-limited to W. Figures A.4(b) and A.4(c) show the spectrum of the modulated signal $S(f)$ for $f_c > W$ and $f_c < W$, respectively.

The envelope of the DSB-PC-AM signal can have the same shape as the modulating signal provided that the following two conditions are both met:

$$|km(t)| < 1, \forall t \tag{A.6a}$$

$$f_c \gg W \tag{A.6b}$$

(A.6a) highlights that with a small enough k, the envelope always remain positive. If (A.6a) is not met, as shown in Figure A.3(c), the DSB-PC-AM signal is then overmodulated and the modulated signal exhibits envelope distortion, i.e., the envelope of the modulated signal does not represent the modulating signal. If (A.6b) is not met, as shown in Figure A.4(c), then the carrier is not oscillating rapidly enough and an envelope cannot be visualized and thus detected. When the above two requirements are both satisfied, an envelope detector, which is a simple demodulator, can be employed.

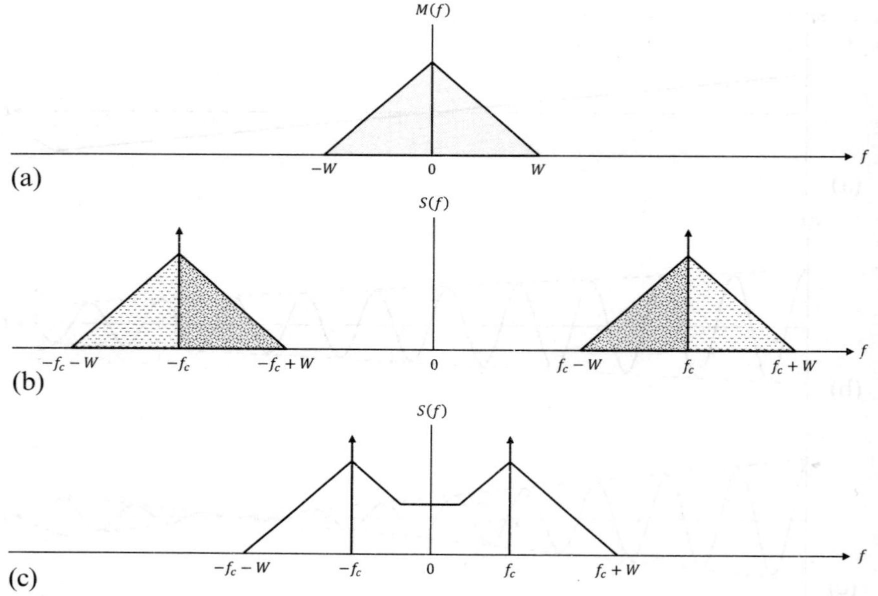

FIGURE A.4 Spectrum: (a) modulating signal, (b) DSB-PC-AM signal for $f_c > W$, and (c) DSB-PC-AM signal for $f_c < W$.

As shown in Figure A.4(b), when the bandwidth of the modulating signal is W, the bandwidth of the corresponding DSB-PC-AM signal is $2W$, as the modulation allows the negative frequencies of the modulating signal to become visible, i.e., measurable. The spectrum of a DSB-PC-AM signal consists of carrier-frequency impulses and symmetrical sidebands centered at $\pm f_c$. The frequency content of the modulated signal $s(t)$ in the frequency band $|f| > f_c$ is called the ***upper sideband*** (USB) and that in the frequency band $|f| < f_c$ is called the ***lower sideband*** (LSB). For the positive frequencies, the USB and LSB are symmetric about f_c, and for the negative frequencies, the USB and LSB are symmetric about $-f_c$. The amplitude and phase spectra of one sideband can thus be determined from those of the other sideband. From the spectrum standpoint, there is thus no need to transmit both sidebands and to require twice as much channel bandwidth. However, bandwidth in the case of DSB-PC AM is wasted so a significant reduction in demodulation complexity can be achieved.

The modulation constraint $|km(t)| < 1$, introduced in (A.6a), implies $-\frac{1}{k} < m(t) < \frac{1}{k}$ or equivalently, $0 < m^2(t) < \frac{1}{k^2}$. The power of the modulating signal $m(t)$ is thus bounded as follows:

$$P_m = \lim_{S\to\infty}\left(\frac{1}{2S}\right)\int_{-S}^{S} m^2(t)dt \leq \frac{1}{k^2} \tag{A.7a}$$

Using (A.4) and (A.7a), assuming the average of the message signal $m(t)$ is zero (i.e., it has no DC component), and utilizing a trigonometric identity, the power of the DSB-PC-AM signal is thus as follows:

$$\begin{aligned} P_s &= \lim_{S\to\infty}\left(\frac{1}{2S}\right)\int_{-S}^{S}(A_c(1+km(t))\cos(2\pi f_c t))^2 dt \\ &= \lim_{S\to\infty}\left(\frac{1}{2S}\right)\int_{-S}^{S}\frac{A_c^2}{2}(1+k^2m^2(t)+2km(t))(1+\cos(4\pi f_c t))dt \\ &= P_c(1+k^2P_m) = P_c + k^2P_mP_c \leq 2P_c \end{aligned} \tag{A.7b}$$

where $P_c = A_c^2/2$ represents the power of the unmodulated carrier wave and P_m represents the power of the message signal. With P_{sb} representing the power of one of the two sidebands, (A.7b) becomes as follows:

$$P_s = P_c + 2P_{sb} \leq 2P_c \tag{A.7c}$$

We can thus conclude:

$$P_{sb} \leq \frac{P_c}{2} \tag{A.7d}$$

This in turn implies:

$$P_{sb} \leq \frac{P_s}{4} \tag{A.7e}$$

As (A.7c) highlights, at least 50% of the total transmitted power P_s resides in a carrier term that is independent of $m(t)$ and conveys no message information. As (A.7e) indicates, no more than 25% of the total transmitted power is required to transmit a single sideband. The conventional (DSB-PC) AM is thus quite wasteful of transmit power.

Since a DSB-PC-AM signal, as reflected in Figure A.4, generates new frequency components, the modulator must therefore be a time-varying and/or nonlinear system. The DSB-PC-AM signals can be generated using various methods, including the switching modulator and the square-law modulator, both of which of course require the use of a nonlinear device, such as diodes, for their implementations. The operation of the square-law modulator is discussed in a problem at the end of the appendix, and our focus here is on the switching modulator.

In a ***switching modulator***, as shown in Figure A.5(a), the sum of the message signal $m(t)$ and the carrier wave $c(t)$, where the carrier amplitude is much larger than the modulating signal, i.e., $A_c \gg m(t)$, is applied to a diode whose

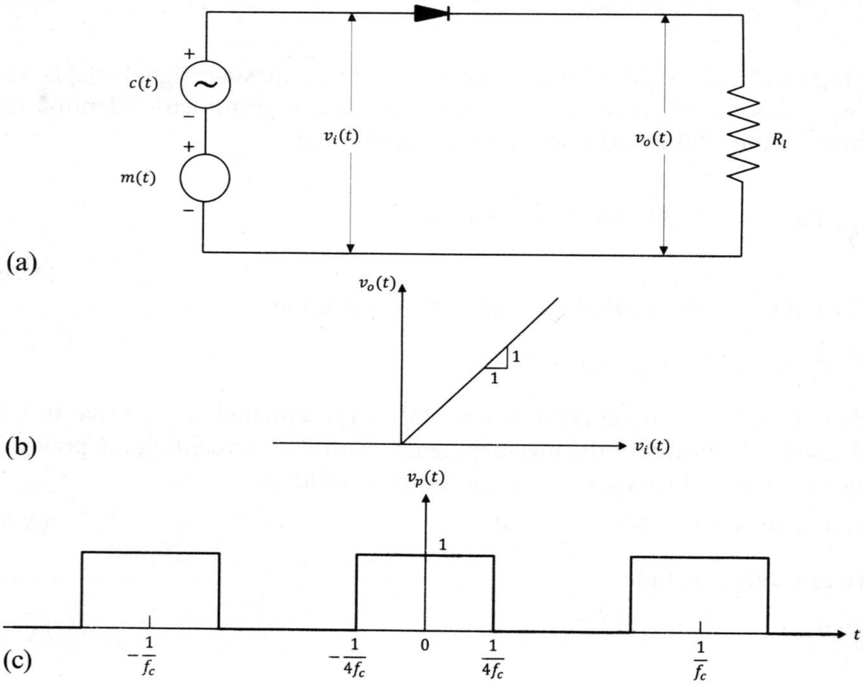

FIGURE A.5 (a) Switching modulator, (b) ideal diode input-output characteristic graph, and (c) periodic pulse train.

input-output voltage characteristic is shown in Figure A.5(b). The diode acts as an ideal switch, i.e., it presents zero resistance when it is forward-biased and infinite resistance when it is reverse-biased. When the input voltage is as follows:

$$v_i(t) = A_c\cos(2\pi f_c t) + m(t) \tag{A.8a}$$

the resulting load voltage is thus simply:

$$v_o(t) = \begin{cases} v_i(t), & c(t) > 0 \\ 0, & c(t) < 0 \end{cases} \tag{A.8b}$$

The load voltage varies periodically between the input voltage and zero at a rate equal to the carrier frequency f_c. This means that the nonlinear behavior of the diode can thus be replaced by an equivalent piecewise-linear time-varying operation. The switching operation may be viewed mathematically as a multiplication of a periodic function $v_p(t)$, as shown in Figure A.5(c), and the input $v_i(t)$. We thus have:

$$\begin{aligned} v_o(t) &= v_i(t)v_p(t) = (A_c\cos(2\pi f_c t) + m(t))\, v_p(t) \\ &\cong (A_c\cos(2\pi f_c t) + m(t))\left(\frac{1}{2} + \frac{2}{\pi}\sum_{n=1}^{\infty}\frac{(-1)^{n-1}}{2n-1}\cos(2\pi f_c t(2n-1))\right) \\ &= (A_c\cos(2\pi f_c t) + m(t))\left(\frac{1}{2} + \frac{2}{\pi}\cos(2\pi f_c t) + \frac{2}{\pi}\sum_{n=2}^{\infty}\frac{(-1)^{n-1}}{2n-1}\cos(2\pi f_c t(2n-1))\right) \\ &= \frac{A_c}{2}\left(1 + \frac{4}{\pi A_c}m(t)\right)\cos(2\pi f_c t) + z(t) \end{aligned} \tag{A.8c}$$

The desired DSB-PC-AM signal, where $k = \dfrac{4}{\pi A_c}$, is obtained by passing the load voltage $v_o(t)$ through a band-pass filter, with bandwidth $2W$ and mid-frequency f_c, so as to remove the unwanted terms represented by $z(t)$. Note that we must have $f_c > 2W$, so the spectrum of the wanted DSB-PC-AM signal on the one hand and the spectra of the unwanted terms on the other hand do not overlap.

There are various devices for the detection of DSB-PC-AM signals, including the square-law detector, which uses a square-law modulator for the purpose of detection, and the envelope detector, which is a simple, yet effective, demodulator for DSB-PC-AM signals. The operation of the square-law detector is discussed in a problem at the end of the appendix, and our focus here is on the envelope detector.

An ***envelope detector***, as shown in Figure A.6, consists of a diode and a simple resistor-capacitor (RC) low-pass filter. During the positive half-cycle of the input signal, the diode is forward-biased and the capacitor C charges up rapidly to the peak value of the input signal. As the input signal falls below the voltage across

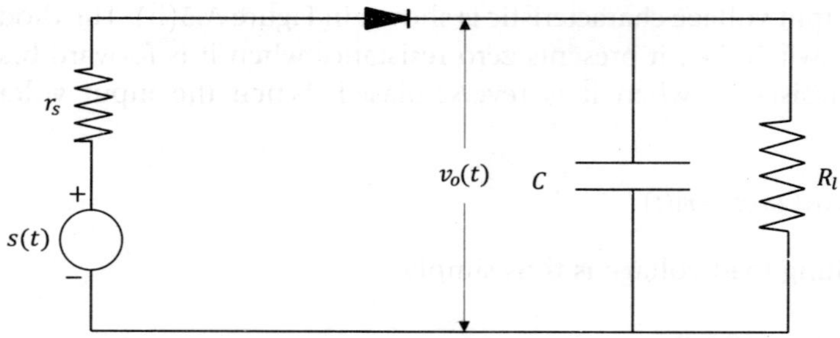

FIGURE A.6 Envelope detector.

the capacitor, the diode becomes reverse-biased and the input disconnects from the output. This is followed by a slow discharge of the capacitor through the load resistor R_l until the next positive half-cycle, when the input signal becomes greater than the capacitor voltage, the diode conducts again. The capacitor charges up to the new peak value of the input signal, and the process is repeated.

We assume the diode is ideal, in that it has zero resistance in the forward-bias region and infinite resistance in the reverse-biased region, and the DSB-PC-AM signal is supplied by a voltage source of internal resistance r_s. The charging time constant must be short compared to the carrier frequency f_c so that the capacitor charges rapidly to follow the voltage to the positive peak value when the diode is in forward-biased region, i.e., we must have:

$$r_s C \ll \frac{1}{f_c} \tag{A.9a}$$

The discharging time constant must be selected to closely follow the variations in the envelope of the DSB-PC-AM signal. Capacitor discharge between positive peaks causes a ripple signal of frequency f_c in the output. If the time constant is too small, the output of the filter then falls very rapidly after each peak and will not follow the envelope of the modulated signal closely. This occurs when the bandwidth of the low-pass filter is too large. If the time constant is too large, then the discharge of the capacitor is too slow and will not follow the fast declining envelope of the modulated signal. Noting the maximum rate of the DSB-PC-AM envelope decline is dominated by the bandwidth W of the message signal, the design criteria for the low-pass filter is thus as follows:

$$\frac{1}{f_c} \ll R_l C \ll \frac{1}{W} \tag{A.9b}$$

By following (A.9b) to design the low-pass filter, the output of the envelope detector closely follows the message signal. As the detector output usually has a small ripple, a low-pass filter is used to remove it so as to smooth the envelope.

A.2.2 Double-Sideband Suppressed-Carrier Amplitude Modulation

In ***double-sideband suppressed-carrier amplitude modulation*** (DSB-SC AM), the modulating signal $s(t)$ is the product of the message signal $m(t)$ and the carrier wave $c(t)$, i.e., we have:

$$s(t) = m(t)c(t) = A_c m(t)\cos(2\pi f_c t) \tag{A.10}$$

Figure A.7 shows a modulating signal $m(t)$ and the corresponding DSB-SC-AM signal $s(t)$. If $M(f)$ is the Fourier transform of the message signal $m(t)$, the Fourier transform of the modulated signal $s(t)$ is then given by:

$$S(f) = \frac{A_c}{2}(M(f - f_c) + M(f + f_c)) \tag{A.11}$$

Figure A.8 shows the spectrum of the modulating signal $M(f)$ and the spectrum of the modulated signal $S(f)$. Apart from a scaling factor, the DSB-SC-AM process translates, i.e., shifts, the spectrum of the modulating signal by $\pm f_c$. As we do not want the spectrum shifted by f_c to overlap with the spectrum shifted by $-f_c$, we require $f_c > W$. The bandwidth occupancy of the DSB-SC-AM signal is $2W$, whereas the bandwidth of the modulating signal is W. The bandwidth requirements for DSB-PC-AM and DSB-SC-AM signals are thus identical. It is also important to note that either one of the two sidebands of $S(f)$ contains all the frequency components that exist in $M(f)$.

DSB-PC-AM and DSB-SC-AM signals are quite similar in the frequency domain, but not so similar in the time domain. The envelope of DSB-SC-AM signal $s(t)$ takes the shape of $|m(t)|$, rather than $m(t)$, and the modulated signal undergoes

FIGURE A.7 DSB-SC AM: (a) modulating signal and (b) modulated signal.

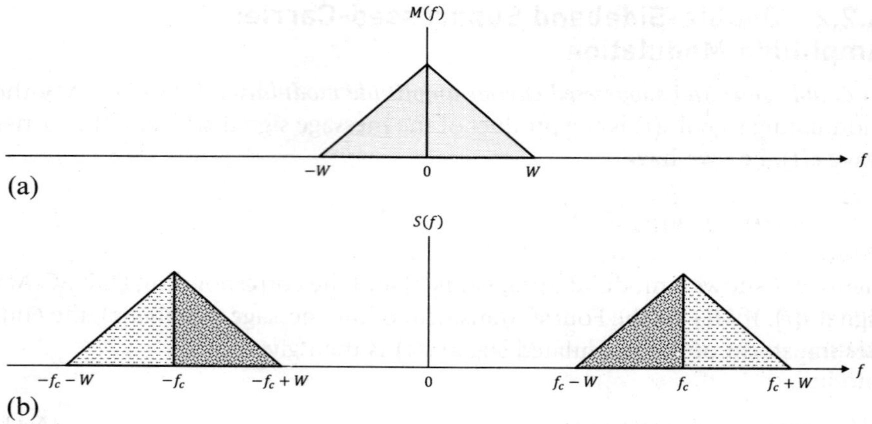

FIGURE A.8 Spectrum: (a) modulating signal and (b) DSB-SC-AM signal for $f_c > W$.

a phase reversal whenever $m(t)$ crosses zero. Full recovery of the modulating signal requires knowledge of these phase reversals, and cannot thus be accomplished by envelope detection.

In DSB-SC AM, vis-à-vis DSB-PC AM, the modulated signal consists of the upper and lower sidebands and not the carrier wave. The transmitted power is saved through the suppression of the carrier wave. The power of the modulated signal is thus as follows:

$$P_s = P_m P_c = 2P_{sb} \tag{A.12a}$$

where P_m represents the power of the modulating signal, $P_c = A_c^2/2$ represents the unmodulated carrier power, and P_{sb} represents the power of one of the two sidebands. (A.12a) in turn means:

$$P_{sb} = \frac{P_s}{2} = \frac{P_m P_c}{2} \tag{A.12b}$$

By comparing (A.12b) and (A.7e), it becomes obvious that DSB-SC AM conserves power significantly.

A DSB-SC-AM signal is simply generated by multiplying the message signal and the carrier wave. This operation is called ***mixing*** or ***heterodyning*** and the device for performing this operation is called the ***product modulator***. There are various forms of a product modulator, including the ring modulator and the balance modulator. The operation of the ring modulator is discussed in a problem at the end of the appendix, and our focus here is on the balanced modulator.

A ***balanced modulator***, as shown in Figure A.9, consists of two DSB-PC-AM modulators so as to suppress the carrier wave. The two modulators must have

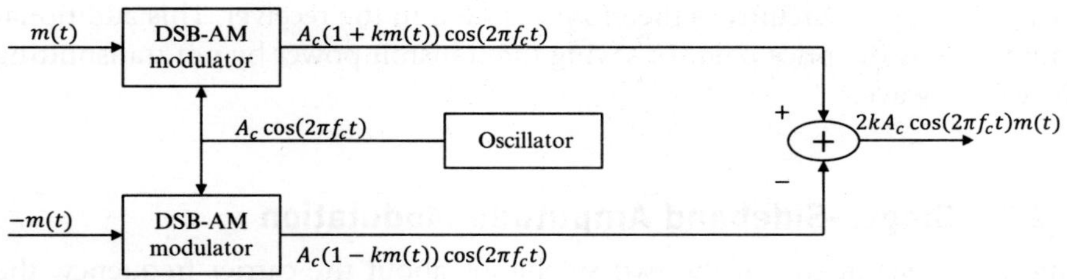

FIGURE A.9 Balanced modulator for DBS-SC AM.

approximately identical characteristics, except for the sign reversal of the modulating signal applied to the input of one of them. The output of a balanced modulator is thus as follows:

$$\begin{aligned} s(t) &= s_1(t) - s_2(t) = A_c(1 + km(t))\cos(2\pi f_c t) - A_c(1 - km(t))\cos(2\pi f_c t) \\ &= 2kA_c \cos(2\pi f_c t)m(t) \end{aligned} \tag{A.13}$$

Except the scaling factor $2k$, (A.13) represents (A.10). As the name implies, the DSB-SC-AM signal does not include the carrier wave. In the demodulation of a DSB-SC-AM signal, the local oscillator signal must then be exactly coherent or synchronized in both frequency and phase with the carrier wave $c(t)$ used in the product modulator. Such a method is known as ***coherent detection***.

If the local oscillator in the receiver has a phase difference φ, measured with respect to the carrier wave used in the transmitter, the output of the product modulator, using (A.10) and a trigonometric identity, is then as follows:

$$\begin{aligned} v_o(t) &= s(t)A'_c \cos(2\pi f_c t + \varphi) = A_c \cos(2\pi f_c t)m(t)A'_c \cos(2\pi f_c t + \varphi) \\ &= \frac{A_c A'_c}{2}(\cos\varphi + \cos(4\pi f_c t))m(t) \end{aligned} \tag{A.14}$$

Figure A.10 shows coherent detection of DSB-SC-AM signal, i.e. when $\varphi = 0$. A low-pass filter, whose cut-off frequency is greater than W but less than $2f_c - W$, can remove all signal and noise components above W, and the resulting signal $\frac{A_c A'_c}{2}\cos\varphi m(t)$ is therefore proportional to the modulating signal when the phase error $\varphi \neq \pm\frac{\pi}{2}$ is a constant. In practice, the phase error is random, and

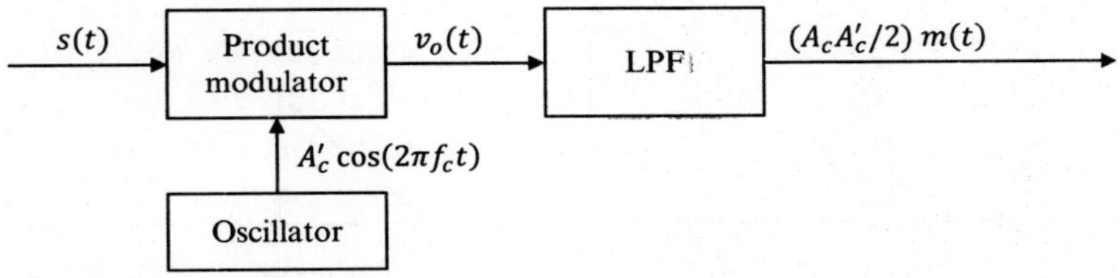

FIGURE A.10 Coherent detection of DSB-SC-AM signal.

a carrier recovery circuitry is therefore required in the receiver. This additional complexity is the price paid for saving the transmit power by not transmitting the carrier wave.

A.2.3 Single-Sideband Amplitude Modulation

Due to the symmetry of the two sidebands about the carrier frequency, the transmission of both sidebands is redundant. In ***single-sideband suppressed-carrier amplitude modulation*** (SSB-SC AM), only one of the two sidebands is transmitted. SSB-SC AM can be employed if the modulating signal has no power near origin, such as speech signals. As shown in Figure A.11, the bandwidth of the SSB-SC-AM signal is W that is the same as that of the modulating signal, and the average transmitted power is as follows:

$$P_s = \frac{P_m P_c}{2} = P_{sb} \tag{A.15}$$

There are fundamentally different methods to generate an SSB-SC-AM signal, including phase shifting using Hilbert transform and frequency discrimination based on selective filtering. The operation of the phase shifting is discussed in a problem at the end of the appendix, and our focus here is on the frequency discrimination.

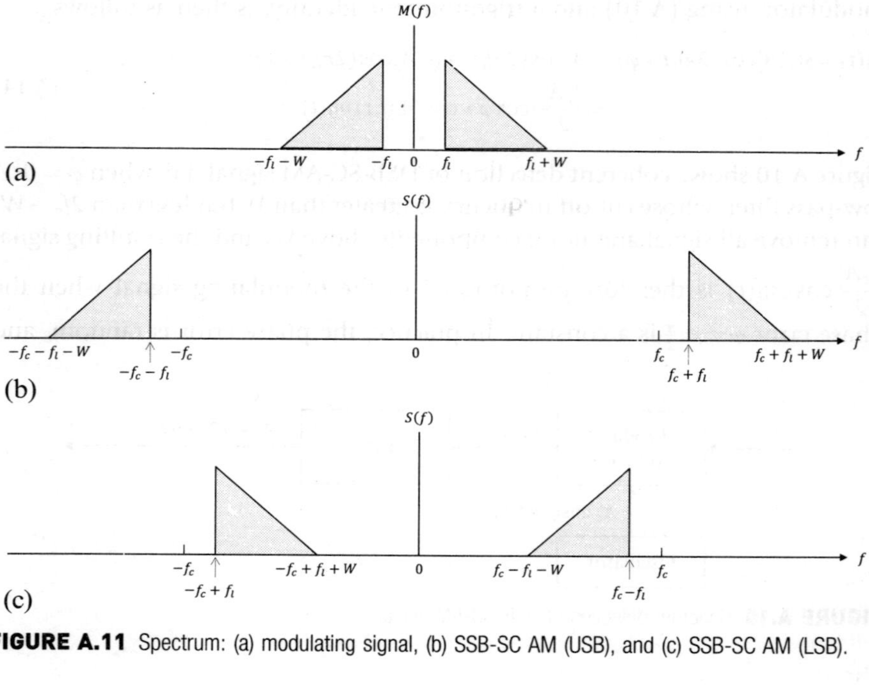

FIGURE A.11 Spectrum: (a) modulating signal, (b) SSB-SC AM (USB), and (c) SSB-SC AM (LSB).

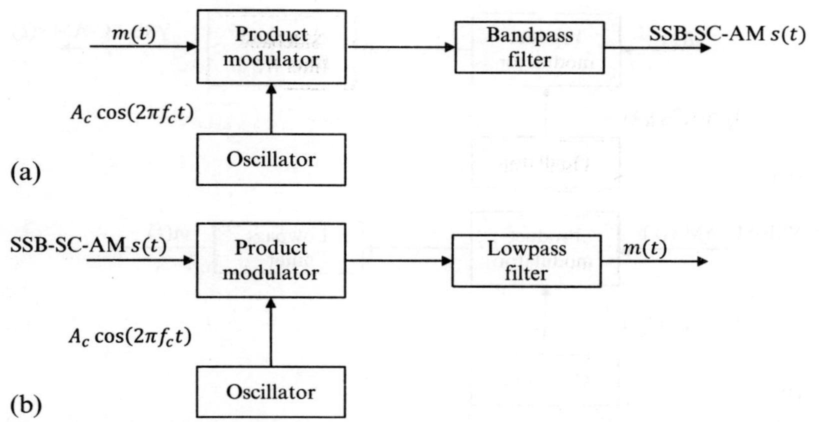

FIGURE A.12 SSB-SC AM: (a) modulator and (b) coherent demodulator.

The modulation and demodulation processes for the SSB-SC-AM signal are functionally simple, but their practical implementations are difficult. In the ***frequency discrimination*** method, as shown in Figure A.12(a), first a DSB-SC-AM signal is generated and then a BPF with stringent requirements is employed to select either the upper sideband or the lower sideband of the DSB-SC-AM signal. The BPF must have a small precise transition band, a passband that passes the desired sideband completely, and a stopband through which the unwanted sideband is rejected in its entirety.

As shown in Figure A.12(b), an SSB-SC-AM demodulation requires a synchronous carrier. Otherwise, with a phase offset, not only the desired sideband is attenuated, but more importantly, the demodulated signal then contains an unwanted component that cannot be removed by filtering. Phase distortion is not considered serious in speech communications, but it has an adverse impact on video and music transmission. An effective approach to avoid phase distortion without using a synchronous carrier in the receiver is the transmission of a pilot tone at the carrier frequency, thus giving rise to SSB-PC AM. This in turn allows the use of simple envelope detection, but at the expense of additional transmit power. This is a trade-off between a reduction in the demodulation complexity on the one hand and an increase in the transmit power on the other hand.

A.2.4 Vestigial-Sideband Amplitude Modulation

A modulation scheme that offers the best compromise among bandwidth conservation, improved low-frequency response, and power saving is the ***vestigial-sideband suppressed-carrier amplitude modulation*** (VSB-SC AM). In VSB-SC AM, the design of the sideband filter is simplified at the expense of a modest increase in the channel bandwidth required to transmit the modulated signal.

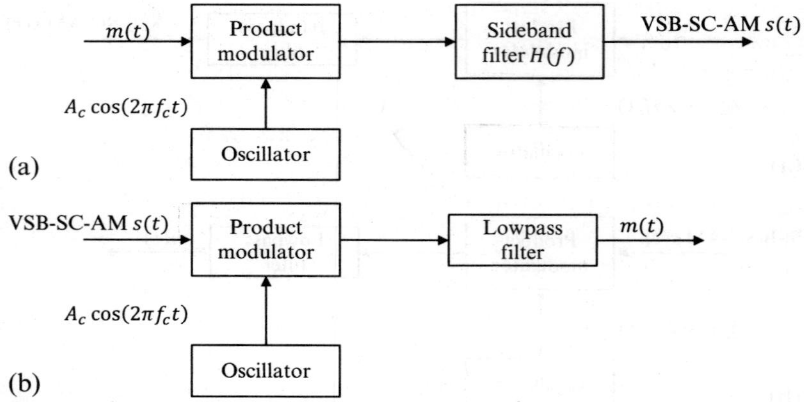

FIGURE A.13 VSB-SC AM: (a) modulator and (b) coherent demodulator.

VSB-SC AM is attractive for signals with significant low-frequency components, such as video signals.

Figure A.13 shows the VSB-SC-AM modulation and demodulation. A VSB-SC-AM signal is derived by filtering a DSB-SC-AM signal in a way that one sideband is passed in almost entirety while only a trace of the unwanted sideband is included. Note that the transmitted vestige of the unwanted sideband compensates for the amount removed from the wanted sideband. An essential requirement for the VSB-SC-AM filter $H(f)$ is that it must have an odd symmetry about f_c and a relative response of 0.5 at f_c. More specifically, as shown in Figure A.14, the transfer function of the sideband filter $H(f)$ must meet the following requirement:

$$H(f-f_c)+H(f+f_c)=2H(f_c)=1, \quad |f|\le W \tag{A.16}$$

where W represents the message bandwidth. Inside the transition band $f_c-\alpha \le |f| \le f_c+\alpha$, the sum of the values of $|H(f)|$ at any two frequencies whose arithmetic mean is f_c is unity, where α is the width of the vestigial sideband.

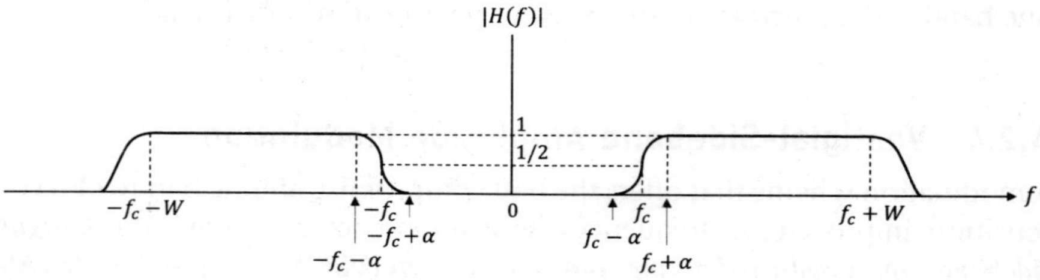

FIGURE A.14 Amplitude response of VSB-AM sideband filter for LSB.

Also, outside the frequency band of interest $|f| > f_c + W$, the transfer function $H(f)$ may meet arbitrary requirements. Note that the VSB-SC-AM sideband filter has a transition band of width 2α, the transmission bandwidth of the VSB-SC-AM signal is $W + \alpha$, where $\alpha < W$. The value of α typically ranges between 15% and 35% of the message bandwidth W. If the vestigial sideband is increased to the width of a full sideband, i.e., $\alpha = W$, the resulting modulated signal becomes a DSB-SC-AM signal, if, on the other hand, the width of the vestigial sideband is reduced to zero, i.e., $\alpha = 0$, the resulting modulated signal becomes an SSB-SC-AM signal. The average transmitted power for a VSB-SC-AM signal is as follows:

$$\frac{P_m P_c}{2} \leq P_s \leq P_m P_c \tag{A.17}$$

which depends on the vestige width α. For instance, when we have $\alpha = 0$, the lower bound in (A.17) is satisfied, and when $\alpha = 1$, the upper bound is met.

Once again to avoid coherent detection, transmission of a large carrier component along with the message is a viable option, thus resulting in VSB-PC AM. For instance, in the NTSC TV broadcast, the received VSB-PC-AM signal is demodulated using envelope detection. Overall, VSB AM is a compromise between SSB AM and DSB AM, unlike SSB AM, it does not require an energy gap at the origin, and unlike DSB AM, the bandwidth is only somewhat greater than that of SSB AM.

EXAMPLE A.1

Suppose the modulating signal is a sinusoidal signal with amplitude A_m and frequency f_m, and the sinusoidal carrier wave has amplitude A_c and frequency $f_c > f_m$. For all amplitude modulation schemes, determine the expressions for the modulated signal in both the time-domain $s(t)$ and the frequency domain $S(f)$.

Solution

Figure A.15 shows the modulating signal

$$m(t) = A_m \cos(2\pi f_m t)$$

and the carrier wave

$$c(t) = A_c \cos(2\pi f_c t)$$

along with the modulated signals in the time domain $s(t)$, and Figure A.16 shows their Fourier transforms

$$M(f) = 0.5A_m(\delta(f - f_m) + \delta(f + f_m))$$

and

$$C(f) = 0.5A_c(\delta(f - f_c) + \delta(f + f_c))$$

along with the Fourier transforms $S(f)$ of the modulated signals.

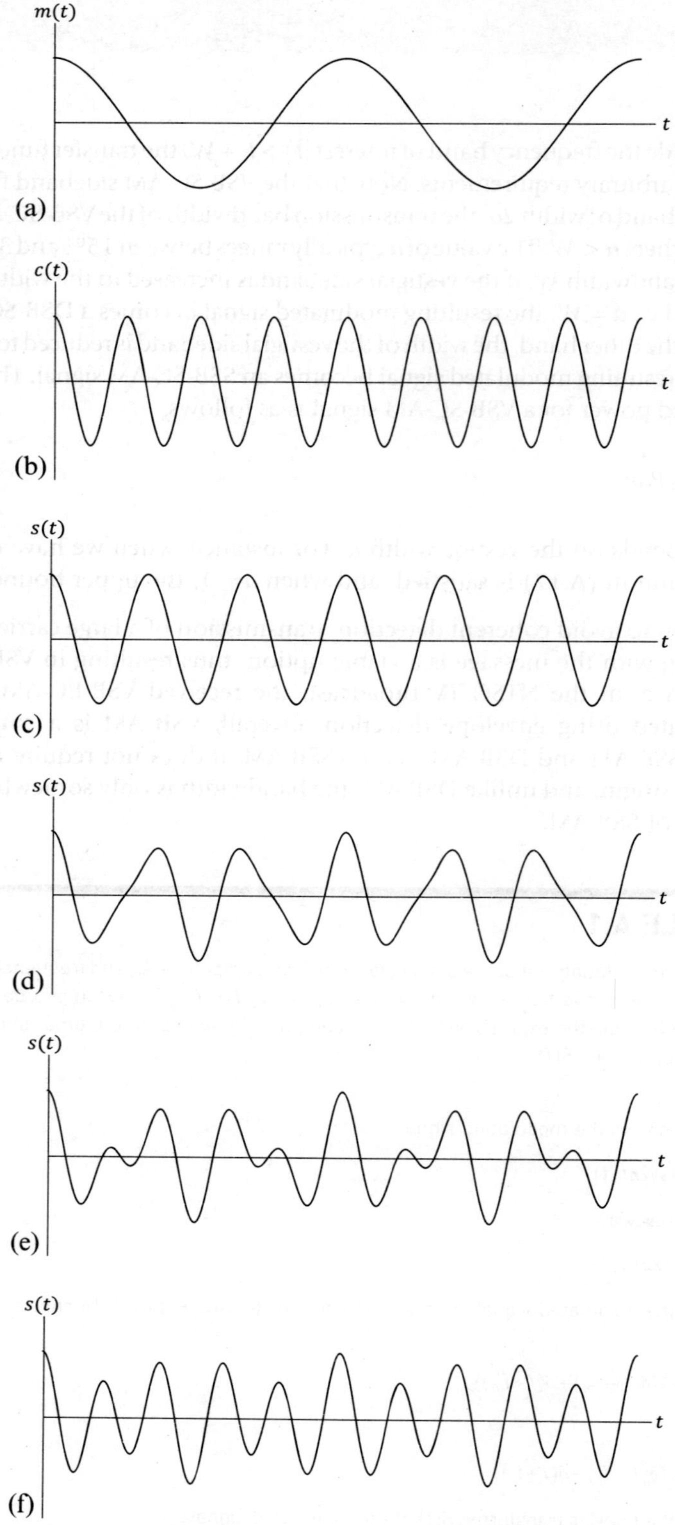

FIGURE A.15 Signals in the time domain: (a) modulating signal, (b) carrier wave,

(Continued)

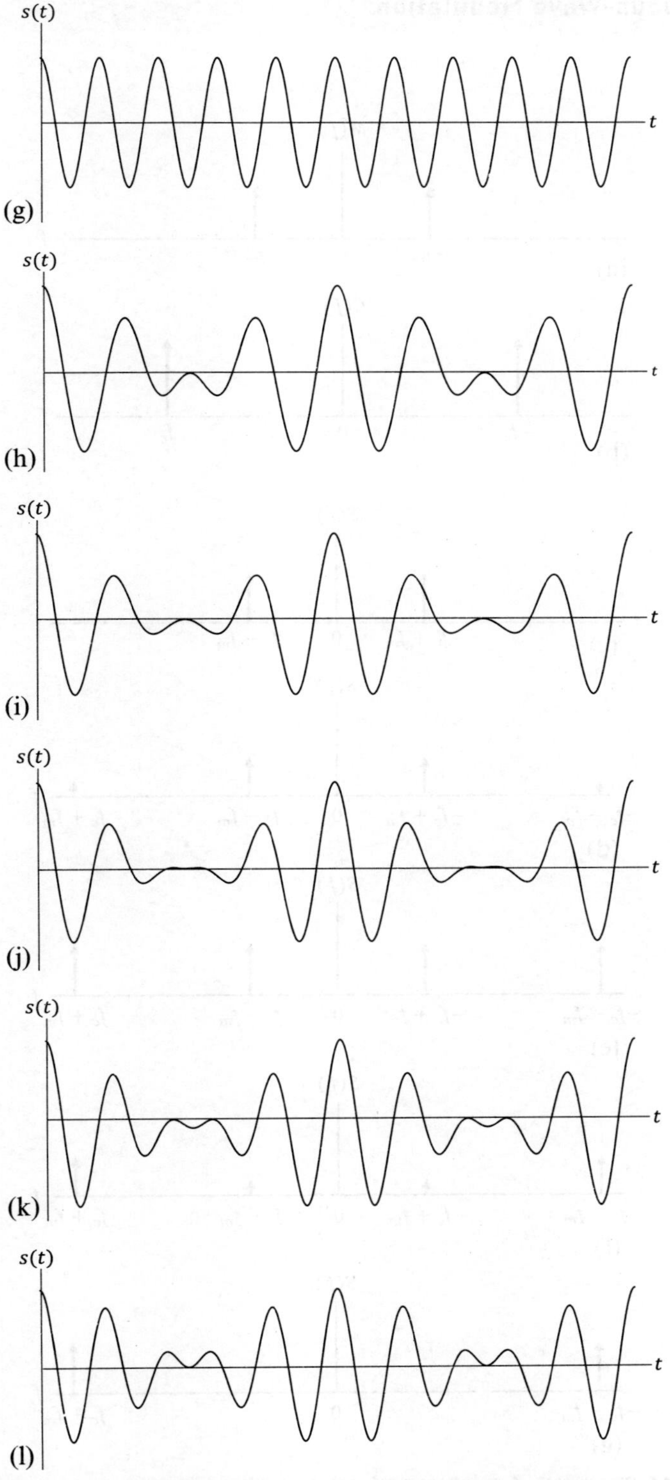

FIGURE A.15, cont'd (c) SSB-SC (LSB), (d) VSB-SC (LSB), (e) DSB-SC, (f) VSB-SC (USB), (g) SSB-SC (USB), (h) SSB-PC (LSB), (i) VSB-PC (LSB), (j) DSB-PC, (k) VSB-PC (USB), and (l) SSB-PC (USB).

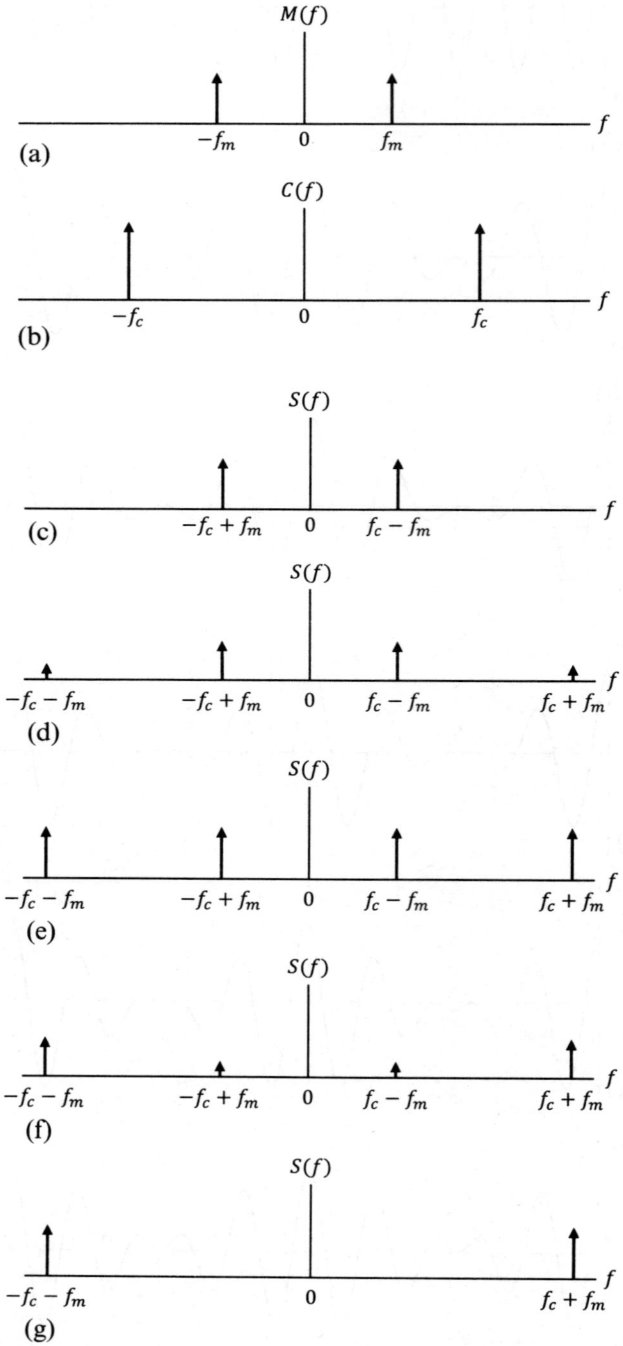

FIGURE A.16 Signals in the frequency domain: (a) modulating signal, (b) carrier wave, (c) SSB-SC (LSB), (d) VSB-SC (LSB), (e) DSB-SC, (f) VSB-SC (USB), (g) SSB-SC (USB),

(Continued)

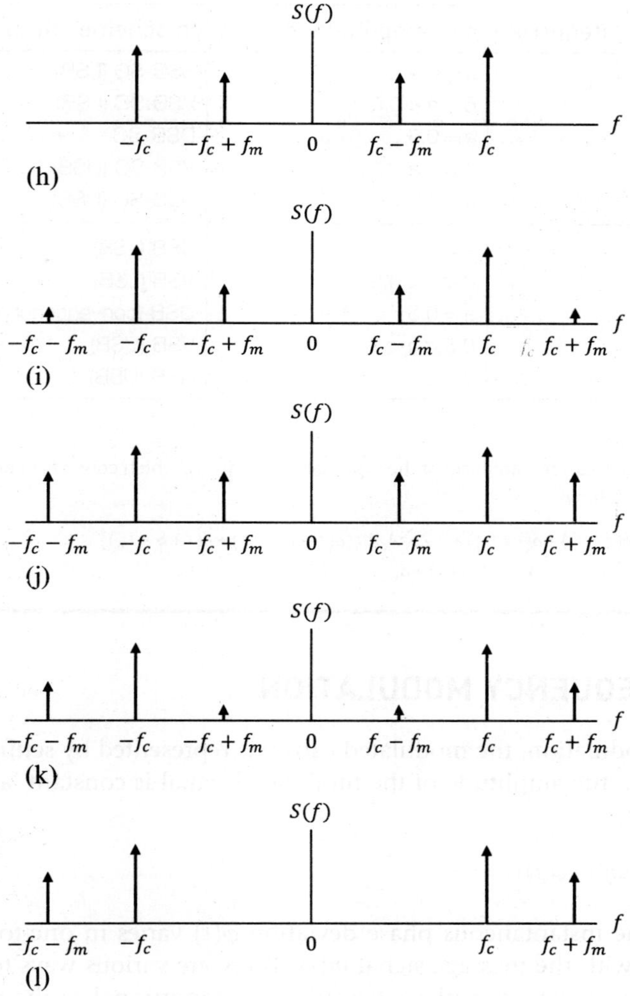

FIGURE A.16, cont'd (h) SSB-PC (LSB), (i) VSB-PC (LSB), (j) DSB-PC, (k) VSB-PC (USB), and (l) SSB-PC (USB).

In deriving the modulated signals in the time domain, we utilize the trigonometric identity $2\cos A \cos B = \cos(A+B) + \cos(A-B)$. For the special case of sinusoidal modulation, the modulated signals $s(t)$ for all amplitude modulation schemes can be thus written in the following common form:

$$s(t) = bA_c\cos(2\pi f_c t) + 0.5aA_cA_m\cos(2\pi(f_c+f_m)t) + 0.5(1-a)A_cA_m\cos(2\pi(f_c-f_m)t)$$

where a, a constant representing the attenuation of the upper-sideband, and b, a constant reflecting the carrier wave transmission, are both defined in Table A.1 for different types of amplitude

Table A.1 Categorization of amplitude modulation schemes in Example A.1

	$a=0$	SSB-SC (LSB)
	$0<a<0.5$	VSB-SC (LSB)
$b=0$ (SC)	$a=0.5$	DSB-SC
	$0.5<a<1$	VSB-SC (USB)
	$a=1$	SSB-SC (USB)
	$a=0$	SSB (LSB)
	$0<a<0.5$	VSB (LSB)
$b=1$ (PC)	$a=0.5$	DSB (conventional AM, $k=0.5$)
	$0.5<a<1$	VSB (USB)
	$a=1$	SSB (USB)

modulation. The Fourier transform of the modulated signal $s(t)$, which consists of delta functions, is therefore as follows:

$$S(f)=0.5bA_c(\delta(f-f_c)+\delta(f+f_c))+0.25aA_cA_m(\delta(f-f_c-f_m)+\delta(f+f_c+f_m))$$
$$+0.25(1-a)A_cA_m(\delta(f-f_c+f_m)+\delta(f+f_c-f_m))$$

A.3 FREQUENCY MODULATION

In angle modulation, the modulated carrier is represented by setting $A(t)=A_c$ in (A.2), i.e., the amplitude of the modulated signal is constant, and we thus have:

$$s(t)=A_c\cos(2\pi f_c t+\varphi(t)) \quad \text{(A.18)}$$

in which the instantaneous phase deviation $\varphi(t)$ varies in one-to-one correspondence with the message signal $m(t)$. There are various ways to vary $\varphi(t)$. In PM, the instantaneous phase deviation is proportional to the modulating signal $m(t)$, and in FM, the instantaneous frequency deviation, i.e., the derivative of the instantaneous phase deviation with respect to time, is proportional to the modulating signal $m(t)$. As mentioned earlier, our focus is exclusively on FM.

A.3.1 Representation of FM Signals

In FM, the instantaneous frequency is equal to the constant frequency of the unmodulated carrier wave plus a time-varying component that is proportional to the modulating signal, as shown by:

$$f(t)=f_c+km(t) \quad \text{(A.19)}$$

where $k > 0$ is the **frequency sensitivity** or **deviation constant** and $km(t)$ represents the **instantaneous frequency deviation**. Assuming the initial phase deviation is zero, i.e., $\varphi(0) = 0$, the **instantaneous phase deviation** is thus as follows:

$$\varphi(t) = 2\pi k \int_0^t m(s)ds \tag{A.20}$$

By substituting (A.20) into (A.18), the ***FM signal*** can therefore be described in the time domain as follows:

$$s(t) = A_c \cos\left(2\pi f_c t + 2\pi k \int_0^t m(s)ds\right) \tag{A.21}$$

If we assume $|\varphi(t)| \ll 1$, for all time t, we then have $\cos\varphi(t) \cong 1$ and $\sin\varphi(t) \cong \varphi(t)$. By using (A.18) and (A.20), (A.21) can be expanded and then approximated as follows:

$$\begin{aligned} s(t) &= A_c(\cos(2\pi f_c t)\cos\varphi(t) - \sin(2\pi f_c t)\sin\varphi(t)) \\ &\cong A_c \cos(2\pi f_c t) - A_c \sin(2\pi f_c t)\varphi(t) \\ &\cong A_c \cos(2\pi f_c t) - A_c\left(2\pi k \int_0^t m(s)ds\right)\sin(2\pi f_c t) \end{aligned} \tag{A.22}$$

(A.22) represents a narrowband FM (NB FM) signal. Note that an NB-FM signal is similar to a DSB-PC-AM signal, the only difference is that the message in NB FM is first integrated, then scaled and modulated on a sine carrier. The NB-FM is not widely used in practice; however, it is often a stepping stone for the generation of wideband FM (WB-FM) signals.

A.3.2 Spectral Analysis of FM Signals

By using a power series to expand (A.18), we can show that the FM signal consists of an unmodulated carrier $\cos(2\pi f_c t)$ plus an infinite number of amplitude-modulated terms, such as $\varphi(t)\sin(2\pi f_c t)$, $\varphi^2(t)\cos(2\pi f_c t)$, $\varphi^3(t)\sin(2\pi f_c t)$, ... Hence, the spectrum consists of an unmodulated carrier plus spectra of $\varphi(t)$, $\varphi^2(t)$, $\varphi^3(t)$, ..., all centered at $\pm f_c$. The spectral analysis of FM, due to its inherent nonlinearity, is thus conceptually quite complicated and mathematically rather intractable. To this effect, we first study the simplest possible case, namely, when the modulating signal is only a single tone. We then generalize the results, to the extent possible, to the more complicated message signals. When the modulating signal is a pure sinusoidal, we have:

$$m(t) = A_m \cos(2\pi f_m t) \tag{A.23}$$

Using (A.19), the instantaneous frequency of the resulting FM wave is then defined by:

$$f(t) = f_c + kA_m \cos(2\pi f_m t) = f_c + \Delta f \cos(2\pi f_m t) \quad \text{(A.24)}$$

where Δf, which is called the ***frequency deviation***, is defined as follows:

$$\Delta f = kA_m \quad \text{(A.25)}$$

The frequency deviation, which represents the maximum departure of the instantaneous frequency of the FM signal from the carrier frequency f_c, is proportional to the peak amplitude of the modulating signal, and is independent of the modulating frequency f_m. Using (A.20), the instantaneous phase deviation of the resulting FM wave is defined by:

$$\varphi(t) = \beta \sin(2\pi f_m t) \quad \text{(A.26)}$$

where β, which is called the ***modulation index***, is defined as follows:

$$\beta = \frac{\Delta f}{f_m} \quad \text{(A.27)}$$

Using (A.18) and (A.26), the FM signal is then given by:

$$s(t) = A_c \cos(2\pi f_c t + \beta \sin(2\pi f_m t)) \quad \text{(A.28)}$$

By using the Fourier series representation, (A.28) can be expressed as follows:

$$s(t) = A_c \sum_{n=-\infty}^{\infty} J_n(\beta) \cos(2\pi (f_c + n f_m) t) \quad \text{(A.29)}$$

where $J_n(\beta)$ is the Bessel function of the first kind of order n and argument β. The Fourier transform of (A.29) is then as follows:

$$S(f) = \frac{A_c}{2} \sum_{n=-\infty}^{\infty} J_n(\beta)(\delta(f - f_c - n f_m) + \delta(f + f_c + n f_m)) \quad \text{(A.30)}$$

Although the modulating signal has only one frequency component f_m, (A.30) reveals that the spectrum of the corresponding FM signal consists of a carrier component plus an infinite number of side components at frequencies $f_c \pm n f_m$, where n is a nonnegative integer. Therefore, the actual bandwidth of the modulated signal is infinite. However, the relative amplitudes of the spectral lines for large n is very small. The number of significant spectral lines is an increasing function of the modulation index β.

When the frequency f_m is fixed and the amplitude A_m is increased, the frequency deviation Δf and the modulation index β are both proportionally increased. This means that the number of significant spectral lines is increased and the frequency between two adjacent spectral components remain unchanged. However, when the amplitude A_m is fixed and the frequency f_m is decreased, the frequency deviation Δf remains unchanged, but the modulation index β is proportionally increased. This means that we have an increasing number of spectral lines crowding into the fixed frequency band $2\Delta f$.

Since the amplitude of an FM signal is always constant, then regardless of the message bandwidth, the ***average transmitted power of an FM signal*** is as follows:

$$P_{FM} = \frac{A_c^2}{2} \sum_{n=-\infty}^{\infty} J_n^2(\beta) = \frac{A_c^2}{2} \tag{A.31}$$

On the other hand, the total power contained in the carrier plus n sidebands on each side of the carrier is as follows:

$$P_k = \frac{A_c^2}{2} \sum_{n=-k}^{k} J_n^2(\beta) \tag{A.32}$$

Based on experimental evidence, if at least 98% of the FM signal power is contained within the transmission bandwidth, i.e., $\frac{P_k}{P_{FM}} \geq 98\%$, the distortion to the message signal is negligible.

With a single-tone modulating signal of frequency f_m, the bandwidth of the modulated signal approaches $2\Delta f$, when the modulation index β is large, and the bandwidth of the modulated signal approaches $2f_m$, when the modulation index β is small. Based on the 98% approximation rule, the transmission bandwidth of an FM signal generated by a single-tone modulating signal of frequency f_m can be approximated as follows:

$$BW_{FM} \cong 2(\Delta f + f_m) = 2f_m(\beta + 1) \tag{A.33}$$

For arbitrary modulating signal $m(t)$, a generally accepted expression for the ***transmission bandwidth of an FM signal*** is as follows:

$$BW_{FM} \cong 2W(D+1) \tag{A.34}$$

where W is the message bandwidth and the ***deviation ratio*** D is defined as follows:

$$D = \frac{\Delta f}{W} \tag{A.35}$$

This relation is known as ***Carson's rule***. Note that if $D \ll 1$, the bandwidth of the modulated signal is approximately $2W$, and the signal is known as a ***narrowband FM*** (NB FM), and if $D \gg 1$, the bandwidth signal is approximately $2DW = 2\Delta f$, which is twice the peak frequency deviation, and the signal is known as a ***wideband FM*** (WB FM).

A.3.3 FM Modulation and Demodulation

There are two methods for generating FM signals: the direct method and the indirect method. In the ***direct method***, the carrier frequency is directly varied according to the modulating signal by means of a ***voltage controlled oscillator*** (VCO). In a VCO, when the input voltage is zero, the VCO generates a sinusoid with the carrier frequency, when the input voltage changes, the frequency changes. There are two approaches to design a VCO. One approach is to use a variable capacitor whose capacitance depends on the voltage applied across it, and the other is to use a variable inductor whose inductance is varied by the current passing through it. The advantage of the direct method is that it can yield sufficiently large frequency deviation with no frequency multiplication, and its drawback is its poor frequency stability, thus warranting additional circuitry for frequency stabilization.

In the ***indirect method***, a narrowband FM (NB-FM) signal, as derived in (A.22), is first generated. Figure A.17(a) shows its implementation, and highlights the similarity of conventional AM signals and NB-FM signals. Next, as shown in Figure A.17(b), the NB-FM signal is converted to a wideband FM (WB-FM) signal using a frequency multiplier that multiplies the instantaneous frequency of the input by some constant n. A frequency multiplier basically consists of a nonlinear device and a band-pass filter tuned to the desired frequency. Use of frequency multiplication normally increases the carrier frequency to an impractically high value. To shift the resulting WB-FM signal to the desired center frequency, a mixer and a band-pass filter can be employed.

There are various methods for FM demodulation. One approach is the phase-locked loop (PLL), which was described in Chapter 8. The signal is fed into a PLL and the error signal is used as the demodulated signal. A PLL can provide a high level of performance, and do not require a costly transformer and can easily be incorporated within FM radio ICs. Another approach is ***Quadrature detector***, which is also suitable for use within ICs. It provides high levels of linearity,

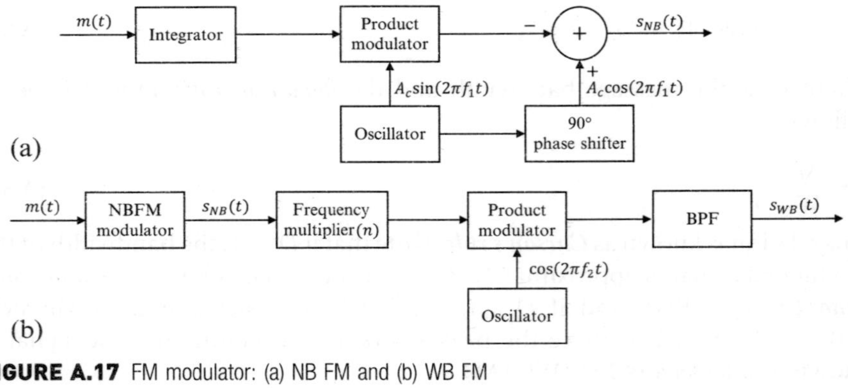

FIGURE A.17 FM modulator: (a) NB FM and (b) WB FM

while not requiring many external components. It phase shifts the signal by 90 degrees and multiplies it with the unshifted version. By low-pass filtering, the original information signal is obtained. There are other approaches, such as software-based FM demodulation by which the received is converted into digital form and thus processed digitally from the beginning.

Our brief focus is, however, on ***frequency discriminator***. If the input to an ideal discriminator is an FM signal, the discriminator output is then proportional to the instantaneous frequency deviation of the input signal, as an ideal discriminator transfer function is a linear function of frequency passing through zero at $f=f_c$, as shown in Figure A.18(a). A simple approximation to the ideal discriminator is an ideal differentiator followed by an envelope detector, as shown in Figure A.18(b). The ideal differentiator performs FM to AM conversion and the envelope detector recovers the modulating signal. Assuming the input to the differentiator is the following FM signal:

$$s_{FM}(t)=A_c\cos\left(2\pi f_c t+\varphi(t)\right)=A_c\cos\left(2\pi f_c t+2\pi k\int_0^t m(t)dt\right) \tag{A.36}$$

the output of the differentiator is then as follows:

$$\begin{aligned} s_{AM}(t) &= -A_c(2\pi f_c+\varphi'(t))\sin\left(2\pi f_c t+\varphi(t)\right) \\ &= -A_c(2\pi f_c+2\pi k m(t))\sin\left(2\pi f_c t+2\pi k\int_0^t m(t)dt\right) \end{aligned} \tag{A.37}$$

The output of the envelope detector is then proportional to $m(t)$, assuming the dc term $2\pi A_c f_c$ is removed. The output of the discriminator is a function of A_c. In order to ensure that the amplitude at the input to the differentiator is constant and not a function of time, a limiter is placed before the differentiator to clip the input signal and convert it to an FM square-wave signal. A band-pass filter is then placed after the limiter to convert the signal back to the sinusoidal form required by the differentiator.

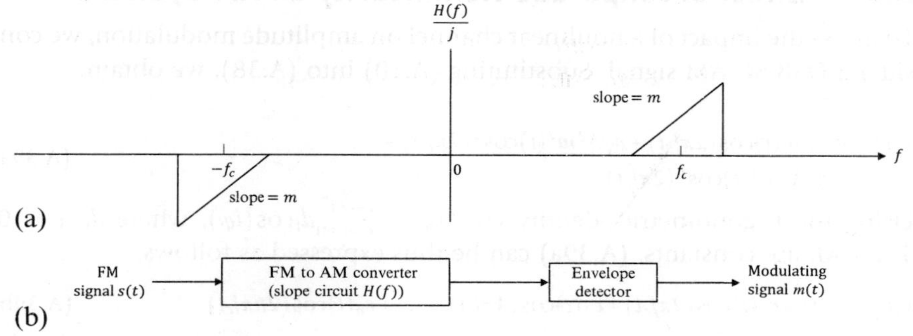

FIGURE A.18 FM demodulation: (a) frequency response of ideal slope circuit and (b) frequency discriminator.

EXAMPLE A.2

Suppose $s(t) = 5\cos(5t + \sin(5t))$ is an FM signal, determine: (a) the total average power, (b) the carrier frequency, (c) the modulation index, (d) the modulating signal, (e) the bandwidth of the modulating signal, (f) the frequency deviation, and (g) the bandwidth of the modulated signal.

Solution

(a) Using (A.21) and (A.31), we have $P = 12.5$.
(b) Using (A.28), we have $2\pi f_c t = 5t$, we thus have $f_c = 5/2\pi$.
(c) Using (A.28), we have $\beta = 1$.
(d) Using (A.21), we have $m(t) = -0.2\cos(5t)$.
(e) Using (A.23), we have $2\pi f_m t = 5t$, the bandwidth f_m is thus $5/2\pi$.
(f) Using (A.27), we have $\Delta f = \beta f_m = 5/2\pi$.
(g) Using (A.33), we have $BW_{FM} = 10/\pi$.

A.4 AMPLITUDE NONLINEARITY IN ANALOG CW MODULATION

Consider a memoryless nonlinear communication channel whose input $x(t)$ and output $y(t)$ are related by:

$$y(t) = a_1 x(t) + a_2 x^2(t) + \cdots + a_n x^n(t) \tag{A.38}$$

where $a_1, a_2, \ldots, a_n$ are constants. Clearly, the first term is the desired term, while the remaining terms represent the unwanted nonlinear distortion. The output spectrum spreads well beyond the input spectrum, and the output signal contains new frequency components not present in the input band. The nonlinearity not only distorts the signal, but also may cause interference with other signals in the channel because of its spectral dispersion (spreading).

A.4.1 Effect of Amplitude Nonlinearity on AM Systems

To assess the impact of a nonlinear channel on amplitude modulation, we consider a DSB-SC-AM signal. Substituting (A.10) into (A.38), we obtain:

$$\begin{aligned} y(t) = {} & a_1 A_c m(t)\cos(2\pi f_c t) + a_2 A_c^2 m^2(t)\cos^2(2\pi f_c t) + \ldots \\ & + a_n A_c^n m^n(t)\cos^n(2\pi f_c t) \end{aligned} \tag{A.39a}$$

Using the trigonometric identity $\cos^M(\varphi) = \sum_{i=0}^{M} d_i \cos(i\varphi)$, where d_i, $i = 0, 1, \ldots, M$, are constants, (A.39a) can be thus expressed as follows:

$$y(t) = c_0(t) + c_1(t)\cos(2\pi f_c t) + c_2(t)\cos(4\pi f_c t) + \ldots + c_n(t)\cos(2n\pi f_c t) \tag{A.39b}$$

Thus, the channel output consists of a total $n+1$ DSB-SC-AM signals with carrier frequencies of $0, f_c, 2f_c, \ldots, nf_c$. Assuming the message bandwidth is W, then by using a BPF of midband frequency f_c and bandwidth $2W$, all terms, except $c_1(t)$, can be removed, provided that the frequency components associated with $c_0(t), c_1(t), \ldots, c_n(t)$ do not overlap. However, the only remaining term, i.e., $c_1(t)\cos(2\pi f_c t)$, consists of the desired term $k_1 m(t)\cos(2\pi f_c t)$ plus distortion terms represented by $k_3 m^3(t)\cos(2\pi f_c t)$, $k_5 m^5(t)\cos(2\pi f_c t)$, $k_7 m^7(t)\cos(2\pi f_c t)$ and other similar terms. As the frequency components of these distortions and those of the desired DSB-SC-AM signal overlap, no type of filtering can alleviate the problem of distortion.

This type of distortion is referred to as nonlinear distortion, and it is not exclusive only to DSB-SC AM, but all amplitude modulation systems experience distortion due to amplitude nonlinearity in the communication channel. To minimize the effects of amplitude nonlinearity in AM systems, the amplifiers must be designed to be highly linear over the required range of operation.

A.4.2 Effect of Amplitude Nonlinearity on FM Systems

We now assess the impact of a nonlinear channel when the input is an FM signal. Substituting (A.18) into (A.38), we obtain:

$$\begin{aligned} y(t) &= a_1 A_c \cos(2\pi f_c t + \varphi(t)) + a_2 A_c^2 \cos^2(2\pi f_c t + \varphi(t)) + \ldots \\ &\quad + a_n A_c^n \cos^n(2\pi f_c t + \varphi(t)) \end{aligned} \tag{A.40a}$$

Using the trigonometric identity $\cos^M(\varphi) = \sum_{i=0}^{M} d_i \cos(i\varphi)$, where d_i, $i = 0, 1, \ldots, M$, are constants, (A.40a) can be thus expressed as follows:

$$\begin{aligned} y(t) &= b_0 + b_1 \cos(2\pi f_c t + \varphi(t)) + b_2 \cos(4\pi f_c t + 2\varphi(t)) + \ldots \\ &\quad + b_n \cos(2n\pi f_c t + n\varphi(t)) \end{aligned} \tag{A.40b}$$

Thus, the channel output consists of a dc component and n FM signals with carrier frequencies of f_c, $2f_c$, …, nf_c. Assuming the message bandwidth is W and the frequency deviation of the FM signal $\cos(2\pi f_c t + \varphi(t))$ is Δf, the frequency deviation of the second term $\cos(4\pi f_c t + 2\varphi(t))$, with the carrier frequency of $2f_c$, is $2\Delta f$. We can extract the desired FM signal by separating it from the second term. Using Carson's rule, the necessary condition can be expressed as $2f_c - (2\Delta f + W) > f_c + (\Delta f + W)$ or $f_c > 3\Delta f + 2W$. Thus by using a band-pass filter of mid-frequency f_c and bandwidth $2\Delta f + 2W$, the FM signal, without any distortion, can be extracted. The only impact is of course the amplitude modification.

We can thus conclude that FM is not affected by amplitude nonlinearity. This immunity allows the use of highly-nonlinear amplifiers and power transmitters at radio frequencies. It is however important to note that an FM system is very sensitive to phase nonlinearity. A common type of phase nonlinearity is known as AM-to-PM conversion, and that occurs when the phase of an amplifier used in the system is a function of the instantaneous amplitude of the input signal. It is therefore important to keep AM-to-PM conversion at a low level; otherwise, the output will contain unwanted phase modulation and distortion.

A.5 NOISE IN ANALOG CW MODULATION

In the analysis of the noise performance in an analog CW modulation system, we assume all system components in both transmitter and receiver, such as modulators, filters, and demodulators, are ideal and introduce no distortion. The only performance degradation is due to noise, which is present in varying degrees in all modulation systems. The effect of noise, however, can be minimized by appropriate filtering. We assume that the front-end receiver noise $n_w(t)$ is additive white Gaussian noise (AWGN). Figure A.19 shows a basic model of a noisy receiver employing an analog CW modulation. Note that the band-pass filter (BPF) is centered at the carrier frequency f_c and has a bandwidth equal to the transmission bandwidth of the modulated signal. The BPF, also known as a pre-detection filter, passes the received modulated signal $s(t)$ without distortion, but limits the amount of out-of-band noise that reaches the detector. The band-pass filtered noise $n(t)$, however, is no longer white, and the low-pass components of this narrowband noise, i.e., $n_c(t)$ and $n_s(t)$, can impact the system performance. The detector output is then low-pass filtered to remove out-of-band noise and harmonic signal terms. The LPF, also known as a post-detection filter, has the same bandwidth as the message signal.

In order to carry out the analysis of the effects of noise on the performance of the receiver and to make a comparative analysis of noise performances of various modulation schemes, a criterion is required. An intuitive measure may be the signal-to-noise ratio (SNR), defined as the ratio of the mean power of the signal to the mean power of the noise.

A key performance metric for the fidelity of the received signal is the ***output*** SNR, defined as the ratio of the mean power of the demodulated signal to the mean power of the noise, both measured at the receiver output. The output SNR depends on the type of modulation employed in the system and the type of the demodulation technique used in the receiver. In order to make a fair comparison of all modulation schemes, they should be all operating under the same environment. More specifically, in order to have a meaningful comparison, the transmitted signal power and the noise power in the bandwidth of

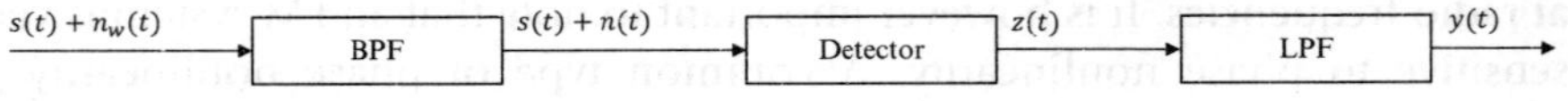

FIGURE A.19 Model of a noisy receiver.

the signal must be the same for all types of modulation. A frame of reference is thus the ***input*** SNR, defined as the ratio of the average power of the modulated signal to the average power of the noise in the message bandwidth, both measured at the receiver input. To assess each modulation scheme, we define a ***figure of merit for the receiver*** as the ratio of the output SNR to the input SNR.

A.5.1 Effect of Noise on AM Systems

Before proceeding to assess the impact of noise on linear modulation, it is important to emphasize that a feature common to all linear modulation schemes is that the SNR at the receiver output can be increased only by increasing the transmitted power.

The average power of the DSB-PC-AM signal $s(t)$ is given in (A.7b). With a narrowband band-pass noise whose double-sided power spectral density of $N_0/2$ in W/Hz, the average noise power in the message bandwidth W is equal to WN_0. The input SNR for DSB-PC AM is therefore as follows:

$$SNR|_i = \frac{P_c(1+k^2P_m)}{WN_0} \tag{A.41}$$

The input to an ideal envelope detector consists of the received modulated signal $s(t)$ and the narrowband noise $n(t)$. Using the narrowband representation of the band-pass filtered noise $n(t)$ in terms of its low-pass in-phase and quadrature components, the composite signal $x(t)$ at the detector input may be expressed as:

$$\begin{aligned} x(t) = s(t) + n(t) &= A_c(1+km(t))\cos(2\pi f_c t) + n_c(t)\cos(2\pi f_c t) - n_s(t)\sin(2\pi f_c t) \\ &= (A_c + A_c km(t) + n_c(t))\cos(2\pi f_c t) - n_s(t)\sin(2\pi f_c t) \end{aligned} \tag{A.42}$$

Assuming the detector is an ideal envelope detector, the output of the detector $y(t)$ is as follows:

$$y(t) = \left((A_c + A_c km(t) + n_c(t))^2 + (n_s(t))^2\right)^{1/2} \tag{A.43a}$$

Assuming the signal power at the receiver input is considerably higher than the noise power, the output of the envelope detector is thus approximately as follows:

$$y(t) \cong A_c + A_c km(t) + n_c(t) \tag{A.43b}$$

The dc term A_c in the envelope detector output can be removed by a capacitor, as it has no bearing on the message signal.

With a low-pass noise whose power spectral density is N_0 and the low-pass signal whose bandwidth is W, the average noise power is then equal to WN_0. The output SNR of a DSB-PC-AM receiver using an envelope detector is thus as follows:

$$SNR|_o = \frac{A_c{}^2 k^2 P_m}{WN_0} = \frac{P_c k^2 P_m}{WN_0} \quad \text{(A.44)}$$

Using (A.41) and (A.44), the ***figure of merit of a DSB-PC-AM receiver*** employing envelope detection is as follows:

$$FoM = \frac{k^2 P_m}{1 + k^2 P_m} < 1 \quad \text{(A.45)}$$

The reason the value of this figure of merit is less than unity lies in the fact that DSB-PC AM wastes transmit power to send the carrier along with the modulated signal.

If the preceding assumption is not true that is the signal power at the receiver input is much lower than the noise power, the situation is then quite different. We have therefore a loss of message signal in that the detector output does not contain the message at all, and it is meaningless to talk about the output SNR. The loss of a message in an envelope detector that operates at a low input SNR is referred to as the ***threshold effect***. By threshold, we mean there is some value of the input SNR above which signal degradation due to noise is negligible and below which the system performance deteriorates quite rapidly.

It is important to note that a threshold effect does not occur when coherent demodulation, instead of envelope detection, is employed. Assuming DSB-SC AM, SSB-SC AM, and VSB-SC AM all employ coherent detection, the figure of merit is the same for all of them. The common figure of merit of unity is superior to that of DSB-PC AM, and their derivations for these three schemes are left as problems at the end of the appendix.

A.5.2 Effect of Noise on FM Systems

The average power of the FM signal $s(t)$ is given in (A.31). With a narrowband band-pass noise whose double-sided power spectral density is $N_0/2$, the average noise power in the message bandwidth W is equal to WN_0. The input SNR for FM is therefore as follows:

$$SNR|_i = \frac{A_c^2/2}{WN_0} \quad \text{(A.46)}$$

The input to an ideal detector consists of the received modulated signal $s(t)$ and the narrowband noise $n(t)$. Using the narrowband representation of the band-pass filtered noise $n(t)$ in terms of its envelope $r_n(t)$ and phase $\theta_n(t)$, the composite signal $x(t)$ at the detector input may be expressed as:

$$\begin{aligned} x(t) = s(t) + n(t) &= A_c \cos(2\pi f_c t + \varphi(t)) + r_n(t)\cos(2\pi f_c t + \theta_n(t)) \\ &= x_e(t)\cos(2\pi f_c t + \varphi(t) + \theta_e(t)) \end{aligned} \tag{A.47}$$

where $\theta_e(t)$ is the perturbation of the carrier phase angle due to noise and also contains the signal, and $x_e(t)$ is the envelope of the composite signal and plays no role, as the response of an ideal detector only depends on its phase $\varphi(t) + \theta_e(t)$.

In order to determine the instantaneous frequency of the carrier wave caused by the presence of the filtered noise $n(t)$, we assume the SNR measured at the discriminator output is large compared with unity and the discriminator is ideal and its output is thus proportional to the derivative of the phase $\varphi(t) + \theta_e(t)$. It can be shown that the output of the detector is then as follows:

$$y(t) = km(t) + \left(\frac{1}{2\pi A_c}\right)\frac{dn_s(t)}{dt} \tag{A.48}$$

This clearly states that the output of the detector consists of the scaled version of the modulating signal $m(t)$ and an additive noise that is a function of the carrier amplitude A_c and the derivative of the quadrature component $n_s(t)$ of the narrowband noise $n(t)$. The differentiation of a function with respect to time corresponds to multiplication of its Fourier transform by $j2\pi f$, and the low-pass filter with a bandwidth equal to the message bandwidth W rejects the out-of-band components of the additive noise. The power spectral density of the low-pass quadrature component $n_s(t)$ of the noise $n(t)$ is N_O, therefore the power spectral density at the output of the receiver is as follows:

$$N_O\left|\frac{j2\pi f}{2\pi A_c}\right|^2 = \frac{N_O f^2}{A_c^2} \tag{A.49}$$

The noise power in an FM system increases as f^2 over the message band. Thus, the message spectral components at higher frequencies are corrupted by more noise than the message spectral components at lower frequencies.

The spectral density of the message signal usually falls off considerably at higher frequencies, whereas the spectral density of the output noise increases significantly with frequency. The message is thus not utilizing its entire bandwidth in an efficient manner. To allow the efficient utilization of the allowed frequency band is that the noise spectral characteristics in an FM system be altered by a ***pre-emphasis filter*** in the transmitter and a ***de-emphasis filter*** in the receiver, as shown in Figure A.20. In effect, we enhance the high-frequency components of the message prior to modulation in the transmitter, and we mitigate the high-frequency components of the noise after demodulation, thus increasing the

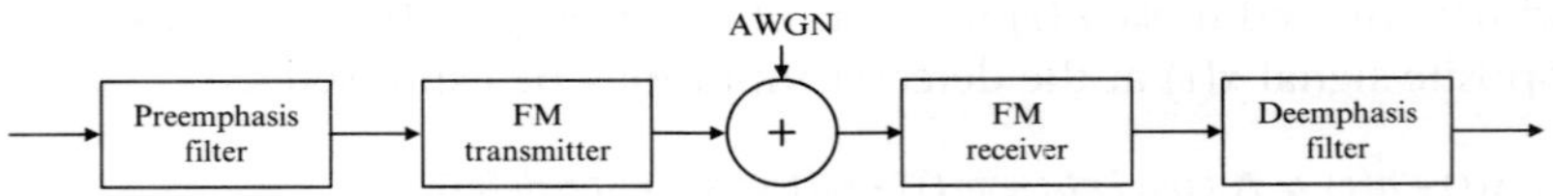

FIGURE A.20 Pre-emphasis and de-emphasis in an FM system.

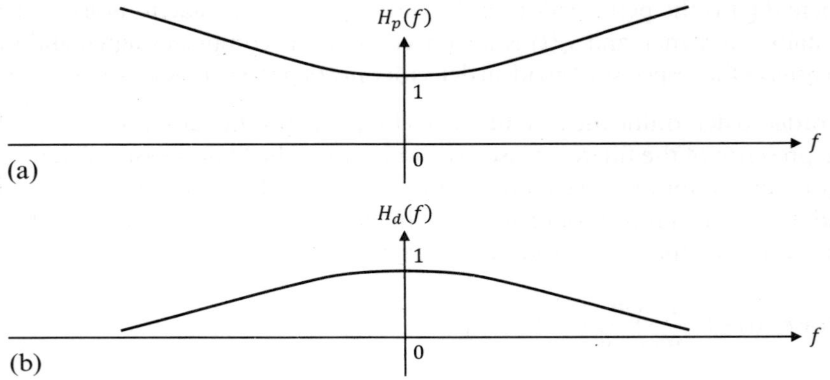

FIGURE A.21 Pre-emphasis and de-emphasis filters characteristics.

output SNR of the system. Typical characteristics of pre-emphasis and de-emphasis filters are shown in Figure A.21.

The average power of the output noise, which is determined by integrating the power spectral density of the noise in (A.49) from $-W$ to W, is $2N_0W^3/3A_c^2$. The average output signal power is also equal to k^2P_m, where P_m is the average power of the message signal $m(t)$. The output SNR of an FM receiver is thus as follows:

$$SNR|_o = \frac{k^2 P_m}{2N_0 W^3/3{A_c}^2} \tag{A.50}$$

Using (A.46) and (A.50), the ***figure of merit of an FM receiver*** is as follows:

$$FoM = \frac{3k^2 P_m}{W^2} \tag{A.51}$$

The figure of merit can be increased by increasing the FM modulator sensitivity k^2 without having to increase the transmitted power. Based on (A.25) and (A.33), it is clear that an increase in k^2 results in an increase in the transmission bandwidth. It is thus possible to trade off bandwidth for SNR in FM systems. This is in clear contrast to amplitude modulation where such a trade-off is not possible.

The preceding analysis is based on the high SNR at the discriminator. However, as the input noise power is increased, the ratio is decreased, and the FM receiver breaks, i.e., the signal cannot be recognized from the noise. There exists a specific SNR, known as the ***threshold*** **SNR**, below which the signal is not distinguishable from the noise. The existence of the threshold effect places an upper limit on the trade-off between bandwidth and power in an FM system. The reason lies in the fact that an increase in bandwidth does not indefinitely brings about a better performance, as it also results in a larger noise power at the input of the demodulator.

A.6 COMMERCIAL RADIO BROADCASTING

Commercial radio broadcasting using electromagnetic radiation over the airways is widely known as AM and FM radio. The frequency allocation and the licensing of airway transmission are regulated by government agencies all over the world, such as the Federal Communications Commission (FCC) in the United States. The standard AM and FM radio receivers are the superheterodyne type. The ***superheterodyne operation*** provides frequency conversion from the variable carrier frequency of the incoming RF signal to a signal with the fixed IF frequency, and thus in turn eliminates the complexity of implementing a high-Q tuned filter in a radio receiver.

A.6.1 AM Radio Broadcasting and Reception

Commercial AM radio broadcasting has been around for almost a century. The AM radio signal, which is in fact a DSB-PC-AM signal, offers a relatively low audio quality due to audio bandwidth limitations and susceptibility to atmospheric and electrical interference. The FCC has allocated the frequency band 540–1600 kHz with 10 kHz spacing for commercial AM radio broadcasting. Noting the bandwidth of the baseband audio signal is limited to approximately 5 kHz, the RF carrier range is thus 535–1605 kHz. However, two stations in local proximity are not assigned two adjacent carrier frequencies. Interference among transmissions from AM radio stations is primarily controlled by a combination of frequency allocation, transmitter power, and transmitting antenna pattern. The permissible average transmit power for an unmodulated carrier ranges from 1 kW to 50 kW. As there are numerous AM radio receivers, it is important to reduce the cost of a receiver. Therefore, DSB-PC-AM radio broadcasting, which is wasteful of both transmit power and channel bandwidth, is employed so that a radio receiver can be equipped with a low-cost envelope detector.

As shown in Figure A.22, the ***AM superheterodyne receiver*** consists of an antenna, a radio-frequency (RF) amplifier, a mixer, a local oscillator, an intermediate frequency (IF) amplifier, an envelope detector, an audio-frequency amplifier, and a speaker. The AM signal transmitted by electromagnetic radiation is received by an antenna and then passed to an RF amplifier. The desired carrier frequency, selected by the listener through a knob, simultaneously tunes

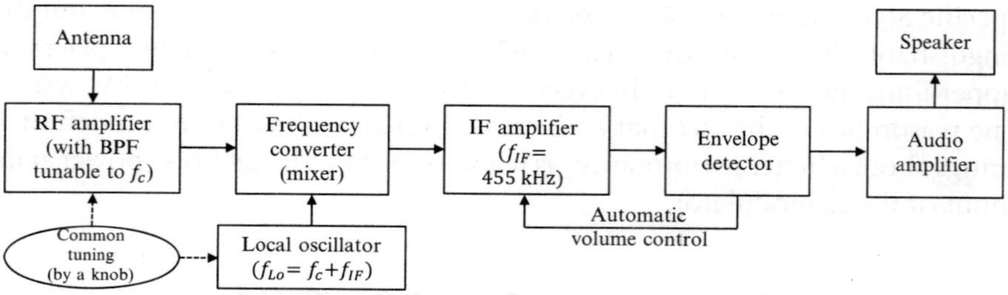

FIGURE A.22 Block diagram of an AM superheterodyne receiver.

the RF amplifier and the frequency of the local oscillator. In all AM superheterodyne receivers, the RF signal is always converted to a common IF signal at a carrier frequency 455 kHz that is $f_{IF} = 455$ kHz. This allows the use of a single-tuned IF amplifier for AM signals from any radio station. The superheterodyne operation, performed by the local oscillator and mixer arrangement, refers to the frequency translation from the variable carrier frequency of the incoming AM signal to a signal with the fixed IF frequency. With the RF tuning range of 540–1600 Hz, the local oscillator must tune 995–2055 kHz, as $f_{Lo} = f_c + f_{IF}$ is the local oscillator frequency. The IF amplifier has a bandwidth of 10 kHz that is the same as the bandwidth of the modulated signal. The output of the IF amplifier is sent to an envelope detector to recover the desired message signal. Since the RF signal often changes slowly with respect to time due to fading, automatic volume control is needed to adjust the gain of IF amplifier. This adjustment is based on the signal level at the envelope detector through a feedback control loop. Lastly, the audio amplifier brings up the power level to that required for the speaker.

Since it is possible that signals from two radio stations to reach the IF amplifier, interference can exist. Suppose there are two signals at frequency $f_{LO} - f_{IF}$ and frequency $f_{LO} + f_{IF}$. When we try to receive our desired station at $f_c = f_{LO} - f_{IF}$, the local oscillator will have to be at f_{LO}. When the local oscillator signal is mixed with the incoming signals, we will also pick up the signal at $f_{LO} + f_{IF}$. This unwanted signal is called the ***image interference***, as shown in Figure A.23.

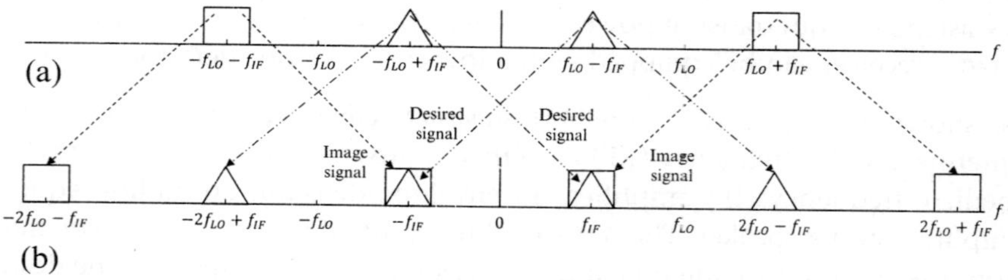

FIGURE A.23 AM radio broadcasting: image and desired signals (a) before mixing and (b) after mixing.

The image interference is solely due to the passive role of a mixer, as it cannot distinguish between the desired signal and its image in that it produces an IF output from either one of them. The possibility of simultaneous reception of two signals exist when the difference between their RF frequencies is twice the IF frequency. For instance, with $f_{IF} = 455$ kHz, the RF signal at 590 kHz is subject to image interference at 1.5 MHz, simply because we have 1500 kHz – 590 kHz = 2 × 455 kHz. The only practical way to ideally eliminate, and practically minimize, the image interference is to use the RF amplification with band-pass filtering to tune to the desired signal and discriminate against the image signal.

A.6.2 FM Radio Broadcasting and Reception

FM radio broadcasting provides high-fidelity sound over broadcast radio. The conventional (monophonic) FM radio has been around since the forties and the stereophonic FM radio since the sixties. The FCC has assigned RF carrier frequencies for commercial FM broadcasting in the frequency band 88–108 MHz. The carrier frequencies are separated by 200 kHz, the peak frequency deviation is fixed at 75 kHz, and power outputs are specified from 0.25 kW to 100 kW. The RF amplifier and the local oscillator are mechanically coupled to provide for a common tuning. All FM radio signals can be brought to a common IF bandwidth of 200 kHz, centered at 10.7 MHz.

The block diagram of an FM receiver is shown in Figure A.24. In an FM system, the amplitude is maintained constant, as the message is embedded in the frequency of the carrier. Any variations in the carrier amplitude can thus be attributed to noise and interference. In an ***FM superheterodyne receiver***, an amplitude limiter between the IF amplifier and the demodulator is thus required to remove any amplitude variations in the received signal by hard-limiting the signal amplitude. The resulting rectangular wave is sent to a band-pass filter, which is centered at 10.7 MHz with a bandwidth of 200 kHz, to produce a sinusoidal signal with constant amplitude. A frequency discriminator is used to perform frequency demodulation. Due to the presence of noise at the

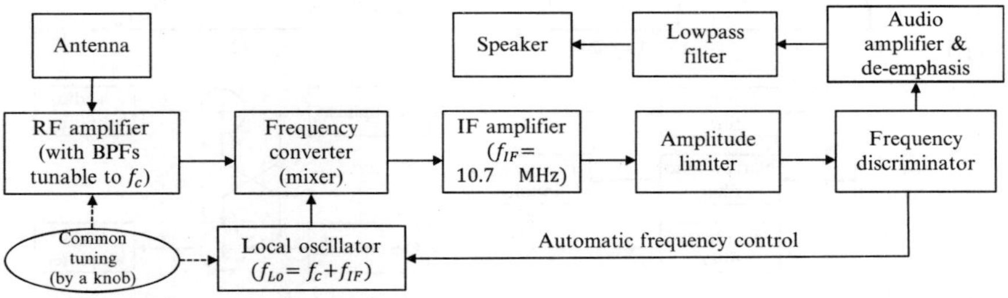

FIGURE A.24 Block diagram of an FM superheterodyne receiver.

receiver input, steps are taken to minimize the noise effects. To this effect, the audio amplifier, in addition to amplification, also performs the function of de-emphasis, as pre-emphasis was employed at the transmitter. Another step is to employ a low-pass filter whose bandwidth is wide enough to accommodate the highest frequency component of the message signal, thus removing out-of-band noise.

FM radio broadcasts employ FM stereo broadcasting to give spatial dimension and natural effect to listeners. In ***FM stereo broadcasting***, two separate audio signals are transmitted by using a form of frequency-division multiplexing. As the stereophonic FM broadcasting came along a couple of decades after the monophonic (conventional) FM system, the FCC ruled that the FM stereophonic transmission had to be compatible with the FM monophonic receivers and operate within the allocated FM broadcast channels. The compatibility requirement meant that the monophonic receivers should also be able to receive the sum of the two independent signals, but of course without the stereo effect.

A block diagram of an FM stereo transmitter is shown in Figure A.25(a). An FM stereo transmitter produces the sum and difference signals of the two audio signals coming from the left and right microphones. The sum and difference signals are both pre-emphasized. The pre-emphasized sum signal is left unchanged in its baseband form, while occupying the frequency band 0–15 kHz. The pre-emphasized difference signal is used to modulate a 38-kHz carrier wave using DSB-SC amplitude modulation, where the carrier is generated

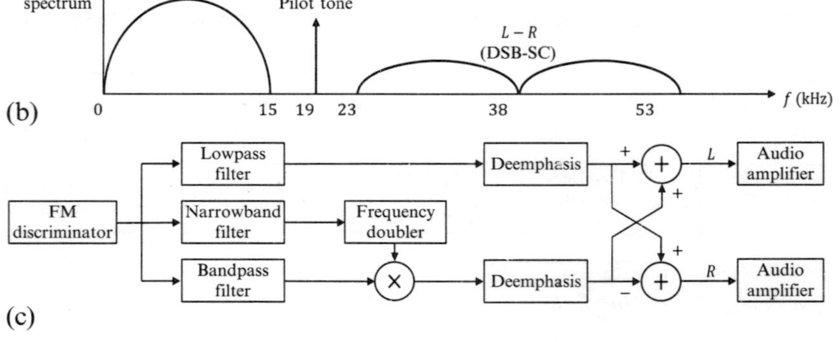

FIGURE A.25 FM stereo broadcasting: (a) FM stereo transmitter, (b) spectrum of FM stereo signal, and (c) FM stereo receiver.

from a 19-kHz pilot tone. The difference signal thus occupies 23–53 kHz. The pilot tone at 19-kHz and the sum and difference signals form a composite signal, as shown in Figure A.25(b). The composite signal frequency modulates a carrier, while the resulting FM signal does not exceed the allocated 200-kHz bandwidth, as required. Note that the composite signal consists of a pilot tone at 19 kHz instead of 38 kHz, since it can be more easily separated from the rest of the composite signal where there are no signal components within 4 KHz of this pilot tone. This 19-kHz pilot can provide a reference for the coherent detection of the difference signal at the stereo receiver. The FM stereo receiver, as shown in Figure A.25(c), is self-explanatory.

A.7 COMPARISON OF ANALOG CW MODULATION SCHEMES

The comparison of analog CW modulation schemes goes beyond the fact that amplitude modulation schemes are linear and angle modulation schemes are nonlinear. There are arrays of measures that can dictate the ultimate choice of a particular modulation scheme over another one. However, we briefly assess modulation systems from implementation complexity, signal bandwidth, transmit power, and channel nonlinearity standpoints.

Implementation – When the carrier wave in AM, along with the message signal, is transmitted, a simple receiver employing envelope detection can be employed. Prime examples are DSB-PC AM (also known as conventional AM) used in AM radio broadcasting and VSB-PC AM used in TV broadcasting. However, the transmission of the carrier wave represents a significant waste of power. A system, in which the carrier wave is suppressed, such as DSB-SC AM, SSB-SC AM, and VSB-SC AM, requires synchronous demodulation. The receiver thus has a complex structure, as it must perform carrier recovery, i.e., generation of a local oscillator that is exactly synchronized in both frequency and phase with the carrier wave used in the transmitter. Also, FM receivers widely used in high-fidelity radio broadcasting (with FM stereo) are rather easy to implement, where there are now several distinct demodulation schemes.

Bandwidth – A system employing a linear modulation (e.g., DSB, VSB, SSB), with or without a carrier wave, requires a bandwidth that is a small fraction of what is required for an angle modulation. For instance, in AM radio broadcasting, the channel spacing is a mere 10 kHz, but in FM radio broadcasting, it is 200 kHz. Of course, the generous use of bandwidth in FM systems is justified as they can bring about a high degree of immunity to channel noise. Of all analog modulation schemes, SSB AM is the most bandwidth efficient, as the transmission bandwidth requirement is the same as the message signal. As SSB AM requires the modulating signal have little or no power near origin, VSB AM is the next most bandwidth efficient and viable option. DSB AM is the least bandwidth efficient of all linear modulation schemes, as it requires a bandwidth that is twice the message bandwidth.

Power – The noise analysis of a wideband FM system is more complicated than that of a system employing linear modulation. In a system employing an amplitude modulation scheme, the SNR at the receiver output can be increased only by increasing the transmitted signal power. Unlike an AM system, the transmitted power in an FM system is completely independent of the modulating signal. Among the linear modulation schemes, a scheme with carrier suppression requires coherent detection that in turn delivers a higher SNR and has no threshold effect. However, for broadcast applications, transmit power efficiency may not be important and carrier suppression is not thus justified, because having low cost receivers is a critical factor. Compared to linear modulation, angle modulation provides substantially improved signal quality at the expense of a significant bandwidth expansion. For instance, WBFM with pre-emphasis/de-emphasis provides the best power efficiency of all systems. FM offers considerable power savings over other schemes. However, threshold effects in FM may somewhat limit the amount of improvement possible.

Nonlinearity – Amplitude modulation is highly sensitive to amplitude nonlinearity in the communication channel, whereas frequency modulation is fundamentally unaffected by such nonlinearity. Frequency modulation is, however, quite sensitive to phase nonlinearity, such as AM-to-PM conversion experienced in radio channels.

Summary and Sources

Appendix was devoted exclusively to an overview of AM and FM. We introduced various AM and FM schemes. For all schemes, bandwidth and power requirements and modem implementations were given. The impact of amplitude nonlinearity and noise on both AM and FM were briefly discussed. We finally focused on commercial AM and FM radio broadcasting.

During the past half century, a number of excellent undergraduate textbooks on communication systems have been published. In their first editions, the focus was mostly on analog communication systems, though the focus turned toward digital communications. There are widely known books on analog communication systems, in which AM and FM have been discussed in detail [1–8].

[1] S. Haykin, *Communication Systems*, Wiley, ISBN: 0-471-02977-7, 1978.

[2] B.P. Lathi and Z. Ding, *Modern Digital and Analog Communication Systems*, fourth ed., Oxford University Press, 2009, 978-0-19-533145-5.

[3] K.S. Shanmugam, *Digital and Analog Communication Systems*, John Wiley & Sons, ISBN: 0-471-03090-2, 1979.

[4] R.E. Ziemer and W.H. Tranter, *Principles of Communications*, sixth ed., John Wiley & Sons, ISBN: 978-0-470-25254-3, 2009.

[5] A.B. Carlson and P.B. Crilly, *Communication Systems*, fifth ed., McGraw-Hill, ISBN: 978-0-07-338040-7, 2002.

[6] H. Taub and D.L. Schilling, *Principles of Communication Systems*, second ed., McGraw-Hill, ISBN: 0-07-062955-2, 1986.

[7] L.W. Couch II, *Digital and Analog Communication Systems*, eighth ed., Pearson, ISBN: 978-0-13-291538-0, 2013.

[8] J.G. Proakis and M. Salehi, *Fundamentals of Communication Systems*, second ed., Pearson, ISBN: 0-13-147135-X, 2014.

Problems

A.1 The square-law modulator is a device for the generation of DSB-PC-AM signals. In the square-law modulator, the sum of the modulating signal and the carrier wave forms the input signal to a nonlinear device. The output signal of the nonlinear device is a linear combination of the input signal and the square of the input signal. The output signal of the nonlinear device is then band-pass filtered. The BPF has a center frequency that is the same as the carrier frequency and a bandwidth that is twice the message bandwidth. Show the output of the BPF is a DSB-PC-AM signal, and determine a requirement between the carrier frequency and the message bandwidth that must be satisfied.

A.2 The square-law detector is a device for the demodulation of DSB-PC-AM signals. In the square-law detector, the modulated signal forms the input signal to a nonlinear device. The output signal of the nonlinear device is a linear combination of the input signal and the square of the input signal. The output signal of the nonlinear device is then low-pass filtered. Show the output of the LPF can be the modulating signal, and determine a requirement such that distortionless recovery of the modulating signal is possible.

A.3 The ring modulator is a device for the generation of DSB-SC-AM signals. In the ring modulator, there are four ideal diodes in the shape of a ring that are controlled by two perfectly-balanced center-tapped transformers. The ring modulator ideally is a product modulator for a square-wave carrier of frequency f_c and the modulating signal. The output of the product modulator is low-pass filtered. Show the output of the LPF can be the DSB-SC-AM signal, and determine a requirement between the carrier frequency and the message bandwidth that must be satisfied.

A.4 The phase discrimination using Hilbert transform is a device for the generation of SSB-SC-AM signals. In the phase discrimination using Hilbert transform, there are two product modulators supplied with two carrier waves in phase quadrature to each other, i.e., one carrier is a sine function and the other is a cosine function. The modulating signal is applied to one of the product modulators and the Hilbert transform of the modulating signal is applied to the other product modulator. Show that the addition or the subtraction of the two modulator outputs can give rise to cancelation of one set of sidebands and creation of the other set.

A.5 Prove that the frequency response of the LPF $H(f)$ for producing a VSB-SC-AM signal must satisfy (A.16).

A.6 Consider a system transmitting a VSB-PC-AM signal, in which the envelope detection is employed. Determine the envelope detector output, and identify two methods by which the distortion due to the use of the envelope detector can be reduced.

A.7 Suppose a modulated (band-pass) signal, which is centered at the frequency f_c and has a bandwidth of $2W$, is an input to a mixer. It is required to translate this modulated signal downward in frequency to a new frequency $f_o < f_c$. For the implementation of a mixer, we may use a multiplier followed by a filter. Determine the frequency of the sinusoidal wave applied to the multiplier and the filter requirements.

A.8 Suppose we have a linear device whose output is a linear combination of the input signal, the square of the input signal and the cube of the input signal. Discuss the performance of this nonlinear device when the input signal is a DSB-SC-AM signal.

A.9 Assuming coherent detector is used, determine the figure of merit for each of the DSB-SC-AM, SSB-SC-AM, and VSB-SC-AM schemes.

A.10 Determine the figure of merit for both DSB AM and FM, provided that the modulating signal is a single-tone signal.

A.11 Using Carson's rule, determine the transmission bandwidth for commercial FM radio broadcasting, provided that the maximum value of frequency deviation is 75 kHz and the bandwidth of the audio signal is 15 kHz.

A.12 Is it possible to apply an FM signal to a square-law device to obtain an FM signal with a greater frequency deviation than available at the input?

A.13 Coherent detection is a method of demodulation for DSB-SC amplitude modulated signals. Is it possible to use this type of modulation scheme to demodulate a conventional AM signal (i.e., DSB-PC AM) as well?

A.14 The envelope of a conventional AM signal (DSB-PC-AM) has the same shape as the modulating signal $m(t)$. This AM signal is squared, and applied to a LPF whose bandwidth is twice as much as that of $m(t)$. Show step by step that the modulating signal can be obtained by finding the square-root of the LPF output.

A.15 Consider a communication channel, transfer characteristic of which is defined by the nonlinear relation, $y(t) = x(t) + x^2(t)$, where $x(t)$ is the input and $y(t)$ is the output. Assuming the input is an FM signal, $x(t) = \cos(2\pi f_c t + \varphi(t))$, find $y(t)$. Is it possible to retrieve $x(t)$ from $y(t)$? If so, how?

A.16 A low-pass signal $m(t)$, with a 10-kHz bandwidth, is modulated by DSB-SC AM technique. Find the value of the carrier frequency so the bandwidth of the modulated signal is 1% of the carrier frequency.

A.17 An FM signal is described by $s(t) = 100\cos\left(2\pi.10^8 t + 10^{-4}\cos(1000\pi t)\right)$. Determine the modulating signal $m(t)$.

A.18 Consider a communication channel, transfer characteristic of which is defined by the nonlinear relation, $y(t) = x(t) + x^2(t)$, where $x(t)$ is the input and $y(t)$ is the output. Assuming the input is a DSB-SC signal, $x(t) = \cos(2\pi f_c t + \varphi(t))$, find $y(t)$. Is it possible to retrieve $x(t)$ from $y(t)$? If so, how?

A.19 Consider the NB-FM signal $s(t) = \cos(2\pi f_c t) - \beta\sin(2\pi f_c t)\sin(2\pi f_m t)$. What is the ratio of the maximum to the minimum value of the envelope of this modulated signal?

A.20 An FM signal $s(t) = A_c\cos(2\pi f_c t + \beta\sin(2\pi f_m t))$ is applied to an RC LPF whose transfer function is as follows: $[j2\pi fRC/(1 + j2\pi fRC)]$. Assume $2\pi fR \ll 1$ in the frequency band occupied by $s(t)$. Show that the voltage is an AM signal.

Computer Exercises

In the following problems, consider a message signal $m(t)$ that is a time-limited sinc function with duration several times longer than its main lobe. A sinusoidal carrier $c(t)$, with a high enough carrier frequency, is modulated by the message signal to produce the modulated signal $s(t)$. By selecting a small enough sampling interval, generate samples of $m(t)$, $c(t)$, and $s(t)$ and plot them. Determine and plot the spectra of the signals $m(t)$, $c(t)$, and $s(t)$. Make all relevant assumptions.

A.21 Assume amplitude modulation schemes are DSB-SC-AM, SSB-SC-AM, and VSB-SC-AM.

A.22 Demodulate the DSB-SC-AM signal using coherent detection.

A.23 Assume amplitude modulation schemes are DSB-PC-AM, SSB-PC-AM, and VSB-PC-AM.

A.24 Demodulate the DSB-SC-AM signal using envelope detection.

A.25 Assume the modulation schemes are narrowband and wideband FM.

List of Acronyms and Abbreviations

AC	alternating current
ACK	acknowledgement
ADC	analog-to-digital conversion
ADM	adaptive DM
ADPCM	adaptive DPCM
ADSL	asymmetric DSL
AEB	amplitude-equivalent bandwidth
AGC	automatic gain control
AM	amplitude modulation
AMI	alternate mark inversion
AMPS	Advanced Mobile Phone System
ARPANET	Advanced Research Projects Agency Network
ARQ	automatic repeat request
ASCII	American Standard Code for Information Interchange
ASK	amplitude-shift keying
AVC	automatic volume control
AWGN	additive white Gaussian noise
B	byte
BASK	binary ASK
BBS	broadcasting-satellite service
BCH	Bose-Chaudhuri-Hocquenghem
BER	bit error rate
BFSK	binary FSK
BIBO	bounded-input-bounded-output
bits	binary digits
BPF	bandpass filter
bps	bits per second
BPSK	binary PSK
BSC	binary symmetric channel
BSF	bandstop filter
BW	bandwidth
CA	certification authority
CATV	community antenna TV
CB	citizen band
CCI	co-channel interference
CD	compact disk
cdf	cumulative distribution function
CDMA	code-division multiple access

codec	coder-decoder
CP	circular polarization
CPFSK	continuous-phase FSK
CPM	continuous-phase modulation
CRC	cyclic redundancy check
CS	checksum
CSMA	carrier-sense multiple access
CSMA/CA	CSMA/collision avoidance
CSMA/CD	CSMA/collision detection
CW	continuous wave
DAB	digital audio broadcasting
DAC	digital-to-analog conversion
dB	decibel
dBmW	decibel reference to 1 mW
DBPSK	differential BPSK
DBS	direct-broadcast satellite
dBW	decibel reference to 1 W
DC	direct current
DECT	Digital European (Enhanced) Cordless Telecommunications
DEMUX	demultiplexer
DES	Data Encryption Standard
DFE	decision-feedback equalizer
DFT	discrete Fourier transform
DM	delta modulation
DMC	discrete memoryless channel
DMS	discrete memoryless source
DMT	discrete multi-tone
DOCSIS	data over cable service interface specification
DPCM	differential PCM
DPSK	differential PSK
DSB	double sideband
DSL	digital subscriber line
DSP	digital signal processing
DSSS	direct-sequence spread spectrum
DVB	digital video broadcasting
DVD	digital video (versatile) disk
ECG	electrocardiogram
EHF	extra high frequency
EIRP	effective isotropic radiated power
ELF	extra low frequency
ESD	energy spectral density
FCC	Federal Communications Commission
FDD	frequency-division duplexing
FDM	frequency-division multiplexing
FDMA	frequency-division multiple access
FDX	full-duplex
FEC	forward error correction
FFT	fast Fourier transform

FHSS	frequency-hopped spread spectrum
FIR	finite-impulse response
FM	frequency modulation
FoM	Figure of Merit
FS	Fourier series
FSE	fractionally-spaced equalizer
FSK	frequency-shift keying
FSS	fixed-satellite service
FT	Fourier transform
G	giga
GEO	geostationary
GMSK	Gaussian MSK
GPS	Global Positioning System
GSM	Global System for Mobile Communications (originally Groupe Spécial Mobile)
HDTV	high-definition TV
HF	high frequency
HFC	hybrid fiber-coaxial
HFD	half-duplex
HP	horizontal polarization
HPF	highpass filter
Hz	Hertz
I	in-phase
IC	integrated circuit
IDFT	inverse DFT
IEEE	Institute of Electrical and Electronic Engineers
IF	intermediate frequency
IFFT	inverse fast Fourier transform
iid	independent, identically-distributed
IIR	infinite-impulse response
IMT	International Mobile Telecommunications
IP	Internet Protocol
IS	interim standard
ISI	intersymbol interference
ISM	industrial, scientific, and medical
ISO	International Organization for Standardization
ISP	Internet service provider
ITU	International Telecommunications Union
ITU-R	ITU-Radio
ITU-T	ITU-Telecommunication
J	Joule
JPEG	Joint Photographic Experts Group
k	kilo
KDC	key distribution center
km	kilometer
LAN	local area network
LDPC	low-density parity-check
LE	linear equalizer
LEO	low-earth orbit

LF	low frequency
LHCP	left-hand CP
LHS	left-hand side
LLC	logical link control
LMS	least-mean square
LNA	low-noise amplifier
LO	local oscillator
LP	linear polarization
LPC	linear prediction coding
LPF	lowpass filter
LSB	lower sideband
LTE	long-term evolution
LTI	linear time-invariant
LZ	Lempel-Ziv
M	mega
m	meter
MAC	medium access control
MAP	maximum a posteriori probability
MASK	*M*-ary ASK
MEO	medium-earth orbit
MF	medium frequency
MFSK	*M*-ary FSK
MIMO	multiple input multiple output
MISO	multiple input single output
ML	maximum likelihood
MLSE	ML sequence estimation
mm	millimeter
MMSE	minimum-mean square error
modem	modulator-demodulator
MPEG	Moving Picture Experts Group
mps	meters per second
MPSK	*M*-ary PSK
ms	millisecond
MSK	minimum-shift keying
MUX	multiplexing
NAK	negative acknowledgement
NBFM	narrowband FM
NEB	noise-equivalent bandwidth
nm	nanometer
NRZ	non-return-to-zero
NTSC	National Television System Committee
OC	optical carrier
OFDM	orthogonal FDM
OOK	on-off keying
OQPSK	offset QPSK
OSI	Open Systems Interconnection
PAM	pulse-amplitude modulation
PAR	peak-to-average power ratio

PC	plus-carrier
PCM	pulse-code modulation
pdf	probability density function
PHz	peta-Hertz
PLL	phase-locked loop
PM	phase modulation
pmf	probability mass function
PN	pseudo-noise
POTS	Plain Old Telephone System
PPM	pulse-position modulation
PSD	power spectral density
PSK	phase-shift keying
PSTN	public-switched telephone network
PWM	pulse-width modulation
Q	quadrature
QAM	quadrature AM
QoS	quality of service
QPSK	quadrature PSK
RF	radio frequency
RFID	RF identification
RHCP	right-hand CP
RHS	right-hand side
RLAN	regional LAN
rms	root-mean square
RS	Reed-Solomon
RSA	Rivert, Shamir, and Adleman
RX	receiver
RZ	return-to-zero
s	second
SC	suppressed-carrier
SCPC	single channel per carrier
SDR	software-defined radio
SER	symbol error rate
SHF	super high frequency
SIMO	single input multiple output
SISO	single input single output
SLF	super low frequency
SNR	signal-to-noise ratio
SONET	synchronous optical network
sps	symbols per second
SQPSK	staggered QPSK
SSB	single sideband
SSMA	spread spectrum multiple access
SSPA	solid-state power amplifier
SX	simplex
TCM	trellis-coded modulation
TCP	Transmission Control Protocol
TDD	time-division duplexing

TDM	time-division multiplexing
TDMA	time-division multiple access
THz	Tera-Hertz
TV	Television
TVWS	TV white spaces
TWTA	traveling-wave-tube amplifier
TX	transmitter
UDP	User Datagram Protocol
UHF	ultra high frequency
ULF	ultra low frequency
USB	upper sideband
UTP	unshielded twisted-pair
UWB	ultra wideband
VA	Viterbi algorithm
VCO	voltage-controlled oscillator
VDSL	very high-rate DSL
VHS	very high frequency
VLF	very low frequency
VoIP	voice over IP
VP	vertical polarization
VSB	vestigial sideband
W	Watt
WBFM	wideband FM
WDM	wavelength division multiplexing
WiFi	wireless fidelity
WiMAX	Worldwide Interoperability for Microwave Access
WLAN	wireless LAN
WRAN	wireless regional area network
wss	wide-sense stationary
ZF	zero-forcing

Index

Note: Page numbers followed by *f* indicate figures and *t* indicate tables.

T

U

V

W

Z